For Simon and Sarah

PREFACE

THE author of any general survey faces problems of style, but they are particularly troublesome in a book which covers as much terrain, chronologically and geographically, as this one does. I have attempted throughout to be accessible, sensible, and consistent, but I am aware that I have probably lapsed on all three counts. All proper names are transliterated into English, except those which are so well known in a different form that it would be silly to change them. When places have changed names, or had alternative names at the time described, I have placed the more familiar name first, with variants in brackets: I apologize if some readers object to the use of, for example, Danzig instead of Gdańsk. Apologies are also due to orientalists who find the absence of markings on Arabic and Turkish names jarring. As a complete non-orientalist, I thought the omission of all markings preferable to an attempt to devise a practice which might have been inaccurate, or at least inconsistent.

I have provided maps with the modest aim of showing simply where the events described took place. For a much more elaborate cartographic treatment of all the developments surveyed in the book, readers are referred to J. Riley-Smith (ed.), *The Atlas of the Crusades* (London, 1991).

In a book of this kind it would be invidious to pick out the work of individual scholars for special mention, as all those whose books and articles are listed under Further Reading have made a contribution. But I willingly thank Peter Edbury, Colin Imber, Werner Paravicini, Michael Heath, Peter Holt, and Tom Scott, for help on specific issues and enquiries. The Inter-Library Loan staff of Leicester University Library have handled a continual flow of requests over several years with efficiency and forbearance. The British Academy and my University's Research Board are owed thanks for grants which made it possible to spend a month in the summer of 1986 reading in Cambridge University Library. Chapter 13 is a heavily revised version of a paper which I read at scholarly meetings in Edinburgh, Nottingham, and London, and incorporates useful criticisms made on those occasions. Individual chapters were read by Geraldine McKendrick and Peter Edbury, who weeded out many errors which would otherwise have proved embarrassing. The

entire book was read by Jonathan Riley-Smith, and most of it by my wife
Valerie; I am profoundly grateful for the suggestions which both made. I
should also like to thank the Press's anonymous reader for a number of
helpful suggestions. In dealing with a book which reached them much
later than expected, the staff of Oxford University Press have, as always,
been helpful and courteous.

Leicester University   N.H.
1991

CONTENTS

LIST OF MAPS

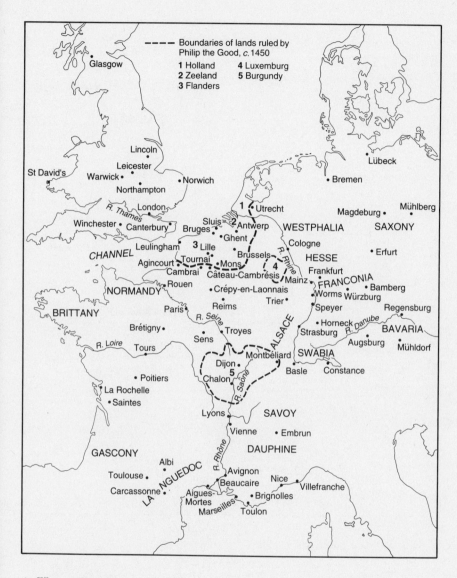

The map contains the following labels:

Legend:
- - - - Boundaries of lands ruled by Philip the Good, *c.*1450
1 Holland   4 Luxemburg
2 Zeeland   5 Burgundy
3 Flanders

Glasgow
St David's
Lincoln
Leicester
Warwick
Norwich
Northampton
London
R. Thames
Winchester
Canterbury
CHANNEL
Agincourt
Leulingham
NORMANDY
Rouen
Cambrai
Paris
R. Seine
BRITTANY
Brétigny
R. Loire
Tours
Sens
Troyes
Poitiers
La Rochelle
Saintes
GASCONY
Albi
Toulouse
LANGUEDOC
Carcassonne
Aigues-Mortes
Avignon
Beaucaire
Marseilles
Toulon
Brignolles
Nice
Villefranche
Lyons
Vienne
Embrun
DAUPHINE
SAVOY
R. Rhône
Chalon
Dijon
Montbéliard
ALSACE
R. Saône
SWABIA
Basle
Constance
Strasburg
Horneck
Speyer
Worms
Würzburg
Mainz
FRANCONIA
Bamberg
Regensburg
BAVARIA
R. Danube
Augsburg
Mühldorf
Frankfurt
HESSE
Erfurt
Cologne
R. Rhine
WESTPHALIA
SAXONY
Magdeburg
Mühlberg
Bremen
Lübeck
Utrecht
1
Antwerp
2
Sluis
Bruges
Ghent
3 Lille
Tournai
Brussels
Mons
Crépy-en-Laonnais
Câteau-Cambrésis
4
Trier
Reims
5

1. Western Europe

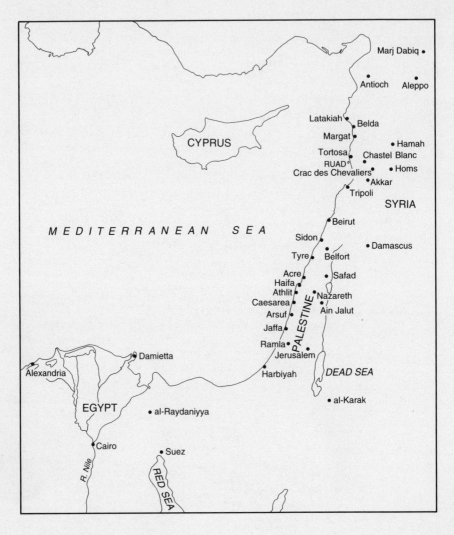

2. Syria, Palestine, and Egypt

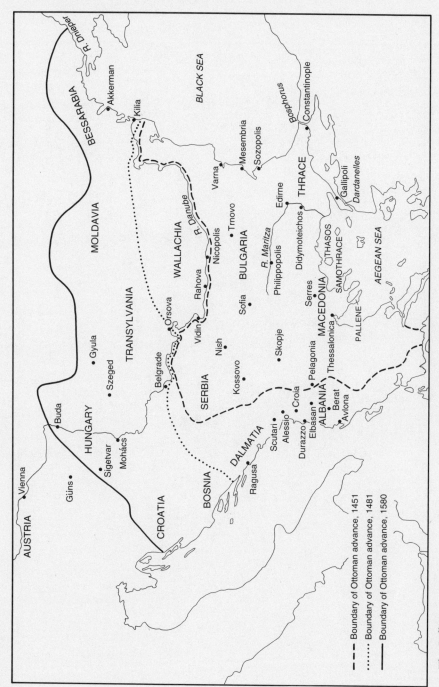

3. The Balkans

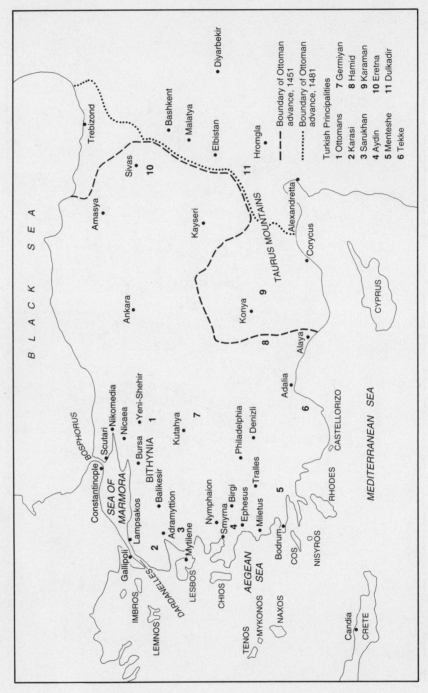

4. Anatolia

Boundary of Ottoman advance, 1451
Boundary of Ottoman advance, 1481

Turkish Principalities

1 Ottomans
2 Karasi
3 Sarukhan
4 Aydin
5 Menteshe
6 Tekke
7 Germiyan
8 Hamid
9 Karaman
10 Eretna
11 Dulkadir

BLACK SEA

Trebizond
Bashkent
Malatya
Elbistan
Diyarbekir
Hromgla
11
Amasya
Sivas
10
Kayseri
Alexandretta
Corycus
TAURUS MOUNTAINS
Ankara
Konya
9
8
Alaya
Adalia
6
CYPRUS

BOSPHORUS
Scutari
Nikomedia
Nicaea
Yeni-Shehir
1
Bursa
BITHYNIA
Balikesir
Kutahya
7
Philadelphia
Denizli
Constantinople
SEA OF MARMORA
Lampsakos
Adramyttion
3
Nymphaion
Birgi
Ephesus
Tralles
Smyrna
Miletus
5
Gallipoli
DARDANELLES
Mytilene
LESBOS
2
Bodrum
COS
NISYROS
RHODES
CASTELLORIZO
MEDITERRANEAN SEA
IMBROS
LEMNOS
CHIOS
AEGEAN SEA
TENOS
MYKONOS
NAXOS
Candia
CRETE

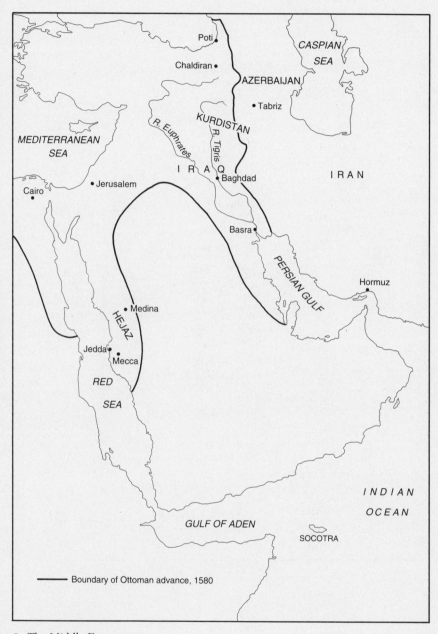

Poti

Chaldiran

CASPIAN
SEA

AZERBAIJAN

• Tabriz

KURDISTAN

R. Euphrates

R. Tigris

MEDITERRANEAN
SEA

I R A Q

Baghdad

I R A N

Cairo

• Jerusalem

Basra

PERSIAN GULF

Hormuz

Medina

HEJAZ

Jedda

Mecca

RED

SEA

INDIAN

OCEAN

GULF OF ADEN

SOCOTRA

—— Boundary of Ottoman advance, 1580

5. The Middle East

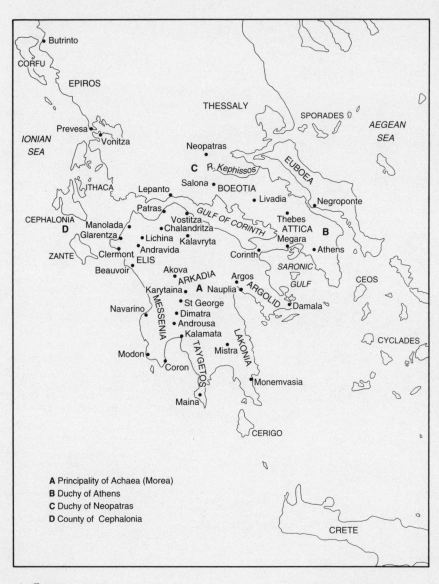

6. Greece

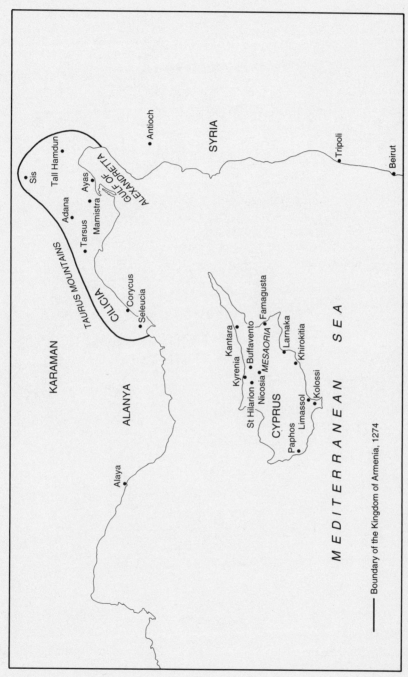

7. Cyprus and Cilician Armenia

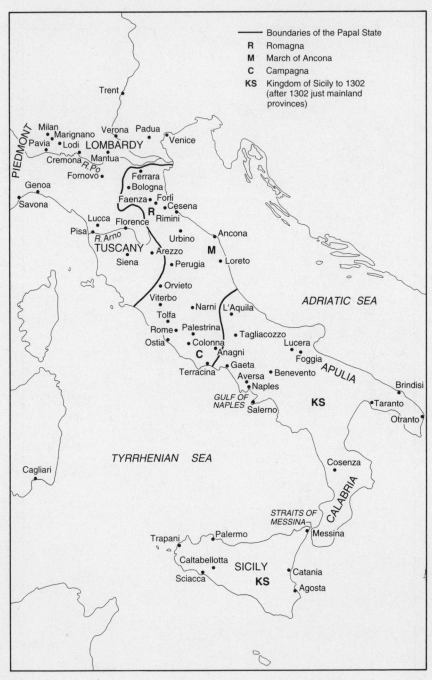

Boundaries of the Papal State
R Romagna
M March of Ancona
C Campagna
KS Kingdom of Sicily to 1302
    (after 1302 just mainland
    provinces)

Trent

PIEDMONT

Milan
Marignano
Pavia Lodi
Cremona Mantua
R. Po
Fornovo

Verona Padua
LOMBARDY
Venice

Genoa
Savona

Ferrara
Bologna
Faenza Forlì
Cesena
R
Rimini

Lucca
Florence
Pisa
R. Arno
TUSCANY Arezzo
Siena

Urbino
Perugia

Ancona

M
Loreto

Orvieto
Viterbo
Narni L'Aquila
Tolfa
Palestrina
Rome Tagliacozzo
Colonna
Ostia C Anagni
Terracina Gaeta
Aversa Benevento
Naples
GULF OF
NAPLES Salerno

ADRIATIC SEA

Lucera
Foggia

APULIA

Brindisi
Taranto
Otranto

KS

TYRRHENIAN SEA

Cagliari

Cosenza

CALABRIA

STRAITS OF
MESSINA
Messina

Trapani Palermo

Caltabellotta
Sciacca SICILY
KS

Catania
Agosta

8. Italy

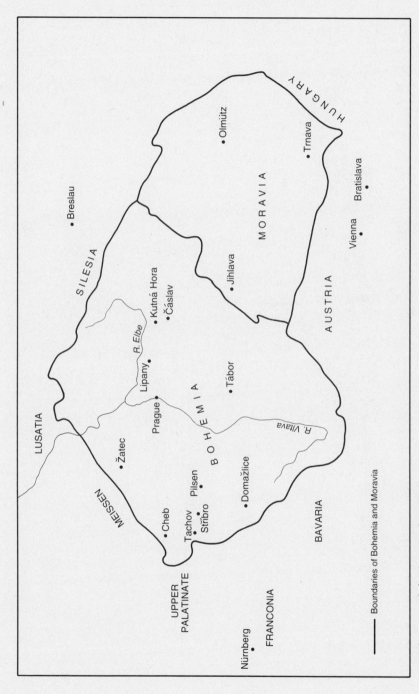

9. Bohemia and the Surrounding Territories

MORAVIA

HUNGARY

Olmütz

Trnava

Breslau

Bratislava

SILESIA

Vienna

AUSTRIA

Jihlava

Kutná Hora
Čáslav

LUSATIA

R. Elbe

Lipany

Tábor

BOHEMIA

Prague

R. Vltava

Žatec

MEISSEN

Domažlice

Cheb
Tachov Pilsen
Stříbro

BAVARIA

UPPER
PALATINATE

FRANCONIA

Nürnberg

——— Boundaries of Bohemia and Moravia

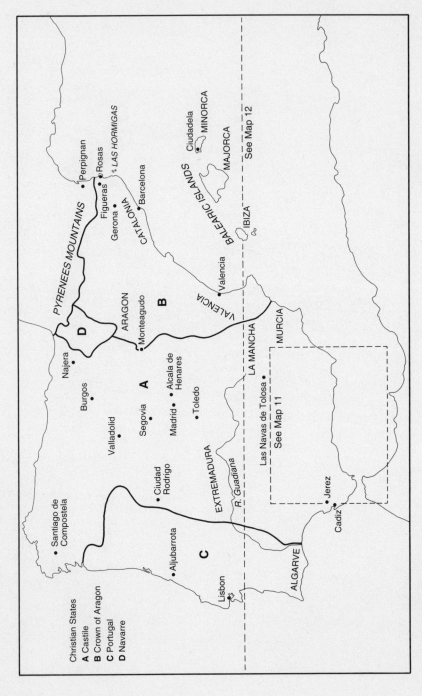

10. The Iberian Peninsula

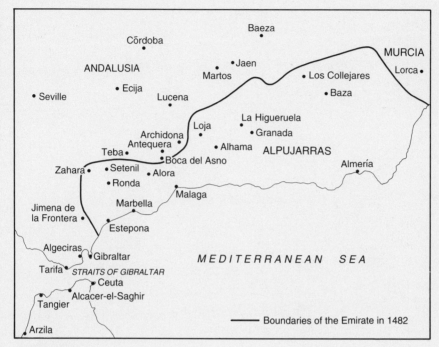

Baeza

Córdoba

MURCIA

ANDALUSIA
Jaen
Los Collejares
Lorca

Martos

Ecija
Baza

Seville
Lucena

La Higueruela

Loja
Granada

Archidona
Antequera
Alhama
ALPUJARRAS

Teba
Boca del Asno

Zahara
Setenil
Alora
Almería

Ronda

Malaga

Jimena de
la Frontera
Marbella

Estepona

Algeciras

Gibraltar
MEDITERRANEAN SEA

Tarifa *STRAITS OF GIBRALTAR*

Ceuta

Tangier
Alcacer-el-Saghir

—— Boundaries of the Emirate in 1482

Arzila

11. Granada

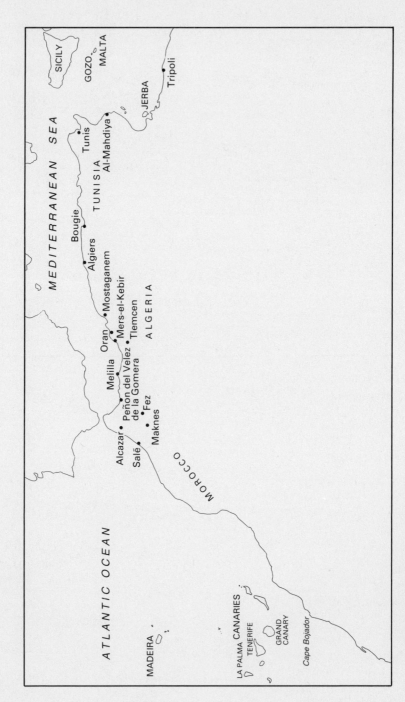

12. The Western Maghrib and Atlantic Islands

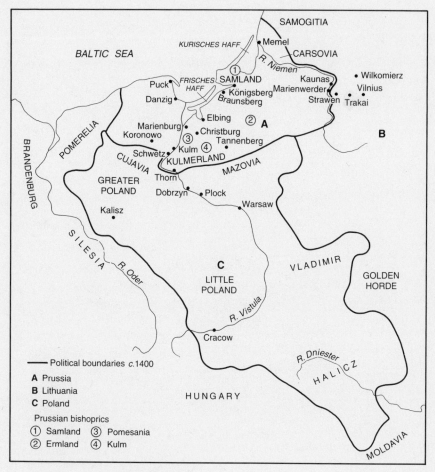

13. The *Ordensstaat* and its Neighbours

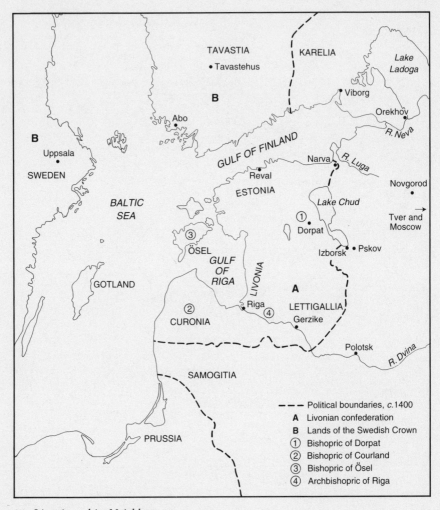

14. Livonia and its Neighbours

Introduction

✠

THIS book began life as a proposal for a short survey of the crusading movement between the Second Council of Lyons and the fall of Granada in 1492. In the course of negotiations with possible publishers the book expanded in several ways. I agreed to take the subject as far as the late sixteenth century, and to write not only about crusading expeditions and projects, but also about the associated processes of conquest and settlement, both Christian (in Spain, the Baltic region, Greece, and Cyprus) and Muslim (in the cases of the Mamluk and Ottoman Sultanates). These changes in time-span and scope in turn necessitated a much longer book. In the event I am pleased that the changes were introduced. It is true that they bring with them the danger of mental indigestion for anyone who is new to the subject. Unavoidably, the shortage of space available to handle complicated and contentious issues has resulted in generalizations, while the sheer size of the historical landscape involved will have led to omissions; reviewers and colleagues will doubtless point these out. But I am convinced in hindsight that to conclude any account of the later crusades earlier than 1580 would be to neglect events of intrinsic interest and significance. It will be apparent from Chapter 10[1] that I now regard the fall of Granada in 1492 as the starting-point for a series of extraordinary developments in Iberian crusading. But the matter goes deeper than that: in a nutshell, it is impossible to regard the crusading movement as a dead or even 'residual' expression of Catholic belief or behaviour in the sixteenth century, before or after (perhaps especially after) the Protestant Revolution. I also think that any account of crusading which does not deal with what the crusaders or their enemies achieved, in terms of government, economy, and society, is incomplete. This applies most importantly to the Mamluks and Ottomans. In affording them as much

[1] Below, 304–21

treatment as space permitted I was influenced by several considerations: that crusading historians are often accused of not paying enough attention to what happened 'on the other side of the hill'; that the failure of the crusades in the East was, to a very large extent, caused by the formidable military organization of the two Sultanates; and, frankly, that both were fascinating subjects to read and write about.

It is necessary to say something about the presuppositions which underpin this book. I am an adherent of the 'pluralist' school of crusade historians, who define crusades as wars proclaimed or supported by the papacy, for which crusade indulgences and privileges were publicized and preached, and whose combatants included men wearing the crusader's cross and fulfilling vows of crusade. Although the pluralist school had antecedents among the earliest serious historians of the crusade movement, it was overshadowed for at least two centuries by a rival approach, which may therefore with justice be dubbed 'traditional'. The main difference between traditionalists and pluralists is that, to decide whether a given expedition was a crusade, the former examine where it was going to, the latter where it originated and how it was organized. Traditionalists regard as crusades only those expeditions which were launched with the intention of defending or recovering the Holy Land. Pluralists, by contrast, look for papal validation, the granting of crusade status, preaching, and evidence of recruitment. If such features are present, then a crusade took place, irrespective of where the war was fought, of the nature of the conflict, and of the offence caused to modern sensibilities, for which the term 'crusade' still carries a cargo of value judgements equalled only by the word 'chivalry'.

The pluralist approach to the crusades was defined and restated in 1977 by Jonathan Riley-Smith in his book, *What were the Crusades?*. Since then a fitful debate has proceeded, in the course of which the main differences between the rival interpretative schools have become clear. It is not simply a question of the role of Jerusalem and the Holy Land. Traditionalists point out that at the same time as multiplying the number of crusades, pluralists may actually diminish the number of crusaders, by excluding contemporaries who did not go through the proper legal procedure of taking the cross: that is the many 'popular', 'peasants'', or 'shepherds'' crusades, of which the so-called 'Children's Crusade' is the best-known example. They argue that it is absurd to refuse to apply the word crusade to expeditions which contemporaries obviously regarded as such: although it is worth noting that it is not easy to find consistent contemporary use of such key words as *cruciata* or *croiserie* for expeditions which were not, to employ an ugly but useful neologism, formally 'indulgenced' by the Church. The corollary, traditionalists argue, is that by laying the definitive emphasis on the validating authority of the papacy, as established by its canon lawyers and buttressed by its own decretals, pluralists are accepting without question a view of papal supremacy within the crusading movement which was tendentious in its own time; it was also patently at odds not only with the general decline of papal influence in the late Middle Ages, but also with the slight role played by the popes (with very few exceptions) in many areas of crusading activity. And by regarding crusading as an institution which was by very definition ecclesiastical, pluralists tend to play down the importance of lay feelings and attitudes. Did contemporaries in the thirteenth and fourteenth centuries accept that crusades against Christian lay powers were necessary and valid? Did they agree that because the Turks were threatening Constantinople and Latin interests in the Aegean world, crusades should be declared against them rather than to recover the Holy Land? Did they acknowledge that, because the rulers of the Lithuanians had undergone baptism and made promises to facilitate the conversion of their people, the regular raids of the Teutonic Knights into Lithuania had lost their *raison d'être*? Did they accept that the *Reconquista* could 'spill over' into North Africa, the Atlantic Islands, and even the Americas? In these, and many more cases, the closely reasoned arguments of the papacy and other churchmen can be followed and stated by the historian with relative ease, but their reception undeniably poses problems.

Much the same applies to the vexed problem of Jerusalem. Some traditionalists rigidly adhere to the idea that contemporaries believed the only true form of crusade to be that launched to effect the rescue of the Holy Land. On occasion, they argue, contemporaries might accept the proposal that crusades could occur elsewhere 'by analogy', in the sense that a threat could be great enough to merit comparison with that to the *terra sancta* itself. But this could only be an *ad hoc* measure: the crusade was rooted in the Holy Land. Other traditionalists, most notably the British historian Christopher Tyerman, accept the pluralist approach in so far as it establishes the legal and institutional equality of all crusades, but argue that contemporaries regarded some crusades as being inherently more meritorious than others: to adapt George Orwell, 'all crusades are equal, but some are more equal than others'. A sort of Football

League Table of crusades is thereby created, those related to the Holy Land occupying Division One, and others against Muslims and pagans Division Two, while the controversial crusades against Christian enemies of the papacy, or of its allies, languish in Division Three. Once again, it is supposedly the level of popularity attained by the varied types of crusade, or the degree of criticism which was directed at them, which enables the historian to detect a gap between the policies of the papal Curia on the one hand, and the response of Christendom on the other.

While it is true that only one chapter in this book is devoted to expeditions to the Holy Land, it is certainly not my intention to play down the importance of Jerusalem in medieval religious thinking, or in the evolution of crusading. As the most holy place on earth, the *sanctissima civitas*, Jerusalem occupied a central position in both. *Crucesignati* in the late Middle Ages undoubtedly believed that the Mamluk possession of the places associated with the Redeemer whose cross they wore was both painful and scandalous. And the ineluctable tendency of victorious crusaders to fantasize about going on to liberate Jerusalem, which we shall examine in Chapter 1,[2] is just one of many striking pieces of evidence that crusading could never be fully dissociated from the Holy Land: as Dr Tyerman has rightly put it, 'the Holy Sepulchre could not be hidden in the shadow of the cross'. But it is equally the case that most crusaders did not aim at Jerusalem, and that there are few signs that they regarded their enterprises as 'cut-price' crusades on these grounds. At different times and in different places, the various theatres associated with crusading enjoyed a widely varying popularity. As more research is done on the social as well as the religious roots of crusading enthusiasm amongst the European laity, the reasons for this variation are likely to emerge as more complex than we have supposed. And we must distinguish between the depth of veneration for the Holy Places, which was unquestionably great, and the desire to participate in a *passagium* to Palestine, which, as contemporaries well knew, was fraught with political and organizational difficulties.

How does my personal stance as a pluralist shape the pages that follow? Naturally it dictates a commitment to discuss activities on every crusading front, and the necessity to try to strike a balance between them. I hope that the latter springs from the inherent significance of a particular crusade, or series of crusades, rather than from personal

[2] Below, 46–8

predilection; though like most writers of general surveys I have probably succumbed to the temptation to write at greater length about developments which have gripped my interest. If the papacy looms large, it is because I believe that, whatever qualifications need to be made, the Curia possessed the *auctoritas principalis* in crusading affairs. Much attention is paid to matters of organization, diplomacy, and funding, because it was on such essential mechanisms that crusading rested. I have deliberately avoided treating the subject as 'an institution in decay' because, despite the manifold difficulties faced by the promoters of crusades, it is absurd to apply the yardstick of decline to a practice which still commanded interest and respect, and some enthusiasm, three centuries after the point at which historians have customarily diagnosed decline. There is some virtue in the argument that crusading changed from being a genuinely popular movement in the late thirteenth and fourteenth centuries, to an affair of courts, diplomacy, and finance between Nicopolis and the Reformation, to a legacy of ideas, associations, and cultural forms in the Early Modern period. But the progression begs many questions.

Certainly the crusading movement underwent great changes, and they are hinted at in this book's subtitle. In 1274 it was still a movement dominated by the French; it rested within the tradition of papal direction and conciliar organization established by Innocent III; and it had as its chief emphasis the relief of the Holy Land. The Second Lyons Council epitomizes these features, which was one reason for picking it as a starting date. The other was that the Council adopted strategic and financial approaches which established or systematized a new pattern in crusading practice, so much so that some historians of the crusades have recently come to invest the Council with more significance than the fall of Acre in 1291. In 1580, by contrast, the main goal of the crusading movement was the containment of the Ottoman Turks, and it served, to a large extent, the interests of the Habsburgs and their Catholic, Mediterranean allies and satellites. Was this necessarily decline? I prefer to regard the crusading movement as having been transformed, and in the process debilitated, by developments in military organization and techniques in the late Middle Ages, before being submerged by the religious revolution of the sixteenth century. This conclusion will not find favour with the traditionalists, most of whom depict the crusading movement as moribund even before the fall of Acre. It is, however, the gist of Chapters 13 and 14, which besides serving to analyse material treated in narrative form in previous chapters, have the function of acting as a general conclusion for the book as a whole.

One of the advantages of the pluralist approach is that it affords ample scope for comparison, and I have tried to compare the various crusading fronts as much as space and current knowledge permit. A similar comparative treatment of the processes of settlement and government is highly desirable, and has been attempted by historians in the cases of Syria, Cyprus, and Greece. It has yielded valuable insights into such matters as the feudal regime, the military problems of the settlers, and the status of the non-Frankish population. But it has not, to my knowledge, been applied to Iberia, North Africa, or the Baltic region, although some authors, such as Felipe Fernández-Armesto, have shown what can be done. Fortunately historians have recently become aware of the importance of considering the medieval frontier regions side by side, and much can be expected in the next few years.

In an earlier book I offered a hostage to fortune by stating that two problematic aspects of the fourteenth century, the influence of the cult of chivalry, and the economic condition of the West, made it impossible adequately to deal with the crusading movement as a whole. In practice the plethora of recently published research on the period from 1274 to about 1400 has made the chapters concerning these years comparatively easy to write. Much greater difficulties reside in the fifteenth and sixteenth centuries, when there are whole areas which call out for critical, up-to-date treatment. Such fundamental topics as the crusading policy of Pope Pius II, the career of Scanderbeg, the crusades against the Hussites, the Hospitallers at Rhodes and in the West, developments in crusade preaching, and the resumption of the *Reconquista*, can be singled out for the fifteenth century; while of the period after the Fifth Lateran Council (1512–17), which effectively marked the end of the medieval phase of crusading, it can be said that nearly everything remains to be done. This book will have more than achieved its purpose if it attracts research historians into these areas. The 'classical period' of crusading (1095–1291) will probably always exert a greater appeal to both historians and readers than the 'post-classical period' which forms the subject of this book. But the latter can assuredly no longer be relegated to concluding chapters or appendices.

1

The Loss of the Holy Land
1274–1370

✠

I N March 1272 the recently elected Pope Gregory X summoned a general council of the Church to discuss the three greatest problems facing the Catholic faith: the threat to Latin Syria, the schism between the Latin and Greek churches, and corruption within the Latin church. The Council, which opened proceedings at Lyons in May 1274, therefore forms a natural point at which to begin consideration both of the downfall of Latin Syria, and (in the next chapter) of papal-Byzantine relations in the late Middle Ages. The Second Council of Lyons does not possess the significance, for the history of the crusades, of the Fourth Lateran Council of 1215, or even the Vienne Council of 1311–12; but as a general council of the Church it was bound to be a major event, and in two respects it was special. It constituted the last attempt by a thirteenth-century pope to launch a crusade which was recognizably cast in the mould of Innocent III's conception of crusading as an expression of papal supremacy in temporal matters. And, more importantly, it can be seen in retrospect as Christendom's last chance to set in motion military activity on a scale sufficient to save the Latin states in Syria from destruction.

Before looking at what took place at Lyons it is thus essential to examine the situation which the General Council was to try to redress (see map 2). The position of the Franks in Syria and Palestine could not be described as favourable at any time after Saladin's great victory at Hattin in 1187. But for some forty years after 1192, when the truce of Jaffa brought the Third Crusade to an end, the Franks' possession of considerable financial resources derived from trade, combined with dissension amongst the Ayyubid successors to Saladin in Syria and Egypt, enabled the Christians to maintain a position of some strength and influence in the politics of the Middle East. This period of relative stability and equilibrium came to an abrupt end in October 1244, when the Franks, together with their Damascene allies, were heavily defeated by the Egyptians and their hired soldiers, the Khwarazmian Turks, at the battle of Harbiyah (La Forbie). *En route* to the battle the Khwarazmians took Jerusalem, which had been in the possession of the Franks since Frederick II's treaty with Sultan al-Kamil in 1229. Harbiyah not only deprived the Kingdom of Jerusalem of its field army, but paved the way for Egypt's occupation of Damascus in 1245. Worse was to follow. Louis IX of France, a dedicated crusader whose reputation will echo throughout this chapter, responded to the disasters in the Holy Land by organizing and equipping one of the finest crusading armies to leave the West. It attacked the centre of Ayyubid power in Egypt and met with defeat in the Nile delta in April 1250.

Between 1250 and 1254 Louis IX stayed in the Holy Land, rebuilding its fortifications and attempting to achieve through diplomacy what he had failed to do through force. By dint of his status and personal authority Louis acted as virtual *de facto* ruler of the Kingdom of Jerusalem, and these were therefore peaceful years in a country whose problems normally included internal dissension on a crippling scale. After Louis's departure Latin Syria collapsed into a state of anarchy. Constitutionally, the Kingdom of Jerusalem was ruled on behalf of its absentee Staufen monarchs, first Conrad and then Conradin, by a series of regents (*baillis*), but their authority was rigidly circumscribed by a legalistic baronage. The situation was worsened by the rivalry between the Military Orders, which pursued semi-autonomous policies towards the Muslims, and by the conflict between the Italian trading republics of Genoa, Venice, and Pisa, which conducted their quarrels within the ports of Latin Syria. Two years after St Louis left for France, the War of St Sabas exemplified the gravity of the situation. A conflict which started as a territorial dispute between the Italian communes gradually involved most of the factional groups within the Kingdom, with the Templars and Hospitallers, the smaller mercantile communities, and the important barons, all taking sides, prolonging the war until 1261. Not only did such conflicts consume the diminishing resources of Latin Syria, but the rivalries which they fed made any sort of consistent policy towards the Muslims impossible, while any one of the many factions might take independent action against the Muslims which would provide the enemy with a *casus belli*.

Whatever importance one attributes to these factors, it was primarily developments within the Muslim lands which dictated the fate of the Frankish states. In May 1250 an event occurred which was to have momentous consequences. In the eleventh century the Seljukid Turks had begun the practice of purchasing Turkish slaves of non-Muslim origin and training them as élite cavalry troops. These Mamluks were an important feature in the armies of Saladin and his successors, and Sultan al-Salih's Bahriyya regiment in particular had excelled at Harbiyah and in the encounters with Louis IX's army. After al-Salih's death in November 1249 the Bahriyya feared that their position would be challenged by the military household of the new sultan, al-Muazzam Turan-Shah. They therefore assassinated him, creating one of their own number, Aybeg, sultan. Although for a time al-Ashraf Musa, a great-grandson of al-Kamil, was nominally sultan, the Ayyubid regime had come to an end in Egypt. Its successor, the Mamluk Sultanate, was to control Egypt until it was destroyed by the Ottomans in the early sixteenth century.

At first the foundation of the Mamluk Sultanate worked to the Franks' advantage: there was conflict between the Bahriyya regiment and Aybeg, who began building up his own Mamluk household, the Muizziyya, as well as between Aybeg and the Ayyubids of Syria. Moreover, in the course of the 1250s the entire political situation in the Middle East was rendered more complicated, and possibly more hopeful for the Franks, by the arrival of Mongol armies. Hülegü, brother of Möngke Khan, took Baghdad in 1258 and Aleppo and Damascus in 1260. Since 1245, when Innocent IV had sent the Franciscan John of Piano del Carpine to the Great Khan's court to convert him to Christianity, some Christians had seen potential converts and allies in the Mongols. None the less, when Hülegü sent his general Kitbuqa southwards to attack Egypt the Franks decided to remain neutral, either because they feared Mongol suzerainty more than the threat of Mamluk conquest, or because they did not want to irritate the Mamluks by allying with Hülegü. Perhaps, too, they hoped that even without Frankish support, the Mongols would inflict enough losses on the Mamluks to make them less of a danger thereafter. It was a disastrous, but understandable miscalculation, for nobody could have foreseen the decisiveness of the Mamluk victory over Kitbuqa at Ain Jalut in September 1260, or the completeness with which Hülegü withdrew to Iran, leaving the Mamluks masters of Syria as well as Egypt.

Shortly after the battle of Ain Jalut its victor, Sultan Kutuz, was murdered, and Baybars al-Bunduqdari became sultan. In the course of the

1260s, after defeating several separatist movements, Baybars embarked on a systematic policy of taking the remaining Frankish castles and ports in the Holy Land. His motivation was less religious than strategic: the fear of a Frankish–Mongol alliance, or simply of a big crusade which might be exploited by the Mongols. In 1263 he sacked Nazareth, but the major offensives began in 1265, with the capture of Caesarea, Haifa, and Arsuf. In 1266 Baybars took the Templar fortress of Safad. In 1268 Jaffa and Antioch fell, besides the castle at Belfort. Acre itself was blockaded and its hinterland periodically raided. Baybars's last big gain was the capture of the Hospitaller fortress of Crac des Chevaliers in 1271. There was virtually nothing the Franks of Palestine and Syria could do to hinder this determined onslaught. Cypriot assistance was valuable, but it was in the West that hope lay, and by a grim coincidence the years of Baybars's greatest pressure were those in which the popes were deploying all available crusading resources to bring about the destruction of Manfred and Conradin of Staufen. A substantial French crusade army was recruited in 1264–5, but its job was to oust the Staufen and place Charles of Anjou, the younger brother of Louis IX, on the throne of the Kingdom of Sicily. A trickle of help did arrive in Palestine, such as the French troops brought in 1264 by Oliver of Termes to relieve the garrison which Louis IX had left at Acre under Geoffrey of Sergines, and the fifty knights under Odo, Count of Nevers, who arrived in 1265. Then, in 1267, Louis IX again took the cross. His expedition, however, set sail to Tunis, whose Sultan the French King hoped to convert before going on to fight Baybars. In August 1270 Louis died near Tunis, and the only element of his crusade which reached the Holy Land was a small force led by Prince Edward of England. Edward at least succeeded, in May 1272, in arranging an eleven-year truce with Baybars. The failure of the West in this critical decade was the greater in that Baybars was very sensitive about the potential danger posed by a crusading army.

When Tedaldo Visconti was elected pope in September 1271 the situation in the Holy Land was thus graver than at any time since Hattin. Indeed, it was the disastrous news arriving from the East that led the cardinals to end a papal interregnum which had lasted nearly three years, and to choose as pope a man who had himself taken the cross and was in Palestine at the time of his election. None the less, the situation was not irredeemable. Granted the total reliance of Latin Syria on western help, there were features in the immediate background to the Second Council of Lyons which pointed to the solid possibility of organizing and dispatching that help. In the first place, not only was the papal Curia presided over by a man who made the crusade to the East the primary aim of his pontificate, but it was also, for the first time for a generation, able to concentrate on the Holy Land without worrying about the threat to its own independence posed by the Staufen. Secondly, there was a group of important western rulers who all showed a real concern for the needs of Latin Syria and who possessed the resources to help it effectively. Edward I of England, who was crowned on return from his crusade in 1274, regarded a new crusade as the ultimate objective of his reign and maintained a consistent interest in the Holy Land. Philip III of France did not inherit his father's obsession with crusading, but he continued to pay the expenses of the French garrison at Acre and co-operated with the Pope in sending troops to Palestine in 1273. Charles I of Sicily showed an interest in the Frankish East which, while it may have been based on considerations of prestige and profit rather than religious enthusiasm, did produce positive results. And James I of Aragon, who had sent a minor expedition to Acre under two illegitimate sons in 1269, came in person to Lyons to express his crusading zeal.

But just as important as the commitment of pope and kings was the continuing popularity of the crusade amongst the population generally. A full consideration of this complex subject will be undertaken in Chapter 13,[1] but it is necessary to mention it briefly now in order to set the Second Council of Lyons and its aftermath in their proper context. In two important respects western society in the 1270s viewed the crusade with a heavy measure of unease and suspicion. First, the failure of both of St Louis's expeditions had created much confusion and resentment: the chronicler Salimbene reported that the friars who had preached the King's first crusade were taunted with its failure, and Joinville remarked that the French nobility was less willing to follow its King on crusade a second time. Secondly, substantial abuses had arisen from the innovations of Innocent III, particularly in regard to Church taxation and the redemption of vows (the payment of a cash sum instead of serving in person or sending a deputy). These developments were important, and they loom large in the memoirs presented to Gregory X in response to his plea for written advice on the crusade: it is, after all, the point of memoirs to present problems which need solving. But when we look at a broader time-span than the Council and its memoirs, we notice other factors which more than balance the reported difficulties. There is the

[1] Below, 394–420.

impressive group of noblemen in the last third of the thirteenth century for whom the crusade was the focal point of their lives—Geoffrey of Sergines, Oliver of Termes, Érard of Valéry, Odo of Grandson, John of Grailly—and who were regarded as exemplars by their contemporaries. There is the fact that criticism of the crusade was less fundamental in argument, even if it was possibly greater in volume, than in earlier periods. And above all, there is the simple fact that, as we shall see in the remainder of this chapter, crusading to the Holy Land continued to be discussed, promoted, and carried out for many decades to come after Lyons, something which would be inexplicable if enthusiasm had reached the low-water mark claimed by some historians.

The Council met, then, in an atmosphere of despondency rather than despair. Its deliberations on the crusade, which occurred in its first two plenary sessions in May 1274, left little trace except in the garrulous and unreliable memoirs of James I of Aragon (who attended the first session), and in the conciliar decree on the crusade, the 'Constitutiones pro zelo fidei', which exist only in mutilated and fragmentary form. None the less, the broad outlines of the Council's approach are clearly discernible. Many of the *Constitutiones*, such as the indulgences granted to those who took the cross or contributed to the crusade with funds, the prohibition of commerce in war material with the Mamluks, and the sanctions proclaimed against rulers who impeded the crusade by their aggression against fellow-Christians, are strikingly similar to clauses in the decrees of the Fourth Lateran and First Lyons Councils, solid reminders that Gregory X, like Innocent III and IV, envisaged the crusade as an occasion, and justification, for wide-ranging papal intervention in temporal matters. Such matters were just as important in the organization of a major crusade as they had been thirty or sixty years earlier—indeed the significance of economic measures against Egypt would loom ever larger as the decades passed—and for the originality of the Second Lyons Council we need to look at two different areas, strategy and finance.

Strategically, the years since Louis IX's first crusade had witnessed a growing interest in the value of permanent garrisons (epitomized by that established at Acre by Louis himself) and of small-scale expeditions of hundreds, rather than thousands, of troops. For example, in a *remembrance* which the Patriarch of Jerusalem drew up in 1267, and in which he listed the requirements of the Holy Land, emphasis was laid on the provision of funds for the payment of mercenaries stationed in Palestine; part of the money was to come on a regular basis from taxes paid by the

Cypriot church. That Gregory X subscribed to this policy of sending small contingents is clear from those which he financed early in his pontificate, and at Lyons James I, the Master of the Templars, and Érard of Valéry all supported the idea of sending an advance party, or *passagium particulare*. This did not mean that a major crusade, a general passage (*passagium generale*), would be unnecessary; it was obviously impossible to defeat the Mamluks decisively without one. But the crusade could no longer be conceived as a single great army, or even, as in the Fifth Crusade, as an army seasonally depleted and reinforced, as some crusaders completed their period of service and departed, while others arrived. It now became an enterprise of at least two separate stages: for eventually, as the *passagium particulare* was recast by strategists in rather grander terms, a third and even earlier stage, the *primum passagium*, came to be added.

This lay in the future, and Gregory X seems to have envisaged his advance parties in such modest form that they did not need to be incorporated in the Council's crusade decree. The *Constitutiones*, or at least those parts which have survived, were concerned only with the general passage, to which it seems that the Pope allocated a six-year preparation period. It is probable that Gregory X adopted this long lead-up partly because the truce with the Mamluks would only expire in 1283, and partly because of the organizational problems which he foresaw. Apart from securing and keeping the commitment of Christendom's rulers to the crusade, the most formidable of these problems was finding the financial resources necessary for the general passage. It is in this area that the Council's second claim to originality lies. Faced with rising expenses, Gregory X had to devise means of radically increasing the funds available for disbursement to those who took the cross. Innocent III, confronted by the same problem some sixty years earlier, had adopted a threefold approach. He had laid extra stress on the provision of paid deputies to serve in the field, so that an individual could take the cross and enjoy the crusader's privileges without serving in person; and he had introduced the practices of systematic vow redemption, and of levying Church taxes for crusading. Gregory X's approach was also essentially threefold. His first measure, the introduction of a miscellany of proposals to raise money from the laity, through voluntary contributions (legacies and alms) and imposed fines (for blaspheming and trading with the Muslims) was not new. His other two certainly were. Gregory greatly increased the burden of Church taxation by levying a compulsory six-year tenth, and by dividing Christendom into twenty-six collectorates so that it would be assembled more quickly and efficiently than hitherto. And he intended to persuade all the rulers of Christendom, 'by warning and exhortation', to levy a universal poll tax of one penny, of Tours or Sterling, which would be collected annually through the six years 1274–80.

Operating within a well-established conciliar tradition, but making financial innovations necessitated by the pressures of the period, the Second Council of Lyons thus laid the foundations for a general passage; the erection of the superstructure depended on the Pope's ability to make secular rulers take the lead. Gregory himself could finance small *passagia*—by the end of 1275 four of these had been sent—but princely initiative, or at least support, was essential to facilitate the collection of the six-year clerical tenth, to collect the poll tax, to weld *crucesignati* and hired mercenaries into viable military units, to organize the transportation required, and above all to provide leadership for the troops in the field. This support appeared to be forthcoming. Philip III and Rudolph of Habsburg, the Emperor-elect, took the cross in 1275, and Charles I of Sicily made a conditional vow. It is possible that the Pope was so encouraged by this response that he brought forward the departure date of the general passage to spring 1277.

Then came Gregory X's death in January 1276. The demise of any pope at such a critical point in crusade planning presents the historian with an insuperable problem of interpretation, and in the late Middle Ages the situation occurred at least three times (with Gregory, John XXII, and Pius II). The subsequent collapse of Gregory's project is sometimes compared with the successful launching of the Fifth Crusade in 1217, despite the death of Innocent III in the previous year; the point being either that popular and princely enthusiasm had declined in the mean time to such an extent that only persistent papal cajoling could get a crusade off the ground, or that Gregory's project would have collapsed even had he lived. The comparison is not really fair, however, since it overlooks the tremendous growth in the importance of secular leadership in crusading matters which occurred between the early and late thirteenth century. The problem in the 1270s was that a number of rulers were genuinely interested in a crusade to the Holy Land, but none would assume the overall leadership as Louis IX had done, probably because they were afraid of the financial implications; the French Crown, for instance, was already well aware of the costs of St Louis's crusading obsession. It was unfortunate that Charles of Anjou, who was best placed to help geographically and in terms of resources, enjoyed a European reputation as a commander, and actually purchased Mary of Antioch's claim to the Kingdom of Jerusalem early in 1277, favoured the anachronistic Staufen approach of peaceful relations with Egypt while pursuing his anti-Byzantine policy. But Charles was open to persuasion. Had Gregory X lived, the Pope might have exerted enough pressure on the pliable Philip III and his Angevin uncle, and collected enough of the sexennial tenth, to secure action on a significant scale.

The Second Council of Lyons left a crusading legacy which persisted into the 1280s. The general passage had, in effect, been postponed, but the tenth was still being collected, and the forthcoming crusade was cited continually by a series of short-lived popes to try to bring to an end the wars between Philip III and Alfonso X of Castile, and Rudolph of Habsburg and Ottokar of Bohemia. The period was dominated by the ambitions of Charles of Anjou. In Palestine his troops, led by Roger of San Severino, held Acre, while in Italy Pope Nicholas III (1277–80) concentrated on trying to reduce Charles's stranglehold on the Papal State. In 1281 the new Pope Martin IV, who as papal legate had worked with Charles for the Capetian conquest of southern Italy, backed the King of Sicily's plan for a reconquest of Constantinople, which would take the form of a crusade against the schismatic Greeks. Had this materialized, it could well have diverted the attention of France's nobility from the Holy Land. But a yet worse combination of events occurred. For at Easter 1282 the Sicilians rebelled against French rule, expelling Charles's troops and welcoming King Peter of Aragon as ruler. The resulting war lasted twenty years and absorbed the manpower and resources of the *Regno*, Aragon, France, and the papacy, all the great Mediterranean powers to which Gregory X had looked with urgency and hope to provide assistance for the Holy Land.

Just as Charles of Anjou's conquest of the *Regno* in the mid-1260s had coincided with Baybars's greatest victories in Palestine, so the efforts of Charles, his son, and their papal suzerains to defend the truncated Angevin *Regno* in the 1280s came at the same time as a renewed Mamluk onslaught. Baybars had died in 1277 and after a period of factional strife Kalavun, like Baybars a veteran of the Bahriyya regiment, seized the Sultanate in 1279. Initially Kalavun faced not only the opposition of Baybars's ousted sons, but also a dangerous provincial rebellion led by Sungur al-Ashqar, the governor of Damascus. Then in 1281 the Mongol Ilkhan Abaqa, whose tentative diplomatic contacts with western rulers were sustaining fruitless hopes for a Christian–Mongol alliance, launched a powerful invasion of Syria. Kalavun repelled the invasion at the second battle of Homs in October 1281, and when Abaqa died in the following year he was succeeded by his brother Tegüder, who was a Muslim. This released Kalavun to carry on with Baybars's policy of gradually destroying the Frankish states. Their exceptional weakness was tempting, and the extent of their political fragmentation was clear from the assortment of individuals—the Masters of the Military Orders, the representatives of Charles of Anjou, the Lady Margaret of Tyre—with whom the Sultan concluded a series of short-lived truces between 1282 and 1285. In 1285 Kalavun took Margat, the last remaining Hospitaller stronghold. Latakia was occupied in 1287, and two years later the Sultan captured Tripoli.

The news of the fall of Tripoli provoked a shock wave in the West. The Kingdom of Jerusalem still enjoyed a truce with Kalavun, but it was only a question of time before Acre was attacked. The Ilkhan Arghun, who dethroned Tegüder in 1284, sent letters and an envoy, the Nestorian priest Rabban Sauma, to the West from 1285 to try and organize combined military operations. Since 1286 Edward I had acted as intermediary between the papal-Angevin party and the Aragonese, and he had taken the cross in Gascony in 1287. Hopes for a Mongol alliance, English pressure—exerted through the indefatigable Odo of Grandson—and the pitiful pleas of a legation from Acre led by John of Grailly, together persuaded Pope Nicholas IV to take immediate steps to protect Acre. He sent money and galleys, and Edward I dispatched Odo of Grandson with a contingent of men; meanwhile Pope and King negotiated the terms of a general passage to be led by Edward. Partly in an effort to placate public opinion, Nicholas also ordered crusade preaching. This was a grave error, because it led to a large and disorderly force of Italian crusaders arriving in Acre in the summer of 1290. Lacking leadership and finding no military activity in hand, they attacked and killed peaceful Muslim peasants and merchants. Kalavun demanded that the murderers be handed over to him and, when this was refused, treated the incident as a *casus belli*. The Sultan died in November 1290, but his son al-Ashraf Khalil pressed on with preparations for the capture of Acre, possibly hoping that this major triumph would consolidate his tenuous grip on the Sultanate. On 5 April 1291 a massive Mamluk army, equipped with large numbers of siege machines, assembled before Acre.

The siege was a short one, for even Acre's formidable double line of walls could not resist the combined efforts of catapults and undermining sappers. On 4 May King Henry of Cyprus arrived with valuable reinforcements, but the city's defenders were still comparatively few. By 16 May the Muslims had occupied the area between the walls, and two days later they launched a general assault on the inner wall. They managed to take the most exposed of the wall's bastions, the Accursed Tower, and from there stormed the gate of St Nicholas, to the south. The Christians had fought with desperate courage, especially the Knights of the Military Orders; the Marshal of the Hospitallers and the Master of the Templars were amongst the dead. But it was now clear that Acre was lost and a chaotic embarkation took place at the harbour. King Henry, the Master of the Hospitallers, Odo of Grandson and John of Grailly were able to escape, but low water prevented many vessels entering the harbour and most of the defenders, clergy, and remaining civilians were either killed or taken prisoner. By nightfall al-Ashraf's troops held all Acre except for the Templars' stronghold, which resisted until 28 May. Like Tripoli, Acre was all but razed to the ground to prevent it serving as a disembarkation point for a recovery crusade.

The remainder of the Holy Land fell easily into Mamluk hands. Shamefully, the virtually impregnable port of Tyre was abandoned by its *bailli*, Adam of Cafran, on 19 May. Sidon and Beirut fell on 14 and 21 July. The Templars evacuated their last fortresses, Tortosa and Athlit, on 3 and 14 August. 'With these conquests', wrote the Arab historian Abu l-Fida, 'the whole of Palestine was now in Muslim hands, a result that no-one would have dared to hope for or to desire.' Those who escaped fled to Cyprus. Here the Military Orders established temporary convents while they considered their future. Ordinary refugees either made their way back to their ancestral homes in the West, or lived on charity in Cyprus. The fate of the latter was shared by those who did not escape but were not considered worthy of slavery; Ricoldo of Monte Croce wrote of their pathetic condition

I see old men, young girls, children and infants, thin, pale, weak, begging their bread, and they long to be Saracen slaves rather than die of hunger . . . Poor wives and old women weep at the foot of the cross, inconsolably mourning their sons and their husbands killed or enslaved by the Muslims.[2]

The enslaved were numerous enough to come to the attention of the papal Curia on several occasions in the decades that followed; it attempted

---

[2] J. Richard, *The Latin Kingdom of Jerusalem*, tr. J. Shirley (Amsterdam, 1979), 456.

to raise funds for their release and exhorted missionaries working in Egypt and Syria to prevent them apostatizing to Islam. Despite this, many did become renegades and some of ability even rose to high office in the Mamluk Sultanate.

In expelling the Franks, the Mamluks imposed a degree of unity on Egypt and Syria unknown since the eleventh century. The two regions came to be termed *al-diyar al-Misriyya* ('the Egyptian homelands') and *al-mamalik al-Shamiyya* ('the Syrian kingdoms'). Syria was divided into six provinces with their capitals at Damascus, Aleppo, Tripoli, Safad, Hamah, and al-Karak. All were potential bases for rebellion against the sultan, especially Damascus, the great power of whose governor was reflected in his title, *malik al-umara* ('king of the emirs'). Provincial revolts were not uncommon occurrences: both Baybars and Kalavun faced rebellions by the governors of Damascus, despite the fact that these were fellow-members of the Bahriyya regiment and owed the Sultans comradely loyalty (*khushdashiyya*). In 1312 the governors of Aleppo and Tripoli deserted to the Mongols, advising Öljeitü on his invasion of 1312–13. The sultans normally attempted to contain this ever-present threat by imposing limitations on their governors' executive powers, and by retaining the right to appoint other key officials in the military and civil administration. The wisdom of this policy was shown when Sultan al-Nasir Muhammad, who spent his time mainly in Egypt, allowed Tengiz al-Husami, his governor of Damascus, to exercise a virtual governor-generalship over the whole of Syria between 1312 and 1340. When relations between the two men deteriorated, Tengiz's dangerous concentration of power forced the Sultan to mobilize an expeditionary force against him. Syria's new provincial status was exemplified by the strict control exercised by officials resident in Cairo over grants of lands and revenues (*iqtas*) to emirs. Thus it was in southern Syria that a full cadastral survey (*rawk*) carried out in 1313–14 paved the way for the redistribution of *iqtas* on a stricter basis. Most of the military households of Mamluks, and hence the centre of political power and factional strife in the Sultanate, remained in Egypt.

It is the persisting importance of these households that explains both the strengths and weaknesses of the Sultanate. As Professor P. M. Holt has written, 'The characteristic and distinguishing feature of Mamluk military society was that it was composed almost wholly of first-generation immigrants, newly converted to Islam.' The Mamluk households, held together by *khushdashiyya* and well-disciplined, were supplemented in wartime by non-Mamluk soldiers (the *Halqa*), at a nominal ratio of one to ten, to form regiments under the command of emirs. In the field the emirs served under the personal leadership of the sultan, whose own household would spearhead operations. This constituted a formidable fighting force. In peacetime, however, the households of the greater emirs, such as the *amir silah* ('sword-bearer') and *amir akhur* ('constable') became autonomous and powerful factions which, especially in combination, could rebel against the sultan. The danger became particularly acute at the death of a sultan, both because the emirs continued to assert the elective, contractual character of the early Sultanate against attempts to make the succession hereditary, and also because every new sultan faced the resentment of his predecessor's household, now stripped of prestige and office. Faction based on household cohesion and loyalty was aggravated by racial hostility when Kalavun began to import Circassian Mamluks to balance the predominant Kipchak Turks.

The political instability of the Mamluk Sultanate was made clear in the two decades following its conquest of Latin Syria. In 1293 al-Ashraf Khalil was killed by his vicegerent in Egypt, the Turkish Mamluk Baydara al-Mansuri. Baydara seized the Sultanate but was himself killed by al-Ashraf's Circassian Mamluks. Al-Ashraf's half-brother, the child al-Nasir Muhammad, was enthroned, showing the growing kudos of hereditary succession, but it was not until 1310 that he wielded real power. Characteristically, this entailed raising thirty-two of his own Mamluks to the emirate in 1310, and forty-six two years later. In the course of the next thirty years al-Nasir Muhammad went further than any other Mamluk sultan towards replacing the 'crowned republic' of his youth with a hereditary autocratic monarchy, a sultanate which would resemble more closely the Islamic model of secular authority. To achieve this he laid greater emphasis on Ayyubid and Seljukid traditions of government, including such emblems of sovereignty as the carrying of a jewelled saddle-cover in procession. The judicial role of the sultan began to overshadow his military responsibilities, and the only legal restrictions on the sultan's power were those derived from his observance of Islamic religious law (the shariah). Al-Nasir Muhammad's great advantage was the development of a predominantly Arabic fiscal administration, which enabled him to execute cadastral surveys in Syria and Egypt, and to make substantial financial savings in a manner which highlighted his control of all *iqtas*, and hence, indirectly, his dominance over the emirs.

Al-Nasir Muhammad's autocracy did not survive his death in 1341.

Since he could not break up the Mamluk household system, which was fundamental to the Sultanate's military organization, all he succeeded in doing, in the long term, was to set up a tension between autocratic aspirations, supported by a traditional Arabic bureaucracy, and the oligarchic factionalism of the Mamluk emirate. The fiscal bureaucracy itself, or rather the wealth which it created, fuelled factional conflict by adding to the value of controlling the Sultanate, by holding it in person or creating a shadow-sultan. Thus, although al-Nasir Muhammad's descendants reigned until 1382, these were decades of confusion and upheaval, in which real power lay with powerful court figures, such as Yalbogha al-Umari, and shifting alliances of magnates. The old Mamluk approach to the Sultanate was immediately reasserted, so that when al-Salih Ismail was installed as sultan in 1342—the fourth of al-Nasir Muhammad's sons to be enthroned in little more than a year—he had to participate in an accession compact with the magnates. Finally, in 1382, a Circassian Mamluk, Barkuk, usurped the Sultanate, holding it (with one brief period in exile), until his death in 1399.

The failure of the Mamluks to develop the authority and role of the sultan in state affairs is striking; it is symptomatic that the Mamluk sultans did not issue *qanuns* (law codes) as the Ottoman sultans were to do. The long-term stability which was a prerequisite for this was simply lacking. There were no effective safeguards, social or religious, against rebellion. *Khushdashiyya* was ephemeral once erstwhile comrades had their own households. In 1261, after the destruction of Baghdad by the Mongols, Baybars installed a refugee Abbasid prince at Cairo as caliph, and thereafter all the sultans were ceremonially invested with their lands by the caliph, but this did nothing to ensure loyalty. When the short-lived Sultan Baybars al-Jashnikir brought out his caliphal diploma of investiture in an attempt to bolster his collapsing authority in 1310 the act met with derision: 'Tell him he's stupid. Nobody takes any notice of the caliph.' The West learnt of this political instability and looked on it as a powerful advantage. Early in 1348, for example, travellers returning from Egypt brought Pope Clement VI news of the struggle in progress between Sultan al-Muzaffar Hajji and the magnates; now was the time, the Pope exclaimed, to reconquer the Holy Land. But a powerful external threat like a crusade would almost certainly have brought a temporary halt to factional conflict. During the years when crusade planning was at its height, in the 1320s and early 1330s, the Sultanate was enjoying its period of greatest stability under al-Nasir Muhammad; and when Peter I of Cyprus attacked Alexandria in 1365 the response of the regent and dominant magnate, Yalbogha, was swift and effective. Above all, as Professor Holt has stressed, the regular periods of chaos at the centre of power are somewhat deceptive. In his words, the Sultanate was 'a remarkably durable structure with a greater and more effective concentration of military and political power than had existed, except briefly and occasionally, under the Ayyubids'. Objectively, it is hard to avoid the conclusion that the Mamluks would have destroyed any crusade of recovery that the West could launch.

After the conquest of Latin Syria the chief preoccupations of Mamluk foreign relations became their own encroachments on Cilician Armenia, and the continuing threat from the Mongols in Iran. Baybars had directed expeditions against Armenia in 1266 and 1275, and al-Ashraf Khalil made conquests there in 1292. Thereafter, as we shall see in Chapter 6,[3] the Armenians were periodically attacked until Sultan al-Ashraf Shaban overran their Kingdom totally in 1375. In the period leading up to this, frequent Armenian appeals for help to their co-religionists in the West meant that Cilician Armenia played an important role in crusade planning, both because of the need to defend the Kingdom and because of its potential as a base for reconquering Syria and Palestine. Lusignan Cyprus was regarded in much the same way, despite the fact that the Mamluks' weakness at sea prevented them attacking the island in the fourteenth century.

As for the Mongols, events in 1299–1303 showed how serious a threat they could still present. In 1299 the greatest of the Ilkhans, Ghazan, who was hostile to the Mamluks despite his own conversion to Islam, launched an invasion of Syria. He preceded it with a suggestion to King Henry II of Cyprus and the masters of the Military Orders that they should contribute troops, a move which led nowhere but confirmed the wisdom of Mamluk strategy in expelling the Franks from the mainland. In December 1299 the Mongol army crushed the Mamluks at Homs, and in January 1300 it occupied Damascus. For the Christians, the next few months were full of hope. Henry II and the Military Orders undertook small-scale military operations on the Syrian and Egyptian coasts, and in response to appeals from Ghazan, who declared himself willing to return the Holy Land to the Christians, Pope Boniface VIII encouraged preparations for a crusade. But Ghazan proved unable to consolidate his successes of 1299. An invasion in the winter of 1300–1 achieved nothing, and in April 1303 the Mamluks defeated a Mongol army near Damascus.

[3] Below, 180–2.

In 1304 Ghazan died, and after an abortive invasion in 1312–13 the Mongols never again presented a danger to Mamluk Syria. The only Christian gain from Ghazan's successes was Ruad, an island off the coast opposite Tortosa, which remained in the hands of the Templars until the Mamluks captured it in 1302. And although Öljeitü, Ghazan's successor, made several overtures to Philip the Fair, Edward I, and Pope Clement V in the new century's first decade, no alliance was forthcoming. Despite the urgings of the Mongols themselves and of their Armenian allies—for whom collaboration with the Ilkhans had long been a fact of life—the overall lesson for the West of the extraordinary events of 1299–1303 was that regaining the Holy Land through military co-operation with the Mongols was not viable. That formidable task was the burden of western Christendom alone, and in the forty years following the disasters of 1291 it was to invest much energy and substantial resources in attempts to fulfil it.

The news of the Mamluk conquest of Acre was received in the West with consternation rather than horror. The news had long been expected, and feelings of grief about the final loss of the Holy Land were mixed up with widespread distaste for the reputation which the great port's residents had come to enjoy for immoral behaviour. There was no emotional shock wave comparable with the reception of the news of Saladin's capture of Jerusalem in 1187, nor was there the immediate organization of a re-covery expedition like the Third Crusade. Characteristically, recrimination was the order of the day, so that Thaddeo of Naples, who was present at the siege and wrote a valuable description of the city's fall at Messina at the end of 1291, criticized the behaviour of Henry II, the Italian mer-chants, and others. But it would be wrong to conclude that contemporaries were unaffected by the disaster, or that they regarded the Muslim occupation of the Holy Land as irreversible. There was a general con-sensus that the regaining of the Holy Land was the solemn responsibility of all Christians, especially their rulers: Thaddeo of Naples concluded his account with an appeal for a crusade. But this responsibility was usually couched in the context of developments which we have already noted: a growing awareness of the serious problems involved, made yet graver by the loss of the last ports; a resulting strategic finesse which took the form of intricate debate about every aspect of crusade planning; and, most strikingly, a dominant tone of caution dictated by a sense of what was at stake.

Such features might suggest that the crusade had become a matter for experts and rulers, a cold agenda for consideration and argument rather than a genuinely popular movement. Luckily, just a few years after the fall of Acre events took place which demonstrated with unmistakable clarity just how strong the yearning to repossess Jerusalem and the Holy Land still was, and how readily western Christians would contribute to its recovery. News of the Ilkhan Ghazan's victory over the Mamluks at the end of 1299, of the severe disruption which this caused to the Egyptian hold on Syria and Palestine, and of Ghazan's generous offer to allow the Christians to hold the Holy Land, caused a sensation in the West. Catholics whose religious sensibilities were already at unusually high pitch because of Pope Boniface VIII's Jubilee Year, saw Ghazan's successes and offer as a gift from God: 'This is the Lord's doing and it is marvellous in our eyes' (Ps. 117: 23). Some chroniclers wrote that the Ilkhan had conquered Egypt as well as Syria, others that he had liberated Christians captured at Tripoli and Acre, or that he had exacted revenge for the massacres there. These seemingly miraculous events excited the comment of contemporaries more than the fall of Acre: for while only one letter has survived which describes the latter, many deal with Ghazan's triumph. Boniface VIII urged those who had taken the cross previously to set out for the newly recovered Holy Land, James II of Aragon wrote to Ghazan to offer him ships, supplies, and troops, and there are indications that members of the Military Orders in the West expected to return to the Holy Land in the spring of 1300. Some took the cross to fight in the Holy Land, and at Genoa a 'passagium quasi particulare' was set in motion. However ephemeral the excitement, jubilation, and short-lived preparations were, they show that if the miasma of defeat and disillusionment was pierced by just one shaft of light, much enthusiasm remained.

In this context, the proliferation of 'recovery treatises', which was an important feature of the crusading movement in the decades following 1291, ceases to be the outpourings of eccentric enthusiasts which it has often been portrayed as, and becomes a literature expressing, in refined and thoughtful terms, the firm aspirations of many contemporaries. The treatises had antecedents, notably the memoirs composed for Gregory X, but their number, and the depth with which some at least dealt with the subject, was a new feature of crusading; they established a tradition which, as we shall see, became significant also in crusading against the Ottomans in the fifteenth and sixteenth centuries. The first treatise, characteristically entitled 'The Book of the Recovery of the Holy Land'

('Liber recuperationis terrae sanctae') and dedicated to Pope Nicholas IV, was completed in 1291, shortly before the fall of Acre, by a Franciscan friar, Fidenzio of Padua. Fidenzio was well qualified to write: his acquaintance with the Holy Land dated back to 1266, when he witnessed the fall of Safad. He had been asked by Gregory X at the Council of Lyons to prepare an advisory tract, and he had since travelled widely throughout the Middle East. In giving heavy emphasis to the need for an effective blockade of Egypt, discussing at length the relative merits of reaching Syria by land (through the Balkans and Anatolia) and sea, and detailing the numbers of horse and foot needed in the crusade army, Fidenzio proved fairly typical of the many who followed him. In the short term, these included King Charles II of Sicily, who responded to Nicholas IV's appeal for advice with a short memoir chiefly concerned with the naval blockade of Egypt, and Galvano of Levanti, a Genoese physician at the papal court.

Enthusiasm and ideas could not, however, find any expression in practice because the twin problems which had bedevilled the crusading movement since the death of St Louis, acute internecine conflict and the absence of strong and committed secular leadership, continued undiminished. The struggle for Sicily preoccupied the papal Curia, especially in the reign of Boniface VIII (1294–1303), who allowed his attention to be diverted to the Holy Land only on receipt of the news of Ghazan's successes, and then briefly. From 1285 France was governed by Philip IV ('The Fair'), who in the early years of his reign showed less interest in the Holy Land than his father had done; in 1290 he even demanded that the Pope allow him to withdraw the French garrison at Acre. It was to Edward I that many looked as the leader of the recovery crusade: in 1282 the Master of the Hospital voiced the expectations of a generation when he wrote to the King that 'of all Christian princes, you have the matter of the Holy Land most at heart, and have most fully shown your concern in deeds . . .'. Edward received most of the English contribution to the Lyons tenth, as well as a new tenth levied by Nicholas IV in 1291, in order to help him assemble an expedition. But Edward left his crusade vow unfulfilled in the face of the mounting domestic and foreign difficulties which characterized the second half of his reign. In 1294 Philip and Edward went to war over Gascony, and even when this ended, in 1303, Philip faced difficulties in Flanders which persisted until the end of his reign. In 1296–7 there was a major clash between Philip and the Pope on the issue of clerical taxation, and in 1301–3 renewed conflict between the two men ended in Philip's collaboration with the Pope's enemies, the Colonna family, to seize Boniface at Anagni. There could be no question of a general or even a 'particular' passage in these circumstances. Instead the crusade was reduced to the status of a propaganda slogan in the wars between the great powers.

The election of Pope Clement V in 1305 ushered in a period of greater hope. The commitment of Nicholas IV and Boniface VIII to the launching of a crusade to recover the Holy Land had probably been as strong as that of Clement, but the new Pope enjoyed political circumstances which were much more favourable than those confronting his predecessors. The long trauma of the Sicilian war had come to a close with the treaty of Caltabellotta (1302), the Anglo-French war was at an end, and Franco-papal relations were slowly mended. In June 1306 the Pope signalled his intentions by summoning the Masters of the Hospital and Temple to the West to give him advice. The Master of the Templars, James of Molay, was somewhat conservative in advocating a general passage without a preliminary 'particular' *passagium*. An army of 15,000 mounted troops and 50,000 foot should, he reckoned, be transported by sea, resting in Cyprus before attacking the Mamluk coastline. In the same year (1307) Clement received a longer treatise written by an Armenian prince, Hetoum of Corycus, who was Prior of a Premonstratensian abbey near Poitiers. Hetoum was more orthodox than Molay in that he supported a two-stage crusade, both *passagia* of which (not surprisingly) would operate from landings in Armenia. Hetoum was the first of the theorists to include a detailed account of the strengths and weaknesses of the Mamluk Sultanate. His treatise enjoyed a wide reputation and many manuscripts survive.

What offered hope that the enthusiasm of the Pope and the ideas of these advisers might lead somewhere was a significant revival of interest in the crusade at the court of Philip the Fair. Possibly this was due to a change in the King's own character: he became gripped by a highly charged piety after the death of his wife Joan in 1305. Certainly the revival was accelerated by the flourishing cult of St Louis, whom Boniface VIII had canonized in 1297. An extraordinary complex of ideas and senti-ments, what has been termed a 'political theology', had come into vogue at Philip's court. It centred on the themes that the French people and their kings had earned peculiar merit and holiness by their services to Christendom in the past, that these justified France's authority and influence in Europe, and that the continued expansion of the Capetian

monarchy would benefit the Christian faith and Church. One consequence of this was that Philip the Fair asserted a claim to untrammelled
leadership of the crusading movement. Crusade projects, not just those
connected with the recovery of the Holy Land but also the schemes of
Philip's younger brother, Charles of Valois, to reconquer Constantinople,
were again greeted with sympathy at the court, while other aspects of
French foreign policy, such as the Flanders war, were viewed in something of a crusade aura. Throughout at least the next three decades, the
crusade came near to becoming the preserve of the French. For the
papacy, already dominated by the French court and soon to settle at
Avignon, on the edge of French territory, this was a dangerous development; but even some non-French cardinals saw it as the cost of repairing
the rift caused by Boniface VIII, and as the only means of securing the
recovery of the Holy Land.

The association of the crusade with French hegemony over the papacy
and Europe generally is clearly visible in tracts written by Frenchmen
who powerfully propagated the ideas just mentioned. William of Nogaret,
Philip's leading counsellor between 1302 and 1313, wrote a short memoir
in 1310 which insisted that if Philip IV was to lead the crusade, he must
be granted lavish funds raised from rigorous Church taxation, money
which must be placed at his disposal so that the French would not (as,
implicitly, in the past) be confronted with massive crusade debts. More
important was the longer tract, 'On the Recovery of the Holy Land' ('De
recuperatione terre sancte'), written in about 1306 by Peter Dubois, a
Norman lawyer. Dubois's tract was in two sections. The first concerned
itself with the organization of a recovery crusade, like Nogaret dealing
chiefly with matters of finance and military recruitment. The second
half, which was intended only for Philip the Fair's eyes, placed the
crusade in the context of French aggrandizement in the West: thus the
Papal State should be entrusted to the French King, who would subordinate the papacy by securing the creation of more French cardinals,
and extend French influence over the western Empire.

Nogaret advocated the suppression of the Order of the Temple and
the seizure of their property as one means of raising money for the
crusade, while Dubois (like others before him) supported the idea of
uniting the Military Orders to cut out waste. These ideas are revealing of
one powerful factor lying behind the arrest, trial, and eventual suppression
of the Order in 1307–12, the wealth which it was believed to hold and
hopes of using this more efficiently for the good of the crusade. Other

factors were the atmosphere of recrimination and betrayal which still lingered from 1291, and which was channelled into the charges of heresy, sodomy, and idolatry levelled against the knight brothers; and, most importantly, the ruthless dynamism and self-assurance of the French government in the last decade of Philip IV's reign, features rooted in 'political theology' but powered by enormous financial needs. The events of the trial we shall consider in a later chapter.[4] Here it is sufficient to note that they cut like a weal across Franco-papal relations in these years, heightening the suspicions of many cardinals about what French intentions really were, and impeding crusade organization on a large scale. The only military activity which materialized in the new century's first decade was thus a limited *passagium* directed not by a secular power, but by the Knights of St John. The expedition originated in Clement V's discussions with the Master of the Hospitallers, Fulk of Villaret, at Poitiers in 1307. It fitted into the new strategy as a *passagium particulare*, and its goals were the relief of Armenia and the enforcement of the embargo on trade with Egypt. At first Philip IV showed interest in the *passagium*, which would be paving the way for his own general passage. But by the time the papal-Hospitaller fleet eventually set sail from Brindisi, early in 1310, Philip had effectively disowned it.

Others were more enthusiastic. Indeed, as news of the *passagium*'s organization circulated it struck a popular chord in much the same way that rumours of the Mongol victories had a decade earlier. Not only did the Hospitallers collect large sums of money donated to their expedition, but in the spring and summer of 1309 thousands of peasants and town-dwellers in England, northern France, the Low Countries, and Germany signed themselves with the cross and made their way southwards towards the Mediterranean ports, their paths marked by characteristic outbursts of robbery and violence. Many arrived at the papal court and begged Clement V to proclaim a general passage. The Pope knew that it would be hopeless to do so without proper preparations, and the movement died out as rapidly as it had arisen. And yet this very absence of planning for a general passage made the Hospitaller *passagium* a rather pointless enterprise. Cut off from any broader programme of action relating to the recovery of Palestine, the expedition appears to have been used by the astute Fulk of Villaret to consolidate his Order's conquest of Rhodes. The sequence of events epitomized the problems attaching to small *passagia*, perhaps the most serious feature of the expedition being

[4] Below, 210–13.

that even such a minor crusade was extremely costly. None the less, the *passagium* was significant. It showed that the future of crusading in the East lay in small-scale, naval activity; it pointed to the redirection of crusading efforts to Anatolia and the Aegean; and it manifested the ability of the Hospitallers to recast their role in terms of naval operations based on Rhodes.

In August 1308, when Clement V was still struggling to establish a viable and respectable approach towards the French initiative on the Templars, he announced the summoning of a general council, which would meet at Vienne in 1310 to consider not only the question of the Templars, but also the crusade and Church reform. The Council, which did not in fact meet until October 1311, was dominated by the fate of the Templars, but the Order's suppression, decreed by the bull 'Vox in excelso' in April 1312, finally cleared the way for the launching of a recovery crusade. A six-year tenth was levied on the universal Church to raise the money needed for the general passage. Like Gregory X, Clement had called for memoranda giving expert and detailed advice, and the strategy which the crusade would pursue received much attention both at the Council and in its immediate aftermath. King Henry II of Cyprus sent two envoys to the Council to present a memoir in which he argued the case for a more aggressive enforcement of the trade embargo, and for a subsequent invasion of Egypt by a crusade army operating from Cyprus. It was also at the time of the Council that William Adam, a Dominican missionary with extensive knowledge of the East, wrote his tract, 'De modo Sarracenos extirpandi' ('How to destroy the Saracens', that is, the Islamic faith). He agreed with Henry II on the importance of the blockade but, in total contrast, wanted the crusade to follow the land route across the Balkans, which would enable it to conquer Constantinople *en route*.

It is clear from the proceedings at Vienne that the era of ambitious papal planning for the crusade, which originated in the reign of Innocent III and still had an echo in Gregory X's 'Constitutiones pro zelo fidei', had passed. Although the Council's provisions relating to the crusade were wide ranging, they did not constitute a programme of preparations, debated and agreed upon mainly by churchmen and imposed on an obedient laity, comparable to those laid down at the great thirteenth-century councils. Even Clement's plan to amass the sexennial tenth into a single, great crusade treasure foundered on the rocks of jealous national feeling. In fact the summoning of Church councils to launch crusades had become unnecessary: provided secular support was forthcoming the Church could be taxed without consulting its prelates, and what mattered was securing binding obligations on one or more of Christendom's rulers through protracted, exhausting negotiations.

Philip IV's power and ambitions dictated the nature of the forthcoming crusade in the same way that they dominated the proceedings at the Council itself. Thus Philip agreed to take the cross in 1313 and to lead the general passage in spring 1319. The King's cross-taking itself became, as one historian has recently commented, 'one of the greatest ceremonies of the French monarchy'. In the course of a chivalric festival which lasted for eight days, at Paris at Pentecost 1313, Philip, his two brothers, and three sons all took the cross, together with Philip's son-in-law Edward II and many English knights. 'Nobody can remember such a great feast taking place in France', was one chronicler's comment. Display had no counterpart in solid preparations, however, and the magnificence of the occasion barely concealed the fact that huge political and financial problems remained. They had not really come to the fore when both Clement V and Philip IV died in 1314.

Two years later the death also occurred of the Catalan missionary and philosopher who was probably the most original and certainly the most wide ranging of crusade theorists, Ramon Lull. Lull was already 59 when he wrote his first work on the crusade in 1291, and he attended the Council of Vienne at the age of 80; in the intervening period his writings on the crusade were plentiful and ran the gamut of contemporary ideas. Thus in the 'Liber de fine' of 1305 he was so discouraged by the failure of plans for a recovery crusade that he proposed concentrating on the expulsion of the Moors from Granada, at the same time maintaining a blockade of Egypt. Four years later, in the 'Liber de acquisitione terrae sanctae', Lull had returned to backing a recovery crusade, though in line with William Adam he proposed that the crusade take Constantinople first, and he wanted simultaneous operations against Granada. Whether he was propounding the crusade to Granada, Palestine, or Constantinople in writing, undertaking missionary activity at Tunis and Bougie, or travelling to the French, Aragonese, and papal courts to put his ideas in person, Lull was a phenomenally active man as well as a very intelligent one. That he changed his views on the crusade is a useful reminder of the sheer complexity of the crusading world in the early fourteenth century, of the difficulty of deciding where resources could most usefully and viably be directed. This was quite apart from the problem, which looms largest in governmental records, of finding and assembling those resources in the first place.

Such difficulties were not generally appreciated. As the years passed and no crusade set sail, while the Vienne tenth was slowly collected and disappeared into the coffers of the Pope and the secular rulers of Christendom, the original suspicions of many that crusading plans had become a pretext for massive fraud were confirmed. John of St Victor mentioned the popular belief that the levying of the crusade tenth had been the whole point of the Vienne Council. Referring to Clement V's bequest of 300,000 florins to his nephew, the Viscount of Lomagne, on condition that the Viscount lead 500 knights to the Holy Land (a condition never fulfilled), another chronicler commented that

The Pope had the money and the Marquis his nephew had part of it, and the King [of France] and the others who had taken the cross did not set out, and the Saracens are still there in peace, and I think they may sleep on undisturbed.[5]

In view of the constant failures which had overcome crusade plans not only since 1291, but since the reign of Gregory X, and of the massive financial gains which they had entailed for their promoters—two complete sexennial tenths levied on the whole Church, in addition to many regional tenths—it is easy to see why such comments were commonplace in the early fourteenth century. But recent scholarship has proved to be rather more sympathetic to the rulers of the time than their contemporaries were. It is now clear that the crusade discussions and planning which continued in a very active way during the reigns of the last Capetian kings of France, Philip V and Charles IV, and the first Valois king, Philip VI, were based on far more than the expectation of financial profit. These years call for close attention, especially since they formed probably the last period when *recuperatio* was seriously proposed by a major western power.

Debate and negotiations were almost continuous from the accession of Philip V in 1317 to the outbreak of the Anglo-French war twenty years later. They were fuelled by many forces: frequent appeals for assistance from Armenia, the obsession with crusading manifested by some French noblemen, in particular Louis of Bourbon, Count of Clermont, the obligations imposed by the cross-taking of 1313 and the French Crown's use of the Vienne tenth, the badgering of the papal Curia, and of course the crusading zeal of the kings themselves. But

[5] J. N. Hillgarth, *Ramon Lull and Lullism in Fourteenth-Century France* (London, 1971), 83.

equally, the obstacles to the realization of these crusade projects were formidable, not only the continual warfare in Flanders and the growing quarrel with England, but severe internal difficulties which showed how superficial was the glittering image of French power presented by court writers. For it is clear that the aggrandizement of the French monarchy under Philip the Fair had been achieved without establishing royal finances on a sound footing, while centralization created massive regional unrest. For all the soaring claims of the propounders of royal absolutism, any projects which involved heavy expenditure had to be debated at general or regional assemblies, where taxes were granted unwillingly and with many reservations. Court politics were characterized by often bitter conflict, especially that between the *parlement* and *chambre des comptes* factions; the former, which nourished the memory of St Louis, looked with favour on crusade plans, while the latter, which saw mainly the appalling cost involved, tended to resist them. More generally, the French economy was already showing symptoms of dislocation, such as the terrible famine of 1316–17, which made its ability to sustain a military operation on the scale of a general passage highly questionable. It is not surprising, therefore, that a key aim of the French in their crusade negotiations with the papal Curia was to share the financial burden involved with other nations.

In the crusading plans of Philip V (1317–22) and Charles IV (1322–8) the need to rescue Armenia played as important a role as the more problematic and longer-term liberation of the Holy Land. This had the advantage of giving emphasis and point to the organization of a *passagium particulare*, and it is during this period that the ideas of theorists relating to the preliminary expedition received most practical attention. Thus in 1318 Philip V appointed Louis of Clermont as his lieutenant in charge of assembling and leading a *passagium particulare*. Its vanguard, a flotilla of ten galleys, was successfully brought together in 1319 but diverted to, and lost in, the struggle between the papacy and its enemies in Italy. Peace in Flanders in August 1319 enabled the King himself to attend to the crusade and in the winter of 1319–20 he held a series of conferences, to one of which veterans from St Louis's second crusade were expected to come. It was probably from views expressed at these meetings that Bishop William Durand of Mende culled the ideas which he expounded in a crusade treatise. No important measures were taken, except for a decision to restrain the costs of government, but the importance of the crusade in royal policy was vigorously reaffirmed.

In the summer of 1320, however, royal attention was absorbed by the uprising of the *pastoureaux* ('the shepherds' crusade'), a movement which, like its predecessor of 1309, expressed the desires of many common people personally to participate in the crusade whose planning they must have heard about. Coming together around Easter from many regions of northern France, the groups first made for Paris, then proceeded southwards towards Toulouse, Carcassonne, and Albi. Here they massacred Jews and attacked some of the wealthy clergy and laity, and were dispersed or killed by the end of the year. The movement was on a larger scale than that of 1309 and its violence scared the secular and ecclesiastical authorities. But, as in 1309, generalizations about the *pastoureaux* are very hazardous because of their sheer heterogeneity. Many of them genuinely wanted to liberate the Holy Land and would have participated in a general passage had such been organized. Some of the *pastoureaux* bore the arms of Louis of Clermont, and members of the lesser nobility may have figured amongst them. But their less respectable elements could not be controlled, and many saw the chaos associated with the *pastoureaux* as a chance to riot, loot, and settle old scores. That the *pastoureaux* actually impeded the *passagium* which they claimed to want was, of course, pointed out at the time by Pope John XXII, but the movement at least shows that royal projects were not harboured in isolation from popular feeling. The problem was how to harness that feeling in more effective ways.

Unable to raise funds for his crusade either from the Pope, who asserted that the proceeds from the Vienne tenth should be sufficient for a *passagium particulare*, or from his own clergy and burgesses, who firmly rejected royal approaches in 1321, Philip V died in 1322 without fulfilling his crusade vow. His brother and successor, Charles IV, became immersed in crusade plans virtually at the start of his reign. In January 1323 he convened an important assembly at Paris which considered news of the latest Mamluk attacks on Armenia. It responded with detailed proposals for a *primum passagium* in 1323, to be followed by a *passagium particulare* in 1324 or 1325. The papal Curia, which had become used to criticizing French plans as too generalized and vague, found this timetable too tight and the associated financial demands too heavy. John XXII asked his cardinals for their written advice and seventeen of their *consilia* remain. Negotiations became bogged down and, while Amaury of Narbonne, the designated leader of the *primum passagium*, managed to assemble six ships for his expedition, they never set sail. By the end of the year Anglo-French relations had deteriorated over a clash in Gascony, and crusade plans petered out. During the remainder of his reign Charles IV displayed occasional concern for the plight of the Armenians and the healing of the rift with Byzantium, but he did not propose anything as concrete as his plans of 1323.

On the whole, Charles's plans in 1323 were moderate and sensible, incorporating the ideas of men like William Durand and Louis of Clermont, who had by this point accumulated several years of experience in the problems of crusade planning. But simply by being specific they showed how appalling were the financial costs involved: for each year of the *passagium particulare* the King reckoned that 1,600,000 *livres* would be needed. Even the *primum passagium* was expected to run up bills of 200,000 *livres*. With costs on this scale, planning needed to be watertight, and the French project was not; for instance, Charles allowed both his uncle, Charles of Valois, and Louis of Clermont, to believe that they would lead the *passagium particulare*. The project reached Avignon at an unfortunate point, since, as we shall see in Chapter 8,[6] the Curia was becoming more deeply committed to crusading against the Italian Ghibellines. The Pope and cardinals thus seized gladly on both the deficiencies of Charles's ideas and the intractable problem of financing them. But even if political circumstances had been more favourable, and the papal Curia wholeheartedly convinced of the King's sincerity and commitment, Charles's plans would still have encountered the central problem that raising cash on the scale required entailed the taxation of the Church outside France, and that this was becoming increasingly difficult for the Curia.

Few realized the implications of this at the time, and it is possible that Charles IV's failure in 1323 induced at the French court the idea that what was needed was a project for a general passage to the Holy Land. This would compel the papal Curia to grant the French massive taxes collected throughout Christendom, on the model of those decreed at the Second Lyons and Vienne Councils; it would also generate greater enthusiasm amongst the French people, facilitating recruitment and the granting of lay subsidies. Such a project was presented to the Pope by the envoys of Philip VI Valois in February 1332. It was the most important of all the French proposals in this period, and it involved the greatest degree of negotiations, crusade preaching, and taxation since the reign of Gregory X. In turn, Philip's failure caused considerable popular

[6] Below, 244.

distress and resentment, to the extent that the Florentine chronicler Matthew Villani saw the French disasters in the early phase of the Hundred Years War as God's punishment of the King for deceiving Christendom. It is therefore on the basis of Philip VI's aborted crusade, rather than the vague plans of Philip V or the active but short-lived proposals of Charles IV, that the commitment of the French monarchy to the crusade can most accurately be judged.

Crucesignatus since 1313, Philip VI's interest in the crusade after his accession in 1328 was at first directed towards Granada. But in the autumn of 1330 Peter of la Palud, the Patriarch of Jerusalem, returning to Paris from a fruitless diplomatic visit to the Mamluk court, delivered a rousing sermon at court calling for a recovery crusade. Despite pressing domestic concerns Philip responded with enthusiasm and persuaded Pope John XXII to set crusade preaching in motion at the end of 1331. There followed, from February 1332 to July 1333, arduous, complicated, and exceptionally well-documented negotiations between Philip's envoys and the papal Curia. The French succeeded in persuading John XXII to levy a six-year tenth throughout Christendom for a *passagium* which would begin in August 1336. It would be led by the King in person as 'Rector and Captain-general' of the Church, a commitment to which his ambassadors bound him in a crowded consistory at Avignon on 16 July. Then on 1 October Philip and many French nobles took the cross in a chivalric gathering near St Germain-des-Près.

It was almost exactly twenty years since Philip IV's similar pageant at Paris, but if those years had been marked by failure and disillusionment, they had also furnished valuable experience and wisdom. The King established a special committee to handle the crusade, and to it were submitted a treatise by Queen Jeanne's doctor, Guy of Vigevano, and, in 1332, the 'Directorium ad passagium faciendum' written by an anonymous Dominican. The *Directorium*'s advocacy of a land route was rejected by Philip's committee, which insisted on the sea route. Its reasons were sensible, and it seems likely that Philip was contemplating a landing in Armenia. Towards the end of 1333 he therefore agreed to contribute to the league which Venice, the Hospitallers, and the Greeks had formed in 1332 to clear the Aegean of Turkish pirates. The league's planned activities, a *primum passagium* in 1334 and a *passagium particulare* to be led by Louis of Clermont in 1335, in effect gave the French plan the traditional appearance of a three-stage crusade. But, important as it considered the first two *passagia* to be, the French government concentrated its efforts on the general passage. In October 1334, for instance, Philip cancelled Louis of Clermont's captaincy of the 1335 *passagium* in order to have him available for the larger expedition.

The biggest headache in the planning of the general passage was of course its financing. Like St Louis, Philip VI tried to exploit all possible sources of revenue, as well as making savings in governmental expenses. Obviously the King relied on the sexennial tenth to cover much of the cost, but it was clear that the tenth, even if it was successfully levied anywhere but in France itself, would be only partly collected by the time the expedition was due to start. Lay subsidies were essential, and Philip's bitterest disappointment was the total failure of his attempt to negotiate a crusade aid with the towns in 1335–6. At the same time as it became clear that the French themselves viewed their King's crusade project with suspicion, relations with England deteriorated and the emergence of Miles of Noyers as chief adviser signalled the triumph of the anti-crusade *chambre des comptes* faction at court. As early as February 1335 Noyers was sent to Avignon to plead with the new Pope, Benedict XII, for an important concession on the tenth; we do not know what it was, but as both sides became heated Noyers was probably asking for permission to deploy the tenth for other uses than crusade preparations. A year later, as it became clear that the deadline for the *passagium* could not be met, Philip sought, and obtained, the cancellation of the project.

When, early in 1336, Philip VI listed his preparations for the *passagium* to Benedict XII, the document reflected the painstaking diplomacy which had been conducted, but military preparations were few: twelve galleys at Beaucaire and other vessels at La Rochelle and off Normandy, 120 warhorses stabled at Chalon-sur-Saône, some provisions purchased. Wage scales had been issued and some men-at-arms had bound themselves contractually to serve the King. This did not constitute the makings of a general passage which could reconquer the Holy Land. Of course it is possible to argue that Philip was holding his hand until the financial basis for the expedition was secure, but in 1333, when he solemnly agreed on the deadline for the passage, he must have known that the parlous condition of royal finances, the failure of his cousin Philip V's earlier attempt to secure a crusading aid, and the slowness with which Church tenths were collected, rendered it impossible to meet from the start. Since Philip stood to gain nothing from failure but public obloquy, this sequence of events cannot be explained in terms of deliberate duplicity, at least not on the King's part. We must accept that, even after twenty years of active crusade planning, there remained a basic underestimation at the French court of the problems involved in mounting a crusade, an inability to match enthusiasm with the efficient and rapid gathering in of resources.

At the same time, however, it is possible to be over-generous to the French. Philip VI's failure to assemble his general passage and Charles IV's inability to organize his *passagium particulare* can be accounted for in terms of the size and cost of these expeditions, but in 1323 even Charles's *primum passagium* had come to nothing. The fact was that the French only managed to reach the stage of action in the 1334 naval league, when the initiative lay with other powers, and that French ineffectiveness in crusade matters contrasts with their rapid mobilization of their resources to meet the English threat a few years later. There was a lack of urgency, and perhaps an incomplete sense of commitment, on the crusade. In a court dominated by faction, constantly faced by money problems, and slowly sliding into renewed conflict with England, this was perhaps inevitable. When it came down to it, the failure of a crusade plan did not threaten either dynasty or kingdom. So when it became clear that attempts to *realize* such a plan might do just that, through subsequent bankruptcy or attacks on France in the absence of the King or some of his leading commanders, let alone military disaster overseas, crusading was abandoned.

One man who was acutely disappointed by the abandonment of Philip VI's project in 1336, just as he had been by Charles IV's failure thirteen years previously, was the Venetian businessman and crusade propagandist, Marino Sanudo Torsello. Sanudo, who was born in 1270, lived for some time in the Venetian quarter of Acre in 1286 and dedicated his adult life to writing about and arguing for a crusade to reconquer the Holy Land, as well as for a more effective defence of the Latin states in the Aegean. His 'Liber secretorum fidelium crucis' ('Book of Secrets of the Faithful of the Cross'), written between 1306 and 1321, is probably the most thorough and practical of all the recovery treatises. It displays both a knowledge of the East and an appreciation of the difficulties of crusade organization. Like Henry II of Cyprus, Sanudo argued for a landing in Egypt, to be carried out initially by a *parvum passagium* of 15,000 foot and only 300 knights, whose work the general passage would complete. The *parvum passagium* was the cutting edge of the crusade and in voluminous writings and personal meetings with those at the French, papal, and Neapolitan courts who were involved with the crusade or the affairs of the eastern Mediterranean, Sanudo attempted to bring urgency and realism to the planning of the years 1321–34. He not only developed and modified his ideas as political circumstances changed, but made sure that they achieved a wide circulation through multiple copies of his writings: John XXII, King Robert of Naples, Charles IV, Louis of Clermont, and others received copies of the *Liber secretorum*.

The entire first book of the *Liber secretorum* was concerned with the economic blockade of Mamluk Egypt. For Sanudo, as for virtually every theorist since the 1270s, this was the essential corollary to military action, and his approach to the embargo was broadly in line with papal policy of the day. The papacy, which since the Third Lateran Council (1179) had vetoed trade with the Muslims in war materials, attempted from the reign of Nicholas IV onwards to prevent all commerce with lands held by the Mamluks. Given the importance of Alexandria and the Syrian ports for the provision of the West's spices, raw cotton, precious metals, and other vital goods, this was an ambitious policy. Its success depended not only on the ability of the papacy to persuade western governments to give the embargo their backing, but also on the provision of policing galleys which could capture those vessels whose owners defied both Church and secular rulers, and, perhaps most importantly, on the discovery of markets outside the Mamluk territories where the West's commercial needs could be met. In the latter respect Sanudo's suggestions, based on a knowledge of the Levant's geography which was probably unequalled in his time, were particularly astute.

Not surprisingly, however, the papacy failed in all three areas. Between about 1300 and 1340 most Catholic governments along the Mediterranean littoral, including Aragon, France, Genoa, Pisa, Naples, and Venice, formally banned trade with Egypt: according to the Mamluk Sultan no Venetian ship entered his ports between 1323 and 1344. But the bans were temporary, partial, unenforced, or riddled with loopholes. The Venetians, for instance, traded indirectly, using the ports of Cyprus, Crete, and Armenia as entrepôts. As for the enforcing of the ban by a resident *custodia maris*, the only powers which had the naval capacity to supply this—essentially the trading cities of Italy and Aragon—were those which stood to lose by it. The Cypriots and Hospitallers, who warmly supported the embargo and benefited from it through the redirection of western trade, faced powerful retaliation from injured parties when they captured Latin galleys. Thus when the Hospitallers seized a Genoese galley trading with Alexandria in 1311, Genoa paid Turkish pirates 50,000 florins to attack the Knights. One historian has recently described this and similar reactions by the West's leading commercial powers as 'a decisive reverse in the economic war against the Mamluks'. Crusading *passagia* from the West which might help to enforce the ban were, as we have seen, few and short-lived. And while some reorientation of commerce in the eastern Mediterranean did occur, mainly towards Armenia and the ports of the Black Sea, these were politically disturbed areas whose facilities could not compare with those of Alexandria. The Armenian port of Ayas (Laiazzo), which built up a rich trade in the embargo's early decades, was sacked by the Mamluks in 1322 and finally lost to them in 1337.

The ban was therefore broken, first by illicit traders with or without the support of their home governments, and then by the papacy itself. Papal policy started with the imposition of stiff fines on those who confessed to having engaged in trade; characteristically, it then moved towards the issuing of licences in advance to those who wished to trade in merchandise unrelated to war. The first licences, which were issued to the Zaccaria family between 1320 and 1328, were linked to the crusade, since the Zaccaria claimed that they needed to trade with Alexandria to meet the heavy expenses of defending their island-fortress, Chios, against the Turks. Licences on a greater scale were not issued until 1343, when all hope of a recovery crusade setting out had faded, and there was no military rationale for weakening the Mamluk Sultanate by depriving it of the products or revenues of commerce. Trade in war materials continued to be banned, but the licensing system became a rather sordid feature of the papacy's fiscal policy for the rest of the century and beyond. Even during the height of the embargo, there are no signs that the Mamluk Sultanate suffered serious inconvenience; it continued to receive war materials, and the vital slave trade with the Black Sea region was apparently undisturbed. The need to prevent Christians trading with Egypt had been as constant a refrain in the recovery treatises as the importance of securing peace between Christian rulers in the West; and both ran so counter to economic and political reality that they stood no chance of success.

Peace in particular became a wistful dream in the decades following 1337, when the Anglo-French conflict and its many ramifications made the very idea of a recovery crusade a vain hope. Writing to Edward III in 1345, Pope Clement VI claimed that 'the right wars for Christian kings and princes are those through which their temporal realms are not lost but expanded, and through which they acquire for themselves the crowns of the everlasting kingdom'. But for Edward at this point the crown of the Kingdom of France was a greater attraction, while Philip VI had recently gained Clement's absolution for the sin of spending all the proceeds of John XXII's crusade tenth on the killing of English Christians. As we shall see in the next chapter,[7] the 1340s witnessed solid crusading achievements in the eastern Mediterranean, but they occurred in the context of the emerging Turkish threat in the Aegean, and they signified a strategic reorientation which is clearly detectable in the naval league of 1334, and of which the Hospitaller *passagium* of 1310 was an early indication. Then the West was struck by the demographic catastrophe of the Black Death in 1348, and the resulting economic depression made even small-scale crusading activity impossible. The relatively auspicious conditions of the 1320s and early 1330s would never be recovered.

None the less, the revival of plans to reconquer the Holy Land did occur, and it originated in an unusual quarter. Peter I of Lusignan, who succeeded his father Hugh IV as King of Cyprus in 1359, was also, by right of his descent from Hugh III, titular King of Jerusalem. Even after 1291 the title continued to be disputed between the Lusignans and the descendants of Charles I of Sicily, who had found it of some use as a bargaining-counter in their attempts to end the struggle over Sicily through diplomacy. Hugh IV had been crowned as King of Jerusalem at Famagusta in 1324, and Peter I was likewise crowned in April 1359. But Peter, heavily influenced by his Chancellor, the crusading fanatic Philip of Mézières, took the title more seriously than his father had done. In June 1362 he sent a letter to the governments of the West declaring his intention of leading a crusade to recover the Holy Land. The immediate circumstances were not unfavourable. Peter had already distinguished himself as a commander by storming the Turkish port of Adalia (Satalia) in 1361, and the active involvement of a Christian power in the eastern Mediterranean was a feature which had been conspicuously lacking in the earlier French projects. In the West, the Anglo-French treaty of Brétigny, sealed in 1360, both brought a temporary halt to hostilities and presented the problem of finding employment for professional fighting men on both sides who did not want to disband and, if not paid to fight, would simply ravage France's countryside and hold its towns to ransom.

In October 1362 Peter left Cyprus for the West to arrange his crusade.

---

[7] Below, 59–61.

At Avignon, in March 1363, plans were formulated which seemed like a rerun of Philip VI's projected *passagium* thirty years earlier. Thus King John II of France, who may have felt compelled to expiate his father's failure, agreed to lead a general passage two years hence. This would be financed by a six-year tenth on the French church. Peter I, John II, and Cardinal Talleyrand, who was appointed legate for the expedition, were given the cross, together with some important nobles. In May Peter, who was realistic enough to know that this expedition would never materialize, secured more valuable terms when Pope Urban V allowed him to recruit for, and lead, a *passagium particulare* to spearhead the French crusade. Peter then embarked on a lengthy recruiting tour which took him to Flanders, Brabant, Germany, England, Paris, Aquitaine, Prague, Cracow, and Vienna. Everywhere he was generously feasted and promises were made to take part in the crusade. The death of King John in April 1364 had relegated the general passage even more firmly to the realm of fantasy when Peter finally arrived at Venice in November. Here he was delayed by the need to settle a major quarrel with Genoa. Not surprisingly, few of the promises made to send troops were kept, and it was to a large extent with troops hired by the King himself that the *passagium* set sail on 27 June 1365.

Peter's trip to the West had not been entirely fruitless: he had been granted some financial assistance by Urban V and the crusade indulgence facilitated his recruitment. With Cypriot and Hospitaller reinforcements, which reached him when he anchored off Rhodes in August, his fleet reached the impressive total of 165 ships. Peter's army may have numbered 10,000 men and 1,400 mounts, a force not far short of the army earlier reckoned by Marino Sanudo sufficient to conquer Egypt. But Sanudo had counted on the back-up of a general passage. What then could Peter achieve? In his bulls on the crusade Urban V had written, with inexplicable confusion, of Mamluks and Turks as though they could be dealt with simultaneously. It is an extraordinary comment on papal policy at this point that Peter could have attacked either the Turks in Asia Minor, or the Mamluks in Syria or Egypt, without infringing Urban's interpretation of the expedition's purpose. In the event the King decided to attack the great port of Alexandria. The assault, which was launched on 10 October, took place when the city's governor was absent on a pilgrimage, and was successful in gaining control of the beaches and the Pharos peninsula outside the city's walls. Then, by a stroke of luck, the walls themselves were scaled at a vulnerable point. By the end of the day Alexandria was in Christian hands.

The taking of Alexandria was an astonishing feat of arms, the greatest blow the West ever struck against the Mamluk Sultanate. According to one Arab source it yielded more than seventy shiploads of booty. But strategically, owing to the absence of plans for a back-up general passage, the success had no future. In a general debate, rather similar to the one which would be held, in strategically analogous circumstances, twenty-five years later at Al-Mahdiya, die-hards like King Peter, Philip of Mézières, and the legate Peter Thomas argued for defending Alexandria against a Mamluk relief army. William Roger, Viscount of Turenne, pointed out that this was an impossible course of action. The bulk of the army preferred evacuation to almost certain death or captivity; by so doing they earned the reputation, which is hardly fair, of being interested only in booty. The fleet set sail on 16 October for Cyprus, from where the crusaders made their way home. News of what had been achieved elicited enthusiasm at the papal and French courts, but despite the pleas of Peter Thomas, the capture of Alexandria was not followed up.

Ever since the contemporary Arab historian al-Nuwairi suggested seven reasons for Peter I's decision to attack Alexandria, the King's motivation has been debated at length. If we accept his own claim that his expedition was a recovery crusade, then his assault fits into the long-standing strategy, expounded most recently by Marino Sanudo, and earlier by Peter's own great-uncle Henry II, of attacking Mamluk power in Egypt, with the aim of either conquering Palestine or exchanging conquests in Egypt for Christian possession of the Holy Land. According to Philip of Mézières, Peter Thomas argued in such terms at the debate held by the crusaders, talking of 'the possession of the city of Jerusalem through the retention of Alexandria'. Certainly the legate wrote of the liberation of the holy city in the desperate appeal for western assistance which he composed after the abandonment of Alexandria. And Peter I himself included the Mamluk surrender of the entire Kingdom of Jerusalem in his list of peace terms proposed in the summer of 1366. But while this interpretation of Peter I's crusade places it clearly within a respectable tradition of strategic thought and action, it also makes the King look foolishly optimistic about what he could achieve with such an army.

In recent years a very different approach has been suggested by Dr Peter Edbury. He has pointed out that, as a result of the relaxation of the papal embargo on Christian trade with Egypt, the Cypriot port of Famagusta underwent severe decline in the first decade of Peter I's reign. Since Famagusta's main rival was Alexandria, one solution was to capture that port and either to incapacitate it by causing massive damage to its trading facilities, or to hold on to it as a Cypriot conquest. For such an ambitious undertaking western resources would be necessary, which explains Peter's visit to the West and his portrayal of his project as a recovery crusade. This new view fits in with Peter's earlier activities, for his capture of the Anatolian ports of Corycus (Gorhigos) and Adalia made similar economic sense, and it is consonant with the many clauses relating to trade which appear in the Cypriot–Mamluk draft treaty of 1367. Nor does it necessarily entail the portrayal of Peter as an unscrupulous manipulator of his contemporaries' crusade aspirations; for the King could well have believed that his conquest or destruction of Alexandria would do such harm to the Mamluks that the reconquest of Jerusalem would quickly follow. But one flaw in this interpretation is that Alexandria played such a central role in Egypt's economy that Peter I must have known that the Mamluks would do all they could to prevent its long-term occupation by another power, while any amount of damage which might be inflicted would not alter Alexandria's fundamental superiority over Famagusta in geographical terms.

Perhaps more likely is the idea that the sack of Alexandria would reopen hostilities between the Christian world and the Mamluks, that this would persuade the Pope to reimpose his embargo and hence force Italian and Catalan merchants to return to trading through Famagusta. If this was Peter's thinking the King did not succeed. Urban V certainly suspended trading licences in August 1366 on hearing of Mamluk war plans against Cyprus, but the embargo failed, and it was only in 1369, when Genoa and Venice were reluctantly compelled by Mamluk intransigence to organize naval action against Egypt, that a renewed embargo could be effectively imposed. This ban in turn was revoked in 1370, when the trading republics reached a peace settlement with the Sultan. As for Peter himself, he continued his policy of aggression against the Mamluks, planning an assault on Beirut in 1366 and sending out a large war fleet in January 1367. There were Cypriot raids on Tripoli and other ports in northern Syria in 1367, and towards the end of the year the King even went to the West again to attempt to raise further support. After Peter's murder in January 1369 there were more Cypriot raids on the Syrian coast, but in 1370 a Mamluk–Cypriot peace treaty was sealed. It brought to a close the last Christian attempt to recover the Holy Land by force: or at least, an expedition which was actively promoted and depicted as such. It seems appropriate, therefore, that the treaty probably included clauses granting Christian pilgrims access to the Holy Places in Palestine on payment of fixed dues. Henceforth this would be the only way any Christian could hope to see such sacred sites.

What of the Muslim guardians of those sites? Popes Clement VI and Urban V had both been cheered by news of factional conflict at the Mamluk court, but as we have seen, such factionalism was an inbuilt feature of the Sultanate and it did little to weaken Mamluk military strength. The Circassian Sultans, all of them sons of Barkuk or members of his household, who ruled from 1399 to 1461, faced the same endemic instability as their fourteenth-century predecessors, and it was aggravated by a growing tendency for the governors of the Syrian provinces to add their weight to rebellions against the sultan. Barkuk's immediate successor, his eldest son al-Nasir Faraj, thus had to lead five expeditions to Syria between 1406 and 1412; this did not, however, save him from being overthrown in 1412 by one of his father's Mamluks, al-Muayyad Shaykh. When Shaykh died in 1421 his attempt to secure the succession of his infant son failed and it was another of Barkuk's Mamluks, Barsbay al-Zahiri, who seized the Sultanate. Barsbay faced powerful enemies, especially the Emir Janibek al-Sufi, and his attempt to bring about the succession of his son was no more successful than Shaykh's had been. Barsbay was thus followed as sultan by two further veterans of Barkuk, Chakmak al-Zahiri and al-Ashraf Inal, both accessions involving violent usurpation.

Yet some of these rulers were, when free of political turmoil at home, as aggressive and vigorous in their foreign policy as any of the earlier sultans. In 1417 Shaykh led an expedition into Armenia which recovered Tarsus, previously lost to the Emir of Karaman, and reasserted Mamluk power in Cilicia and Elbistan. A year later another Mamluk army even made a brief conquest of Kayseri, the capital of Karaman. These triumphs were overshadowed by the successes enjoyed by Barsbay, who dispatched expeditions to Cyprus in 1424, 1425, and 1426. As we shall see, in the last of these King Janus himself was defeated and captured, and Cyprus subsequently reduced to tributary status. Barsbay also strengthened the Mamluk protectorate over the Hijaz, occupied Jedda to exercise firmer control of commerce passing through the Red Sea, and consolidated Mamluk borders in northern Syria. Chakmak, like Barsbay, showed the naval power of the Sultanate, in his case by sending three unsuccessful expeditions to attempt the conquest of Hospitaller Rhodes, in 1440, 1442, and 1444.

After 1461, however, symptoms of decay began to manifest themselves in the Sultanate. Its roots were economic. The Black Death had cost Syria and Egypt probably a third of their population, and there were twelve severe epidemics between 1416 and 1513. The effects of plague were aggravated by the destruction caused by periodic civil conflict and, in Syria, by the devastation inflicted during the brief but savage invasion of Tamerlane in 1400–1. The long-term damage caused to the Sultanate's agrarian and manufacturing economy by plague and warfare resulted in falling revenues; the land-tax in Egypt, for example, yielded less than two million dinars in 1517, by comparison with nine million three centuries earlier. And this fall in income coincided, in the latter part of the fifteenth century, with soaring military expenditure as the Mamluks engaged in a series of wars in the marcher lands of northern Syria, first to secure their protégés in Elbistan (1468–9), and then with their new rivals in this area, the Ottoman Turks. The two great conflicts with the Ottomans (1485–91 and 1516–17) involved particularly heavy costs, and in the intervening years the sultans faced heavy expenditure in building ships to defend the Red Sea against the Portuguese, who had established themselves in the Indian Ocean after rounding the Cape of Good Hope in 1497.

To fight these essential wars, the government initiated a number of highly unpopular fiscal measures, including sales taxes, which probably accelerated commercial decline. One consequence of the desperate hunt for money was that the sultans had less to distribute to their own household Mamluks in the form of largesse, and this is one reason for the signs of mounting insubordination in the sultan's own household which become visible from about 1450. In the past, sultans had been able to ride the storms of periodic rebellion by their emirs and provincial governors because of the loyalty they could expect from their own households. The withholding of this loyalty made the sultan more vulnerable to rebellion by his magnates. The weakening of the sultan's power was reflected too in the difficulties which the government encountered in keeping control of nomadic tribesmen, both the Buhayra and Sharqiyya of Lower Egypt, and, more importantly, the Hawwara of Upper Egypt, on which the more densely populated Nile delta depended for grain.

Financial difficulties, the faltering authority of the sultan, mutinous royal Mamluks, and, above all, the structural conservatism of Mamluk military society, together explain the Sultanate's most striking weakness in its last years: its inability effectively to introduce firearms into its armies. There were many obstacles to this, notably the lack of copper and iron ore in the

Mamluk territories, the appalling economic conditions, and the political instability which made consistent innovation impossible. But the fierce opposition mounted by the royal Mamluks, which was deeply rooted in the Mamluk élite generally, tipped the balance. The Mamluks, themselves less efficient as cavalry due to the decay of training facilities and discipline, viewed with alarm and disgust the efforts of Sultans al-Nasir Muhammad and Kansawh al-Ghawri to cast more field cannon and train arquebusiers. The latter in particular were seen as a threat to the status as well as the income of the Mamluks. By refusing to handle arquebuses, bullying the sultan's arquebusiers, and declining to change their traditional battle tactics to provide a role for artillery and hand-guns, the Mamluks played a crucial part in preventing the updating of their armies which was essential to defeat the Ottoman janissaries, foot-soldiers armed with hand-guns. The consequence was the great Ottoman victories at Marj Dabiq in August 1516 and al-Raydaniyya in January 1517. The Sultanate was destroyed and both Egypt and Syria were incorporated into the Ottoman Empire.

By that time, as we shall see, the growth of Ottoman strength and the Sultanate's seemingly boundless ambitions had long since come to dominate the crusading movement, and the West's chief response to the Ottoman absorption of the Mamluk lands was to lament the enormous accretion of power which it represented. But it would be inaccurate to conclude from this that the ideal of recovering Jerusalem had ceased to play any role in crusading; for while the active planning of recovery crusades came to an end in 1370, the reconquest of the Holy Land continued for centuries to exercise the imagination of at least some Catholics. Only five years after the Mamluk–Cypriot treaty had been sealed a number of favourable political factors came together and persuaded Pope Gregory XI to revive hopes of a crusade to Palestine. The atmosphere of optimism was short-lived, and by October 1375 the Pope was writing to Queen Joanna of Naples, who had displayed enthusiasm for the crusade, to persuade her to contribute instead to the war against the Turks. Philip of Mézières continued right up to his death in 1405 to argue passionately for a recovery crusade, focusing on the idea of creating a chivalric Order, the Knighthood of the Passion of Jesus Christ, which would help reconquer, and then garrison, the Holy Land. Philip's fascinating moral allegory, 'The Dream of the Old Pilgrim' ('Le Songe du vieil pèlerin', 1389) contained detailed advice on the organization of a recovery crusade. In 1420 a Cretan merchant called Emmanuel Piloti wrote a recovery treatise as detailed and earnest as most of those composed a century earlier. In 1505 King Manuel of Portugal was presented with a marble altar-stone supposedly derived from Christ's tomb, by an envoy of Kansawh al-Ghawri, who had come to protest against Portuguese aggression in the Indian Ocean. It was probably this which incited Manuel, between 1505 and 1509, to pursue tentative negotiations for the planning of a recovery crusade with the English, Castilian, and papal courts.

Even after the Ottoman conquest of Egypt and Syria the idea of a recovery crusade was occasionally revived. In 1609, for example, a Christian resident at Cairo argued that the difficulties which the Ottomans faced in their wars in Hungary and Persia, and the rebellions in Anatolia, presented sented an ideal opportunity to take Alexandria, seize Cyprus, or co-operate with the disaffected Emir of Sidon, and so regain the holy places. Some years earlier Philip III of Spain had been presented with what must surely be the most bizarre of all recovery projects, a proposal that his troops reconquer Jerusalem in association with the Spanish *conversos* (converted Jews, whose Christian faith was under suspicion):

Here it was proposed that the King entrust the conquest of the Kingdom of Jerusalem to that nation [i.e. the *conversos*], by naming a king of that caste and helping this enterprise with a major portion of his troops. With these forces and those they could gather in the whole world they could easily become masters [of the Holy Land] and thereby relieve Spain [of the *conversos*].[8]

Of greater significance than these infrequent proposals for a crusade specifically intended to liberate the Holy Land was the consistency with which that goal is brought into the context of the crusade against the Turks. There are one or two indications that Clement VI allowed himself to consider the liberation of the Holy Land when he appointed Humbert of Vienne leader of the Smyrna crusade in 1345. Fifty years later, during the negotiations which led to the Nicopolis crusade, Charles VI of France wrote of the liberation of the Holy Land as one of the crusade's several objectives. Similarly, the crusade to the Holy Land was linked to that against the Turks at the Council of Constance, while in 1439 the Greek theorist of the anti-Turkish crusade, John Torcello, optimistically reckoned that the reconquest of the Holy Land would follow the defeat of the Turks within less than a month. During the preparations for the Varna crusade, in 1443–4, Pope Eugenius IV and Bartholomew of Genoa, a Franciscan friar, described the recovery of the Holy Land as the expedition's ultimate goal. In 1451 John Germain outlined to Charles VII of

    [8] S. W. Baron, *A Social and Religious History of the Jews*, XV, *Resettlement and Exploration*, 2nd edn. (New York, 1973), 178–9.

France a plan of campaign which would culminate in the recovery of Jerusalem via the reconquest of Anatolia, Cilician Armenia, and Antioch, or alternatively by a naval invasion launched from Constantinople, or through peaceful negotiations with the Mamluks. After the extraordinary crusading victory over Mehmed II at Belgrade in 1456 both the crusaders' leader, John of Capistrano, and Pope Calixtus III believed that the time had come to recover the Holy Land as well as Constantinople. At Rome in 1490 Peter Mansi, Bishop of Cesena, appealed to the nations of Europe not only to defeat the Turks, but also to 'recover yourselves that holy city of Jerusalem, the sacred sepulchre of our Saviour'. Four years later Charles VIII of France proposed both to repel the Ottomans and to recover the Holy Land.

Forging a link between what were, in practice, two very different types of crusade continued to be commonplace in the sixteenth century. The Greek humanist John Lascaris wrote in 1508 of the reconquest of the Holy Land following that of Constantinople. In an appeal for help at the Fifth Lateran Council in 1513 the Hospitaller Giovanni Battista of Gargha exhorted Christian princes to recover both Constantinople and Jerusalem. In 1518 Francis I offered his services 'for the recovery of the Holy Land and for the increase of the faith and Christian religion'. When the treaty of London in the same year brought peace between England and France, Pope Leo X saw it as the opportunity to launch a crusade to regain Jerusalem: 'Be glad and rejoice, O Jerusalem, since now your deliverance can be hoped for.' Pius V alluded to Cyprus's position as 'an avenue of approach' to Palestine when he argued for the defence of the island in 1570. And after the great naval victory over the Turks at Lepanto in 1571, the French humanist Mark-Anthony Muret preached a sermon in Rome in which he declared that the time had come to free Jerusalem. Nor was it only the anti-Turkish crusade which received such treatment: we shall see that Ferdinand of Aragon regarded the ultimate goal of his Tunisian crusade of 1510 as the recovery of the Holy Land.

These instances, which could easily be multiplied, illustrate what was clearly an important impulse to look beyond the crusade against the Turks (and occasionally the Moors of Granada or North Africa) towards the liberation of the Holy Land. What should one make of it? Clearly it disproves the idea that the liberation of the Holy Land disappeared from view once the Ottoman threat loomed large, before or after the conquest of Constantinople. One cannot agree with those who argue, with Professor K. M. Setton, that after 1453 'the recovery of Constantinople rather than of Jerusalem . . . now became the crusading ideal of such Europeans as were moved to contemplate war against the infidel'. And the pilgrim Felix Fabri was quite wrong when he gloomily remarked, in the late fifteenth century, that 'the Holy Land has been so utterly lost to us that no-one so much as thinks about recovering it': some clearly did. But the opposite viewpoint—that Jerusalem and the Holy Land continued to hold a central place within the crusading movement even after the active planning of recovery crusades had ceased—seems to me to be equally erroneous. If that were the case all anti-Turkish crusades would be linked to the recovery of the Holy Land, which they were not. In the instances when they were, it was for one of several reasons. Speakers like John Germain and Peter Mansi were, characteristically, couching their appeals in terms of the rich historical traditions of the crusading movement, in which the expeditions to the Holy Land were of central importance; it was natural for them to link the crusade which they were advocating with those of the past. Similarly, French kings such as Charles VI, Charles VIII, and Francis I could not conceive of crusading without thinking of the example of their predecessors, whose efforts had been largely directed towards the Holy Land. And optimism in the wake of a great victory like Belgrade or Lepanto not surprisingly made the thoughts of men like Calixtus III turn towards the enslaved Holy Land.

Both past success and present ignominy thus kept the ideal of recovering Jerusalem firmly within the living tradition of the crusading movement long after 1370, but they did not allow it to dominate that tradition, or distort overmuch the fruitful new paths which it was following. Reconquering Christ's patrimony was the supreme goal of any crusade, which would, if achieved, give its organizers and participants unequalled glory; but it was in the backs of people's minds, not the foreground of their thinking and planning. Nobody, least of all the thousands who went on pilgrimage there, could forget that the Holy Land was in infidel hands and must, if the chance presented itself, be recovered, but most would have agreed with the realistic thinking which Gregory XI expounded in his letter to Joanna of Naples in 1375: that the Mamluk occupation had been a fact of life for a long time, and that there were more urgent tasks awaiting the efforts of Christians.

2

Greeks, Turks, and Latins: The Crusade in Romania, 1274–1396

✠

WHATEVER the strategic complexities which resulted from the idea of attacking Mamluk power in Egypt, and from the need to defend Armenia and Cyprus, crusading in the south-eastern Mediterranean remained essentially straightforward owing to the continuity of its foremost goal: the recovery of the Holy Land. The same cannot be said of the crusading activity which took place in the fourteenth century in the north-eastern Mediterranean, the area to which contemporaries gave the name *Romania*, and which roughly comprised the lands constituting the Byzantine Empire at the time of the Fourth Crusade (see maps 3 and 4). Latin interests here were complex and contradictory, and papal policy lacking in clarity; above all, there was no tradition of crusading comparable in richness and chivalric connotations with that which had developed in connection with the Holy Land. Despite this, it was in *Romania* that the crusading movement displayed its greatest vitality in the fourteenth century. And for all the complexity of texture, an evolution of ideas and goals is visible in this period, as the West moved from an initial concentration on countering the revival of Byzantine power towards attempts to organize resistance to the Turkish maritime principalities in Anatolia, finally recognizing the Ottomans as Christendom's greatest enemies.

A useful starting-point for the consideration of this evolution is the Greek recovery of Constantinople in July 1261. This put an end to the Latin Empire, the inherently weak state which had been created by the leaders of the Fourth Crusade after their capture of Constantinople in 1204. Byzantine revival had originated both in Epiros and at Nicaea, but the Emperor of Nicaea, Michael VIII Palaiologos, defeated his rival, Michael Doukas, at the battle of Pelagonia in 1259, and it was Michael VIII's troops who took the capital two years later. The Palaiologan restoration prolonged the life of the Byzantine Empire for nearly two centuries, in the course of which it enjoyed a remarkable cultural renaissance and religious revival. But economically and militarily the restored Empire was weak from the start. Michael VIII held little more than a thin stretch of land in Asia Minor, Thrace, Macedonia, and some of the Aegean islands. The rich trade which passed through Constantinople yielded comparatively little revenue since it was largely in the hands of the Genoese who, by the terms of the Nymphaion convention of 1261, paid the Emperor no customs duties. To finance essential rebuilding work in Constantinople, and the construction of a new Byzantine fleet, Michael VIII had to devalue the gold coinage. This debilitated Empire faced powerful enemies. The Turks in Anatolia, the independent kingdoms of Bulgaria and Serbia, and the rival Doukas dynasty at Epiros all posed threats periodically throughout the reign of Michael VIII.

It was the West, however, which most concerned Michael VIII, for the exiled Latin Emperor, Baldwin II, found there not only sympathy but promises of active support for the recovery of Constantinople. Despite his concern about the advance of Baybars in Syria, and the Staufen Manfred in Italy, Pope Urban IV would not, at first, accept that the Latin Empire was a lost cause. The papal Curia had not wanted the Fourth Crusade to take Constantinople, but it had accepted the creation of a Latin Empire as a way of ending the schism between the Catholic and Orthodox churches, and had preached crusades in its support. When he received news of the fall of Constantinople Urban IV therefore proclaimed a crusade on Baldwin's behalf. Like its successors, it was couched in terms of a war against schismatics for the recovery of Catholic territory, with the subsidiary theme of facilitating the crusade to the Holy Land. But even with the guarantee of naval assistance from the Venetians, whose highly favourable trading position at Constantinople had been lost in 1261, a crusade against Michael VIII called for the help of a major western power, and this was lacking. Baldwin himself hoped that King Manfred of Sicily might provide this help, but his efforts to make peace between Manfred and the Pope only alienated Urban, and in the course of 1263 the Curia was led to postpone hopes of retaking Constantinople while dealing with the more immediate Staufen threat. None the less, in the spring of 1264 Urban had a crusade preached on behalf of the Latin Principality of Achaea, which was threatened by the Greeks.

Charles of Anjou's victory over Manfred at Benevento in 1266 was a key event in the development of the anti-Byzantine crusade. Charles continued the Norman-Staufen policy of hostility towards the Greeks, making it much more dangerous than it had been by the combined French and Sicilian resources which he had at his disposal. As the Greek historian Nikephoros Gregoras put it, 'Charles, motivated not by small but great ambitions, implanted in his mind like a seed the resolution of taking Constantinople.' At Viterbo in May 1267 Charles and the Emperor Baldwin sealed a treaty which became the cornerstone of Angevin hostility towards the Palaiologoi in the following decades. Charles would provide 2,000 cavalry to fight for Baldwin. In exchange the King would be given one-third of the conquered territory, besides suzerainty over Achaea. To effect a dynastic link between the two men, it was agreed that Charles's young daughter Beatrice would marry Baldwin's son Philip. By a treaty sealed a few days previously, Charles had agreed with Prince William of Achaea that Charles's son Philip would marry William's daughter and heiress, Isabella. Charles thus planned not only to acquire substantial lands in *Romania*, but also to ensure that his descendants ruled over most of the territory in Christian hands.

But while the anti-Byzantine crusade had gained the backing of a resourceful and brilliant secular ruler, it had lost that of the papal Curia. Charles consistently claimed that his goal was 'to undertake the pious task of restoring the noble limb severed by the schismatics from the body of our common mother, the Holy Roman Church', and his treaties with Baldwin and William were sealed in the papal residence at Viterbo. But Clement IV's approval stemmed from his need to retain Charles's good will in the struggle against the last Staufen, Conradin, rather than from whole-hearted support for the project itself. Papal hopes for a military restoration of the Latin Empire by means of a crusade were counter-balanced by two powerful factors. One was concern about the resulting growth of Angevin strength, which might dominate the Church's temporal power in Italy. The other was the possibility that the schism could be ended through negotiations, an idea which Michael VIII had encouraged since 1261 in order to stave off the threat of a crusade. Michael added the appealing bribe that if Church Union could be achieved he would personally lead troops against Baybars. Just a few days before the sealing of the Viterbo treaties, the Pope wrote to Michael VIII of a pincer thrust against the Mamluks by the Greeks from one direction and Louis IX of France from the other. For the Curia both coercion and negotiation had their attractions, but both were highly problematic. During the next 50 years both options would be extensively pursued.

In the years following his Viterbo treaties Charles of Anjou pursued a vigorous policy of establishing footholds in Greece and the Balkans which he could exploit in the context of papal approval and a full-scale crusade against Michael VIII. His successes included the occupation of Durazzo in 1271 and the overlordship of Albania in 1272. But the crusade eluded him. Clement IV's death in 1268 was followed by a lengthy interregnum, during which Angevin military resources were diverted to Tunisia by Louis IX's second crusade. Then came the election of Pope Gregory X, who was attracted by the prospect of Greek assistance for Palestine and reopened Clement's correspondence with Michael VIII about Union. Charles of Anjou and the Emperor Baldwin were persuaded to postpone their execution of the Viterbo treaty, and the massive preparations made in southern Italy for an assault on Greek territory could not be implemented. With Gregory X desperate to make use of Byzantine resources for his crusade to Palestine, and Michael VIII prepared to offer any concessions to forestall an Angevin attack, Union was achieved with deceptive ease at the second and fourth sessions of the Lyons Council in June and July 1274. The two key moments were the acceptance by Michael VIII's envoys of papal primacy in jurisdictional and magisterial matters, and of the *filioque* clause, the controversial Latin addition to the Apostolic Creed which the Greeks had long condemned as unorthodox.

In the years that followed, however, the hopeful atmosphere which had briefly characterized Greco-Latin relations at Lyons dissolved. News of the Union caused a storm of hostility towards the Emperor at Constantinople, the Unionist Patriarch John Bekkos ruefully commenting that 'men, women, the old and the young . . . consider the peace a war and the union a separation'. Michael VIII's discussions with the papal Curia about a Greek contribution towards the crusade against the Mamluks virtually ended with Gregory X's death in January 1276. Pope Nicholas III was more insistent than Gregory had been about the implementation of Union within the Empire, but he continued to withhold his permission from Charles of Anjou's invasion plans. Charles decided to proceed notwithstanding, and in 1279 and 1280 he ferried large numbers of troops across the Adriatic and began a siege of the key fortress town of Berat in Albania. Here he sustained a serious defeat in spring 1281. But the set-back at Berat was compensated for by two great

Angevin successes elsewhere. At Orvieto in July the Venetians, exasperated by the steady deterioration of their relations with the Greeks, concluded an offensive treaty against Michael VIII with Charles and his son-in-law, the titular Emperor Philip, who had succeeded his father Baldwin in 1273. The Venetians would supply forty armed galleys, the essential seapower for an assault on Constantinople, which Charles had hitherto lacked. Then in the autumn of 1281 the newly elected French Pope Martin IV excommunicated Michael VIII. In March 1282 crusade indulgences were granted to all·who would take part in the Veneto-Angevin expedition, for which Charles of Anjou received some of the proceeds from the sexennial tenth levied at Lyons, together with other crusade funds.

Had it set sail, Charles's expedition would have been an important crusade. But on Easter Sunday 1282 the Sicilians rose against Angevin rule and Charles's preparations were diverted into the first phase of the War of the Sicilian Vespers. Michael VIII's tireless diplomatic activity and massive subsidies to Charles's enemies had helped pave the way both for the rebellion and for the Aragonese invasion which supported it. For the rest of the century there could be no question of an anti-Byzantine crusade; but, with Michael's son Andronikos II (1282–1328) pursuing a policy of animosity towards the West, neither could there be fruitful moves towards negotiated Union. Relations entered a period of stagnation until the marriage in 1301 of Catherine of Courtenay, granddaughter of Baldwin II and titular Latin Empress, and Charles of Valois, Philip IV's younger brother, provided the dynastic conditions for a renewal of Charles of Anjou's schemes, this time in the context of a leading cadet branch of the French royal house. For some years warfare in Flanders and southern Italy prevented Charles harnessing the essential French and papal backing for a crusade against Andronikos II, but in 1306 his plans began to take shape, in much the same way that Charles of Anjou's had in 1281. Thus a treaty with Venice provided Charles with the ships he would need, while Pope Clement V granted Charles crusade preaching, taxes, and other privileges. Most importantly, Charles had the permission of Philip IV to raise an army in France.

Charles of Valois lacked the resources in manpower and money which had been available to Charles of Anjou, but in 1307 it seemed possible that he might compensate for this by securing the services of an élite military force already stationed in *Romania*, the Catalan Grand Company. This mercenary army had arrived in Constantinople in 1303 at the invitation of Andronikos II. After fighting for the Greeks in Anatolia they rebelled against their employers and entrenched themselves, first in Thrace and subsequently in Macedonia. In their conflict against the Byzantines the Catalans raised the banner of St Peter, and depicted themselves as loyal Catholics combating schismatics. It was therefore comparatively easy for Charles of Valois's envoy, Theobald of Cépoy, to enlist the Company in his service. A year later Charles formed an alliance with the King of Serbia, Stephen Uros II, and he also received overtures from noble malcontents within the Byzantine Empire. But what looked like an overpowering threat turned out, as so often, to be a house of cards. Instead of acting as the spearhead of the Valois crusade, the Catalans moved southwards into Thessaly and the Frankish Duchy of Athens, where, as we shall see in Chapter 5,[1] they destroyed the forces of the Burgundian ruler and installed themselves. In the West, Charles had difficulties collecting his crusade taxes and lost his title as Emperor when his wife died in 1308. The Venetians, frustrated by Charles's failure to fulfil his side of the treaty, concluded a twelve-year treaty with Andronikos II in 1310.

In April 1313 the young Catherine of Valois, sole offspring of the marriage between Charles and Catherine of Courtenay and titular Latin Empress, was married to Philip of Taranto, a younger son of King Charles II of Naples. The union had been proposed by Pope Clement V and Philip the Fair as the best means of bringing about the long delayed reconquest of Constantinople, since Philip of Taranto had lands in the Balkans and Greece which might serve as the springboard for action. A year previously, the Pope had granted Philip crusade indulgences, and some of the proceeds from the Vienne tenth, to assist a planned expedition to Achaea which would defend it against the Greeks advancing from their holdings in the south. Thus the initiative in the anti-Byzantine crusade returned to the Kingdom of Naples, but to a *Regno* severely weakened by the loss of Sicily, and to a cadet branch of the ruling house. Philip the Fair, and later Philip V, were ready to promise their Angevin kinsmen French support, but papal and Neapolitan commitments in Italy deprived the new titular Emperor of the resources necessary to plan a major expedition. So although he made initial advances to Venice in 1320, Philip concentrated on consolidating his position in Achaea. Even crusade theorists, some of whom, including Ramon Lull, Peter Dubois, and William Adam, had earlier espoused the cause of reconquering Constantinople, were by the 1320s losing interest in it. The anti-Byzantine crusade had effectively come to an end.

[1] Below, 161–4.

How significant a feature of the crusading movement had it ever been? It is tempting to dismiss these projects as a crude hotchpotch of Angevin and Valois dynastic ambition, Venetian commercial greed, and Latin religious intolerance, dressed up in crusade clothes by a compliant papacy. But that would be simplistic. Naturally these elements were present, and historians have quite rightly viewed both Charles of Anjou and Charles of Valois as the latest in a long line of western rulers and princes, stretching back to Robert Guiscard and Bohemund of Taranto at the time of the First Crusade, who were irresistibly attracted by the wealth, prestige, and self-assurance of Byzantium, and who were equally anxious to portray their ambitions as a form of holy war. But the plans of the period 1261–*c*.1320 were also characterized by less self-seeking features: a sense of outrage at the continuation of a damaging schism, shock at the loss of a great patriarchal city, and a genuine conviction on the part of many that the repossession of Constantinople would facilitate the recovery of the Holy Land. Throughout the late Middle Ages, as we saw at the end of the last chapter, crusading enthusiasts had a grasp of geography which was tenuous enough to permit the belief that not only Constantinople but even North Africa were milestones to Palestine. Naturally this belief was stimulated, indirectly, by Michael VIII's well-publicized assurances that he would send an army to accompany Gregory X's crusade. It is notable that Clement V, Charles of Valois, and Louis of Clermont, all passionate enthusiasts for 'recuperatio terre sancte', were also supporters of the anti-Byzantine crusade. Whether these plans for reconquest had any popular appeal is an impossible question to answer since none of their proponents ever launched a major campaign of crusade preaching. It is also largely irrelevant, as nobody wanted a *passagium generale*: what was needed was a comparatively small force of professionals paid for by church taxes, effectively a *passagium particulare*, and the anti-Byzantine crusade should be envisaged not on the scale of the recovery of the Holy Land, but on that of the relief of Armenia and Cyprus.

The 1320s, which witnessed the end of active crusade planning against the Greeks, also saw the resumption of papal-Byzantine negotiations for Union. In 1324 Andronikos II sent the Genoese Bishop of Caffa to the West to reopen talks, and in the following years the crusade theorist Marino Sanudo Torsello eagerly took up the cause on the Emperor's behalf. In 1326 more envoys came from Constantinople to both Avignon and the French court, and although popular animosity towards the Latins forced Andronikos II to call a halt to this tentative *démarche* in 1327, there were further negotiations under his grandson Andronikos III (1328–41), notably the mission of the Calabrian monk and humanist Barlaam in 1339. What propelled the Greeks into undertaking these talks was no longer fear of the West, but hopes of gaining western assistance in defending their lands against the Turks. In these circumstances the crusade in *Romania* moved away from the glittering prize of Constantinople itself, towards the western coast of Anatolia and the Aegean islands and trade routes.

It was impelled to do so by the aggressive naval activities of the Turkish *ghazi* emirates. In the early thirteenth century the Seljukid Sultanate of *Rum* (Anatolia) organized a number of marcher governments, commanded by emirs, along its borders with Byzantium. With a population composed of semi-nomadic Turcoman tribes grouped around hereditary leaders (beys), and refugees or exiles from Seljukid rule, these marcher principalities were virtually autonomous and fundamentally unstable, their chief feature being their vigorous engagement in frontier warfare with their Greek neighbours. When the Seljukid Sultanate was first challenged by the Khwarazmians in 1230, and then subjugated by the Mongols in 1243, the emirates both became less susceptible to central control, and received large numbers of displaced persons who added to their militancy. In 1277 the Mongol *Ilkhanate* reacted against rebellion by its Seljukid dependants by taking over direct rule of Anatolia, but the centre of Mongol power in Persia was too distant for this rule to be effective, and there were constant revolts against overlords felt to be oppressive and resented as non-Muslims. Gradually, in the last decades of the century, the entire peninsula began to break up into independent Turkish principalities (*beyliks*).

Inland, the most important of these was Karaman, which from 1314 was based at the former Seljukid capital of Konya (Iconium) and whose rulers came to regard themselves as the heirs to the sultans. To its north-west the principality of Germiyan established its capital at Kutahya, while those of Dulkadir and Eretna originated in the first half of the fourteenth century in the upper Euphrates and on the north-eastern borders of Anatolia. At the same time the marcher principalities of western Anatolia began to take identifiable shape. The first was that of Menteshe, which, like many of the new principalities, was named after its founder. As early as the 1260s Menteshe, a coastal bey, grouped several seaports in the southwest under his personal rule, and by 1282 he had expanded northwards as far as Tralles and Nyssa. Then, in the early fourteenth century, no fewer than three beys sent from Germiyan to wage war against the Byzantines succeeded in founding principalities on land won from the Greeks: Mehmed, the son of Aydin, that of Aydin; Sarukhan Bey that of Sarukhan; and Qalam and his son Karasi, that of Karasi.

The formation of hereditary *beyliks* or emirates gave Menteshe, Aydin, Sarukhan, and Karasi political cohesion, but it did not for some time change the distinctive frontier culture of these regions. *Ghazi* groups (*ghazi boluks*) led by renowned warriors, often coming together from several *beyliks*, continued to seek every opportunity to gain booty (*ghanima*) and prestige by fighting the infidels, their exploits being celebrated in epics. Heterodox religious sects flourished. But at the same time the beys presided over courts in prosperous towns like Denizli, Balikesir, and Birgi, which impressed al-Umari and Ibn-Battuta in the 1330s. They controlled ports like Ephesus (Ayasolug) and Miletus (Balat) which played an important part in commerce between Anatolia and the West. The profits from this enabled the beys of these maritime principalities to hire discharged Greek sailors, construct large numbers of galleys and other vessels, and to deploy them against western ships and lands in Greece. *Ghazi* warfare, with its distinctive organizational and cultural features, thus took to the sea, al-Umari deploying the term 'sea *ghazis*' to describe those who fought. Between about 1310 and 1330 the Venetians and others thus began to suffer attacks like those which the Byzantines and Armenians had endured for decades. The Turks, whose military operations had been almost entirely land-based for two centuries, made an explosive entry into the Aegean world. Umur Bey of Aydin in particular became famous for his naval exploits: in about 1330 al-Umari saw Umur's war as possessing the consistency and ferocity of a *jihad*, and in the 1460s the Turkish poet Enveri celebrated Umur's exploits in a chapter in his *Dusturname*, which remains one of our best sources for the character of the *ghazi beyliks*. In 1318 Venetian official documents began to take notice of Turkish attacks, and in 1325 the Republic first considered forming a league (*societas*) of threatened Latin powers to deal with them. Two years later the Venetian Senate decided to send letters to its leading officials in Crete, Negroponte, and Constantinople instructing them to begin talks about such a league with Andronikos II, the Master of the Hospitallers, Martin Zaccaria, lord of Chios, and others.

It was from this Venetian initiative that the anti-Turkish crusade sprang, and it is notable that its characteristic form, the naval league made up of the contributions of several Christian powers, was there from the start. The papacy was not averse to granting crusade indulgences for fighting Turks; it did so as early as 1322 in the context of defending the Peloponnese, and consistently regarded the struggle against Turkish aggression in the Aegean and elsewhere as an *opus* or *negotium fidei* (work or matter of the Faith), which possessed just as much crusading validity as the struggle against the Mamluks. But the Curia of Pope John XXII was too preoccupied with its wars in Italy and, by the early 1330s, with Philip VI's proposals for a *passagium generale*, to take the lead. The Venetians, however, pressed ahead, and in September 1332 they were rewarded with success. A five-year league was formed, consisting of ten Byzantine, six Venetian, and four Hospitaller vessels. No action resulted in 1333 but during the winter of 1333–4 Philip VI, Hugh IV of Cyprus, and John XXII agreed to contribute to the squadron, which reached a total, on paper, of forty galleys. The ships proceeded to the East in 1334 and in September inflicted a defeat on the fleet of the Bey of Karasi in the gulf of Adramyttion.

The 1334 league was in some ways disappointing. A renewal of operations was planned for 1335, but nothing came of it. In these circumstances Marino Sanudo Torsello's prediction that the Turks would hide in their ports while the fleet was in the East and emerge after its departure to do fresh harm came true. There were other problems. The division of Turkish naval strength into a number of mutually antagonistic emirates, which was a boon in so far as it stopped the Turks concentrating their power, also made it hard to know where to strike. No defeat had been inflicted on the most dangerous of the maritime beys, Umur, and his seapower and range of operations grew alarmingly in the late 1330s and early 1340s: he was able to muster 350 vessels for an expedition to the mouth of the Danube in 1341, and two years later led an army 15,000 strong. Although he had been a signatory to the 1332 agreement, Andronikos III had not taken part in the league, the first sign of the difficulty of organizing effective Latin–Greek co-operation. Soon after 1334 the *basileos* came to terms with Umur, even accepting the latter's suzerainty over Chios and Philadelphia. And, as we saw in the last chapter,[2] the league had been clumsily fitted into the theoretical role of a *primum passagium* in Philip VI's crusade plans. The anti-Turkish crusading league had yet to achieve independent status in the crusading

---

[2] Above, 34–5.

movement; in this respect the 1334 league, like the Hospitaller *passagium* of 1309–10, played a transitional role.

More important were events which took place ten years later. In 1341 Hugh IV of Cyprus and the Master of the Hospitallers sent envoys to the papal court to beg for assistance against mounting Turkish aggression. They arrived at an opportune moment. The new Pope, Clement VI, was an expansive and energetic personality. He wanted to direct Christian energies in a crusade and had himself, as a negotiator for Philip VI, become familiarized with the complex but heady plans of the early 1330s. With the long-term postponement of plans for the recovery of the Holy Land, the effective failure of the papal embargo on trade with Egypt, and the Anglo-French conflict depriving Clement of any access to English and French clerical revenues and crusading enthusiasm, it made sense for the Pope to seize the offered initiative in *Romania*. Clement therefore responded positively to the pleas for help and sent a legate to Venice to form a new league. In 1343 arrangements were finalized for a league which would be based mainly on papal, Hospitaller, Cypriot, and Venetian contributions. To finance the galleys which he agreed to provide, Clement VI levied taxes on selected Church provinces and decreed crusade preaching to raise extra funds. These crusade measures, together with the agreement of the league's participants that it would last for three years and operate solely in *Romania*, represented the emergence of the anti-Turkish naval league as an autonomous form of crusade activity, and one of the most characteristic of the late medieval and Early Modern periods. In various combinations it would enjoy an existence of more than two centuries, achieving its greatest success in 1571 at the battle of Lepanto.

As a military operation Clement VI's league was small scale: probably fewer than thirty galleys took part, compared with the hundreds which fought in the great Veneto-Genoese naval wars of this period. In addition, the league shared with its successors the constant bickering over finance, leadership, and strategy which seemed to be inseparable from Christian co-operation. None the less, it was strikingly successful. The galleys assembled at Negroponte in the spring of 1344, and inflicted a serious defeat on the Turks at Pallene on or about Ascension Day (13 May). Then on 28 October the Christians attacked and took Umur Bey's chief port, Smyrna (Izmir). This success, which seems to have been owed largely to Umur's absence from Smyrna at the time of the assault, was a *coup de main* not dissimilar to the capture of Alexandria in 1365; but unlike the great Egyptian port, Smyrna remained in the hands of its captors. Even after the break-up of Clement VI's league a garrison continued to hold Smyrna, led by a captain appointed by the Pope. The captain and his soldiers were supposed to be paid by the former members of the league, and although payment was slow, partial, and usually in arrears, the very existence of this Christian foothold on the Anatolian coast was a reminder of what Clement's league had achieved, and a stimulus to his successors to try to renew it. Finally, faced with the imminent loss of Smyrna to Turkish attack in 1374, Pope Gregory XI transferred custody of the port to the Hospitallers, who held it until Tamerlane's conquest in 1402.

The news of the capture of Smyrna caused considerable excitement when it reached the West at the end of 1344. Even the deaths of the league's leaders in a disastrous sortie in January 1345 did not dampen the resulting optimism. This led to one of the most pathetic crusading ventures of the period, the expedition of Humbert II, the Dauphin of Viennois. Humbert's interest in the league derived not from fear of the Turks or hope of material advantage, but from a long-standing obsession with chivalric values—he founded the secular Order of St Catherine—and an indisputable piety. Initially at least, the Curia did not regard an expedition led by Humbert, whose military reputation was dubious, with any enthusiasm. In May 1345, during prolonged festivities at Avignon, Humbert persuaded Clement VI to appoint him 'captain of the holy Apostolic See and leader of the whole army of Christians against the Turks'; but these grandiose titles gave him neither the financial backing of the Church nor any real authority over the forces of the league. The situation was complicated by the wave of crusading enthusiasm which swept parts of the West in 1344–6. Prompted by exaggerated rumours of a great victory over the Turks, by miraculous signs of God's favour, and, at L'Aquila in southern Italy, by a vision of the Virgin, several thousand people took the cross, especially in the north Italian cities. Clement VI encouraged this, interpreting the enthusiasm, and Humbert's leadership, as a divinely bestowed opportunity to follow up the foothold at Smyrna with a major expedition: what would in effect constitute a *passagium particulare*. But the Pope seems to have given little thought to what this expedition would do in Anatolia, and Humbert could not control the crusaders, very few of whom were bound to him by ties of allegiance or contracts.

The result was a dismal failure. Humbert set out from Venice in mid-November 1345, but he failed to take the rich and strategically important island of Chios, which was seized by a Genoese fleet under Simon Vignoso. Humbert went on to Smyrna, arriving in late June 1346. The substantial Christian forces there suffered from inadequate provisions and disease, and they could not dislodge the Turks from the port's fortress. Apart from strengthening Smyrna's fortifications and conducting a few sorties, there was little that Humbert could usefully achieve. The Venetians, having lost Chios to the Genoese, were half-hearted about further action and the Dauphin, himself now ill, sailed to Hospitaller Rhodes and spent the winter there. Humbert had sworn to remain in the East for three years, but in November 1346 Clement VI allowed him to return home early. A truce was to be negotiated with Umur. In May 1347 Humbert was back at Venice. His departure was followed by another naval victory over an allied Turkish fleet, this time near Imbros, and although there were negotiations with the Turks and a draft treaty was worked out in the winter of 1347–8, Clement desperately tried to keep the league in activity. In August 1350 the Pope even announced the formation of a modified league, with contributions from the Venetians, the Cypriots, and the Hospitallers. But this renewal was frustrated by the outbreak of the Third Veneto-Genoese war (1350–5), and Clement's league was suspended.

Thanks to a Latin superiority in naval warfare which would continue into the fifteenth century, Clement VI's league was able to achieve several heartening victories in isolated naval engagements with the Turks. And by merely holding Smyrna the crusade dealt a crippling blow to Aydin, which now had difficulty reaching the Aegean, and lost its predominance amongst the *beyliks*. This was no mean achievement. However, the league proved unable to exploit its unexpected capture of Smyrna to extend its grip on the Anatolian littoral. No doubt this failure was due partly to Humbert of Vienne's dilatory and pliable leadership, but three factors of a more general nature were surely of greater significance. The first was the debilitated economic conditions and acute political divisions of the West itself; as the Pope himself acknowledged in anguished letters to Humbert, these prevented Church taxes being collected and stopped *crucesignati* setting out to fight. This in turn highlights the point that Clement VI's success in originally promoting the league hinged on its limited size: it did not call for the amassing of resources which had so hindered earlier projects for the recovery of the Holy Land. The second factor was a basic division of goals amongst the partners in the league. Clement and, in so far as we know their wishes, the Hospitallers and Cypriots, wanted the league to last for several years, and thus serve as a long-term deterrent against Turkish naval aggression. But the Venetians favoured a burst of hard-hitting action which would compel the Turks to negotiate, as well as securing useful gains for the Republic; at this point they would rely on diplomacy, either in conjunction with their allies or independently. By 1353 they had negotiated a sound commercial agreement with Hizir Bey, Umur's brother and successor. Thirdly, beyond defeating the Turks at sea Clement VI's strategy was vague, and prone to optimism and misguided liberality: this was shown not only in his agreeing to the 'upgrading' of the crusade in 1345, but also in his earlier instruction to his legate, Henry of Asti, to send help to the beleaguered Armenians. Had this been done, it would have constituted the division of naval resources which were already perilously small.

None of these factors would have mattered so much had Clement's league, and its successors, operated within a context of Greco-Latin co-operation, along the lines envisaged in 1332 when Andronikos II subscribed to the prototype of the 1334 *societas*. But both of the prerequisites for such a context, a strong and vigorous government at Constantinople and a feeling of mutual trust and shared goals between Greeks and Latins, were conspicuously lacking. The deep-rooted internal malaise already apparent in Michael VIII's reign only worsened in those of Andronikos II and III. Andronikos II's rigorous economies, which included the drastic reduction of the army and the total disbanding of the navy, added to the Byzantine Empire's vulnerability without solving its fiscal crisis: massive debasement continued and the Emperor could not effectively tap either the landed wealth of the nobility and monasteries, which passed governmental taxes on to the already overburdened peasantry, or the trade passing through imperial territory, which was monopolized by the customs-exempt Italians. In wars against Venice (1297–1302), the Catalan Grand Company, and the Turks, Andronikos II reigned in an atmosphere of constant crisis, aggravated after 1321 by the rebellion of his grandson Andronikos III.

By contrast, the victory of Andronikos III in 1328 inaugurated a brief period of relative success, marked by the reconquest of Thessaly and Epiros. There were signs that the Byzantines might be able to effect a reorientation of the Empire away from Anatolia, now almost wholly lost to the Turks, towards Greece and Thrace. Had this been achieved, it would have given the Empire greater geographical unity, strengthening its internal lines of communication and probably accelerating the emphasis on its Greek nature which was already a notable feature of Byzantine cultural and religious life. But the Emperor's death in 1341 provoked a terrible civil war between his leading counsellor, John Cantacuzene, and Andronikos's wife, Anne of Savoy, who was defending the rights of their eldest son, the nine-year-old John. In the course of the ensuing conflict Cantacuzene employed Turkish troops, and by the time a political settlement was reached in 1347 the Turks had thus won a vital foothold in Europe. In addition, the Serbs had overrun Thessaly and Epiros, the financial resources available to the Emperor had been yet further depleted, and the Byzantine economy ravaged by war and plague. In terms of territory, the Empire now consisted of little more than the four cities of Constantinople, Thessalonica, Adrianople, and Didymoteichos, with parts of Thrace, Philadelphia and a few isolated fortresses in Asia Minor, and the southern Morea. The collapse of Byzantine power, even from the position maintained by Michael VIII, had been remarkable; and it was dramatically demonstrated by the humiliating naval defeat which the Greeks suffered at the hands of the Genoese in 1349. The Empire had shrunk from the status of a second-rate power to that of a third-rate one.

Naturally this heightened the appeal of Church Union and the concomitant Latin aid. But negotiations were plagued by mutual mistrust, and hence by a basic problem of timing; for the Greek envoys argued that only the appearance of western assistance in the form of a crusade would persuade their people that the Latins were trustworthy and thus win them over to Union, while the papal Curia believed that the Greeks would renege on any agreement once western help had solved their immediate difficulties. As Pope Benedict XII put it: 'If the Greeks are strengthened . . . by ourselves and others of the faithful before the said Union [is achieved], they will afterwards turn their backs on us and the Church.' This problem helped to frustrate the important mission led by Barlaam in 1339, after which there were few contacts between Constantinople and Avignon until John V Palaiologos became sole Emperor in 1354. The gap, caused partly by the internal convulsions of the civil war and Clement VI's unwillingness to become involved in it, constituted a missed opportunity of some importance, since these were the years of greatest papal interest in the affairs of *Romania*. By 1348, when John Cantacuzene reopened negotiations and even specified the numbers of troops whom he would contribute to a crusade, Clement was talking of disengaging his resources from the struggle in the Aegean. This new *démarche* therefore came to nothing, and in any case the league's own activities demonstrated that a simple linking of Byzantine and Latin interests in *Romania* was impossible. In the first place, the Greeks harboured residual fears that a crusade might act as a disguise for western aggression, and in the second, the chief concern of the Byzantine government was not the piracy of the coastal *beyliks*, but the threat posed by the inland principalities in the immediate vicinity of Constantinople.

By 1350 it was clear that the most dangerous of the emirates was that founded at the end of the thirteenth century in eastern Bithynia by Osman. Later Ottoman chroniclers, intent on glorifying the ruling dynasty, used mainly oral traditions to concoct an impressive genealogy for Osman. They developed the idea that he was directly descended from the mythical Oguz Khan; they also claimed that Osman had been the designated heir to the Seljukid Sultan Ala ed-Din II, and that Osman had experienced a prophetic dream which his father-in-law, the dervish Edebali, had interpreted in terms of God granting Osman rulership of the world. In reality few facts are known for certain about Osman before he started to become a threat to the Byzantines in the first decade of the fourteenth century, and thereby began to figure in the pages of their chroniclers. The earliest surviving royal inscription in the first Ottoman capital, Bursa, attests that Osman's son, the Sultan Orhan, bore the title '*mujahid*, Sultan of the *ghazis*, *ghazi* son of a *ghazi*', and it may be that from the start the Osmanlis placed a greater emphasis on holy war than other marcher beys did; but if this was so it was not because they possessed an inherent sense of mission, but because they had the huge practical advantage of sharing a border with the Christian Byzantines. This enabled them to attract followers and maintain a powerful expansionist drive. In addition, it is likely (though virtually impossible to prove) that from the mid-1330s the partial containment of the maritime *beyliks*' expansionist drive by the crusading leagues assisted the Ottomans by channelling *ghazi* recruits northwards and away from the coast.

In 1302 Osman inflicted his first big defeat on the Greeks, at Baphaeon near Nikomedia. He went on to occupy Melangeia, survived attempts first by the Catalans and then by the Mongols to oust him, and by about 1310 had effective control of the lands adjoining the Sea of Marmora and the south-western coast of the Black Sea. His major objective was the city of Bursa, but this was too well fortified and garrisoned for the Turks to take until the rebellion of Andronikos III stopped the Byzantines sending reinforcements to the city, leading to its fall in 1326. With Bursa as capital, the Ottoman principality began to take shape under Orhan (1326–62). Mongol suzerainty was renounced, coins minted, and a basic administration established, staffed largely by jurists from the inland cities of Anatolia. Bursa was already 'a great important city with fine bazaars and wide streets' when Ibn Battuta visited it in 1333, and Orhan went on to build an impressive complex of buildings there. At the same time he virtually completed the Turkish erosion of Byzantine Anatolia. A big expedition led by Andronikos III in person was routed at Pelekanon in 1329, and Nicaea fell two years later. Nikomedia was taken in 1337, Scutari in 1338. Inroads into the rival *beylik* of Karasi brought Orhan's troops to the Straits of Gallipoli.

A crucial event in Ottoman history was of course the crossing of these straits, and we have already seen that it was the war between Anne of Savoy and John Cantacuzene which furnished the opportunity to achieve this. In 1345 John's Turkish ally, Umur of Aydin, was unable to provide him with troops because of the recent Christian capture of Smyrna, and the Emperor turned instead to Orhan. The Ottoman Sultan responded by leading more than 5,000 men into Thrace. By an irony of history, it was thus a crusade which indirectly provided the circumstances for the Ottoman penetration of Europe. Initially the Ottomans served John Cantacuzene reasonably well, so that in 1346 the Emperor married his second daughter, Theodora, to Orhan. But in the longer term the Turks proved scarcely more amenable as allies than the Catalans had been, and Cantacuzene had to allow them to raid at will throughout Thrace. More importantly, in exchange for Ottoman help against Serbian and Bulgarian attacks, Cantacuzene had to cede Orhan the fort of Jinbi on the Gallipoli isthmus. From 1353 Orhan's eldest son, Suleyman, began to use the base at Jinbi to establish permanent conquests, and in 1354 a valuable alliance with Genoa gave the Ottomans the naval assistance they needed. In the same year an earthquake destroyed many of the fortifications of Gallipoli and enabled the Turks to occupy and refortify it. Large numbers of *ghazi* warriors were now brought across to Europe, and in 1356 John V Palaiologos, unable to oust the Turks, was forced to recognize their conquests. From this point onwards the city of Constantinople was virtually cut off from the West: 'Are not all of us within the walls caught as if in the net of the barbarians?', was Demetrios Kydones's comment. In staving off the massive threat posed by Stephen Dushan's Serbian Empire, John Cantacuzene had thus inadvertently paved the way for the Ottoman conquest of Constantinople a century later.

The rapidity of the Ottoman advance in north-western Anatolia and Thrace in the 1350s, together with a decline in the threat posed by the southern emirates after the death of Umur Bey in 1348, persuaded Clement VI's successor, Innocent VI, to broaden papal policy in *Romania* and concede the idea that crusading aid might be directed further north. This was facilitated by the definitive victory of John V Palaiologos over John Cantacuzene in 1354, for John V proved to be more committed to Union than any Byzantine Emperor since Michael VIII. At the end of 1355 he sent a chrysobull to Avignon in which he suggested a remarkable solution to the familiar deadlock about whether Union or Latin aid should come first: this was that Innocent should organize a two-stage crusade, the first and lesser *passagium* not only paving the way militarily for the big crusade, but also showing the Greeks that their co-religionists could be trusted and hence persuading them to accept Union. The two-stage crusade, originally designed to deal with the problems of crusading to the Holy Land, was thus proposed as a remedy for the very different problems of *Romania*. The chrysobull also contained extravagant promises about the enforcement of Union in Constantinople and far-reaching guarantees intended to allay western suspicion about the Emperor's sincerity.

Even if Innocent VI believed these promises, he was effectively hamstrung by the West's debilitated condition and by its chronic state of war. An attempt in 1356–7 to revive Clement VI's naval league got as far as the drawing up of provisional terms for the arming of a handful of galleys, but subsequently foundered. Then in 1359 Innocent made what was, given the limited resources at his disposal, a major effort: Peter Thomas, the Bishop of Coron, was appointed legate in the eastern Mediterranean, crusade preaching was ordered in Italy and the Latin territories in the East, and a tenth was levied to help pay the new legate's expenses. At the same time important measures were taken for the better management of Smyrna's defence, but Innocent's choice of Peter Thomas, who had carried out an important embassy to Constantinople in 1357, shows that the Pope was not averse to the extension of crusading activity northwards, where it was most needed. It is not surprising, therefore, that while Peter Thomas made an inspection of Smyrna's defences on his arrival in the East, he quickly sailed to the Dardanelles with the galleys provided by the Venetians and Hospitallers. Combined Byzantine and western forces stormed and sacked the Turkish fortress town of Lampsakos, opposite Gallipoli.

Since the taking of Lampsakos probably represented the first occasion since the twelfth century that Byzantine and crusading forces co-operated in the field, it was an event of some significance; but in the absence of negotiations for Union, which had petered out in 1357 and did not resume until 1364, it could have no sequel. Peter Thomas' was preoccupied in the following years by affairs at Smyrna, on Crete, and, increasingly, in Cyprus. He supported King Peter I in his aggressive policy towards the Turks of southern Anatolia, and Peter I used the galleys which Cyprus was contributing to the league in his occupation of Corycus in 1360, and his seizure of Adalia in the following year. With the initiative in the hands of Peter I, crusading activity in the eastern Mediterranean was drifting southwards, and in 1363, as we saw in the previous chapter,[3] Peter persuaded Pope Urban V to sanction a renewal of former plans to recover the Holy Land. The crusade which resulted was irrelevant to the needs of the Greeks. In these circumstances the Latinophile group at Constantinople, led by the Grand Logothete Demetrios Kydones, encountered growing opposition from the Orthodox party which promoted the alternative idea of the Balkan Slavs assisting Byzantium in its plight.

Some outside help was clearly essential, for the growth of Turkish power in Thrace was alarming. In 1361 they took Didymoteichos. Orhan died in 1362 and was succeeded by Murad I (1362–89), the first great Ottoman ruler. During the early years of his reign Murad expanded the borders of his Anatolian holdings towards the east, but he concentrated his efforts on Thrace. With no seapower and little infantry at his disposal, Murad could not beseige Constantinople, but he took a series of major towns, including Philippopolis in 1363. Murad was still a *ghazi* leader, albeit on an unusually large scale, and attempts to interpret his activities in these years as a systematic strategy of conquest are unconvincing; but it was obvious that the Sultan, because of the size of his territories, their position straddling Europe and Asia, and the aggressive drive which lay behind them, presented a uniquely potent threat. Urban V thus made a clumsy attempt to fit an anti-Turkish campaign into his plans for a *passagium generale* to the Holy Land; more importantly, the Pope tried in 1365–6 to persuade a number of different Catholic powers, including Louis of Hungary, Peter of Cyprus, Count Amedeo VI of Savoy, and the Genoese, to go to John V's assistance. It was in order to beg for such help in person that John V undertook an extraordinary journey in the

[3] Above, 39–40.

winter of 1365–6 to the court of Louis of Hungary at Buda. Returning empty-handed from this visit, the Emperor suffered the even greater humiliation of imprisonment by the Bulgarians.

This was the situation when, in June 1366, Amedeo VI of Savoy, the only ruler to answer Urban V's call, set sail from Venice at the head of a modest force. Amedeo's crusade originated in the Franco-Cypriot project formulated at Avignon in 1363, but by the time the Count was able to muster his small army of 3,000–4,000 men the general passage had long been abandoned and Peter of Cyprus had withdrawn from Alexandria. The Venetians falsely informed Amedeo that Peter I had made peace with the Mamluks, bringing hostilities in the south to a close. Amedeo therefore sailed instead to *Romania*, a natural destination since John V was his cousin. He appears to have hoped that King Louis of Hungary would lead an army with which he could co-operate, but when he arrived at Negroponte at the beginning of August there was no news of Hungarian preparations, and Amedeo wisely took local advice to attack Gallipoli, the principal disembarkation point for the Turks in Europe. Gallipoli was taken in August and Amedeo then sailed on to Constantinople. His achievement was already considerable, but there was more to come. Hearing of his cousin's imprisonment in Bulgaria, Amedeo sailed up the coast of the Black Sea, took the ports of Mesembria and Sozopolis, and laid siege to Varna as a means of putting pressure on the Bulgarians. John V was released, joining Amedeo on the coast, where they wintered together before returning to Constantinople in the spring of 1367. The Count left for the West in June 1367.

Clearly it will not do to exaggerate the importance of Amedeo's crusade, but his success was notable, especially when it is compared to the fate of Humbert of Vienne's expedition twenty years previously; and since Amedeo owed his success largely to his own willingness to co-operate with the Greeks, it affords a glimpse of what might have been achieved had such co-operation been more frequent. As it was, Amedeo's crusade, in conjunction with the mounting Turkish threat, gave the pro-Union lobby at the Byzantine court the stimulus it needed. So although a major Greek embassy to the papal Curia in 1367 met with a disappointing response, John V decided to undertake a visit to the West to make a personal profession of faith. The Emperor arrived at Naples in early August 1369 and entered Rome some weeks later. In October John V made a declaration of faith, both in person and in writing, in which he accepted the beliefs taught by the Roman church and acknowledged papal primacy. This was an important event, and had both protagonists been in a position to do what they claimed, it might have been a turning-point in history. But John V proved unable, in the years that followed, to persuade his clergy and people to follow his example, while Urban V could muster little assistance from the West. Letters flowed out from the papal chancery, but Peter of Cyprus was assassinated in 1369, Louis of Hungary was no more ready to help than he had been in 1366, and the Genoese and Venetians would not take action by themselves.

It was probably in 1369, the same year that John V made his fruitless visit to the West, that Byzantium suffered its greatest blow yet in Thrace when a force of Turks seized Adrianople. Murad moved his capital to the city, renamed Edirne, thus signifying his intention to make his existing holdings a springboard for expansion into the Balkans. Constantinople and the residual Byzantine lands along the Sea of Marmora were left as a prize to be taken when circumstances permitted. For the remaining twenty years of Murad's reign Ottoman conquests in Europe seem to have followed a strategic pattern dictated by the roads, valleys, and mountain passes of the south-eastern Balkans. In the centre the Turks pushed up the Maritza valley; to the east, they followed the Black Sea coast and passes through the eastern Balkan range; to the west, Turkish forces led by Evrenos Bey, a renegade Greek, had as their main objective Byzantium's second city, Thessalonica. Murad enjoyed the great advantage of a splintered and mutually antagonistic opposition. The Serbian Empire had broken up after the death of Stephen Dushan in 1355, and now offered less resistance in the west than might have been expected. The Bulgars too were disunited, and they faced the attacks of Louis of Hungary, who seized Vidin from them in 1365. Louis himself, whose lands included parts of Wallachia, Moldavia, and Croatia as well as Hungary and Transylvania, displayed little concern at the Ottoman threat and faced internal problems which hindered the efficacious deployment of his vast resources. He failed to make use of the crusade privileges which Urban V granted him in 1366 to fight the Turks, and when he did assemble an army two years later it was in order to renew hostilities with the Bulgars.

In 1371 two prominent Serbian princes, Ugljesa and Vukasin, organized an army to march on Adrianople. On 26 September it engaged the Turks at Crnomen on the Maritza river, about twenty miles west of Adrianople, and suffered a severe defeat. Pope Gregory XI was appalled, believing that the Turks would now flood into Macedonia, Albania, and Thessaly, even perhaps Achaea and southern Italy. In line with established papal policy in *Romania*, Gregory made an attempt to organize a united response by all the threatened Christian powers, summoning them to a congress at Thebes. The congress never met, and the Pope was reduced to negotiating with individual powers, especially the Genoese, Louis of Hungary, and the Hospitallers. Louis was granted crusade preaching against the Turks in 1373 but once again failed to make use of it. The Fourth Veneto-Genoese War kept the West's leading naval powers out of the anti-Turkish conflict between 1376 and 1381. All that Gregory XI proved able to arrange was a minor Hospitaller *passagium* which, when it finally set sail in 1378, was deflected into landing in Albania and achieved nothing of note. In fact it was becoming clear that crusading in *Romania* had to change in nature if it was to deal with the Ottomans. Naval leagues like those maintained by Clement VI and Innocent VI, and expeditions like those led by Humbert and Amedeo, were on too small a scale to inflict any real damage. A general passage overland was needed, preferably in conjunction with considerable naval activity in the Aegean, the Dardanelles, or the Sea of Marmora. In this context the failure of the Hungarians to co-operate, either with Amedeo's *passagium* in 1366, or with the Hospitallers in the 1370s, was symptomatic of troubles to come.

The Turks did not fulfil papal fears by flooding into Greece and Italy in the years following Crnomen: instead Murad continued his patient strategy of piecemeal expansion in all three directions. In the centre the Sultan captured Sofia in 1385 and Nish in 1386, sending his raiding partics as far as Bosnia. In the north John Sisman, Tsar of the Bulgars, was forced to accept Ottoman suzerainty. Meanwhile the Greeks endured the erosion of their few remaining territorial holdings. John V Palaiologos became a tributary of Murad in 1372–3 and was thereafter compelled to provide troops for the Sultan's campaigns. Murad regained Gallipoli in 1377, while Evrenos Bey occupied Serres in 1383 and took Thessalonica in 1387. At this point a Serbian prince called Lazar succeeded in co-ordinating Christian resistance and inflicted defeats on the Ottomans in 1386 and 1388. Others joined him, John Sisman renouncing Murad's suzerainty and even the Wallachians promising help. For the first time the Ottomans encountered the problem of war on two fronts, for in 1387 Murad had to fight against the powerful principality of Karaman, whose rulers were justifiably alarmed at recent Ottoman gains in central Anatolia. Murad defeated his Turkish enemies, partly through the novel use of firearms, then returned to Europe. Early in 1389 Ottoman troops overran

Bulgaria as far as the Danube, reducing Sisman to suzerainty again. Then, on 15 June, the coalition of Balkan princes engaged Murad's army at Kossovo. The Sultan was killed during the battle, but his son Bayezid smoothly took over command and the Ottomans won one of their greatest victories.

For the Christians, Kossovo was more terrible than Crnomen, for it showed that the Ottomans could defeat a united Christian army (though it was true that the allied forces were plagued by internal squabbling), even when their commander died in the middle of the battle. In addition, by confirming the Turks' occupation of Bulgaria and facilitating their rapid conquest of most of Serbia, Kossovo set the seal on the Ottoman conquests in the Balkans. Despite his ability to mobilize considerable resources and his commitment to *ghaza* warfare in the cause of Islam, Murad I had been reluctant to bring lands there under direct rule; he generally preferred to establish firm suzerainty over Christian rulers with whom he shared borders, thus gaining valuable military contingents and avoiding the danger of over-extending his frontiers and lines of communication. Bayezid reacted to Lazar's coalition by imposing direct rule, but this meant neither the expropriation of the local aristocracy nor compulsory Islamization. In the course of time massive Turkish immigration, initially into Thrace and the Maritza valley, made the eastern Balkans a predominantly Muslim region: the town of Skopje, which was captured in 1391, had by 1455 twenty-two Muslim quarters compared with only eight Christian ones. But in most of Serbia and Bulgaria the Ottoman conquest brought much less far-reaching change. Professor Inalcik noted that as late as the mid-fifteenth century a large proportion of land in parts of *Rumeli* (as the Ottomans called their Balkan lands) was held by Christian nobles of military origin and proven loyalty to the sultans. Christians paid a special tax but there were no constraints on worship or persecution of the clergy. This policy was based not solely on religious tolerance, but on convenience and the desire to prevent local discontent which might foster rebellion in connivance with a crusade. It was outstandingly successful.

These massive territorial gains in the Balkans, together with those achieved in Anatolia, accelerated in the early years of Bayezid I's reign changes in Ottoman military and political organization which had begun under Murad I. The most important of these was the transformation of the army. The Turkoman *ghazi* cavalry who fought for the Ottomans because of religious zeal and the hope of booty were increasingly used as advance troops, raiders (*akinjis*) placed on the borders of the Sultanate to prepare the way for further conquest. Salaried cavalry (*musellems*) and infantry (*yaya*) were already in use under Orhan, and as the Ottoman territories grew these were gradually settled on conquered lands. For this purpose the sultans adapted the Seljukid *iqta*, the 'fief' receiving the new name *timar*. Provincial administration was essentially an offshoot of this military system, since the *timar*-holders were given responsibility for keeping the peace and collecting taxes within the localities, and were eventually grouped into a hierarchical structure of *alays*, *sancaks*, and *eyalets*, whose forces were commanded by *alay* beys, *sancak* beys, and *beyler* beys (governors). Ottoman society thus acquired its fundamental division into two classes: the *askeri* (ruling, military class) and the *reaya* (subject, civilian class).

But the most distinctive feature of Ottoman military organization was the growth alongside the *akinjis* and *timar*-holders of a third force. Murad I began the practice of training slaves won through capture in war as élite regiments of infantry (*yeni ceri*/janissaries = new force) and cavalry (*sipahis*). These *kapi-kulus* grew in number during Bayezid's reign, thanks to his encouragement of the *devsirme* system, a periodic levy of able Christian children for the service of the Sultan. The Ottomans owed many of their military victories to the *kapi-kulus*. In addition, the existence of a large body of troops obedient only to the Sultan was a powerful disincentive to provincial rebellion (although it diminished in time, as the *sipahis* were increasingly granted *timars* and assimilated with the Turkish aristocracy). Ottoman centralization also owed much to its readiness to learn from a number of models, especially the classical Arab, Turkish, and Byzantine, which all contributed to the radical change from an informal and personal tribal leadership to a complex and structured administration. For example, the position of sultan itself, thanks to the influence of the many Byzantine and Bulgarian princesses who married into the ruling dynasty, acquired some of the ceremonial aloofness of the *basileos*. The Seljukid office of vizier was developed to handle government business both in the provinces and in the central administration, the grand vizier becoming the chief executive officer in about 1360. And long-standing Arabic fiscal techniques were brought into play to regularize the growing number of *timars*.

In addition to promoting these large-scale changes in Ottoman government, Bayezid I was forced, during the early years of his reign, to engage in virtually ceaseless campaigning in Anatolia and the Balkans.

In 1390 the Sultan defeated and annexed the principalities of western Anatolia, Aydin, Sarukhan, and Menteshe, together with the remnants of Hamid and Germiyan. A settlement was reached with Karaman, and Bayezid then turned back to Europe. He strengthened the Ottoman hold on the region adjoining Constantinople, placing the city under virtual blockade in 1394, encouraged Evrenos Bey to invade Thessaly and send raiders into the Morea, and defeated the Bulgars, who had rebelled again. In 1393 John Sisman's capital of Trnovo was taken, the Tsar was captured (he suffered execution two years later), and the whole of Bulgaria brought into the Sultanate. Fresh campaigning against Qadi Burhan al-Din, the powerful Sultan of Sivas, resulted in more gains and the organization of the province of *Anadolu*, incorporating all the Ottoman lands in Asia Minor. This rapid movement back and forth between Asia and Europe earned Bayezid the title Thunderbolt (*Yildirim*), but the size of the Sultanate was starting to cause serious logistical problems, which were aggravated as Bayezid reacted to rebellion by his vassal-princes by annexing their lands. In addition, his gains brought him into direct contact with two powerful new neighbours, Tamerlane in Anatolia and the Kingdom of Hungary in Europe. King Sigismund of Hungary (1387–1437) took the lead in co-ordinating Christian resistance to Bayezid in the Balkans. He also made great efforts to arouse interest in his cause in western courts. The result was the most important crusade organized against the Turks in the fourteenth century, and the most severe crusading defeat since the days of St Louis.

Sigismund's appeals for help were successful largely because of a remarkable revival of interest in crusading at the royal courts of England and France. Since 1378 the ability of the West to send assistance to its fellow-Christians in *Romania*, already severely impaired by the Anglo-French conflict, had been further weakened by the Great Schism in the papacy. Not only had the Roman and Avignonese obediences been preoccupied with their own quarrel, they had also made vigorous attempts to channel crusading energies into the resolution of that struggle by military means. As we shall see in Chapter 8,[4] the political and dynastic dispute between England and France thus acquired an edge of religious animosity as each side regarded the other as the abetter of schism. From 1384, however, with the first truce in the Anglo-French war since 1369, an atmosphere of reconciliation began to predominate at the French and English courts. During the crusade planning of the 1360s the idea had

[4] Below, 247–8.

been popular of the crusade forming an outlet for professional soldiers discharged by the two monarchies. This practical approach to the problem of peace was now revived, and on to it was grafted a broader-based, idealistic programme of ending the Schism and sealing the Anglo-French peace, by launching a crusade which would unite Christendom and epitomize the shared chivalric culture of the two nations. As Charles VI of France put it in a highly significant letter to Richard II in May 1395:

by virtue of this peace between us . . . our mother, Holy Church, crushed and divided this long time by the accursed Schism, shall be revived in all her glory through the prayers of the most gentle Virgin Mary. Then, fair brother, it will be a fit moment . . . that you and I, for the propitiation of the sins of our ancestors, should undertake a crusade to succour our fellow Christians and to liberate the Holy Land . . . And so through the power of the Cross we shall spread the Holy Catholic Faith throughout all parts of the East, demonstrating the gallantry of the chivalry of England and France and of our other Christian brothers.[5]

Dr John Palmer has shown that a key role in promoting these ideas was played by Philip of Mézières, former Chancellor of Peter of Lusignan and tutor to the young Charles VI. From the mid-1380s onwards Philip wrote a series of works relating to the crusade. More importantly, his crusading Order, the *Nova religio passionis* ('New Order of the Passion'), functioned as a formal means for the chivalric nobility of England and France to express their commitment to the crusade: most of the eighty or so knights who enrolled in it, or promised their support, between 1390 and 1395 came from the two monarchies, and they included many of the most important English and French magnates. Four prominent members of the Order, John of Blaisy, Robert le Mennot, Louis of Giac, and Odo of Grandson, were dubbed by Philip his 'four evangelists', and three of them played a significant part in diplomatic exchanges between the two courts. But the commitment and personality of Philip, his writings, and even his chivalric Order, would have exerted much less influence had they not existed within a distinctly favourable background. The crusading enthusiasm of many individual nobles at this time is shown by the Duke of Bourbon's crusade to Al-Mahdiya in 1390, and by the Earl of Derby's expeditions to Prussia in 1390 and 1392, which we shall examine in future chapters.[6] Such enthusiasm, however, was common to much of the late thirteenth and fourteenth centuries: what

[5] J. J. N. Palmer, *England, France and Christendom, 1377–99* (London, 1972), 180.
[6] Below, 286, 355.

was unique about this period was the sustained and altruistic backing given to it by government, especially in the years following the truce of Leulingham in 1389. Dr Palmer has gone so far as to remark that the 1390s 'have left more traces of genuine good feeling and of active and even enthusiastic co-operation than . . . any other period of the Middle Ages'.

The beginnings of active crusade planning can be traced to 1392, with tentative initiatives by Charles VI and his uncle, Philip the Bold of Burgundy, whose enthusiasm for the crusade dated back nearly thirty years. In the following year a small Anglo-French force was sent to Hungary, and in 1394 Richard II, Philip the Bold, and Louis of Orleans sent separate embassies to Sigismund's court. In July 1394 Philip wrote of a crusade which would be led by himself, Louis of Orleans, and John of Gaunt, and which would set out early in 1395. It was only in the course of 1394 that its objective was fixed as Hungary rather than Prussia, but this uncertainty about the expedition's goal did not prevent its leaders making extensive preparations. Philip the Bold succeeded in raising the money needed for the Burgundian contribution, primarily by levying special taxes on his territories, while both Gaunt and Orleans seem to have got royal support. By the end of the year Gaunt had re-cruited 1,500 men-at-arms for his force, Venice had made a provisional agreement to provide naval assistance, and Sigismund was committed to fielding an army in the spring of 1395. The Pope of the Roman obedience, Boniface IX, issued crusade bulls in June and October decreeing preaching in the Balkans, Austria, and Venetian lands; his example was later followed by his rival, Benedict XIII. The foundations had been well laid for a major Anglo-French expedition.

The year 1395, however, brought disappointments which transformed the nature of the crusade. The Hungarians, who had agreed to send envoys to Venice early in January to complete arrangements, proved dilatory, and it was not until May that their ambassadors met the Dukes of Burgundy and Orleans at Lyons. By this point a campaign in 1395 was out of the question, and a revolt in Gascony combined with an Anglo-French dispute over Richard II's marriage to induce Gaunt to delegate the leadership of his troops to his illegitimate son, John Beaufort. Louis of Orleans pulled out altogether and Philip the Bold entrusted the leadership of the Burgundian forces to his eldest son, John of Nevers. Thus the crusade lost its character as a symbol of Anglo-French amity, as well as the experienced war leadership of Gaunt and Philip the Bold.

It became a Burgundian enterprise, John of Nevers's household of some 150 men-at-arms forming the core of an army composed chiefly of knights from Burgundy and other French principalities. Other promin-ent leaders included John of Boucicaut, Philip of Artois, and John of Vienne (the Marshal, Constable, and Admiral of France), Enguerrand of Coucy, Henry of Bar, and James of Bourbon. Their combined experience of crusading, whether in *Romania*, North Africa, or Prussia, was immense. After elaborate preparations at Dijon, John of Nevers led the bulk of the expedition from Montbéliard at the end of April 1396.

Travelling via Regensburg and Vienna, the Franco-Burgundian army reached Buda in late July. Here it was joined by other units which had journeyed eastwards independently, notably Enguerrand of Coucy's contingent. Any description of the campaign and battle which followed is vitiated by the weakness of the sources. Western narrative accounts are either, like Froissart's, ill-informed and fanciful, or they are coloured by the need to explain an appalling defeat, and therefore present the crusading army as an immoral and badly disciplined rabble which brought catastrophe on itself. Ottoman sources are laconic, their writers, with the benefit of hindsight, portraying the crusade as a minor episode compared with the threat looming from Tamerlane in Anatolia. Inter-pretative problems start with the advice which King Sigismund is said to have proferred at Buda, that the army should take up a defensive posi-tion, thus forcing Bayezid's troops to carry out a long and tiring march. If such advice was given, it did not take account of the difficulty of keeping a large fourteenth century army, crusading or otherwise, intact and provisioned in a stationary position. The strategy adopted, of ad-vancing deep into occupied territory in Bulgaria, met this requirement and forced the Sultan to take the field against his opponents as quickly as possible. It was not an unwise strategy, and if the Christian campaign achieved nothing else, it compelled Sultan Bayezid to lift his siege of Constantinople, giving the Byzantine capital a valuable breathing-space. Thus the first steps in the campaign consisted of successful assaults on the Turkish fortresses of Vidin and Rahova, and they were followed by the investment of the key Danubian fortress of Nicopolis. It was here, on 25 September, that the decisive battle took place between the Franco-Burgundian and Hungarian forces, and a relieving army led by Sultan Bayezid, who had reluctantly relaxed his blockade of Constan-tinople to deal with the invasion. Each side probably numbered between 10,000 and 20,000 men.

After summarizing the conflicting accounts of the battle of Nicopolis given by the leading narrative sources, including that of the Bavarian John Schiltberger, who was captured in the battle, Professor K. M. Setton observed that

Froissart, Boucicaut's biographer, and the chronicler of S. Denis all claim to have derived their accounts of the battle from eyewitnesses. There is no reason to doubt them, and no reason to doubt that Schiltberger was captured at Nicopolis. In the hand-to-hand combat of the era, however, neither commanders nor common soldiers really knew who was winning . . . Battles did not take place on a given spot; they extended over a mile or two or more. An eyewitness knew what was happening to him and to those around him, but he knew little else. As time passed he learned more from other 'eyewitnesses', and each time he told his tale it grew taller.[7]

This judicious note of caution notwithstanding, the crucial mistake made by the Christians in the battle seems clear enough: that the French cavalry insisted on being in the vanguard of the Christian attack, despite Hungarian advice that it be kept in reserve to deal with Bayezid's heavy cavalry, the *sipahis*, whom the Sultan could be expected to shelter behind his infantry and lightly armed troops. The result was that the western men-at-arms had to fight their way through two lines of Turks before encountering the main body of Ottoman horse, who outnumbered and slaughtered their tired opponents. Christian defeat was made certain by the desertion of Sigismund's Wallachian and Transylvanian auxiliaries. One of the Sultan's Christian vassals, the Despot of Serbia Stephen Lazarevic, defeated the Hungarian forces. Christian losses were heavy. Sigismund escaped, but amongst the dead were John of Vienne and William of la Trémoille, the Marshal of Burgundy, while the captured included John of Nevers, Marshal Boucicaut, Philip of Artois, and Enguerrand of Coucy.

There can be no doubt that Nicopolis was not only one of the most crushing crusading defeats *per se*, but also ranked amongst the most important in terms of its long-term repercussions. If Crnomen and Kossovo showed that the Ottomans could crush the rulers of the Balkan states in pitched battle, whether they fought independently or in conjunction, Nicopolis represented an alliance between western crusaders and Hungarian troops meeting with the same fate: predictably, the author of

[7] K. M. Setton, *The Papacy and the Levant (1204–1571)*, i, *The Thirteenth and Fourteenth Centuries* (Philadelphia, 1976), 355.

Marshal Boucicaut's biography claimed that the Hungarians deserted their French comrades during the battle. So although the existence of 'front-line' Christian states directly imperilled by the Turks and well-acquainted with their military ways should have made the organization of crusades and their management easier, the reality turned out to be very different. In addition, as Dr Palmer has observed, the Nicopolis crusade had been envisaged as the advance guard, effectively the *passagium particulare*, for a second, bigger expedition which would be led by Charles VI and Richard II in person, as outlined in Charles's letter quoted above. He has argued that the Wilton Diptych, a masterpiece of late medieval English art, portrays Richard vowing to lead this general passage alongside Charles VI. The defeat at Nicopolis made this second crusade impracticable; moreover, it was ammunition for English opponents of Richard's policy of peace with France, with which the crusade plans had been associated. So although, as we shall see in the next chapter,[8] a certain amount of French and English aid, in both men and money, was sent to the Emperor Manuel II in the years following Nicopolis, there was no further attempt to organize a combined Anglo-French expedition. The Lancastrian revolution of 1399 finally put an end to the unique atmosphere of idealism and co-operation which had underpinned the planning of the early and mid-1390s. The political background to the Nicopolis crusade was irrecoverable.

The only bright feature of the aftermath to Nicopolis relates to Burgundy's involvement with the crusading movement. For Philip the Bold, the severity of the defeat was aggravated by the need to ransom John of Nevers and other important figures captured in the battle. Finding and transferring the 200,000 ducats agreed on in June 1397 as their joint ransom placed a large strain both on the Duke's relations with his subjects (who had only recently paid special taxes for the campaign itself) and on Burgundian bureaucracy; at least one debt incurred in connection with the ransom was still outstanding in 1403, and it has been estimated that the total cost of the ransom arrangements probably reached half a million francs. Yet one of the most remarkable aspects of the Nicopolis crusade is that these sums could be found without any long-term damage to Burgundian state finances: the contrast with the financial problems faced by the French court when attempting to assemble crusades earlier in the century is striking. Crusading had not become less expensive in the mean time; rather, there had appeared a state whose

[8] Below, 80–1.

rulers enjoyed financial resources commensurate with the costs involved. Just as important was the fact that the Burgundian court did not become disillusioned with crusading as a result of Nicopolis: indeed, John of Nevers was fêted as a hero when he returned early in 1398. The warm reception which John received at Rhodes, *en route* for the West, created friendly ties between Burgundy and the Hospitallers which paid dividends for the latter in the 1440s. Similarly, the crusading enthusiasm of John's son, Philip the Good, was to be one of the most hopeful features of the mid-fifteenth century. With Nicopolis, the focus of French crusading energy thus moved from the royal court to that of the Burgundian dukes.

3

The Ottoman Threat
1396–1502

✠

His personal status as a *ghazi* leader enhanced by his great victory at Nicopolis, Sultan Bayezid I was able immediately to resume his twin strategies of unifying Anatolia and tightening the noose on Constantinople (see map 4). In 1397 the Sultan occupied Konya and destroyed the state of Karaman, after defeating Alauddin Ali Bey at the plain of Akcay. In the following year the death of Qadi Burhan al-Din enabled Bayezid to establish his suzerainty over the former's large territories in central Anatolia. The Ottomans were now in direct contact with the Mamluk lands, and in 1398–9 the Sultan penetrated the Euphrates Valley, taking Malatya and Elbistan. By 1400 most of Cilicia was in Ottoman hands, and Anatolia was virtually united. At the same time the siege of Constantinople, begun in 1394, was renewed. Its most important feature was the construction of a fortress, Anadolu Hisar, on the Asian side of the Bosphorus, in order to control Byzantine access to the Black Sea. Famine conditions prevailed in the city in 1397.

With hindsight it is clear that Bayezid could only have taken Constantinople if he had concentrated all his resources on the task, but the danger appeared grave enough to the Emperor Manuel II, and in 1397–8 he sent urgent appeals to the West. It is interesting that even in the wake of Nicopolis these met with some response, for in 1398, 1399, and 1400 the Roman Pope Boniface IX ordered crusade preaching to raise funds for the Emperor, and in 1399 Charles VI of France sent Marshal Boucicaut with a 'task force' of about 1,200 men to aid in the defence. Most of these troops returned with Boucicaut in December after a few months' desultory campaigning in the vicinity of Constantinople. But a small garrison remained in the city, and Manuel was encouraged to undertake a personal visit to the West. The Emperor reached Venice in May 1400 and arrived in Paris on 3 June. He crossed the Channel in December and spent Christmas at the English court, before returning to Paris in February 1401. It was only some two years later that he made the return journey to Constantinople. In the autumn of 1400 an envoy also toured the Spanish courts on Manuel's behalf asking for aid. The presence of the Byzantine Emperor in the West on what was essentially a begging mission aroused curiosity and compassion. The Welsh chronicler Adam of Usk commented 'I thought within myself how grievous it was that this great Christian prince from the farther east was being forced by the infidels to visit the more distant islands of the west to get help against them.' For Manuel, however, the trip was all but fruitless: Charles VI, Henry IV, and Martin I of Aragon failed to keep their generous promises of assistance, and the funds raised by crusade preaching mostly went adrift. What saved the Emperor's capital from the threat of Turkish conquest was help from a very different quarter; for on 28 July 1402 Bayezid was decisively defeated and captured near Ankara by the army of the Tatar war-lord Tamerlane.

Born in 1336 to a member of the ruling Cagatay dynasty at Kes, south of Samarkand in Transoxania, Tamerlane had established himself as ruler of Transoxania before, from 1381 onwards, waging a series of brilliant and ruthless campaigns against the Iranians and Iraqis. Towards the end of 1394 his extraordinary successes had brought him into contact with both the Mamluks and the Ottomans. During the next five years Tamerlane was busy in Central Asia, India, and eastern Iraq, enabling Bayezid to win at Nicopolis and to make his Anatolian conquests. But in 1400 the Turcoman princes of eastern Anatolia, who had accepted Tamerlane's suzerainty as a defence against the Ottoman advance, appealed against the Sultan's pressure. The rivalry between Bayezid and Tamerlane was not only territorial: Tamerlane regarded himself as the representative of the lawful descendants of Genghis Khan taking disciplinary action against an upstart frontier dynasty, and as the standard-bearer of militant Islam (his seizure of Christian Smyrna in 1402 may have been an attempt to establish *ghazi* credentials). In 1400 Tamerlane occupied and sacked Sivas before marching south and crushing the Mamluk forces in Syria. Two years later he advanced into western Anatolia and defeated Bayezid's army at the battle of Ankara; the imprisoned Sultan died, possibly by his own hand, in 1403. Tamerlane proceeded to dismantle Ottoman Anatolia and reconstruct the Turcoman principalities, giving pride of place to

Karaman. The Ottoman lands which were left were divided between Bayezid's sons, Suleyman ruling from Edirne, Isa Celebi from Balikesir and Bursa, and Mehmed Celebi from Amasya. Inevitably, the three became rivals, and it was only after a complicated period of civil war that Mehmed I emerged as sole ruler of all the Ottoman lands in 1413.

What enabled the Ottoman state to survive both the disastrous events of 1402 and the partition and civil strife which ensued? Most importantly, the institutions implanted by Murad I and Bayezid I. Their development of a provincial system of government, and of a *timar*-holding class of warriors (including the heavy cavalry, or *sipahis*), called for a degree of central control and regulation. To establish it, Bayezid employed administrators from formerly Seljukid centres in Anatolia, and from Iran and Egypt. It was probably under Bayezid that registers of taxes (*defters*) due from the regions of the Empire began to be kept. As we saw in the previous chapter, Bayezid also developed the *devsirme* system introduced by Murad, with a resultant growth in the numbers of *kapi-kulus*. Legally slaves of the sultan, the *kapi-kulus* were in practice an élite whose reliance on, and devotion to, the sultan, made them excellent agents of central government. There was an in-built tension between the *kapi-kulus* and the *timar*-holding aristocracy of the provinces, and the rivalry between the two groups has been viewed, perhaps with some exaggeration, by certain historians as the central theme of Ottoman history in this period. Be that as it may, during the interregnum (*Fetret*), *kapi-kulus* and aristocracy had a common interest in the restoration of unity and order, as the *kapi-kulus* needed them for their own advancement, and the legal titles to *timars* rested on the maintenance of the *defters*. From their undamaged base in *Rumeli*, the Ottomans were therefore able to rebuild their position in *Anadolu*. Centralization and recovery were further facilitated by the death of Tamerlane in 1405, and the inability of the Byzantines, Genoese, and Venetians to profit from Ottoman division beyond the extraction of concessions from rival princes, in exchange for help or neutrality. The West, meanwhile, was preoccupied with ending the Great Schism; as so often in the decades to come, Ottoman weakness and quiescence were viewed as a chance to forget about crusading, rather than as a golden opportunity to drive the Turks from Europe.

This is not to say that recovery was either rapid or easy: most of the reign of Mehmed I (1413–21) was taken up with campaigning in both Anatolia and the Balkans. In 1414–15 the Sultan regained much land in the south of Anatolia, captured from Aydin, Menteshe, and Karaman.

But in 1416 a man claiming to be Mehmed's brother Mustafa (*Duzme* Mustafa = Mustafa the Pretender) led a rebellion in Rumelia, and Venice defeated an Ottoman naval force near Gallipoli. Mircea, Prince of Wallachia, encouraged Mustafa and Seyh Bedreddin, a disloyal *qadi* who caused trouble in Anatolia and Rumelia before Mehmed caught and executed him in 1419. In 1420 Mustafa too was defeated and fled to Constantinople, which had done its best to keep the hornets' nest buzzing. Mehmed also had to placate Tamerlane's son, Shahrukh, employing the familiar argument that his campaigns against the revived Anatolian principalities were necessary because their rulers were preventing him from waging the holy war in the Balkans.

If Mehmed's reign is usually depicted as one of recovery, that of his son Murad II (1421–51) has the traditional label of a period of preparation for the great conquests of Mehmed II. The start of Murad's reign was troubled, like that of his father's, by rebellions, the renewed revolt of *Duzme* Mustafa in Rumelia, and that of Murad's younger brother (also called Mustafa) at Hamid in Anatolia, where he was supported by the princes of Germiyan and Karaman. Murad defeated *Duzme* Mustafa, laid siege to Constantinople in 1422, as punishment for the aid the Greeks had given the pretender, then crossed to Anatolia, where he arrested and executed his brother. Following this, Murad annexed the principalities of western Anatolia and went to war with Venice (1423–30). That the Ottomans had recovered and once again posed a threat to the existence of Byzantium was shown by the siege of Constantinople in 1422 and, more importantly, by the capture of Thessalonica, the Empire's second largest city, in 1430.

By the 1430s Murad felt strong enough to listen to the counsel of those who wanted a renewal of the advance in the Balkans (see map 3). The death of Sigismund of Hungary in December 1437 encouraged Murad personally to lead an army into Transylvania in 1438, and in the following year to annex the Despotate of Serbia. In 1440 the Sultan made the first of several unsuccessful attempts to capture Belgrade. The Ottomans now faced the most powerful Christian state in the Balkans, the Kingdom of Hungary. Its troops were effectively led by the governor (*voivode*) of Transylvania, John Hunyadi, who in 1441 and 1442 inflicted crushing defeats on the Turks. Christian armies had never before defeated the Ottomans so decisively, and there was great excitement in the West. Hunyadi's success lay partly in his deep familiarity with Turkish tactics and his skilful exploitation of Ottoman weaknesses, particularly in launching attacks on Ottoman garrisons in autumn when the feudal contingents had been demobilized. Stephen the Great of Moldavia was to adopt the same approach. Hunyadi also used battle tactics borrowed from the Hussites. But the Ottomans were themselves good learners, and as a result of their many campaigns against Hunyadi they introduced firearms as quickly as possible to the janissary corps. Murad II also organized a cannon corps (*Topcu Ocagi*).

Thus it was that in the late 1430s, after more than thirty years of virtual dormancy, the crusade against the Turks again became a major western concern, in the twofold context of relieving the Greeks and supporting the Hungarians. This revival was, however, much complicated by the fact that it occurred when relations between the reunited papacy and the exponents of conciliarism were reaching crisis point. Manuel II had sent envoys to the Council of Constance (1414–18), and Pope Martin V had responded with enthusiasm to their offers of negotiations about Union. Proposals for sending aid to the Greeks were discussed at the Council of Basle between 1434 and 1437. By the end of that time it had become clear that the Emperor John VIII and the Patriarch of Constantinople would have to choose between Pope and Council in negotiating Union in exchange for aid; in turn, whichever succeeded in attracting Greek envoys and bringing about Union would find its position in the West powerfully enhanced. Eventually the Greeks opted for the Pope (Eugenius IV), chiefly because conciliar authority was strange to them, Basle could not pay the expenses of their envoys, and they believed that the Pope would be in a better position to organize a crusade. It was ironical that the Greek church, which had for centuries opposed the extreme claims of papal supremacy, played a key role in consolidating the Pope's position *vis-à-vis* his conciliar rivals in the West.

In February 1438 the Emperor John VIII arrived at Venice and made his way to Ferrara, where the Pope had reconvened the Council. It was at Florence, where the Council moved in February 1439, that the act of reunion of the Latin and Greek churches was finally achieved in July 1439. The reunion was thus a double triumph for Eugenius IV, since it finally ended a schism whose roots went back to the eleventh century, and its negotiation at a Council summoned by the Pope and his supporters marked the resurgence of papal authority within the western church. In practice the triumph quickly turned sour in both respects. At Constantinople, the storm of hostility which greeted news of the Union was reminiscent of the problems which Michael VIII had faced after the

Second Council of Lyons. And in the West, the conflict between Eugenius and the rump of the Basle Council (together with the antipope, Felix V, whom the Council created in 1439) continued to create problems for the crusade, since the Council's adherents interpreted Eugenius IV's crusading plans as a trick to gain money and prestige, and co-ordinated resistance to them. Even Aeneas Sylvius Piccolomini, who as Pius II was to be the most enthusiastic crusading pope of the century, saw Eugenius's plans in this light.

Papal supremacy entailed commitment by the Curia to the organization of a crusade of relief. To this Eugenius responded with greater energy than any pope since Gregory XI, both by renewing the administration of indulgences to raise money for the immediate defence of Constantinople (October 1439), and also by outlining plans to send papal galleys, and to urge imperial, Hungarian, and Albanian action against the Ottomans. Hopes for military activity in 1440 were doomed by Eugenius's need to defend the Papal State against Filippo Maria Visconti of Milan, and by rivalry for the Hungarian throne between Ladislas, the infant son of Albert II of Habsburg and his wife Elizabeth of Hungary, and King Wladyslaw III of Poland. But in February 1442 the Pope recognized the gravity of the situation in the East by appointing one of the most able and influential of his cardinals, Julian Cesarini, as legate in eastern Europe to co-ordinate action against the Turks. By the end of the year the prospects for a crusade to relieve Constantinople, once again under siege by the Turks, seemed good. Cesarini had restored peace in Hungary by persuading the Habsburgs to accept Wladyslaw's rule, and Hunyadi's successes had made a Christian recovery of Wallachia seem possible. Optimism was in the air: Bartholomew of Genoa, the Franciscan vicar-general in the East, thought in February 1443 that the expulsion of the Turks from Rumelia was feasible. The train of circumstances now began which led to the worst crusading defeat of the century, the battle of Varna.

Eugenius's plan was to send galleys to the Dardanelles in the summer of 1443, to ease the pressure on Constantinople, and prevent Turkish reinforcements crossing from Anatolia, while the Hungarians advanced into the heartland of Rumelia. Comparatively few galleys would be needed and their brief, to stop the Turks crossing the Straits either at Gallipoli or in the Bosphorus, would be much simpler than in the case of earlier flotillas sent to the East. Nevertheless, this attempt at co-ordinating land and sea forces had failed time and again in the fourteenth century and it was to be no more successful on this occasion. The main reason was Venice's lack of commitment to the papal strategy; the Republic did not believe that a decisive blow could be delivered to Ottoman power in the Balkans without a general crusade. It feared that it would end up losing its trading rights while at the same time facilitating a renewal of Hungarian influence in Dalmatia, where it had only recently been eliminated. Venice therefore refused to provide galleys for a campaign in 1443; moreover, the Republic held up the preparation of Eugenius's ships, which it was fitting out. The Pope was also partly to blame for the delay: he entered a coalition formed against Francis Sforza of Milan, alienating the Venetians and Florentines, Sforza's allies, whose clergy he was taxing to pay for the papal ships. The result was that by September, when the Hungarians and Poles finally crossed the Danube, no ships were ready to be sent, and the strategy collapsed.

None the less, the land campaign, whose unusual length of four months earned it the contemporary name of 'the long campaign' (*longum bellum*) was a triumph. An army of about 25,000 men was assembled, the nucleus composed of Hunyadi's Transylvanians, but with contingents from every Balkan country threatened by the Turks, as well as Czech and Moldavian mercenaries, and Italian, French, and German volunteers. Led by Hunyadi, Wladyslaw, Cesarini, and the exiled Serbian Despot, George Brankovic (whose experience of Balkan warfare went back to the battle of Kossovo in 1389), the army set out late in the campaigning season, mainly because it was only on 1 September that Wladyslaw sealed a truce with the leader of the Habsburg faction in Hungary. The crusaders captured the cities of Nish and Sofia and marched on Edirne. It was not the Turks, but lack of provisions and the bitter cold of late December, which forced the army to retreat. Even then it inflicted two defeats on the pursuing Turks and reached Belgrade safely in late January 1444. Not until the Russo-Turkish wars of the nineteenth century would a Christian army penetrate so deeply into Ottoman territory again. Had western galleys guarded the Straits and prevented Murad from crossing to bolster the defence of Rumelia, the victories would have been even more dramatic.

Fearful of a repeat performance of this terrible campaign, which might result in the loss of Edirne, and threatened by Karaman, Murad II was ready to make important concessions to Wladyslaw and George Brankovic. This, however, would not save the Greeks, and Eugenius pressed for another campaign in 1444, this time, he assured Cesarini, with naval support. This was now viable, since the Venetians were impressed enough by the 'long campaign' to equip the papal galleys and provide some of their own. Dubious about whether the promised galleys would materialize, and facing heavy opposition to renewed war from both the Hungarian and the Polish nobility, Hunyadi and Wladyslaw kept their options open. At a Diet at Buda in April the King vowed to renew the conflict, but in May he and Hunyadi sent envoys to Murad's court at Edirne. They came back with attractive terms for the return of captured towns and a ten-year truce. The proposed restitution of the Despotate of Serbia would make it much more difficult for the Turks to attack Hungary even when the truce expired. But nothing was said about the Greeks, and the terms were vehemently and eloquently opposed by Cesarini. On 1 August, at Szeged, Wladyslaw solemnly ratified the truce. Three days later the King forswore his oath, announcing that 'notwithstanding any treaties made or in the making', he intended to take the field against the Turks. It is likely that in the intervening days news had arrived of Murad's departure for Anatolia to fight Ibrahim Bey of Karaman, which would deplete the Rumelian garrisons and make the chances of success much greater. But if Murad's terms had failed to secure Hungarian neutrality, they had at least robbed the crusading army of Serbian support, for George Brankovic ratified a separate peace with the Turks on 15 August.

During these summer months the papal squadron had finally set sail. In the end twenty-two or twenty-four galleys had been armed, eight or ten by the Pope, four by Philip of Burgundy, eight by Venice, and two by Ragusa. Genoa steadfastly refused to provide any ships, and none was sent in the end by King Alfonso I of Naples, despite a firm commitment to help. The ships were under the command of Cardinal Francis Condulmer, the Pope's nephew, but since all but two of the galleys were manned by Venetians, it was Venetian interests, represented at sea by Alvise Loredan, which dictated their movements. The flotilla reached the Straits of Gallipoli in July, but it was only two months later, on 20 September, that the Hungarians crossed the Danube at Orsova. Their army contained about 5,000 men fewer than in 1443, but with the fleet guarding the Straits, uprisings in Albania, attacks on Turkish positions by Byzantine troops under Constantine Dragases in the Morea, and Shiite religious disturbances and janissary pay-riots breaking out in Edirne, the chances of dealing Ottoman power in Rumelia a highly damaging blow were excellent. The Venetian Senate, a body of men not given to optimism, remarked in May 1444 that 'such a propitious timing and such well-disposed circumstances are unprecedented in our lifetime'.

The Christian position was helped by confusion within the Ottoman government. Murad seems to have gone through a period of self-doubt and depression after the defeats of 1443 and the death of his favourite son. He renounced the throne in favour of Prince Mehmed and retired to Bursa as soon as he had made peace with Ibrahim Bey. But in response to the burgeoning crisis he agreed to return, and crossed the Bosphorus above Constantinople in late October 1444 with 30,000–40,000 men. No attempt was made by the fleet to stop him, or to sail into the Black Sea to link up with the crusading army, which had marched to the port of Varna with that intention. The paralysis which overcame the galleys at this critical point, and which led to bitter recriminations later, has never been satisfactorily explained. Probably the Venetians believed that Wladyslaw had ratified the truce, which was shown them by Turkish officers, and that they would be fighting alone; but it is possible that Loredan had secret orders not to prevent a crossing anyway, or that the flotilla simply fell prey to the old problems of confusion and prevarication. When the two armies met at Varna on 10 November 1444, the crusading troops were probably outnumbered two to one. After an exceptionally hard-fought, day-long battle, in which Wladyslaw was killed, the armies disengaged without victory on either side; but losses had been so terrible that the Christian camp disintegrated.

The Varna campaign has led to great debate amongst historians, especially in establishing the perjury or innocence of Wladyslaw at Szeged in August 1444. Hungarian historians in particular have attempted to show that the King did not ratify the terms of the truce with the Turks, but his solemn oath of 1 August is attested by a wide range of reliable sources. In any case, it has been pointed out that an oath taken to an infidel was invalid, and that the King could easily have secured a papal absolution, while the Turks themselves were sometimes guilty of betraying truces. The problem with the Szeged oath was that it was followed by the decisive defeat of a crusading army, and that later commentators (including Martin Luther, in his detailed refutation of the charges in the bull *Exsurge Domine*) used the Varna campaign as proof that crusading was an illicit form of Christian activity. In Hungary a legend formed that Wladyslaw survived the battle and spent the remaining years of his life as a wandering hermit to expiate the perjury which, he believed, God had punished by inflicting this crushing defeat on him.

Historians from the Balkan countries occupied by the Turks have commonly viewed the years 1442–4 as the last chance to expel the

Ottomans from Europe and avoid centuries of repressive and backward government. This is to ignore the fact that Macedonia and Thrace were by this time predominantly Turkish in population. Nevertheless, the crisis facing Murad II in 1443–4 was exceptionally grave, and this makes it important to understand why the Christian strategy failed, despite all the advantages which the crusaders enjoyed. Two difficulties, both deep-rooted, call for special notice. One was the numerical inferiority of the Christian army, the result of the absence of the Serbs and the reluctance of the Hungarians and Poles to field troops or provide funds, given the favourable terms offered by Murad. Linking the needs of the Greeks and the eastern Europeans, which seemed natural to the Pope, ran contrary to the real differences between their situations; it was not in the best interests of the Hungarians to fight in 1444. The second difficulty was the utter lack of co-ordination between naval and land forces, hopes for which underpinned the whole strategy espoused by the papal Curia since 1439, coupled to the formidable problems involved in assembling the squadron of galleys at all. This second point, familiar from the previous chapter, hardly needs stressing, except to remark that even when Hungarian and Venetian political interests *seemed* to be reconciled, only half the battle had been won, as it was still necessary to co-ordinate their military contributions.

After Varna hopes of doing anything on behalf of Constantinople faded. The Venetians made peace with the Turks in February 1446, and the defence of the Balkans reverted to the local Christian rulers. Hunyadi, who survived the battle, and became regent of Hungary for Ladislas of Habsburg, immediately planned another campaign against the Turks. In 1448, backed by crusade indulgences issued by Pope Nicholas V, he marched south through Turkish-occupied Serbia with the goal of linking up with the Albanians. The combined army of Hungarians and Wallachians encountered Murad's forces at Kossovo. As at Varna, the Christians were outnumbered, and in the course of a two-day battle (18–19 October), Hunyadi was defeated by Murad on the same ground that the Serbs had suffered defeat fifty-nine years earlier. As a result Ottoman control of the lands south of the Danube was affirmed and Murad regained suzerainty over Wallachia. The Greeks of the Peloponnese were no more successful. In 1415 Manuel II had attempted to secure the Morea against Turkish attack by building a great wall, the Hexamilion, across the six-mile neck of land from the Saronic Gulf to the Gulf of Corinth. In December 1446 this was breached by artillery, and the Morea then subjected to a terrible raid, punishment for the hostile activities of the Despot Constantine. From this point onwards the autonomous existence of the Morea hinged almost solely on Ottoman good will.

The only successful resistance to Murad II was mounted in Albania. Here the chieftain George Castriota Scanderbeg held the Turks at bay for twenty-five years and provided a ray of hope for western observers of the decaying situation in the Balkans. Scanderbeg's resistance began in November 1443, when he seized the fortress of Croia (modern Kruje) after the Turkish defeat at Nish. After Varna Murad made several attempts to regain Croia, but his troops were defeated both in pitched battle and in the guerilla warfare of which Scanderbeg became a brilliant practitioner. In 1448 Murad led a large expedition into Albania and took Sfetigrad after a three-month siege. In May 1450 the Sultan laid siege to Croia, casting cannon on the spot from metal which he had brought with him. The situation seemed hopeless and by October Scanderbeg was threatening to surrender the fortress to the Turks unless Venice took over its defence. But continual harassment of the siege camp from Scanderbeg's troops, and the approach of winter, compelled Murad to withdraw before the end of the month. When the Sultan died in February 1451 most of Albania was still free of Turkish occupation, and a month later, by the Treaty of Gaeta, Scanderbeg became the vassal of Alfonso of Naples, gaining valuable Arago-Neapolitan aid with which to continue his struggle.

Scanderbeg had two great assets in waging this conflict. One was Albania's mountainous terrain, which proved ideal for the type of warfare he was fighting. The second was his own acquaintance with Turkish military techniques, gained during the many months which he had spent on campaign with them in his twenties as his father's hostage at Murad's court. The name 'Scanderbeg' itself was formed from the name and title (Alexander Bey) conferred on him by Murad, and his retention of the name reflected his respect for the power and prestige of his enemy; despite this, the war was marked by savagery on both sides, to a degree rare even by Balkan standards. The precise character of the long conflict (1443–68) has always aroused controversy; that it still does was shown by the many articles published in 1968 to commemorate the fifth centenary of Scanderbeg's death. To his own countrymen, Scanderbeg has always been a national hero fighting against the threat of Turkish enslavement; modern Albanian historians, ignoring the facts, have even claimed that he was of peasant stock. To Catholic historians, he was a 'fanatical, single-minded crusader', and a loyal son of the Church. Ottoman historians have customarily portrayed him as a bandit-leader, a defender of entrenched feudal privilege against the fairer social regime which the Turks introduced in the Balkans. Forming an objective picture of Scanderbeg has not been helped by the fact that his earliest biographer, the near-contemporary Marinus Barletius, invented correspondence as well as distorting events, while an eighteenth-century biographer, Giammaria Biemmi, forged more material. It is true that Scanderbeg's resistance was probably motivated, in the first instance, by a judicious evaluation of the advantages to be gained by fighting against the Turks rather than working for them; and that his protestations of crusading zeal were intended to secure western aid. But his own conversion to the Catholic faith appears to have been genuine, and he did succeed in achieving, and sustaining, a broad-based consensus of Albanian interests for his defence of the country's independence.

Scarcely easier to assess is the degree of assistance which Scanderbeg received from the West. The papacy was generous with praise and encouragement, but its financial subsidies were limited: Albania was, after all, only one sector of a very long anti-Turkish front. It is possible that the Curia only provided Scanderbeg with about 20,000 ducats in all, which would have paid the wages of just twenty men over the whole period of the conflict. Certainly, during the winter of 1466–7, when the situation in Albania was critical, Scanderbeg spent several pitiful weeks at Rome trying to persuade Paul II to give him money; at one point the Albanian was unable even to pay his hotel bill, and he commented bitterly that he should be fighting the Church rather than the Turks. Only when Scanderbeg had actually left for Naples did the Pope send on 2,300 ducats (to be fair, Paul's parsimony had a political explanation, his fear of the territorial ambitions of Scanderbeg's lord, Ferrante, and his ally, Venice). The court of Naples, whose policy in the Balkans hinged on Scanderbeg's resistance, was more generous with money, armaments, and supplies, and Scanderbeg was warm in his praise for Alfonso and Ferrante. Ragusa and Venice helped when it was in their interests to do so. But it is probably fair to say that Scanderbeg financed and equipped his troops largely from Albanian resources, richly supplemented with Turkish booty.

The only western power which displayed any real interest in the crusade during the last years of Murad II was Philip the Good's Burgundy (see map 1). Philip's crusading enthusiasm, which played a dominant role in the middle decades of the century, appears to have derived from a number of influences: the Franco-Flemish tradition of crusading to which he was heir; the desire to revenge his father's defeat and capture at Nicopolis; and the perception that an active part as organizer and sponsor of a major crusading effort would assist his political pretensions in western Europe. It was sustained by a remarkable proliferation of chivalric literature, crusade tracts, and apocryphal texts at the Burgundian court. As early as 1421 Philip, in conjunction with Henry V of England, sent Guillebert of Lannoy on a reconnaissance mission to the East. Nine years later there occurred two key events which would keep his attention focused on the crusade: his founding of the chivalric Order of the Golden Fleece, which although not explicitly linked to the crusade tended to be associated with Philip's crusading ideas; and his third marriage, to Isabella of Portugal. Isabella was an extremely forceful personality who leavened the Burgundian crusading tradition with that of Portugal, itself recently renewed by her brother, Henry the Navigator. The Duchess consistently directed her husband's thought to crusading in the Mediterranean, and it has been suggested that her realism and astuteness gave Philip's rather grandiose schemes such practicality as they possessed. It was probably her initiative, for instance, which brought about the marriage between her nephew, John of Coimbra, and Charlotte of Lusignan, heiress to the Kingdom of Cyprus, in 1456, the aim being to provide Burgundy with a naval base in the eastern Mediterranean.

In 1432 Philip encouraged Bertrandon of la Broquière and several other Burgundian nobles to go to the East, in effect a second reconnaissance party, and six years later he ordered the construction of a Burgundian fleet, including a *grande nave* and a carvel, at Sluis, Brussels, and Antwerp. Expert Portuguese shipwrights assisted, and at this stage the ships may have been intended to help the Portuguese attack Moorish Tangier. But in May 1441, in response to a Hospitaller appeal, Geoffrey of Thoisy was dispatched with four ships, including the *nave*, to help defend Rhodes. The Duke went in person to Sluis to see off his ships. Thoisy went via Lisbon, Ceuta, and Barcelona to Villefranche and Rhodes, returning to Villefranche early in 1442 to refit. Thoisy, who had accompanied Bertrandon of la Broquière to the East, was to play a leading role in Philip's crusading endeavours, and the importance of Duchess Isabella is clear from the fact that one of her officials handled the payment of the expedition's costs, while a third of the sailors who manned the *nave* were Portuguese.

In the early summer of 1442 Philip's court was visited by a Byzantine embassy pleading for aid, led by Theodore Karystos. The Duke decided to use Thoisy's ships, together with others built or hired at Nice and Venice, as a Burgundian contribution to the Pope's planned flotilla. The four galleys hired at Venice were placed under the command of Waleran of Wavrin. They sailed in July 1444, and after failing to stop Murad's army crossing the Bosphorus, wintered at Constantinople. Here Wavrin was joined by Thoisy, who had raided Muslim shipping off the North African coast before helping the Hospitallers to break the Mamluk siege of Rhodes in the summer. That the Burgundian contribution to the flotilla was divided in this way, part of it spending crucial months at Rhodes rather than in the Straits, is symptomatic of the disorganized nature of Philip's crusading ideas, which reflected the strategic chaos of these years generally. As so often with Burgundian involvement in the crusading movement, one has the impression that any form of fighting against Muslims or pagans, whether they were Moors, Mamluks, Turks, or Lithuanians, was enough to make the ducal court feel that it had achieved its goal.

Events in 1445 showed little improvement. In the spring Thoisy took his ships along the south coast of the Black Sea. His open engagement in piracy led to his arrest at Poti, on the Georgian coast, and his release had to be negotiated by the Emperor of Trebizond. Wavrin, more fruitfully, arranged a joint campaign with John Hunyadi on the Danube, and a meeting took place as planned in September, at Nicopolis. But the Turkish army would not fight, and Wavrin arrived back in Constantinople in November. Both Thoisy and Wavrin now returned to the West, leaving the *grande nave* to rot before the walls of Constantinople as mute testimony to the fiasco of Eugenius IV's crusade. Although Burgundian ships continued to operate in the eastern Mediterranean and Black Sea in 1447–9, they were essentially acting as pirates, causing a flow of Genoese complaints to Philip. With Pope Nicholas V refusing to take any initiative on the crusade other than occasionally issuing indulgences, Philip the Good's considerable expenditure on his Mediterranean ships was all but wasted. Probably more effective was the Duke's dispatch of 300 men-at-arms to assist Constantine Dragases in the Morea in 1444.

Surprisingly, however, even these disappointing events served to strengthen Philip's interest in the crusade in the eastern Mediterranean. He exchanged envoys with Alfonso of Aragon on the subject, tried to persuade Pope Nicholas V to take a greater lead, attempted to make peace between England and France, and expressed interest in acquiring Genoa, which would make an ideal base for a Burgundian crusading flotilla. In May 1451 the Duke solemnly undertook the leadership of a crusade to the East. He was encouraged by the enthusiasm of one of his leading advisers, the Bishop of Chalon John Germain, and in general there was an atmosphere of buoyant hopefulness at the Burgundian court in 1451–2. Judging by surviving writings of Germain, it was based on such tenuous factors as Hunyadi's continuing resistance, the successful defence of Rhodes in 1444, the reunification of Christendom in both East and West, and the Ottoman dispute with Karaman. Murad II's death in 1451, and the succession of the 19-year-old Mehmed II, reinforced this atmosphere, as nobody expected the new Sultan to be dangerous. Such optimism could scarcely have been more misplaced.

Mehmed II's succession sealed the fate of Constantinople, for Mehmed was determined to conquer the city as the first step in a planned expansion of the Ottoman state to the banks of the Danube and Euphrates rivers. This was how the new Sultan himself was said to have put the case for conquest:

The *ghaza* is our basic duty, as it was in the case of our fathers. Constantinople, situated as it is in the middle of our dominions, protects the enemies of our state and incites them against us. The conquest of this city is, therefore, essential to the future and the safety of the Ottoman state.[1]

Like Ferdinand and Isabella in their assault on Granada three decades later, Mehmed was proceeding on a mixture of pragmatic and ideological grounds. He saw the need to eliminate a hostile enclave whose rulers were sheltering a pretender, his distant cousin Orhan, and were constantly appealing for a crusade in their assistance. But the conquest would also signify his return to a strategy of aggressive holy war, which had been abandoned by his father after the set-backs of 1443, and was still opposed by the Grand Vizier, Chandarli Pasha. With Constantinople and the Bosphorus safely in their possession, the Turks could initiate a thrust into Central Europe without having to worry about Christian fleets forcing apart their Asian and European provinces.

The decision was a risky one, for it entailed concentrating Ottoman strength on a difficult siege at a time when Mehmed had powerful enemies on his borders, Karaman and Hungary. Ibrahim Bey of Karaman was neutralized, however, by a brisk campaign in the autumn of 1451. As for the Christian powers, Mehmed intended to act so quickly that the Hungarians and Venetians would not have time to organize relief. In

---

[1] H. Inalcik, 'The Rise of the Ottoman Empire', in P. M. Holt, *et al.* (eds.), *The Cambridge History of Islam*, i (Cambridge, 1970), 295.

April 1452 work was begun on a fortress on the European shore of the Bosphorus, Rumeli Hisar, to complement Bayezid I's fortress, Anadolu Hisar, and stop Christian ships entering the Black Sea. In February 1453 troops from Edirne occupied the shores of the Sea of Marmora and siege artillery was put in place. This included three cannon of enormous size, one of which, designed by a Hungarian or Rumelian called Urban, had required sixty oxen to pull it from Edirne. In the following month Anatolian forces crossed to Rumeli Hisar while galleys cruised in the Sea of Marmora. By early April 1453 Constantinople was under siege.

The Emperor Constantine XI had pitifully little with which to withstand this massive concentration of men and *matériel*. The population of the city had shrunk to probably 40,000 or 50,000 by this point. His defenders numbered perhaps fewer than 6,000 men, including contingents of Venetians and Genoese (under John Giustiniani Longo), who fought with great courage. Even with the great land walls built by Theodosius II, and the iron chain which forbade the Turks access to the waters of the Golden Horn, all the Emperor could hope to achieve was to last out until he was relieved. But Hunyadi was not prepared to help, and Venice responded only belatedly and slowly to the crisis. By 22 April the Turks built a road and wheeled trolleys which enabled them to transport their ships overland from the Bosphorus to the Golden Horn, so that the garrison had to defend the entire circumference of the vast city. A month later the Sultan, worried about the possibility of a relief force arriving, calculated that his cannon had destroyed enough of the walls to risk an all-out assault. On 29 May the attack was launched, and after the repulse of two Turkish onslaughts the decisive breakthrough was made at about 4.00 a.m. by the janissaries. Constantine XI was killed and the city taken. The resulting sack was appallingly destructive of church property and works of art, though only about 4,000 Greek civilians were killed, a strikingly small number by twentieth-century standards.

Mehmed intended that Constantinople become the capital of his Empire, and his policy towards the city and its captured population was astute. Islamic law compelled him to permit his troops to sack the city, but he called a halt after one day, and throughout the remainder of his reign he devoted much energy to the rebuilding and repopulating of Constantinople. Greeks from elsewhere were forcibly resettled in the capital or attracted there by economic privileges. Most importantly, Mehmed's appointment of George Scholarios as Patriarch in January 1454 showed at an early stage that the Sultan intended to treat the

Orthodox church with respect and give it the role of representing Greek interests. This was the first step in the creation of the *millet* system, by which religious minorities in the Ottoman Empire enjoyed a degree of self-government under their own leaders, in exchange for loyalty and service to the Sultan; the Armenians, Jews, and others were later granted similar rights. Still, by 1477 Constantinople was a predominantly Muslim city—there were almost three times as many Muslim households as Greek ones. By that date it was also thriving, thanks to its unrivalled location as a commercial, administrative, and cultural centre at the heart of Mehmed's lands. Houses, markets, aqueducts, and roads were rebuilt, a prominent role in providing capital being played by the *waqfs*, Islamic charitable trusts.

The conquest of Constantinople not only provided the Ottoman Empire with its natural capital, it also had an important impact on Ottoman imperial ideology, which was considerably refined during Mehmed's reign. Before 1453 that ideology combined three principal themes. The first was the *ghazi* idea, which continued to exercise a massive influence in the fifteenth century, but changed in nature. In the fourteenth century the popular *ghazi* ideal had thrived in the context of living oral traditions about heroes engaged in lucrative frontier warfare. But as the vast majority of the troops in the Ottoman armies were, by the mid-fifteenth century at the very latest, either *timar*-holders who served as a contractual obligation, or professional *kapi-kulus*, the old *ghazi* traditions became, in practical terms, irrelevant. By the time of Mehmed II the *ghazi* warriors from the frontiers, the *akinjis*, played a rather insignificant role in military campaigns, and only when the central bureaucracy broke down, in times of crisis, did they exert any political influence. Instead, writers such as Ahmedi and Nesri portrayed a much more ascetic form of *ghaza*, one more in line with the ideals of the shariah, and, above all, associated with the person of the sultan. The capture of Constantinople, envisaged for centuries as the highest goal of the *mujahid*, led the Ottoman sultans to place enormous emphasis on their pursuit of *ghaza*. In the *feth-name* (victory bulletin) which he sent to the Sultan of Egypt after the fall of the city, Mehmed even attempted a delineation of their respective functions in terms of the Mamluk's protection of the pilgrimage routes, and the Ottoman's waging of holy war.

The other two main themes of Ottoman ideology were legitimizing and genealogical. As we saw in the previous chapter, the legitimizing argument hinged on the basic idea that Osman inherited sovereignty over Seljukid territory from Sultan Ala ed-Din II; and an Ottoman genealogy was compiled in the fifteenth century which aimed to prove that the dynasty was descended through the senior branch of the Oguz (the Muslim Turks of western Asia), and had always been rigorously orthodox Sunni Muslims. To these three themes of holy war, legitimacy, and genealogical purity was now rapidly added the idea that with the conquest of Constantinople the Sultan inherited Roman universal sovereignty; this was the easier to accept thanks to Islam's traditional emphasis on the indivisibility of political authority. As the Greek, George of Trebizond, flatteringly wrote to Mehmed in 1466: 'No one doubts that you are the Emperor of the Romans. Whoever is legally master of the capital of the Empire is the Emperor and Constantinople is the capital of the Roman Empire.' The conquest of Constantinople fused with the *ghazi* tradition, which dominated Mehmed's thinking, to make his reign one of astonishing vitality and aggression. According to one observer, the Sultan remarked 'The world empire must be one, with one faith and one sovereignty. To establish this unity, there is no place more fitting than Constantinople.'

It was also in the reign of Mehmed II that the Ottoman Empire began to take on its distinctive shape in terms of government. The figure of the Sultan was central, his role being to enforce the shariah, the path of God's decree. In theory this meant that the Sultan should be available personally to hear all complaints; in practice, given the size and expansion of the Empire, it meant that the Sultan tried to create a governmental system which would be as perfect a reflection of his will as possible. Mehmed made two important contributions towards the realization of this goal. First, he placed increasing emphasis on the *kapi-kulus* in all spheres of official life. After the momentous dismissal of Chandarli Pasha in 1453 all Mehmed's ministers, with one exception, were drawn from amongst his personal slaves. They became *qadis* (judges), governors of provinces, tax collectors, and, most importantly, janissaries. The janissary corps, which Mehmed reformed by increasing pay, improving weapons (especially firearms), and doubling in numbers (from 5,000 to 10,000) became the cutting edge of the Sultan's authority in the provinces; in consequence, the role of the beys was reduced. The members of this massively expanded ruling class were known as 'Ottomans' (*Osmanlilar*); together with the dynasty itself they constituted the core of an Empire which by this time had ceased to have any racial or national homogeneity.

Mehmed's second innovation was legal codification. Traditionally religious law (shariah) had been regarded as adequate. But it was argued that in the highly diversified and closely governed Empire that was emerging in the second half of the fifteenth century, justice called for codified, secular law. It is possible that Byzantine law codes, especially that of the sixth-century Emperor Justinian, provided models, but more important was the Seljukid tradition, which elevated the role of the sultan into a fully fledged secular ruler with legislative authority. Mehmed thus issued a series of three codes of law (*qanun-name*). The first (1453–6) detailed the obligations of subjects (*reaya*) and established a code of criminal law. In 1477–8 this was followed by a *qanun-name* which described the official hierarchy created by the Conqueror. Finally, in the very last years of Mehmed's reign, came a code dealing with economic organization.

If it was the Sultan's duty to protect the *reaya* against injustice, he also had the task of expanding the borders of Islam through war against the infidel. The *ghazi* theme may have become rather more of a justificatory idea, and rather less a driving obsession, by the mid-fifteenth century, but it was reflected in the Empire's social organization, and it was the chief determinant of economic policy, which centred on the creation of wealth in order that the military establishment could prosper. The direction of Ottoman advance was strongly influenced by commercial advantage. For example, the century-long struggle between the Ottomans and the Karamanids hinged on control of the spice markets of southern Anatolia; conversely, the long period of cordial relations between the Ottomans and the Mamluks resulted partly from the benefit they mutually derived from the thriving trade between Egypt and Asia Minor. Most importantly, a thrust to dominate the Black Sea and its littoral, a region of massive human, agricultural, and mineral resources, formed a key Ottoman policy from the reign of Mehmed II.

The Sultan took steps to encourage mercantile activity through road-building, the provision of security and facilities for travellers, and the issuing of trading privileges. Together with Constantinople, Edirne and especially Bursa became important international trading centres. Within the towns manufacturing, chiefly of textiles (cotton, silk, mohair) was closely regulated through the craft guilds, working with the local *imam* to enforce Islamic law on economic matters (the *hisba*). The *hisba* did hinder economic development in some respects (for instance, in its ruling that property be distributed amongst all a deceased person's heirs, so that capital accumulation for more than a single generation was difficult), and Ottoman economic policy stopped short of true mercantilism. But the Empire was characterized by the healthy development of its inter-regional trade, and by its central position between the West, the Inner

Asian lands, Mamluk Egypt, and the Steppes bordering on the Black Sea. As western observers ruefully noted, there was a rich economic underpinning to the grand ambitions of Constantinople's conqueror.

No event since the fall of Acre caused as much dismay in the West as the news of Mehmed II's capture of Constantinople. To distress at the slaughter and enslavement of the Greeks, and the loss of the fourth, and last, eastern patriarchate to Islam, the voices of lament added two other themes, the destruction of Greek culture, so dear to the humanists of Italy, and the accretion of Ottoman power, which enormously added to the danger the Turks posed to the West. As Aeneas Sylvius Piccolomini (later Pope Pius II) put it in a famous letter to Nicholas V:

I grieve that S. Sophia, the most famous church in all the world, has been ruined or polluted. I grieve that saints' basilicas without number, built with wondrous skill, should lie beneath the desolation or defilement of Mohammed. What shall I say of the countless books, as yet unknown to the Latins, which were there? Alas, how many names of great men will now perish. Here is a second death for Homer and for Plato too . . . Now Mohammed reigns among us. Now the Turk hangs over our very heads. The Black Sea is closed to us, the Don has become inaccessible. Now the Vlachs must obey the Turk. Next his sword will reach the Hungarians, and then the Germans.[2]

A flood of projects and exhortatory appeals (*exhortatoria*) began to appear, and continued through into the sixteenth century, dwelling on the threat which the Ottomans now posed not to the Greeks or even to the Christian states in the Balkans, but to western Christendom, starting with the Italian peninsula. It was widely reported that Mehmed II wanted to conquer 'Old Rome' just as he had 'New Rome'. As Cardinal Bessarion, a leading exponent and propagandist of the crusade, put it, 'The Turk thinks that he can achieve nothing worthier, nothing which would add more glory to his name, than leading an army into Italy, and adding to his dominions a province accustomed to dominating.' Lionello Chieregato, the papal legate sent to plead the cause of the crusade at the French court in 1488, pointed out that 'the holy apostolic see has not sent us here to argue the cause of Jerusalem, Asia or Greece, as in the days of your ancestors, but to beseech you on behalf of Italy, the towns, cities and peoples subject to the holy Roman church'. Humanists fancifully considered that the Turks (*Turci*) wanted to overrun Italy not just because of its riches but also

---

[2] K. M. Setton, *The Papacy and the Levant (1204–1571)*, ii, *The Fifteenth Century* (Philadelphia, 1978), 150.

because they hoped to find the graves of their Trojan ancestors (the *Teucri* who came to Italy with Aeneas after the sack of Troy).

From 1453, therefore, the crusade became a simple matter of self-interest.

We believe that we are facing a common enemy. Let us fight this common war not listlessly, not slowly, not grudgingly, not as we do when somebody else's property is at stake, as has been the case hitherto; but vigorously, quickly, generously, as we do when our own affairs reach the point of crisis.[3]

This was the theme which the papal Curia tried to press home in its crusade bulls, arguing that Christian powers which were engaged in fighting the Turks, such as the Venetians or Hungarians, were Christendom's 'front-line' states, the *antemurale Christianitatis*. But if all the sources of the second half of the century display a keen awareness of the severity and proximity of the Ottoman threat, they also show that the reaction of the main Christian powers was characterized by a fatal combination of inertia and disunity. The disparity between what was promised and what was done became greater than ever before. Rulers continued to harbour the illusion that the Turks were not particularly good soldiers, and that if they did attack Italy or Germany they could easily be turned back. The enemies of Venice even argued that the Turks performed a useful service in keeping the Republic occupied. Aeneas Sylvius Piccolomini's commentary was, as usual, colourful and perceptive:

Christendom has no head whom all obey. Neither the supreme pontiff nor the emperor is given his duc. There is no reverence, no obedience. Like characters in fiction, figures in a painting, so do we look upon the pope and the emperor. Every city-state has its own ruler. There are as many princes as houses . . . What order will there be in the army? What military discipline? What obedience? Who will feed so many people? Who will understand the different languages? Who will hold in check the different customs? Who will endear the English to the French? Who will get the Genoese to join with the Aragonese? Who will reconcile the Germans with the Hungarians and the Bohemians? If you lead a few men against the Turks, you are easily defeated. If you lead many, you are confounded.[4]

As so often, the prospects for an expedition to recover Constantinople initially appeared good. On 30 September 1453 Nicholas V issued the

---

[3] Bessarion, 'Orationes contra Turcas', in J. P. Migne (ed.), *Patrologiae cursus completus: Series graeco-latina*, clxi, col. 675.

[4] Setton, *The Papacy and the Levant*, ii. 153.

bull 'Etsi ecclesia Christi', a major initiative to stir Christendom into action. Predictably, its greatest impact was at the court of Burgundy. Philip had been warned of the Ottoman preparations to take Constantinople, but his attempt to put together a crusade of relief had been wrecked by the rebellion of Ghent in 1452. Only when Ghent was pacified, in July 1453, could the Duke again think of the crusade. The fall of Constantinople made a deep impression on his court: the *Informations* of the Florentine merchant James Tedaldi, with their first-hand description of the Turkish siege and their call for a crusade before the Sultan could consolidate his new conquests, were circulated widely in Burgundy, while William Dufay was moved to compose his four-voice motet 'The Lamentation of our holy mother church of Constantinople'.

At Lille in February 1454, Philip organized the banquet known as the Feast of the Pheasant, the most impressive example of the Burgundian flair for spectacle and extravagance, and a calculated attempt to whip up enthusiasm amongst the nobility. At the height of the sumptuous display a live pheasant was brought into the hall, and Philip solemnly swore on the bird (which was presumably drugged to keep it quiet) that he would undertake a crusade provided that at least one other ruler also took the field. The vows of more than 200 Burgundian nobles to accompany their Duke were recorded, and when Philip went to Regensburg in April to attend an Imperial Diet at which the crusade would be high on the agenda, the organization of his expedition was well under way. *Reichstag* consideration of the crusade was postponed at Regensburg, but at Frankfurt in autumn 1454 a crusade was agreed on. During the winter of 1454–5 *aides* were collected throughout the Burgundian lands, and by December 1454 Charles of Charolais, Philip's heir, could confidently write of his father setting off in the following spring. There were busy negotiations about the crusade with the papal Curia, France, and especially the Iberian powers, on whom, given the the lukewarm response of Charles VII and the Germans, Philip came increasingly to depend for assistance. Then the deaths of Nicholas V and the Bishop of Utrecht on the same day in March 1455 necessitated a postponement, since the character of the expedition was not yet fully settled, and Philip could not resist the temptation to exploit the papal and episcopal interregna by invading the territory of Utrecht.

Other rulers besides Philip appeared to respond with enthusiasm to Nicholas V's call to arms. Alfonso of Aragon and Naples engaged in negotiations on the crusade with Philip the Good, sent important aid to

Scanderbeg, and took the cross on All Saints Day 1455. In the summer of 1456, when exhorted by Aeneas Sylvius Piccolomini to take part in the forthcoming crusade, Alfonso claimed that he and his nephew Alfonso V of Portugal would attack the Turks in 1457 at the head of a fleet of 400 ships and an army of 50,000 men. The Emperor Frederick III also took the cross in autumn 1455. The Peace of Lodi, concluded on 9 April 1454, released both Venice and Milan for the crusade. Meanwhile, the new printing presses took on the role of both alerting people to the Turkish threat to Hungary, and of facilitating the advertisement of indulgences on an unprecedented scale and intensity. Towards the end of 1454, for instance, the famous pamphlet 'A Warning to Christendom against the Turks' ('Eyn manung der cristenheit widder die durken') was printed at Mainz, while John Gutenberg printed copies of Nicholas V's encyclical letters of plenary indulgence for the crusade in 1454–5.

Nicholas V, moreover, was succeeded by Calixtus III, a 77-year-old Catalan who was dedicated to crusading. According to the Franciscan Gabriel of Verona, the Pope had no time for anything else:

The Pope conducts other affairs with a single word, but this matter which relates to the faith he thinks about and concerns himself with continually. He is always discussing it, turning it over in his mind; he hardly sleeps and eats, and people are all wondering at such great enthusiasm in so old a man for this arduous and difficult business.[5]

Despite the fall of Constantinople, the Pope's strategy was little different from that of Eugenius IV a decade earlier: to encourage Hungarian and Albanian resistance to the Turks while organizing a naval attack from the West. For the latter, Calixtus sought the help of the maritime powers, especially Aragon–Naples and Portugal; Venice, at peace with the Turks since 1454 and embittered by Eugenius IV's failure to pay for the galleys he had hired in 1443–4, would do nothing to help. But Calixtus also resolved to make a larger, and better-financed, papal contribution than Eugenius had. This meant a financial commitment way beyond the income of the debilitated Renaissance papacy, and Calixtus both spent the substantial reserve left by Nicholas V and sought out every means of raising cash. This included setting in motion a degree of preaching and tax collection probably unknown since the fourteenth century; it caused enormous resentment and engendered a formidable crop of tricksters posing as pardoners. Calixtus even ordered the gold and silver ornamentation

---

[5] Setton, *The Papacy and the Levant*, ii. 164.

to be stripped from Nicholas V's precious books and converted to money with which to fight the Turks. Gabriel of Verona remarked that:

Everything he can get, he turns to this account. I was present once while he was at the table, and seeing the golden salt-cellar, which had belonged to his predecessor Nicholas, he cried, 'Take it away, take it away. Use it against the Turk; earthenware is good enough for me.'[6]

Eccentric as such behaviour appeared, Calixtus's economies enabled him, by the late spring of 1456, to arm sixteen galleys at a cost of 150,000 ducats. They were placed under the command of a legate, Cardinal Ludovic Trevisan. It was clear that they would be needed. In 1454 and 1455 Mehmed had brought Serbia firmly under his control, had inflicted a defeat on Scanderbeg at Berat, and had won over, albeit temporarily, Scanderbeg's best general, Moses of Dibra. In 1456 the Sultan launched a massive attack on Belgrade, the key fortress city in the Danube valley. In September 1455 Calixtus had sent Cardinal John of Carvajal as his legate to Hungary. Carvajal had the difficult task of reconciling Ladislas V with his cousin Frederick III, and Hunyadi with his enemy Ulrich of Cilli, as well as organizing Hungarian resistance. At the Diet of Buda in February 1456 the legate gave the Franciscan friar John of Capistrano a special commission to preach the crusade. The result was spectacular. A brilliant and inspiring preacher (he was later canonized) working against the background of an immediate threat to Hungary and Christendom generally, Capistrano enjoyed greater popular success than any preacher since the thirteenth century. Many thousands of crusaders, mainly Hungarians, but including some Austrians, Germans, Poles, Dalmatians, and Bosnians, marched with Capistrano to relieve Belgrade, to which Mehmed II had laid siege on 7 July.

As the historian Johannes Hofer rightly remarked, what followed was one of the most extraordinary episodes in military history. Ladislas and his court had fled to Vienna; the Hungarian barons refused to fight; Carvajal was desperately trying to recruit a real army at Buda. Hunyadi had few troops, apart from Capistrano's poor and lightly equipped crusaders, with which to defend Belgrade against the strongest army yet fielded by the Turks in Europe, armed with massive cannon, commanded by the Sultan in person, and flushed with the successes of 1453–5. Mehmed hoped to take Buda itself before the end of the campaigning season. Hunyadi despaired of the situation, arguing for the city's surrender

---

[6] Setton, *The Papacy and the Levant*, ii. 164.

to spare the lives of its inhabitants, even at the cost of opening up Hungary to the Turks. To this logical argument Capistrano opposed his faith in divine help, and Hunyadi was so impressed by the friar's character that he agreed to make an attempt to defend Belgrade.

On 15 July Hunyadi's men and the crusaders together succeeded in breaking the Turkish naval blockade of the city. During the night of 21–2 July the crusaders and the civilian population of Belgrade fought off a massive Turkish assault on the city's battered walls. Mehmed decided to retreat, but during the afternoon of 22 July the crusaders made a rush from the walls which captured Mehmed's batteries as the Turks were organizing their withdrawal. Capistrano's iron nerves and indomitable faith had saved Belgrade, and probably Hungary too. Turkish losses had been severe: James of Promontorio de Campis, a Genoese nobleman who resided at Mehmed's court and was present at the siege, put them at twenty-eight cannon, 100 galleys, and more than 13,000 men. It was the greatest crusading victory over the Turks in the fifteenth century, one of Mehmed II's worst defeats; and it was won not by a professional army but by a mainly civilian force commanded by a 70-year-old friar who could not even speak the languages of the men he led. It is not surprising that contemporaries thought that such an event could only be explained as God's work.

Success at Belgrade, albeit darkened by the deaths of both Hunyadi and Capistrano from the plague in August and October 1456, to some extent compensated for the shattering blow of 1453; the victory was repeatedly cited in the decades to come as proof that the Ottomans were not invincible. But it owed nothing to the flotilla assembled at such heavy cost by Calixtus III. For Ludovic Trevisan's galleys, which left Ostia in late June, and were supposed to launch a diversionary attack on the Turkish littoral, were detained at Naples, waiting for Alfonso's promised contribution. It was not until 6 August, two weeks after the victory at Belgrade, that Trevisan's ships, together with a few Aragonese galleys, proceeded to the East. Still, they recovered the islands of Lemnos, Samothrace, and Thasos in the Aegean, won a battle over the Turks at Mytilene in August 1457, and harried the coasts of Cilicia, Syria, and Egypt, before returning towards the end of 1457. The Pope was so impressed by these achievements that he had a commemorative medal struck. This run of Christian successes was completed by Scanderbeg's greatest victory, at Albulena, in September 1457. By the time of his death in 1458 Calixtus was writing of the recovery of Constantinople and the

Holy Land, and of the destruction of Islam. But the following years revealed how pathetically misguided such optimism was. The damage inflicted on Ottoman military resources had been comparatively slight. In 1459 Mehmed was able to take the final stage towards incorporating Serbia into his Empire. After expeditions in 1458 and 1460, the Sultan occupied the Morea, with the exception of the Venetian footholds at Modon, Coron, Navarino, and Lepanto. And in 1461 he overran the Greek Empire of Trebizond, on the southern coast of the Black Sea.

Even had Pius II, Calixtus's successor, not been deeply involved in crusade planning thanks to his active participation, as Frederick III's Secretary, in the Diets at Regensburg, Frankfurt, and Wiener Neustadt in 1454-5, these advances would have fixed his attention on the encroaching Ottoman threat. As it was, Pius himself claimed in his invaluable *Commentaries* that 'among all the purposes [he] had at heart none was dearer than that of rousing Christians against the Turks and declaring war upon them'. Readers of the *Commentaries*, with their massive concentration on Italian affairs, might be tempted to dismiss this as fine words, but the Pope's dedication to the cause of the crusade was a strong one. There is no denying that it was also complex in nature. At times Pius's vanity, extravagance, and sense of drama seem to dominate his crusade activities, as in his unblushing comments on the praise which he received for his eloquent speeches on the subject, or in the extraordinary stage management with which he brought the head of St Andrew to its new home in Rome after the Turkish conquest of the Morea, during holy week in 1462 (an event strongly reminiscent of the Feast of the Pheasant eight years earlier). At other times he pin-pointed the hopelessness of his task with bleak clarity, displaying the moral heroism of a man who persevered in what he saw as his duty, although he knew that the chance of success was slim. For all his faults, he was without doubt the greatest crusade pope since Gregory X.

Pius decided that the only way to bring about a united Christian response to the Turks was to preside over a congress of Christian powers, which he summoned to meet at Mantua in June 1459. Pius was banking on securing a binding agreement on joint action. This was a new approach, previous assemblies having been either small gatherings of a few rulers, or great Church councils which included the crusade as one of many items on their agendas. Pius was naturally anxious to avoid the latter, which could only become a platform for a renewed conciliarist attack on his authority; indeed, one of the reasons for his vigorous seizure of the initiative on the crusade was to complete the destruction of conciliarism. The Congress at Mantua started late and with inadequate representation, eliciting from the Pope the bitter comment that 'if we continue thus, it will be all over with us'. Even when they materialized, English diplomatic representation was derisory, while the French envoys wanted to discuss only the Angevin claim to Naples. Florence, which was energetically building up a thriving Levantine trade at the expense of Venice, was uninterested in a crusade, declaring it to be the job of the Germans and Hungarians. Castile was interested only in securing a full range of crusade privileges for its war against Granada. None the less, after a three-hour speech by Pius on 26 September, the Pope was able to exact a unanimous decision for war against the Turks. This was followed by much close discussion of strategy, recruitment, finance, and other essentials. By the close of the Congress, in January 1460, Pius reckoned to have promises for an army of 88,000 men, to be financed by taxes levied in the Italian states (except for Venice and Genoa), and with the hope of French, Venetian, Castilian, and Portuguese aid.

It is hard to tell how much of this Pius himself believed. If he placed any reliance on what had been achieved at Mantua, the next two years disenchanted him, as none of the promises was kept. Much hinged on the Empire, which as Hungary's neighbour might be expected to show most concern for its fate. But as Cardinal Bessarion, Pius's legate to Germany, found out in Vienna in the autumn of 1460, the Germans would do nothing but talk. Bessarion was scathingly critical: 'We need arms, arms I tell you, and strong men, not words; an army well supplied, not neat and polished oratory; we need the enduring strength of soldiers, not the bombast of fine speeches.' Meanwhile the Pope himself became involved in the war over the Kingdom of Naples between King Ferrante and the Angevin party, which poisoned his relations with France. Only two events in the aftermath of Mantua gave any cause for hope. One was the discovery of alum at Tolfa, in the Papal State, by John of Castro in 1461. This meant both that an embargo could be placed on the import of Turkish alum, and that papal funds for the crusade could be dramatically increased. The other was Venice's drift into war with the Turks in 1462–3. At least the Pope could count on one power which would support the crusade, provided of course that it served Venetian interests.

Aside from this the situation was bleak. It became increasingly clear that the leading powers were simply stalling on the crusade, waiting for the old and sick pope to die and the expedition to be formally abandoned.

In March 1462 Pius expressed his own feelings of disappointment and frustration at a meeting with six loyal cardinals:

We longed to declare war against the Turks and to put forth every effort in defence of religion, but when we measure our strength against that of the enemy, it is clear that the Church of Rome cannot defeat the Turks with its own resources . . . We are far inferior to the Turks unless Christian kings should unite their forces. We are seeking to effect this; we are searching out ways; none practicable presents itself. If we think of convening a council, Mantua teaches us that the idea is vain. If we send envoys to ask aid of sovereigns, they are laughed at. If we impose tithes on the clergy, they appeal to a future council. If we issue indulgences and encourage the contribution of money by spiritual gifts, we are accused of avarice. People think our sole object is to amass gold. No one believes what we say. Like insolvent tradesmen we are without credit. Everything we do is interpreted in the worst way, and since all princes are very avaricious and all prelates of the Church are slaves to money, they measure our disposition by their own.[7]

Despairing of joint action, Pius had thought of the one way to secure military action. As Philip the Good had committed himself, at the Feast of the Pheasant, to taking the field if one other prince did so, the Pope himself would lead the crusade. Others would follow Philip, or be shamed into action. 'It is not good to say "Go"; perhaps they will listen better to "Come".' This was the simple, or simplistic, project which Pius attempted to put into action over the next two years.

With Venice at war with Mehmed from July 1463, and Philip the Good renewing his commitment to the crusade after a serious illness, the project had some initial thrust, although the goals of its protagonists were so disparate as to be irreconcilable in practice. Preaching and tax collection were put in motion, and in the autumn of 1463 Pius presided over a congress of Italian powers which discussed the practicalities. Milan and Florence voiced the common fear that the proposed crusade would increase the danger of Venice dominating the Italian political scene. The Pope's response showed that he placed priority on the Ottoman menace: 'To buildings already in flames you bring no water but you are in a hurry to plan for those that may some day catch fire.' Cardinal Bessarion worked hard to promote the crusade in the Venetian dominions. On 22 October Pius solemnly, and rather grandiloquently, declared war on Mehmed in his bull *Ezechielis prophetae*. More importantly, the Pope, Venice, King Matthias Corvinus of Hungary, and Philip of Burgundy concluded a treaty of alliance against the Turks. This envisaged the total destruction of

---

[7] Setton, *The Papacy and the Levant*, ii. 235.

Ottoman power in the Balkans and the division of the conquered lands between Venice, Hungary, Scanderbeg, and others. The Florentine ambassador at Rome said that whereas it had previously been predicted that the crusade 'would go up in smoke', the combination of the four powers now made its departure viable: 'as long as the Pope and the Duke of Burgundy live, this expedition ought to succeed to the great honour of Christendom'.

Throughout the winter of 1463–4 the Pope made military preparations in Italy while Philip of Burgundy organized his contribution. The ceremonial sword which the Pope traditionally sent each Christmas to a Christian prince of whom military activity against the infidel might be expected, was dispatched to Matthias Corvinus. Philip the Good seemed determined finally to fulfil his vow. The preparations initially set in train in 1454–5 were renewed and pressed with vigour, an active part being undertaken by William Filastre, Bishop of Tournai and Chancellor of the Order of the Golden Fleece. Geoffrey of Thoisy and Waleran of Wavrin, veteran executants of the Duke's crusading policy, wrote memoranda of advice to add to those commissioned in the mid-1450s. At Christmas 1463 Philip convened an assembly at Bruges of *crucesignati*, and prominent prelates and lords, at which he announced his intention of embarking at Aigues Mortes in May 1464. Observers considered that the Duke really would set out this time, Louis XI of France commenting, rather brutally, to a Milanese ambassador that '[Philip] was a prince who had always had his own way, never having had to share power with a companion or equal, and that he was not of great intellect.' Then, in February 1464, the expedition received a serious blow when Louis XI persuaded his Burgundian vassal that his departure on crusade would expose France to the threat of an attack by the English, 'who have done more harm here than the Turks have in the lands they have conquered'. Philip, already uneasy at the prospect of actually going on crusade, was happy to take this way out, the pill being sugared by Louis's assurance that once peace was reached with England he would send a French crusade army of 10,000 men. The Duke therefore delegated leadership of his vanguard to his natural son, Anthony, asserting that he would follow when Anglo-French relations were more settled.

Despite this set-back, which Pius II bitterly resented, the crusade still seemed to be viable. Anthony of Burgundy set out with 3,000 men, embarking at Sluis in May 1464. They stopped off at Ceuta to assist the Portuguese against a Moorish attack, before proceeding to Marseilles.

On 18 June 1464 Pius himself took the cross in St Peter's, then set out to Ancona, where the Venetian fleet was expected to transport the crusaders across the Adriatic, after which they would fight alongside either Matthias Corvinus or Scanderbeg. Besides the Burgundians, several other bodies of crusaders were making their way to Ancona, including a small force sent by Francis Sforza under his son Tristan. As usual the Venetians were late, and when they arrived they had only twelve galleys, albeit commanded by the Doge in person. It scarcely mattered as Pius died of a fever on 15 August. The Burgundian contingent received the news at Marseilles, and it was ordered to return. Pius's crusade died with him. From the beginning it appeared an incredible undertaking, and more than one historian has remarked on the haphazard character of its organization. Yet the Pope's own enthusiasm, the commitment of Philip the Good and the interest shown by the Venetians, meant that it got as far as the recruitment of crusaders, the hiring and armament of ships, and the movement of the various elements towards their assembly at Ancona. No other fifteenth-century expedition launched outside the Balkan states achieved so much.

Philip the Good died in 1467 without fulfilling his crusade vow, and although his successor, Charles the Bold, showed a great deal of interest in the crusade, mounting French pressure on the Burgundian state meant that it ceased to be a potential crusading power. That left Scanderbeg, Matthias Corvinus, and Venice. Scanderbeg's struggle with the Turks was briefly interrupted when he went to southern Italy to fight for his lord, Ferrante of Aragon, in 1461; here his habit of killing all his prisoners shocked the Neapolitans, who were used to a gentler style of warfare. War with the Turks was resumed in 1462, and the Albanians received valuable Venetian help from 1463. In 1466 Mehmed II made his most ambitious attempt to take Croia, with a huge army, estimated at 150,000 men. He failed, but during the siege constructed, in the course of just a month, a fortress nearby at Elbasan. Thereafter this fortress, under the command of Balaban Pasha, posed a constant threat both to Croia and to Venetian shipping. Scanderbeg could not take it as he had no siege machinery, and although he inflicted another defeat on the Turks in 1467, the signs are that his situation was deteriorating when he died at Alessio in January 1468.

During this series of campaigns in Albania, Matthias Corvinus sustained his vigorous defence of the Danube frontier, assisted by generous financial subventions from Pope Paul II. In 1468, however, Matthias was drawn into the crusade against George of Podiebrady, the heretical King of Bohemia, which distracted him from the struggle against the Turks for several years. The Danube border stabilized as the Hungarians built up a defence system of powerful fortresses, supported by an increasingly militarized frontier society. Venice, on the other hand, remained locked in combat with the Turks until 1479. The Republic had a powerful ally in Uzun Hasan, prince of the Turcoman Ak-Koyunlu (White Sheep) and, from 1464, ruler of vast lands stretching as far as Persia. In 1468 Mehmed destroyed most of Karaman, but its ruler, Pir Ahmed, fled into the Taurus mountains and co-operated with Uzun Hasan in harassing Ottoman garrisons. Mehmed was compelled to fight on two fronts, and although Scanderbeg's death rid him of a major nuisance, the Venetian fleet operated in the Aegean with devastating effect in 1469. Mehmed responded by seizing Negroponte (Euboea) in July 1470, the worst blow Venice had yet suffered at Turkish hands.

Pope Sixtus IV viewed the loss of Negroponte as a severe one, sending out no fewer than five legates *a latere* to work for a crusade, and allocating large sums for papal galleys to assist the Venetians. But Venetian hopes rested largely on Uzun Hasan, with whom, after a long period of negotiations, the Republic and the Knights of St John formed an alliance in 1472. Venice undertook to provide Uzun Hasan with the firearms and cannon which he needed to meet the Ottomans on equal terms. The Venetian and papal galleys, commanded by Peter Mocenigo and Cardinal Oliver Carafa, attacked Adalia and Smyrna, while Uzun Hasan raised an army which raided deep into Anatolia. But Uzun Hasan failed to keep a rendezvous with the Venetian ships bringing him equipment. In August 1473 he was defeated by Mehmed near Bashkent, and a year later accepted peace terms. This enabled the Sultan to clear the Taurus of hostile Turcomans and complete the conquest of Karaman (1474). Mehmed was also able to give the Venetians more attention, laying siege to Scutari in 1474 and 1478. In January 1478 Uzun Hasan died, and five months later Croia finally fell to the Turks. The situation seemed hopeless, and in January 1479 Venice sealed a peace which ceded Mehmed Negroponte, parts of Albania, and other possessions, and committed the city to an annual tribute payment of 10,000 ducats, in exchange for trading rights within the Ottoman Empire.

During the later stage of the war with Venice Mehmed was also engaged in conflict with the powers bordering the western shores of the Black Sea. By 1475 a formidable coalition had developed in response to

Ottoman ambitions in the area: Stephen the Great of Moldavia, Casimir IV of Lithuania-Poland, Prince Ivan III the Great of Muscovy, the Tatar Golden Horde, and the Crimean Khanate. In January 1475 Ottoman troops under Hadim Suleyman Pasha were routed at Rahova. But Mehmed succeeded in winning over the Crimean Tatars, who from this point onwards were steadfast and valuable allies against the rising power of Muscovy. This enabled Mehmed to defeat Stephen of Moldavia in battle at Akdere in July 1476, and to ravage his principality. The Sultan then turned on Matthias Corvinus, and beat back his attack. Two years later Albania was finally incorporated into the Ottoman Empire. In just three years (1475–8), Mehmed had changed a situation which threatened Ottoman domination of the trans-Danubian lands, into one of total success and further gains. Following close on the Sultan's victory over Uzun Hasan, these successes in the Balkans demonstrated the concentration of military power which Mehmed had achieved in two decades.

The Veneto-Ottoman peace of 1479 represented victory over the greatest Christian maritime power, signifying the emergence of the Ottomans as a formidable force at sea as well as on land. Their seapower dated back to the building of an arsenal at Gallipoli by Bayezid I in the 1390s, so that at the siege of Constantinople in 1453 Turkish galleys already had a key part to play, much to the astonishment of the Greeks. But it was only after 1453, with the construction of a second arsenal at Galata, and the harnessing of Greek naval expertise, that seapower became an important factor in Ottoman expansion, featuring in the conquest of Trebizond in 1461 and that of Negroponte in 1470. Ten years later Mehmed felt confident enough to launch two simultaneous amphibious operations, an attack on the Hospitallers of Rhodes and a landing at Otranto in Apulia, with the aim of conquering at least the south of the Italian peninsula. This was rash, especially as the two campaigns coincided with land operations on several of the Sultanate's borders. But although Mesih Pasha's attempt to expel the Hospitallers failed in the summer of 1480, Gedik Ahmed Pasha succeeded in August 1480 in capturing Otranto. Leaving a garrison behind him, Gedik Ahmed crossed to Albania to make preparations for further advances in 1481.

Events had confirmed the papal Curia's worst fears: the Turks were striking at the heart of Christendom. Sixtus IV issued a rousing appeal for a crusade to recover Otranto.

How perilous it has become for all Christians, and especially the Italian powers, to hesitate in the assumption of arms against the Turks and how destructive to delay any longer, everyone can see . . . and so if the faithful, and especially the Italians, want to keep their lands, homes, wives, children, liberty, and the very faith in which we are baptized and reborn, let them believe us that they must now take up arms and go to war.[8]

The Pope himself undertook to maintain twenty-five galleys, and despite the promises of others, it was papal and Neapolitan forces alone which retook Otranto on 10 September 1481. This did not prove to be difficult: Turkish plans for expansion in Italy had collapsed with the death of Mehmed II, aged 49, on 3 May, and resultant confusion about the succession. But although Sixtus saw the Christian victories on 1480–1 at Rhodes and Otranto, and the Sultan's death, as the opportunity for a great crusade, a *tempus acceptabile* granted by God, there was no response.

Mehmed's death was followed by convulsions within the Ottoman Empire almost as severe as those caused by Tamerlane. There had been a build-up of resentment against the Sultan's juridical innovations, and the fiscal policies needed to pay for his virtually ceaseless aggression. The Sultan had levied a heavy tax on his periodical reminting of the silver coinage, farmed out provincial monopolies on essential items, and confiscated much land held by individuals and *waqfs* to create new *timars*. This discontent was channelled into the personal rivalry for the throne of the Conqueror's sons, Bayezid and Jem. The outstanding flaw in the Ottoman political system was the absence of any provision for a peaceful succession. No such provision could lawfully be made since the disposition of political authority was in God's hands. Even Mehmed II had contented himself with ruling that the prince who emerged victorious, with God's help, could kill his rivals: religious authorities agreed that this was licit since it would restore peace. Since princes were customarily sent to regional capitals in Anatolia at the age of 12, and were there able to build up local power-bases, full-scale civil war, like that between Bayezid and Jem, was hard to avoid.

Bayezid led the reaction against his father's policies, and defeated his brother in battle near Yeni-Shehir in June 1481. Jem fled to Cilicia and Cairo, but managed to organize fresh forces and tried a second time to fight Bayezid. Defeated again, he fled to Rhodes in July 1482. From here Jem went to France, remaining in Hospitaller custody. His aim was to encourage a crusade which would place him in power. He was quite

---

[8] Setton, *The Papacy and the Levant*, ii. 364.

prepared to make far-reaching concessions in exchange for western help, and until his death in 1495 Jem was the key factor in relations between Bayezid II and the West. As long as the pretender lived, Bayezid was happy to pay 45,000 Venetian ducats a year to Jem's hosts to keep him in the West, and pursued a conciliatory policy generally. In 1489 he even offered Charles VIII of France the crown of Jerusalem if Charles would consent to keep Jem captive and assist the Sultan against the Mamluks. To those who espoused a crusade, on the other hand, Jem represented a unique asset, and one which would not last for ever.

It was not only Jem that made Bayezid markedly more friendly towards the West, at least at first, than his father had been. The new Sultan also needed peace with the western powers in order to pursue wars elsewhere. His first serious military operations were against Stephen the Great of Moldavia, who used Jem's revolt to attack Ottoman Wallachia in 1481. Bayezid seized Kilia in July 1484, while his allies, the Crimean Tatars, took Akkerman in Bessarabia in August. The Ottoman conquest of these outlets to the Black Sea was a severe blow to Moldavia and Hungary, as well as to Venice and Genoa. Bayezid himself is said to have remarked that he had 'won the key of the door to all Moldavia and Hungary, the whole region of the Danube, Poland, Russia and Tatary, and the entire coast of the Black Sea'. The Sultan then turned to his southern frontier. Mehmed's conquests had brought the Ottoman and Mamluk lands in Cilicia into direct proximity, and territorial clashes were aggravated by the help Jem had received at Cairo. War broke out in 1485 and was brought to a close by mutual exhaustion in 1491. For the remainder of the 1490s the main field of Ottoman military activity was the Balkans, where Bayezid faced powerful enemies in Maximilian of Habsburg, who was crowned Emperor in 1493 and claimed to be an avid crusader, and King John Albert of Poland (1492–1501). Another attempt to capture Belgrade was abandoned when John Albert launched a major attack in the summer of 1497, hoping to break the Ottoman alliance with the Crimean Tatars, Moldavia, and Moscow. But the Polish army was defeated at Kozmin and John Albert came to terms in 1499.

Within the Empire, Bayezid reacted against the harshness of his father's policies, and by returning expropriated properties and ruling in accordance with the dictates of the religious law, he earned the title of *Bayezid-i Adli* (Bayezid the Law-abiding). None the less, he faced great internal discontent even after Jem's flight, especially in the hostility of nomadic Turcoman tribesmen who resented the government's increasing interference in their affairs, and its active encouragement of a cereal economy. Many were also attracted by the ideas of the growing Safavid movement (after Shaykh Safi al-Din, 1252–1334), a militant Shiite heresy in open opposition to the shariah of Sunni Islam. Called the Red Heads (*kizilbas*) from their distinctive red headwear, these groups formed natural followers for pretenders and rebels like Ismail Safavi, a blood-relative of Uzun Hasan, who made incursions into Ottoman territory from his base in Iran during the later years of Bayezid II's reign. Ismail resumed Uzun's policy of attempting to forge an anti-Ottoman alliance between Iran and the West.

Crusade activists welcomed such overtures, and were encouraged by news of the *kizilbas*, but they realized that their chief hope lay in Jem. Between 1489 and 1495 there were two major attempts in the West to use the advantage afforded by the person of Jem to launch a crusade. The first was made by Pope Innocent VIII (1484–92). It seemed obvious that Bayezid II would eventually renew his father's assault on Italy, and in 1489, after several years in which his sponsorship of the crusade was limited to the issue of indulgences and the levy, or attempted levy, of taxes, Innocent summoned a congress to meet in Rome to organize a crusade. The Congress, for which of course Mantua was no promising precedent, met in March 1490 and some good sense was shown in the consideration of the various practical problems involved, including the organization of the three armies reckoned to be needed, and the co-ordination of their efforts to best effect. But the Pope's conclusion, that an army of 95,000 men and 75,000 horses would be necessary, was the stuff of fantasy. The only Christian powers which might have taken a lead were Venice and Hungary. Venice regarded the renewal of war with the Turks with horror, while the premature death of Matthias Corvinus in 1490 ruled a Hungarian initiative out of the question. Innocent VIII's congress was long remembered, and cited, as proof of the futility of debating the crusade at a time when none of Christendom's rulers showed any real interest in assuming the initiative.

The second, and more important, attempt to launch a Jem-centred expedition originated with the French Crown. First embroiled in the conflict with Lancastrian England, then preoccupied with internal recovery and the dismemberment of Burgundy, the French court and nobility had played a virtually negligible role in the crusading movement since Nicopolis. But the accession of the youthful Charles VIII brought with it a resurgence of French interest in crusading. In September 1494 Charles set out on an expedition to Italy which placed the peninsula at the centre of the European power struggle for decades. The King loudly asserted that his expedition had the dual goal of recovering the Kingdom of Naples, lawfully his through his descent in the Angevin line, and of using the *Regno*'s Adriatic ports to launch a crusade against the Turks in the Balkans. We could dismiss this as thin propaganda, akin to that of his father Louis XI, were it not for the King's undoubted piety and idealism. Pope Alexander VI viewed the French invasion of Italy with alarm, giving Ferdinand of Naples a tenth to defend the *Regno* and even requesting Bayezid II to persuade the Venetians to attack the French. But on the last night of 1494 French troops entered Rome, and on 27 January Jem, who had been in papal custody since 1489, was handed over to the French.

Moving southwards, Charles VIII encountered no Neapolitan resistance, and all seemed set for a rapid occupation of the Kingdom and the crossing of the Adriatic in galleys promised by Ludovic Sforza of Milan. There were significant anti-Turkish uprisings in Greece and Albania in anticipation of the French army's arrival. Charles entered Naples in triumph on 22 February 1495. But three days later Jem died, probably of pneumonia, and when Sforza went back on his promise and Venice refused to provide naval help, French crusade plans collapsed. Charles continued to talk about crossing to fight the Turks, but at the end of March 1495 Alexander VI, Sforza, Venice, the Emperor Maximilian, and the Spanish sovereigns formed the anti-French League of Venice (its purpose also, ostensibly, to fight Bayezid), and the French army had to retreat. After the inconclusive battle of Fornovo in July Charles withdrew into Piedmont.

Early in 1499 Jem's corpse arrived in Istanbul, proof for Bayezid that he had nothing more to fear from his brother. For some years, both in response to internal pressure for a renewal of the holy war, and as a result of minor clashes between the two powers, Bayezid had been building up his fleet for another war with Venice. War finally broke out in July 1499, and went disastrously for the Republic. In August Lepanto fell to the Turks in a joint land–sea assault, commanded by the Sultan in person. In the following year the Turks took Modon, Coron, and Navarino, while the *akinjis* raided freely in Croatia and Dalmatia. Venice desperately sought allies. Apart from granting crusade indulgences to the Republic's soldiers and sailors, there was little Alexander VI could do; indeed, the derisory response to his attempts to organize a crusade show just how ineffectual the Renaissance papacy had become in crusading affairs.

Venice's Italian enemies were openly jubilant at her defeats. The Bishop of Torcello, Stephen Taleazzi, prepared three crusading tracts which considered the problem from all angles but concluded with the realistic assessment that nothing would be done in the end anyway. In June 1500 the Pope issued the crusade bull 'Quamvis ad amplianda', which attempted to levy a universal tenth on the Church, and he tried to persuade Louis XII of France to take the lead. Otherwise, Alexander wrote, Italy would be 'done for' ('de Italia actum erit'). Venice secured Hungary's entry into the war in May 1501, and a Franco-Venetian fleet operated in the Aegean in the summer of the same year, but in August 1501 the Turkish capture of Durazzo completed a run of appalling Venetian losses. By 1502 Bayezid reckoned that he could make no further progress, and he made peace with Venice in December. Peace with Hungary followed in 1503.

The Veneto-Turkish peace of 1502 marks a logical point at which to end a chapter which has focused on the alarming growth of Ottoman power in the fifteenth century. The war of 1499–1502 brought about the furthest extent of the Turkish advance westwards under Bayezid II, more than compensating for the withdrawal from Otranto in 1481. It also demonstrated the emergence of two factors which would be very important in the sixteenth century. One was the dominance of Ottoman sea-power. Formidable enough if one considers just the fleets sent out from Istanbul, it was powerfully augmented by the corsairs who had begun to raid Christian shipping from the North African ports, and who were given Ottoman patronage in exchange for sharing their expertise and knowledge of the Mediterranean. Kemal Reis, the most famous of these sea-*ghazis*, entered Ottoman service in 1494 and carried out important reforms in the Turkish navy which contributed greatly to the victory over the Venetians. 'Reversing centuries of frontier history,' Professor A. C. Hess has written, 'the Ottomans had achieved naval supremacy in the eastern Mediterranean'.

The second significant feature of the Venetian war was Bayezid II's active search for western allies. The Sultan had built up close contacts with Christian powers during the years of his brother's custody in the West, and he fully appreciated the opportunities which the Italian wars of the 1490s opened up for useful alliances. Milan and Naples were enlisted on the Ottoman side against Venice, and although their assistance proved less valuable than anticipated, the important precedent was established of active military co-operation between Christian powers and the Sultanate, rather than the simple neutrality which had formerly been the rule.

Juristic commentators, such as the Spanish Rodrigo Sánchez of Arévalo, had begun to argue that such co-operation was legitimate if a Christian state was fighting for its life. The seed was thus sown which would eventually flower into Ottoman integration into the pattern of European alliances. Paradoxically, this occurred at precisely the same time that the overwhelming power and aggressive ambitions of the Turks made the persistence of crusading ideas inevitable, however much those ideas were reshaped by the new political and social configurations of the Early Modern world.

4

The Anti-Turkish Crusade and European Politics, 1502–1580

✠

Until a few years ago most historians would have said that the inclusion of a chapter on events in the sixteenth century in a book about the later crusades was at best superfluous, and at worst misguided. They would have argued that popular and governmental commitment to a crusade against the Turks was negligble by 1500; that calls for a crusade, no matter how frequently or forcefully made by individual enthusiasts or the papal Curia, were therefore anachronistic, meriting serious study only by antiquarians; and, most importantly, that narrating the great conflicts which occurred in the sixteenth century between the Ottomans and their western enemies, especially the Habsburgs, in terms of a religious war is as misleading as applying that description to, say, the Allied campaigns against the Turkish armies in the First World War. It is the achievement of Professor K. M. Setton to have shown how inaccurate this view was. In two massive volumes, a total of 1,179 double-columned pages, he recently surveyed Turkish relations with the West between 1502 and 1571 in exhaustive detail. By simply describing what took place, Professor Setton demonstrated that, while these relations accommodated many new features characteristic of an age of profound change, they also formed a continuation of crusading history, in terms of basic ideas and institutions as well as terminology. No great chasm separated the world of King Philip II of Spain and Pope Pius V from that of Philip the Good of Burgundy and Pius II; the one evolved from the other and shared many of its features. Lepanto (1571) was a great crusading victory, Alcazar (1578) a terrible crusading defeat, and some account of at least this first phase of the long Habsburg–Ottoman struggle must now feature in any history of the later crusades which claims to be comprehensive (see maps 3, 4, and 5).

Having said that, there is no doubt that the crusade in this period calls for a rather different perspective from that against which even the movement in the fifteenth century can be viewed. Generally speaking, three patterns ran through these decades, and will therefore predominate in the pages that follow. First, there was the organization of military expeditions in crusading form, taking place through a familiar pattern of projects, diplomatic negotiations with the Curia, the formation of naval leagues, the issuing and preaching of indulgences, and the levy of taxes. The stimulus was the ever-present Turkish threat. In the second place, the crusade played a large role in European politics in the shape of a cluster of major propaganda themes: this again will be familiar. Indeed it is striking that there seems to have been just as great an emphasis on crusading ideas in sixteenth-century propaganda as in earlier periods, and maybe even more so. Instead of taking this as their cue to dismiss the Early Modern crusade as a propaganda exercise, historians should take cognizance of the fact that it would hardly have been worth while constructing this complex and detailed tissue of claims and counter-claims had the crusade become wholly detached from popular feeling.

The third theme, which as we have seen only really made its appearance towards the end of the fifteenth century, is the entry of the Turks as a major force on the European political stage, in the sense that the Ottomans actively sought western allies, encouraged the activities of dissident internal groups which would work to their advantage, and kept in close touch with the complex events taking place in the West. Naturally this new theme itself fed and helped to sharpen crusade propaganda: but the point to emphasize is that increasing contacts with the Turks, of a diplomatic and military nature, coexisted with simultaneous and large-scale crusade planning, and that the former did not show the latter to be nonsensical or pointless. In fact there was much more anti-Turkish crusading in this period than active military co-operation between the Ottomans and Christian powers, partly because co-operation proved exceptionally difficult to organize in an effective manner. These are areas which call for further investigation and will doubtless receive it. What is certain is that the crusade in the sixteenth century is a fascinating subject which warrants serious treatment at the hands of the historian.

For the Ottomans, the opening decade of the new century was a difficult period for, although they emerged victorious in the war against Venice, they faced crisis in Anatolia as the rebellion of the *kizilbas* came to a head. The Red Heads' spiritual leader, Shah Ismail Safavi, had a firm power-base in Iran, actively encouraged *kizilbas* defiance of the Ottoman provincial administration, and himself launched invasions of eastern Anatolia in 1502 and 1507. In 1508–9 Ismail conquered Baghdad and became more aggressive in his persecution of Sunni Muslims. Bayezid II was reluctant to take action against Ismail or the *kizilbas*, but in 1511 a rebellion in south-western Anatolia (Tekke) under Shah-Kuli enjoyed great success, winning over many Ottoman troops and posing a threat to Bursa. Bayezid sent the Grand Vizier, Ali Pasha, with a powerful army and near Kayseri in August 1511 Shah-Kuli was killed and his army defeated, at the cost of Ali Pasha's life. Throughout these years Ottoman court politics were dominated by the struggle for power and the right of succession between Bayezid's five adult sons; in 1512, with the support of the janissary corps, Selim emerged as victor. Claiming that a more forceful sultan was needed to deal with the Safavid threat, Selim forced his father to abdicate in April. In the following month Bayezid died, probably poisoned by Selim.

After defeating a rebellion by his brother Ahmed in 1513, the new Sultan turned to deal with the threat posed by Shah Ismail. He made careful preparations. Venice and Hungary were kept out of the conflict with substantial concessions; an offensive alliance was concluded with the Mamluks; and a massive pogrom was carried out against Ismail's supporters and agents in Anatolia. Proclaiming his campaign a *ghaza* against Shiite heretics, an important innovative move in Ottoman ideological thinking, Selim invaded the upper valley of the Euphrates in the summer of 1514. Ismail wanted to avoid battle, allowing Selim's formidable supply difficulties to make him retreat, but *kizilbas* exiles demanded the chance to fight, and the two armies met at Chaldiran in Azerbaijan on 23 August. Superior Ottoman firearms won the day and Selim occupied Tabriz, but the bulk of the Turkish army was still a seasonal fighting force and Selim was unable to prolong the campaign long enough to take possession of northern Iraq. None the less, the Ottomans had dealt a decisive blow to Ismail's power and influence, and between 1515 and 1517 Selim annexed the whole of the eastern Anatolian plateau as far east as Diyarbekir. As so often in Ottoman history, a crisis had proved to be the stimulus to massive territorial gains.

But this was, in a sense, just the prologue to yet greater conquests. Even before their gains of 1515–17, the Ottomans were led to contemplate the invasion of Egypt by the glaring weaknesses of the Mamluk Sultanate, aptly described by Professor Hess as 'inferior in modern military technology, isolated in exterior politics, internally divided, economically dependent on exterior structures, and defenceless in naval men and material'. The decay of Mamluk power, which we examined in Chapter 1,[1] was both demonstrated and accelerated by Portuguese naval domination of the Indian Ocean and Red Sea, achieved in the new century's first decade. Key events in this were the Portuguese occupation of the island of Socotra in the Gulf of Aden, and their capture of Hormuz in the mouth of the Persian Gulf. Faced with an unprecedented threat to their commercial revenues, the Mamluks responded by building a navy, which the Portuguese promptly sank in 1509. The Mamluk Sultan Kansawh al-Ghawri desperately appealed to Istanbul for help and, provoked by Portuguese assistance to Shah Ismail, the Ottomans sent vital munitions, naval supplies, and experts to Egypt in 1511–12. Clearly the Mamluks were no longer able to defend the holy cities of Mecca and Medina from possible Portuguese attack, or, for that matter, to resist Ottoman aggression. And as Ottoman rule was established in Dulkadir and northern Iraq, there were border clashes between the two states, which strengthened the argument of the hawks at the Ottoman court that the new lands could only be effectively held if Cilicia and Syria too came under Turkish control. These factors, together with Selim's own ambitious and bellicose nature, propelled the Ottomans into their greatest and most daring military venture.

In the spring of 1516 Kansawh al-Ghawri, anticipating an Ottoman attack, led an army northwards to Aleppo. North of the city, at Marj Dabiq, Selim met him in battle on 24 August 1516. More decisively than at Chaldiran, Ottoman firearms and discipline proved their superiority. Kansawh died on the battlefield. Following this single battle the Ottomans occupied all Syria and Palestine in a matter of weeks: leading provincial officials, in particular the governor of Aleppo, Khair Bey, had already negotiated in secret with Selim, and the heterogeneous religious and racial groups of the area had less to fear from the new regime, with its established approach of granting limited rights of self-government, than from the increasingly chaotic and corrupt rule of the Mamluks. Tumanbay seized power in Cairo after Marj Dabiq, and Selim hoped to avoid war by offering him the governorship of Egypt, but Tumanbay had himself proclaimed Sultan in October. Selim therefore crossed Sinai in January and inflicted another heavy defeat on the Mamluks at al-Raydaniyya (23 January 1517). Cairo was taken after three days of street fighting. After the capture

[1] Above, 43–5.

and execution of Tumanbay in April the Ottoman conquest of Egypt was secure, and in July the guardianship of the holy cities was placed in Selim's hands. Even granted the exceptional frailty of the Mamluk Sultanate, the conquest of Syria and Egypt in less than a year was an extraordinary achievement, especially for a power operating from Anatolia: at the battle of al-Raydaniyya the Ottoman army was many hundreds of miles from its base-line. Without the guarantee of naval support the entire undertaking would have been impossible, a fact which historians critical of Bayezid II's reign would do well to bear in mind.

When Selim I died in 1520 he had, in the course of just eight years, added more territory to the Empire than any of his predecessors. His conquests were important for the Ottoman state in three ways. In the first place they naturally brought about an enormous increase in Ottoman resources. The Sultan rapidly established stable government in the two new areas, grouping the many Turcoman and Kurdish tribes of the eastern Anatolian plateau into 'peoples' (*ulus*), and instituting a governor (*beyler* bey) with exceptional powers in Egypt. Residual local discontent, and the distance between Istanbul and Cairo, made the latter post a potentially dangerous one—the second governor, Ahmed Pasha, did in fact rebel in 1524—but in general the speed with which the Ottomans incorporated the new lands, so as to start extracting revenues from them, is striking. Figures from 1528 show that the province of Diyarbekir was then providing Istanbul with twenty-five million aspers, while Syria and Egypt brought in about 100 million; in the same year the Balkan provinces provided about 200 million. In the case of the new territories much of this money came from long-distance commerce, but it has recently been stressed that the Ottomans were rather more interested in the fiscal and commercial exploitation of their vastly expanded internal economy than in the siren-call of India and Inner Asia: what they wanted above all was continental territory, which they could divide into *timars* or tax directly to pay for their huge building programmes in Istanbul, Edirne, and Bursa, for the wages of the janissary corps (which under Selim grew greatly), and for escalating expenditure on artillery and the navy.

One consequence of Selim's conquests was thus that the tremendous aggression which had characterized Mehmed II's reign could be renewed, financed this time by the resources of the Fertile Crescent. The second was that the Sultanate's enforcement of an unprecedented degree of political and religious unity within Islam had the effect of giving Ottoman state ideology its finishing touches. By extinguishing its Mamluk rival and gaining guardianship of the holy cities, the Sultanate became by far the greatest Islamic power and the only major Sunni one. Its new status and responsibility were reflected above all in its emphasis on the sultan's possession of a 'great' or 'exalted' caliphate. Sultans since Murad I had called themselves caliph, a title which could be assumed by any Muslim ruler who was enforcing the shariah; what was new was the Ottoman claim to the pre-eminence of their caliphate. For instance, in response to appeals for Turkish help from Muslim rulers in India and Central Asia, Suleyman I described himself as 'Caliph of the Face of the Earth'. Technically such appeals had to be answered, so that the most important effect of this stress on the sultan's possession of a unique religious position within Islam was to reinforce the already powerful Ottoman expansionist drive. As before, this was fuelled by an emphasis on the role of the sultan as a *ghazi* leader, and facilitated by a centralized and absolutist government, and by the organization of Ottoman society into military and non-military classes. For most of the sixteenth century this society was remarkably stable and peaceful, forming a great contrast with social conditions in the West. The only serious internal problem facing the sultans was the continuing opposition of the nomadic Turcomans to centralization and taxation, which found expression in periodic uprisings, called *celali* revolts after the inspirational Safavid preacher Celal.

It was clear, then, that expansion would continue, but the third consequence of Selim's conquests was to make the direction of expansion highly problematic, a matter for intense debates within the Ottoman court which we can follow only in their broad outlines. To existing areas for possible expansion—Hungary, the shores of the Black Sea, Safavid Persia, and Iraq—Selim's conquests added two more, the Red Sea and Indian Ocean on the one hand, North Africa on the other. In the Red Sea Ottoman naval power had already encountered the Portuguese when it had rendered assistance to the Mamluks. A strong commitment to the security of Muslim shipping in the Red Sea did not, however, escalate into a major conflict with Portugal in the Indian Ocean: by the end of 1525 the Sultan had decided that a force of just twenty-five ships and 4,000 men was sufficient to achieve his goals in South Arabia. Historians have frequently castigated this approach as an illustration of the Ottoman failure to appreciate the importance of the spice trade; in fact it merely shows that the Portuguese and Turks had quite different objectives in the area, the former wanting to create a commercial and oceanic empire, the latter a land-based one with strong internal communications. From this point of view North Africa, especially the Central Maghrib, seemed much more promising. The acquisition of Egypt directed Ottoman attention towards Tunisia, Algeria, and Morocco, where, as we have seen, they had already built up links of patronage with the resident pirates. In his last years Selim sent troops as far as the borders of Tunisia, and it was clear that the Ottomans had the capacity both on land and at sea to make a powerful impact on the North African littoral as far west as the Straits of Gibraltar. A second area of potential conflict between the western powers and the Turks was thus added to the Balkans, so that even though the anti-Turkish crusade did not reach the Indian Ocean, it was still a more extended movement than previously.

Although Selim's campaigns against the Safavids and Mamluks meant that Turkish resources were mainly directed against non-Christian powers in the years following the Veneto-Ottoman peace of 1502, the crusade still played an important role in European politics, both because the long-term threat remained and because of the propaganda value still attaching to crusading ideas. The immediate goals of Pope Julius II (1503–13) were the reconquest of the Romagna and the reduction of Venetian power in northern Italy. An important theme of papal diplomacy, therefore, was the familiar idea that the Venetians had to be defeated before a crusade could be launched, while the anti-Venetian diplomatic talks at Savona in 1507, and the discussions which resulted in the League of Cambrai in 1508, were conducted under the guise of crusade negotiations. This placed Venice in the extraordinary position of claiming to be 'Christendom's first line of defence' against the Turks, at the same time as the Republic's envoys at the Ottoman and Mamluk courts were arguing that the city was keeping the western powers from launching a crusade. The French made much of this, so that John Lemaire de Belges, in his 'La Légende des Vénitiens' (1509), described the Venetians as 'forerunners of Antichrist and agents of Mohammed'. Similarly, before he reached agreement with Louis XII at Cambrai, the Emperor Maximilian asserted that before going on crusade it was essential to expel the French from Milan, where they constituted a greater threat to Christendom than the Turks. Appropriately, the same remark about the priority of defeating the French, who were guilty of cruelty worse than that practised by the Turks, was addressed by Henry VIII to Maximilian a few years later, when the Emperor had urged Henry to make peace with France for the sake of the crusade. Meanwhile rulers on the periphery of this great contest, such as Manuel of Portugal and James IV of Scotland, continued to come forward with sincere, though fanciful, proposals for a crusade; to these projects, often conceived during leisurely winter evenings and forgotten about when spring came, Fernand Braudel gave the apt title 'dossiers d'hiver'.

Hopes for genuine crusade planning became somewhat stronger with the accession of Pope Leo X in 1513. In 1511, responding to the threat of a French and German schism, Julius II had summoned a general council of the Church, placing the organization of a crusade on its agenda in wholly traditional style. The result was the Fifth Lateran Council (1512–17), the last Church council before the onset of the Reformation. At its sixth session, in April 1513, the case for a crusade was forcefully made in the presence of the new Pope, and although the work of the Council was overshadowed by the continuing conflict in Italy, in September 1513 Leo issued the first crusade indulgences against the Turks for many years. At the Council's tenth session, in May 1515, the opening discourse was given by the indefatigable Archbishop Stephen Taleazzi, who had first preached a sermon about the crusade in 1480; in 1500, as we saw in the last chapter,[2] Taleazzi had expressed scepticism about the chance of a crusade being launched, and nothing had changed in the mean time. Maximilian expressed anxiety at the extent of Ottoman conquests, and in the negotiations which followed the French victory at Marignano in September 1515 the new King of France, Francis I, claimed that he wanted to lead a crusade; but neither ruler went any further. As on so many previous occasions, in the absence of any real concern shown by western rulers all that the Council could do was to levy a three-year tenth on the Church for a crusade which nobody expected to materialize. The contrast with the crusading achievements of the Council's thirteenth-century namesake is striking; for all the eloquent and impassioned speeches it generated on the subject of the Turkish advance, the Council represented the low point in the medieval papacy's leadership of the crusading movement.

No pope could have remained inactive faced with the extraordinary advances made by Selim and their implications for Christendom, but Leo X's response was noticeably energetic. In November 1517 he issued new indulgences, called for suggestions from the West's rulers, set up a working-party of eight cardinals to consider the details of an expedition, and granted Francis I a tenth for the crusade. The cardinals quickly produced a report, which was sent to the French and Imperial courts for comment. One interesting feature of the report was the suggestion that

[2] Above, 116.

Christendom's princes form a 'brotherhood of the holy crusade' (*fraternitas Sanctae Cruciatae*) to preserve and enforce the crusade's *sine qua non*, peace in the West. The French reply at least displayed common sense, but the German plan was little more than the expression of Habsburg *Hauspolitik*, a complex project for three years of co-ordinated assaults on North Africa, the Balkans, and Greece. As Professor Setton remarked, 'the German document is too fatuous to take seriously as a plan for the crusade. It almost assumes that the Turks would stand idly by while Maximilian's tortuous scheme was worked out to dismember their empire over a three-year period.' None the less, in March 1518 Leo imposed a five-year truce on Christendom, and sent out four legates to try to enforce it. The Anglo-French treaty of London of October 1518 showed that rulers were responding at least to the call for peace, if not to that for a crusade, while the death of the Emperor Maximilian in January 1519 led both of the leading aspirants to the Empire, Francis I and Charles of Spain, to assert their crusading zeal as part of their electoral campaigns. French fleets were dispatched eastwards in 1518 and 1520, the last significant gesture of French hostility towards the Turks for many decades. In fact the crusade as a serious military venture aroused more publicity and discussion in the years 1517–20 than it had for decades. One clear sign of this is the proliferation of crusade tracts, including the reappearance of a curious Franciscan project first put forward in 1474, which suggested an army of 500,000 men paid for by monasteries, convents, and those parishes in the hands of the mendicant Orders.

In the autumn of 1520 news reached the West that Sultan Selim had died, and crusade plans were shelved in the expectation that his successor, Suleyman, would present less of a problem. This optimism was just as misguided as similar hopes of Mehmed II had been at his accession in 1451, for Suleyman 'the Magnificent' proved to be Christian Europe's most dangerous Turkish enemy since the Conqueror. It was Suleyman who benefited from the conquests which Selim had scarcely time to enjoy, and from the start of his reign he showed that he believed westwards expansion to be just as important as the continuing struggle against Safavid Persia. The new Sultan's most important western adversary was Charles V, whose election as Emperor in June 1519 rounded off the gathering into his hands of the most formidable group of territories held by a single Christian ruler since Charlemagne: Austria and the original Habsburg lands (through his paternal grandfather Maximilian); Franche Comté, Luxemburg, and the Netherlands (through his paternal grandmother

Mary, daughter of Charles the Bold); the Crown of Aragon and the *Regno* (through his maternal grandfather Ferdinand of Aragon); and Castile and its American dependencies (through his maternal grandmother Isabella).

Together with the imperial title, this great legacy would seem to have made Charles the military match for Suleyman; as ruler of Germany, Naples, and Spain he certainly had good reason to act as Europe's chief anti-Turkish protagonist, quite apart from the ideological commitment— which Charles took very seriously—inherent in his possession of the imperial title. Moreover, from his Austrian, Burgundian, and Iberian ancestors Charles inherited a combined crusading tradition richer even than that enjoyed by Francis I. But Charles faced problems which prevented him applying his power with anything like the concentration and continuity which the Sultan could take for granted. These arose partly from the geographical and political diversity of his own lands, partly from the ramshackle nature of imperial authority, but most importantly from two developments which proved exceptionally useful to Suleyman: the Protestant Reformation and the persistent enmity of France, which feared encirclement by Habsburg might and at times secured the support of England, the papacy, and other powers wary of Charles's ambitions. As a result the struggle between Suleyman and Charles, which dominated the middle decades of the century, often appears a rather unequal contest; it is significant that whenever the Sultan had to neglect his western borders to fight in the east, Charles's problems prevented him using the chance to recover lost ground.

Suleyman began his reign in a spectacular fashion by capturing Belgrade in August 1521 and expelling the Hospitallers from Rhodes in December 1522. With these triumphs the Sultan firmly established his own reputation as a *ghazi*, exacted revenge for two of Mehmed II's most humiliating reverses, and cleared a path for westwards expansion, initially by land, and within a decade by sea as well. The loss of Belgrade was especially serious as it signalled the collapse of Hungary's frontier system. Meanwhile Charles V and his ally Henry VIII of England were engaged in driving the French from northern Italy, while at the Diet of Worms (April 1521) the German Estates adopted their traditional line of refusing to provide assistance to Hungary. At the same Diet Martin Luther was placed under the imperial ban and his views condemned, a turning-point in the spread of Protestant dissent. Well might Pope Clement VII declare, at his first consistory in December 1523, that the three greatest problems facing Christendom were the Turkish threat, warfare between

Christian princes, and the Lutheran schism. In 1525 Charles V defeated and captured Francis at the battle of Pavia, which broke French power in Italy and led to the highly favourable Treaty of Madrid (January 1526). The Emperor's reaction to Pavia was that it would enable him to deal with Suleyman, and the treaty included the customary clauses relating to the organization of a crusade. The 'main intention' of Charles and Francis, according to the treaty, was that of 'attaining a general peace and consequently organising an expedition against the Turks'. But as usual Charles's success led to the creation of an anti-Habsburg alliance, on this occasion the League of Cognac, whose adherents (France, Venice, Clement VII, and Florence) predictably claimed that one of its chief goals was a 'general expedition of Christian princes against the Turks, the enemies of the Christian name'. The French had become adept at this game: on an earlier occasion Francis I had proposed a Valois–Habsburg treaty to conquer England and divide Italy, under cover of a simultaneous crusade project which would distract the attention of the pope and other Christian powers.

In these circumstances King Louis II of Hungary could expect no help from Charles V, and the mobilization of German resources in favour of Louis and Charles's brother Ferdinand, ruler of Austria and imperial *Staathalter* in Germany, remained problematic. Even after the fall of Belgrade the German Estates displayed limited concern about Suleyman's advance, pressing for a resolution of the growing religious problem to come first. Protestant leaders were suspicious of what the Emperor would do with any men or money they granted to him, and by 1526 two of them, the Landgrave of Hesse and the Elector of Saxony, were arguing that the provision of aid should be made contingent upon imperial concessions on the religious issue. None the less, in the summer of 1526 the situation in Hungary, which was facing a massive Turkish invasion, was so critical that the Diet of Speyer granted 24,000 men in response to Ferdinand's pleas. This grant came too late to prevent the disaster which overtook Hungary. In July the Grand Vizier, Ibrahim Pasha, took several fortress towns north of Belgrade. And on 29 August Louis II and his army were defeated in the battle of Mohács. Louis died during the retreat, and after nearly a century as Christendom's chief *antemurale* against Ottoman expansion, his Kingdom degenerated to the level of a buffer-state between Habsburg and Ottoman lands. There followed an Ottoman occupation of Buda, and although Suleyman soon withdrew, Hungary's long-term plight was worsened by a disputed succession, in which

Ferdinand of Austria, whose claim lay in his marriage to the childless Louis's sister, was opposed by John Zápolya, *voivode* of Transylvania, who led the anti-German faction. Zápolya accepted Turkish suzerainty and naturally joined the anti-Habsburg coalition which had formed in 1526.

With Zápolya dependent on Suleyman's support, and the French court in regular contact with Istanbul, the Ottoman integration into European politics was clearly proceeding rapidly. At the same time, as noted at the start of the chapter, propaganda use of the crusade idea was continuing, and both Charles and the anti-Habsburg powers went to great lengths to depict their opponents as holding up a major crusading effort. In 1526–7 Suleyman was fully occupied in suppressing a series of dangerous *celali* uprisings in Anatolia and Cilicia, giving Ferdinand the chance he needed to defeat Zápolya and be proclaimed King of Hungary. Suleyman reacted in 1529 by launching another invasion of Hungary. He established Zápolya as King at Buda in September, and as a punitive gesture for Ferdinand's intervention in Hungary, went on to lay siege to Vienna. Germany was struck with alarm as Turkish raiding parties penetrated deep into Bavaria and Bohemia. But Vienna's fortifications proved to be too strong and after three weeks the Sultan withdrew. Amongst the forces which marched in relief of Vienna were troops provided by the Protestant princes, who rallied to the defence of Germany; it was the last time they would do so without tying their assistance to religious concessions. None the less, victory at Vienna was not the only event in 1529 which led Charles V to believe that his exalted view of how Christendom should be governed and defended might be capable of implementation, for in the Treaty of Barcelona, in June, Clement VII reached agreement with the Emperor on Italian affairs, and two months later, at Cambrai, Francis I made peace.

This proved to be no more than a hiatus in Charles's problems. Francis I depended on continuing Turkish pressure, which he was prepared to incite and guide, to stave off what he saw as the threat of Habsburg domination of all Europe, and to enable his troops to regain his lost lands in Italy. 'I cannot deny', he was quoted as saying, 'that I keenly desire the Turk powerful and ready for war, not for himself, because he is an infidel and we are Christians, but to undermine the Emperor's power, to force heavy expenses upon him and to reassure all other governments against so powerful an enemy.' After 1519 any interest which the French King displayed in the anti-Turkish crusade was thus either propaganda or, as in the case of the Anglo-French alliance of October 1532, functioned as the disguise for an anti-Habsburg initiative. From 1531, moreover, the Protestant princes of Germany, grouped into the Schmalkaldic League, adopted a clear policy of linking aid to concessions. And while Clement VII clearly felt a responsibility towards the Hungarians and Croatians, who sent him numerous appeals for help, his own fears of Habsburg might, coupled with his lack of money, prevented him doing much to assist; as a papal secretary recorded of one consistory in July 1531, 'many things were said, but no decisions taken'. In 1532, responding to a provocative Habsburg siege of Buda at the end of 1530, Suleyman fielded a massive army in another attempt to take Vienna, or to force Charles to risk a pitched battle in defence of the city. According to the French ambassador in Rome, panic had set in there, and the Pope was contemplating flight to Avignon. But Ottoman strategy failed, as Charles refused to fight, and the Turks were held up for so long by the garrison at Güns, in Hungary, that they had no time even to reach Vienna before the onset of autumn and their lack of supplies compelled them to retreat.

Suleyman's invasions of 1529 and 1532 led the Pope to make financial concessions to Charles V on an unprecedented scale, rising to a half of Church revenues in Spain in 1533. This extraordinary grant reflected the severity of the crisis as perceived at Rome and Vienna (though not, understandably, in Spain). By this point, however, the crisis had already passed, for the 1532 campaign proved to be the last in the sequence of ambitious Ottoman thrusts into Central Europe which had started in 1521. Suleyman apparently realized that until Hungary was fully incorporated into the Empire, incursions into Austria would entail a short campaigning season with perilously extended lines of communication, and carried with them the danger of pushing the Protestant princes into the arms of the Habsburgs. In addition, Suleyman wanted to campaign against Safavid Persia. After difficult, and particularly well-documented negotiations, which nearly stalled thanks to Charles V's insistence on calling himself King of Jerusalem, the Sultan made peace with Ferdinand in 1533. Suleyman accepted the Habsburg's rule over the north and west of Hungary in exchange for Ferdinand's recognition of the Sultan's suzerainty. Both sides then set about constructing the formidable frontier system of fortified villages and marcher lordships which set the later pattern for the Habsburg–Ottoman border. For Charles V, success over the Turks in 1532 was won at the cost of granting the Protestants the religious peace of Nürnberg, the precursor to the Augsburg Peace of

1555. Between these two dates, the Protestant leaders skilfully and ruthlessly exploited the Ottoman threat to extract a series of important concessions from the Emperor.

His hands freed in the Balkans, Suleyman turned to Safavid Persia, which had shown that it remained a threat to his Empire by sponsoring the *celali* revolts of 1526–7 and conducting negotiations with Charles V, besides continuing the persecution of Sunni Muslims in Mesopotamia. In October 1533 Ottoman armies under Suleyman and the Grand Vizier invaded Azerbaijan and Iran. By the end of 1534 Suleyman had occupied Tabriz and Baghdad. Tabriz was subsequently lost, and the permanent conquest of Azerbaijan was prevented by the skill of the Shiite Kurds in defending the mountainous terrain. But the southwards advance was more successful: Basra capitulated in 1538, and Ottoman rule reached the shores of the Persian Gulf. These substantial additions to the Empire were accompanied by problems of assimilation which persisted throughout Suleyman's reign; but they also brought more great trade routes under the Sultan's control, consolidated his reputation as the champion of Sunni Islam, and confined Safavid rule to Iran, from where the encouragement of dissent within the Empire became much more difficult.

The pause in the Balkan theatre of operations caused by the 1533 truce was the signal for greater attention to be paid by both sides to the naval war which was in progress in the central Mediterranean, as the Habsburgs challenged Ottoman power in Algeria. Since 1502 two Greek brothers, Uruc Reis and Hizir Reis, had risen to prominence as leaders of the corsairs who represented Ottoman sea power west of Greece. Hizir, or Khayr al-Din 'Barbarossa', as he became known, came to an agreement with Istanbul whereby he would win Algiers with Ottoman help, and rule over it as *beyler* bey. He gained control of the town in 1525 and expelled the Spanish garrison from their fort in 1529. This compelled Charles V to invest greater resources in his navy, in order to cut the new province's lines of communications with Istanbul. The conflict naturally centred on the narrow sea-lanes between Sicily, Malta, and Tunis. One vital step was the Emperor's settlement of the Hospitallers at Tripoli and on the strategically placed island of Malta in 1530, moves fully in accordance with the Iberian tradition of using the Military Orders to provide frontier garrisons. Equally important was Charles's hiring of the Genoese admiral Andrew Doria, the only Christian naval commander whose ability matched that of Barbarossa. During the critical summer of 1532 Doria ravaged the Greek coast and captured Lepanto and Coron, and this led the Sultan to summon Barbarossa to Istanbul and create him Grand Admiral, in charge of a much enlarged Ottoman fleet. Barbarossa's appointment signified the re-emergence of a strident naval lobby at the Ottoman court after a decade in which the leaders of the janissary corps, exponents of land-based expansion, had exerted the dominant influence on policy.

Barbarossa's brief was to recapture Coron and Lepanto and, in the longer term, to co-operate with the French; by this means Suleyman hoped to stop Charles acquiring the breathing-space to attack Ottoman lands while the Sultan was occupied on his eastern frontier. Barbarossa was successful in retaking Coron and Lepanto, and added the port of Tunis to his conquests by expelling the Hafsid Sultan Mulay Hasan. The seizure of Tunis became an immediate necessity for Charles V. An imperial armada of over 400 vessels left Cagliari in Sardinia in June 1535 to retake the port. Charles led the expedition in person, and in July his troops retook first the arsenal fortress at La Goletta, and then Tunis itself. It was the first major clash in a great galley war which would last nearly forty years. From the beginning this war was officially regarded as a crusade, for the new Pope, Paul III, permitted the crusade to be preached for Charles's expedition, granted crusade taxes for it, and himself supplied six galleys, in the tradition established by fourteenth-century popes.

One of the chief beneficiaries of this naval conflict was Francis I. As we have seen, the Ottoman thrust into Central Europe had always carried with it the danger of the German Protestant princes rallying to the Habsburgs in defence of their country. The Mediterranean war tied down Charles's resources just as effectively without the accompanying hazard, and this encouraged Francis to try and make his own links with Istanbul rather stronger than hitherto. By contrast, he viewed any sign of crusading activity, such as the Holy League of 1538, as implicitly anti-French and did his best to hinder it, making any French participation contingent upon the return of all his north Italian possessions. One year after the recapture of Tunis, Francis's envoy at Istanbul, John of La Forêt, negotiated the first Franco-Ottoman treaty. 'The Capitulations', as the treaty has come to be called, were commercial in nature, with clauses guaranteeing low customs duties and juridical rights for French merchants residing in the Ottoman Empire. It has been questioned whether this commercial treaty was implemented, but it is highly probable that La Forêt's negotiations did lead to a specific, though necessarily top-secret, agreement for military co-operation between the two powers. The following years certainly witnessed some attempts at a joint Franco-Ottoman military strategy against Charles. Thus in July 1537 Barbarossa landed troops, briefly as it transpired, in Apulia, apparently hoping for simultaneous French operations in northern Italy; while a French fleet made contact with Turkish troops besieging Corfu. Nothing came of this, however, and in the summer of 1538 Francis I again made peace with Charles V, promising, true to form, to take part in a crusade against Suleyman.

At this point a crusade was in active progress. In 1536 Ottoman troops began making inroads into Croatia and the Adriatic islands, and war therefore broke out again between Venice and the Turks in the following year. As usual when it was fighting the Turks, Venice appealed for papal assistance. In 1536 Pope Paul III couched an ambitious plan for a Council at Mantua to resolve the dispute with the Protestants and to organize a crusade; but the Lutheran princes and cities refused to attend the Council, and in the end it was indefinitely postponed. Instead, in February 1538, that other time-honoured approach to the problem of the Turks, a naval league, was adopted, with Charles V, Venice, and the Pope agreeing on offensive action. Vessels supplied by the three powers assembled at Corfu in September, but their co-operation was seriously hindered by animosity between the Venetian commanders of the papal and Venetian galleys, and the imperial Admiral, the Genoese Doria. On 27 September 1538 the Christian fleet engaged Barbarossa off Prevesa, on the Epirote coast of Greece, and suffered a heavy defeat. The league dissolved and Venice negotiated peace with Suleyman in October 1540, surrendering its last fortresses in Greece and agreeing to pay an indemnity of 300,000 ducats. The first attempt to combat the Ottomans at sea by joint action had met with ignominious, and (as ever) costly, failure, and had enabled Barbarossa to avenge his defeat at Tunis. In 1541 the Habsburg cause suffered a further set-back when an attempt to take Algiers was frustrated by a violent storm.

Prevesa was not the only Ottoman victory in 1538; such were Suleyman's resources that he was able to conduct major military operations in two other areas at the same time as the naval war proceeded in the Mediterranean. The Sultan himself suppressed a rebellion by the vassal prince of Moldavia, annexing southern Bessarabia and bringing the Empire to the banks of the Dnieper in the same year that it reached the Persian Gulf. Meanwhile the governor of Egypt commanded a fleet which sailed from Suez in response to an appeal for help from the Muslim ruler of Gujarat in western India. The Ottoman hold over the Red Sea was strengthened, but

Portuguese diplomacy prevented the Turkish expedition achieving any-thing of note in India. This widespread military activity was followed by two years of concentration on internal affairs, with the issuing of new *qanun-name* (codes of law) for matters of justice and finance, and the regulation of a vast range of governmental activity.

Meanwhile the Habsburg-Ottoman duel had reverted to the Balkans, where the death of John Zápolya in 1540 tempted Ferdinand to try to recapture lost territory. This was a mistake, for it provoked Suleyman in 1541 to concentrate his forces in a major expedition into Hungary, the central part of which he annexed to the Empire as the *beylerbeyilik* of Buda. Ferdinand was left with only the northern and western highlands, and after his attempt to retake Buda in 1542 was repulsed and several of his fortresses taken by the Turks, he agreed to a truce in 1545, renewed in 1547. During these years Suleyman made his most strenuous attempt to make his alliance with Francis I an active military partnership. In August 1543 Barbarossa's galleys joined the French Mediterranean fleet in an assault on Imperialist Nice, and the Ottoman fleet then wintered at Toulon, whose inhabitants were compelled by their government to provide accommodation for the Turks. These extraordinary events shocked public opinion and were probably regretted by Francis I, especially as his military gains were slight. The Imperialists had already begun to point out the contrast between Francis's cordial relations with the Sultan and his persecution of French Protestants. The existence in 1543–4 of a Turkish colony at Toulon, complete with mosque and slave market, was as great a propaganda gift as had been the Staufen toleration of their Muslim military colony at Lucera, in southern Italy, three centuries previously. Suleyman too was dissatisfied with the way events had gone, believing that the French had supplied inadequate provisions to his navy, and the new Franco-Habsburg peace, signed at Crépy-en-Laonnais in September 1544, was a factor in leading him to agree to the Habsburg–Ottoman truce in the following year. Suleyman used this to return to problems of internal government, and to renewed campaigning against the Safavids.

The Habsburg–Ottoman truce of 1545, which brought a five-year break to the conflict between the two powers, marks a convenient point at which to pause and consider the place of the crusade within European politics after forty years of political and religious turmoil. In 1547 Charles V profited from the lull in his wars with Suleyman and France to lead an army against the Protestant Schmalkaldic League, defeating its forces at Mühlberg in April. The victory was almost as fruitless as Pavia had been, for by this time a military solution to Lutheranism was no more viable than a negotiated reconciliation; after fresh fighting, in which the Protestants received the help of Henry II of France, the Religious Peace of Augsburg (1555) not only brought several decades of peace to Germany, but made it clear that the Church was in irreparable schism. Any future German action against the Turks would have to take the form of an alliance between Catholic and Protestant princes, with the crusade being preached, at best, in those lands held by Catholic rulers. The chances of any major European power except the Habsburgs, Venice, and the papacy taking part in a crusade were slight, for England too was now Protestant, and France was attached to Istanbul in an alliance which continued, albeit fitfully, under Henry II.

Amidst this religious upheaval, the Curia continued its efforts to co-ordinate opposition to the Turks. The Council of Trent, which Paul III convoked in May 1542, was intended to deal as much with the Turks as with the Lutherans; but the Council, which eventually became the great instrument of the Counter-Reformation, had less chance of organizing a broad-based international expedition than even such pathetic predecessors as Pius II's Congress at Mantua and Innocent VIII's Council at Rome. As we shall see in a future chapter,[3] this does not mean that Christendom (*Christianitas*) had ceased to exist as an identifiable group of nations sharing certain basic religious and cultural values; but its political manifestation, the medieval *respublica christiana*, had been dealt a death-blow. The future of the anti-Turkish conflict, and therefore of the anti-Turkish crusade, lay first with papal grants of crusade indulgences, taxes, and privileges to Catholic 'front-line' states such as Austria, Venice, and Poland, and secondly with the organization of naval leagues of Christian powers. These constituted valid and significant forms of crusading activity, but there is no denying that the confinement of crusading to the Catholic, and chiefly Mediterranean powers, was a far cry from the original conception, still propounded by Pope Leo X, however ineffective-ly, in the early decades of the sixteenth century.

In 1550 war between Ferdinand of Austria and the Turks recom-menced with Habsburg intervention in the affairs of Transylvania, which was ruled as an Ottoman vassal-principality by Zápolya's son, John Sigismund. Suleyman responded by sending Mehmed Sokollu, governor

[3] Below, 454–5.

of Rumelia, to Transylvania with a large army. Local hostility to the Austrians, increasingly conflated with Calvinist resistance to Habsburg-backed Catholicism, enabled Mehmed in 1551–2 to win back most of the principality. Apart from border raiding, the Balkan front now became of little importance, the struggle becoming firmly focused on the central Mediterranean. Here hostilities began again with the imperialist capture of Al-Mahdiya in September 1550, and an increase in Hospitaller raids on Muslim shipping from their base at Malta. Barbarossa's successor as Admiral, Turgut Reis (Dragut), captured Tripoli in 1551, and there were landings at Agosta (Sicily) in 1551, and at Gaeta in 1552, the latter creating fears that an attack on Rome itself was imminent. Three years later the Pope ruefully commented that the Turks 'know our homelands and our shores better than we do'. Since Prevesa the Turks had held the initiative at sea, and although a new Franco-Ottoman alliance (1553) was no more successful in terms of military co-operation than the previous one, Charles V's abdication in 1555–6 created extra problems for the Habsburg defence; Charles's eldest son Philip II received all the lands in Spain, Italy, and the Netherlands, while the imperial title went to Ferdinand. To make matters worse, in May 1555 the virulently anti-Habsburg John Peter Carafa was elected as Pope Paul IV. In December 1555 Paul agreed to an anti-Habsburg treaty with the envoys of Henry II of France, and at one point in 1557 this extraordinary Pope even threatened to call in the Turks to fight on his behalf, asserting that 'it would have been lawful and indeed praiseworthy for us to call the Turks, Moors, and Jews [sic] for our defence . . .'. Even after the Pope had patched up his quarrel with the Habsburgs, the organization of a crusade against the Turks continued to be a hopeless cause, until the major Franco-Habsburg peace of Câteau-Cambrésis in April 1559, and Paul IV's death in August, restored conditions which were somewhat more favourable.

Fortunately for Christian Europe, the 1550s were a difficult decade for Suleyman too. War against the Safavids continued with a series of expensive campaigns, until the Sultan acknowledged that further acquisitions were impossible and made peace in 1555. Naval conflict against the Portuguese led to the defeat of Seydi Ali Reis off Hormuz in 1554 and Ottoman exclusion from the Persian Gulf, though the trade route through the Red Sea remained in Turkish hands. Meanwhile the victories of Ivan IV (the Terrible) over the Crimean Khanate made the Sultan realize that a powerful new enemy, Muscovy, had emerged to the north and east of the Black Sea. Most importantly, internal problems of an economic and political nature had to be confronted. Inflation and high taxation were symptoms of troubles to come, while a struggle took place between Suleyman's sons for the right of succession, a familiar conflict in the last years of most Ottoman sultans but no less debilitating each time it occurred. Suleyman's execution of his son Mustafa in 1553 on the charge of treason was followed by a serious uprising in Rumelia in 1555. A 'false' (*duzme*) Mustafa rallied dissident janissaries and *timar*-holders against the Sultan before being defeated and executed by Prince Bayezid. Bayezid and his surviving brother, Selim, then raised armies and fought, the victory of Selim in 1560 finally securing him the succession.

These problems had not prevented the continuation of the Ottoman advance in North Africa. The Spanish forts (*presidios*) there had been neglected for decades in favour of the wars which Charles V waged in France and Italy, and when the Turks attacked Bougie in 1555 the garrison surrendered without firing a shot. The regency government of Joan, Philip II's sister, responded by fielding an army which was routed at Mostaganem in 1558. In the same year a galley fleet of about 150 vessels landed in Minorca, where the Turks took and burned the city of Ciudadela. Towards the end of 1559 Philip II responded to these set-backs by making an attempt to retake Tripoli, which appeared to be a relatively easy target. The new Pope, Pius IV, was encouraging, supplying three galleys to the fleet of some fifty which set out from Malta in February 1560, as well as granting the expedition a crusading indulgence. The result was a disaster for the Christians. Dragut Reis reinforced Tripoli before the arrival of the fleet, and it was decided to try to seize the island fortress of Jerba instead. This was achieved, but almost immediately a Turkish relief force arrived under Piali Pasha. The Christian fleet was routed, with the loss of about nineteen galleys and twelve round-hulled ships, and the 6,000-strong garrison on Jerba was besieged. After an eighty-two-day siege, during which it suffered terribly from thirst, the garrison was forced to surrender on 31 July. Together with the sea battle, this netted the Turks many thousands of prisoners, including hundreds of Philip II's most skilled and experienced soldiers and seamen. The great victory confirmed Suleyman's naval supremacy, although his internal problems stopped him making full use of it.

Between 1561 and 1564 the Turks undertook no large-scale military operations against the Christian West either at sea or in the Balkans. As Professor Setton has noted, their quiescence was an important factor in enabling the Council of Trent to concentrate on internal reform, and, in the course of its crucial Third Period, to 'redefine the basic doctrines of Catholicism'. When, in March 1565, a Turkish fleet of about 150 oared vessels left the Bosphorus for an assault on Hospitaller Malta, so inaugurating the final and critical phase of the Mediterranean galley war, the Ottomans faced a Catholic Europe which was more united and self-confident than it had been for decades, and which displayed again at least some of its old enthusiasm for the Holy War. To give just two examples. In 1561 Pope Pius IV authorized the foundation of a new Military Order, the Knights of St Stephen, by Duke Cosimo I of Florence; the Order's goal was specified as the naval defence of the Mediterranean against the Muslims. And the numbers of *aventureros*, volunteer noblemen for the most part (including, interestingly, young Frenchmen), who flocked to the relief of Malta in 1565, impressed contemporaries. After the election of Pius V in January 1566 this revived and militant Catholicism was led by a Pope who was a firm believer both in the crusade and in the organization of crusading leagues. This meant that the years leading up to the Holy League of 1571 were characterized by a significant revival of the papacy as an active crusading power; its ability to make Christian rulers take action was no greater than it had been for centuries, but it proceeded with a concentration, commitment, and altruism which had largely been absent since the days of Pius II, with whom Pius V has often, and rightly, been compared.

Like Pius II, whose embittered comments on this subject we saw in the last chapter,[4] Pius V could not make bricks without straw; and straw, in this context, still meant Habsburg Spain and Venice. Venice had been let down so badly in 1537–40 that it would not take part in any joint action unless its own territories of Cyprus and Crete were threatened. As for Spain, between the disastrous events of 1560 and the reopening of major hostilities in 1565 Philip II found his ability to concentrate on the defence of his Mediterranean possessions impeded by the burgeoning revolt of the Netherlands. As early as 1560, Professor Parker has shown, Spanish policy in the Netherlands was being influenced by the conflict against the Turks; and by the time Malta was under siege it was clear that events in the Low Countries presented Philip with a problem of priorities as severe as that faced by his father, and one that was to be substantially worsened by Philip's deepening involvement in the French Wars of Religion. Although each side made overtures, there was never active co-operation

[4] Above, 107.

between the Dutch rebels and the Turks, any more than there was between the German Protestant leaders and Suleyman; but the mere fact that they were simultaneously sapping Spanish resources was enough. Between 1568 and 1570 a further dimension would be added when the Moriscos of the Alpujarras region rebelled against Christian rule, forcing Philip to divert troops to their suppression and to guard against the possibility (always more apparent than real) of their acting as a 'fifth column' in the event of an Ottoman invasion of Spain. As Professor Hess has written, the Ottomans, Dutch rebels, and Moriscos added up to '[a] deadly interplay of frontier wars that strained Spanish energies'. To anyone acquainted with the problems of priorities faced by the thirteenth- and fourteenth-century papacy in maintaining an active and viable crusade policy, the Habsburg dilemma is very familiar.

The Turkish failure to take Malta in 1565, which we shall examine in Chapter 7,[5] gave the Christians their first big victory since the relief of Vienna a generation earlier. In the following year, however, in one of those extraordinary recoveries at which they excelled, the Turks not only mounted a major expedition into Hungary, capturing the forts of Sigetvar and Gyula, but sent a powerful fleet under Piali Pasha which took Chios, the last remaining Genoese colony in the eastern Mediterranean, before raiding in the Adriatic. The Sultan himself led the army and it was in the field that Suleyman died, in September 1566. The Grand Vizier, Mehmed Sokollu, was able to secure a peaceful succession by his sole surviving son, Selim II. Selim's reign only lasted for eight years, but it was characterized by external policies no less ambitious than those of his father. One such was Mehmed Sokollu's project to conquer Astrakhan and build a canal between the Don and Volga rivers. A fleet would be transferred to the Caspian Sea and the military potential thus secured both to block Muscovy's southwards advance and to encircle and crush Persia. The difficulties involved in building the canal proved insuperable, but a fleet was hauled overland to the Volga (itself no mean achievement), and attacked Astrakhan in 1569. The attack failed, and in the ensuing debate about where to attack next the protagonists of war in the Mediterranean defeated those who favoured further expansion in the Balkans or Iran. In the Mediterranean, Selim's thoughts were directed towards an assault on Venetian Cyprus rather than the alternative of North Africa. This was partly because of Ottoman fears that the Venetians and Spaniards were drawing closer together, and partly because of increasing Christian piracy

[5] Below, 231–2.

in the eastern Mediterranean, using Cyprus as a base. But just as important was the seductive argument that the conquest of this rich and famous island would constitute the major victory with which each new sultan liked to start his reign; one Venetian source related the decision to Selim's desire to provide a rich endowment, arising from victory over the infidels, for a mosque which he proposed building at Edirne.

Whatever the precise reason for it, Selim's invasion of Cyprus lit the fuse which led to Lepanto. An important preliminary was the renewal of the Franco-Ottoman *entente*, in October 1569. This new 'Capitulations' agreement was, as before, primarily commercial, and this time the Ottomans did not try to secure active military co-operation, both because of previous disappointments, and because the maelstrom of France's internal politics would have made it impossible. In February 1570 the Sultan presented Venice with the choice of surrendering Cyprus or going to war. Pius V and Venice immediately started pressing Philip II to enter a Catholic League, its aim being to take the offensive against the Turks. It was argued that Selim was counting on taking Cyprus while the Spaniards were fully occupied with the suppression of the Moriscos and the rebels in the Netherlands, and that a vigorous response would take the Turks unawares. None the less, the negotiations for the League, which was modelled on that of 1537–8, proved exceptionally complex and difficult; there were generations of mutual suspicion to contend with. It was rumoured that even the Doge, Peter Loredan, lacked the spirit to fight, and would prefer giving up Cyprus to engaging in another war with the Turks. Philip II made his entry into the League contingent upon massive financial concessions from the Pope, and attempted to make the proposed league serve his interests in North Africa as much as those of Venice in the eastern Mediterranean. Royal advisers pointed out that it made sense to undertake conquests in Tunisia and Algeria while the Ottomans were tied down by their invasion of Cyprus; in particular, it was important to retake Tunis, which the Turks had seized late in 1569. The role of Pius V in bringing these reluctant partners together has rightly been stressed. By rampant simony the Pope was able to fund a number of galleys himself, besides granting crusade indulgences to all who fought against the Turks. Ottoman troops were landed in Cyprus at the beginning of July, and on 9 September they took Nicosia. Although the League was not yet formalized, a total of nearly 200 galleys were assembled off Crete, under the command of Mark-Anthony Colonna and John-Andrew Doria. But Doria had received strict orders from Philip II not to engage the enemy, and when news reached the fleet of the fall of Nicosia campaigning was abandoned.

Despite this set-back, which gave rise to a predictable salvo of recriminations, the tortuous negotiations about the League continued throughout the winter of 1570–1. They were effectively fuelled by fears of what Selim would next attempt: Philip II even ordered the evacuation of the Balearic Islands. Finally, in May 1571, agreement was reached, and Venice ended the tentative peace negotiations which it had been conducting with the Turks. The terms of the treaty, which were signed in Rome on 25 May, provided for an expedition of some 200 galleys, 50,000 infantry, and 4,500 light horse to serve in 1571. There would be operations too in the following years; the details of these would be agreed upon each autumn at a special meeting in Rome. For the 1571 campaign Philip undertook to bear a half of the total cost (initially estimated at three million *escudos*), Venice a third, and Pius V a sixth. Don John of Austria, the illegitimate son of Charles V who had recently suppressed the Morisco revolt in Andalusia, had already been appointed as commander-in-chief; he would take decisions jointly with Mark-Anthony Colonna and Sebastian Venier, the Venetian captain-general. Colonna and Don John both received papal banners, and Pius V engaged in frantic diplomatic activity to try and bring other powers into the planned operations; this was not successful.

Thanks mainly to the slowness of the Spanish, it was not until 16 September 1571 that the forces of the League set sail from Messina. By this time Famagusta had fallen to the Turks, and, with disputes between the Venetians and Spaniards nearly breaking up the fleet, it looked as though the events of 1570 would be repeated. But on 6 October the fleet of Muezzinzade Ali Pasha was sighted in its winter quarters in the Gulf of Corinth, and on 7 October the battle of Lepanto was fought. It was, by any standards, a massive engagement, 208 Christian galleys against about 275 Turkish vessels. It has been estimated that over a quarter of a million mature trees were felled to build the two fleets, and Fernand Braudel pointed out that the number of men who fought, about 100,000, were the equivalent of the population of a very large town. Using traditional Turkish tactics, Ali Pasha attempted to outflank the Christian fleet. But the attack of his right wing was contained by the Christian left (mainly composed of Venetians), and the Turkish galleys were finally driven ashore. The Turkish left, unable to engage Doria's Genoese and papal galleys, which moved to seaward, joined in the struggle which had developed in the centre. Here the fighting was hardest, but Ali Pasha's death, and Don John's capture of the Turkish flagship, turned the tide, while Doria's belated arrival completed the Turkish rout. Christian losses were heavy, fifteen to twenty ships and perhaps 8,000 men. But those of the Turks were devastating: about eighty of their vessels were destroyed or crippled and 130 captured. More than 30,000 Turks, many of them veteran sailors and janissaries, were killed.

Lepanto was a Christian naval victory on an unprecedented scale and it sparked off an astonishing outpouring of celebration in the form of church services, commemorative paintings and medals, and popular literature: between late October and the end of December 1571 alone, at least 190 separate items were printed in relation to it. In 1572 7 October was designated as the feast-day of St Mary of the Victory (S. Maria della Vittoria), an expression of the Marian devotion which characterized both the crusading movement and the Counter-Reformation. It is undeniable that the victory boosted Christian morale and destroyed the myth of Ottoman invincibility. According to Cervantes, in *Don Quixote*, the battle 'revealed to all the nations of the world the error under which they had been labouring in believing that the Turks were invincible at sea'. In other respects, however, the battle's long-term significance has been convincingly challenged. In the first place, the battle did not stop Selim completing his conquest of Cyprus, or enable Venice to recover the island. Secondly, far from capitalizing on its success, the League rapidly collapsed. It was solemnly renewed in February 1572, when Pius granted more indulgences to those who fought, but the campaign in that year proved to be a repetition of the 1570 débâcle. Venice claimed that it had spent twelve million ducats on the war, and although the Republic authorized yet another campaign in February 1573, in the following month it agreed to a humiliating peace with the Turks. Cyprus was formally surrendered and an indemnity of 300,000 ducats was to be paid. The League had achieved little for Venice except for worsening the city's reputation for deserting its Christian allies. The response which Philip II made to the Venetian ambassadors who had the unenviable task of telling him about the Republic's treaty with the Turks shows how bad this reputation already was:

The king listened to us, always most attentively, and the longer he observed the unfailing modesty of our discourse as we ran through our argument, and our speech took that affectionate form of delivery which so grave a matter required, the more closely his Majesty looked at us, keeping his eyes fixed in our direction. He showed no emotion except that, when toward the end he learned that the conditions of peace had been accepted, there was a slight ironical twist of his lips. He smiled ever so faintly. It seemed as though his Majesty wanted to say, without interrupting us, 'Oh-ho, you've done it, just as they all told me you would'.[6]

If the failure of the Holy League to exploit its victory greatly reduced the long-term significance of Lepanto, even more striking was the extraordinarily rapid recovery of Ottoman sea power. Lepanto was a terrible blow to the Turks—one Ottoman historian believed it to be the greatest disaster since Noah's construction of the first ship, while another wrote that Selim II was so upset by the news that he could not sleep for three days and nights—and it is clear that they placed the highest priority on immediate recovery. In May 1572 the French ambassador at Istanbul, Francis of Noailles, wrote to Charles IX that

in five months they have built 150 vessels [i.e. one a day] with all the artillery and equipment needed and, yes, they have resolved to continue at this pace for an entire year . . . Already their general is prepared to set out to sea at the end of this month with two hundred galleys and one hundred galliots, of corsairs and others, without the Grand Seigneur [sc. Sultan]'s having used a single écu in his treasury for this huge expense. In short, I should never have believed the greatness of this monarchy, had I not seen it with my own eyes.[7]

The Ottomans had been able to call on the virtually undamaged resources of their North African and Black Sea galley units to achieve this feat, and they had used a great deal of green wood, at the cost of a limited life expectancy for the new fleet. None the less, the achievement was an astonishing manifestation of the Sultanate's power. There was no need even to hold up work on the great mosque which Selim was building at Edirne, and Mehmed Sokollu was not so far from the truth when he boasted that 'if an order was issued to cast anchors from silver, to make rigging from silk, and to cut the sails from satin, it could be carried out for the entire fleet'. The new fleet soon proved its worth. In October 1573 Don John used the Spanish contribution to the Holy League to seize Tunis, and in July–September 1574 a Turkish armada of about 300 vessels retook the port and its outpost of La Goletta. The Spaniards were expelled from Tunisia, and the Ottoman hold on North Africa was consolidated, Turkish recovery from Lepanto forming a sharp contrast with the bankruptcy which Philip II suffered in 1575.

[6] K. M. Setton, *The Papacy and the Levant (1204–1571)*, iv, *The Sixteenth Century from Julius III to Pius V* (Philadelphia, 1984), 1093.
[7] Ibid. 1075.

Four years after the fall of Tunis the Christian cause endured an even greater defeat in the struggle for supremacy in North Africa. In 1576 the new Sultan, Murad III, attempted to complete his control of the North African littoral by giving his support to a *coup d'état* in Morocco, which had long resisted the Ottoman advance. With Turkish troops and guns, an exiled member of the ruling Saadi family, Abd al-Malik, was able to oust the reigning Sultan, Muhammad al-Mutawakkil, from Morocco and establish a government closely tied to Istanbul. Muhammad al-Mutawakkil fled to the Portuguese court, where he found a sympathetic response to his plight. The young King Sebastian had already evinced a determination to extend Portugal's Moroccan outposts, notably in a foolhardy expedition to Ceuta and Tangier in 1574. In addition, he could hardly ignore the threat of Ottoman ships appearing off West Africa, raiding Portugal's coast, and disrupting his Atlantic trade. Most importantly, the situation appealed to his obsession with the crusade, usually written off as the irresponsible fanaticism of an unintelligent man, but less surprising when one considers Sebastian's ancestry. Sebastian therefore started planning a large-scale expedition to Morocco. Naturally he expected help from his cousin Philip II, whose lands were threatened by the new Ottoman gains as much as Portugal was. Bankrupt, heavily committed in the Netherlands, and sceptical of Sebastian's military ability, Philip promised only very limited support. None the less, by 1578 Sebastian's forthcoming crusade had become the major obstacle to the peace negotiations which Philip was conducting with Murad III; although almost exclusively a Portuguese expedition, it thus represented, indirectly, the latest stage in the Habsburg–Ottoman struggle.

Sebastian's expedition was all but a summation of the military blunders which had been so prominent throughout crusading history. The core of the army, which embarked in disorder at Lisbon in June 1578, was a levy of 10,000 Portuguese, poorly armed, trained, and motivated; and the army was encumbered by large numbers of non-combatants and a vast baggage train. Having landed his army at Tangier, Sebastian decided to march inland to reach a ford over the river Loukkos. At Alcazar the march of his demoralized and exhausted troops was halted by the strong army collected by Abd al-Malik, including 4,000 arquebusiers and thirty-four cannon. Some of these vital munitions had been supplied by Elizabeth I of England, a fact which Habsburg propagandists did not fail to point out. On 4 August, under a scorching sun, the Portuguese army was destroyed in a six-hour battle during which Sebastian, Muhammad al-Mutawakkil and Abd al-Malik were all killed. Alcazar confirmed the triumph of the Ottomans in the struggle for North Africa and presented the danger of an invasion of Iberia. But the threat failed to materialize. The Ottomans baulked at the logistical problems involved and settled instead for war against Persia, while Mulai Ahmed, who succeeded his older brother Abd al-Malik as Sultan of Morocco, directed his energies against the negro state of Songhai in the western Sudan.

In fact Alcazar worked to Philip II's advantage, in that he was able to occupy a rulerless and disorientated Portugal in 1580 at the cost of only 100 Spanish dead. And in March 1580 a truce was agreed on between Spain and the Ottomans. It was subsequently renewed and signified the disengagement of the two great powers, and the release of their resources for warfare elsewhere. Morocco meanwhile had come to form a substantially neutral buffer-state. As Professor Hess put it, 'All along the military frontier in the western Mediterranean, rulers had concluded that an appeal to religious warfare would not substantially change the space of respective civilizations.' The decision to disengage was based not only on the dwindling prospects for major territorial gains, but also on the shrinking profits from coastal raiding as both sides tightened up their maritime defences, and, perhaps above all, on the escalating cost of galley warfare. Building the ships, paying and feeding their huge crews, and replacing losses sustained through military action, storms, and ordinary wear-and-tear, represented a massive burden. From Ottoman sources, Dr Imber has suggested a wartime expenditure of 500,000 ducats to keep a Turkish galley fleet at sea for one season. This is probably a conservative estimate, for in 1570 it was estimated that the Venetians would have to spend 2,500,000 ducats each year on their war with the Turks, and, as we have seen, three years later Venice claimed to have spent nearly five times that amount. Few gains warranted expenditure on this scale, and by the mid-1570s, Professor Guilmartin has commented, 'the fiscal and logistic burden of maintaining a galley fleet powerful enough to accomplish anything of note strategically had grown so large as to be prohibitive'.

Victory in North Africa enabled the Turks to embark on their greatest struggle yet with Safavid Persia. War was proposed by Lala Mustafa Pasha and Sinan Pasha with the goals of occupying the Caucasus and Azerbaijan, and of stopping the Safavids from stimulating internal dissent and harbouring refugees and exiles; it was vigorously opposed by the Grand Vizier, Mehmed Sokollu, on the grounds of its appalling expense and the well-known logistic difficulties involved. Murad III yielded to the idea that his growing financial problems, and the unrest of the janissary corps, would both be solved by conquest and the resulting creation of new *timars*. He therefore accepted the advice of the hawks and plunged into a war which had catastrophic long-term consequences. At first Ottoman advances were spectacular. By 1590 the Ottomans and their allies, the Uzbegs of Central Asia, had inflicted such damage on Shah Abbas I that he signed the treaty of Istanbul, ceding to Murad vast tracts of the Caucasus, Kurdistan, and Azerbaijan. But this success was deceptive, for Shah Abbas spent the next few years assiduously preparing for a counter-attack. When this came in 1603, the reformed Persian army smashed the Uzbegs and won several victories over the Ottomans, whose resources were already fully stretched in the Balkans. Shiite uprisings in the newly conquered territories and *celali* revolts in Anatolia added to the Turks' problems, and by the time this second phase of the conflict was brought to a close in 1618, Mehmed Sokollu's prediction that the eastern war would be a mistake had been amply confirmed.

The end of conflict in the Mediterranean in 1580 left the long Balkan frontier as the region where crusading activity might be expected to occur. Between 1593 and 1606 the Austrian Habsburgs fought the gruelling 'Long War' with the Turks. In military terms it was indecisive, but certain aspects of the treaty of Zsitvatorok, which concluded the war, demonstrated that the Ottomans had suffered a defeat; particularly important was the Sultan's unprecedented acknowledgement that the Emperor was his equal in rank. Pope Clement VIII certainly saw the 'Long War' as a crusade, and papal and Italian troops took part in it. Clement pursued a traditional policy of attempting to organize a holy league centring on contributions from the Austrian and Spanish Habsburgs. Given the solidity of the Danubian frontier, the Pope began to investigate other options for driving the Turks back, some of which are recognizable from previous periods (for instance, hopes for a resistance movement amongst the conquered Christian peoples in the Balkans), while others were new (such as plans for Russian help). Without a detailed investigation into the crusading aspects of this war, as into the great Veneto–Ottoman war of 1645–69, and the Holy League of 1684, it is quite impossible to make the sort of balanced assessment of the seventeenth-century crusade which Professor Setton's volumes have made possible in the case of the decades before 1580.

Some aspects of this assessment require comparative comment and are best left until the final chapters of this book; but it is hoped that the claim expressed at the start of the chapter about the importance of the sixteenth-century crusade has already been validated. Put at its simplest, elements of continuity, in language, ideas, institutions, and structures, are as impressive as those of discontinuity and change, which have tended to dominate historians' attention until now because they are so striking and apparent. We have seen that crusade preaching was authorized, and indulgences issued, invariably now in printed form, on many occasions, such as by Leo X at the Fifth Lateran Council, by Clement VII on behalf of the struggle in Hungary, by Paul III in support of Charles V's Tunis expedition in 1535, by Pius IV for the ill-fated Jerba campaign of 1560 and the relief of Malta in 1565, and by Pius V for the Holy League. Catholics in the sixteenth century did not lack opportunities to take the cross or gain the crusade indulgence by sending soldiers or donating alms, even if they were subjected to crusading appeals less frequently than their ancestors had been. The regular issuing of indulgences, moreover, formed just one aspect of a crusade policy which the popes of the Renaissance and especially the Counter-Reformation continued to pursue, some more actively than others, but all (except for Paul IV) with some measure of vigour and commitment. Other familiar aspects of this policy were peacemaking and attempts to enforce a trade embargo on the Ottomans in strategic materials. Above all, the financial institutions of the crusade continued to lead to detailed and acrimonious wrangling between secular powers and the Holy See. Numerous crusade tenths were granted to Francis I, Charles V, and Ferdinand of Austria, for actual or proposed expeditions against the Turks in the century's early decades, and virtually the only practical measure taken by the Fifth Lateran Council was the levy of a three-year tenth on all Christendom.

It was in the context of the vastly expensive galley war which Venice and Philip II waged against the Turks that traditional crusade finance played its most important role. From the mid-1530s the annual grant by the Curia of a tenth, or a double tenth, became essential to Venice's defence of the Adriatic, even though its proceeds represented a relatively small proportion of the Republic's total expenditure. Spain came to rely not only on the tenth, usually levied as a *subsidio*, but also on the *cruzada* (the administration of indulgences by the monarchy in exchange for money) and the *excusado* (the grant to Philip II of an agreed proportion of the tithe paid by the laity). It has been estimated that one year's yield from the 'three graces', as these sources of revenue came to be known, would alone have paid Philip II's contribution to the expenses of the Lepanto campaign. It can safely be said that only revenues linked to the crusade, admittedly in the rather peculiar forms which they had come to assume in Early Modern Spain, enabled Philip II to sustain his many financial burdens in the 1560s and early 1570s, without going bankrupt earlier than he did. Lepanto was thus the last big crusading victory not only in terms of its political background, in that the Holy League was the creation of patient and selfless papal diplomacy, and in terms of the distinctive ethos of Holy War which characterized the battle, but also in the sense that the funding of this massive Christian fleet rested on institutional foundations which went back more than three centuries, to the taxes inaugurated by Pope Innocent III, or introduced in the Spanish kingdoms during the thirteenth-century *Reconquista*.

But the long-term insignificance of Lepanto reminds us that the anti-Turkish crusade, in the sixteenth century as in the earlier periods of the emergence and rise of the Ottomans, proved to be a singularly ineffective instrument for resisting Turkish power. The reasons are to be found partly in Christendom's enormous internal problems, and in the declining efficacy of the crusade as a means of organizing Christian military resources; but mainly in the sheer prowess of the Turks, their ability first to retain much of the vigour and aggression of their *ghazi* origins when their conquests had necessitated a high degree of administrative organization and control, and secondly to concentrate their military power in a manner which was virtually the exact opposite of their disunited and strife-ridden Christian enemies. It is one of the ironies of crusading history, therefore, that the first symptoms of long-term Ottoman decline made themselves felt at precisely the point that disengagement in the Mediterranean was occurring.

Only ten years after the naval reconstruction of 1571–2 displayed the full extent of the Sultanate's military resilience, financial strength and administrative capability, the first cracks began to be visible in the great edifice of Ottoman government and society. Ottoman decline was a complex process and all we can do, or need to do, here is point out some of its main features and consequences. Perhaps at the root of decline were the twin problems of massive population growth and runaway inflation. It has been estimated that the population of the Empire doubled in the course of the sixteenth century, and while the government siphoned off some of the extra mouths in forced deportations to newly conquered lands (such as Cyprus after 1570), most peasants either remained in their place of birth, competing for limited land and employment, or migrated

to already overcrowded towns and cities. Famines became frequent
occurrences. Meanwhile inflation, caused by the infusion of American
silver via Europe, eroded the value of fixed-income *timars* and, together
with increasing specialization in warfare, which led the sultans to call on
their services less frequently, caused poverty, loss of status, and political
disaffection amongst the military aristocracy. The resulting instability
amongst both the *reaya* and its supposed protectors began, in the
century's last quarter, to destroy the equilibrium which was the Islamic
ideal of social order, and which the Ottoman state had for a time almost
achieved.

It is arguable that even if the Ottoman government had responded with
energy to these problems, they would have proved insoluble. As it was,
intense factional conflict at court combined with the appalling burden
of protracted warfare on two fronts to aggravate the crisis. Professor
Kortepeter has stressed that the decline in the sixteenth century of the
devsirme system, allied to the destruction of the ablest in frequent and
bloody *coups d'état*, robbed the Empire of the talented and innovative
administrators who might at least have proposed viable remedies. And
the vast increases in taxation necessitated by the wars against the Persians
and Austrians—tax levels quintupled between 1576 and 1600—led to a
series of provincial revolts. The widespread diffusion of firearms had a
crucial role in hastening the process of decentralization, as well as
contributing to social disorder and brigandage. These social, economic,
and political factors all came together in the worst of the *celali* revolts,
which rocked Anatolia between 1596 and 1610. Disbanded soldiers and
deserters co-operated with rebellious *timar*-holders to compel villages
and towns to support them in prolonged resistance to the central
government. Anarchy accelerated the migration to the cities (dubbed 'the
Great Flight' by Turkish historians), and caused irreparable damage to
the Anatolian economy.

The proliferation of muskets which made such rebellions more serious
was the result mainly of an effective Ottoman response to the greater use
of firearms by their German enemies in the Balkans during the last decade
of the century. This too was ironic, since one of the most striking features
of Ottoman decline was a perceptible slackening in the innovativeness
and readiness to copy others which had been such important factors in
the Empire's earlier success. Turkish siege cannons, often designed and
fired by Christian engineers, had played a major role in the Sultanate's
expansion between 1453 and *c*.1520; thereafter the Turks ceased to

follow the important changes taking place in the West, and increasingly Ottoman siege artillery struck western observers as unwieldy and ineffective. Much the same was true of Ottoman field artillery. Worst of all, the Ottomans suffered heavily by continuing to build mainly galleys when naval technology was shifting towards the iron-gunned sailing vessel, aptly described by Carlo Cipolla as 'essentially a compact device that allowed a relatively small crew to master unparalleled masses of inanimate energy for movement and destruction'. Even in the sixteenth century, the Ottoman galleys were often successful in the narrow and relatively calm waters of the Red Sea, but were generally outfought, or destroyed by adverse weather conditions, in the more open Persian Gulf and Indian Ocean.

Confronted by superior military technology during a war against the Russians in the eighteenth century, the Ottomans would resort to exactly the same criticism, the frustrated language of the loser, that the Mamluks and Safavids had earlier used against them: 'Let them leave their abominable batteries and encounter us like brave men, hand to hand, and we shall see whether these infidels can resist the slaughtering sabre of the True-Believers.' Undefeated by the crusades launched against them by the Curia during the Renaissance and Counter-Reformation, the Ottomans would thus eventually fall victim, like the Mamluks before them, to internal decay and their own failure to adapt. But this could hardly have been foreseen in 1580, when Turkish power was solidly entrenched in the Balkans and North Africa, and the Habsburg–Ottoman truce marked the close of a war which was distinguished by a string of the Empire's most remarkable successes. Even though Alcazar was not, as Fernand Braudel claimed, 'the last Mediterranean crusade', King Sebastian's disastrous expedition is an appropriate event with which to conclude a sequence of chapters on the anti-Turkish crusade.

5

Latin Rule in Greece and the Aegean
1274–1580

✠

THE conquest of Constantinople by the Fourth Crusade in 1204 led to the creation of an intricate tissue of Latin states in *Romania*, and it is their later fortunes which form the subject of this chapter (see map 6). The most prestigious of the creations, the Latin Empire of Constantinople, was also the weakest. Surrounded by enemies, and failing, despite their strenuous efforts, to attract the settlers they needed for long-term viability, the Empire's rulers staggered from crisis to crisis while searching in vain for a western protector. The *coup de grâce*, Michael VIII's reconquest of Constantinople in 1261, completed the shift in western interests towards the southern and western part of *Romania* which had begun with the collapse of the ephemeral 'Kingdom of Thessalonica' in 1224; military aid from Latin Christendom could be dispatched more rapidly towards southern Greece, and the Venetians could deploy their naval superiority with greater effectiveness there and in the Aegean and Adriatic islands. The most important of the surviving states were the Principality of Achaea, which occupied the classical Peloponnese (or Morea, as both Franks and Greeks termed it), and the Duchy of Athens. The Peloponnese was overrun by William of Champlitte and Geoffrey of Villehardouin in 1204–5, and ruled by Geoffrey's descendants. Athens was conquered by Boniface of Montferrat in 1204 and consigned as a fief to the Burgundian lord Odo of la Roche. Odo and the dynasty which he established came to govern Attica, Boeotia, and the Argolid. Seventeen islands in the Cyclades were seized in 1207 with comparative ease by a group of Venetian entrepreneurs led by Mark Sanudo, who partitioned the islands as fiefs amongst his followers, retaining Naxos and several other islands for himself, and ruling with the title Duke of the Archipelago.

In the Ionian Sea, the collapse of Byzantium in 1204 enabled Matthew Orsini to consolidate his existing possession of Cephalonia, Zante, and Ithaca, which became the County of Cephalonia.

These conquests were the achievements of individual French and Italian adventurers. Their shape and limits were dictated less by design than by the military resources at the disposal of the conquerors, and the toughness of the resistance mounted by the local Greek aristocracy. By contrast, the contours of Venice's territorial gains in the years following 1204 were considered and implemented with care. The Venetians were entitled to three-eighths of the conquered Empire, and their doges adopted the title 'lord of one quarter and one half [of a quarter] of the Empire of Romania'. But, in accordance with their traditional approach, the Venetians were anxious to avoid acquiring lands which might prove difficult and expensive to defend. Their only major acquisition was Crete. The island had been granted to Boniface of Montferrat by the Emperor Alexios IV Angelos in 1203, but the Republic purchased his claim in August 1204, and sent a fleet to begin the arduous task of conquering Crete in 1206. Venice also took over the harbour area of Constantinople itself, and it established bases, for strictly commercial purposes, at Negroponte in Euboea, and at Modon and Coron (the 'two eyes of the Republic') in the southern Morea. Apart from these few instances of direct rule, the Venetians were content with the exercise of suzerainty over the rest of Euboea and the County of Cephalonia.

In terms of social texture and political structure, the Latin states of *Romania* which still existed in 1274 fell into three broad categories: the feudal principalities of Champenois Achaea and Burgundian Athens; the island lordships of the Aegean and Ionian Seas; and the Venetian colonial domain. Much is known about Achaea, thanks in part to two remarkable sources, the narrative 'Chronicle of the Morea' and the 'Assizes of *Romania*', the Principality's feudal law code. Both sources survive in fourteenth-century guise: the oldest version of the 'Chronicle' (that in French) probably dates from 1341–6, and the 'Assizes' from about the same period. None the less, they throw much light on the thirteenth century. The feudal regime established by Geoffrey I of Villehardouin, and maintained by his son Geoffrey II, constituted a fairly elaborate hierarchy. The prince's immediate inferiors were the 'high barons', about a dozen feudatories who shared high justice with the prince and could only be judged by their peers. Ranged below the 'high barons' were the 'lieges', who enjoyed favourable terms of tenure and presided over their own courts. The 'men of simple homage' had few legal prerogatives, and although they owed less military aid, their tenurial position was in other respects more onerous. The men of simple homage included the sergeants, non-noble mounted soldiers whose fiefs were generally worth half a knight's fee. As commoners they could not be expected to swear fealty and therefore just rendered homage for their fiefs.

This system was successful, initially at least, in meeting the military needs of Achaea. The Morea's well-ordered and healthy agrarian economy proved an attractive prospect, particularly in the western provinces of Elis and Messenia. The process of enfeoffment was therefore rapid and extensive, leading the author of the Greek version of the 'Chronicle of the Morea' to remark that 'the knights who had one fief each and also the sergeants who were enfeoffed I do not name because of the amount of writing it would require'. The international Military Orders—the Templars, Hospitallers, and Teutonic Knights—all acquired lands in the Peloponnese, although the military service they owed was nominal. The prince had a field army of between 500 and 600 western knights, making his Principality one of the most significant military powers in the eastern Mediterranean. It was Prince Geoffrey II's timely arrival on the scene which saved Constantinople from capture in 1236, and when William II of Villehardouin joined Louis IX's crusade in 1249 he led a contingent of 400 mounted men. The high barons and lieges built castles which met the Morea's defensive requirements. And although the 'Assizes of *Romania*' portray the prince's authority as severely limited by the prerogatives of the high barons and lieges, in practice the Villehardouins were forceful rulers. This was partly because they retained as much as a quarter of the Morea for their domain, including the important market centre of Andravida, the Principality's main port at Glarentza, and the four castles of Corinth, Clermont, Beauvoir, and Kalamata. The prince had an up-to-date administrative household and his court, which normally resided at Andravida, became renowned throughout the West as a centre of chivalric culture. Geoffrey II reputedly kept a household guard of eighty knights with golden spurs. As a modern historian, himself echoing contemporary comments, has put it, Villehardouin Achaea was 'the mainstay of Latin rule [in Greece], the brilliant vindication of the founding of a New France on Hellenic soil'.

The *nova Francia* consisted, however, of a comparatively thin layer of French knights and sergeants, and Italian traders, superimposed on the Greek population, whose chief classes were the landed aristocracy (*archontes*), and the dependent peasantry (*paroikoi*). The personal status of the *paroikoi* had declined so much during the twelfth century that the Latin conquerors were able to treat them as villeins. The relations of the new rulers with the *archontes* was perhaps the Principality's most distinctive feature. The French version of the 'Chronicle of the Morea' relates that the *archontes* 'reached an agreement with the man from Champagne to the effect that Greek noblemen who held the land's fiefs, lands, and villages should each retain and hold them according to his quality, and the surplus be distributed amongst our people'. Many *archontes* were thus immediately incorporated into the new feudal regime as men of simple homage. After 1262, if not earlier, some were knighted and were therefore able to create vassals of their own and become lieges. Adjustments were made to the tenurial status of the *archontes* to take account of Byzantine practices; for example, article 138 of the 'Assizes' permitted equal succession to a fief by the sons and daughters of Greek vassals. The process of integration was more gradual and limited than the above quotation would imply, and no Greek appears to have gained access to the baronial group; it also, of course, left the vast majority of the Greeks, the *paroikoi*, untouched. Nevertheless, it was a remarkable achievement, given the background of hostility between the races, and the immense differences separating the new feudal practices from the deeply rooted traditions of Byzantine politics and society.

The advance of the *archontes* accelerated in the fourteenth century, when losses in action had severely depleted the ranks of the Frankish fiefholders and created openings for them. Two Greek aristocratic families in particular achieved a remarkable degree of success. Stephen Koutroules held the high-ranking post of *protovestiarius* in Achaea in 1336, while his son Nicholas was one of the most powerful feudatories in 1379. John Misito held several fiefs in 1324, when he was captain of the important castle of Kalamata, and his son Nicholas succeeded him in 1327. Both Nicholas and another member of the family, John II, were rich and influential fiefholders in the Principality. It was for one such feudatory, probably a member of the court of Erard III le Maure, lord of Arkadia, that the Greek version of the 'Chronicle of the Morea' was written in the second half of the fourteenth century. The work is written in the Greek dialect of the Morea, but it is heavily influenced by French and Italian. It is permeated by Frankish values and prejudices, especially in its emphasis on chivalric and feudal practices, and in the antagonism which it displays towards both the Palaiologan emperors and the schismatic

Orthodox church. In no other region that they conquered did the crusaders achieve this degree of assimilation with the existing aristocracy, except possibly in the case of Prussia; and there, as we shall see, the Old Prussian nobility were simply submerged by German colonial society, at the cost of losing their former traditions. By contrast, the *archontes* of Achaea managed to perform a delicate balancing act, remaining conscious of their Greek identity (to the extent of commissioning a Greek version of the 'Chronicle'), while embracing Frankish ways. Professor Peter Topping aptly described the result as a 'Franco-Greek synthesis'.

Much less is known about Burgundian Athens than about Villehardouin Achaea. It is unlikely that the Achaean feudal pyramid was replicated by the la Roche dukes, who did not need to reward an inner group of followers with baronial status, and managed both to retain more land as ducal domain, and to exercise greater authority over their vassals. There are no signs that the archontic class of Attica or Boeotia received fiefs on Achaean lines, and the Orthodox church was treated less favourably than in the neighbouring Principality, where the maintenance of the Greek church and clergy was often guaranteed in written privileges issued at the time of the Frankish conquest. Economically, Burgundian Athens prospered. The Duchy had a very old silk industry at Thebes, produced food for export, and attracted Italian traders. The feudal army was substantial, and there was a prestige attached to the title of Duke of Athens which still resonated in the writings of Boccaccio and Chaucer in the fourteenth century. According to the French version of the 'Chronicle of the Morea', the ducal dignity was confirmed by Louis IX when Guy of la Roche visited the French court in 1259, in the wake of a war between Achaea and Athens; though this may be an attempt to catch for the title some of the aura surrounding Louis's name. Peter III of Aragon's description of the Acropolis in 1380 as 'the richest jewel there is in the world and such that all the kings of Christendom could not create its equal', shows that by this point Athens's classical beauty met with western appreciation, even from those who had never been there.

As Freddy Thiriet showed, the main characteristics of Venice's government of its possessions in *Romania* were centralization, and the duplication of Venice's own political institutions. The Duke of Crete, the *baillis* of Negroponte and Constantinople, and the castellans of Modon and Coron, were elected by Venice's Greater Council, and although they were expected to make important decisions without referring back, such decisions had to be ratified at Venice. These governors acted in accordance with briefs given them at the time of their appointment, and they were rigorously accountable for their actions while in office to the 'syndics for eastern affairs'. They were subject to the guidance of a small group of advisers (*consiliarii*), normally numbering two, a group which mirrored the Doge's Council at Venice and acted as a constraint on the governors' power. When the number of resident Venetians warranted it, Venice authorized the creation of further imitative organs, a Senate or 'Council of Twelve' and a Greater Council (*maggior consilio*), although these did not share the power of the governor and his *consiliarii*. The impression of a 'little Venice' being created is therefore misleading in so far as it implies a degree of decentralization, along the lines which characterized Genoa's overseas colonies. The only effective way for Venetians living in the Levant to protest against misgovernment was by sending ambassadors to Venice. They had no influence even in the organization of their own defence, since the 'Captain general of the Gulf', who was entrusted by the Senate with the overall responsibility for the safety of the sea lanes crucial to Venice's commerce, was answerable only to the home government.

The importance to Venice of its possessions in *Romania* lay in two main spheres. The more important was that of facilitating Venetian trade. The significance of maintaining a privileged position at Constantinople lay in that city's continuing role in the dispatch westwards of cereals, alum, raw silk and silk fabrics, precious metals, and spices, in exchange for finished metals, wool, and arms. For a short time there were almost as many Venetians resident at Constantinople as at Venice itself. But Negroponte, Modon, and Coron also played key roles in furnishing safe harbours, arsenals, and repair workshops for Venetian ships, acting as focal points in maritime policing, relaying vital information, and contributing active help in times of crisis. Negroponte was well placed for distributing western cloth to the Balkan states in exchange for grain, besides providing facilities for the shipping to Venice of grapes and salt from the Duchy of Athens and the Argolid. The port of Candia (modern Iraklion) in Crete became an essential entrepôt for Venice's trade with Cyprus, Syria, Cilician Armenia, and the Anatolian emirates, and to some extent Alexandria. The other sphere of importance was that of the direct provision of food supplies for Venice. The Republic came to value Crete above all as a dependable source of grain, wine, oil, timber, salt, and cheese. The cultivated land around Modon and Coron also sent foodstuffs to Venice, although most surplus production here was needed to feed the crews of ships berthing at the two ports.

In terms of the promotion of settlement, only Crete called for active attention. Venice's record there was a mixed one. The Republic decided to implement a programme of colonization, granting knights' fiefs (*cavallerie*) to Venetian nobles and sergeantries (*sergenterie*), each one-sixth of a *cavalleria*, to commoners; both groups owed military service, and each colonist had a contract defining his rights and obligations. Between 1211 and 1252 approximately 3,500 Venetians settled on Crete; the depth of Venice's commitment to the programme is shown by the fact that the city's population at this time totalled only about 60,000. This successful settlement was achieved largely at the expense of the Cretan *archontes*. Their estates were confiscated to provide fiefs, they were excluded from the councils established to represent the colonists, and their higher clergy were expropriated to provide livings for Venetian clerics. Even voluntary admission into the Latin church did not remedy their inferior social status, and intermarriage was strictly prohibited. The contrast with Greco-Frankish relations in Achaea has often been pointed out, and it is highlighted by the dozen major Greek uprisings on Crete with which Venice had to deal between 1212 and 1367. These were so commonplace that some notarial deeds contained exclusion clauses relating to 'periods of open warfare between the Latins and the Greeks'. Even after the most serious of the revolts, that of Alexios Kallergis in 1282–99, had brought about an amelioration of the *archontes'* economic status, the exclusion of the Greek aristocracy from Crete's Greater Council continued. It was the growth of social and economic ties between colonists and Greeks, rather than policy decisions made by Venice, which slowly restored the island's stability; and as we shall see, this local *rapprochement* brought fresh problems for the home government.

The nature of Latin rule in the Greek islands remains shadowy. The Sanudi dukes were vassals of the Latin emperors, and in 1236 the Emperor Baldwin placed them under the intermediate suzerainty of the princes of Achaea. But these ties imposed relatively few burdens or constraints on the Sanudi, nor did their own lordship weigh heavily on the other island lords. Effectively they were independent rulers, as were the Orsini counts of Cephalonia. Dynasties such as the Sanudi at Naxos, and the Ghisi at Tenos and Mykonos, acquired compact domains whose revenues, from agriculture, fishing, mineral resources, and tolls on passing trade, were enough to finance ambitious attempts at aggrandizement. Thus Mark Sanudo tried to seize Crete in 1212, and captured Smyrna from Theodore Laskaris, the Greek Emperor of Nicaea, in 1213.

But gradually local feuds, like that between the Sanudi and Ghisi, came to dominate their attention. Relations with their Greek subjects were better than in mainland Greece, and intermarriage more common. The Orthodox church was tolerated to a greater extent than in either Athens or Achaea. The Orsini in particular achieved a remarkable degree of Hellenization, their contacts with the neighbouring Greek Despotate of Epiros being as close and intimate as those with their fellow Latins in Greece or Italy.

By 1274 most of these areas of Latin rule had begun to be threatened by the revival of Byzantine power. After his reconquest of Constantinople in 1261 Michael VIII Palaiologos naturally turned his attention to the other states established by the Latin interlopers. He immediately dispatched a naval expedition to Crete to incite a rebellion there. This proved unsuccessful, and in 1277 the *basileos* was forced to recognize Venetian sovereignty in Crete. Similarly, initial Byzantine success in regaining many of the Aegean islands proved illusory in the face of superior western seapower and the resilience of the island lords. It was in Achaea that the Greek recovery was most dramatic. In 1259 Michael VIII had inflicted a major defeat on William II of Villehardouin and his Greek ally, the Despot Michael II of Epiros, at the battle of Pelagonia. William II was captured and, as his ransom, agreed at the end of 1261 to cede to Michael VIII the key strongholds of Monemvasia, Mistra, and Maina, situated in the south of the Morea in the peninsulas of Lakonia and Taygetos. These formed the springboards from which a Byzantine advance northwards was begun.

Although the initial stage of this advance was marked by Byzantine defeats, William II knew that his family could only hold Achaea by securing a western protector. After his conquest of the Kingdom of Sicily in 1266, Charles of Anjou seemed perfect for this role: he was a powerful and proximate ruler of proven ability and known ambition, a member of the French royal house and a protégé of the papacy, which was as committed to the defence of Achaea as it was to the recovery of the Latin Empire of Constantinople. The treaty of Viterbo, sealed in May 1267 by Charles and William, marked the beginning of more than a century of Angevin intervention in the affairs of Latin Greece. The price of Charles's aid was a marriage between William's daughter and heiress, Isabella, and Charles's son Philip. William was to retain the Principality in his lifetime, but should Philip die before fathering children, Achaea would revert to Charles and his heirs on the Sicilian throne. A few days later another treaty was finalized at Viterbo which committed Charles to helping the exiled Latin Emperor, Baldwin II, recover Constantinople from Michael VIII. In one clause of this treaty Baldwin vested in Charles suzerainty over Achaea and its feudal dependencies, chiefly the islands of the Archipelago, Corfu, the Orsini islands in the Ionian Sea, and Latin holdings in Epiros.

The wide-ranging repercussions of the two Viterbo treaties, in terms of Angevin, and later Valois, plans for an anti-Byzantine crusade in association with Venetian naval support, have been reviewed in Chapter 2.[1] Here we shall focus on the political and military consequences of Angevin suzerainty for embattled Achaea. William proved a valuable vassal, turning the tide of battle for Charles at Tagliacozzo in 1268, and winning for his lord the port of Avlona in 1269, in order that Angevin pretensions to rule in Albania could be implemented. In exchange, a flow of Angevin commanders, troops, and supplies across the Adriatic prevented the Greeks making further gains in the Principality. The Byzantine military thrust was redirected towards Thessaly, Euboea, and Albania. The loss of Kalavryta in about 1277 was serious, but at the time of his death in 1278 William II still held the north and west of the Principality, while the Argolid continued to be ruled by the Duke of Athens. Philip of Anjou had died a year earlier without children, and in accordance with the harsh terms of the first Viterbo treaty Isabella was now dispossessed and Charles took over direct rule of Achaea. He governed through seneschals, first Galeran of Ivry and then Philip of Lagonesse, until the Sicilian rebellion in 1282 led to the recall of Philip and a general relaxation of the Angevin grip. For some years the Latin Morea enjoyed the comparatively benign rule, as *baillis*, of William II of la Roche, the Duke of Athens, and Nicholas II of St Omer, co-seigneur of Thebes. William and Nicholas tried to contain the Byzantine threat to Messenia by building the castles of Dimatra and Navarino (Port-de-Jonc). Then in September 1289 Charles II of Sicily handed Achaea back to Isabella of Villehardouin, her husband Florent of Hainault, and their direct heirs, under Angevin suzerainty. Isabella agreed that, in the event of Florent's death, she would not remarry without her suzerain's approval. This remarkable volte-face in Angevin policy was stimulated less by Charles's chivalrous reaction against his father's ill-treatment of Isabella, than by his awareness of how much resentment had been caused in Achaea by a decade of absentee rule.

Florent of Hainault's rule in Achaea between 1289 and 1297 has sometimes been viewed as marking a return to the political stability and prosperity of the early Villehardouin period. The Byzantine advance in the Morea had all but ended with the death of Michael VIII in 1282; the

[1] Above, 51–5.

efforts of Andronikos II were absorbed by his struggle against Greek claimants to his throne in Epiros and Thessaly. Florent therefore made peace with Andronikos and for most of his reign maintained cordial relations with the local Byzantine commanders. According to the French Chronicle of the Morea, the Frankish–Byzantine peace caused the country to become 'so fat and so plenteous with all things that its people did not know the half of what they possessed'. Florent was even able to bring aid to the beleagured Despotate of Epiros, Achaea's traditional ally. On the other hand, there are signs that the years immediately before Florent's arrival marked a turning-point in the struggle for power in the Peloponnese, notably in the Greek capture of the central basin of Arkadia. The balanced feudal regime established by the Villehardouins was also being distorted by the arrival of French and Italian knights from the *Regno* who married the widows or daughters of fief-holders killed in battle. The newcomers showed little patience with existing customs. An ominous sign of things to come occurred in 1292, when the Catalan admiral Roger of Lauria carried out a large-scale raid on Greece, attacking Byzantine and Latin possessions, defeating an Achaean force at Navarino, and sacking the archiepiscopal city of Patras.

Above all, relations between Isabella and her Angevin lords remained unsatisfactory. In 1294 Charles II vested immediate suzerainty over Frankish Greece in his son, Philip of Taranto, retaining a somewhat vague overlordship for the Crown. Three years later Prince Florent of Hainault died, and despite the fact that she was over 40 and had a daughter, Mahaut, by Florent, Isabella wanted to marry again. In 1301 she wed Philip of Savoy, a dangerous rival of the Angevins in Piedmont, without consulting Charles II. The King was furious and accepted the union with bad grace, at the intervention of Pope Boniface VIII. But five years later, after Philip had refused to support an Angevin campaign in Epiros, Charles deposed him for violating his feudal oath. Isabella, who was considered to have forfeited both her own rights to the Principality, and those of Mahaut, appealed in vain against the royal verdict. Achaea passed again under direct Angevin rule, this time exercised by Philip of Taranto. For the next twenty-five years Philip's ambitions loomed large in the politics of Latin Greece. Charles II granted his son the title 'Despot of *Romania*' in recognition of the fact that he enjoyed political overlordship of all Frankish Greece from Durazzo to the Cyclades. But although Philip's position looked strong, in practice he was dependent on the support he received from his father and, following Charles II's death in

1309, from his brother King Robert. Moreover, Philip was pulled in two different directions by his main goals in Greece, the defence of Achaea against the Byzantine advance, and the re-enforcement over Epiros of the vassal status which his grandfather had established in 1279, and which had since lapsed. For example, Philip led an important expedition to Achaea in the summer of 1306, which retook several castles and offered hope of a decisive turn-about in the Principality's fortunes. But the Prince never returned to the Morea, and a succession of Angevin *baillis* could not hold on to what he had won.

The history of Frankish Greece in the forty years following the treaties of Viterbo was thus shaped to a large degree by the political fortunes of the House of Anjou. By contrast, the fourteenth century witnessed the arrival of substantially new forces on the scene, in the shape of the Turks and the Catalan Grand Company. The former arrived in Greece in 1263 as mercenaries in the army sent by Michael VIII under the command of his brother Constantine. Their desertion to the Franks in the following year was instrumental in bringing about a major Byzantine defeat, and the grateful Prince William II baptized and dubbed two of their leaders, endowing them with fiefs. But it was not until the early fourteenth century that the maritime *beyliks* of Anatolia were able to make piratical forays as far as Greece. The Catalans made a much bigger initial impact, although in the long term their role was to be minor compared with that of the Turks. The Grand Company was formed of troops who fought for Frederick of Aragon-Sicily in the War of the Sicilian Vespers. When that conflict ended in 1302 the Company's leader, Roger of Flor, offered the services of his followers to Andronikos II. The *basileos*, who had just been defeated by Osman's Turks at Baphaeon, granted good terms of employment, and the Catalans sailed to Constantinople, sacking Ceos *en route*. The chaos which the Catalans then brought to *Romania*, and the extraordinary mixture of greed, ambition, and panache which characterized their activities, bears a striking resemblance to the career of Cortes's *conquistadores* in Mexico.

At first the Company served Andronikos II well, driving the Turks back from the southern shores of the Sea of Marmora and relieving Philadelphia. But thereafter relations between Greeks and Catalans deteriorated, and Roger of Flor was murdered at Adrianople in April 1305. Retaining its cohesion, and led now by Berenguer of Rocafort, the Company moved westwards, from Gallipoli through Thrace to Macedonia. Its progress was marked by pillaging on an unprecedented scale. In

1307–8, as we have seen, Rocafort conducted abortive negotiations with Theobald of Cépoy, an envoy of Charles of Valois, who hoped to use the Company to conquer Constantinople. Then Rocafort was overthrown and the Catalans marched southwards into Thessaly. In 1310 they agreed to fight against the Greeks on behalf of Walter I of Brienne, who had succeeded his cousin Guy II of la Roche a year earlier as Duke of Athens. The Company won much of southern Thessaly for Walter, but the Duke then made the error of refusing to pay the Catalans their wages. Instead he enfeoffed several hundred and ordered the rest to leave his lands. A conflict then ensued to decide, as Professor Setton has put it, 'who would go and who would stay'. On 15 March 1311 the Company and its Turkish auxiliaries met in battle with Walter's feudal host near the river Kephissos. Although the French were numerically superior and included the élite of Frankish Greece's knighthood, the Catalans employed marshy terrain to break up their charge and inflicted a crushing defeat on them. The Duke and many hundreds of his knights were killed, and the Duchy passed, with very little further resistance, into Catalan hands.

The creation of a Catalan Duchy of Athens represented a milestone in the history of Latin Greece for two reasons. First, the arrival of the Catalans signalled the break-up of the political system established after the Fourth Crusade. Despite the frequent hostilities between the states created after 1204, and the conflicts between the Angevins and their Villehardouin vassals in Achaea, relations between Greece's Latin rulers had hitherto been characterized by an underlying consensus and unity. They were common beneficiaries from the partition treaties of 1203–4; they were connected by ties of marriage and suzerainty, of which some at least constituted a workable clientage network; and their position was safeguarded by the papacy, which in the thirteenth century stood at the height of its influence as a legitimizing authority. By contrast, the Catalans were regarded, especially at the papal, French, and Angevin courts, as dangerous interlopers whose government lacked legal authority. For decades following their conquest of Athens they were politically isolated and excommunicated, ranked alongside the Byzantines, and in due course the Turks, as irreconcilable foes of the Latin establishment in Greece. The exiled Brienne dynasty pulled all the strings available to it to secure a French reconquest. Walter II, son of the last Duke, was a dangerous adversary. His maternal grandfather, Walter of Châtillon, was Constable of France, his wife Beatrice the daughter of Philip of Taranto, and he was himself a powerful feudatory of King Robert of Naples. In

1330–1 he recruited an army of 800 French knights and 500 Tuscan foot to invade the Duchy. Following the pattern set by Clement V, who in 1312 had granted crusade indulgences and taxes to an expedition planned by Philip of Taranto against the Byzantines, John XXII preached a full-scale crusade in Walter's support. The Catalans declined battle and Walter's invasion was a débâcle, but it was not until 1341 that the papal Curia followed Venice's lead and initiated a *rapprochement* with the Catalans; in the mean time many had despaired and joined the Orthodox church. As late as 1371 Walter II's nephews, the Enghiens, attempted to reconquer Athens for their family. By this point the Catalans had become respectable enough for Pope Gregory XI to choose their capital, Thebes, as the rendezvous for his planned congress of rulers of *Romania* to debate the region's defence against the Turks. Ironically, the Catalans were now too weak to perform the crusading role which Gregory outlined for them, but in their heyday they had conclusively demonstrated the weakness of Latin Greece, paving the way for other outsiders, notably the Navarrese Company, to carve out possessions there by the application of *force majeure*.

The second change brought about by the Catalans was in the nature of their rule. Society and government in their Duchy differed sharply from the feudal pattern which had previously dominated mainland Greece; its concomitant chivalric culture had been dazzlingly manifested as late as the spring of 1304 at the great tournaments which Philip of Savoy held at Corinth. The Catalan Grand Company itself was a remarkable example of the medieval genius for forming coherent yet flexible legal corporations. Once its members left the service of King Frederick of Sicily they formed an independent and sovereign *societas*, capable of making conquests, owning property, and bestowing fiefs. Following the death of Roger of Flor the Company possessed its own seal, depicting St George killing the dragon, as well as statutes in the form of articles ('els Capitols de la Companyia'). After 1311 the personal nature of the Company's bonds naturally dissolved as its members formed communes in the Duchy's chief towns, channelling their energies, loyalties, and intense legalism into landholding, commerce, and government. Truces with Venice in 1319, 1321, and 1331 reveal the 'Corporation of the Army of Franks in *Romania*' still acting as a body, and a General Council met irregularly until 1381. But the distinctive form of government in the Duchy had become the municipal corporations of Athens, Thebes, and Livadia, with their elected officials and assemblies of citizens; the feudal law of

Burgundian Athens was displaced by the Customs of Barcelona. Anxious to preserve their group identity, and living as small groups in a fluid urban milieu, the Catalans could not afford to show sympathy towards their Greek subjects: the marriage of Latin women to Greeks was prohibited, that of Greek women to Catalans frowned upon. There occurred none of the assimilation which by this point had become such a striking feature of Achaean feudal society.

The Catalans realized from the start the precarious nature of their rule in Athens. Surrounded by enemies and lacking a leader of status, they initially persuaded one of their own captives, Roger Deslaur, to rule them, and when he proved inadequate they turned to the Sicilian royal House. In 1312 the dignity of Duke was vested, subject to carefully defined conditions, in the Infante Manfred, Frederick of Sicily's 5-year-old son. A vicar-general was to rule at Thebes until Manfred came of age. Although the problem of communications always hampered the vicars-general, the following decades saw them gradually extending the prerogatives of ducal lordship. Don Alfonso Fadrique, King Frederick's natural son, was particularly effective between 1317 and 1330, in the course of which the Catalans acquired the Duchy of Neopatras. Sources for the later history of Catalan Athens and Neopatras are poor: we do not even know the names of the Sicilian vicars-general for the years between 1331 and 1354. But it seems clear that conditions were deteriorating. Catalan aggression was turning inwards and fuelling division, and the Duchy was increasingly subjected to Turkish attack, which sapped its economic prosperity. The link with Sicily proved to be as disappointing as that of Achaea with Naples. After the premature death of the Infante Manfred in 1317 the ducal title passed erratically through the royal family, residing during the years 1355–77 with the weak King Frederick III, who was in no position to do anything to assist his subjects in Greece. In 1362 the Marshal of the Company, Roger of Lluria, led a rebellion against Sicilian rule, which ended only when Roger himself was appointed vicar-general, probably in 1366. By the early 1370s the Catalans were desperate to transfer their allegiance to the Crown of Aragon, which they hoped would prove a more efficacious overlord. After the death of Frederick III without male heirs, Peter III of Aragon did lay claim to Athens and Neopatras, but although the King showed concern for the Duchies' well-being, he could do little more to help the Catalans there than Frederick had.

The government of neighbouring Achaea continued in this period to be dominated by the vicissitudes of Angevin suzerainty. In 1313 Philip of

Taranto was married to Catherine of Valois, in an attempt to give some substance to French hopes of realizing the Valois claim to Constantinople. Catherine had been engaged to Duke Hugh V of Burgundy, and the price which Philip had to pay for his bride was the government of the Morea. The arrangement was complicated. The Principality was returned to Mahaut of Hainault, Isabella of Villehardouin's daughter by Florent, although it remained under Angevin suzerainty. Mahaut married Hugh V's brother, Louis; in return, Louis renounced to Hugh all his claims to Burgundy. The return of Achaea to Mahaut was accompanied by the same conditions that had been attached to her mother's match with Florent in 1289, in particular that her remarriage would require the approval of Philip of Taranto. Louis was immediately faced with the need to repel an attempt by the Infante Ferdinand of Majorca, with the backing of Frederick of Sicily, to conquer his Principality. Ferdinand's ambition to imitate the Catalan success in Athens ended in his defeat and death in the battle of Manolada in July 1316. But just four weeks after his great victory Prince Louis himself died. As so often in the history of Latin Greece, premature mortality had wrecked a carefully considered project to ensure long-term stability on a firm dynastic basis.

King Robert of Naples now conceived the plan of bringing Achaea once again under direct Angevin rule by compelling Mahaut to marry his youngest brother, John of Gravina. Mahaut, who was as strong-willed as her mother had been, frustrated the project by secretly marrying a Burgundian knight, but this enabled Robert to declare that she had forfeited her rights to Achaea. Once Burgundian claims, left over from the brief rule of Louis, had been settled, the way was open for the investiture of John of Gravina as Prince of Achaea, which took place at the papal court at Avignon in 1322. Nine years later Mahaut died in Angevin captivity at Aversa. In the thirteenth century Achaea had suffered from being a pawn in the far-reaching ambitions of Charles I of Anjou; its experience of Angevin rule after 1322 proved no happier, since Robert retained massive commitments in Italy, while possessing fewer resources with which to finance them. There was little to spare for Achaea. John of Gravina led an imposing expedition to the Principality in 1325, but he failed to make any gains from the Greeks. After a fruitless siege of Karytaina John returned to Naples in the spring of 1326. The only tangible result of his expedition was his landing at Cephalonia, *en route* for the Morea; here he deposed the Orsini and instituted direct rule, along the lines practised in Corfu since 1267.

After 1326 Angevin intervention in Achaea waned. When Philip of Taranto died at the end of 1331 his 5-year-old son Robert inherited suzerainty over Achaea. In the following year John of Gravina exchanged his title for lands and claims further north, and until 1364 Achaea was ruled directly by Robert as Prince; his mother, the titular Empress Catherine, acted as regent until Robert attained his majority. Catherine spent large sums on Achaea, notably during a prolonged visit between 1338 and 1341, but her government of the Principality was perforce largely absentee. It weakened after the death of King Robert in 1343, when both she and Robert of Taranto became preoccupied with the turbulent politics of the *Regno* in Queen Joanna I's early years. The discontent of the Morea's barons with Angevin rule led to a series of attempts to find alternative rulers. In 1321 they tried to persuade Venice to accept Achaea. Twenty years later overtures were made to John Cantacuzene, and in 1344 a group of prominent barons approached James II of Majorca, who had a claim of sorts as a descendant of William of Villehardouin. In 1356–7 Pope Innocent VI tried to arrange the transfer of the Principality to the Hospitallers, but Robert refused to countenance the plan.

During this phase of Angevin rule the Principality experienced a radical change in the constitution and way of life of its landholding class, as the original French dynasties died out or were represented only by heiresses. Increasingly, estates were acquired through sale or marriage by Italian families, particularly the Florentines, Venetians, and Genoese. The barony of Chalandritza, for example, was granted by Louis of Burgundy to two of his knights, Odo and Aimon of Rans, when the founding Trémolay line became extinct at the death of Nicholas of Trémolay. Odo died and Aimon sold the fief to Martin Zaccaria, the lord of Chios. A few years later, in 1327, Martin acquired the fief of Damala by marriage to Jacqueline of la Roche. But even Martin's success in the Principality was overshadowed by that of the Acciaiuoli of Florence. Their privileged position as bankers to the Neapolitan court enabled them to acquire Achaean fiefs, initially Lichina and Mandria, as repayment of the loans which proved crucial to the implementation of Angevin policy in the Peloponnese. Between 1332 and 1342 they lent John of Gravina and Catherine of Valois 40,000 gold ounces for their financial outgoings in Achaea. Nicholas Acciaiuoli's rise to power and wealth as creditor, adviser, and feudatory during the regency of Catherine of Valois, particularly in the years 1332–8, was spectacular. In 1348 he became Grand Seneschal of the *Regno*, and for the rest of his life he was the main influence on Robert's rule in Achaea, dying a year after the Prince in 1365.

The entrenchment in the Morea of families such as the Zaccaria and Acciaiuoli sounded the death knell for the feudal and chivalric society created by the Villehardouin princes of Achaea. When the newcomers arrived, the Byzantine conquest of so much of the rural interior had already effected a shift from a castle-dwelling, agrarian class of knightly fiefholders, towards a feudal élite which clustered in the ports and coastal regions, and owed service for both estates and money-fiefs. The Italian fiefholders were thoroughly urbanized and engaged in mercantile and banking activities which the feudal nobility of the Villehardouin era would have despised. They did not preside over courts, and although they were deeply attracted by the cult of chivalry, they had little time to sponsor the chivalric activities cherished by their predecessors. Instead of serving in person for their fiefs they furnished hired troops, often fewer than was specified in the 'Assizes of *Romania*'. The feudal system depicted in such detail in the 'Assizes' was thus increasingly at odds with reality. Despite this, the 'Assizes' were clearly considered to form a valuable guide to feudal customs in Achaea and elsewhere in Greece, since they were applied by Venice to its own lands in *Romania*; indeed, they survive in a Venetian translation of the late fourteenth century.

In a famous letter written in 1338, Nicholas Acciaiuoli assured his father that the family firm could expect a tenfold return on its Achaean investments. The comment has sometimes been taken as indicating that members of the new Italian landholding class implemented a more exploitative, and ruthless, agrarian regime in the Morea than their predecessors had done. The generalization is hard to test; indeed, gauging the economic condition of Achaea in the fourteenth century is exceptionally difficult. By 1356 Nicholas Acciaiuoli himself was bemoaning the dwindling prosperity of the Principality. Similarly, a detailed inquiry into the condition of the estates owned by Mary of Bourbon, Robert of Taranto's wife, in 1360–1, proved to be gloomy reading. On the other hand, Achaea continued to export grain and wine, albeit on an irregular basis, throughout the century, and the revenues accruing from the ports of Glarentza, Patras, and Vostitza remained buoyant. The cost seems to have been the decline of such manufacturing centres as Thebes and Corinth, as *Romania*'s economy became geared to supplying food and raw materials for Italy, and providing a market for its finished products. As late as the mid-fifteenth century, however, Pope Pius II could consider the Peloponnese to be 'a region most convenient for the whole world's trade, a veritable abode of merchants, abounding in wine, wheat and everything requisite for human existence'. It is hardly possible that the political *malaise* afflicting the Principality, as well as the disruptive presence of so many mercenaries, did not damage Achaea's economy; but the barons' desperate appeals for a takeover by another power seem to have been motivated less by their declining prosperity than by the grave external threats which they faced.

One of these consisted of the Byzantine forces in the southern Peloponnese. By 1300 the Empire's holdings in the south had developed into a strong province. It had a flourishing port at Monemvasia and a secure capital at Mistra. The Greeks of Mistra both beat off the attacks of Philip of Taranto and John of Gravina, and continued to advance northwards into Arkadia. Andronikos Palaiologos Asen took the castles of Akova, Karytaina, and St George in 1320, inflicting a serious defeat on the Franks in an ambush near St George in September. By this point only three of the original twelve baronies of Achaea—Patras, Vostitza, and Chalandritza—remained in Frankish hands. The Morean Byzantines also shared in the cultural renaissance enjoyed by the Empire in the fourteenth century, notably in the construction of beautiful churches at Mistra. Mistra's heyday came after 1348, when John VI Cantacuzene appointed his son Manuel to the governorship and made the province into a Despotate. Manuel proved to be a very capable ruler. Relations between Franks and Greeks improved, and the Despot's court became the political focal point of the entire Peloponnese. Manuel's subjects benefited from a thriving economic life, and the stable and effective government which they enjoyed contrasted sharply with conditions in the neighbouring Principality.

By the mid-fourteenth century, in fact, it was becoming clear that all the Christian powers in Greece faced a common enemy which made co-operation imperative. The growing threat of organized piracy practised by the maritime *beyliks* of Anatolia, and the crusading leagues which formed the Latin Christian response, have been surveyed in Chapter 2.[2] Venice's commitment to the leagues reflected in part its consciousness of the threat to Negroponte and its island holdings, while the failure of the Angevin court to participate was symptomatic of the bankruptcy of its Greek policies. By 1350 piracy and raiding had already curtailed the prosperity of the Aegean's island lordships, and brought about the

[2] Above, 56–67.

evacuation of the smallest islands. The danger posed by large-scale raiding to mainland Greece was demonstrated by a raid into the Gulf of Corinth, in spring 1349, by a fleet of eighty ships; such activities were a formidable spur to co-operation, and some years later a coalition comprising the *bailli* of Achaea, Manuel Cantacuzene, Venice, and the Hospitallers inflicted a defeat on the Turks off the coast of Megara. Similarly, the Angevins spent some effort on improving coastal defence: when the people of Corinth appealed for help in 1358, Prince Robert responded by handing the whole area over as a new barony to Nicholas Acciaiuoli, and allowed Nicholas to commute the feudal service for all his lands in Greece into the provision of defensive measures for the region. But the naval threat could not be contained, and from the battle of Crnomen (1371) onwards it was joined by the possibility of a land-based Ottoman invasion from the north.

The hope that these twin perils might be countered by common action, which formed the basis for Gregory XI's policy at the start of his reign, was dashed by events within Greece in the last three decades of the fourteenth century. These years formed probably the most confused period in the whole history of Latin rule in Greece. After the death of Robert of Taranto in 1364 the title of prince passed to his brother, Philip II, but he died without heirs in 1373, and Queen Joanna then took Achaea under her own rule. In 1376 the Queen leased the Principality to the Hospitallers for a five-year period in exchange for an annual rent of 4,000 ducats. Under papal prodding, the Order of St John was beginning to assume the responsibility for defending Latin Greece; but its policies, both in Achaea and in Epiros and Albania, were also motivated by the territorial ambitions of its masters, which soon outstripped their resources. In 1378 the Hospitaller commandant in the Morea, Gaucher of la Bastide, hired the services, for eight months, of two companies of Navarrese and Gascon mercenaries. Their leaders were Mahiot of Coquerel and John of Urtubia, and they had originally been recruited by Louis of Évreux in 1375–6 to press his dynastic claim to Albania by occupying Durazzo. The new arrivals were not as well-organized and effective as the Catalan Grand Company had been, but they enjoyed a great advantage in the political confusion which now characterized Latin Greece, and their significance was soon registered.

Early in 1379, their contract with the Hospitallers at an end, John of Urtubia led one group of mercenaries eastwards into Catalan territory. They conquered Thebes, driving a wedge between the Catalan Duchies of Athens and Neopatras. Their comrades remained in Achaea, seizing and pillaging lands virtually without hindrance, after the Hospitallers' lease on the Principality expired in 1381 and the Order withdrew. The assassination of Queen Joanna in 1382 brought to an end Achaea's connection with the Angevins, and the members of the Navarrese Company became, largely by default, the effective rulers of the Latin Morea. The Company's headquarters lay at Androusa, in northern Messenia, from where they conducted sporadic hostilities against the Greeks of Mistra. After the death of Mahiot of Coquerel in 1386, they were ably led by a Gascon, Peter of St Superan, and what they held was still attractive enough for their rule to be challenged by a number of western claimants. These included the Les Baux family of Naples, Louis II of Clermont, and Amedeo of Savoy. But a document drawn up in 1391 reveals that the Navarrese still controlled the western Morea, as well as the castle at Vostitza. In 1396 St Superan even persuaded the impecunious King Ladislas of Naples to sell him the hereditary title of Prince of Achaea for just 3,000 ducats. This cut-price acquisition, by a mercenary captain from Gascony, of a title previously held by scions of the illustrious House of Anjou, is the most telling example of what the unstable politics of Latin Greece could place in the hands of an able and ambitious man.

Apart from the Navarrese, the most dynamic forces in Greece in the late fourteenth century remained two Italian families, the Tocchi and Acciaiuoli. William Tocco and his son Leonard were officials of Philip I and Robert of Taranto in Corfu during the period of direct Angevin rule there, and in 1357 Robert rewarded Leonard by creating him Duke of Leucadia and Count of Cephalonia and Zante. The waning of Angevin power left Leonard Tocco in control of the southern Ionian islands, and his son Charles not only retained this position but managed in the early fifteenth century to add to it the Despotate of Epiros. Meanwhile the Acciaiuoli were ably represented by Nerio, an adopted son of Nicholas, whose chief possession was the barony of Corinth. In 1374 Nerio seized the Catalan castle of Megara. He encouraged and perhaps sponsored the Navarrese attack on Thebes in 1379, and in 1385 overran what was left of the Catalan Duchy of Athens after Urtubia's onslaught. In May 1388 the last remnant of Catalan rule in Athens ended when Peter of Pau's Aragonese garrison surrendered the Acropolis after a long siege. Nerio later persuaded Ladislas of Naples to grant him the coveted title Duke of Athens, but the success of the Acciaiuoli hinged on Venetian rather than Neapolitan support. Liberated in 1381 by the Peace of Turin from the gruelling ordeal of its last major war with Genoa, Venice was reluctantly assuming greater commitments in Greece as the only resourceful Latin power left in the region. Its acquisitions in the 1380s and 1390s rivalled those of the early thirteenth century. In 1383 Euboea passed almost wholly into Venetian hands. In 1386 the Venetians seized Corfu and the Epirote port of Butrinto from Naples, and in 1388 they purchased Argos and Nauplia. After the death of Nerio Acciaiuoli in 1394 Venice also assumed control at Athens, incorporating the city within its possessions under the rule of a *podestà*. In Albania, Durazzo, Alessio, and Scutari became Venetian possessions.

It looked as if Venice had left things too late. In 1387 the Ottomans captured Thessalonica, and in the same year the Turkish general Evrenos Bey carried out a great raid of the Morea. Technically he was responding to an appeal for help from the Despot Theodore of Mistra, and in the decades to come the Ottomans could usually rely on one of the warring Christian rulers of Greece to call in their troops. Two years later the crushing Serbian defeat at Kossovo made a full-scale invasion of Greece seem inevitable. In 1393–4 the Turks conquered Thessaly, and the Catalan territories of Neopatras and Salona. In the winter of 1394–5 Evrenos Bey reappeared, this time in alliance with the Navarrese, to attack the Despotate of Mistra. His premature withdrawal was probably the result of Sultan Bayezid's preparations to meet the Nicopolis crusade, and the breathing space thus gained enabled Venice to reach a peaceful settlement with the Navarrese. But in 1397 Latin Greece suffered its worst yet Ottoman attack, which culminated in the sack of Argos in June. The Despot Theodore was so convinced of imminent doom that in 1397 he persuaded the Hospitallers to accept Corinth, which he had seized after Nerio Acciaiuoli's death. In 1399–1400 Theodore, who was making hasty provision for exile at Venice, even negotiated the sale of his entire Despotate to the Order. The Master of the Hospitallers, Philibert of Naillac, had revived his Order's earlier project of installing itself in Greece, and this appears to have caused Bayezid some anxiety.

Like Constantinople, Greece was saved from Ottoman conquest at this point by Tamerlane's victory at Ankara in 1402. This gave Latin rule two extra generations of life, although they were overshadowed throughout by the fear of a Turkish resurgence. The Latin Morea had now become too weak to withstand any external pressure. When Peter of St Superan died in 1402 Centurione Zaccaria, one of Achaea's leading barons, usurped power. Following St Superan's precedent, he purchased legitimacy from

Ladislas of Naples, although unlike the mercenary leader, Centurione actually paid the money. Centurione ruled with the help of Venice, which strengthened its commercial structure by acquiring the ports of Lepanto (Naupaktos) in 1407, Patras in 1408, and Navarino in 1417. But the government of Achaea remained feeble and divided, and the search for an outside protector, preferably someone who would reunite the Peloponnese, was resumed. In 1422 the Hospitallers declined an invitation from both Latins and Greeks in the Peloponnese to renew their involvement in the region's political affairs. A cautious proposal from the Venetians for overall Venetian rule, in 1422–3, also met with no success, and in the event it was the Greeks of Mistra who unified the Morea through force of arms, by dealing the death blow to the remains of the Latin Principality.

The context was a twofold one. First, despite the traumatic invasions by Evrenos Bey, Mistra remained a relatively prosperous and vigorous polity. The credit for this was largely due to the Despot Theodore I (1383–1407), who encouraged large numbers of Albanians to settle in the Peloponnese in order to replace Greeks killed by plague or enslaved by the Turks. One estimate puts the Albanian proportion of the peninsula's population at more than a third by the mid-fifteenth century. In 1415–16 the Emperor Manuel II spent a busy year in the Morea, putting the defence and administration of the Despotate in order. In particular, he supervised the reconstruction of the Hexamilion, Justinian's great wall across the isthmus of Corinth, which was intended to stop the Turks flooding into the Peloponnese. Secondly, 1423 witnessed the renewal of Turkish attacks in the form of a great raid on the Peloponnese by Turakhan Bey, whose troops easily scaled the Hexamilion. The raid showed the urgent need to create a united front, and in 1427 the Greeks began to conquer the lands of the most important remaining western rulers, Charles II Tocco and Centurione Zaccaria. Glarentza fell, and two years later Patras returned to Greek hands. With the exception of Venice's fortified trading stations at Modon, Coron, Navarino, Lepanto, Argos, and Nauplia, the whole of the Peloponnese was restored to Byzantine rule. The process of reconquest initiated by Michael VIII more than a century and a half before was thus completed.

Athens meanwhile had experienced a remarkable revival of Acciaiuoli strength in the person of Anthony, an illegitimate son of Nerio who showed himself to be as ruthless as his father. In 1402 Anthony, who had inherited Thebes and the castle of Livadia from Nerio, seized Athens from the Venetians. He defeated a substantial force led by the *bailli* of

Negroponte, and in 1405 compelled the Republic to accept this *fait accompli* when he was recognized as Duke of Athens, under a light Venetian suzerainty. The protection subsequently afforded by the Republic, Anthony's adroitness in remaining on good terms with the Turks, and the range of fiefs, church offices, and commercial contacts in the Duchy, attracted many Florentines to Greece during the thirty-three years of Anthony's rule. Florence's trade with the East was growing fast as a result of its conquest of Pisa in 1406, and purchase of Livorno in 1421, and although the *signoria* established no political ties with the Acciaiuoli rulers of Athens, it has been suggested that the family's influence was a factor in stimulating Florentine interest in the crusade plans formulated after the fall of Constantinople. Burgeoning commercial ties went hand-in-hand with early humanist interest in Classical Greece: one of the fullest accounts of political and social life at the courts of Latin Greece in these last decades was written by the antiquary Ciriaco of Ancona, who visited Greece three times.

The defeat of the crusading army at Varna in 1444 was as disastrous for Greece as Nicopolis would have been, but for Tamerlane. It made the Ottomans acutely aware of the danger of the West using Greece as a base from which to attack Turkish lands, and it freed their hands to ensure that this would not happen. Two years after Varna Sultan Murad II in person led an army southwards from Thessaly in a terrible razzia which netted thousands of captives. The Turkish failure to take either the citadel at Patras, or Mistra itself, underscored the fact that the Ottoman conquest of Greece would demand the protracted deployment of resources which could not be spared for long enough until Constantinople had fallen. But after 1453, with no crusade (or Tamerlane) appearing to offer a temporary respite against Sultan Mehmed's programme of conquest, events took a predictable course. The Turks occupied Athens in 1456, ousting the last Duke, Franco Acciaiuoli. Greek historians in Ottoman service reported Mehmed's fascination with Athens, whose charms had been described to the Sultan, rather unwisely, by Ciriaco of Ancona. Under the terms of his capitulation Franco Acciaiuoli was allowed to retire to Boeotia, where he survived for four years before the suspicious Mehmed ordered his murder. The definitive conquest of the Peloponnese was achieved in two great campaigns in 1458 and 1460. The rugged terrain, and the determined opposition mounted by the Greeks, made this one of the most gruelling wars the Ottomans ever conducted, and as in contemporary Albania, they attempted to break down resistance with calculated frightfulness.

There remained Venice's extensive island possessions, so that after 1460 the history of Latin rule in Greece shades imperceptibly into that of Venice's long fighting retreat in the eastern Mediterranean. Laying aside Cyprus, which we shall consider in the next chapter,[3] the key events related to Euboea, the Archipelago, and Crete. When war between Venice and Mehmed broke out in 1463, the Venetians exploited the tenuous nature of their enemy's hold on Greece with energy and skill. Uprisings were provoked, coastal towns raided, and ambitious assaults mounted on Patras and Mistra. Pope Pius II believed that the Venetians hoped to conquer and colonize the whole Peloponnese, a course of action 'urged upon them by an overcrowded city which could no longer endure itself . . . They thought they ought to send out a colony and that there was no better place to send one than the Peloponnese.' If such a plan was seriously entertained, it proved illusory. When he was again able to turn in person to Greece, Mehmed concentrated on conquering Euboea. This project hinged on taking the fortress-city of Negroponte. It has been pointed out that the Sultan invested as much time and care in laying siege to Negroponte in 1470 as he had in besieging Constantinople seventeen years previously; and that despite this, the siege lasted almost as long. The city's fall caused immense distress at Venice: 'Now it seemed that Venetian grandeur was abased and our pride extinguished', wrote Dominic Malipiero. The disaster brought Euboea into Turkish control, confirmed Mehmed's earlier Greek conquests, and enabled the Sultan to direct his growing naval power towards the Ionian islands and Italy. From this point onwards Venice was generally on the defensive. As we saw in Chapter 3,[4] the city lost Lepanto, Modon, Coron, and Navarino to Bayezid II at the end of the century.

For all its naval strength, the Republic's military difficulties on the mainland were largely replicated in the islands. Following the death of John Sanudo in 1361 the Venetians were drawn into the Duchy of the Archipelago's dynastic politics in order to exclude the Genoese and Florentines. They probably backed the *coup d'état* carried out by Francis Crispo in 1383, which resulted in his family replacing the Sanudi as lords of Naxos and dukes of the Archipelago. The Republic also established firmer links with the dynasties controlling other islands, and assumed direct rule when lordships fell vacant, as did Tenos and Mykonos when the Ghisi family died out in 1390. But once Mehmed had embarked on his programme of galley building, Venice could not defend all the islands

[3] Below, 198–202.   [4] Above, 115–16.

in the Cyclades group against the Turks. After periods of tributary subsistence, varying in length, the islands gradually fell into Ottoman hands. Naxos itself survived the longest. In 1564 the last Duke, James V, was overthrown by his subjects, who would no longer tolerate the penalties which accompanied Christian rule within the Ottoman state system. There followed one of the most curious episodes of Ottoman history, when Sultan Selim II gave Naxos to a favourite, the Portuguese Jew Joseph Nasi. Following Lepanto the Crispi were briefly restored to power, but thereafter the islands came under direct Ottoman rule. Venetian losses in the Aegean were not, however, duplicated in the Ionian Sea, where the Turks proved unable to take the island fortresses of Corfu, Cephalonia, Zante, and Cerigo.

Throughout the late Middle Ages Crete remained the jewel in Venice's colonial crown, 'caput status nostri Levantis', as the Senate put it in 1470. Its strategic importance in the Republic's trading grew as Venice organized its convoy system for Levantine commerce, and as other Venetian possessions began to be overrun by the Turks. The government of Crete, however, continued to pose great problems for the Republic. The revolts by the *archontes* which had punctuated the thirteenth century did not end when the Venetians settled the grievances of Alexios Kallergis. There were dangerous rebellions in 1333 and 1341, though these were overshadowed by the revolt which broke out in August 1363. On this occasion the Venetian colonists themselves were driven by maladministration, crushing fiscal burdens, and constraints on their economic activity, to proclaim an independent republic under the patronage of St Titus. The rebels even engaged in negotiations with the native Greeks, for whom they now felt more sympathy than for their metropolis, to try to secure their collaboration. Venice, thoroughly alarmed, equipped a substantial expedition which landed near Candia in May 1364. The professional mercenaries hired by the Republic defeated the rebel forces, took Candia, and beheaded Mark Gradenigo, the revolt's leader. But as soon as the mercenaries departed the Greek *archontes* in turn rebelled, and it was not until 1367 that Venetian authority was restored in full. The suppression of the Greek phase of the revolt was particularly brutal, and the island's garrison was augmented to prevent any recurrence of these events.

The great revolt of 1363–7 taught Venice the dangers of neglecting Crete, and the later fourteenth and fifteenth centuries were a period of fairer government and greater prosperity for Venetians resident there. Irrigation was systematically promoted, and the development of sugar plantations proved especially lucrative. The conditions of the Greeks also improved, many *paroikoi* gaining the means to buy their freedom. Greeks from Thessaly, Constantinople, and the Morea fled to Crete to escape the Ottoman advance; Candia, long an entrepôt for goods bound for the West, became one also for humanist scholars with their sights set on Italy. Some refugee scholars and artists stayed in Crete, while other Greeks who were born there developed the island's cultural traditions. Crete in the fifteenth century thus helped to bridge the Byzantine and Italian renaissances. In more general terms, too, the degree of fusion which occurred between Crete's Latin and Greek inhabitants, mainly through mixed marriages and conversions to both the Catholic and Orthodox churches, makes Crete comparable to the Peloponnese as a land where a partial synthesis was achieved of conquerors and conquered. In the case of Crete it was, above all, the passing of time which made this possible: for despite devastating razzias and the occasional threat of full-scale invasion, the Ottomans did not take Crete in the period covered by this book, even during their great expansionist drive in the mid-sixteenth century.

With the exception of Crete and a few other Venetian holdings, the period of Latin rule in Greece thus lasted for about two and a half centuries, the last fifty years of which constituted a breathing-space afforded by the crisis which beset the Ottomans in 1402. Essentially the Latins filled a gap between the collapse of one centralized and bureaucratic empire ruled from Constantinople, and the eventual creation of its successor-state. The chronic instability of Latin Greece, and the inability of western rulers to do more than fill the political vacuum between Byzantines and Ottomans, are related above all to Greece's geographical position. The Balkan states were generally fragmented and politically backward, and the ambitions of the most coherent and able—such as Stephen Dushan's Serbia and Louis the Great's Hungary—lay elsewhere. The only western power which might have governed Greece effectively was the Kingdom of Sicily; and we have seen that after 1282 the *Regno*'s monarchs could not give their lands across the Adriatic a prominent place on their political agenda. Without a substantial, sustained military commitment, all the Angevins' elaborate permutations of feudal overlordship and dynastic linkage became exercises in futility. If anything, Catalan Athens fared worse under Sicily and Aragon than Frankish Achaea and its dependencies did under Naples. The persistent reluctance of Venice to assume greater commitments than it already possessed prevented the Republic stepping into the breach; and the internal weaknesses and many other commitments of the Hospitallers would not permit them to play the dominant role which they were, at times, tempted to assume.

The forceful monarchies and Military Orders which organized both conquest and settlement in Iberia and the Baltic region were thus conspicuous by their absence in Latin Greece. This placed the country in the hands of miscellaneous French and Italian dynasts, and groups of free-lance mercenaries from Catalonia, Navarre, and Gascony. We have seen that there was a multiplicity of such families and groups. They were powerfully attracted by the prestige and vulnerability of Greece, which held out the prospect of a pleasant, though never luxurious, way of life right up to the eve of the Turkish conquest. But such rulers were prevented from making a deep and long-term imprint by their own limited resources, the vagaries of dynastic succession, and the challenges mounted by others like themselves. In such circumstances, rural and urban settlement on the massive scale experienced in Valencia and Andalusia, or Prussia and Finland, was out of the question. Last but not least, the constant refrain of popes and crusade theorists, that Latin Greece was an invaluable springboard for crusades to the Holy Land and other parts of *Romania*, enjoyed little response in the West, which failed to rescue its fellow-Catholics from the fatal consequences of their political turmoil and military weakness.

6

The Kingdoms of Cilician Armenia
and Cyprus, 1274–1573

✠

WHEN Acre fell in 1291, the remaining Latin establishments in the eastern Mediterranean comprised not only the Frankish states and colonies of *Romania*, but also the Kingdoms of Armenia and Cyprus (see map 7). Like Frankish Greece, these Kingdoms originated as by-products of the crusading movement, and their defence by western Catholics was an important goal of the papacy's crusading policy in the fourteenth century. By 1274 Cilician Armenia, a non-Frankish country, was economically debilitated, politically chaotic, and immensely vulnerable to Islamic attack. In 1375 it was extinguished altogether by the Muslims. For most of the century preceding this, Cyprus, protected by the sea, had presented a very favourable contrast to its embattled northern neighbour. The island's Frankish royal house and nobility enjoyed deep-rooted governmental stability, occasionally marred by dynastic and constitutional conflict; and until the mid-fourteenth century Cyprus's economic prosperity was striking. But by 1400 the most independent, constructive, and brilliant period of Cyprus's medieval history had ended. Invaded, exploited, and politically disrupted, fifteenth-century Cyprus increasingly resembled the Kingdom of Armenia a century earlier. In Cyprus, as in Syria and Greece, Frankish government began well but ended in disunity and disaster.

The Kingdom of Cilician (or 'Lesser') Armenia dated from January 1198, when Prince Leo II was crowned by Conrad of Hildesheim, Chancellor and envoy of the Emperor Henry VI. The Armenians, whose original homeland had been in eastern Anatolia, had only settled in the Taurus mountains in the decades leading up to the First Crusade. Here, and in the coastal plain to the south, the Rupenid family built up a flourishing principality in the face of the contesting claims of Byzantium, the Turks, and the Franks of Antioch. Leo II was the finest in a line of able rulers. He vigorously encouraged Cilician Armenia's orientation towards the Latins in both West and East. Italian merchants were attracted to trade there, the Hospitallers and Teutonic Knights were granted lands and castles, and dynastic marriages were arranged. By assisting Frederick Barbarossa on the Third Crusade Leo earned the gratitude which, together with his support for imperial policy in the East, won him the crown in 1198. The cost was Union of the Armenian and Latin churches. Most of the Armenian bishops resisted this, but it was virtually forced on them by Leo II. Apparently the King persuaded them that the Union could be formal, a view the easier to accept as the Armenians had an essentially federalist conception of the Church. Trouble was thus stored up for the future, but by the death of Leo II in 1219 Lesser Armenia had become a latinized state. Under Leo's successor, Hetoum I, the Assizes of Antioch were even translated into Armenian for use in the Kingdom.

Cilician Armenia's difficulties began with the arrival of the Mongols in Greater Armenia, Georgia, and Anatolia in the 1230s. Initially, the Mongols were advantageous to Hetoum: in 1247 he sent his brother, the Constable Smbat, to submit to the Great Khan, Göyük, and the King in person submitted to the Mongols in 1253. Mongol aid then helped Hetoum to defeat the Seljukids of Konya, and the King became the leading exponent of the seductive idea of a Latin–Mongol alliance against the Muslims. But after the defeat of the Mongols at Ain Jalut in 1260, and the waning of Mongol power and interest in Syria, the early benefits of the Mongol presence were more than outweighed by the disruption of the existing balance of power which they had effected. After Ain Jalut Hetoum achieved some outstanding successes, especially the capture of Behesni in 1262 and the defeat of the Karamanid Turcomans in Seleucia in 1263. But a few years later Baybars appeared in northern Syria, his reputation resting on his past and future victories over the pagan Mongols and their non-Islamic allies. While Hetoum made his way to Tabriz to plead for Mongol aid, Baybars invaded Cilicia in 1266 and destroyed its army, led by the Constable Smbat. For twenty days the Mamluk forces ravaged the prosperous coastal plain, sacking the four chief towns, Mamistra, Adana, Ayas, and Tarsus. Irreparable damage was done, and the vulnerability of the Kingdom to attack from Syria was made clear, especially once Baybars had taken Antioch in 1268. Hetoum negotiated the release of his son Leo from Mamluk captivity, took him to the court of the Ilkhan Abaqa to secure Mongol ratification of his succession, and then retired to a monastery.

The reign of Leo III, which began so inauspiciously, scarcely improved. He suffered continual Turcoman raids, another Mamluk invasion in 1275, and baronial revolts. When a Mongol army finally appeared in 1281 and invaded Syria with Armenian support, Sultan Kalavun crushed it near Homs. Four years later Leo finally secured peace with Egypt at the price of an annual tribute of a million dirhams. In 1289 Leo died, and was succeeded by his son, Hetoum II. The new King pitifully bought off a Mamluk attack in 1291, but in the spring of 1292 the patriarchal see of Hromgla, on the upper Euphrates, was taken and sacked. In 1293 an invasion of Cilicia was prevented only by a doubling of the tribute owed and the cession of key fortresses. Thereafter the only circumstance which could work in the Kingdom's favour—internal dissension in the Mamluk Sultanate—gave it a few years of peace. Hetoum cast around for allies, including Byzantium. Appeals to the West multiplied—five letters were dispatched to Edward I between 1291 and 1307—but brought negligible help. In 1296 the King had to contend with the rebellion of his brother Smbat, who partially blinded him. In 1298 came a fresh Mamluk invasion. Hetoum recovered power in 1299 and led 5,000 men to assist the Ilkhan Ghazan in his campaign in Syria. Mongol success gave the Armenians a flicker of hope in 1300, but further expeditions in 1300–1 and 1303 failed. Worse still, in 1304 Ghazan adopted Islam as the official faith in all his lands, and relations between Cilicia and the Mongols deteriorated: Hetoum abdicated in 1305, and when he and the new King, his nephew Leo IV, visited the Mongol emir Bilarghu in 1307, they and their entourage were massacred. After this, the Kingdom's Mongol overlords became capricious and unreliable, and raids by Tatar warbands, over which the Ilkhans had little control, added to the insecurity of the Armenians. In the early fourteenth century Marino Sanudo Torsello placed the Tatars amongst the formidable list of enemies whom the Armenians had to contend with—the others being the Mamluks, the Turkish emirs of Anatolia, and Christian pirates.

In these circumstances survival itself was an achievement, and the persistence of the Kingdom for more than a century following the great invasion of 1266 has to be credited in part to the strengths and resilience of the Armenians, as well as to external factors. The Hetoumid tradition of abdication does not mean that the kings lacked forcefulness or ability as commanders and diplomats. They led substantial forces, played their political hand well, and used the periods of Mamluk weakness or diversion to consolidate, or to reconquer what had earlier been lost: the fortress of Tall Hamdun, for example, was regained twice in the late thirteenth century. The Mamluk invasions were destructive, but they were partially balanced by Lesser Armenia's growing commercial import-ance to the West after the losses of 1289–91 in Syria. The port of Ayas in particular attracted the Italians and Catalans. It was the only significant Christian harbour on the Levantine littoral, and became a major centre of East–West trade. Marco Polo, who visited Cilician Armenia after the invasion of 1266, was impressed by the prosperity which parts of the country still enjoyed. And despite the harm done to Cilician Armenia's cultural and religious life by such events as the sack of the cathedral city of Sis in 1266, and of Hromgla in 1292, its scholars continued in the fourteenth century to produce original and elegant works of theology and history. As in the case of Byzantium under the later Palaiologoi, the fact that people lived under conditions of acute instability and peril did not stifle their creativity.

As at Constantinople, however, internal dissension was aggravated and given form by the issue of religion. The Union achieved in 1198 had survived the thirteenth century only in the sense that relations were never formally severed: in discussion with a papal legate in 1261, for example, a prominent representative of the Armenian church had simply denied the pope's primacy. But the success of the Hetoumids' pro-Latin policy hinged on their ability to satisfy all the papacy's demands on rite and doctrine; only then could the Armenians hope for western help, which was one of the Kingdom's few remaining hopes once the Mongols had become Muslims. This enabled baronial factions to exploit popular anti-Latin feelings to their own advantage, and undermine the power of the Crown. Kings Oshin (1307–20), Leo V (1320–41), and Guy of Lusignan (1342–4: called Constantine IV by the Armenians), all encountered resistance when they tried to bring the Armenian church closer to Rome. All three were murdered. Nor did their Latinophile policy bring aid on the scale they hoped for. The Avignonese papacy issued crusade indul-gences, sent some money, and organized a grain shipment during a famine in 1336. But as we have seen, its crusading plans were tied in the early fourteenth century to the aspirations of the French court, which was obsessed with the Holy Land, and took an interest in Armenia only as a strategic base for Palestine's reconquest. When practical crusading revived in the 1340s, it was directed against the *Beylik* of Aydin, not that of Karaman, which was one of Lesser Armenia's greatest problems. For most westerners, even those dedicated to the crusade, the Kingdom was of peripheral significance compared with Cyprus, Latin *Romania*, or Byzantium. For all their dynastic connections with the ruling houses of Cyprus, Naples, and Barcelona, the Hetoumids and their people were regarded as outsiders, and their religious practices of dubious orthodoxy. Even the Kingdom's commercial ties with its co-religionists declined after 1322, when Ayas was sacked by the Mamluks. After 1337 the port was permanently in Egyptian hands.

The failure of the alliance with the Mongols, and the disappointing trickle of support which came from the West, left the Kingdom dependent on its own resources, and these waned with the repeated assaults on royal authority which marked the first half of the century. After the death of Guy of Lusignan in 1344 the throne was usurped by Constantine V, the son of a former Marshal of the Kingdom, Baldwin. Constantine abandoned the *rapprochement* with Avignon as fruitless and attempted to placate the Mamluks. But he was not anti-Latin: it is possible that his cession of Corycus to Peter I of Cyprus encouraged the Cypriots and Hospitallers to capture Adalia in 1361. This was the last Christian success in the region for some decades. There is numismatic evidence that Peter I accepted an offer of the crown of Armenia made to him after the death of Constantine V in 1363, though he did not visit the country. In practice Constantine was succeeded by another usurper, Constantine VI, who was assassinated in 1373. Leo VI, an illegitimate scion of the Lusignan line, was crowned King in September 1374, but in the following year a Mamluk army took Sis, sacked the city, and captured the King. After seven years of captivity Leo was released, and travelled to the English and French courts in an attempt to raise an expedition to recover his Kingdom. Ironically he arrived at a time when the atmosphere in these courts was more sympathetic towards crusading than it had been for decades, and Leo's visit was one stimulus towards the organization of the Nicopolis crusade. The King died in 1393, and his title passed to the Lusignan kings of Cyprus.

Cyprus's status as a kingdom, like that of Cilician Armenia, was a gift of Henry VI, who in 1197 had Aimery of Lusignan crowned at Nicosia by Bishop Conrad of Hildesheim. Aimery's petition for the crown, and the imperial suzerainty which went with it, was part of his policy of stabilizing an island which had acquired a reputation for turbulence. Since Richard I of England won it from the Greek usurper Isaac Doukas Komnenos in 1191, Cyprus had already passed through three sets of hands. A revolt against Richard led him to sell it to the Templars, who in turn faced a rebellion which caused them to consign it in 1192 to the dispossessed King of Jerusalem, Guy of Lusignan. Guy and his brother Aimery, who succeeded him in 1194, proved to be effective rulers. Guy started the colonization of the island by advertising generous terms of enfeoffment for both knights and sergeants. Mainland nobles, their estates lost to Saladin and regained only in part by the Third Crusade, regarded the island as an attractive alternative, and Guy reputedly granted about 500 fiefs in all, 300 of them to knights. Most of the land needed for this appears to have been in an abandoned state, or public domain, so Guy did not have to seize the estates of the Greek *archontes* and was able to pacify them. Frankish burgesses were also attracted to reside in the main towns. Guy's generosity depleted public lands and rents to such an extent that Aimery had to pursue a policy of recovery, which brought him a solid annual revenue by the time of his death in 1205. By then a Latin church had also been established on Cyprus, with an archbishopric at Nicosia, and three suffragan dioceses at Paphos, Limassol, and Famagusta.

Thirteenth-century Cyprus was protected by the sea from the advance of both the Mongols and the Mamluks. Its rulers were thus in a position to fulfil Innocent III's hope that a Latin Cyprus would assist the crusading movement in the East, besides acting as a transit point, and as a source of food supplies. For dynastic reasons also, its history became closely tied to that of the mainland Kingdom. Aimery married Queen Isabella of Jerusalem in 1197, and was therefore King of both countries for eight years. His son Hugh I led a Cypriot force in the early phase of the Fifth Crusade, dying at Tripoli in 1218, where he had gone to witness the marriage of his sister Melisende to Count Bohemund IV. Hugh left an infant son, Henry I, for whom his mother Alice and two of the most important barons of Cyprus, Philip and John of Ibelin, acted as guardians. When Frederick II appeared in Cyprus in 1228, he interfered vigorously in the affairs of both Kingdoms, in Cyprus by right of his imperial suzerainty, and in Jerusalem as regent for his young son Conrad, heir to the throne there. The Ibelins resisted the Emperor, and both Cyprus and Jerusalem experienced bitter warfare, although the fighting on Cyprus ended in 1233, when the imperialist forces submitted. In 1247 Innocent IV annulled the imperial suzerainty over the Lusignans, who thus regained their independence while retaining their royal status. Henry I continued his father's policy of assisting crusading expeditions and becoming involved in Syria's affairs. He sent 300 men to fight at the battle of Harbiyah in 1244, and himself led a Cypriot contingent to Egypt during Louis IX's first crusade.

Cyprus's dynastic entanglement with Jerusalem became more complicated in 1257, when Bohemund VI of Antioch persuaded the latter's authorities to accept the claims of Henry I's young son, Hugh II, to be King. From 1264 the regency for both Kingdoms was held by Hugh II's cousin, Hugh of Antioch-Lusignan, and after the premature death of Hugh II in 1267, and the death of Conradin of Staufen in the following year, the former regent became King of both Cyprus and Jerusalem. Hugh III did all he could to stem Baybars's advance, so much so that in 1271 the Cypriot knights objected to the principle that they were bound to perform military service on the Syrian mainland for their fiefs. The King found it impossible to meet the triple task of defending Latin Syria, governing Cyprus, and countering the rival claim of Charles of Anjou to the kingship of Jerusalem; his son Henry II faced less internal resistance, thanks to the collapse of Angevin power after 1282, but militarily he could do little in Latin Syria. He arrived at Acre during the final siege on 4 May 1291, and left when it was clear that the Mamluk assault had succeeded, on 18 May. Cyprus then played out the final role in its relationship with the mainland Frankish states, as a place of refuge for the exiles who escaped the Muslim conquest.

While this series of kings, from Aimery to Henry II, was attempting to bolster the Frankish establishment in Syria and to enforce their own right to govern there, the economy, government, and church of Cyprus were achieving settled and recognizable form. The agrarian economy and regime have been well described by Jean Richard. He has emphasized the island's varied topography, ranging from the fertile and well-watered northern plain to the dry plain of the Mesaoria and the cultivable highlands of the western region. Cereals were grown almost everywhere during the winter, with yields of 7.5 to 1 on barley in good years, and the possibility of extracting an annual cotton crop as well, if the harvest was early enough. Statistics, admittedly dating from the much later Venetian occupation, reveal good crops of beans, onions, olives, carobs, grapes, and other vegetables and fruits. Cyprus also produced much cotton and sugar, and animal husbandry flourished. Hunting Cyprus's extensive game (including wild sheep) became the favourite pastime of the Frankish aristocracy. Irrigation was, for most of the island, a constant burden which provoked disputes over land rights; but the productivity of the land throughout the centuries of western occupation was striking. Significantly, the king's financial year began on the day he leased out his villages (*casals*). The high level of production which was attained enabled the king and nobility to sell for export a large proportion of the produce from their estates: in Professor Richard's words, 'the lords' granaries and cellars were the source of their wealth, and the merchants beat a path to their door'. Important commercial privileges were granted to the Genoese in 1218, and to the Pisans and Catalans in 1291. The Venetians appear to have had no privilege before 1306, although they may have continued to use the trading rights granted to them in the period of Byzantine rule.

Cyprus's agricultural production thus became geared to the needs of the Italian cities, and to some extent of the constricted towns of Latin Syria. In particular, much of the sugar and cotton produced was geared towards export rather than home consumption. This did not, however, entail either monoculture or the deprivation of the Cypriot population. The widespread growing of cereals kept prices relatively low, and the legal status and economic condition of the peasantry appear to have improved steadily under Frankish rule. A seigneurial regime was established, the lord's court being in many cases a complex of buildings including stables, granaries, wine-cellars, and flour or sugar mills. The peasants attached to the *casals* fell into two groups. The *paroikoi* were tied to the land and subject to a number of obligations, chiefly levies in money (*chevage* and *dimois*), a proportion of their crops (*partizon*), and labour services (*anguaires*). *Francomates* or *eleutheres* had achieved emancipation, but still owed their lords a portion of their produce, and money dues. The proportion of *francomates* to *paroikoi* increased, so that while in 1355 the majority of the peasants were still tied to the land, by the end of the fifteenth century there were more *francomates* than *paroikoi*. Since freedom was won in most cases by purchase, the drift is a testimony to the ability of the peasantry to accumulate financial reserves despite the heaviness of their obligations, which derived not only from their seigneurs but also from communal services in their villages. The movement from direct exploitation towards leasing lands is further evidence of the difficulty which lords faced in maintaining the number of *paroikoi* attached to their *casals*.

The legal and governmental institutions of the Kingdom of Cyprus were modelled on those of Jerusalem: indeed, at their coronation the kings swore to observe 'the assizes of the Kingdom [i.e. of Cyprus] and of

King Amalric and King Baldwin his son and the ancient customs and assizes of the Kingdom of Jerusalem'. This was natural in so far as the chief legists of thirteenth-century Palestine, whose treatises comprised the Assizes of the Kingdom of Jerusalem, were as heavily involved in the affairs of Cyprus as in those of the mainland, while the kings of Cyprus after Hugh II were also kings of Jerusalem: the two crowns were formally incorporated by Hugh III in 1267. Even after 1291 the Lusignan kings continued to bear the title, and to receive a separate coronation as King of Jerusalem. The latter, which took place at Famagusta, traditionally followed their coronation as King of Cyprus at Nicosia. And it was at Famagusta, which was accorded the legal status of a city in the Kingdom of Jerusalem, that each king honoured a number of men with the titles of high-ranking officials in the defunct Kingdom. Like Jerusalem, Cyprus had a High Court, which convened at Nicosia and exercised jurisdiction in all cases involving fief-holding. It also had a group of royal officials modelled on those of Jerusalem—notably the seneschal, constable, marshal, and chamberlain—and maintained a separate law for town-dwellers and non-noble Franks.

The monarchy's position in respect to Cyprus's fief-holders was a complex one. The latter inherited the 'assise sur la ligece', the law which had been held to legitimize resistance to excessive demands by the Crown. But the Cypriot monarchy managed to make certain inroads into the comparatively weak legal position formerly endured by the Crown in Jerusalem; it had no great territorial fiefs to contend with; and it possessed, in the royal domain and regalian rights, a financial basis which gave it great advantages in its dealings with the feudal nobility. Throughout the thirteenth and fourteenth centuries the domain was extensive, while rights over market taxes, salt pans, fisheries, and above all the minting of coins, were retained and exploited. Greek financial institutions were adapted, though the monarchy's chief fiscal organ, the *Segrète*, was probably modelled on that of Jerusalem. Financially buoyant, the monarchy was able to allow public dues to slip into the hands of its vassals and the Church, and did not suffer real financial difficulties until the last three decades of the fourteenth century. It was in a position to hire mercenaries, and built a fleet of royal galleys at Famagusta.

As Jean Richard has noted, the public law established by the Franks in Cyprus through the *assises*, whether for fief-holders or *burgenses*, existed side-by-side with the private laws of the non-Frankish Christians, chiefly Greeks but also Armenians and Syrians (Famagusta was for the most part inhabited by the latter). These communities had their own legal practices which received little interference from the Franks, in the same way that the structure of village life was permitted to exist alongside the new seigneurial regime. Unlike the Morea, Cyprus affords no examples of Greek nobles entering the feudal hierarchy in the thirteenth century, though relations between the two groups were not hostile: Cyprus did not experience the revolts which punctuated the period in Crete. In the later fourteenth century some Greeks achieved knighthood, although the numbers who entered the Cypriot nobility have in the past been exaggerated. Intermarriage between Greeks and Latins was common by 1400, while at least some nobles spoke Greek. In the political upheavals of the fifteenth century what has been described as 'a process of cultural and social osmosis' took place. By 1455 James of Fleury could complain that 'the government of this Kingdom has fallen entirely into the hands of Greeks and people of no consequence'. By this point, as in Latin Greece, the continued application of laws dating back to the thirteenth century (and believed, in Cyprus, to have their origins in the twelfth) was largely a formality, which disguised a transformation in social structure as well as a change in the racial make-up of the upper class. By the early sixteenth century the Greek chronicler Georges Boustronios could employ the term 'Cypriots' to denote both Greeks and Latins.

The idea that the Latin establishment in Cyprus, in its early phase, enjoyed relations with the Greeks which were somewhere between the partial integration achieved in Achaea and the bitter resistance met in Crete, is supported by ecclesiastical developments in the thirteenth century. Initially many of the estates of the Greek church were despoiled to establish a Latin church on the island, and in the early period of the occupation an attempt was made to subordinate the Orthodox hierarchy to the Latin one, and even to replace it entirely. Slowly, and with much ill will on both sides, a situation of compromise and *laissez-faire* developed. One notable landmark was Pope Alexander IV's *Bulla Cypria* of 1260, in which the constitution of the Orthodox church was regulated. Nothing better than a *modus vivendi* could be hoped for, and there were disturbances in the fourteenth century, notably in 1314, when a mob tried to burn down the palace of the Latin Archbishop of Nicosia. But it has been pointed out that the most serious incident, the execution of thirteen Greeks in 1231 for heretical assertions, involved outsiders on both sides: it is also notable that on this occasion, due to the war which was raging between the Ibelins and the adherents of Frederick II, the secular power could not intervene to dampen down the mutual hostility. In 1314, by contrast, no punishments were imposed, even on the ringleaders. The government consistently attempted to achieve the peaceful coexistence of the two churches, especially in the decades following 1261, when it feared that Michael VIII, having regained Constantinople, might try to stir up a rebellion on the island by fomenting religious unrest.

The disasters of 1291 formed a major event in the history of Lusignan Cyprus. The King lost the remaining parts of his prestigious, if troublesome, mainland realm; Cyprus had to absorb thousands of refugees, many of them destitute; and the perceived threat from the triumphant Mamluks compelled the government to invest rather more resources than hitherto in fortifying the island against attack—the town wall and citadel of Famagusta both date from Henry II's reign. But there were gains too. The King could now concentrate on governing Cyprus. And as we shall see, Cyprus enjoyed a commercial windfall as a result of Latin Syria's final collapse, besides the expertise and capital brought by those who made a more timely withdrawal from Syria's coastal towns. This did not mean that Cyprus's long-standing connections with the mainland or with crusades to the Holy Land had ended. Apart from the fictional perpetuation of the Kingdom of Jerusalem which has already been noted, there was a sentimental nostalgia expressed in the tradition, observed in 1335 and 1394, that Cypriot noblewomen wore black cloaks in mourning for Syria, whenever they went out of doors. And Cyprus's kings were naturally interested in recovery projects, both because of their own dynastic claims, and because of the inevitable implications of a large-scale *passagium* for Cyprus. Thus Henry II was heavily involved in the coastal raids around the turn of the century, and submitted an interesting crusade memorandum to Pope Clement V in 1311–12; while Peter I organized and led one of the great *passagia* of the fourteenth century. It is important, however, not to exaggerate or misconstrue the connection between Cyprus and the Holy Land crusade. It is true that two crusade theorists, Peter Dubois and Emmanuel Piloti, proposed in a rather highhanded way that the Lusignans be replaced by rulers who would make a more effective contribution towards a crusade to recover the Holy Land. But it cannot be said that the *raison d'être* of Latin Cyprus, or of its monarchy, was participation in crusading endeavours (as was the case, for example, with the Military Orders). Cyprus was an independent state whose rulers, for a variety of reasons, occasionally chose to become involved in such matters.

It was therefore mainly coincidental that at the very time when Peter Dubois suggested the ousting of the Lusignans, and the Templars were facing an onslaught which arose partly from their inactivity in the East, Henry II was overthrown by a rebellion led by his brother Amalric. In April 1306 Amalric, with powerful backing amidst the court aristocracy, informed the King that his misgovernment had compelled the Kingdom's most important feudatories to take power out of Henry's hands and entrust it to himself, as governor and regent. The King resisted, and after intervention by the heads of the Military Orders an agreement was reached which assigned an annual pension to Henry, the Queen mother, and other relatives. This was confirmed in 1307, but Amalric was unable to compel his brother to sign documents which would have made the regent's position more secure. In 1310, concerned at the build-up of loyalist support amongst ordinary knights, Amalric sent Henry across to Ayas, to be guarded by his brother-in-law King Oshin. Raymond of Pins, Clement V's nuncio, managed to persuade Henry to appoint Amalric governor for life, but on 5 June 1310 Amalric was murdered by a disgruntled favourite. The loyalist cause now gathered momentum, although a third brother, Aimery, tried to secure Amalric's position for himself. Agreement was reached that Henry could return from Armenia provided that Amalric's widow and her children were allowed to seek exile there, and in August 1310 Henry landed at Famagusta. Traitors such as Aimery, and Balian and Philip of Ibelin, were imprisoned; and thanks largely to Amalric's fortuitous and still unexplained murder, Cyprus emerged relatively unscathed from a major dynastic crisis.

Henry II died in 1324, by which point the commercial prosperity of his Kingdom was striking. To a certain extent it was based on the inherent productivity of the island, which, apart from foodstuffs, also exported fine textiles and embroideries, precious pottery, and worked items of gold and silver. But the papal attempt to ban all trade with Mamluk Egypt and Syria also helped. As we saw in Chapter 1,[1] the ban itself was less than effective; but because it occurred at the same time that a shift in the Asian trade routes was in any case bringing goods northwards to northern Syrian and Cilician ports, it worked to Cyprus's advantage. Italian and Catalan merchants brought western products to Famagusta and bought spices there, while local merchants, Muslim or non-Latin Christians, traded between Famagusta and the ports of Syria. The overall effect was to make Famagusta, like Ayas, a key entrepôt in East–West trade. The

[1] Above, 37–8.

practice was described succinctly by the fifteenth-century author, Leontios Makhairas:

And there was great wealth there: all rich lords such as were Sir Francis Lakha the Nestorian and his brother Sir Nicholas Lakha the Nestorian . . . For the merchant ships of the Christians which came from the West did not venture to do their business anywhere else but in Cyprus; and all the trade of Syria was done in Cyprus. For thus were the commands and prohibitions of the most holy pope on pain of excommunication . . . And because Syria is near Famagusta, men used to send their ships and convey their wares to Famagusta, and they had agents there for the sale of their goods, Francis Lakha the Nestorian and his brother. And when the ships of Venice, of Genoa, of Florence, of Pisa, of Catalonia and of all the West arrived, they found the spices there and loaded their ships with whatever they needed and went on their way to the West.[2]

Ludolf of Sudheim, a priest who visited Cyprus in about 1340, concurred with Leontios Makhairas about the riches which flowed into the hands of the nobility and merchant class from this trade: 'In Cyprus the princes, nobles, barons and knights are the richest in the world.' And an English traveller of 1344 noted the presence at Famagusta of not only merchants from Italy and Catalonia, but also Muslims from the Mamluk Sultanate, 'dwelling in palaces which are there called loggias, living in the style of counts and barons; they have abundance of gold and silver'. Such impressions helped to create the western image of Lusignan Cyprus as an exotic, semi-oriental kingdom.

Dr Peter Edbury has argued convincingly that Henry II and his successors were not only aware of the causes of this prosperity, but skilfully promoted them. They may have established Famagusta itself as a staple by discouraging the development of other Cypriot ports, especially Limassol, and it is possible that the coolness of their relations with Cilician Armenia, despite their dynastic ties with its kings, was rooted in the rivalry of Ayas. They certainly supported with vigour the papal ban on Christian trade with Syrian and Egyptian ports, using their newly developed naval strength to arrest those guilty of breaking the ban. Both in his memorandum of 1311–12, and in advice presented to the Pope in 1323, Henry II referred to the need to enforce the blockade before a crusade could be successful. His own commitment to the recovery of his former kingdom, and the military benefits to his existing one of a weakened Mamluk Sultanate, are not in doubt; but he must also have

[2] Leontios Makhairas, *Recital concerning the Sweet Land of Cyprus entitled 'Chronicle'*, ed. and tr. R. M. Dawkins (Oxford, 1932), para. 91.

appreciated the economic advantage accruing to Famagusta. The situation had already begun to swing against Cyprus by the late 1330s, when the trade routes were again beginning to favour Alexandria, and the papal ban was being breached by the licensing system. But by then Famagusta's reputation, facilities, and dynamic merchant class, together with Cyprus's own exporting potential, were sufficient to give the port several more decades of relative prosperity; the Mamluk occupation of Famagusta's erstwhile rival, Ayas, in 1337, also helped.

The principal cost of Famagusta's golden age, which thus lasted for about half a century after 1291, was the resentment of the Genoese, who held the oldest trading privileges with Cyprus and were most injured by Henry II's attempted enforcement of the papal ban. It is apparent that Cypriot–Genoese relations were already strained by 1306, when one of the charges brought against Henry by Amalric was that of not combating Genoese aggression; Amalric went on to grant extensive privileges to Genoa's greatest rival, Venice. Relations grew worse as the century progressed, and more incidents and disagreements occurred on the interpretation of Genoa's privileges. The Genoese, for example, wanted the privileges extended to cover the descendants of inhabitants of former Genoese quarters in Frankish Syria, which would have robbed Cyprus of jurisdiction over many Syrian merchants. In 1299 Genoa proclaimed a boycott on trade with Cyprus, and in 1316, responding to a Genoese pirate's raid on the coastal district of Paphos, Henry II arrested all the Genoese in Nicosia and kept them in prison for some years. The two powers needed each other, as the number of Genoese arrested by the King (some 460) attests; but by the mid-fourteenth century Genoa's relations with the Lusignan kings were becoming ominously similar to those of Venice with Byzantium in the period preceding the Fourth Crusade.

Attempts to regulate Cyprus's relations with the Italian trading powers formed one of the main themes running through the reign of Hugh IV (1324–59), Henry II's nephew. The 1306 treaty with Venice was renewed with a few changes in 1328, and treaties with Genoa were concluded in 1329 and 1338, though there were fresh disagreements in 1344. In much the same way that Henry II had supported the recovery projects put forward in the West during his reign, Hugh IV showed some enthusiasm for the new orientation of crusading towards *Romania* from the early 1330s onwards. The exact scope and motivation of the Cypriot contribution are, however, hard to assess due to the weakness of the chronicle sources for Hugh's reign. He would not support his kinsman, Guy of Lusignan, when the latter was King of Lesser Armenia, but he was prepared to deploy his galleys against the Turks, perhaps because he viewed the latter as a potential threat to Cyprus's trading prosperity. The King received a congratulatory letter from Benedict XII in 1338, referring to a Cypriot success at sea. And it was Hugh's initiative, acting through Bishop Lambertino of Limassol, which began the negotiations leading to Clement VI's naval league in 1343. Cypriot galleys fought in the league, and there was a Cypriot contribution to the league formed in 1350. Seven years later Hugh again agreed to furnish galleys. Hugh's readiness to initiate military action, or to support that of others, was expensive, leaving his successor with limited reserves to pursue his own crusading goals. In general Hugh's anti-Turkish policy has not been given the credit it deserves by historians, who have been captivated by a contemporary description of Hugh as a man of peace, and have attempted to draw a contrast between his reign and that of his son Peter I. This is not to deny, however, the general peacefulness of his long and relatively uneventful reign, or the benefits which Cyprus drew from it: it is probable that most of the architectural patronage of the Lusignans occurred under Hugh, who was noted also for his learning, and delight in good craftsmanship.

The central events of the reign of Peter I, his capture of Adalia in 1361, journey to the West to promote a crusade in 1362, and capture of Alexandria in 1365, have received attention in Chapter 1.[3] This of course is indicative of the fact that, with Peter I, Cyprus moved briefly from the wings to centre stage in the crusading movement. The King had personal goals and interests which make him unique in his line, his foundation of the Order of the Sword before acceding to the throne being the most remarkable. But it is increasingly apparent that much of what Peter did made sense within the context of the difficulties faced by Henry II and Hugh IV, and the policies which they pursued. This applied most clearly to his relations with the Genoese. Although Peter renewed Genoa's privileges in 1363, a typical clash of jurisdictions at Famagusta in the same year led to Genoa instructing all its nationals to leave Cyprus. The conflict imperilled the planned crusade, which was in its last stage of preparation, and it was only in April 1365 that a new treaty, granting the Genoese unprecedented rights, was accepted by both sides. But any jubilation experienced at Genoa about its improved position at Famagusta must have dissolved when news arrived of the sack of Alexandria, which was

[3] Above, 39–41.

almost as great a blow to Genoese trade as to that of Venice. Genoese exasperation with the Lusignans therefore grew in proportion to the importance of Famagusta for their trade in the East.

As we saw in Chapter 1,[4] the decision to attack Alexandria has also been reinterpreted recently in terms of long-term Cypriot concern about the declining role of Famagusta as a result of the failure of the papal ban on trade with Egypt, and the tremendous advantages enjoyed by Alexandria. According to Dr Edbury's plausible new approach to Peter's policy, the initial assault was made with the goal of either holding on to the port and controlling its revenues, or destroying it and redirecting trade towards Famagusta. Both having failed, Peter attempted, in his peace negotiations with the Sultan, to secure privileges for Cypriot merchants which would place them in a more advantageous position than hitherto: perhaps even make it cheaper for western merchants to buy goods after they had been shipped from Alexandria to Famagusta, thereby restoring the latter's position as an entrepôt. A similar approach, it has been argued, lay behind the seizure of Adalia in 1361. The port's capture not only constituted a damaging blow to Turkish power on the southern coast of Asia Minor, but established a replacement for Ayas, a Christian-held port—held, moreover, in conjunction with Famagusta rather than as a rival to it. And Peter's activities after 1365, including his planned attack on Beirut, and his raid on Tripoli and the ports of northern Syria in 1367, also fit this pattern of a war of commercial competition and aggrandizement.

Faced by the decline of Famagusta, which was bound to affect royal revenues, Peter thus perceived the solution to be large-scale, aggressive warfare against both Turks and Mamluks. Such warfare not only bore heavily on Cyprus itself, but it needed the support of western resources, and these had to be garnered by expensive fund-raising tours of Christendom. As a consequence the King's reign was one of fiscal adventurism: parts of the royal domain were alienated, and people were allowed to purchase exemption from the poll tax in exchange for a lump sum. There was opposition to such measures in the royal council, but, more importantly, the nobility objected both to the extent of military service which was being demanded of them, and to the King's practice of hiring mercenaries, who enjoyed preferential terms. Returning from a second, fruitless, tour of the West in September 1368, Peter stimulated this resentment by a series of arbitrary and irrational actions. These culminated

[4] Above, 41–2.

in a clear breach of the *assises* in January 1369. The leading vassals, genuinely concerned about the King's behaviour and the defence of their legal position, tried to persuade Peter's two brothers, John and James, to represent them. Matters came to a head on 16 January 1369 when, in circumstances scarcely clearer than those of Amalric's murder in 1310, a group of barons burst into Peter's bedroom and killed him. The conspirators did not allow the initiative to slip out of their hands, but assembled a meeting of the High Court on the same day and established a committee of 16 barons to draw up a definitive text of the *assises* based on the lawbook of John of Ibelin (1265–6), whose interpretation of the King's obligation to abide by feudal convention had underpinned their resistance against Peter's misrule.

Peter I's son, Peter II, was 12 in 1369, and a regency was therefore held by his uncle John for three years. Although the Kingdom finally emerged from its war against Egypt in 1370, these were years of political strain, as the Queen mother Eleanor held John responsible for her husband's death and plotted his assassination. After a dispute between the Genoese and the Venetians at Peter II's coronation as King of Jerusalem in October 1372, a riot broke out in which the Genoese suffered heavy losses. Queen Eleanor irresponsibly appealed to Genoa to intervene in force to avenge Peter I's death, and the Genoese government judged the situation ripe to allow their long-standing grievances to come to a head. The Venetians, who might have gone to Cyprus's aid, were preoccupied with other concerns. In March 1373 a squadron of seven galleys was dispatched from Genoa, and this was reinforced in October by a fleet of thirty-six ships. By a clever ruse, Famagusta was occupied and the King captured. In December the Genoese, still benefiting from Eleanor's obsession with avenging Peter's death, occupied Nicosia. Kyrenia, the island's strongest fortress, was brilliantly defended by the dead King's second brother, James, and the Genoese were able to oust him only by compelling Peter II to send an order for James to proceed to the papal court to lodge a complaint. *En route* for the West James was overtaken and imprisoned by the Genoese. In October 1374 a peace treaty was sealed at Nicosia. Its terms were amongst the heaviest imposed in any medieval treaty, indicating both the extent of Genoa's success, and its determination to retain its new position of supremacy. Apart from an annual tribute of 40,000 florins, and a single payment of 90,000 florins for the expenses of the Genoese fleet, Peter II was obliged to pay an indemnity of 2,000,000 florins over a twelve-year period. During that time Famagusta was to remain wholly in Genoese hands.

The defeat and humiliation of Lusignan Cyprus in 1373–4 has to be attributed in large measure to its acute internal dissensions, and in particular to the feckless double-dealing of the Queen mother. Eleanor was prepared to accept Genoese supremacy in order to avenge her husband's death: this despite the fact that her own infidelity to Peter had helped cause his erratic behaviour in 1368–9. In a bizarre scene reminiscent of a Jacobean tragedy, she finally scored her revenge on Prince John in 1375 when, at a banquet held in the very room in which Peter was murdered, she suddenly uncovered a dish to reveal Peter's bloodstained shirt; this was the signal for hidden retainers to emerge and murder John. The destruction and economic dislocation caused by the fighting of 1373–4, occurring at a point when the island's commercial prosperity had in any case passed its peak, inaugurated the long-term decline of Cyprus. Quite apart from the necessity of regaining Famagusta from the Genoese, 1375 brought the Mamluk occupation of Cilician Armenia, and it was likely that the Mamluks would soon turn their attention to Cyprus to exact revenge for 1365. There was a heavy price to pay for the superficial brilliance of Peter I's reign.

To oust the Genoese Cyprus naturally turned to Venice, and in 1377 an anti-Genoese alliance was formed between Cyprus, Venice, and Visconti Milan. The only result was an abortive attack on Famagusta in 1378. After the death of Peter II in 1382 the throne passed to his imprisoned uncle, James, but he was not allowed to return to Cyprus until a revised, and yet harsher, treaty had been worked out, in 1383. A new indemnity of 852,000 florins was to be paid over a period of eleven years, and Famagusta was transferred to Genoa entirely: rather than, as formerly, being held in pledge. Faced with the need to impose heavy taxation to meet these terms, and by an outbreak of plague in 1392–3, James I could make no major attempt to regain Famagusta. His son Janus, who succeeded him in 1398, had, as his name suggests, been born during his father's imprisonment at Genoa, and had been brought up there as a hostage. He was determined to expel the Genoese, and laid siege to Famagusta with 6,000 men and thirteen hired Catalan galleys in the spring of 1402. Venice would have liked to help, but did not dare to oppose Genoa's governor, Marshal Boucicaut, who represented Charles VI of France. Boucicaut came East with a fleet in April 1403 and compelled Janus to raise the siege, and to agree to a new treaty of peace and commerce in July. Another indemnity, this time of 150,000 ducats, was imposed. Relations between the King and the Marshal were superficially good: Janus even provided two galleys for Boucicaut's raids on Beirut and Tripoli. But in 1404 the King again besieged Famagusta, this time with cannon purchased from the Venetians (who also, characteristically, sold artillery to the city's defenders). Unsuccessful again, Janus made peace with Genoa in 1410.

In view of Cyprus's military weakness and the need to regain Famagusta, peaceful relations with the Mamluks were imperative. They were endangered by piracy on both sides, but the Sultanate's attitude was not generally hostile, and negotiations brought about a settlement of outstanding issues in 1414. Janus, however, maintained a foolishly cavalier stance, and responded to a Mamluk raid on Limassol in 1424 by attacking the Syrian coast in strength in the following spring. Sultan Barsbay answered with an attack on the south coast in the summer of 1425, in which Larnaka was sacked and Limassol burnt. There was little that Janus could do to defend the island, and Barsbay, recognizing an easy target, sent a force of about 500 Mamluk cavalry and several thousand infantry in 1426. The resulting campaign was even more disastrous than that of 1373-4. The Muslims retook Limassol on 3 July, and four days later King Janus led his troops into battle against the invaders at Khirokitia. The Cypriots performed poorly and were cut to pieces. The King was captured. The Mamluks entered Nicosia on 11 July and pillaged it mercilessly before sailing to Egypt with an estimated 6,000 captives. In the circumstances of total disorder which followed something akin to a *jacquerie* occurred; an Italian mercenary captain was able to set himself up as ruler of the whole district around Paphos. Public order was painfully restored and after humiliating treatment by the Mamluks in Cairo, Janus was ransomed for 200,000 ducats. The King returned to Cyprus in May 1427. Leontios Makhairas commented that Janus never laughed again; he had good reason not to, for Cyprus now lay under Mamluk suzerainty, with an annual tribute payment of 5,000 ducats. These additional costs naturally came on top of the existing debts to Genoa, which were renegotiated in 1428. Desperate measures were needed to meet these expenses, and when Janus died in 1432 he was said to have left plate and jewels worth only about 50,000 ducats.

Janus's active if disastrous reign was followed by comparative lethargy under his son John II (1432–58). There were periodic rumours of another Mamluk attack, with the goal of conquering the whole island, and Cyprus lost Corycus to the Turks of Karaman in 1448. Aware of the fact that Cyprus, like Rhodes, was now in constant danger, the papal Curia had by mid-century adopted the practice of regularly issuing indulgences for its relief. Nicholas V made a grant in 1451 which resulted in probably the earliest example of a printed indulgence (Mainz, 1454) while indulgences sold in France in 1452 were intended to subsidize John's refortification of Nicosia. The King's personal ineffectiveness was compounded by his marriage in 1442 to Helena, the daughter of Theodore II Palaiologos of Mistra. The match was symptomatic of the integration of the Latin and Greek populations which, as noted above, characterized fifteenth-century Cyprus; but Helena was domineering, and in the 1450s Cypriot dynastic politics became as violent and colourful as in the period of Eleanor of Aragon. The political situation worsened after the deaths of John II and Helena in 1458. John's illegitimate son, James, decided to challenge the lawful succession of John's daughter Charlotte. Making his way to Cairo, James bribed the leading emirs to lobby the Sultan for his appointment as ruler instead of Charlotte, on the grounds that a woman should not hold the island's lordship. In September 1460 a formidable fleet of eighty ships sailed to Cyprus with an invading army on James's behalf.

James's attempt to usurp power with open Muslim aid was scandalous, and Pope Pius II treated the defence of Cyprus against this invasion as a crusade, granting Church taxes to Charlotte's husband, Louis of Savoy, and issuing indulgences to all who contributed to the loyalist cause. The Master of the Hospitallers saw the invasion as the latest phase in a perilous onrush of Muslim power both north and south of Rhodes, recently manifested in the Mamluk siege of Rhodes in 1444 and the Ottoman conquest of Constantinople in 1453. The invasion was, however, totally successful, bringing into James's hands, by autumn 1464, not only all the territory held by Charlotte and Louis, but also Famagusta. The indomitable Charlotte, refusing to accept that her cause was lost, resided at Rhodes for another ten years in the hope of organizing a reconquest. She then moved to the West, where she lived, mainly at Rome, until her death in 1487. As late as 1478 she went to Egypt to pursue a tortuous scheme for regaining control of Cyprus.

James II had succeeded in defeating one of Cyprus's two enemies, the Genoese, by adopting the sponsorship of the other, the Mamluks. Unpalatable as this approach was to the Pope and other exponents of the crusade, it was realistic and, to some extent, viable: other Christian rulers, in Greece and the Balkans, tried the same with the Ottomans, with varying degrees of success. The recovery of Famagusta enabled James, during his short reign (1464–73), to initiate a partial revival of royal power. Former loyalists were easily reconciled, and supporters, especially from Sicily and Catalonia, were rewarded with the estates of men who had fallen during the civil war. It was natural for James to move closer to Venice, some of whose merchants and bankers had already expanded their interests on Cyprus during John II's reign. In 1468 the King married, by proxy, Catherine Cornaro, a member of one of the Republic's most distinguished patrician houses. James had by this point been recognized by the Venetian Pope Paul II, which enabled him to be crowned, so Catherine became Queen of Cyprus. But Venice went further towards consolidating its new position on Cyprus: by formally adopting Catherine as 'the daughter of St Mark', it set up a symbolic familial claim to her possessions and rights, so that if she and her husband were to die childless, the Republic would possess a dynastic claim to Cyprus itself. Four years after the proxy marriage Catherine sailed eastwards and was married in person to James. In July 1473 James died, aged only 33, and although Catherine had a son, James III, he too died a few days before his first birthday, in August 1474.

By then circumstances had compelled Venice to act with urgency to protect the situation which luck and good management had enabled it to create in Cyprus. A Catalan faction at the court resisted the growth of Venetian influence, placing its hopes in James II's illegitimate children, to whom the King had bequeathed Cyprus in the event of his heir's premature death. In November 1473 the Catalans carried out a *coup d'état*, murdering Catherine's uncle, Andrew Cornaro, and arresting Catherine. Venice sent galleys and, although the rebellion had already collapsed, the Republic decided in March 1474 to assume the government of Cyprus. A *provveditore* would command a garrison of 100 cross-bowmen, who would be placed at Famagusta and Kyrenia, and two nobles would act as permanent 'counsellors' to Queen Catherine. The nominal government exercised by Catherine continued for fifteen years, with a steady growth of Venetian interference. In response to reports of mismanagement of the Kingdom's finances, the Venetians took its revenues out of the hands of the *Segrète* in May 1479, giving them instead to two chamberlains (*camerarii*) appointed by the Republic. And in 1481 a committee of three was created to handle the affairs of Cyprus at Venice itself. In 1488, however, Venice decided that direct government was essential, both because it was the only way to ensure the efficient defence of the island against the Turks, and also because of fears that Catherine might secretly remarry and endanger the prospect of ultimate Venetian inheritance after her death. Despite Catherine's objections, the handover of sovereignty was formally effected at Famagusta on 26 February 1489, when the Queen handed the standard of St Mark to Venice's captain-general, who then had it raised. Catherine returned to her native city and was pensioned off with a small lordship at Asolo. Its revenues, together with a sum drawn from Cypriot income, equalled an annual grant of 8,000 ducats, a cheap price for the acquisition of the Kingdom.

Venice radically reshaped the government of Cyprus, to bring it into line with that of the Republic's other colonial possessions. The *assises* remained in force, and the Lusignan viscounties of Nicosia and Famagusta were maintained as courts of first instance in the two towns and their environs. But the High Court, which was too closely associated with the Lusignan regime and might have become a focus of opposition to Venetian rule, was abolished. All cases which would have gone to it, as well as appeals from the viscounts' courts, and cases involving the death sentence, went to three Rectors, who were based at Nicosia. They were appointed by Venice, to which appeals against their sentences had to be sent. One Rector was the Lieutenant, who headed the administration, and the other two were his counsellors, who advised and supervised him. Famagusta had a Captain, who acted as the commander of Venetian forces stationed on the island, although in wartime a *proveditor-general* was sent out to take over this job. As in Crete, the Republic tried to counter the impression of rigid centralization by establishing a 'Great Council' at Nicosia, made up of noble Cypriots and resident Venetians; but its powers of appointment and consultation were limited. Similarly, a degree of self-government was permitted at both Nicosia and Famagusta, where the amorphous urban assemblies which had existed under the Lusignans became fully fledged town councils.

The Venetian government of Cyprus soon became subject to heavy criticism by contemporaries on the grounds of inefficiency and corruption, but an attempt to check these by regular inspection by Syndics, instituted in 1497, made little headway. Financial mismanagement was acute and brought constant complaints to the metropolis. According to these, the former estates of the royal domain were sold off recklessly, clerical benefices auctioned in a scandalous way, and *paroikoi* enabled to buy their freedom. Venice certainly made a handsome profit from Cyprus. Figures from the late sixteenth century specify the total annual revenue as 546,000 ducats. No fewer than 300,000 ducats came from the salt monopoly, while tax revenue afforded only 90,000 ducats, and revenue from public *casali* brought in 156,000. The latter figure is surprisingly high, considering the turbulence of the last century of Lusignan rule, and the claim that the colonial officials were alienating estates; if accurate, it reflects the strength of the monarchy's position in the thirteenth and early fourteenth centuries. Venetian costs, in 1561, were only 184,331 ducats. In good years, therefore, Venice could expect a gain of over 360,000 ducats from Cyprus.

There were also indirect gains. Venice valued the prestige accruing from the fact that its colonial possessions included a kingdom, and sedulously maintained the island's royal status. More important was Cyprus's ability to produce much of the grain, cotton, sugar, oil, and saffron required by Venice. The Republic took unprecedented steps to regulate the island's economic life by instituting grain quotas, encouraging cotton plantations, catching runaway *paroikoi*, and demanding labour services from the *francomates*. This, in Professor Richard's words, 'converted an economy essentially Cypriot into an economy increasingly colonial'. As the series of grievances presented to Venice in 1490 by Cypriot envoys make clear, the grain quota was especially resented on the grounds that when drought, or the growing menace of the locusts, seriously affected the crop, the island was barely self-sufficient. There were violent grain riots in 1565. Both the free and the unfree peasant classes suffered, and the general standard of living on Cyprus fell in a way which it had not done since the Frankish conquest. The nobility meanwhile incurred a loss of income and self-esteem from their exclusion from most important public offices. And according to grievances submitted in 1490, the port of Famagusta was in decline, needing urgent measures of government support. Venetian rule brought some benefits to Cyprus, and is currently receiving more favourable judgements from scholars than was formerly the case. But the prevailing view remains that it was not one of the more prosperous or creative periods in Cypriot history. While there was relatively little popular unrest, it is striking how little support the Venetian *regimento* received against the Turks when they invaded.

The threat of Ottoman attack, one of the reasons for Venice's occupation of Cyprus in 1489, hung over the island throughout the period of Venetian government. The Ottoman conquest of Syria and Egypt in 1516–17, and the fall of Rhodes in 1522, made it seem certain that an invasion of Cyprus would follow: though on both occasions Venice considered it politic to congratulate the Sultan on his victories. When the Turks attacked Corfu in 1537 Venice sent a *proveditor-general* to Cyprus in expectation of an imminent attack. In 1539 the Turks raided and burnt Limassol. Then the peace of 1540 gave Venice a breathing-space, which the Republic tried to prolong by a policy of systematic bribery at the Sultan's court. The main defensive moves made by Venice lay in the sphere of fortifications, though its record in this respect was a mixed one. Work on updating the walls of Nicosia was begun in 1567, and it involved reducing the four-mile circuit by about a quarter. Buildings left outside the new ramparts, which had eleven bastions, were levelled, including the old royal palace and many churches. Famagusta received much attention between 1492 and 1528, by which date 178,000 ducats had been spent on materials and wages. More work was done in 1544 and 1558, and visitors were highly impressed by Famagusta's defences, although the garrison was repeatedly described as inadequate, demoralized, or poorly provisioned. The castles of St Hilarion, Buffavento, and Kantara were demolished so that the Turks could not make use of them, and Venice considerably strengthened the fortifications at Kyrenia. Limassol was left with its old walls.

For decades Venetian Cyprus was a beneficiary of the formidable range of different commitments and goals which competed for resources at the Ottoman court after the conquests of Selim I. But in 1570 the island's attractions and vulnerability finally gave the exponents of invasion the edge over those who preferred campaigning against Persia, a renewal of the advance in North Africa, or intervention on behalf of the embattled Moriscos in Spain. A fleet under Piali Pasha sailed from Istanbul in April, and more ships with artillery and munitions followed in May, while troops and more munitions made their way southwards to the Anatolian coast. After the embarkation of the army, the assembled fleet, probably about 350 sail in all, left for Cyprus at the end of June, landing at Salines on the south coast on 3 July. More troops were landed on 22 July and the commander, Mustafa Pasha, laid siege to Nicosia a few days later, choosing to take the weaker of the two large cities first. After a month's siege Mustafa had cause to worry that the débâcle at Malta five years earlier might be repeated, and he sent to Piali Pasha for reinforcements. The Turks were gambling on the expectation that no relief force would appear in the immediate future, and the gamble succeeded: on 9 September an assault on the walls, the fifteenth since the siege began, effected entry at several of the bastions, and by nightfall Nicosia had fallen.

The defence of Nicosia had been handled with extraordinary incompetence by the Lieutenant, Nicholas Dandolo, and Famagusta's superior fortifications and garrison, ably led by the Captain, Mark-Anthony Bragadin, and the field commander, Astorre Baglione, presented Mustafa with far greater problems. The defence of the city was one of the most heroic episodes of the period, rivalling that of Malta in 1565. Famagusta was invested in mid-September, but despite the huge numbers of troops involved—possibly as many as 250,000—it remained untaken in the following spring. However, the absence of a relief force from the West, and the constant arrival of Turkish replacements and siege materials from Syria and southern Anatolia, meant that by mid-July 1571 representatives of the civilian population were pleading with Bragadin for the voluntary surrender of the city. Great assaults launched each day from 29 to 31 July finally compelled the defenders, whose ammunition and food supplies were almost literally nil, to surrender on 1 August. Mustafa's fury at the tenacity of the Christian resistance is clear from the outburst which he directed at Bragadin: 'Tell me, you hound, why did you hold the fortress when you had not the wherewithal to do so? Why did you not surrender a month ago, and not make me lose 80,000 of the best men in my army?' The horrifying martyrdom subsequently suffered by Bragadin—he was flayed alive—similarly reflects Turkish anger in the face of one of the most costly of their military successes. But the capture of Famagusta brought with it the rest of Cyprus, and in the peace treaty sealed in March 1573 Venice renounced her claim to the island, consenting also to pay a heavy war-indemnity to the Sultan. Only the loss of Crete would have been of comparable severity: as the Grand Vizier was reported to comment on hearing the news of Lepanto, two months after Famagusta's surrender, if the Republic had shorn his beard, he had severed one of its arms.

With the Turkish conquest of Cyprus, all three of the Christian kingdoms established in the eastern Mediterranean by, or in association with, the crusades, had come to an end. The cluster of royal titles passed into the region of heraldry and genealogy, though thanks to international rivalry, and occasional plans of Christian reconquest, there were political ramifications too. The most consistent and convincing claim was exerted by the Ducal House of Savoy, which had gained the titles through agreement with the exiled Queen Charlotte in 1462 and 1485. Faced with this juristically sound claim, Venice fell back on the argument that the Mamluk Sultan had possessed the legal right to override Charlotte's claim in favour of James II. The Duke of Savoy joined the League of Cambrai in 1509 in the hope of regaining Cyprus through Venice's defeat, and Duke

Victor Amadeus's employment of the title of King of Cyprus in 1633 provoked a breach of diplomatic relations between Savoy and the Republic which lasted for thirty years. Later dukes of Savoy, who became successively kings of Sardinia and Italy, continued to assume the titles of kings of Jerusalem, Armenia, and Cyprus until the abdication of Humbert II in 1946. But for the Syrians, Armenians, and Greeks such claims and disputes were an irrelevance: they remained under Ottoman rule until the British occupation of Cyprus in 1878 produced the first inroad into the Turkish domination of the Levant.

7

The Templars and the Hospitallers,
1274–1565: *Disaster and Adaptation*

✠

O F the three great international Military Orders whose chief function, in 1274, was the defence of the Holy Land, the most successful in the late Middle Ages was the Teutonic Order. Its achievements in colonizing and governing Prussia and Livonia, and in waging a prolonged war against Lithuania, will be recounted in Chapter 11.[1] The older Orders of the Hospital and the Temple followed very different paths. The Knights of St John found the task of adaptation to changing circumstances after 1291 a painful one. Although they quickly succeeded in finding a new base for their operations at Rhodes, more than a century passed before they evolved a new role as a front-line power in Christendom's struggle against the Turks; and that role was essentially a reactive one, the result of Ottoman successes and the gradual realization, at Rhodes and in the West, of the island-fortress's strategic importance. As for the Templars, the trial and suppression of their entire Order between 1307 and 1312 represented a catastrophic sequence of events whose causality and significance remain highly problematic.

In their attempt to explain the destruction of the Templars, historians have naturally paid considerable attention to the activities and reputation of both the Templars and the Hospitallers during the decades leading up to the trial. This has meant examining the role played by the two Orders in the last years of Latin Syria, and assessing the changing public image of the Orders in the West. It is clear that the Orders exercised an impact on the political life of the Frankish states in Syria which grew as the thirteenth century progressed. This occurred both because of the weakness and confused condition of the monarchy in the Kingdom of Jerusalem,

[1] Below, 328–33, 337–44.

and because the Orders' western estates and incomes made them less vulnerable than the Crown and the feudal nobility to the territorial losses inflicted by the Muslims. The Orders' relative share of military responsibility thus increased, and in return they expected a greater say in the decision-making process. As early as 1231 Pope Gregory IX claimed that without the Hospitallers and Templars the Holy Land 'would be in no way governable'. Internally, their masters helped to resolve disputes, and were present at the High Court when key issues were discussed. Externally, they conducted their own negotiations with the Muslims, had to be specifically included in the terms of truces, and were prominent in arranging the dispatch of news and pleas for help to the West. The masters were capable of acting in harmony, but all too often they assumed opposing sides in the disputes which punctuated the century, most notably on the succession to the throne and regency, the rivalry of the Italian mercantile republics, and relations with Muslim neighbours. For all their positive action, the main image reaching the West was one of mutual animosity, and resultant damage to the Christian position. The dangers involved were clear to the Orders themselves. Thus at the time of the Second Council of Lyons the Master of the Templars stressed the need for 'peace and concord' between the Temple and the Hospital, 'lest material for gossip be provided to others, to the detriment of both Orders'.

Much the same can be said of the Orders' military activity in Syria. From the departure of Louis IX in 1254 onwards, their great castles represented the most serious obstacle in the path of the Mamluk conquest of the Holy Land, and to a large extent the pace of the Muslim advance can be measured in terms of the fall or capitulation of these fortresses: Hospitaller Arsuf in 1265, Templar Safad in 1266, Templar Belfort in 1268, Templar Chastel Blanc and Hospitaller Crac des Chevaliers, Akkar, and Belda in 1271, and Hospitaller Margat in 1285. The Hospitallers and Templars fought in the unsuccessful defence of Tripoli in 1289, and both Orders were prominent in the final siege of Acre; the Master of the Templars was killed, the Master of the Hospitallers seriously wounded, and the Templars defended their palace for several days after the rest of the city had fallen. Despite this fine record, many in the West were sceptical, in the years before 1291, about the usefulness of the Orders' military work. Philip of Nanteuil, who was captured by the Muslims at Gaza in 1239, asserted that the Knights of the Orders had shown cowardice there.

Such complaints, which were more than countered by anecdotes of the brethren's courage, were less important than the impact of the Orders' consistent policy of declining to assist crusaders to achieve the conquest of land which could not be held afterwards. This approach stretched back to the Third Crusade, but it was misconstrued by many: in particular, Frederick II's publicists made a great deal of the opposition mounted by the Orders to the Emperor's peaceful recovery of Jerusalem in 1229. It was noted at the Council of Lyons in 1274 that the Master of the Templars appeared reluctant to commit his Order to a major military undertaking. Some, including Richard of Mepham, Dean of Lincoln, saw this reluctance as incompatible with the Orders' possession of massive western estates. Like many others before and after him, such as Matthew Paris and Marino Sanudo Torsello, Richard exaggerated the extent of the Orders' western resources, but his critical viewpoint was shared by those in authority, for in 1278 Pope Nicholas III demanded that the Orders' military establishment in the East correspond to their resources in the West. Other contemporaries, perturbed by stories of the Orders' rivalry, expounded the idea of amalgamation. This proposal was made at Lyons, although it was opposed not only by the Orders themselves, but also by the Spanish kings, who believed that in Iberia a unified Order would constitute a potential threat to their authority, and feared for the survival of their native Military Orders.

Discussion of the Orders' failings, and plans for their reform, intensified after 1291, in the twofold context of the need to account for the collapse of Latin Syria, and the planning of a recovery crusade. The theme of efficiency was taken up by many commentators. Rostanh Berenguier of Marseilles was particularly caustic in his attack on the idleness of the Templars, recommending the Order's dissolution. This was exceptional; most critics opted for amalgamation. Such was the view of Charles II of Sicily, Peter Dubois, and many of the Church councils which met in response to Nicholas IV's request for advice. Charles II even wanted to bring all the western Hospitaller Orders into the new 'super-order'. Ramon Lull, who toyed with the idea of ending rivalry by stationing the Orders on different fronts (North Africa and *Turquia*), came down in favour of their amalgamation in a new Order which would be called 'the Order of the Holy Spirit'. The Pope even claimed that the 'common voice' demanded amalgamation. In so far as a *communis vox* existed, Nicholas was probably right in thinking that it opposed the continued existence of the two Orders as separate institutions. It has been noted that none of the enthusiasts for union pursued the practical implications of the idea, and that the papacy did nothing apart from occasionally urging the proposal on the Orders themselves. But it is equally the case that in the years following 1291 popular feeling, normally conservative, was primed for change. It was, in Anthony Luttrell's words, 'an epoch of crises and confusions', a backcloth which does not in itself explain the fall of the Templars, but without which it surely would not have been possible. In this sense the fall of Acre and the trial cannot be separated; and historians have remarked on the ease with which Peter Dubois effected the transition from accusing the two Orders of 'mala fides' (i.e. treachery) in his 'On the Recovery of the Holy Land' (1305–7), to commenting on the 'error Templariorum' (i.e. their suspected heresy), in 1308.

Amalgamation was not the only proposal put forward. Churchmen, facing heavy taxation in association with plans for a recovery crusade, took up again the idea of the Orders' efficient utilization of their western estates: after the Council of London in 1292, for example, the Archbishop of Canterbury advised the Pope that 'taxed according to the value of their goods, in income and produce, they should be compelled to maintain, on a permanent footing, as many able fighters for the acquisition and defence of the Holy Land, as they can reasonably support from their resources'. The role of the Orders in the organization and leadership of the recovery *passagium*, and in the government and defence of the reconquered Jerusalem, also received much attention. Charles II of Sicily argued that funds raised for the crusade should be entrusted to the Master of the single, new Order, and Ramon Lull was prepared to place the command of the *passagium* itself in his hands. The idea was mooted of combining this magistracy with kingship itself. In his 'Liber de fine' (1305), Ramon Lull coined the expression 'warrior king' (*rex bellator*) for the man who would be both the head of the amalgamated Order and the King of the reconquered Jerusalem. Criticism was certainly expressed, and it was made clear that a better and more responsible performance was expected in future: but for all who considered the problem of recovering and holding the Holy Land, the Orders—in whatever form—had an important role to play. They were being challenged to adapt and improve.

Their response was on the whole disappointing. The two Orders retreated to Cyprus in 1291, and the organization of their headquarters there naturally absorbed their energies initially. There are signs that the Hospitallers concentrated on building up a naval squadron, while James of Molay, the last Master of the Templars, toured the West in 1294–5, and directed naval raids against the Mamluk coastal towns. The Templars defended Ruad, an island off Tortosa, until it was stormed in 1302. The Orders had little to show for the decade following 1291, although in fairness it is hard to see what they could have achieved without the help of the recovery crusade which was being discussed in the West. When, in 1306, Clement V asked both James of Molay and the newly elected Master of the Hospitallers, Fulk of Villaret, for advice on the crusade, he received two sensible memoranda. In particular, both men grasped the importance of maintaining a trade embargo on Egypt. Molay and Villaret were thus not out of touch with recovery thinking, and they were prepared to invest their Orders' resources fully in the *passagium*. But amalgamation was rejected by Molay in a *mémoire* in which he emphasized the proven advantages of plurality, notably that it stimulated healthy competition between the two Orders. The arguments advanced by this conservative, fighting aristocrat were closely reasoned, but disastrously isolated from popular feeling. As Peter Partner has put it, 'as the Templars approached their last days their mood seems to have been passive and negative'.

Granted that the Orders had a poor image in the eyes of contemporaries, and that the Templars in particular failed to project their Order in an attractive manner, the trial remains largely unexplained until the protagonists, Philip IV and his government, are brought into the picture. All religious Orders lose their initial impetus; many pass through a phase of unpopularity and self-doubt. And past views of a crescendo of criticism levelled against the Orders after the fall of Acre have been grossly exaggerated. The Orders retained some defenders in the last decades of the thirteenth century, just as they had been bitterly resented by some in the early twelfth. It is a long way from the standard accusations of pride, avarice, and luxury which formed the staple diet of critics of the Templars, to the charges of apostasy, idolatry, and sodomy which were brought against the Order in 1307. Not even the most severe critics of the Templars had ever accused them of heretical beliefs. Above all, the fact that the Hospitallers did not come under fire in the same way in 1307 is strong evidence that one of the Orders was picked out for attack. It is true that the Templars had a marginally worse reputation, and were weaker in that they lacked their rivals' relatively strong conventual command-structure, while the Hospitallers exercised a charitable function which compensated for their attenuated military activity. None the less, the extinction of one Order and the survival of the other cannot be explained primarily by reference to the Orders themselves.

Why then did Philip unleash his attack on the Templars? According to royal officials, the King was approached in 1305 by Templars who denounced certain practices in their own Order; he investigated the matter through spies, who confirmed the reports. It is extremely unlikely that the bizarre practices detailed were in reality widespread in the Order, though it is possible that some innocent but obscure rituals were misinterpreted by participants, wilfully or by mistake. It is reasonable to suppose that the French government seized on the reports because the confiscation of Templar property in France would ameliorate its severe financial problems. In 1306, when Philip attempted to increase his tax revenues by a harsh currency reform, the ensuing riot forced him, ironically, to take refuge in the Templar fortress in Paris. By this point the French government had for some years been practising the expedient of despoiling well-off but vulnerable social groups, notably the Italian bankers and the Jews. The latter were in fact arrested, their property seized, and then expelled, in 1306, in what almost looks like a dress rehearsal for the onslaught on the Templars.

To this background of acute financial need and customary brutality should be added the issue of sovereignty, the growing feeling that everybody resident in France should be subject to governmental control, which the Templars were not. Indeed, the government feared that although the richest Templar estates lay in France, the Order was drifting into the political orbit of England and Aragon, France's leading enemies. An attack on the Templars would prepare the way for greater exertions of control in the case of other Orders, as well as that of the secular clergy, with whom Philip's ministers had already had several harsh clashes. Finally, using the charge of heresy would allow the government to deploy the machinery of the Inquisition, the only way to legitimize an attack on an Order of the Church.

If this makes Philip's actions sound calculated and cynical in the extreme, it does not take into account the curious ethos which prevailed at the French court in the second half of Philip's reign, or his undoubted crusading aspirations, which were described in Chapter 1.[2] For the same exaltation of the monarch's role and rights which resulted in the obsession with sovereignty also created a burdensome sense of the King's responsibility for the spiritual well-being and harmonious regulation of the realm. Malcolm Barber has demonstrated the emphasis placed by the government on the claim that the Templars had offended against the

---

[2] Above, 25–9.

divine order in a particularly shocking manner; at the very least, Philip was bound to remember his promise, at his coronation, that he would implement the decrees of the Fourth Lateran Council 'concerning the extirpation of heretics from his Kingdom'. The strong tide of anti-clerical feeling in France in this period made it relatively easy to believe the truth of rumours about the Order, especially in a society terrified about the power of the demonic. And the laity's sense of deep-rooted, even conspiratorial, corruption within the Church made it seem plausible that the Templars could be guilty of virtually the same offences which had allegedly been committed by Pope Boniface VIII. Again, Philip's serious commitment to the crusade, whatever his prevarications, and dynastic interests in it, made him as disturbed as anyone by the idea that the Templars had not only failed the cause, but had betrayed it. The enigmatic personality of Philip the Fair, and the difficulty of ascertaining the extent to which the King directed his government's policies, make it impossible now to be certain of his true feelings on the Templars. None the less, any account of the French actions which omitted these important background factors would be inaccurate and unfair. The Order's innocence cannot seriously be questioned. But this is not the same as saying that the French government set about its destruction in a spirit of cold and conscious duplicity, no matter how far-fetched and hypocritical French pronouncements during the trial sound.

The French attack was launched on Friday, 13 October 1307, when all the Templars in the Kingdom were arrested. Technically the action was carried out at the behest of the Inquisitor, William of Paris, but it still constituted a clear and astounding breach of the Order's accumulated privileges, which placed it under papal protection. Philip's justification was that he acted under 'vehement suspicion', and it was essential that this suspicion now be confirmed by the French Templars in order to placate the Pope. The arrested brethren were therefore questioned and, under torture, nearly all confessed to the crimes suggested. This was hardly surprising as few were knights and the majority middle-aged men, while the tortures employed were savage. Significantly, one of the most indignant denials of the charges was voiced by a German Templar, Corrand of Mangoncia, who was captured while returning to the Empire. He was not under the same political and social pressure as the French Templars, who suddenly found the weight of their own government and Church against them. Modern historians have quite rightly stressed the psychological shock this must have caused. The most important confession was that of the Master himself, which was made on 24 October in circumstances which remain unclear. The feeble and contradictory leadership which Molay provided throughout the next few years was not the least important reason for the trial's disastrous outcome.

The next stage, the dissolution of the Order, had to be decreed by the Pope. In this respect Philip encountered a resistance which, in the light of Clement V's previous concessions, he had no reason to expect. Early reactions to the French charges, expressed by James II of Aragon and Edward II of England, were frankly incredulous, but Clement's initial response was one of fury. He insisted that the persons and goods of the French Templars be assigned to two cardinals representing the Roman Church. Papal anger was directed less at Philip's actions, however, than at his unorthodox methods. Clement realized that he could not reverse what the King had done without gravely insulting him: all he could do was to rectify the procedure followed. Accordingly, on 22 November 1307, in the bull *Pastoralis praeeminentiae*, Clement himself ordered the arrest of all Templars throughout Christendom. In the following months Philip's government worked hard to regain the initiative. Most dramatically, an assembly of the French Estates at Tours, in May 1308, gave its backing to royal policy. A few days later Philip met the Pope at Poitiers. Clement was virtually a prisoner until the King decided that he had got what he wanted, and the stand which the Pope took in this situation was courageous, more so than most historians have given him credit for. Royal ministers went as far as they dared towards threatening the Pope personally with the charge of favouring heresy, and in July–August 1308 Clement set up his own twofold enquiry into the Order: episcopal and inquisitorial investigations throughout Christendom, and a single, eight-man commission to enquire into the Order as a whole. The bull 'Regnans in coelis' announced the convening of a general council, which would meet at Vienne in October 1310, to consider the results of both sets of enquiries. Neither Pope nor King had won the struggle. Philip's hope for a speedy dissolution of the Order, which would prevent the Templars rallying, and hide the methods used by Nogaret and his torturers, had been quashed; but equally, the papal commission was heavily influenced by the French government. Its president was Giles Aycelin, Archbishop of Narbonne and a prominent counsellor of Philip the Fair.

The slow progress of both the provincial enquiries and the papal commission lacks the drama and tension of the years 1307–8. They followed rather predictable courses. The French Templars were caught in the inquisitorial catch-22 that, as self-confessed heretics, they could be treated as relapsed heretics if they subsequently denied their guilt. This ruling was deployed by Philip in 1310 when it appeared that the Templars were mounting a dangerously convincing defence before the papal commission. Philip of Marigny, Archbishop of Sens and brother of the royal Chamberlain, burned fifty-four Templars to death at Paris on 12 May. They protested their innocence to the end; as one chronicler noted, the people observed this 'with great admiration and immense surprise'. Outside France, the trials were a shambles. In England especially the Templars emerged as innocent of any serious unorthodoxy, and the Archbishops of Mainz and Trier actually ruled in the Order's favour. The gulf between French policy and the broader feelings of Christendom was embarrassing above all to the Pope. Nor did his situation improve when the Council of Vienne assembled, a year later than planned, in October 1311. A vigorous pro-Templar lobby developed which argued that the Order should be allowed to present a defence. Philip responded by calling a meeting of the Estates at Lyons in February 1312, to reassert the condemnation of the Templars; and in March he demanded that Clement suppress the Order immediately. But the arrival of the King in person with an armed force, on 20 March, was necessary before Clement took the required action. On 22 March the bull 'Vox in excelso' decreed the suppression of the Order, 'not by way of judicial sentence, but by way of provision'. The suppression was thus in accordance with an earlier comment by the Pope that 'if it cannot be destroyed by the path of justice, let it be destroyed by that of expediency, lest our dear son the King of France take offence'. The dissolution was based on the papal plenitude of power, the Council, as Walter of Hemingborough commented, neither consenting nor expressly contradicting'. It was richly ironic that *plenitudo potestatis* was employed to effect a suppression which, more than any other single event in this period, demonstrated the weakness of the papacy in its relations with the French government.

There remained the question of individual Templars and their property. The brethren were allowed pensions, to be drawn on the rents or produce of their former lands. Most were prepared to accept this comfortable though humiliating retirement, but in March 1314 the trial went through a remarkable final scene at Paris when the Master and the Preceptor of Normandy, on being informed of their sentences—perpetual impris-onment—withdrew their confessions. Both were burnt, in haste, on a small island in the Seine. The disposition of Templar property is the only bright feature in a series of events which is otherwise composed of viciousness, bungling, and weakness. Throughout the trial Clement had insisted that the Templar estates should be conserved for the benefit of the crusade to regain the Holy Land. By the time of Vienne the Pope had come to favour their cession to the Hospitallers. Clement's determination to pursue this path, despite the opposition of many cardinals, most of the prelates at the Council, and Philip the Fair, forms one of the several extraordinary and unexplained aspects of the trial. Perhaps the Pope believed that the foundation of a completely new Order would take too long, and that in the mean time Templar property would be frittered away. A certain amount of Hospitaller lobbying probably also occurred. The result was that the bull *Ad providam*, of 2 May 1312, granted to the Knights of St John all Templar lands and rights outside the Iberian peninsula: property and rents donated by Christians over the course of two centuries to the crusading cause were thus retained for that purpose.

It is clear that, as Anthony Luttrell has put it, 'the triumph of Foulques de Villaret and the Hospital was as spectacular as the failure of Jacques de Molay and the Temple'. The inevitable losses involved in the transfer, the new administrative costs borne by the Hospital, and the fact that the Order found itself burdened with crippling debts shortly after the Council of Vienne, should not disguise the fact that, as one Hospitaller expressed it in 1313, Clement had given the Order a gift greater than the Donation of Constantine. It is impossible accurately to quantify the Hospital's gains. Perhaps of greatest significance was the acquisition of the Temple's estates in Cyprus, which were transferred quickly and without major losses in 1313: food from these later proved invaluable when there was famine on Rhodes. The French estates were not occupied until 1318, when the Order finally came to an agreement with the French court about the costs which the latter claimed to have incurred during the trial; the settlement cost more than 300,000 *livres*. This sum, together with the revenues from the Templar estates for the years of their occupation, constituted the financial benefits accruing from the onslaught of 1307, though the military, legal, and administrative costs sustained by the government must have been substantial. In other countries, too, opposition to the transfer occurred: few rulers were ready to lose the chance of profiting from the windfall represented by the Templar tragedy, whatever their attitude during the trial itself. In Iberia the Kings of Aragon and Portugal persuaded the Curia to allow the cession of the many Templar estates to new military Orders, that of Montesa in

Valencia, and that of Christ in Portugal. In 1331 the Castilians too came around to petitioning for a new Order, but John XXII informed them that their request had been made too late. All in all, however, the transfer of property took place relatively quickly, for by the early 1320s the bulk was in Hospitaller hands.

During the early stages of the trial of the Templars, the Hospitallers in the East were conquering Rhodes; indeed, Clement V prematurely confirmed them in the possession of the island on 5 September 1307, just nine days before Philip IV sent out secret orders to his *baillis* and *sénéchaux* for the arrest of the French Templars. The events are so close together that, as in the case of the Teutonic Order's definitive move to Marienburg in 1309, historians have often viewed the Hospitallers' move to Rhodes as an attempt to avoid the Templars' fate by establishing an independent base and a new military role. The invasion of Rhodes was clearly not in itself a response to events in France, since the Order's secret agreement with the Genoese adventurer Vignolo degli Vignoli, for their joint conquest of the Rhodian archipelago, was sealed in May 1306, before the wave of rumours about the supposed errors of the Templars had become alarming; but the energy with which the Order pursued the conquest of the island, in the years following 1307, was surely due in part to news of the trial. Fulk of Villaret's deep involvement in the planning of the *passagium* which eventually sailed to the East early in 1310, was, again, almost certainly intended to show that his Order had recovered from the years of inactivity following 1291, even if in practice he deployed the crusade's resources simply to complete the conquest of Rhodes. The years between 1307 and 1313, which witnessed important crusades in Spain, Italy, and the East, the crusade discussions and decrees at Vienne, besides the Templar crisis and the decisive reorientation of the other international Orders, are amongst the most complicated and densely packed in the history of the crusading movement. The interaction of these events was manifold and much still needs to be unravelled. But it would be unfair to deny Fulk the credit of reacting with intelligence and vigour to the Templar trial.

It is not hard to see why the Order was attracted by Rhodes. Cyprus was unsuitable as a long-term base partly because the relationship between the Order and the Cypriot Crown was unclear and likely to remain so, and partly because the Order could not avoid getting involved in Cypriot politics. During the *coup d'état* engineered by Amalric in 1306 the Hospitallers, who at first worked with the Templars as mediators between Amalric and King Henry, eventually came around to supporting Henry. The Grand Preceptor worked for his release from Armenian custody in 1310, and Henry appointed Fulk of Villaret as his viceroy in the summer; the resolution of the crisis was due in large part to the Hospitallers' intervention, but it was burdensome and did little for their reputation in the West. By contrast, the Rhodian archipelago offered political independence: at the time of the conquest it was contested by Greeks, Turks, Venetians, and Genoese, but none of them could seriously challenge a Hospitaller occupation on legal grounds. Rhodes itself was fertile, and the islands were well placed to benefit from trade, as well as to function as a communications centre between *Romania*, Cyprus, and the West. Above all, Rhodes was ideal as a base for Hospitaller intervention in both spheres of crusading activity dominant in the early fourteenth century. From here the Order could take part in a recovery *passagium*, raid the Syrian coastline, and harass Christian ships trading illegally with Egypt (Ramon Lull argued the advantage of a Latin occupation of Rhodes in the latter respect in 1305); but Rhodes, just twelve miles away from Anatolia, also placed the Order on the edge of *Romania*, so that it could fight the Turks and Byzantines. It was hard to imagine a better base.

The conquest of the island began in June 1306, when a joint Hospitaller-Genoese expedition sailed to nearby Castellorizzo. The Hospitallers attempted the capture of Cos and of the town of Rhodes. Andronikos II, whose troops held the town, reacted energetically by dispatching reinforcements. But the town surrendered, probably in 1308, and two years later Fulk of Villaret completed the conquest of the island. By 1311 the situation was stable enough for the Order to hold a chapter general at Rhodes; it and a successor three years later regulated the island's defence. Fulk immediately set about deploying the Order's new strategic position to good effect: some strongholds on the mainland were seized, Christian vessels trading with Egypt were captured, and a defeat was inflicted on the Turks in the Cyclades in 1312. A report was sent to the Council of Vienne about the latter, claiming the deaths of 1,500 Turks.

Fulk also initiated the colonization of Rhodes. In 1313 a magistral bull specified the terms of feudal tenure which the Order would grant to men from different social ranks—knights, undubbed nobles, and commoners—who came from the West and agreed to provide military service. An attempt was even made to augment the Order's still feeble naval arm by offering good tenurial terms to anybody who would provide a war galley, or a vessel of another kind. The bull enjoyed little if any western response.

Italians already present in the East accepted fiefs, such as the Assanti brothers of Ischia, enfeoffed with the whole island of Nisyros in 1316 in return for the provision of a galley, and Vignolo degli Vignoli's brother Fulk, who was enfeoffed with the village of Lardos in 1325. But while Italians and others flocked to the town of Rhodes, either as merchants or as lawyers, notaries, and craftsmen, the rural hinterland exerted much less attraction. In 1335 the chapter general held at Rhodes therefore allowed the Master to begin leasing lands in exchange for an annual rent. This proved to be more successful, over 20 grants or confirmations of land outside the town of Rhodes being made in 1347–8 alone. Latins and Greeks leased land, without any obligation to provide military service, and in most cases without residing on their estates, which were considered purely as an investment. After an abortive attempt to replicate the pattern of feudal settlement familiar to it from Cyprus and Syria, and most recently implanted in Villehardouin Achaea, the Order thus resorted to a system of land exploitation which resembled that of contemporary Greece. There, as we have seen, the feudal *assises* were becoming increasingly divorced from reality. The Order was disadvantaged in so far as it had to rely, for its military establishment, on serving brethren, mercenaries, and, *in extremis*, a call to arms to all free adult males subject to its jurisdiction, whether Latin or Greek. But it may well have gained in terms of its relations with the Greeks, who were not placed under the overlordship of a foreign, settler class, and did not rebel against the Hospital. The Order helped to sustain these good relations by taking no steps to coerce the Greeks into abandoning the Orthodox church.

The Order assiduously fostered the mercantile prosperity of its new acquisition while building up its own administration and defences there. Like the Teutonic Knights in Prussia, the Hospitallers were competent traders, sending sugar westwards from their own lands and purchasing cloth for eastern markets. The master's chancery developed, and courts were established to handle civil and criminal cases. The castle at Rhodes was strengthened, and landward and seaward walls provided for the town. Hospices (*auberges*) were built for serving brethren from the various priories, and a hospital was established to maintain the Order's tradition of caring for the sick. Western merchants and pilgrims were impressed by what they saw. There was also, for some years after the conquest, a sustained attempt to co-operate with other Latin powers in the Aegean against the Turks at sea, which resulted in victories in 1318, 1319, and possibly 1320. But the expense of all this activity, coming so soon after the cost of the campaigns to conquer Rhodes, and the *passagium* of 1309–10, nearly bankrupted the Hospitallers. By 1320 they owed over 580,000 florins, more than twice the ordinary annual revenue of the papacy.

Master Hélion of Villeneuve spent thirteen years in the West dealing with these debts, finally liquidating them in the mid-1330s by raising responsions (the annual payments made by the priories to the Convent), selling estates, and levying special taxes. The timing of this financial crisis and its resolution proved unfortunate, for it compelled Hélion to display reluctance to commit his Order to supporting the series of *passagia* being discussed by the papal and French courts. By the time the Hospital was again solvent, the Anglo-French war had broken out and *passagia* plans were shelved. In the late 1330s, when the Order had amassed a massive credit with the Pope's bankers, Benedict XII's personal disinclination to promote the crusade was bolstered by his fear of what would happen to his own finances if the Order's credit was withdrawn. Then in the 1340s, when the Hospitallers' healthy financial position had enabled them to be comparatively vigorous in their support of Clement VI's naval league, the bankers themselves went bankrupt, taking the Order's reserves with them. To a greater extent than historians have commonly recognized, the direction and tempo of the crusading movement in the second quarter of the fourteenth century were dictated by the condition and interaction of Hospitaller and papal finances.

Even after the Hospitallers had succeeded both in conquering and settling on Rhodes, and in liquidating the debts run up during the magistracy of Fulk of Villaret, they continued to face grave problems. These problems, which placed severe constraints on what the Order could achieve at Rhodes, fell into three categories: its internal difficulties, its relations with the papacy and secular powers in the West, and its inability to elaborate and implement a fully satisfactory role in the eastern Mediterranean. Internally, the main problem throughout the fourteenth century was the Convent's unsatisfactory relations with the priories. Amongst the senior brethren of the Convent itself the period was one of stable government. The only major crisis occurred at the end of Fulk of Villaret's reign, when the Master's corruption led the brethren at the Convent to attempt his assassination in 1317. On failing they elected a substitute master, and the schism was only ended two years later by papal intervention. Thereafter elections and magistracies proceeded without serious upsets. But all the masters who succeeded Fulk, until the election of John Fernández of Heredia in 1377, were rather undistinguished men. And to extract men and money from the priories they had to engage in a battle against what Anthony Luttrell has characterized as 'endless indifference and corruption'. Many Hospitallers regarded their vocation simply as an agreeable and respectable form of the monastic life, spending their careers exclusively on their preceptories' lands; the more ambitious served at Rhodes to get a good appointment in the West, and thereafter regarded the Convent's demands as intrusions. The latter tendency was criticized by Philip of Mézières in 'The Dream of the Old Pilgrim'. Responsions were thus unpaid or permanently in arrears, reforming decrees of chapters general were ignored, and some priories lost contact with Rhodes to such a degree as to be virtually autonomous. In the course of the century the Hospitallers of Brandenburg achieved quasi-independence, in the sense that they were all but released from the authority of both the masters and the priors of Germany. Ironically, the early career of John Fernández of Heredia, later a highly competent if unscrupulous Master, best illustrates these dangers, in that he accumulated three priories, and deployed the protection and favour of the papal Curia to defy the orders of the Master. Even commentators who were reasonably well acquainted with the Convent failed to appreciate the debilitating conditions under which it had to work: Marino Sanudo Torsello, for example, quoted the annual total of 180,000 florins due from responsions as if they were guaranteed income.

But just as alarming as the priories' insubordination was their own internal condition, which contrasted sharply with the achievements of the Convent at Rhodes. Throughout the century, but especially after the disasters of the 1340s, the priories faced economic problems; in many countries, particularly the French priories, these were compounded by the dire consequences of warfare and brigandage. The findings of the episcopal inquests ordered into Hospitaller estates by Pope Gregory XI in 1373, some of which have recently been published, reveal the full grimness of the situation. They also show that the majority of the Hospitallers, whose actual numbers had fallen dramatically since the 1330s, were priests rather than knights or sergeants, and that most were in early or late middle age. In these circumstances their sense of alienation from Rhodes becomes more understandable. Indeed, it is remarkable that the Great Schism was not used by quasi-independent priors to effect a total break from the Convent, which supported the Avignonese popes, by supporting the Roman obedience. This failed to occur even in countries firmly attached to the Roman obedience, such as England, and even when there was an 'anti-Master' appointed by the Roman obedience, between 1383 and 1395. The schism in the Hospital was in fact ended in 1410, seven years before that in the papacy itself.

One reason why the priories resisted the financial demands of the Convent was that they were always subject to similar demands on the part of their local secular rulers. We have seen that one background factor in Philip the Fair's attack on the Templars was his resentment of their claim, as a religious Order, to be less than fully subject to his sovereignty. The fourteenth century witnessed a considerable increase in the manifold pressure exerted on the priories to erode their privileges of exemption and to make the brethren undergo the same burdens as any other social group. Such pressure was exerted regardless of calls for money coming from Rhodes, and it materialized at two distinct levels. First, there were governmental demands for a say in the appointment of important office-holders, individuals who were often in charge of key fortresses or large revenues, and who could prove highly dangerous if they were inimical towards the secular power. There were also attempts to tax the Order's preceptories and commanderies, and a constant struggle to bring them within the jurisdiction of the secular courts. But a scarcely less significant, though worse documented, form of harassment came from minor officials whose activities could, if they provoked too shrill a reaction from prior, master, or pope, be disowned as *ultra vires*. In this respect the arrests of the Templars in 1307, and the seizure of their property, formed a particularly large-scale and co-ordinated example of a type of governmental brigandage which was practised constantly, and in most western countries.

It was perhaps at its most severe in the Crown of Aragon, although there is a danger that the remarkably rich (and forthrightly expressed) surviving documentation creates a distorting picture. The Aragonese not only pressed the theme of sovereignty and its concomitant rights as hard as any government, but they also upheld the tradition that the Hospitallers should take part in royal campaigns against the Moors or in defence of the Crown, either by sending men or by donating cash. When they were slow in doing so the Aragonese threatened to confiscate estates. King James II was cynical in his evaluation of what the Hospital was doing at Rhodes, and never accepted the claim that the island's defence represented a renewal of the Order's crusading role: in 1325, for example, he refused to permit the export of Aragonese coin to pay off the Order's debts on the grounds that the Holy Land was no longer in Christian hands. So serious was James's hostility towards the Order that it encouraged the King's marriage to Mary of Lusignan in 1315, hoping that this would make James more sympathetic towards the Latin East; but Mary died childless in 1322.

In its attempt to keep control over the priories, and to defend them from being crushed or taken over by the local lay powers, the Convent came to rely more than formerly on the papal Curia. The assistance which the papacy rendered to the Hospitallers was one of the most impressive features of its crusading policy in the fourteenth century. John XXII, who ended the schism of 1317–19 and effectively aided Hélion of Villeneuve in repaying the Order's debts, rendered a comparable service in cajoling the priors to pay their responsions, and defending the Order against assaults on its privileges. A tradition of assisting the Convent was established which John's successors, especially Urban V and Gregory XI, maintained and developed. The tradition continued into the Great Schism and beyond: in particular, the profits which the Order drew from the special indulgences which were granted to it from 1390 onwards constituted one of the main reasons why its financial situation improved in the late fourteenth century. By 1392 indulgences had already brought in more than 25,000 florins, which compared favourably with the 38,500 florins coming to Rhodes each year from all the priories in the West. Papal help was not always forthcoming or effective. Nevertheless, starting with *Ad providam*, the relationship between the Order and the papal Curia was unprecedentedly close. A number of fourteenth- and early fifteenth-century frescos and manuscript illuminations portray Hospitallers in attendance on popes; in one the Master, Philibert of Naillac, is shown crowning Pope Martin V at the Council of Constance in 1417.

There was of course a price to pay. Papal policy towards the Order was affected by the venality and favouritism which afflicted every feature of papal activity in this period. The notorious John Fernández of Heredia sheltered behind the support of Innocent VI and Urban V; it must have been galling that this pluralist was chosen to convey the Curia's dissatisfaction with the Order's unreformed condition to the Convent in 1354. Like other rulers, the popes could not resist the temptation to use the Hospitallers as officials, so that able men were lost for years at a time to the Order's own service. The Hospitallers were supposed to be exempt from clerical taxation for crusading; but many papal bulls levying tenths and annates ruled that their exemption was temporarily annulled. Papal

collectors, who were usually members of the frequent
clergy, set about exacting the Hospital's contribution v
and determination. Most importantly, the Curia expec
show gratitude for its help, especially for the grant of the
This meant not only helping to implement the Curia's c
the East, but also instituting internal reforms deemeu ...
undertaking initiatives of its own against the Muslims.

In 1343 and 1355 Clement VI and Innocent VI wrote strong letters of
complaint to the Master. Both popes called for internal reform and a
greater commitment to military action. Innocent's letter was especially
sharp. The Hospitallers did not enjoy such great wealth so that they could
luxuriate at Rhodes. Instead, they should move the Convent to the
mainland, which would place them in a better position to fight the Turks.
They should imitate the Teutonic Knights, who had once been a junior
partner but whose wealth now equalled that of the Hospitallers. This
comparison with the Teutonic Order must have been particularly irritating
to the Hospitallers, who were well aware of the success of their sister-
Order in recruiting western knights as volunteers for its campaigns, but
could not hope to match it at Rhodes. If the Hospitallers did not improve
their performance, Innocent threatened (as Clement VI had in 1343), he
would take back the Templar lands and use them to found a new Military
Order. *Ad providam*, it was implied, had been mistaken generosity.
Gregory XI went much further than cajoling letters: his inquest of 1373
was intended to ascertain the true strength of the Order and initiate
military action in accordance with it. When, as we have seen, the results of
the inquest proved that the priories were in a dire condition, the Curia,
like many governments since, ignored the unpalatable results of its own
enquiry and continued to demand more than the Order could provide.

As the preceding pages have shown, criticism of the Order by the papal
Curia, inimical rulers such as James II of Aragon and Philip the Fair, and
crusade theorists like Marino Sanudo and Philip of Mézières, did not take
into account the formidable problems which the masters faced in maintaining, controlling, and channelling their resources. None the less, it is
hard to deny that a lack of consistency and purpose is visible in the
Order's activity at Rhodes during its first century there. To a large extent
this was due simply to the slowness and hesitancy with which the
crusading movement underwent its fundamental evolution, from the
proposed recovery of the Holy Land towards the defence of Latin
Romania and the Balkans against the Turks. If the Curia, as late as the

60s, could suddenly revert to the idea of recovering Jerusalem, it is hardly surprising that the Hospitallers found the elucidation of their role difficult. Quite apart from this strategic crux, there were intractable problems attached to the crusade against the Turks. Which emirates should be fought, how, and with what precise goals? To what extent should assistance be dispatched to the Armenians and the Byzantine Greeks? And should the Order acquire a footing in Latin Greece, whose strategic importance was undeniable, but whose acute political instability was offputting?

It is not surprising that the Hospitallers' response to these questions was equivocal. Fulk of Villaret showed enthusiasm for recovery projects, but after him there is little evidence that the senior conventual brethren gave much credence to the papal and French planning. They also ignored Clement V's request that they fight the Catalans in Greece, and responded only intermittently to papal appeals that they assist the Armenians. It was the Turks in Anatolia who commanded their attention. There was a lull in the Hospitallers' naval activity in the 1320s and 1330s, but once the series of Latin naval leagues against Aydin and Menteshe began, the Order could be relied upon to make a contribution. It was a partner in, and host to, the negotiations which formed the league of 1332, which in its expanded form won a victory in 1334. It supplied several galleys to Clement VI's league of 1343, and joined the league formed in 1350, which failed to achieve anything because of the Veneto-Genoese war. The Order was also one of the powers charged with financing the defence of Smyrna, and in 1359 a Florentine Hospitaller was allowed to conduct the defence and fortification of the outpost on a private-enterprise basis. In the same year Hospitaller galleys again took part in a naval action against the Turks, and the Order provided troops and ships to Peter Thomas in 1359, and to Peter of Cyprus's attack on Adalia in 1361. A hundred brethren led by the Admiral, Ferlino of Airasca, fought at Alexandria in 1365, and the Order provided assistance to Peter I for his campaigns in 1366 and 1367.

These three decades of willing and generally successful participation in naval leagues contrasted with the period of expensive failure which followed. In 1374 Gregory XI, appalled by the corruption which had long marked the government of Smyrna, insisted on placing the port entirely in the hands of the Hospitallers. Between 1373 and 1378 the Pope and the Order worked towards the dispatch of a wholly Hospitaller *passagium* to *Romania*; John Fernández of Heredia, elected Master in 1377 against the wishes of the Convent, directed the expedition towards Epiros, where the Order had recently acquired Vonitza. The port had strategic value in the defence of Latin Greece against the Ottoman advance, but the *passagium* was ambushed and destroyed. This involvement in Greece, which had attracted the Order since the 1350s, continued. As we saw in Chapter 5,[3] in 1376 the Hospitallers leased Achaea from Queen Joanna of Naples, but their rule was challenged by their own Navarrese mercenaries, and in 1381 they pulled out of the Principality. The expenses of Smyrna, the *passagium*, and the Achaean débâcle, left the Order heavily in debt. And in addition to the collapse of their ambitious plans in Epiros and the Morea, the Hospitallers failed through inactivity either to protect Cyprus against Genoese aggression in 1373—despite the fact that the young Peter II's guardian was a Hospitaller—or to assist Armenia in its death agony in 1375.

Heredia was, however, a brilliant Master, and he set about reconstructing the Order's policies with energy after the reverses of 1378–81. The debts were liquidated within a decade, and the Hospitallers contributed galleys to the naval league which formed part of the background to the Nicopolis crusade. Hospitallers sailed up the Danube to take part in the battle. More importantly, they undertook the defence of Corinth in 1397, and the role which they played in defending the Morea was irksome enough to Sultan Bayezid I for him to insist on the Order quitting Greece as part of his negotiations with the Despot Theodore in 1402. In the same year the garrison at Smyrna mounted a valiant though unsuccessful resistance against Tamerlane when he besieged the port in December. Master Philibert of Naillac, who succeeded Heredia in 1396, played an important role as mediator in the Cypriot-Genoese conflict, and was instrumental in helping Boucicaut to achieve his successes at Alaya, Tripoli, and Beirut in 1402. The Order's attempt to establish a foothold in Greece, however, met with renewed failure, and faced with the opposition of Anthony Acciaiuoli and Theodore of Mistra, the Hospitallers evacuated Corinth in 1404.

Deprived of both Smyrna and Corinth, the Hospitallers began to invest more money in the defence of the Rhodian archipelago. The walls of Rhodes itself were strengthened, and in 1407–8 the building of a major new castle was begun on the mainland at Bodrum, opposite Cos. Bodrum, whose strategic importance was limited, was constructed largely as a publicity and fund-raising exercise. With Smyrna lost, it constituted

[3] Above, 169–70.

proof that the Order was still engaged in war against the Turks, retained a foothold in enemy territory, and could harbour Christian slaves who managed to escape from the infidel. From this point of view the castle was highly successful, attracting tax exemptions, financial contributions, and papal indulgences which would probably not have been forthcoming if they had been solicited for the defence of Rhodes alone. Both for Bodrum and in the case of major crises like the siege of Rhodes in 1480, papal indulgences were a welcome source of revenue in the fifteenth century: the proceeds were especially good in 1480 because Sixtus IV was persuaded temporarily to suspend all other indulgences in the Order's favour.

With many Latin outposts in the East falling to the Ottomans, Rhodes's importance as a trading centre grew, especially for the Florentines, who were now penetrating the area for the first time in large numbers. The Order continued to co-operate with the Genoese and Venetians when these asked for naval assistance against the Turks, and it showed undiminished interest in Christian Greece. But conventual morale remained low, and uncertainty about the Order's role and future was acute. There are signs that the latter even extended to the value of Rhodes itself. The Order threatened to abandon Rhodes altogether when faced by the hostility of Pope John XXIII in 1412, and eleven years later it actually approached Venice with the idea of exchanging the island for land of equal value in Greece, preferably Euboea. It may have been only after the first Mamluk attack on Rhodes in 1440 that the Hospitallers developed a full sense of the strategic importance of their island, and a renewed determination to defend it, notwithstanding the many problems involved.

Passing the magistracy of Philibert of Naillac (1396–1421), a note of caution is necessary. Thanks to the efforts of Joseph Delaville le Roulx and, more recently, Jonathan Riley-Smith and Anthony Luttrell, the general development and much of the specific activity of the Hospitallers between 1274 and 1421 is remarkably clear. But the subsequent period, for which the documentation is paradoxically much richer, has received very little scholarly attention since the seventeenth century. Aside from the great sieges of Rhodes and Malta, the Order's relations with neighbouring powers and with rulers in the West remain unclear; and its internal condition and development are largely obscure. As Dr Luttrell has commented, 'the history of the Order from 1421 to 1565 awaits its historians'. To a greater extent than in any other part of this book, what follows can only be regarded as a tentative account of events.

The Order's history was bound to be shaped in large part by the continuing rise of the Ottoman Turks, and especially by their emergence as a naval power. But it was only after Mehmed II's conquest of Constantinople in 1453 that this dominated Hospitaller thinking. In the first half of the century the Mamluks were perceived as the more serious threat. Under Naillac Hospitaller relations with Egypt were favourable. A treaty sealed in 1403 restored the status quo established in the peace of 1370, and the Hospitallers were enabled to maintain a hospital at Jerusalem, keep consuls at Jerusalem, Ramla, and Damietta, and generally to oversee Latin pilgrimage traffic to Palestine and Sinai. Such a role could only boost the Order's image in the West. Nevertheless, Hospitaller fear of Mamluk seapower led the Order to maintain the aggressive stance which it had held in the period of Boucicaut's campaigns against the Mamluks. That fear was justified in 1426 when Barsbay launched his great attack on Cyprus, in the course of which the Hospitaller commandery at Kolossi was devastated. It was only a matter of time before the Mamluks also attacked Rhodes. The onslaught materialized in 1440, when a Mamluk squadron of eighteen galleys was beaten off by Master John of Lastic. Four years later came a more serious attack, in which the town of Rhodes itself was placed under siege for more than a month. It was the first serious test of the Hospitallers' hold on the archipelago for more than a century, and they were fortunate to receive the assistance at this critical point of Geoffrey of Thoisy and the Burgundian crusade flotilla. The Mamluk withdrawal was followed by the restoration of peace in 1445. But the Hospitallers now took urgent precautions against another attempted siege, whether by the Mamluks or the Ottomans. By 1449 watch was being kept for an approaching fleet by day and night, and John of Lastic continued the strengthening of the town's walls which had been begun by his predecessor, Anton Fluvian.

After 1453 an Ottoman attack, deploying the artillery which had proved its worth at Constantinople, was naturally expected. But Mehmed held back from a full-scale offensive, initially because he wanted to press home his advance in Greece and the Balkans, and later, perhaps, because he feared a repetition of the humiliating reverse which he had suffered at Belgrade in 1456. Tribute, with its clear connotations of political over-lordship, was the traditional first stage in Ottoman conquest. It was demanded from the Order in 1454 but refused. The Turks then sacked Cos in 1455, though their inability to capture its castle was a clear indication of the Order's defensive strength in the archipelago. A compromise on the payment of tribute, in the form of an annual 'gift' to the Sultan from the Order, was reached in 1462, but in 1464 Ottoman pressure for tribute *per se* was renewed, and by 1470, when the Order sent two galleys to the defence of Negroponte, relations had become consistently hostile. The Hospitallers joined the league assembled by Popes Paul II and Sixtus IV, which in 1472 sacked the Order's former outpost at Smyrna, as well as Adalia, Silifke, and Corycus.

Resounding successes like these could still result from the co-ordination of Latin seapower, and it was in this context that the Hospitallers were at their most effective. But the naval strength of the Turks was formidable enough by the 1470s to give them unquestioned dominance against the Order when it fought alone. Throughout the mid-1470s Turkish flotillas raided the islands of the Rhodian archipelago each spring, compelling the peasants to take shelter in the series of castles maintained by the Order. As Professor Lionel Butler remarked, there were a number of good reasons for Mehmed to attempt the acquisition of Rhodes itself: the fame attached to its former Greek city; the excellence of the harbour and the fertility of the island; its commercial importance; and its strategic value as a base for operations against rebellions in southern Asia Minor. And of equal significance were the indirect benefits which would accrue to the Sultan from such a victory: ending the activities of the Order; eliminating a nest for Christian pirates and a potential bridgehead for a crusade; and securing a propaganda *coup* over the Mamluk Sultanate, which had failed in 1444. As in the case of the Mamluks, therefore, an Ottoman attack on Rhodes was virtually inevitable.

The financial health of the Order as it awaited this onslaught was not good. To meet an anticipated Mamluk attack after James of Lusignan's invasion of Cyprus in 1460, Master James of Milly had to levy a special tax of over 100,000 florins on each of the priories. It was no easier to extract men and money from the priories in the fifteenth century than earlier. The flamboyantly rhetorical letters which John of Lastic wrote to the Prior of Auvergne in 1454, and Master Peter of Aubusson to all the priors in 1480, in which they declared their willingness to die for the faith and asked their brethren to do the same, clearly had the purpose of shaming into action men who normally turned a deaf ear to appeals. Indeed, Aubusson commented in his letter that 'in answering our pleas some have proved more obdurate and idle than we could have believed possible'. The expenses facing the Convent were immense: the hospital grew in size in the mid-fifteenth century, partly because of the increasing numbers of pilgrims passing through Rhodes; and although a bequest of 10,000 florins from Master Anton Fluvian facilitated the rebuilding which began in 1440, the running of the hospital probably imposed a greater burden than at any time since 1291. Master Peter Raymond Zacosta (1461–7) undertook the fundamental and expensive task of adapting the walls of Rhodes to the offensive power of artillery.

Difficulty in controlling the priories, and financial problems at Rhodes, were not the only respects in which the Order's internal condition displayed continuity: the Order's relations with its Greek subjects remained good, it continued its extraordinary love–hate relationship with the Genoese and Venetians (the latter launched a punitive raid on Rhodes in 1460 in connection with a commercial incident), and it still suffered the erosion of its rights and privileges at the hands of western rulers. But in other respects important changes within the Order can be discerned. First, the seven *langues* into which the Convent was divided—those of Provence, Auvergne, France, Italy, Spain, Germany, and England—increasingly expressed national and regional rivalries which reflected those of their western homelands. Although the resulting tensions did not become as acute as those which prevailed within the Teutonic Order, they showed that no international Order was immune to the period's hardening lines of allegiance and loyalty. In 1462 the *langue* of Spain was subdivided into those of Castile-Portugal and Aragon-Navarre, and a major office was assigned to the *pilier* (chief) of each *langue*. Competition between the *langues* was further stimulated by the decision to allocate to each *langue* a specific section of the fortifications to defend. A second change was the increase in importance of the Order's naval arm, whose officer, the admiral, had by 1480 come to rival the marshal in prestige. And in the second half of the century there occurred a perceptible growth of sentiment about Rhodes itself. The Order, or at least the Convent, began to see the island not only as a unifying force within a Christendom increasingly torn by national dissension—'our city of Rhodes is shared by, and open to, all Christian nations'—but also as a defining attribute of its own character. As Aubusson put it in 1480, Rhodes had become a 'firm rock and foundation of our Order'.

Aubusson's own importance in the Order's history demands comparison with that of Fulk of Villaret or John Fernández of Heredia. His reputation rests solidly on his conduct of the defence of Rhodes in 1480. Throughout the late 1470s the Master made preparations for an attack: grain supplies were accumulated, the walls strengthened yet further, and

Hospitaller Knights persuaded to come to Rhodes from the West. When Mehmed's fleet finally set out to besiege Rhodes in the spring of 1480, the defensive force probably numbered about 3,500 men. Of these only a few hundred were serving Knights of the Order, the rest being Greek and Latin residents of the archipelago, hired troops, and pilgrims from Europe caught in Rhodes by the siege. On 23 May the Turks landed their troops, probably between 10,000 and 15,000 men, and they sealed off the city by land and sea. The siege followed a straightforward course: the Turks concentrated their efforts on the Tower of St Nicholas, an isolated but strategically vital fortress at the end of the harbour mole, and on the weakest sector of the city wall, at its south-eastern boundary. The most determined assault on the Tower, carried out during the night of 18–19 June, failed totally, despite the fact that the 300 stone balls shot at it had reduced its western side to rubble. And an assault on the Wall of the Jews on 28 July was repulsed. One Ottoman source attributed this to the fact that the Turkish commander, Mesih Pasha, demoralized his troops at the crucial point by forbidding the plundering of the captured city; while a Hospitaller account of the battle explained the Turkish retreat in terms of a miraculous intervention by the Virgin and St John the Baptist. Whatever the true explanation, the failure of this assault was decisive. The Turks abandoned the siege.

There can be little doubt that the defeat of the Turks in 1480 was due primarily to the fact that Mehmed was simultaneously waging important campaigns in southern Italy, Hungary, the lower Danube, and Persia, so that the available troops were too few for the conquest of Rhodes. The decision to attack had been a rash one, and the Sultan showed that he did not blame his commander by immediately giving him the key governorship of Gallipoli. The Order was saved from a fresh expedition in 1481, led by the Sultan in person, by Mehmed's death. In 1482, moreover, they played host to Jem, and until he died in 1495 were therefore able to recover from the siege. This sequence of good fortune gave the Hospitallers an extra forty years at Rhodes. But Aubusson's exploitation of the situation was also important. During the siege itself he provided resourceful and inspiring leadership, conducting the defence of St Nicholas's Tower with immense skill and himself leading the Knights in their repulse of the Ottoman attack on the wall. After the siege he set about with energy restoring the damage done, constructing four polygonal boulevards in the walls in order that the proven defensive worth of the Order's artillery could be more effectively deployed in future sieges. There seems to have been no European prototype for these great structures: they were invented by the Master on the basis of his own studies in mathematics and engineering, conjoined with his observations in 1480. The fortifications at Bodrum were also strengthened, and Aubusson found money to complete the building of the new hospital in 1489, and to construct a church, St Mary of the Victory, to celebrate the repulse of the assault on 28 July.

The Master's other contributions were manifold, so much so that it is tempting to see the Order as it entered the sixteenth century as virtually reshaped by his energy and vision. He was quick to seize the various opportunities presented by the arrival in July 1482 of Jem, the pretender to the Ottoman throne: a treaty of perpetual peace with Jem in August was followed by a treaty with Sultan Bayezid II in December. By the terms of the latter the Order secured an annual grant of 35,000 ducats for the expenses of playing host to Jem, and in 1484 Bayezid sent the Master, as a conciliatory gift, the right hand of St John the Baptist. In 1489 Pope Innocent VIII thanked Aubusson for transferring Jem to his custody by making him a cardinal, and by granting to the Hospitallers the possessions of the Orders of the Holy Sepulchre and of St Lazarus, which had been dissolved. In 1484 peace with Egypt was renewed. The Order's security and prestige in the East had dramatically improved, as had its reputation in the West. Aubusson appears to have played a hand in the publicization of the victory of 1480, which the new art of printing facilitated enormously. Even Louis XI, whose interest in the East was not strong, ordered celebrations of the Knights' success. The idea that Rhodes had been saved on 28 July 1480 by miraculous intervention gained popular currency; so, more importantly, did the belief that the island-fortress and its guardians had now proved their worth and deserved support as Christendom's greatest bulwark against the Turks. At a time when attention was fixed on the spectacular achievements of the Castilians in Granada, Aubusson thus reminded the West of what his brethren were doing at the opposite end of the Mediterranean. In a letter written in 1496, he referred to 'our Order, whose function it is in this portion of the Levant to resist [the Grand Turk's] most insolent power'. When the Grand Master died in 1503, his cardinal's vestments were laid on one side of his body, and the armour he had worn in 1480 on the other.

After Jem's death in 1495 the Order's position again became subject to the vagaries of Ottoman court policy on where Turkish power should be directed. Piracy between Christians and Turks grew under the sponsorship of both the Sultan and the Grand Master, and in 1501 the Hospitallers supplied several galleys to the latest naval league formed under papal auspices. But neither Bayezid II nor Selim I attempted a full-scale attack on Rhodes. The Hospitallers' main enemies in the East in the first decade of the new century were the Mamluks, whom they decisively defeated in a sea battle near Alexandretta in 1510. Seven years later the Ottomans extinguished the Mamluk Sultanate, and when Selim I died in 1520 it was clear that another great siege of Rhodes was imminent. A hasty attempt was made to bring the fortifications up to date by the Vicenzan engineer Basil della Scala. The new Sultan, Suleyman the Magnificent, began his reign by conquering Belgrade, and then turned to Rhodes. His siege in 1522 was prepared and executed much more methodically than had been that of 1480. The only power which might have assisted the Hospitallers, Venice, was neutralized by a treaty in December 1521, and the army which landed on Rhodes in July 1522 was very large, and commanded by Suleyman in person. The Grand Master, Philip Villiers of L'Isle Adam, led a strong garrison, probably more than 7,000 men, and the improved fortifications proved their value by holding the Turks at bay in repeated attacks through the late summer and autumn. But the Grand Master knew that the situation was ultimately hopeless. No help was coming from the West, and the Sultan, who could not afford failure, was prepared to winter on Rhodes. The surrender of Rhodes was negotiated in December, and in the first days of January 1523 the Order evacuated the island, ending an occupation which had lasted more than 200 years.

Sailing via Crete and Messina, L'Isle Adam and the survivors of the siege arrived in western Europe in March 1523. It was essential to find a new island base from which the struggle against the Turks could be resumed, and at the end of the year Charles V offered the Order the islands of Malta and Gozo, provided that it also assumed the onerous defence of Tripoli. The offer was not viewed with enthusiasm: a commission sent to inspect Malta reported it to be 'merely a rock of soft sandstone', barren, with no running water, very little wood, and about 12,000 inhabitants, who were mainly miserably poor. There were two excellent harbours, but they were overlooked by hills which would make their defence extremely difficult. There were other snags to the offer aside from the islands' deficiencies and the need to defend Tripoli. The Order would be bound by the terms of the investiture to assist Spain or Sicily if they were attacked, which the French *langue* found unacceptable, and it had to accept the Spanish right to nominate the Bishop of Malta. It was only in 1530, after hopes of reconquering Rhodes with the help of a native rebellion had proved groundless, that Charles V's offer was accepted, 'in order that they may perform in peace the duties of their Religion [Order] for the benefit of the Christian community, and employ their force and arms against the perfidious enemies of the Holy Faith'. The Emperor's emphasis on the war against the Turks was significant, for the Protestant Reformation was already damaging the Order's provincial network and making a resumption of its justificatory role crucial. In October 1530 the exiles sailed to Malta, anchoring in what later became the Grand Harbour.

The following three decades were amongst the most challenging in the Order's history. At a time when the Protestant Reformers were depriving it of its lands in England, Brandenburg, Sweden, and Denmark, the Convent had to shoulder the triple burden of defending Tripoli, contributing to the naval war against the Turks, and providing their main settlements on Malta with a basic defensive structure. These settlements comprised the walled town of Mdina (Città Notabile), in the centre of the island, and the twin promontories of Isola San Michele and the Borgo, which jutted northwards into Grand Harbour, and between them enclosed the port of galleys. The Hospitallers were able to do little more than build a wall along the southern side of the Borgo, of which each *langue* received a separate section to defend, as at Rhodes; they also constructed a fort, St Michael's, in the Isola, and another fort, St Elmo, at the end of Mount Sciberras, which closes in Grand Harbour to the north. By mid-century it had become clear that in the struggle for control of the Central Mediterranean which was in progress between the Spaniards and the Turks, the Order occupied a position whose strategic importance equalled or surpassed that of its former base. Indeed, in 1550 Charles V and Philip II, for whom the Maghrib ranked low in their order of priorities, tried to supplement the Order's commitment at Tripoli by persuading it to take on Al-Mahdiya. But Tripoli was lost to the brilliant naval commander Dragut Reis in 1551, and the Spanish disaster at Jerba in 1560 placed the Order in the Christian front-line. In the spring of 1565 Suleyman sent an armada to attempt the conquest of Malta.

This third great Ottoman siege of the Order's headquarters was characterized by acute dissension amongst the Ottoman commanders, the general of the land forces Mustafa Pasha, and the Admiral Piali Pasha. The siege lasted from May until September. Against the advice of Piali Pasha (the victor of Jerba) and Dragut Reis, Mustafa took the erroneous decision to concentrate on capturing Fort St Elmo. This took a month to achieve, giving Philip II's viceroy in Sicily, Don García of Toledo, the time to organize a relief expedition and, more importantly, to secure his master's permission to send it. In the mean time the Hospitaller defence was ably handled by Grand Master John of La Valette. The Turks lost heavily in taking St Elmo, one fatality being Dragut Reis, but in July and August they launched ferocious attacks on the Isola and Borgo. One of the most severe, on 7 August, was only broken off when a small group of Hospitallers from Mdina raided the Turkish camp, causing a panic in the assault force. Demoralized, and weakened by hunger and disease, the Turks abandoned the siege as soon as news reached them of the arrival of Don García's relief force on 7 September. Appropriately, it was the eve of the Nativity of the Virgin, and later tradition, echoing that of 1480, had the Turks withdraw because they were dazzled by a vision of the Virgin and St John. After a half-hearted attempt to engage the Spaniards on 11 September, the Turks embarked their men and sailed away.

The fact that Malta was relieved points immediately to the chief difference between the Order's new base and their beloved Rhodes, which in 1565 they still hoped to recover (La Valette had been one of the exiles of 1523). 'Malta is the key to Sicily', Don García wrote to Philip II, 'and if it is lost, the defence of your own possessions will have to be at such immense expense that I do not know how it can be borne.' Only this extreme argument persuaded the King to risk the danger of a naval engagement with the Turks so soon after the catastrophe at Jerba. None the less, the point was not lost on the Hospitallers that at Malta, for all its disadvantages, they were much less isolated and self-dependent than they had been at Rhodes, especially in their last century there, when the only Christian power from which they could even hope for major assistance was Venice. At the same time, the ease with which the Sultan had conducted the massive siege of Malta showed that any idea of returning to Rhodes, now deep inside the Ottoman Empire, was hopeless; and this perception was reinforced by the conquest of Cyprus a few years later. Malta, moreover, not only presented an indomitable obstacle to Ottoman control of the Mediterranean seaways, but was well placed for battling the autonomous or semi-independent Muslim corsairs operating from the Barbary coast. It also seems clear that, as in the case of the 1480 siege of Rhodes, the victory of 1565 strengthened the Order's proprietorial feeling for the island itself.

La Valette capitalized on the good will which his Order enjoyed in the aftermath of the siege by soliciting donations to build a new city on the hilly northern side of the Grand Harbour, which would make the Hospitaller position much more defensible in future. *Valletta Umilissima*, begun in March 1566, and incorporating the latest features of European defensive engineering, represented the Order's reconciliation to its new base. From here the Hospitallers resumed the 'guerre de course' and charitable work which made them, as late as the first half of the eighteenth century, the most significant institutional survival of the crusading movement. There are few more striking examples in history of a corporate body retaining its essential goals and characteristics while successfully adapting, albeit with much prodding from others, to a series of changing circumstances. For all their failings and inadequacies, the Hospitallers' prolonged and stubborn defence, first of Rhodes and then of Malta, commands respect. In the last resort the Knights merited the famous eulogy bestowed on them by the Byzantine Emperor Manuel II: 'They are men for whom nothing is more important than what is conducive to good courage, warfare and a noble spirit. To them it is far better to die with glory than to offer their enemies the opportunity of exulting and inflicting wounds on the backs of men who are in retreat.'

8

The Enemy Within:
Crusading against Christians

SOME of the most important crusades in the late Middle Ages were waged against men and women who had been baptized as Catholics. In some cases they comprised groups holding heterodox beliefs, against whom the normal procedures established by the Church for the investigation and suppression of heresy had failed, or could not even be applied. In others they were individuals in possession of secular authority, whose political opposition to the papacy was construed as posing a serious threat to the integrity and faith of the Church. Both forms of crusade, and especially the latter, aroused controversy in their day; and they still provoke lively disagreement amongst scholars of the crusading movement. In this chapter we shall therefore need not only to examine the crusades themselves, but also to give some attention to their historical origins and the polemic to which they gave rise.

In the 1320s the publicist Augustinus Triumphus, posing the question 'Should the Pope send crusaders against tyrants who resist him?', played Devil's Advocate with the reply 'Since they are Christians, tyrants are signed with the cross. Consequently they must not be overthrown by people signed with the cross (*crucesignati*).' Christ's soldiers should not fight against those who had been received into His Church. Augustinus's answer to this criticism was essentially the same as that put forward about seventy years previously by the great canonist Hostiensis, who had written:

If it seems correct that we should promote the crusade overseas (*crux transmarina*), which is preached in order to acquire or recover the Holy Land, then we should use all the more vigour in preaching the crusade on this side of the sea (*crux cismarina*), against schismatics, which is aimed at the preservation of ecclesiastical unity . . . For the son of God did not come into the world or suffer the cross to acquire land but to redeem the captive and to recall sinners to repentance . . .[1]

In essence this argument, which justified all crusading against Christians, was simple: the function of the crusade was to defend Christians and their Church from attack. Such an attack could be launched by malignant Christians, whether they were guilty of heresy, or of rebellion against papal authority, just as easily as it could by pagans; indeed, it would be more severe since the aggressors would be operating within the heart of Christendom itself and would have more chance of disrupting the pastoral and judicial work of the Church.

This was a valid viewpoint and, contrary to what historians once thought, it was expressed at a remarkably early stage in the history of the crusading movement. In the first half of the twelfth century the language, and some of the features of crusading, were in fact applied to Christendom's internal enemies, especially those guilty of schism and brigandage, more rapidly, and to a larger overall extent, than they were to the German frontier with the pagan Slavs. In the years immediately following the First Crusade supporters of Church Reform in the West compared the defence of the Church, which Jerusalem had long been held to symbolize, with the capture of the city itself, while in the late 1130s the chronicler Orderic Vitalis depicted Count Helias of Maine claiming that protecting his own subjects from attack was as meritorious as going on crusade. In 1135 the Council of Pisa granted a full crusade indulgence for fighting against King Roger of Sicily and the Antipope, and four years later indulgences were guaranteed to all who fell while fighting the bands of brigands (*routiers*) who were troubling southern France. Yet while the Germans' struggle against the Slavs was validated as a crusading front during the Second Crusade, no full-scale crusade against Christians seems to have been proclaimed until the reign of Innocent III. Then in 1199 came the release of crusade indulgences for Innocent's war in Sicily against the German adventurer, Markward of Anweiler, a grant usually portrayed as the first crusade against a Christian lay ruler. And nine years later the Pope declared a crusade against the cathars and their protectors in Languedoc, the first crusade against heretics.

It remains hard to be sure what persuaded Innocent to take steps which his predecessors over the course of nearly a century had failed to take,

---

[1] N. Housley, *The Italian Crusades: The Papal–Angevin Alliance and the Crusades against Christian Lay Powers, 1254–1343* (Oxford, 1982), 63.

although clearly tempted to do so. Three factors can be pinpointed which certainly played a role in his decisions in 1199 and 1208, though the precise significance of each, and the relationship of one to another, remain problematic. First, the crusade itself was a much more stable and better-defined institution by 1199 than it had been at the time of the Second Crusade. The Decretists (early canon lawyers) had given much-needed attention to the functions of the crusade, the responsibility of the papacy for its proclamation, and the nature of the crusade vow itself. In essence, this made it comparatively easy for Innocent both to declare crusades against Christians, and formally to justify his actions. It also introduced the need for the Curia to formulate a crusading policy, especially to relate the 'internal crusade' to that in the East.

Important as they were, these juridical developments would have led nowhere had local conditions in Languedoc and southern Italy not persuaded Innocent that military action on the scale of a crusade was imperative. In Languedoc, this meant the threat posed by a powerful and missionary cathar church, coupled with the failure of the region's political overlord, King Philip II of France, to take the lead in suppressing it. The resulting war, the Albigensian Crusade, lasted twenty years and undoubtedly exerted a great influence on papal thinking about the *crux cismarina*. The lessons of the crusade caused the Fourth Lateran Council (1215) to frame the decree *Excommunicamus*, which established a mechanism for the use of the crusade against any secular lord who neglected to purge his lands of heresy when asked to do so by the Church. Just as important, the crusade induced at the papal Curia an ongoing and deep concern about heresy spreading in conjunction with political opposition to the Church. This meant that charges of heresy often entered into conflicts between the Curia and secular powers which were, in origin, territorial in nature. Historians have been quick to condemn such charges as trumped up, failing to appreciate either the extent to which politics and religion overlapped, or the atmosphere of fear which prevailed at the Curia in the thirteenth and fourteenth centuries in relation to the danger of heresy, and which regularly burgeoned into a feeling of crisis.

This is not to say that territorial disputes were unimportant: indeed, the third factor which lay behind Innocent III's actions in first deploying the *crux cismarina* was his determination to give solid expression to the papacy's claims to direct rule over the patrimony of St Peter in central Italy, and to an effective suzerainty over the Kingdom of Sicily (see map 8). These claims were long-standing: in the case of central Italy they dated back to donations made by the Frankish kings in the eighth century, while a claim to suzerainty in the south lay behind the investitures of the Norman princes and kings, beginning in 1059. What enabled Innocent to make a determined attempt to enforce them was the fortuitous death of the young Emperor Henry VI in 1197, which removed imperial opposition to papal claims in Italy and left the *Regno* in the hands of Henry's infant son Frederick. By his death in 1216 Innocent had created a viable principality in central Italy, and had acted with vigour to place the *Regno* more firmly under papal authority. For the rest of the thirteenth and fourteenth centuries a major plank of papal activity was the maintenance or restoration of this temporal power, and it involved the repeated deployment of the crusade against those rulers who impeded the Curia's agents and allies. To some extent the obsession with land as sacred *patrimonium*, which always characterized crusading in the Holy Land, had been transferred to Italy: it was no coincidence that Innocent III gave the fullest articulation to the idea that the pope exercised a 'vicariate of Christ' on earth, and that the Papal State was referred to as 'the inheritance of the Lord', and 'the patrimony of the crucified one'. But for the most part the importance of defending the papacy's temporal possessions was phrased in terms akin to Hostiensis's argument: that these lands were crucial to the effective government of a centralized Church, and hence to the Church's mission of saving souls.

This was a fairly abstruse argument, and there was a danger that Innocent III and his successors, in embracing the idea of an 'internal crusade', would work counter to popular opinion. The danger was less apparent in the case of crusading against heretics than in that of crusading against lay powers: some contemporaries who appreciated the overriding need to destroy the cathar threat did not view the defence of papal lands and rights in the same light. That this was true is clear from the criticism which, as we shall see, was levelled at the popes. It also explains the strenuous efforts which the Curia made to broaden the basis of such crusades by describing the material damage which its enemies were inflicting on the Italian church, and the way in which they hindered planning for a crusade to the East by tying down the resources of the papacy and its allies in Italy. Because of the inherent paradox of crusading against Christians, and the skill displayed by the pope's political enemies in making propaganda use of it, people always had to be convinced of its necessity.

Innocent III's grant of crusade indulgences against Markward of

Anweiler in 1199 began a pattern of crusades associated with the *Regno* which persisted throughout the thirteenth century. In 1239 Pope Gregory IX declared a crusade against the Emperor Frederick II, the erstwhile protégé of Innocent III who had, ironically, become one of the most powerful opponents the medieval papacy encountered. Thanks to Frederick's possession of the *Regno* as well as the Empire, the crusade against him was broadly based, with fighting in Italy and Germany. But it was inconclusive, and after the Emperor's death in 1250 crusade indulgences had to be issued almost immediately against his son Conrad IV. After Conrad's death four years later his half-brother Manfred built up his position in southern Italy and came to pose as serious a threat to the papacy's temporal power as his father had done. The desperate Curia invested Charles of Anjou, brother of St Louis, with the Sicilian Crown. Charles led a substantial army of French and Guelf (pro-papal) crusaders against Manfred, defeating and killing him at the battle of Benevento in 1266. Two years later the last of the Staufen, Conrad IV's son Conradin, invaded Italy from Germany, and was defeated by Charles at Tagliacozzo. The capitulation of Frederick II's Muslim colony at Lucera in 1269 brought to an end thirty years of crusading against the Staufen and their supporters.

When the Second Council of Lyons assembled in 1274 the recent history of the *crux cismarina* thus made a striking contrast with that of the *crux transmarina*: to Clement IV, the intellectual and rather neurotic pope who presided over the Angevin invasion of 1265–6, Charles's victories had proved that God supported papal policy in Italy. Although Charles's activities in central and northern Italy caused some concern at the Curia, they could not be compared with the stranglehold exerted by Frederick II and Manfred; and as we have seen in previous chapters, Charles had ambitions in Palestine and *Romania* which were to a large extent in accordance with papal policies there. However, these ambitions contributed to Charles's downfall, through the enemies which they made and the heavy taxation which they entailed in the *Regno*. The Sicilians in particular suffered from a combination of fiscal oppression and governmental neglect, and at Easter 1282 they rebelled against French rule. In the background to the revolt lay an anti-Angevin conspiracy, its chief protagonists the Byzantine Emperor and King Peter II of Aragon, who had married Constance of Staufen, Manfred's daughter, when the latter was at the height of his power in 1258. Peter II thus had dynastic reasons for hostility towards the papal-Angevin settlement, and when the Sicilians offered his wife the crown of the *Regno* he accepted, landing at Trapani with his army in August 1282.

The resulting struggle, the War of the Sicilian Vespers, lasted twenty years. From all points of view, the duration of hostilities, the number of important powers which became involved in it, the geographical spread of the conflict, the scale of its battles on land and sea, and the expenses incurred by the combatants, it was a big war. From January 1283, when Pope Martin IV granted crusade indulgences against the rebels, the conflict took the form of a series of crusades. This was virtually inevitable. There could of course scarcely be a more pro-Angevin pope: as Simon of Brie, Clement IV's legate in France, Martin had played a key role in organizing the Angevin invasion of 1265–6, especially in cajoling the French church into paying for the expedition through taxes. Simon's election as Pope in February 1281 was all but engineered by Charles, and we have seen that he granted his vassal crusade indulgences for his planned *passagium* to Constantinople. But Martin IV's undoubted partisanship should not disguise the fact that the Sicilian revolt, coupled with the Aragonese intervention, presented the Curia with little choice but to declare a crusade. Unless Sicily was restored to Angevin rule the political settlement which had cost so much to achieve twenty years previously —and nobody knew better than Martin IV what the cost had been— would be destroyed, and the papacy's temporal power all but nullified. The situation was just as grave as it had been in the worst days of the Staufen threat: indeed, Martin's bulls make it clear that he regarded the war as a continuation of the earlier struggle.

In February 1283 the Aragonese crossed the Straits of Messina and took the war into Calabria. It was clear that Angevin resources alone would not be sufficient to defeat the rebellion, and the Pope sent a legate to the French court to offer the throne of Aragon to King Philip III's younger son, Charles of Valois. Negotiations were successful and in February 1284 Philip accepted the Crown of Aragon on behalf of his son. In retrospect this papal transfer of a great kingdom to a foreign prince without even consulting its inhabitants appears painfully high-handed. The popes had enjoyed feudal suzerainty over Aragon since 1204, but it was a formal overlordship, and the emphasis of Martin's deposition of Peter II was on a general papal authority to transfer kingdoms because of wrongful actions by their rulers, coupled with an implicit reference to the decree *Excommunicamus*. Once again, however, Martin IV's actions are explicable as much in terms of the difficulty of the overall situation as in those of his French patriotism; for Peter II had no enemies in Iberia strong enough to overthrow him, and Philip III would only undertake the invasion and occupation of Aragon if victory would bring with it a substantial accretion of Capetian power. Politics and geography thus conspired to lead Martin IV into an attempt to repeat the great French successes of 1265–8.

These events briefly shifted the focus of the war from southern Italy to the Franco-Aragonese frontier. Philip III recruited a crusading army of about 8,000 men and crossed the Pyrenees in the spring of 1285. The expedition was one of the Capetian monarchy's biggest military undertakings, and it proved to be disastrous. Peter II declined battle and the French army spent more than two months besieging the fortress of Gerona. No sooner was Gerona taken than news arrived of the destruction of much of the French fleet at Las Hormigas by Catalan galleys commanded by Peter II's brilliant Admiral, Roger of Lauria. Roger proceeded to land troops at Rosas and cut Philip's supply route. It was now autumn and the crusading army, under constant harassment by Catalan irregulars (*almugavars*), retreated across the Pyrenees. On 5 October Philip died of fever at Perpignan. Events had gone no better in Italy: in a naval battle in the Gulf of Naples in June 1284 Charles of Anjou's son and heir, Charles of Salerno, was captured together with most of the Neapolitan fleet. Charles of Anjou himself had suffered reverses in Calabria and abandoned the province before dying at Foggia early in 1285.

With the failure of Martin IV's project for a French conquest of Aragon, the war entered a decade characterized by continued fighting in southern Italy and complex negotiations to restore peace. While Charles of Salerno was in captivity the embattled *Regno* was governed by regents, Count Robert of Artois and Cardinal Gerard Bianchi. They received the full support of the Curia in stemming the Aragonese advance, and even attempted an invasion of Sicily in 1287. In the following year Charles was released, and he was crowned in 1289 by Pope Nicholas IV. Charles II was granted bulls renewing crusade preaching, but the new King of France, Philip IV, was not prepared to maintain hostilities with Aragon, and without the weight of French power behind the papal-Angevin alliance the two sides were too evenly balanced for a military solution. In 1291, under pressure from his nobility, Alfonso III of Aragon sealed the treaty of Brignoles. This ended the Franco-Aragonese war and left Sicily, now in the hands of Alfonso's younger brother James, to its fate. Alfonso's premature death in June 1291 robbed the treaty of effect, for

James succeeded him as King of Aragon and initially resolved to hold on to Sicily. But in practice James was no more able to do this than his brother had been, and in 1293 he reached agreement with Charles II at Figueras for the surrender of Sicily in exchange for massive compensation.

For more than two years after the death of Nicholas IV in April 1292 the Curia had been able to do little to influence the struggle for Sicily; there had been a two-year interregnum, followed by the extraordinary reign of the unworldly hermit-pope, Celestine V. When Celestine resigned the new Pope, Boniface VIII (Benedict Caetani), resumed a more vigorous policy. At the Caetani palace at Anagni, in June 1295, Aragon's disengagement from Sicily was finalized and a peace settlement between Philip IV, Charles II, and James II was arranged, to be sealed by a series of dynastic marriages. But the Sicilians would not accept the restoration of Angevin rule, and they persuaded James II's younger brother, Frederick of Aragon, to take the crown. The Angevins, supported by fresh crusade bulls against the Sicilians, cleared the mainland, but despite help now furnished by James II (including galleys commanded by Roger of Lauria), the reconquest of Sicily eluded them. A major invasion in 1299–1300 failed to regain more than Catania and a few fortresses. Confronted by this stalemate in Sicily and by anti-papal (Ghibelline) uprisings in northern and central Italy, Boniface VIII once again turned to France, calling in an army under Charles of Valois. In May 1302 these troops reached Sicily, where they engaged in combined operations with the Catalan-Angevin fleet and Angevin soldiers led by Charles II's son, Robert. The allies besieged the south-coast port of Sciacca, but no progress was made, disease broke out in the army, and at the end of August Robert made peace with Frederick at the village of Caltabellotta.

The peace of Caltabellotta ruled that Sicily would revert to the Angevins at the death of Frederick of Aragon. Boniface VIII insisted that until then the island should be held as a fief of the Church (with the title 'Kingdom of Trinacria' so that the mainland provinces could retain that of Kingdom of Sicily), subject to Frederick's payment of a heavy annual tribute of 15,000 florins. In the event, Frederick quickly became an ally of the Ghibelline powers and hostilities between himself and Angevin Naples reopened. King Robert of Naples, who succeeded Charles II in 1309, launched several big expeditions against Sicily without success. But although Frederick and his heirs failed to pay their tribute money, and tied down Angevin resources which the Curia desperately needed further north, Boniface VIII's successors refused to reopen the crusade against

Sicily. They realized that the Angevins simply lacked the strength fully to subdue the island, and they were terrified of a repetition of the financial nightmare which the long war had become. For together with contemporary conflicts in Flanders and Gascony, the War of the Vespers epitomized the soaring costs of large-scale military endeavour, and the strain which they imposed on all concerned, whether rulers and subjects, employers and paid troops, bankers and borrowers, or military allies. In fact the crusade against the Sicilians played a decisive role in transforming the apparatus of extended Church taxation for crusade purposes which was tentatively established by Gregory X at the Second Lyons Council, into a reasonably efficient, if bitterly resented, structure.

One of the most important long-term consequences of the protracted Sicilian war was thus the solid bureaucratic shape which it gave to the papacy's taxation of the western Church for crusade purposes. Another was the fact that it made the Curia more keenly aware of threats to its temporal power, and readier to respond to these with the weapon of the crusade. It has been suggested that the second consequence followed on naturally from the first, in that the proclamation of a crusade made possible, or greatly facilitated, the levy of taxes generically associated with crusading; in reality, thanks to the length of time it took to gather in money through clerical taxation, this was only the case when the Curia was committed to a long war. On other occasions the quicker resort to the crusade, which became a prominent feature of the period after 1282, was the result partly of the loss of Angevin military backing on the scale which could be expected before the Vespers, and partly of greater sensitivity about temporal power *per se*, and the 'status Romane ecclesie' generally. The importance of both factors was made clear in two lesser crusades of the period, those against the Colonna in 1297 and the Venetians in 1309.

The crusade against the Colonna family, especially the Cardinals James and Peter Colonna, was in one sense the culmination of a fairly typical clash of territorial ambitions between the Caetani and Colonna families in the Roman Campagna. In this instance, however, the clash overlapped with a severe division of opinion about papal policy (the Colonna Cardinals wanted to leave Sicily in Aragonese hands), and was placed by the Colonna in the context of doubts about the legitimacy of Boniface VIII's election. The open breach which occurred in May 1297, when Stephen Colonna seized a Caetani treasure convoy, therefore rapidly escalated into a Colonna denial of Boniface's authority, and the Pope's condemnation of the rebels as schismatics. A short but grim period of warfare in the Campagna followed, including the declaration of a crusade in December. The castle at Colonna itself fell in July 1298, and the great fortress of Palestrina was surrendered in October. The Colonna sought terms and their power in Campagna was dismantled. The crusade graphically illustrated how far the ripples from the Sicilian war spread, and the tension which they created within the Curia.

The crusade against the Colonna resulted from a threat to the Roman church coming, unusually, from within; that against the Venetians which Clement V declared in 1309 was the response to a more characteristic, external, danger to the fabric of the papacy's temporal power. The death in 1308 of the *signore* of Ferrara, Azzo VIII of Este, was seized by Venice as the chance to assert control over the city, by backing the succession of Azzo's natural son, Fresco. Ferrara lay within the Romagna, the northernmost and most turbulent province of the Papal State, and Clement V supported Azzo's brother Francesco. In April 1309 the Pope dispatched one of his favourite cardinals, Arnold of Pellegrue, as legate to restore papal sovereignty over Ferrara, including amongst Pellegrue's powers that of preaching a crusade. Through a mixture of able leadership, luck, and Venice's domestic problems, Pellegrue was successful, and the campaign was effectively over by the autumn of 1309. The severity of Clement V's response to Venice's intervention is somewhat surprising. The city was not a traditionally Ghibelline power and the crusade made available relatively few extra resources in men or money: more significant was the papal declaration that Venetian vessels and goods could be lawfully seized. Possibly Clement was more attuned to thinking in crusading terms at this point in his reign because of the expeditions in Spain and the East which were being assembled; certainly he regarded the Venetian seizure of Ferrara as a grave challenge to the Curia's temporal power, the worst, he asserted in 1311, for twenty years.

Arnold of Pellegrue's success in beating off this challenge, coming as it did in the aftermath of the failure to reconquer Sicily and the humiliating assault on Boniface VIII at Anagni, was undoubtedly important in raising morale at the Curia. As a crusade fought under the war leadership of a powerful cardinal-legate, in defence of the Papal State against the territorial aggression of an Italian regional power, the campaign of 1309 ushered in a pattern which characterized most of the crusades waged by the papacy against Christian rulers during its Avignonese exile (1305–78). The chief political determinants of this pattern emerged in the wake of Henry VII's *Romzug* of 1310–13. On the one hand, there was a group of tyrants (*signori*) in Lombardy and Tuscany who were engaged in the difficult process of regional state-building and were eager to incorporate cities from the Papal State into their lands; for political and cultural reasons such men, including the Visconti dynasty at Milan, Raynaldo Bonacolsi at Mantua, Cangrande della Scala at Verona, and Castruccio Castracani at Lucca, were Ghibellines, who maintained contact with claimants to the imperial crown in Germany. Within the Papal State itself there were *signori* of smaller towns, like the Montefeltro at Urbino, who rebelled against papal sovereignty. On the other hand, there were traditional Guelf powers, like Florence and Naples, which enjoyed important economic ties with the papacy and each other, as well as sharing political goals. Both Ghibellines and Guelfs saw the usefulness of military co-operation, and in practice this bound the local conflicts together into an intricate patchwork of military activity.

The deployment of the crusade in this struggle hinged largely on papal decisions to invest heavily in attempts to impose stability on to central and northern Italy, in order that the Curia could return from its exile at Avignon. The first such attempt was made by Pope John XXII, who in 1319 sent Cardinal Bertrand du Poujet to Italy as his legate. For the next fifteen years Poujet conducted large-scale military operations against the tyrants in Lombardy and Romagna. At the end of 1321 John XXII issued crusade indulgences both for Poujet's campaigning against Matthew Visconti and the Estensi lords of Ferrara, and for the struggle which papal officials were waging against rebels in the eastern provinces of the Papal State. Three years later new bulls were issued against the sons of Matthew Visconti, Raynaldo Bonacolsi, and rebel communes in the March of Ancona. The papal forces, together with troops supplied by Florence and King Robert of Naples, enjoyed some successes, such as the defeat of Matthew Visconti and Frederick of Montefeltro in 1322, but these were local or short-lived. In general the Ghibelline *signori* were too many and too resilient, and their military leadership too able, for even the combined efforts of the Guelf triad to subdue.

The struggle in Italy was complicated by a new papal-imperial dispute. In 1322 Louis of Bavaria defeated his rival for the German crown, Frederick of Austria, at Mühldorf. Louis refused to accept John XXII's claims regarding his candidature and was excommunicated in 1324. The arrival of the Emperor-elect in Italy three years later to secure his coronation brought the situation in the peninsula to the point of crisis. Early in 1328 Louis was crowned at Rome and inaugurated a short-lived schism by creating an antipope. Together, the Emperor, the various Ghibelline *signori*, and King Frederick of Sicily seemed capable of holding Bertrand du Poujet's forces in check, invading the *Regno*, and forcing Florence to come to terms. A crusade was declared against Louis in January 1328 and renewed during the following year. Internal tensions and the death of its ablest commander, Castruccio Castracani, impaired the effectiveness of the Ghibelline coalition, and Louis left Italy in 1330. But at this point of triumph one of the recurring weaknesses of Avignonese policy in Italy became apparent. The Curia had powerful allies, and the financial resources to field large armies of its own, but it was liable, partly because of its distance from Italy, to make serious political miscalculations. In this instance John XXII gave his support to a plan for the creation of a north Italian kingdom, to be held as a papal fief by King John of Bohemia, the son of Henry VII. The idea brought Ghibelline Milan and Guelf Florence into temporary alliance, and caused the destruction of all Bertrand du Poujet's gains in Lombardy. When John XXII died in December 1334 the first major series of Italian crusades since the War of the Vespers had failed to achieve their objectives: Bologna, the key to papal control of the Romagna, had been lost just nine months previously, and there could be no question of the Curia returning to Italy.

It was not until 1353, when Innocent VI sent Cardinal Gil Albornoz to Italy as legate, that the Curia made another sustained attempt to restore order in the Papal State. Albornoz was tenacious, ruthless, and a great castle-builder: he built or strengthened seventy-two fortresses in the Papal State. Lands thus reconquered and held down were subjected to widespread administrative and legal reforms. Albornoz succeeded in pacifying the Papal State's western provinces in 1354–5, but in the Romagna he encountered the strong opposition of Francis Ordelaffi, lord of Cesena and Forlì, and of the Manfredi family of Faenza. In the winter of 1355–6 Innocent agreed to the preaching of a crusade against Ordelaffi and the Manfredi, and in 1356 the Manfredi went over to the papal side. At this point Bernabò Visconti became so alarmed at Albornoz's successes that he sent assistance to Ordelaffi in the shape of Conrad of Landau's army of mercenaries. The preaching of a crusade against Landau's troops in 1357 signified a new development in the Italian political scene. The crusade was not particularly important in itself—Albornoz bought the German commander off in August—but it was the first in a series of crusades proclaimed against one of the period's greatest scourges, the mercenary companies.

Autonomous, well organized, soundly equipped, and often brilliantly led, the companies were a new feature of European warfare, brought into existence by its growing professionalism. They presented commanders like Albornoz with an irresolvable dilemma: hiring the companies was the only way to achieve important military goals, but once dismissed, the companies turned on their former employers and either pillaged the area or extracted huge sums of 'protection money' to leave a locality. They were thus able to profit from the inherent instability of Italian politics, and during the 1360s the Curia alternated between two contrasting policies. On the one hand, it attempted to use the companies to gain the upper hand over its enemies. The Visconti *signoria* was now recognized as the chief obstacle to the pacifying of the Papal State, and Urban V tried to destroy it by declaring crusades against Bernabò Visconti in 1363 and 1368. On the other hand, Urban tried to bring the Guelf and Ghibelline powers together in a league to expel the companies from the peninsula. The latter policy characterized the years 1364–8, when there was peace with the Visconti, and it was hoped that the companies could be persuaded to take part in the crusades to the East which were being planned or executed by such rulers as Peter of Cyprus, Amedeo of Savoy, and Louis of Hungary. In France too the period after the peace of Brétigny (1360) was marked by appalling harassment of the French countryside and towns by dismissed troops, and the Curia regularly granted crusading indulgences to people who died defending their lands against the *routiers*. Only after the renewal of Anglo-French hostilities in 1369 furnished the companies with legitimate employment again did relative peace return.

In 1361 the city of Avignon itself was threatened by the companies, and Innocent VI in desperation declared a full-scale crusade against them. Episodes like this, together with other *routier* threats to Avignon in 1357, 1363, 1365, 1366, and 1375, confirmed the Curia in its belief that any expense was worth while to restore its authority in central Italy and so facilitate its return there. In 1367 Urban V went to Viterbo, but he found Rome unsafe, and in 1369 there was a serious rebellion at Perugia. The city hired the company of Sir John Hawkwood, and although the revolt was suppressed, with crusade preaching against both the Perugians and their hired soldiers, Urban fled back to Avignon in 1370. Seven years later Gregory XI entered Rome, but it cannot be said that either Albornoz, or any of his many successors as legate under Urban V and Gregory XI, had brought to the Papal State the degree of central control and internal order attained in other territorial states of northern Italy. In addition, they had failed to break the hold of the Visconti lordship in western Lombardy, while the final disintegration of the Guelf alliance, which had never regained the strength which it enjoyed in the 1320s, occurred in 1376 with the outbreak of war between the Pope and Florence.

When Gregory XI died in March 1378 the cardinals, under pressure from the Roman mob, elected an Italian, Bartholomew Prignano, as Pope Urban VI. Urban rejected the oligarchic government which had prevailed at Avignon, and his determination to rule alone, aggravated by his unstable personality, drove the cardinals in September to declare his election invalid and to elect one of their number as Clement VII. The Great Schism, which tore Latin Christendom apart for the next thirty-nine years, gave rise to the last major series of crusades against Christian lay powers. In November 1378 Urban VI proclaimed crusade indulgences against Clement's supporters, and following this the popes of both obediences regularly attempted to encourage their adherents by declaring crusades against their rivals' supporters. Historically, the association of schism and crusade was a natural one. Quite apart from crusades against the Orthodox Greeks and Russians, what appears to have been the earliest application of a crusade indulgence to warfare between Christians (1135) occurred in the context of the Anacletan Schism, and we have seen that Boniface VIII's crusade of 1297–8 against the Colonna Cardinals arose partly from their schismatic rejection of his authority.

In terms of the body of opinion and theory which was soon formulated about the best means to bring the Schism to an end, crusading against the rival obedience was seen as the practical application of the *via facti* ('voie de fait'), the achievement of that goal by military means. But to raise large armies both obediences needed the assistance of secular rulers; and since the origins of the Schism lay not in doctrinal divergence but in the constitutional deficiencies of the Roman church, allegiance, in the case of many European countries, was dictated by existing political configurations. Particularly important was the allegiance given to Clement VII, who resumed the Curia's earlier residence at Avignon, by France and its allies. England reacted by supporting Urban VI, with the result that in both countries the national animosity already characteristic of the Anglo-French war was sharpened and justified by the belief that the enemy was schismatic. As William of Courtenay, the Archbishop of Canterbury, put it in 1383, 'the Church cannot have peace without the realm, nor can the well-being of the realm be secured except through the Church, and it is both meritorious to fight for the faith, and fitting to fight for one's lord'. The result was a form of 'national crusade' similar to the wars waged by the kings of Spain and eastern Europe against the Moors and Lithuanians, with the difference that the enemy was Christian.

If the Great Schism did not produce the extraordinary spectacle of armies of English and French soldiers, *crucesignati* against each other, clashing on the battlefield, it was mainly because it straddled the central and least violent decades of the Anglo-French war, between the Reconquest of Charles V and the campaigns of Henry V. As it was, crusade preaching was utilized by the rival governments in the context of the several expeditions which they sponsored between 1382 and 1386 in the hope of 'outflanking' the national enemy, or of gaining additional resources for the struggle. They all ended in fiasco. Thus in 1382 Clement VII granted crusade indulgences to Frenchmen who joined the banners of Louis of Anjou for his great expedition to the Kingdom of Naples, whose Clementist ruler, Joanna, had been ousted by the Urbanist Charles of Durazzo. Louis achieved little and died in Italy in 1384. In 1383 Henry Despenser, the warlike Bishop of Norwich, secured the permission of the royal council to lead a crusade to Flanders to aid an Urbanist revolt against the French. His army enjoyed initial successes but retreated ignominiously when a French relief army appeared. Then three years later John of Gaunt, titular King of Castile through his marriage to Constance in 1371, led a crusading army to Castile to attempt its conquest. It was a fruitless expedition, and after a patched-up settlement with his enemies Gaunt left Iberia in 1387.

By this point the English and French courts were disillusioned with the *via facti* as a means of ending the Schism and gaining the upper hand in their own dispute; as we saw in Chapter 2,[2] they soon turned to the crusade against the Ottomans as the culmination of an alternative programme of peace and unity in Christendom. Unable to rely on the resources of Europe's leading military powers to fuel their conflict, the rival obediences found commanders and manpower wherever they could. Typical was an attempt by Urban VI to persuade William I of Guelderland, a crusading enthusiast, to lead a crusade against the Clementist French in 1388, which appears to have come to nothing. Similarly, in 1397 Urban's successor at Rome, Boniface IX, put forward an abortive plan to bring an English force to Italy led by John Holland, the Earl of Huntingdon. In 1409 the Council of Pisa, which was attended by cardinals from both obediences, tried to end the Schism by deposing both the

---

[2] Above, 73–5.

Roman Pope, Gregory XII, and his Avignonese rival, Benedict XIII, and electing its own pope, Alexander V. The ploy failed as neither Gregory nor Benedict would accept the Council's decision. Benedict XIII came to depend almost exclusively on Spanish support; this brought about his involvement in the struggle for the Aragonese succession between Ferdinand of Antequera and James of Urgel, in the course of which (1413) Benedict proclaimed a crusade against James. But it was Alexander V's successor, the belligerent John XXIII, who proclaimed what seems to have been the last of the Schism's many 'internal crusades', when he granted indulgences against his enemy King Ladislas of Naples in 1411. Ladislas made peace with John XXIII in 1412, but in 1413 the King seized Rome. The crusade against Ladislas was renewed in the spring of 1414, on the eve of the Council of Constance. Three years later the Council brought the Great Schism to an end with the election of Cardinal Oddo Colonna as Pope Martin V. Relations between popes and councils became very bad in the following decades, but the only occasion on which they degenerated to the level reached during the Schism was in 1447, when Nicholas V attempted to enlist French support against the Basle Council and its Antipope, Felix V, by offering Charles VII crusade indulgences if he would invade Savoy, Felix's homeland and his chief source of support.

One of the most pressing problems confronting Martin V in 1417 was the spread of Hussite unorthodoxy in Bohemia (see map 9). Since the destruction of catharism in the thirteenth century heresy had not posed a threat serious enough to warrant crusade preaching on a large scale. There had been a short and localized crusade against the followers of the Joachimite preacher Fra Dolcino in Piedmont in 1306–7, but for the most part the Curia relied on the machinery of the Inquisition, granting partial indulgences to laymen who assisted its work; sometimes these volunteers grouped into confraternities, such as the 'Company of the Cross' which the inquisitor Conrad of Germany founded at Bologna in 1450. That Hussitism could not be dealt with in the same manner was due to the deep roots of doctrinal unorthodoxy itself, the heresy's gradual association with Czech national sentiment, and the structural and personal weaknesses of royal government under the Luxemburg dynasty.

The Bohemian reform movement, from which Hussitism germinated, originated in the reign of King Charles IV (1346–78), when the preachers Conrad Waldhauser and John Milič fiercely denounced the abuses of the Church and called for religious revival. Both men were summoned to the

Curia at Avignon, and in the normal run of events the call for change, which was widespread in Europe at this time, would not have led to heresy in Bohemia, let alone the need to attempt its suppression by crusading. What made the situation in the Czech lands uniquely explosive was a confluence of factors in the period following 1378. First, the Great Schism both exacerbated corrupt practices within the papacy and in the Church at large, and weakened the normal machinery for the investigation of unorthodox beliefs; the outcry against abuse thus became more vociferous and less subject to control. Secondly, the vigorous and pious Charles IV was succeeded by Wenceslas IV, a king whose personal deficiencies were compounded by the strong support given to the reform movement by the well-entrenched Bohemian nobility. Thirdly, the philosophical and theological ideas of the English heresiarch, John Wyclif, began to find an eager reception at the University of Prague, partly because they gave intellectual rigour and coherence to Bohemian reform thinking, and partly because of the national rivalry within the University between the dominant Germans and the Czech masters. The former espoused nominalism, and the Czechs seized on Wyclif's ultra-realism as a means of attacking and even ousting their enemies: 'Haha, Germans, haha, out, out', one Czech wrote in the margin of a Wyclif manuscript.

John Hus was born in about 1369 and graduated at Prague University as MA in 1396. By this point Prague, and Bohemia generally, were extremely turbulent, and Hus became the focal figure in the reform movement because he bridged the academic and non-academic worlds: he became Dean of the University's Arts Faculty in 1401, and in the following year was appointed resident preacher at the Bethlehem chapel, a popular centre for lay reform. The 3,000 sermons which Hus preached at the chapel during the next twelve years were delivered in Czech, a symptom of the growing polarization between Czech reformers and German opposition, which was destroying the racial harmony Charles IV had tried hard to maintain. Hus brought together the main strands of the doctrine which his enemies later christened with his name, above all that Christian belief should be based on concentrated and constant study of the Bible, that religious practices and institutions not in accordance with the tenets of Scripture should be ended, and that the Christian's faith should be strengthened by frequent, ideally daily, participation in the eucharist. From the latter derived one of the most characteristic and persistent demands of the Hussites, that laymen, like priests, should take communion in both forms ('in utraque specie', hence the word often used to describe Hus's followers, utraquists).

In 1408 Archbishop Zbyněk of Prague finally took action against the propagation of Wycliffite ideas, partly because of pressure exerted by the Roman Pope Gregory XII. Even at this late stage the spread of unorthodoxy in Bohemia could have been contained, in the same way that English Lollardy was suppressed, but for the political ambitions of Wenceslas IV. The King wanted to transfer Bohemia's allegiance from the Roman obedience to the Council of Pisa, in order to secure the Council's support against his rival for the Empire, Rupert of the Palatinate. To get the influential backing of Prague University for this step he needed to end the hegemony of its German masters, whose personal interests favoured Bohemia's continuing allegiance to the Roman obedience. By the decree of Kutná Hora, in January 1409, Wenceslas therefore gave the Bohemian 'nation' (i.e. the Czech masters) a majority of votes within the University. The decree had far-reaching consequences: Archbishop Zbyněk, who refused to abandon the Roman obedience, resigned in 1410; the last chance to stop the reform movement becoming heretical by the use of normal procedures had passed; and an enduring fusion of reforming sentiment and national feeling had come about.

When agents of Pope John XXIII arrived in Prague in 1412 to preach the crusade against Ladislas of Naples, they seemed to Hus and his supporters to epitomize the papacy's corruption. Hus's condemnation of the crusade led to his major excommunication in 1412, and two years later he was summoned to defend his views at the Council of Constance, under the security of a safe-conduct. Here the full unorthodoxy of Hus's beliefs emerged, and he was condemned and burned in July 1415. It was a disastrous step, for Hus's followers immediately regarded him as a martyr, and his cruel death outraged and united a broad cross-section of the Bohemian community; 452 nobles of Bohemia and Moravia set their seals to a letter to the Council in September 1415 asserting that Hus had been unjustly killed. Developments in Bohemia during the five years that followed the execution were complicated, but it was obvious that the country was sliding into religious revolution. The decrees of the Council were flouted and the practice of utraquism became common. In southern Bohemia there took place a number of extraordinary open-air masses on hill-tops, signs of an extremist wing developing within the reform movement; its adherents rejected such basic features of Catholic belief as purgatory and the intercession of the saints.

Today it is clear that like the Protestant Reformation, which it resembled to a far greater degree than it did earlier medieval heresies, the Hussite movement was a broad-based and shaky coalition. Apart from the important pockets of Catholic allegiance which long persisted, especially on Bohemia's western rim, between Pilsen and Cheb, the utraquists themselves ranged from conservative critics of the Church, including nobles and academics, to the radical reformers, some of them also social revolutionaries, who founded the town of Tabor, south of Prague. Indeed, Hussitism's gravest weakness was that whenever the threat from outside lapsed, internal discord erupted into civil war, as in 1424 and 1434. Foreign observers at the time, however, saw the movement as a monolithic and serious threat to both religious orthodoxy and social order; they were obsessed with Tabor, a centre of fervent theological debate and liturgical innovation which one historian has described as 'the great incubator of heresy'. Cardinal Henry Beaufort, echoing earlier papal pronouncements, wrote of a 'rabble flowing to Bohemia to add evil to evil from amongst the wretches in every kingdom whose aim is to subvert and throw down both faith and human society', and he claimed that the Hussite leaders were fighting 'not only the faith but alle polytyke rewle and gouernance, steryng the peple to rebellione and disobeisaunce of her lordes and gouernours'. The terror of radical Hussitism spreading, which Professor George Holmes has aptly compared to the fear of Bolshevism in the years after 1917, helps to explain both the high level of expenditure which Pope Martin V was prepared to devote to anti-Hussite measures, and the readiness of Bohemia's German neighbours to raise armies to destroy the heresy. The eagerness of the German authorities in this respect formed a curious contrast to the consistent lethargy which they displayed in the face of the Ottoman advance.

What made such intervention by the papacy and the German princes both possible and necessary was the political situation which developed in Bohemia in 1419–20. King Wenceslas was able to do little to prevent the spread of utraquism, or the seizure of ecclesiastical property which went with it, and which formed part of its appeal to the Czech nobility. A half-hearted attempt at disciplining the reformers in 1416 failed, and when another such attempt was made three years later it provoked a crisis. In July 1419 John Želivský, a radical utraquist, led a riot in Prague in which thirteen of the city's Catholic magistrates were thrown out of the Town Hall's windows (the first 'defenestration of Prague'). Wenceslas died of shock and his brother, Sigismund of Hungary, the Emperor-elect, succeeded him. This event enabled the Hussite leaders to formulate a series of religious and political demands in the early autumn of 1419, and to make their allegiance to Sigismund contingent on his accepting them. The demands included the exclusion of all Germans from administrative posts in Czech areas, and the hearing of court cases in Czech.

Misjudging the situation, Sigismund decided to go to Bohemia at the head of a large army. To raise it he held a *Reichstag* at Breslau (Wroclaw) in the early months of 1420. As early as 1414 the conciliarist Dietrich of Niem had suggested that a crusade might be necessary to destroy Hussitism, and in 1418 Martin V had empowered Cardinal John Dominici to preach a crusade should Sigismund intervene in Bohemia. At the Breslau *Reichstag*, in March 1420, Sigismund welcomed a papal legate, Bishop Ferdinand of Lucena, who proclaimed a crusade against the 'Wycliffites, Hussites, other heretics, and those favouring, accepting, and defending such heresies'. Sigismund's experience of crusading armies was not a happy one and he could only have resorted to this step with great trepidation. In fact the precise political context of the Hussite crusades was all-important: Sigismund had to impose his authority on an extremely unstable and fractious country; his Hungarian resources were limited and, in any case, largely tied down in containing the Ottomans; he therefore needed to call on the help of the German princes, which he was entitled to do since he was Emperor-elect and the Crown of Bohemia lay within the Empire; and to rouse the princes into action he was prepared to accept the Pope's appeal that heresy be suppressed by military means. The problem was that these means were to prove woefully inadequate, five great crusades ending in failure or disaster.

Sigismund's expedition in 1420 was the first of these débâcles. The threatened invasion had the effect of rallying the Hussites, and the government of Prague assumed responsibility for co-ordinating resistance with a message in which Martin V's crusade bull was condemned as 'a vile and venomous serpent's egg hatched by this church, who has long before shown herself to be not a mother but a vicious stepmother to the Czech people'. This was the first in a significant series of manifestos in which the two themes of reform and national sentiment were fused in the crucible of common defensive action. In the campaign which followed a decisive role was played by the Taborites, commanded by the finest Hussite general, John Žižka, and by soldiers from another radical settlement at Mount Oreb, the Orebites. Sigismund initially tried to take Prague but in July suffered a defeat to the east of the city, at Vitkov Hill. He was crowned

king in St Vitus's Cathedral in Hradčany Castle, which was held by the
Catholics, but then withdrew south-eastwards to Kutná Hora, an important German settlement. Here the crusaders incurred a more serious
defeat on 1 November. In March 1421 the King retreated from Bohemia.
Just as grave for Sigismund as these military set-backs was the consolidation of the Hussite movement which occurred at the Diet of Čáslav in
June 1421: the adoption of the 'Four Articles of Prague' as an expression
of Hussitism's basic tenets, and the repudiation of Sigismund's claim to
rule.

In the late summer of 1421 a second crusade was launched, at the
initiative of a new legate, Cardinal Branda of Castiglione, and of the
German electors, especially the three Archbishops of Mainz, Trier, and
Cologne. One army, commanded by Frederick of Meissen, won a victory
over a Hussite army led by John Želivský in August, but a larger German
force invading from the Upper Palatinate was routed after an unsuccessful
siege of Žatec in September–October. Sigismund had planned to invade
Moravia at the same time as these attacks in the north, but it was only in
October 1421 that his army took the field. It was a substantial force and
was commanded by the able Florentine *condottiere* Pipo Spano. The
crusaders gained Kutná Hora but were repulsed by John Žižka in terrible
winter fighting at the beginning of 1422. A third crusade under Margrave
William of Meissen and the Elector Frederick of Brandenburg was
launched in the autumn of 1422. Circumstances were propitious, for
fighting had broken out between the Taborites and the moderate reformers; John Žižka himself had moved from the Taborite to the Orebite
brotherhood in 1422 because the former had become too extreme. But
the crusade's leaders were so cautious that they achieved little, and the
expedition had petered out by the end of the year.

Caution was a natural response to the repeated set-backs of 1420–2,
though the unreliability of contemporary commentators on the subject of
figures makes it impossible to form an accurate assessment of German
losses. The defeats were due partly to the lacklustre leadership, indiscip-
line, and bad co-ordination which dogged most of the crusade armies.
But of equal or greater importance were the excellent generalship of John
Žižka and the tactical innovations of the Hussites. Their religious revolution was saved by a military one. Especially important was their use of a
mobile barrier of wagons as a shelter. The Hussite war wagon began as an
improvised defence for Žižka's vulnerable infantry, one which he may
have seen in use in Poland. But when the wagons were given additional

protection, and the rectangle they formed was strengthened by ditches, a virtually impregnable shield resulted, which could be rapidly dismantled when the counter-attack began. The war wagons made it possible to use artillery in the field, and the skilful co-ordination of cannon, handguns, and crossbows became a hallmark of Hussite tactics. Another important innovation, battle flails, also started life as an improvisation, derived from the numbers of peasants in Žižka's army who were initially armed only with the flails which they used to thresh grain.

The impressive military ordinance which Žižka drew up, probably in July 1423, laid heavy emphasis on proper organization and obedience to orders; even his battle song, 'You Who Are the Warriors of God', made basic points about military discipline:

> You all must remember the password
> As it was given to you.
> Always obey your captains.
> Each shall help and protect the other.
> Each shall look for and stay with his own battalion.

The same song, interestingly, expressed neo-crusading ideas:

> Christ will reward you for what you lose,
> He promises you a hundred times more.
> Whoever gives his life for Him
> Will gain life eternal.
> Blessed everyone who stands by the truth.[3]

Solidly based as it was on this combination of tactical finesse, skilful organization, and religious zeal, the military superiority of the Hussite forces did not end with Žižka's death in 1424. His followers at Mount Oreb, who now called themselves 'the Orphans', continued to win battles, while the Taborites were led by another brilliant commander, Prokop the Bald.

After the failure of the third crusade against the Hussites there followed a four-year lull. Then, in January 1427, Frederick of Brandenburg agreed with the Bishops of Bamberg and Würzburg to organize another expedition; this they termed a 'spiritual tournament' (*spirituale torneamentum*). Martin V appointed Cardinal Henry Beaufort, the powerful Bishop of Winchester, as legate for the new crusade and detailed plans were formulated at a *Reichstag* held at Frankfurt in the spring. It was the most ambitious of the crusades, planned as a fourfold attack on Bohemia.

[3] F. G. Heymann, *John Žižka and the Hussite Revolution* (Princeton, NJ, 1955), 497–8.

In the event only two armies materialized, those of Archbishop Otto of Trier and Frederick of Brandenburg. In July the crusaders laid siege to the strategically important town of Stříbro, in western Bohemia, but they fled in confusion when a Hussite army approached. Wagons which had been brought in the hope of imitating Hussite tactics were commandeered to effect a quicker getaway. Not only was the crusade itself a total débâcle, but the Hussites used the opportunity to besiege and take the town of Tachov, which contained the second-strongest royalist fortress in western Bohemia.

Beaufort, who had done all he could to stop the rout, was appalled at the unreliability of the German princes and the lack of spirit of their troops. While an unsuccessful attempt to revive the crusade was being made in Germany, the idea was therefore put forward of broadening the basis of opposition to the Hussites by bringing in other European powers. During the early months of 1428, when Beaufort was at the court of Philip the Good, plans were evidently discussed for a joint English, French, and Burgundian crusade, strikingly reminiscent of that projected in the early 1390s in response to the Turkish threat. Detailed and ambitious memoranda were drawn up by Guillebert of Lannoy in 1428–9, and although Burgundian intervention came to nothing, Beaufort secured the permission of the Lancastrian Regency Council to raise an English army to fight in Bohemia. Once again there was a strong echo of earlier events, in this instance Bishop Henry Despenser's 1383 crusade to Flanders, as Beaufort set about arranging crusade preaching and recruiting his force of 250 spears and 2,000 archers. But after Talbot's defeat at Patay in June 1429 the troops were needed in France. The horrified Martin V had to instruct Beaufort to stop using his legatine insignia while fighting Charles VII's soldiers.

In the three years following the disaster of 1427, as plans for bringing other powers into the anti-Hussite conflict failed, while Sigismund was fully preoccupied with the struggle against the Turks in Serbia, the military initiative passed to the Hussites. Abandoning their hitherto defensive stance, they used this chance to launch a series of devastating raids into the lands of their Catholic neighbours. These razzias were given the chivalric epithet 'beautiful rides', and they were carried out with the threefold purpose of sustaining the radical brotherhoods of Tabor and Oreb through the collection of booty, exacting revenge for the damage inflicted on Bohemia by the crusaders, and putting pressure on Sigismund to give in to the political and religious demands of the Hussite leaders. In

Silesia the attacks were so destructive that they were a major factor in bringing about a secular collapse in the region's rural economy. After the failure of negotiations with Sigismund at Bratislava in the spring of 1429, the armies of Tabor and Oreb executed the greatest of the 'beautiful rides', five armies ranging at will through Saxony-Meissen, Franconia, and the Upper Palatinate. To save Nürnberg from attack, Frederick of Brandenburg made far-reaching concessions to the Czech commanders. In the following year the Hussites defeated a Hungarian army near Trnava, and with Polish help made substantial gains in Silesia, as well as some religious converts. By the end of 1430 it was clear that the Hussites must either be destroyed or allowed their demands.

Neither Sigismund nor Martin V was yet prepared for the latter course of action. The Pope appointed Cardinal Julian Cesarini as legate to prepare a fifth crusade, and in February and March 1431 an impressive *Reichstag* at Nürnberg decided on the recruitment of a massive army, 33,000 strong. As in 1427, it was to be supported with artillery and battle wagons modelled on the Hussite example, and on this occasion the crusade's organizers tried to ensure better discipline with a detailed military ordinance, possibly also based on Hussite precedents. In late May 1431 Sigismund made an unsuccessful attempt to reach an agreement with the Hussites at Cheb. Cesarini's energy and charisma were the principal motive forces in bringing about the invasion of Bohemia in July by four separate armies. For the first time there was a degree of co-ordination between the two armies invading from the Palatinate and Bavaria, the Silesian–Lusatian force approaching from the north, and the Austrians, under Sigismund's son-in-law Duke Albert V, in Moravia. The German armies represented many of the leading princes and cities of the Empire. The Austrian troops made some gains in Moravia, but the main army under Frederick of Brandenburg and Cesarini displayed the same fatal weaknesses which had plagued previous crusades. In August it was routed by the Hussites near Domažlice, in circumstances of paralysis and confusion not very different from those of 1427.

In view of the painstaking preparations which had preceded it, it is not surprising that this latest disaster caused almost irreparable damage to the policy of ending the Bohemian crisis by force. A week before the crusade invaded Bohemia the Council of Basle opened, and in 1433 leading utraquists accepted an invitation to attend and argue their position. Bohemia was war-weary, and its nobility and urban patriciate were alarmed by the political pretensions of the radical brotherhoods.

But the Hussite leaders at first pressed for obligatory utraquism through-out Bohemia and Moravia, which the Council rejected because it would include Catholic areas such as the *Landfrieden* of Pilsen. The resulting impasse was broken by developments within Bohemia. As on previous occasions, the absence of external attacks allowed dissension amongst the Hussites to erupt into open conflict, and in May 1434 the field armies of the radical brotherhoods were crushed at Lipany by an army representing the Czech nobility and its supporters. The way was now open for Sigismund to come to terms with the moderate utraquists at Jihlava in Moravia in July 1436, when he accepted the 'Compacts of Basle', a watered-down version of the 'Four Articles of Prague'. These grudgingly permitted the lay chalice to all who wished it, but were silent or vague on other Hussite demands like infant communion and lay preaching. The compromise enabled Sigismund to enter Prague and rule Bohemia until his death in December 1437.

Sigismund's political problem had been solved but the religious issue remained open, for the Compacts were not ratified by either Pope or Council. The great utraquist Archbishop of Prague, John Rokycana, presided over a church in a condition of autonomy and semi-reformation, in which Catholics and moderate utraquists worshipped alongside radical Taborites, at least until the subjugation of Tabor in 1452. After the extinction of Sigismund's dynastic line in 1457, George of Podiebrady, a utraquist landowner from eastern Bohemia, was elected king. The Curia under Pius II put pressure on George to abandon the Compacts, and Pope Paul II was tempted by the internal opposition which the King faced, and by the ambition of George's son-in-law, King Matthias Corvinus of Hungary, to attempt once again to apply a military solution to Hussitism. Appeals for a crusade came from Breslau, and indulgences were granted in 1465 to stiffen Catholic resistance. Then at Christmas 1466 Paul II deposed George and denounced him as a heretic, and soon after ordered the preaching of a full-scale crusade against him in Germany and Silesia. Preaching was probably just as intensive for this crusade as for the earlier anti-Hussite ventures. From 1468 until his death in 1471 George fought an inconclusive war against Matthias, who was supported by Bohemia's Catholics. The nobles of Bohemia then elected a weak king, Wladyslaw of Poland, and in 1478 the Kingdom was partitioned between Wladyslaw and Matthias. But the Compacts remained the foundation of religious practice in many parts of Bohemia. The papacy had therefore failed to suppress doctrinal error by force. Its only consolation was that earlier fears of Hussitism spreading beyond Bohemia had not materialized, partly because of its close association with Czech nationalism, and partly because the Hussites lacked the great advantages which printing would give to the Protestants.

The failure of the Hussite crusades showed, of course, that successful crusading against heretics depended on favourable political and military conditions. But even when such conditions existed, the crusade was a problematic weapon to use. This was clearly demonstrated by a crusade launched against the Waldensians in the French Alps in 1488. The Waldensians followed the teachings of a twelfth-century preacher, Valdès. He himself had been orthodox, but his ideas had been subjected to a radical interpretation which the Curia had condemned as heretical. In the Alpine towns and villages, where they were densely clustered, the Waldensians possessed their own church, as well as lay magistrates who organized a communal resistance to the Inquisition. During the mid-1480s John Baile, Archbishop of Embrun, was taking methodical action, but this was necessarily slow, and in April 1487 Pope Innocent VIII appointed Albert Cattaneo, Archdeacon of Cremona, as special inquisitor for the Dauphiné, Savoy, and Piedmont. Cattaneo had permission to preach a crusade, and at the end of 1487 the French court instructed its governor of the Dauphiné to support this action. Troops supplied by the governor, together with crusaders wearing a white cross on their right shoulders, engaged in military operations both east and west of the Alpine passes in March and April 1488. Although the crusaders were victorious, it cannot be said that their crusade was a success. It was not effectively followed up by the Inquisition, and Waldensian beliefs persisted in the Alps into the sixteenth century. And although the operations were small-scale—only about 160 suspected Waldensians were killed—they were of necessity brutal, arousing considerable local sympathy for the heretics. Furthermore, the victims of the crusade claimed that the legal proceedings had been irregular, and in 1509 the *grand conseil* at Paris quashed all the earlier sentences and ordered the restitution of property seized.

By this point crusading against Christians had ceased to be the major constituent of the crusading movement which we have been examining so far in this chapter. A few grants of indulgences can be found, such as those which Sixtus IV issued against Basle at the end of 1482, when the city became a centre for heterodox preaching. As in the past, too, there occurred some instances of over-zealous legates who took measures of which the Curia itself would not have approved. In July 1460, for example, Pius II's legate to England, Francis Coppini, raised the papal standard at the battle of Northampton, and granted the Yorkist troops the crusade indulgence, because the Earl of Warwick had convinced him that the defeat of Henry VI was essential if England was to participate in Pius's planned crusade. Although ardently pro-Yorkist himself, Pius was not prepared to go this far in their support and later had Coppini tried on grounds of favouritism. But it is striking that the Curia in the post-conciliar period seems to have chosen not to use the crusade against its political opponents within Christendom, even though the wars which it was waging in Italy were no less continuous, intensive, and costly than in the fourteenth century. As we saw in Chapter 3,[4] the Curia was becoming obsessed with the Ottoman threat, and it may have resolved to restrict crusading elsewhere.

In the sixteenth century, by contrast, there occurred something of a revival of 'internal crusading', both in the context of the papacy's involvement in dynastic warfare, and in that of the period's religious upheavals. Julius II made some grants of indulgences to his own troops fighting in Italy; it was these grants which Erasmus excoriated in his brilliant satire, 'Julius exclusus'. The Pope also granted the soldiers of Henry VIII crusade indulgences for the English King's planned invasion of France in 1512. In rich contrast, England's role in the Reformation meant that an anti-Henrician crusade was being discussed in 1533–4. Similarly, in 1546 Gianmaria Del Monte, an experienced canonist and Paul III's legate at the Council of Trent, considered the possibility of declaring a crusade against the Protestant princes of the Schmalkaldic League. Five years later, as Pope Julius III, Del Monte wrote of his intention to preach a crusade against Henry II of France because of Henry's alliance with the Ottomans, while in 1556 the unbalanced Paul IV threatened Charles V and Philip II with a crusade. More importantly, as we shall see in Chapter 10,[5] the Spanish Armada of 1588 was conceived as a 'Counter-Reformation crusade', and as late as 1600 the Earl of Tyrone and his followers were granted crusade indulgences to assist their rebellion against Elizabeth I. This is an impressive list of actual or projected crusades, and it will doubtless grow longer as more instances come to light. But they remain isolated examples. Few of them had military consequences, and they cannot be compared with the many important crusades outlined in the previous pages. It would probably be

[4] Above, 99–100.   [5] Below, 319–20.

fair to characterize the period from the wars against Frederick II in the 1240s, to the anti-Hussite expeditions of the 1420s, as the heyday of the *crux cismarina*.

It was during these two centuries, therefore, that the papacy had to incorporate its crusades against Christians into its overall crusading policy. Most importantly, this entailed establishing an order of priority between the *crux cismarina* and the *crux transmarina*, and the Curia's approach was that the crusade within Christendom must be concluded before a crusade against the Muslims in the East could be launched. This was of course in line with Hostiensis's argument, quoted at the start of the chapter, that the threat from within the Church was more serious than that from without: but in practice this rather severe viewpoint was softened by the claim that the *crux cismarina* prepared the way for a crusade to the East. Not surprisingly, this claim found its fullest expression during the War of the Sicilian Vespers, both because the surviving Christian holdings in Palestine and Syria were falling at this time, and also because the ports, galleys, and other resources of the *Regno* would be exceptionally valuable for a rescue crusade to the Holy Land. Thus when organizing the crusade against Peter II of Aragon in 1283, Martin IV accused Peter of frustrating the implementation of the crusade decreed at the Second Lyons Council; and in 1300 Boniface VIII placed the Italian expedition of Charles of Valois in the broadest of contexts: 'When Sicily has been stabilized, and the other rebels in Italy subjugated and restored to obedience to ourselves and the [Holy] See, it will be possible more usefully and efficaciously to provide opportune aid for the Holy Land.' But the same themes of priority and linkage were expressed again and again in the late Middle Ages. There is, for example, Pope Gregory XI's very concise statement of policy in 1372, when he wrote to King Louis of Hungary that 'depositio tyrannorum est dispositio passagii': 'deposing the tyrants [i.e. the Visconti] is a preparatory measure for the *passagium* [against the Turks]'. And almost a century later Pius II, replying to criticism from the cardinals that his wars in Italy had stood in the way of the crusade against the Turks, asserted that 'We fought for Christ when we defended Ferrante [of Naples]. We were attacking the Turks when we battered the lands of Sigismondo [of Malatesta, lord of Rimini].'

What did this policy mean in practice? In the first place, the Curia proved reluctant to promote expeditions to the East at a time when it wanted to conserve crusade resources for the *crux cismarina*. Thus in 1363 Urban V assured Cardinal Albornoz that 'we will not permit the preaching of the cross for an overseas expedition . . . until the matter of the said heretic [Bernabò Visconti] has been brought to a successful conclusion . . . '. Secondly, the vows of people who had taken the cross for service against the Muslims were sometimes commuted so that they would fight instead against Christian enemies of the Church. Such commutation was a leading feature of the anti-Staufen crusades, and although it later became less common, there are some instances for the fourteenth century. Similarly, when *crucesignati* redeemed their vows, the proceeds were on occasion used to finance the *crux cismarina*. But by far the most striking and persistent characteristic of papal policy was the siphoning off into crusades against Christians of money which had been given for crusades to the East. Some of this constituted sums donated in the form of alms and legacies. At various points during the War of the Vespers money given for the crusade to the Holy Land, in the *Regno*, France, and England, was diverted into the struggle against the Sicilians. But such amounts were overshadowed by the Curia's use against Christian enemies of clerical tenths which had been levied and collected for the crusade to the East. The most spectacular instances of this related to the six-year tenths decreed at the Second Council of Lyons in 1274 and the Council of Vienne in 1312. Large amounts of the Lyons tenth disappeared into the financing of the Sicilian war, while much of the Vienne tenth subsidized John XXII's crusades against the Ghibelline powers in Italy. In 1319 John even assigned to the Italian conflict ten galleys built or hired with the proceeds of the Vienne tenth and intended for service in the East. Attempts were made to justify such actions. John XXII wrote to Philip VI of France in 1332 of the pope's authority, in cases of emergency, to redirect money from one pious purpose to another; and Innocent VIII argued in 1487 that it was justifiable to deploy money raised against the Turks in order to engage rebels in the Papal State, since the latter could have formed dangerous alliances with the Ottomans. But the Curia knew that it was vulnerable to the charge of wholesale fraud. John XXII himself implicitly acknowledged this when he claimed that money used from the Vienne tenth would eventually be made good.

It is important to consider criticism of the *crux cismarina* against this background because much hostile comment was directed not at the crusades themselves but at this policy and its consequences. The distinction is subtle but crucial. It is undeniable that numerous voices were raised in protest both at the order of priorities adopted by the Curia, and at the misuse of crusade funds so often associated with it. The voices belonged to four groups of individuals. First, messengers from the Latin East who came to the West, in circumstances of crisis, to beg for aid were disturbed to find that their needs were not given priority at the Curia. Secondly, western rulers who wanted to lead a crusade East, like Edward I of England in the 1280s, and several French kings in the fourteenth century, put pressure on the Curia to change its approach. In this they were encouraged by crusade propagandists like Marino Sanudo Torsello and Philip of Mézières; Marino Sanudo in particular was eloquent and active in arguing that papal policy should be reversed. Thirdly, the tax-paying clergy objected strongly to the duplicity practised by the Curia in diverting crusade tenths and subsidies. And fourthly, the Christian enemies of the Curia found in its own policy a stick with which to beat it. Naturally they asserted too that they were eager to lead, or join, an expedition to the East if given reasonable peace terms by the pope. This was a constant refrain of the Aragonese kings during the War of the Vespers and of the Italian Ghibellines in the Avignonese period, as well as their supporters, such as Bartholomew of Neocastro during the Sicilian war, and Marsilius of Padua at the court of Louis IV. Individuals with no specific political axe to grind, but with strong antipapal sentiments, such as the Ghibelline poet Ottokar of Steiermark, also took the Curia's crusading policy to task, some of them even laying responsibility on the popes for the disasters which were occurring in the East.

Historians have been slow to recognize that this large and articulate chorus, expressing disapproval of certain prominent aspects of the papacy's crusade policy, shrinks dramatically in size when one looks for critics of the validity of the *crux cismarina* itself. It is the fourth group, the Curia's enemies and their adherents, which then dominates the sources. They all asserted that crusading against Christians was a fundamental perversion of the crusade, but apart from this the arguments which they deployed varied considerably, in accordance with their religious stance and beliefs. The orthodox Sicilians and Aragonese, who were consistently careful to avoid the charge of showing contempt for the papacy's spiritual authority (*contemptus clavium*), claimed only that the Curia was waging an unjust war and hence misusing that authority. As Bartholomew of Neocastro put it, 'We fear Holy Church and, since we are Christians, we accept her as our mistress and mother. But we hate the priests, because they are our enemies and hate us, not because of our sins but because they love the French.' By contrast, some of the Ghibelline *signori* argued that the spiritual authority of the popes was negated by its misuse, and described the crusade indulgences as worthless. The Hussites went further: they regarded the crusades declared against them as symptomatic of a corrupt papacy, which some of their extremists portrayed as the Antichrist of the Book of Revelation. In this they followed Hus's own condemnation of Pope John XXIII's crusade against Ladislas of Naples, as well as the bitter criticism levelled against the Bishop of Norwich's Flanders crusade by Wyclif and the Lollards. As the 'Lollard Conclusions' of 1394 put it, 'it is indeed robbery of poor folk when lords get indulgences from punishment and guilt for those who aid their army to kill a Christian people in distant lands for temporal gain'.

Whatever the precise line of attack which they employed, the Curia's enemies possessed certain distinct advantages in criticizing the use of the crusade against them. All crusades in the late Middle Ages involved atrocities, such as the killing of innocent people, but those committed in the course of crusading against Christians were acted out within Christian countries rather than on the periphery of Christendom. They were therefore better publicized and caused more distress, and this tended to reinforce doubts about the wisdom of sanctioning such activity. It has been observed that the second half of the fourteenth century witnessed a sharper perception of the horrors of warfare, especially in the context of the Anglo-French conflict and the wars fought by papal armies in Italy. As Christopher Allmand put it, 'not so much the existence of war as the manner of fighting it . . . aroused the criticism of an increasingly outspoken body of persons'. The crusade generally benefited from this growing sensitivity in so far as writers like Philip of Mézières advocated dispatching the most brutal agents of war, the *routiers*, to fight the infidels; but the *crux cismarina* suffered, because the shedding of Christian blood at clerical command was increasingly distasteful. This seems to have been particularly the case during the Hussite expeditions, in which the crusaders regularly ignored the contemporary laws of war in an attempt to coerce the utraquists into submission. As a chronicler at Magdeburg noted during the first Hussite crusade, 'whoever was taken prisoner on either side, for him there was no other outcome but an inhumanly bitter death'.

Most crusades against Christians were unsuccessful, and this too worked to the advantage of the Curia's enemies and critics, who depicted military failure as a sign of divine disapproval. 'You must know, father', Bartholomew of Neocastro has a Sicilian hermit say to Pope Nicholas IV, 'that as often as you have taken up arms for the French, the invincible power of Jesus Christ has fought for the Sicilians.' Similarly, as disaster followed disaster in the Hussite crusades, the idea gained ground that God did not favour the crushing of the utraquist heresy by force. As we have seen, the fifth Hussite crusade was a last attempt at a military solution before discussions with the heretics started at the Council of Basle. This points to what was probably the biggest difference between crusading against Christians and that against non-believers. In the case of the former, since the antagonists shared a common political culture, the alternative of a lasting, peaceful settlement always seemed feasible, provided that both sides would make some concessions. For these reasons *crux cismarina* could never become simply another form of crusading: it was always *sui generis*.

This does not, however, mean that it was unpopular. If the widespread criticism of the Curia's crusade policy had reflected a rejection of *crux cismarina* in itself, or if the propaganda of the Curia's enemies had won the day, we would not find the degree of acceptance which greeted the preaching of such expeditions. Measuring the result of preaching is always a difficult procedure, and analysing the motivation of people who responded by taking the cross or donating money is, perhaps, even more hazardous. To give one relatively minor but illuminating example, the most recent student of the 1488 crusade against the Alpine Waldensians has concluded that its most prominent supporters, far from being altruistic *milites Christi*, were 'a gang of institutionalized plunderers, who exploited the heresy laws ruthlessly for their own gain'. As a result of their activities the proverb was formed that 'their heresy was in their wallets; and if they had been poor, they would never have been accused of such things'. But notwithstanding these problems of assessment and inter-pretation, three points about the response to the preaching of the *crux cismarina* can be made.

One is that, while the sources for our period do not reveal the degree of popular enthusiasm which had marked some earlier crusades against Christians (such as that against the Romano *signoria* in northern Italy between 1255 and 1260), there are a few instances which do bear compar-ison; most importantly, the extraordinary response to the preaching in England of the Flanders crusade in 1382–3, and the popularity of indul-gences granted for engaging the *routiers* in fourteenth-century France and Italy. Secondly, the response which was encountered on other occa-sions was, as far as we can see, as great as that for contemporary crusades against Muslim powers: comparing, for instance, the War of the Vespers with *passagia* to the Holy Land, the Avignonese crusades against the Ghibellines with the Smyrna expedition, and the Hussite wars with crusading against the Ottomans. Thirdly, there is no evidence that those who took the *crux cismarina* regarded their crusade as being inferior to an equivalent expedition against the Muslims in the East or in Spain, or against the pagan Slavs. On the contrary, service in a crusading expedition against Christians, like these other forms of crusade, was assimilated into the chivalric culture of the period as a valued and laudable expression of knightly prowess. French men-at-arms in the later thirteenth century equated their service with the Angevin forces in Italy with participation in St Louis's crusades. In 1363–5 the young Thomas Beauchamp considered Urban V's anti-Visconti crusade as one of several crusade fronts on which he might fight. John Holland, the Earl of Huntingdon, who fought in John of Gaunt's crusade of 1386–7 and negotiated with Boniface IX for another anti-Avignon crusade in 1397, also played a prominent part in the discussions which lay behind the Nicopolis expedition, and was a patron to Philip of Mézières. Clerics like Cardinal Julian Cesarini and the Franciscan Observant Angelo Carletti of Chivasso preached the crusade against heretics and Turks with equal enthusiasm and commitment.

Of course it can be argued that individuals who eagerly embraced the theory and practice of the *crux cismarina* were as exceptional as those who condemned them. Given a setting as diversified, intellectually alert, and constantly changing as late medieval Europe, any general conclusion on what 'public opinion' thought of crusading against Christians runs the risk of being simplistic. A wide spectrum of response was possible, within not only nations, social groups, and families, but individuals: a man may have accepted Boniface VIII's argument that the recovery of the Holy Land hinged on that of Sicily, but objected to that Pope's crusade against the Colonna; another may have agreed with Hus that John XXIII's crusade against King Ladislas was testimony to the Church's internal corruption, while later supporting the crusade against Hus's own followers. But the older view that this form of crusading was essentially a deviation from the true type of crusade, or a perversion of the crusade ideal, is untenable in the light of its historical evolution, its strong institutional similarity to other forms of crusading, and, above all, the popular response to its preaching. Arguments *e silentio* are always suspect in medieval history, but there can be no doubt that a much richer and more representative body of criticism would exist had the *crux cismarina* met with the kind of response historians once supposed.

9

The Iberian Peninsula: The Rewards and Problems of Conquest, 1274–1415

✠

WHEN the Council of Lyons assembled in 1274 Castile, Aragon, and Portugal, the principal Christian states of Iberia, could look back on a recent crusading history which stood in sharp contrast to the run of disasters which their contemporaries had experienced in the Holy Land and *Romania* (see map 10). Following the decisive defeat of the Almohad army at Las Navas de Tolosa in 1212, at the hands of a mainly Castilian and Aragonese force, the territorial impasse which had characterized the *Reconquista* since the time of the Second Crusade was broken. The rulers of all three peninsular kingdoms made substantial gains. King James I of Aragon seized the Balearic Islands between 1229 and 1235, and overran the Kingdom of Valencia in 1232–45. Sancho II and Alfonso III of Portugal effectively completed the Portuguese *Reconquista* by extending their lands as far south as the coast of the Algarve. Most spectacularly, Ferdinand III of Castile brought under direct control Extremadura, Murcia, and much of Andalusia, including the great urban prizes of Córdoba (1236) and Seville (1248). From 1246 the Emirate of Granada endured tributary status to Castile, and as early as 1227 Ferdinand entertained hopes of carrying the war across the Straits of Gibraltar into Muslim North Africa. Within two decades about a third of the peninsula and its population had been transferred from Islamic to Christian hands, and the balance of power between the two contesting religions had been fundamentally and irrevocably altered.

The aftermath of these spectacular events played a dominant role in shaping Christian–Muslim relations in Iberia throughout the decades covered by this chapter. The conquests were a formidable act to follow, and according to the Castilian 'Primera crónica general' the dying

Ferdinand III told his heir, Alfonso X, that he would do very well if he managed simply to hold on to what had been won. Securing extra gains of a substantial nature was to prove virtually impossible because of the innate strengths of Granada and a resurgence of Islamic unity and aggressiveness in Morocco. Moreover, assimilating what had been won was difficult, especially for the Castilians, while relations between the Christian states could never be better than uneasy, thanks to the massive growth of Castile. Henceforth all Christian alliances against the Muslims— the *sine qua non* for a major crusading effort—proved to be short-lived and vexatious in character. In 1299 James II of Aragon informed Pope Boniface VIII that only by partitioning his overweening neighbour could the final defeat of the Moors be achieved. Renewed crusading activity certainly occurred in the later thirteenth and fourteenth centuries, and was sometimes on an important scale; but much of this period's interest lies in the absorption of what the 'conquest generation' had achieved, and in the emergence of a new political configuration in Iberia.

The *Reconquista* has been well characterized as 'at once a crusade against the infidel, a succession of military expeditions in search of plunder, and a popular migration', and to be successful in the long term the crusaders' conquests had to be followed by a large influx of Christian settlers. The need was less pressing in areas where the Muslims sur- rendered after the agreement of capitulation documents which allowed them to retain their lands under Christian lordship, as was the case for much of Valencia. But even in Valencia rebellions led the kings of Aragon to attempt repopulation by Christians. This was not as easy as it had once been, despite such enticements as the indulgences offered by Pope Gregory IX to all who would populate the lands conquered by James I. In the 1270s James I complained that while the security of Valencia called for a minimum of 100,000 Christian households, only 30,000 had come. So while the urban centres of the Kingdom came to contain chiefly Christian inhabitants, the Valencian countryside continued to be popu- lated mainly by Mudejars, Moors living under Christian government. Given this fact, one of the most impressive features of the Valencian reconquest is the rapidity with which the regular and secular Church was implanted there: by the mid-1270s a full parish network existed, and Professor Robert Burns has brilliantly described 'the waves of friars, contemplatives, military monks, canons, parish priests, and nuns, trans- ported like a numerous garrison into this borderland', giving 'tangible shape to the Christian self-image, making it a living thing'. In conquered

Majorca, too, Catalan settlement was generally restricted to the island's towns and lowland areas.

Castile, whose size had doubled, faced an even more daunting task. In towns and their surrounding areas economic attractions brought many southwards, and detailed *repartimientos* reveal a pattern of successful colonization in the form of smallholdings (*heredamientos*), at the demographic expense of Old Castile. In other, less favoured, regions the Castilian government was compelled to bestow huge blocks of land (*donadíos*) on two groups which benefited more than any others from this phase of the *Reconquista*: the Military Orders and the great noble families. The chief Iberian Orders had been founded in the late twelfth century as a means of providing assistance for the hard-pressed urban militias holding the Guadiana basin against the Almohad threat: Calatrava in 1164, Santiago in 1170, Alcántara shortly before 1176. They had proved more useful in garrisoning strongholds and resettling border areas than in providing troops for Christian field armies, and this undoubtedly encouraged the Castilian monarchy to grant them enormous estates in La Mancha and Extremadura, as well as parts of Andalusia and Murcia. The authority of the three Orders was regularly recognized in royal charters and laws, in which the king spoke of 'my land and that of the Orders', and it was displayed in the ability of the Military Orders to prevent any other monastic Orders from gaining a foothold in these upland areas. Both the nature of the terrain and the relatively few settlers who came southwards encouraged the Orders to develop the pasturage potential of their new lands, in what Professor C. J. Bishko described as 'an explosive expansion of the ranching industry of the plains'. The long-term result was profound: Castile's economy became geared to the export of raw wool to Flanders, and the import of cloth and other manufactured goods in exchange. The Aragonese monarchs too were generous in their grants of land to the Orders in the economically less attractive northern zone of Valencia.

The Castilian monarchy was well aware of the dangers of making these very large grants to the three Military Orders, and took steps to stop them abusing their power. One such was Alfonso X's strengthening of the 'Real Concejo de la Mesta' in 1273, which gave royal protection to the various arrangements adopted by Castilian towns for the seasonal migration of their flocks to the grasslands of La Mancha and Extremadura. This was an answer to attempts by the Orders to prevent northerners sharing their winter grasslands. But although the masters of the Orders inevitably became involved in Castile's political struggles, they never posed the kind of danger which the nobility did. This was mainly because of the Crown's close control over appointments to masterships, so that kings succeeded in getting their own kinsmen or protégés elected to these posts, or in prolonging vacancies to their own benefit. For example, the Master of Santiago between 1342 and 1358 was an illegitimate son of Alfonso XI; the same king had the Master of Alcántara put to death in 1339; and in 1354 Peter I had one master of Calatrava deposed and chose his successor. In fact, by making the masterships posts of such value the Crown robbed the Orders of any independence of action they still possessed. In 1408–9 the regent Ferdinand acquired the masterships of Alcántara and Santiago for his sons; as both were minors this enabled Ferdinand to control the revenues involved. Similarly, the Orders' corporate spirit was subordinated to the national identity of their brethren, so that Calatrava split into Aragonese and Castilian branches during the war between the two countries in 1356–66. Thus the vast additional resources gained by the Orders in the second half of the thirteenth century were not capitalized on as fully as one would expect.

The same cannot be said of the nobility. Royal grants of estates, lordships, and towns in the conquered lands of the south were augmented in the later thirteenth century by purchases from smallholders abandoning their land. The Andalusian magnate clans thus acquired a political and economic stranglehold which they were still exerting in the Córdoba region a century and a half later. In terms of both local dominance and court politics the Castilian nobles, especially such great clans as the Haro, Lara, Castro, and Cameros families, were placed in an advantageous position which the monarchy's dynastic problems enabled them to exploit; for it has been pointed out that 'not one of the nine reigns from 1296 to 1504 remained unaffected by either the serious problems posed by a minority or the dangers of a disputed succession'. Thus in 1322, during the minority of Alfonso XI, the *cortes* complained that 'Diego López and Alfonso Fernández . . . entered by night the royal town of Vea, threw out those who lived there, took all they had, made a fortress there and [still] hold it'. In these circumstances it is not surprising that a key institution of late medieval Castile was the series of *Hermandades* (brotherhoods), groups of lesser nobles, towns, and bishops which grouped together for mutual protection, usually against the attacks of the *ricos hombres* (greater nobles).

The power and intransigence of Castile's nobility largely explains the paradoxical position of the Castilian Crown in the late Middle Ages. For in comparison with Aragon's ruling House of Barcelona, Castile's kings seemed to enjoy two signal advantages: they had access to revenues possibly four or five times greater, and they faced a consultative body, the *cortes*, which never became as articulate or powerful as either the Aragonese *cortes* or the Catalan *corts*. The *Siete partidas* of Alfonso X (compiled from 1265 onwards) was a great attempt to systematize Castilian legal practices, and represented the peninsula's main contribution to the general European trend of assertive monarchy. But these were superficial strengths. The Crown was unable to get its hands on the many sources of revenue which it theoretically controlled, and throughout this period desperately sought new ones. The *Siete partidas* remained an ideal law code which could rarely be applied; and in practice Castile was almost as particularist as the formally federated Crown of Aragon. Above all, the *cortes* was weak because the nobility did not need to express its claims through such a representative body. Noblemen negotiated directly with the king from a position of growing strength in their territorial bases. The comparative weakness of the country's towns played into their hands, as did the Crown's financial needs and the constant willingness of Aragon and Granada to foment discontent in Castile. As Alfonso X put it in a letter to his heir, 'They [i.e. the nobles] act as they do so as to keep kings under pressure and take what is their own from them. They look for ways in which they can disinherit and dishonour them . . . they want always to have a foot [in Granada], as well as one here.'

The greatest consequence of the 'conquest generation' was of course the placing under Christian rule of many thousands of Muslims; even more than before, those areas of Iberia under Christian rule thus became home to three religions, Christianity, Islam, and Judaism. Relations between them were complex, and it is useful to divide them into their several aspects: the legal status and economic conditions of the Mudejars; the approach adopted by the Christian rulers towards the practice of Islam and Judaism; the question of acculturation; and the implications of the second and third of these for Spanish attitudes towards crusading. About none of these aspects can it be said that a consensus of views exists amongst historians. To begin with, such was the variation in the Mudejars' legal and economic position between Portugal, Andalusia, Valencia, Majorca, and Murcia, and even between different parts of these regions, that virtually any generalization is capable of disproof. At first glance treatment of the Mudejars does not appear oppressive, with the exception of those areas where sustained resistance led to the Moors being expelled wholesale under the laws of war. Leading scholars of the large Mudejar communities in Aragon and Valencia, Professors John Boswell and Robert Burns, have emphasized the degree of self-government and the resulting sense of community which they enjoyed, as well as the fact that the fiscal burdens imposed on them were, at least initially, no greater than those borne by their Christian neighbours. The Mudejars of Aragon were called on to provide troops to fight against the invading French crusaders in 1285, while individual Mudejars rose to high positions, influence, and wealth in government service. If many Majorcan Moors were expelled or enslaved, others purchased indemnity or release from slavery, and there is evidence of continuity in the predominantly Mudejar communities of the island's poorer uplands and central mountain region. In Castile, too, Mudejar towns were granted privileges of self-government, furnished soldiers, and were even given economic advantages in the hope of attracting immigrants from Granada. In 1305 Ferdinand IV acknowledged 'the many and great services' performed on the Crown's behalf by the Mudejars of Murcia.

But both Boswell and Burns have expressed serious reservations about an over-favourable picture of this aspect of Mudejar life. Boswell has pointed out that almost all the documented instances of legal and fiscal benefits granted can be balanced by other evidence of discrimination, and, more importantly, that the Mudejars were a uniquely vulnerable social group in times of stress. And Burns has reacted with characteristic vigour against the idea that his detailed studies of the Valencian Mudejars are generally optimistic by stressing that the political and cultural way of life of these communities was being inexorably eroded: 'the bottom line for Mudejars was that they inhabited a colonialist, survivalist subculture'. This erosion was reflected in the wave of Mudejar rebellions which occurred in both Aragon and Castile in the last decades of the thirteenth century, rebellions which naturally themselves led to worsening conditions.

The position of the Mudejars was perhaps at its best in their ability to practise their religion. In all the Christian kingdoms of Iberia their communities were allowed to maintain mosques, together with their support structure of schools, courts, and charitable foundations. Even after the Council of Vienne prohibited the public invocation of Mohammed's name in Christian countries, there were innumerable exceptions in Aragon and Castile. It was an approach rooted in practical considerations:

in 1329 Aragonese envoys, dispatched to the Curia to request crusade privileges, were instructed to counter papal demands for the expulsion of Muslims with the reminder that James I had conquered Valencia by guaranteeing freedom of worship. Much the same rights were enjoyed by Jews, who are known to have maintained synagogues in at least 118 places in the peninsula. This tolerance was supported by sanctions against Christians who attacked Muslims or Jews, and by royal edicts forbidding conversion by force. Clauses in the *Siete partidas* were characteristic:

We decree that Moors shall live among Christians in the same way that . . . Jews shall do, by observing their own law and not insulting ours . . . Although the Moors do not acknowledge a good religion, so long as they live among Christians with their assurance of security, their property shall not be stolen from them or taken by force . . .

Christians should endeavour to convert the Moors by causing them to believe in our religion, and bring them into it by kind words and suitable discourses, and not by violence or compulsion.[1]

Eminent figures of the late thirteenth and early fourteenth centuries, including the Catalan missionary Ramon Lull and the Castilian Prince Don John Manuel, shared this view that the Mudejars could be converted by discussion and reasoning.

Convivencia, the practice of three religious faiths existing in close proximity, has long been recognized as a distinctive feature of Iberian society in the central Middle Ages. It cannot be denied that in many ways individual believers of the three religions worked together without antagonism, and occasionally with personal friendship and sympathy for each other's beliefs. This applied even in circumstances with religious implications. Professor J. N. Hillgarth has cited instances of Muslim minstrels being hired to play in churches during night vigils of the great festivals, of Christian women bringing their Jewish and Muslim friends to mass, and of Christians acting as witnesses in contracts between Jews. But there is a big difference between the practice of tolerance and the principle of toleration. The latter is essentially a post-Enlightenment concept and it was alien to medieval thinking. Similarly, a major gap existed between individuals co-operating, and groups or communities interacting. 'Medieval minority-communities . . . were not modern minorities striving to assimilate in all but a single element such as color, residual ethnicity, or compartmentalized or privatized religion. Each in

---

[1] J. Muldoon (ed.), *The Expansion of Europe: The First Phase* (Philadelphia, 1977), 95.

his community shrank from the other, despised the inseparable religio-cultural package the other represented, and actively resisted assimilation.' Professor Burns's verdict may be extreme, but it forms a welcome corrective to the rosy view of thirteenth-century Iberia as a paradise of tolerance. As another Hispanist has put it, the Christian and Muslim communities remained 'geographically close yet mentally closed'.

This view of *convivencia* as a mixture of acceptance and disdain, in which the latter grew as the Mudejars' position declined, leads into the vexed issue of acculturation. In this respect it is useful to refer to three models proposed by anthropologists: cultural fusion (the wedding of two groups to form a new, third group); the assimilation of one cultural group by another, more dominant one; and pluralism (arrested fusion or incomplete assimilation), the cultural equivalent of *convivencia*. No modern Hispanist would claim that thirteenth-century Spain produced cultural fusion, but the assimilation of the Mudejars and their Islamic culture occurred only after a long period of *de facto* pluralism. In acculturative terms this period was undoubtedly rich. Borrowings from Islamic culture were manifold, not only because of constant contacts with the Mudejar communities, but also because the triumphant Christians had become self-confident enough to borrow with ease. Acculturation is a complicated subject, partly because the imitative process, by its very nature, leaves little evidence, but three characteristic and striking examples of Christian borrowing are worth citing. One is Mudejar architecture and decoration, which proved influential throughout the peninsula, except in Catalonia and Portugal, and was copied by Christian architects and workmen. The second is the spread of public baths, already known in Christian towns in the early thirteenth century, but exceptionally common by 1300. And the third is Castilian loan words from Arabic, many of which first appeared in compilations written at the court of Alfonso X.

How did this affect Spanish attitudes towards crusading? Foreigners who travelled in Iberia were shocked by the degree of *convivencia* and acculturation they witnessed, simply because they were so impressed by the employment of Muslims in posts of government, by the permitted functioning of Muslim places of worship, and by superficial borrowings of dress, custom, and behaviour. But the reality, as we have seen, was less favourable for the Mudejars, and in any case crusade and *convivencia* were not irreconcilable, because they were solutions to different problems: government by Islamic powers and the existence of a conquered Muslim population. *Convivencia* might be damaged by the local anti-Islamic feelings unleashed by crusade preaching, but it survived, simply because it was necessary. Tensions were inevitable anyway because, as Professor Boswell put it, 'the Mudéjares were an imperfectly assimilated element in a culture dedicated to stability, homogeneity, and tradition', and tensions were both commonplace and bearable in late medieval society. Only the very altered circumstances of the later fourteenth and fifteenth centuries would bring about a fundamental deterioration in the Mudejar position.

As for crusading, it is clear that enthusiasm affected Iberia just as much as it did other parts of Europe, with an added sharpness derived from the excitement of the peninsula's recent past, allied to the continuing threat from Granada and North Africa. Indeed, it has been argued that in Portugal, where crusading ideas only took firm root in the early thirteenth century, national commitment was stronger in the fourteenth century than ever before, reaching its climax at the battle of Salado in 1340. And in neighbouring Castile, more than anywhere else in Europe, proponents of the cult of chivalry stressed the value of fighting against Islam. As the Prince Don John Manuel had the eponymous hero of his 'Libro de Patronio' declare, 'the best way [for a noble] to save his soul, according to his estate and dignity, is to die fighting the Moors'. Shifts of emphasis naturally occurred. The Virgin displaced St James (Santiago) as the central figure in the cultic veneration of Castilian *crucesignati*. And as the idea of a national chivalry began to take shape, the crusader's religious duty was increasingly expressed in terms of public service, as in John of Mena's *Coronación*, written in the mid-fifteenth century to celebrate a Castilian victory over the Moors. But the enthusiasm remained.

Historians have long recognized that crusading activity during the period covered by this chapter fell into two phases: one of relatively frequent campaigns, which lasted until the Castilian abandonment of the siege of Gibraltar in 1350, and the other of much more limited fighting, which spanned the entire second half of the century. While even the first phase did not produce fighting on the scale of the 1230s and 1240s, it was an important period of the *Reconquista* which included one of its greatest pitched battles, fought on the banks of the Salado river in 1340. What distinguished it from the period of Ferdinand III and James I was the passing of military initiative into Moorish hands. In this respect the watershed was the 1250s and 1260s. At the start of his reign Alfonso X actively planned to take the war into North Africa: a dockyard was built at Seville and ships commissioned, and crusading indulgences secured for the offensive. Henry III of England toyed with the idea of taking part, but failed to persuade the Pope to commute his vow of going to the Holy Land. None the less, by 1260 Alfonso had taken steps towards neutralizing Granada, Tunis, and Egypt, and in that year a fleet of thirty-seven ships attacked and took Salé. Much to Alfonso's fury it did not attempt to garrison the port but returned almost immediately. Two years later Alfonso was preparing for a renewed attack, possibly now aimed at Ceuta, when widespread Mudejar uprisings, encouraged by Granada, occurred throughout Andalusia and Murcia. They were suppressed with the help of crusade indulgences, but the rebellions demonstrated that the 'home front' was not secure enough for Castile to proceed into Africa before conquering Granada.

The attack on Salé was ill-timed in terms of the Maghribian political scene. Since the early thirteenth century Almohad power in Morocco had been undermined by the Banu Marin, a branch of the Zanata Berbers. Nomadic pastoralists, the Banu Marin made important gains in western Morocco between 1217 and 1239, but it was the death of the Caliph Sa'id at the hands of another Berber tribe, the Zayanids, in 1248, which gave them their breakthrough, enabling them to occupy Maknes and Fez. When Alfonso's ships attacked Salé, Abu Yusuf Ya'qub was deep in conflict with the Zayanids. He saw the threat which Castile's newly acquired strength could pose and realized that the solution was sending assistance to Granada; he also appreciated the value of *ghazi* status in his conflict with the Zayanids. The chronicler Ibn Idari described Abu Yusuf rebuilding the walls of Salé with his own hands: 'He did not cease to devote himself, from now on, to the Holy War.' Historians disagree about the motivation of Abu Yusuf and his followers, and in this respect there are obvious comparisons with early Ottoman history. For the emirs of Granada the political disadvantages of allowing the Berbers to cross the Straits were clear; they generally preferred to stave off Castilian attacks by bribing Castilian nobles, but the more hard-pressed or reckless emirs did call in the Banu Marin (or Marinids). Thus in 1275 Abu Yusuf himself led a force into Andalusia, crushed a Castilian army, and raided as far as Seville. Another Marinid army appeared in 1278, and again in 1282–3. On the latter occasion Abu Yusuf acted as the ally of Alfonso X against his rebellious son Sancho.

As the preceding sentence indicates, the political configurations of the 1280s and the following decades were complicated. Even when Sancho IV succeeded his father in 1284 and Castilian policy regained consistency, the alliance of Castile and Aragon against Granada and Morocco was made a rare event by the fear felt by the lesser powers for their stronger neighbours. In 1292, for example, Granada helped Sancho IV to take the strategic port of Tarifa from the Moroccans, while during the troubled minority of Ferdinand IV, Aragon allied with Granada to seize Murcia. In these circumstances it was naturally hard to persuade the papal Curia to issue crusade indulgences, and in 1294, when he prepared to lay siege to Algeciras, Sancho IV resorted to ordering the preaching of old bulls of Innocent IV and Clement IV. Castile's immediate objectives were, however, clear enough: the Straits ports of Tarifa, Algeciras, and Gibraltar must be taken and held against the Marinids before anything else could be undertaken against either Granada or Morocco. And if Aragon's hostility to further Castilian expansion was to be neutralized and the vital services of the Catalan fleet secured, its kings must be offered the prospect of a substantial share in the gains. This was possible since the kings of Aragon were still interested in southwards expansion, even though their chief goals lay further east, notably in Sicily, Sardinia, and Tunis. Thus the two countries made important agreements at Monteagudo (1291) and Alcalá de Henares (1308), which partitioned North Africa between them and guaranteed Aragon a sixth of conquered Granada.

The agreement of 1308 envisaged assaults on Almería by James II of Aragon, and on Algeciras by Ferdinand IV; it was the nearest the peninsula's Christian kings had come for some decades to a major combined assault on Granada. The agreement included the Marinid Sultan, who hoped to use the general attack to regain Ceuta, seized by Granada in 1306. Nevertheless, Clement V was persuaded to grant the joint Christian-Muslim offensive crusade status, and to allow James and Ferdinand to levy tenths on their clergy to finance it. The result was a fiasco. The Catalan fleet seized Gibraltar for Ferdinand but the Marinids deserted the alliance as soon as they regained Ceuta, and both Christian sieges failed. The experience was traumatic for Aragon, and James and his successors concentrated henceforth on objectives in the central Mediterranean; they fostered their interests in the Maghrib by peaceful means, especially a protectorate over Hafsid Tunis, and assisted Castile only at times of crisis. An ingenious proposal for a joint-Spanish offensive against Granada, timed to coincide with a crusade to the Holy Land, was put forward by the Aragonese at the Council of Vienne, but it had an exclusively financial rationale. The papacy too was from this point onwards much more sceptical in responding to proposals from Spanish envoys for crusades, placing limitations on its grants of indulgences and taxes, and frequently complaining that promises and guarantees had not been kept.

There were other features of the débâcle of 1309–10 and the immediately following years which proved to be of long-term significance in shaping the fourteenth-century *Reconquista*. One was the limitations imposed on Castile's activity by its internal problems, demonstrated by the quarrelling of the Castilian magnates at the siege of Algeciras, and by their intense conflicts for power during the long minority of Alfonso XI (1312–25). The other was the innate strength of Granada. The Emirate's ability to withstand attack puzzled contemporaries. In 1309, for example, James II declared that 'it was our great shame that the King of Granada, having so little power, should stand so long, with great dishonour to Jesus Christ and to us and harm to all Spain'. But Granada's survival did not only hinge on Christian weakness and Marinid assistance. It enjoyed three signal advantages derived from its own nature. One was its mountainous landscape, which was skilfully utilized through the construction of up-to-date fortifications and watch-towers which made offensive operations difficult to sustain, and ambushes against invading armies easy to mount. The second was the diplomatic ability of the Emirate's Nasrid rulers, who played off Morocco, Castile, Aragon, and Portugal to their own advantage. Generally the emirs aimed to sustain an Iberian balance of power without reference to religious divisions, though they were prepared to bring in outside help *in extremis*. Whatever their policy, the emirs were enabled to pursue it by the substantial revenues they derived from Granada's rich agricultural resources, supplemented by taxes on trade. The Genoese in particular found in the Emirate many of the products, including silks, sugar, saffron, and dried fruits, that Venetian and Turkish hostility made it increasingly hard for them to ship from the East. Granada's third advantage was its embattled, defensive social ethos; both long-standing residents of the region and the large numbers of exiles from the recently conquered lands to the north could never forget that if the Emirate fell they would have to flee to Africa. In this atmosphere holy war could easily be preached, and while this naturally operated against the pragmatic approach favoured by most emirs, it also gave Granada a great boost in wartime. Conquering this relatively small territory would therefore be a formidably difficult and expensive undertaking.

In 1325 Alfonso XI of Castile attained his majority. He was the most successful king in the *Reconquista* between Ferdinand III and the Catholic Monarchs, applying himself to the problem of Moroccan intervention and its focal point, the Straits ports, with a consistent energy absent in the reigns of his immediate predecessors. Alfonso's success hinged largely on his ability to channel the restless forces of his nobility away from rebellion into crusading, a recurring goal of Castile's monarchs in the late Middle Ages which was epitomized in John of Lucena's comment in 1463 that 'there is no trouble around the house when the pigs are gone to the woods'. Why Alfonso XI proved more able in this regard than others is not easy to say. One reason was probably the immediate background of national set-backs and humiliations: the defeat and deaths of Alfonso's regents in a bungled attack on Granada in 1319, the loss of Baeza in 1324 and Martos in 1325. With its nobility united, albeit temporarily, under the leadership of a vigorous king, Castile's resources vastly outmatched those of Granada, and Alfonso was purposeful enough in his initial preparations to secure a flood of papal crusade grants, from 1328 onwards. Outsiders expressed strong interest in the burgeoning conflict, and in 1329–30 it seemed possible that a sizeable expeditionary force might cross the Pyrenees to join the Castilians; in 1331 even Philip VI of France considered crusading in Spain as an alternative to his problematic general passage. A number of foreigners fought for Alfonso XI at the siege of Teba in the summer of 1330. They included Sir James Douglas, who was *en route* for Jerusalem, where he was to bury the heart of Robert Bruce, but was killed at the siege together with three of his companions.

The desperate Muhammad IV appealed to Morocco. At this point the Marinids were emerging from a period of acute dynastic conflict and Sultan Abu al-Hasan undertook to intervene in force, even though this would divert troops from his planned conquest of Tlemcen. In 1333 his soldiers retook Gibraltar. Pope John XXII granted Alfonso fresh crusade preaching and clerical tenths, but internal discord compelled the King to seal a truce with Yusuf I of Granada in 1334. When the truce expired in 1339 matters rapidly reached crisis point. Two years previously Abu al-Hasan had conquered Tlemcen, bringing Algeria under his control. He could now concentrate on Spain, and the death of his son Abu Malik in a raid on Jerez stimulated him to dispatch a massive army to Spain in 1340. Its crossing was facilitated by the defeat of the Castilian fleet in April. The Berber troops, joined by those of Yusuf I, besieged Tarifa in September. Peter III of Aragon, who feared the rising naval strength of the Marinids, sent galleys which proved invaluable, and Pope Benedict XII, in a departure from his general parsimony in crusading matters, granted crusade preaching and taxes on a lavish scale. Alfonso moved to relieve Tarifa, accompanied by Alfonso IV of Portugal, and reached the Salado river, near the port, on 29 October. Here a battle was fought on the following day. The Castilians engaged the Moroccans and the Portuguese the troops of Yusuf I, but it was a surprise attack on the Muslim rear by the Tarifa garrison which seems to have been decisive in breaking the Muslim battle front. Abu al-Hasan fled to Algeciras and thence to Morocco.

A comparison between the aftermaths of the battles of Las Navas de Tolosa and Salado bears out the points made earlier about the strength of Granada. For compared with the collapse of the Almohad empire and Ferdinand III's massive conquests, the results of the victory of 1340 were not spectacular. In retrospect it is possible to see that Salado was a decisive battle, simply because it discouraged the Marinids from making renewed interventions in Iberia. But in order to seal the victory it was necessary to take the various ports in the Straits, and this was no easier after Salado than before it. Alfonso XI's acute financial problems, barely helped by the vast booty he won in 1340, meant that it took him two years even to besiege Algeciras, and at least once during the gruelling two-year siege it seemed certain that the King would have to abandon it. Papal grants of crusade preaching, tenths, and a direct payment of 20,000 florins from the *camera*, proved valuable in finally bringing about the fall of Algeciras in 1344. But once the port was won, the need for internal reforms forced the King to postpone the logical next step, the siege of Gibraltar, until 1349. And then the arrival of the Black Death, which killed Alfonso on Good Friday 1350, doomed the siege to failure.

Alfonso XI's achievements were primarily those of Castile, and his troops were raised from traditional Castilian sources, chiefly the royal household, town militias, contingents led by the magnates, and the Military Orders. But it is important to take cognizance of other contributors to the battle of Salado and the taking of Algeciras. This meant chiefly the naval help of the Catalan fleet and the troops who came from Catalonia and Portugal; it has correctly been stressed that although neither Aragon nor Portugal possessed a land frontier with Granada by this point, crusade enthusiasm was still a potent force in the two countries, linked to hopes at both royal courts of expansion into North Africa. Philip, King of Navarre, the small northern state which in political and cultural terms bridged Castile and France, fought and died at the siege of Algeciras. The importance of extra-peninsular aid is harder to assess. Reference has already been made to abortive plans for a general expedition to Spain in 1329–30. The project was actively promoted by the King of Aragon, who sent an envoy to several courts to arrange the crusade, possibly in the hope of exerting indirect pressure on the Pope to grant him financial concessions; Alfonso XI himself did nothing to encourage the project. The Salado crusade was preached outside the peninsula, and at Algeciras, according to some sources, a stream of nobles arrived from France, Germany, and England, making a valuable contribution to the siege. The Earls of Derby and Salisbury both went, and although they had the important diplomatic mission of wooing Alfonso XI for the English cause in the war against France, they also played an energetic military role in the siege. English participation was notable enough for Chaucer to include the siege as one of the several crusading feats of his Knight in 'The Canterbury Tales'. From this point onwards sources, both Castilian and extra-peninsular, note the presence of non-Iberians at many of the engagements in the *Reconquista*, and although their military contribution was clearly small (a point Spanish historians have tended to stress), the trend demonstrates the central place still held in contemporary views of the crusades by the struggle which was in progress in southern Spain. Victories and set-backs there were constantly discussed in the context of events in the East, especially at the papal court.

This having been said, it was naturally on conditions within Castile that the pursuit of the *Reconquista* hinged. And after 1350 these became even less favourable than beforehand. The financial underpinning of Alfonso XI's campaigns had always been fragile, and the economic crisis which afflicted the century's middle decades made any kind of warfare more burdensome: prices and wages in Castile doubled between 1351 and 1369. But it was political conditions which mattered above all. The Granadan policy of Alfonso's successor, Peter I, is not easy to assess since our main source for his reign, the *Chronicle* of Peter Lopez of Ayala, was written as propaganda in the service of the King's enemies. Its depiction of Peter as philo-Islamic, so similar to accusations which were later levelled against Henry IV, is clearly distorted, and historians now see his policies as being an unsuccessful continuation of his father's. In 1354, for example, Peter asked Pope Innocent VI for crusade privileges to help Castile support the Moorish Emir of Montesclaros, in North Africa, in his conversion to the Christian faith; this initiative, probably an attempt to undermine the already waning power of the Marinids, could easily have been made by Alfonso XI. Like Alfonso, Peter was expansionist, but he failed to rally Castile's nobility behind him, and he shunned the proven toughness of Granada or Gibraltar. Instead he directed his military resources against what he envisaged as the softer target of Aragon. War between the two countries broke out in 1356 and lasted for ten years.

The conflict was disastrous for both participants. Aragon, already exhausted by war with Catalonia's chief trading rival, Genoa, suffered heavy defeats; these drove Peter III into the arms of France, which was eager to enlist his alliance against the Anglo-Castilian coalition. In 1366 French mercenary companies commanded by Bertrand du Guesclin assisted Peter I's illegitimate brother, Henry of Trastámara, to overthrow Peter. The defeated King, helped by the troops of the Black Prince, returned to Castile in 1367 and smashed Henry's French army in April at the battle of Nájera. But the withdrawal of the English enabled Henry to defeat his half-brother in 1369, after which the captured King was murdered. Peninsular politics had become geared into the Anglo-French war, with the result that the civilian population endured the worst features of that conflict; and this northwards shift of Castilian energy gave Granada an invaluable breathing space in which to recover from the blows inflicted by Alfonso XI. Muhammad V even recovered Algeciras in 1369, though he proved unable to hold the city, which he destroyed and abandoned. Interestingly, it was amongst Henry's French mercenaries that the idea of crusade continued to exert some appeal. They were encouraged by Pope Urban V to visualize their expedition as a crusade against the Moors, and in March 1366 Henry even bestowed the crown of Granada on Bertrand du Guesclin at Burgos. It was not the first time in the *Reconquista* that crusading attitudes were stronger amongst non-Iberians than amongst the Spaniards themselves.

Trastámara propaganda led contemporaries to believe that Henry's final defeat of the 'philo-Islamic' Peter would be followed by the resumption of the *Reconquista*. In this they were disappointed, for whatever his own feelings about Granada, Henry had too many enemies and interests elsewhere to spend much time in the south. An unfavourable peace treaty with Granada was sealed in June 1370 and the new King spent the ten years of his reign shoring up his position in Castile. A planned campaign against Granada in 1375, to which Henry managed to attract Louis of Bourbon, the French crusading enthusiast, was abandoned in the face of Portuguese hostility. In 1384 Henry's successor, John I, gambled on conquering Portugal. This led to renewed Trastámara conflict with England, and to the great Castilian defeat at the hands of an Anglo-Portuguese army, at Albujarrota in 1385. As we saw in the previous chapter,[2] crusading made an appearance in this dynastic struggle in the shape of grants of indulgences made to the opposing sides by the rival popes of the Schism. Urban VI thus proclaimed a crusade against John I in 1382, while Clement VII supported John with indulgences against John I of Portugal. With virtually no papal grants of indulgences against the Moors since Alfonso XI's death in 1350, it is possible that more Iberians took the cross in the second half of the fourteenth century to fight against fellow-Christians than to wage war against Muslims. Characteristically, there was general disapproval in Castile of the large-scale razzia led by the Master of Alcántara against Granada in 1394, which ended in disaster.

What brought this prolonged period of stagnation to a close was a renewal of Muslim aggression towards the end of the century. Piracy and coastal raids by both Christians and Muslims were commonplace in this period, but in 1397 a particularly heavy raid by North African galleys on Torralba caused Valencia and Majorca to organize a reprisal expedition, which was granted crusade status by Pope Benedict XIII, himself Aragonese, in March 1398. The Christians took and sacked Tedelic in August 1398. Then in 1401 Granada launched a full-scale raid on Castilian territory, and in the following decade hostilities reached a pitch comparable with the days of Alfonso XI. In 1406 Muhammad VII's troops invaded Murcia and Jaen, sustaining defeats but ravaging the countryside until, in October, they were turned back near Quesada at the battle of Los Collejares. A meeting of the Castilian *cortes* at Toledo granted a very large *servicio* of forty-five million *maravedís* for war, specifying its use for a combination of naval and land operations. The death of Henry III at the end of 1406 meant that the expedition's leadership passed to his brother Ferdinand, co-regent with Henry's widow, Catherine of Lancaster, for the minor John II.

Although he faced constant insubordination from Castile's nobility, as well as difficulties in co-operating with Catherine, Ferdinand opened the campaign in the late spring of 1407. To emphasize its character and importance he carried the sword of King Ferdinand III. A naval victory in August was followed by the fall of Zahara on 3 October. Ferdinand then

[2] Above, 248.

proposed an assault on Ronda, but the nobles would not support this, and as a compromise the army besieged Setenil. This proved a failure, and the Castilians withdrew, much against Ferdinand's wishes, on 25 October. After further hard negotiating with the *cortes* on subsidies, and lengthy preparations during the winter of 1409–10, Ferdinand returned to the offensive by besieging the fortress of Antequera in April 1410. Antequera's dominance of both the north–south and the east–west routes made it the key to any large-scale conquests in the Emirate. Ferdinand was only able to conduct such an ambitious operation because his control over the nobility had improved markedly since 1407, largely due to his acquisition of the masterships of Santiago and Alcántara in 1408–9. A Granadan relief army was defeated at Boca del Asno in May, and in September the city finally fell. The victorious Ferdinand gained the sobriquet 'of Antequera' from the siege.

The success at Antequera was not immediately followed up. The *cortes* of 1411 voted another forty-eight million *maravedís* for the continuation of the war, but most of the money was siphoned off by Ferdinand to further his dynastic interests in Aragon, where he became King in 1412. But the campaigns of 1407 and 1410, and the background of enthusiasm which made possible the *cortes* grants of 1406 and 1411, were watersheds in the *Reconquista*. They indicated the revival of Castilian interest in crusading, and they also demonstrated the military forms such crusading would from now onwards assume. The former hinged, as always in the peninsula since the thirteenth century, on the commitment of the court, and Trastámara interest in crusading was rooted partly in the failure of their Portuguese project, and partly in their response to the danger which could still be posed by Moorish aggression. While not ignoring Ferdinand's dynastic ambitions, his most recent biographer had no doubts about the depth and sincerity of his crusading zeal; certainly his dispatch to Seville reporting the victory at Boca del Asno was packed with grateful references to the help he had received from God, the Virgin, and St James. But a broader, if gradual, reawakening of crusade enthusiasm in Castile can also be detected from this point onwards. One of its symptoms was the popularity of 'frontier romances' (*romances fronterizos*), which depicted the border with Granada as a theatre of chivalric holy war. And for the first time a connection now occurred between crusade and the enforcement of religious orthodoxy within Castile, for 1391 witnessed the first major anti-Jewish pogroms, while in 1412 discriminatory laws were passed against Jews and Mudejars. This connection between the decline of *convivencia* and enthusiasm for crusading is problematic; the two even contradict one another, in so far as the pogroms tended to be associated with economic depression, which was hardly conducive to the heavy financial demands exerted by crusading. None the less, a pattern existed in Castilian crusade enthusiasm in the late Middle Ages, and Ferdinand's campaigns clearly represented an upswing.

As for Antequera and the future, the siege prefigured those conducted by the Catholic Monarchs in many respects. Ferdinand adopted a clear and purposeful strategy, aimed at cutting off Granada's western provinces by advancing as far as the coastal port of Málaga. The siege was conducted by a more professional army than Castile had hitherto possessed, the result of the military reforms initiated by the Guadalajara *cortes* of 1390: the court's financial negotiations with the *cortes* were now accompanied by precise figures of the numbers and types of troops to be employed. Naval operations were co-ordinated with the siege, so that Castilian galleys raided Ceuta, Almería, and Estepona. Like the Catholic Monarchs, Ferdinand made intensive use of cannon and siege engines, notably the great *bastidas* ('belfries' or towers), which were built at Seville and transported to Antequera on 300 carts. Above all, victory was won, as in the 1480s, by many months of hard and persistent work, in which groups of foreign volunteers played a colourful if peripheral role. The Count of La Marche, a son-in-law of the King of Navarre, fought for Ferdinand with a company of eighty knights in 1407, as did the Burgundian adventurer Guillebert of Lannoy, who also fought at Antequera three years later.

The economic and financial features of Ferdinand's campaigns in 1407 and 1410 also prefigured those of the Catholic Monarchs seventy years later. The assembly, billeting, control, and provisioning of Ferdinand of Antequera's troops imposed the same strain on public order and resources in Andalusia that the later campaigning of King Ferdinand would bring about there. And the co-regent's campaigns represented a similar financial burden for the monarchy and nation. Thanks to the large amount of artillery called for, the *cortes*'s original estimate of the cost of Henry III's planned expedition of 1407 was over 100 million *maravedís*, and at one point Ferdinand almost called off the siege of Antequera because his funds were exhausted. It is striking, therefore, that another recurrent feature of the later campaigns, the regular issuing of bulls of crusade, either did not occur in relation to Ferdinand's war, or has left no documentary trace. The latter seems more likely, in that Benedict XIII had complied readily enough with Ferdinand's requests that his sons be granted the masterships of the Military Orders. The Pope certainly granted Ferdinand *tercias*, the 'third' of church tithes which the Curia had become accustomed to grant to those rulers of Castile who engaged in crusading in the south. And in 1416 he granted indulgences for the defence of Antequera against a Granadan counter-thrust. Interestingly, Benedict's rival, John XXIII, attempted to bribe Ferdinand to bring Castile into his obedience by offering him crusade preaching.

Five years after the fall of Antequera another Christian military success occurred which also firmly pointed the way to future developments, the Portuguese capture of Ceuta. Naturally this event fitted into a long-standing pattern of Iberian interest in undertaking conquests in Morocco, its most important precedent being Alfonso X's plans in the mid-thirteenth century. But there was also a broader, and more recent, Maghribian context. Following in the tradition established by Louis IX in 1270, when he besieged Tunis with a crusading army, a major French crusade attempted in 1390 to capture the Hafsid port of Al-Mahdiya. The Genoese, encouraged by their capture of the island of Jerba in 1388, approached the French court in the winter of 1389–90 with the proposal that they transport an army to take Al-Mahdiya. Coming in the wake of the Anglo-French truce of June 1389, this proposal had great appeal, both to the chivalric nobility and to the court, which was seeking closer links with Genoa in the hope of establishing a French protectorate there. Louis II of Bourbon, Charles VI's maternal uncle, was therefore permitted to lead the expedition, although his recruitment in France was limited to 1,500 men. The enterprise was, exceptionally, recognized as a crusade by both Clement VII and his rival, Boniface IX. The fleet, estimated by the most reliable French source as twenty-two galleys and eighteen transports, sailed from Genoa in July 1390. A successful landing was achieved and Al-Mahdiya was invested. But after a siege of nine or ten weeks, and the arrival of Muslim relief forces, a treaty was negotiated and the crusaders withdrew. The expedition was regarded by its French participants (and, more surprisingly, by their contemporaries) as a resounding success on the grounds that armies led by three Muslim emirs had been kept at bay. Its main importance was that it revived French interest in crusading, thereby paving the way for Nicopolis. The Genoese came out best, though the view that they had 'duped' the French should be reconsidered in the light of France's acquisition of Genoa in 1396, for which the crusade may well have proved useful.

Like the French army at Al-Mahdiya, the Portuguese expedition to Ceuta received crusade indulgences, though they were not preached until after the fleet had set sail in order to preserve secrecy as long as possible. These two campaigns were the initial steps in what later became a massive investment of Christian military resources in North African expansion, most of it also undertaken in crusading form. For geographical reasons that investment was made largely by the Portuguese and, in its later stages, by the Castilians; but Al-Mahdiya has the merit of showing that it was not only the Iberian nations which were attracted by holy war in the Maghrib, even if they did come to dominate it. It is also useful to compare Al-Mahdiya and Ceuta on the vexed question of the motivation behind the expansion. That solid commercial reasons existed for attempting conquest in the case of both ports, based on the growing importance of the Maghrib in Europe's trade, cannot be doubted. Europeans brought eastern goods, and their own manufactured products, to such ports as Tangier, Ceuta, Melilla, Oran, Algiers, Bougie, and Tunis, in exchange for a variety of local raw materials, grain and other foodstuffs, and gold. The last in particular was essential to provide for the increasing number of Europe's gold currencies, and in seizing Ceuta the Portuguese hoped to establish a direct grip on the trade routes to the sub-Saharan regions, particularly the famed, gold-exporting Kingdom of Mali, as well as to combat Muslim raids on their shipping as it passed through the Straits. The timing of their attack was linked to the growing weakness of the Marinids, thanks to their chronic political instability, a weakness which the Nasrids of Granada had long been exploiting.

But the importance of the crusading impulse should not be under-estimated when considering either Al-Mahdiya or Ceuta. This is self-evident in the case of French enthusiasm for the Genoese project; the account of the crusade given in John Cabaret's life of Louis of Bourbon affords some of the most striking proof of the chivalric appeal of holy war. And yet the circumstances behind the Ceuta crusade were not dissimilar. Writing in about 1450, the Portuguese chronicler Zurara portrayed Prince Henry the Navigator persuading his father to undertake the conquest of Ceuta in terms of the chance to fight infidels. Zurara's version of events has long been criticized as rhetorical and panegyric (as well as written long after the event), but his account seems accurately to reflect the atmosphere at the court of King John I. Professor P. E. Russell suggested that chivalric mores, with their strong crusading aspirations, had a firm grip there because of the influence of John's wife, Philippa of

Lancaster. The new dynasty of Avis wanted to impress its contemporaries. The best way to do this was by a feat of arms which both fitted in with Portugal's crusading traditions and excelled the recent achievement of France's chivalric élite. One year after the conquest, the Council of Constance gave the Portuguese the chance publicly to boast that in taking Ceuta they had seized, on Christendom's behalf, 'the door and the key' to all Africa. As the dubbing of Crown Prince John after the storming of Arzila in 1471 shows, chivalric ideas continued to shape the Portuguese conquest of Africa well into the fifteenth century.

This 'exporting' of the Reconquest beyond the peninsula brought about a substantial revision of the traditional justification of Iberian crusading. Contemporaries sometimes argued that North Africa too had once been a Christian land; in practice, however, the rationale of recovery (*recuperatio*), still dominant (though not exclusive) in the fourteenth-century bulls of crusade, was gradually superceded by the theme of *dilatatio*, the expansion of the Christian faith through a linked programme of conquest and conversion. The beginnings of this reorientation in papal thinking are most clearly visible in Pope Clement VI's abortive grant of the Canary Islands to Louis of la Cerda in 1344; almost a century later it was again in relation to the Canaries that Eugenius IV declared that his greatest desire was 'to expand the Christian faith in our lifetime'. French crusading in Tunisia again provides interesting comparisons with the Iberian experience in the western Maghrib and the Atlantic islands. For one explanation of Louis IX's attack on Tunis in 1270 was that the King had been informed that the Emir of Tunis needed Christian protection to announce his conversion to Christianity; and in 1390 the Genoese argued their proposal to Charles VI in terms of compelling the Emirs of Tunis, Tlemcen, and Bougie, who depended on Al-Mahdiya for grain supplies, to become Christians:

And we have no doubt . . . that if Africa was in Christian hands—and we shall seize it, God willing—then these three infidel kings and their countries will either be destroyed, or will adopt the Christian faith, which would be a great achievement for your lordship.[3]

As we shall see in the next chapter,[4] the change of approach accelerated, under force of circumstances, as the Age of Discoveries progressed.

---

[3] Jean Cabaret d'Orville, *La Chronique du bon duc Loys de Bourbon*, ed. A. M. Chazaud (Paris, 1876), 218.
[4] Below, 309.

It has been pointed out that between 1350 and 1460 Castile and Granada were at war for only twenty-five years. In view of the heavy cost of defending the frontier in wartime—twenty million *maravedís* a year in the early fifteenth century—the alacrity with which both sides sought truces and treaties is unsurprising. What were the characteristics of frontier-life during the long stretches of official peace, which occurred in particular during the second half of the fourteenth century? Not surprisingly, the views of modern Hispanists about frontier relations vary in much the same way, and for much the same reasons, as on the parallel question of *convivencia* within the Christian kingdoms. Professor Angus MacKay has emphasized the role of the frontier in the process of acculturation; this was noticeable, for instance, in military techniques, in that the frontiersmen on both sides adopted similar tactics of rapid raiding executed by lightly armed and highly mobile cavalry, against whom defensive systems of scouts, warning beacons, and widely scattered fortified places were employed. And he has pointed to the existence of peace-keeping mechanisms: the magistrates ('alcaldes entre cristianos y moros'), and expert scouts ('rastreros'), who dealt with frontier incidents or complaints, and the 'alfaqueques' who ransomed or exchanged captives. Such 'hinge men' were essential along a rambling and mountainous frontier, where boundaries were not marked and travellers frequently got lost. Their activities were specifically sanctioned and protected in truces between Castile and Granada. Against the crusading tone of the genre of frontier ballads, which almost always related military actions taking place during 'official' war, has to be set documentary evidence that in periods of peace between Castile and Granada 'fairly amicable coexistence' characterized the frontier. Thus, 'while the frontier world was at times undoubtedly affected by [religious] militancy and zeal, at other times the religious situation was also characterized by confusion, fluidity, and even tolerance and respect'. There was even a local saint, San Ginés de la Jara, who was revered by Christians and Muslims alike, and performed miracles for the latter.

Not all Hispanists accept this picture of the frontier. While nobody would now argue that the frontier was one of unremitting hostility fuelled by religious animosity, the religious divide none the less made it different in kind from borders between the peninsula's Christian states. The same sort of 'Cold War' existed which had previously characterized relations between Latin Syria and its Muslim neighbours. Professor C. J. Bishko has highlighted the important role of the frontier nobles, towns, and Military Orders in waging an intermittent 'private war' whenever the frontier's 'relative, uneasy peace' broke down, and Luis Suárez Fernández described the 'feigned peace, which was broken at every moment by raids and surprise attacks'. In one frontier ballad a Christian narrated how he had been captured during a Moorish raid which occurred 'between peace and war' ('captivaron me los moros entre la paz y la guerra'). It was symptomatic of this state of affairs that the export from Castile to Granada not only of war materials but also of horses and mules was forbidden because of their military value to the Moors.

By painting this warfare in the colours of chivalric *mores*, replete with splendour and courtesy, the authors of the *romances fronterizos* mythologized it in much the same way as their contemporaries did in describing the *Reisen* against the Lithuanians. In reality, like the *Reisen*, it was brutal and destructive fighting, and the economy and society of the frontier regions were distorted as a result. Together with what has been described as 'the climate of insecurity born of endemic brigandage sustained by warfare', frontier hostilities thus had the effect of restricting agricultural practices in much of Andalusia and Murcia, perpetuating a booty economy forgotten further north, and making the impact of famine and plague more severe than elsewhere. In addition the frontier remained, as in previous periods, a place where obscure members of the lesser nobility could achieve wealth and renown by fighting. And the Christian communities along the frontier were not immune to crusading fervour: on several occasions in the fifteenth century the popes granted crusade indulgences in response to requests from Andalusian nobles and towns for spiritual rewards for those proceeding to fight the Moors.

There were thus potent economic, social, and religious elements aggravating the variety of *casi belli* which existed on all medieval frontiers. A rough and ready *convivencia* may have been the practice for decades at a time on parts of the border, but it was always precarious. Seen in this light, the peace-keeping mechanisms seem rather more fragile than when first examined, and the evidence for acculturation in military techniques gloomy proof of hostility rather than evidence of a *modus vivendi*. It used to be thought that the revival of crusading enthusiasm in fifteenth-century Castile represented the spread northwards, through the popularity of the *romances fronterizos*, of frontier habits or attitudes. This seems to be confusing cause and effect and now appears unlikely; but it is equally unlikely that the escalation in hostilities which resulted from Castile's renewed interest in crusading radically altered the established way of life on the frontier.

10

The End of the Reconquista: *Granada and Beyond,* 1415–1580

✠

THE pivotal point of this chapter is the series of campaigns waged between 1482 and 1492 by the 'Catholic Monarchs', Ferdinand and Isabella, which culminated in the conquest of the Emirate of Granada and the ending of Muslim power in Spain (see maps 10 and 11). Recent research has confirmed the political significance of these events, while in its scale and intensity the Granada war ranks alongside the Varna campaign and the wars against the Hussites as one of the greatest crusades of the fifteenth century. Thanks largely to the work of Professor M. A. Ladero Quesada, the character of the war itself is now clear; but both the background to the crusade, and its long-term results, remain highly problematic. In the case of the former, the difficulty lies in deciding whether or not the crusade represented a radical change in Castilian policy towards Granada and, more broadly, attitudes towards *convivencia*. And in the case of the crusade's long-term results, the dominant question is the fate of Iberian crusading ideas, institutions, and attitudes after the completion of the *Reconquista*. Continuity is apparent in some features of Spanish government and society in the sixteenth century, such as Castile's advance into North Africa and the resultant struggle with the Ottomans, and the survival into the Early Modern period of both the Iberian Military Orders and the 'Bula de la cruzada'. But investigation of the subtler links between the crusade and the Spanish conquest of the New World, and Habsburg imperial policy generally, forms one of the most tantalizing aspects of the history of later crusading.

The difficulty of making an accurate assessment of Castile's policy towards Granada in the decades between the fall of Antequera in 1410 and the outbreak of war in 1482 forms part of the larger problem of evaluating the long reigns of John II (1406–54) and Henry IV (1454–74). Both monarchs have traditionally suffered in comparison with Ferdinand and Isabella, and the current tendency to stress their positive achievements, and to establish links between their goals and those of the Catholic Monarchs, certainly makes sense in the case of crusading. It is true that John II was a weak and pliable king, but he faced formidable internal opposition in the *Infantes* of Aragon, Ferdinand of Antequera's sons John and Henry. As Professor Hillgarth has written, Ferdinand had left these men 'so powerful in lands and offices that they could obstruct any king's liberty of action'. Indeed, in the reigns of John II and Henry IV the preoccupation with power and personal gain, which had long characterized Castile's greater nobility, reached their height: as one chronicler put it, 'they wanted justice and more than justice against their opponents, but none for themselves'. None the less, between 1431 and 1437, when royal policy was most concentrated in the hands of Alvaro of Luna, John's enigmatic favourite, the Castilian government used the advantage of civil war within Granada to wage a series of ambitious campaigns against the Emirate. Jimena de la Frontera fell in March 1431, and in the following July the Castilians won a major victory at La Higueruela. The war fought in this and subsequent years was on a considerable scale: in one reverse at Ecija in 1434 the Order of Alcántara lost 800 cavalry and 400 foot, and in the following year the Order sustained one of its worst-ever defeats in the *Reconquista*. This was a far cry from frontier skirmishing. By the time a truce was signed in 1439–40 territorial gains had been secured which made possible raiding throughout the Vega of Granada and the districts (*campos*) of Ronda and Málaga, threatening the economic existence of the Emirate. Many of these gains were lost to Muhammad X in the following years.

The campaigns of the 1430s were characterized by the dramatic reawakening of papal interest in the *Reconquista*. Grants of indulgences and *tercias* by Martin V were followed by a series of privileges given by Eugenius IV, including crusade indulgences and a tax on Castile's clergy in 1431, new indulgences and clerical subsidies two years later, and more crusade preaching in 1437. The most significant feature of these grants was the adoption of a standard rate of payment for gaining the indulgence, fixed initially at eight ducats by Martin V and subsequently reduced to five florins by Eugenius IV (1433) and then to three florins by Nicholas V (1448). As Professor Jose Goñi Gaztambide put it, 'the introduction of a fixed rate for those who wanted to gain the indulgence was bound to increase the economic returns from the bull', and the revenues which accrued to the Castilian Crown, although not quantified, were clearly substantial. Luna obviously appreciated them, and if the main reason for fighting Granada was his hope of imitating Alfonso XI's success in channelling the rebellious energy of Castile's nobility into holy war, the decision was no doubt facilitated by the papal grants.

The outbreak of civil war in Castile in 1438 brought the earlier period of warfare with Granada to a close, but in the final years of John II's reign Luna reverted to his earlier policy and secured a series of new concessions from Pope Nicholas V. These included grants of crusade preaching in 1448, 1449, 1451, and 1452, while in 1453 the Pope transferred the administration of the Order of Santiago to John II. Shortly afterwards the administration of both Santiago and Calatrava was granted to John's successor, Henry IV. Although he was a Valencian, Calixtus III was no less generous to Castile than Nicholas had been. It was characteristic that his first crusade bull for the peninsula was issued on the very day of his coronation; it contained what has been described as the earliest reference to St James (Santiago) in a papal bull of crusade. And in April 1456 Calixtus took the significant step of declaring formally that the indulgences could be applied to souls in purgatory. Given the medieval preoccupation with lineage, this further heightened the proceeds to be gained from crusade preaching, especially since Calixtus also reduced the payment expected for the indulgence to the very low rate of three Aragonese florins or 200 *maravedís*. Indeed, the contemporary chronicler Alonso of Palencia believed that the Pope's extension of indulgences to the deceased brought in a million ducats.

It is clear that the growing financial attractiveness of crusade bulls led to increasingly insistent Castilian demands, and that these in turn stimu-lated papal interest in the *Reconquista*, if only to keep an eye on what was being done with the grants. But there seem to have been other reasons for the consistent interest displayed by the fifteenth-century Curia in the war against Granada. Eugenius IV hoped to use his grants to dissuade Castile from supporting the Council of Basle against him, while Nicholas V and Calixtus III viewed the Spanish crusade against the all-encompassing background of the Ottoman advance. Castile could not at this stage be expected to participate in an anti-Turkish crusade; but Castilian successes against the Moors could be cited to encourage or humiliate other Christian powers to take action against the Turks. This applied above all to

Alfonso V of Aragon, who after his conquest of the Kingdom of Naples in 1443 was ideally placed to fight the Ottomans. Thus in 1456 Calixtus III was persuaded by the Castilian envoy, Rodrigo Sánchez of Arévalo, to extend to Spaniards fighting the Moors all the privileges granted by Nicholas V to the anti-Ottoman crusade; and in the autumn of 1455 Alfonso V took the cross, proposing to attack the Ottomans, Mamluks, and Hafsids of Tunis while Henry IV simultaneously assaulted Granada. Similarly, there were occasional attempts at forging a financial link between the two crusading fronts, as in 1460, when Pius II allowed the preaching of indulgences for the war against Granada to continue, provided that half its proceeds were donated to the crusade against the Turks. Pius later claimed that his reaction to Castile's capture of Gibraltar in 1462 was 'extraordinary satisfaction, since among so many calamities to Christendom there was at least this one piece of good news'. In this way the connection between the two fronts, which had been made at periodic intervals since the late eleventh century, was renewed in the early fifteenth century; and following the fall of Constantinople in 1453 the growth of Ottoman naval strength led the Curia slowly to evaluate the two arenas in a common strategic context, one which became inevitable as the frontiers of the Ottomans and the Castilians converged.

It is a moot point whether the regular crusade preaching which thus occurred in Castile from the 1430s onwards created, or at least contributed to, popular dissatisfaction with the fact that neither John II nor Henry IV attempted the total destruction of Granada. Expectations ran high and failed to take into account the problems involved. In 1455, for instance, Rodrigo Sánchez predicted that Henry IV would cross into North Africa and conquer the province of Tangier, achieving the reunification of the ancient Gothic (i.e. Vizigothic) monarchy. It has often been remarked on that one of the demands made by the nobles who rebelled against Henry IV was that the King should wage more effective war against the Moors. This was unfair, in that Henry launched a series of selective but destructive raids on Granada between 1455 and 1458, captured Archidona and Gibraltar in 1462, and exerted such pressure on the Emirate generally that its collapse appeared imminent. Henry's desire to avoid large-scale, indiscriminate raiding parties was explained in terms which neatly combined humanitarian and financial motives:

Because he was pious and not cruel, more a friend of the life of his [followers] than the spiller of their blood, he said that . . . the life of men had no price or equivalence, and it was a great error to risk them, and because of this it did not please him that his [followers] went out on skirmishes . . . And in such expeditions, [too] much money was spent; he wished [rather] to expend his treasures [in] damaging the enemies little by little . . .[1]

In so far as their criticism of Henry was more than simple propaganda, the rebel nobility seem to have resented the absence of opportunities for gaining chivalric renown and booty which resulted from such tactics.

There is a similar difficulty in assessing the accusations of 'Islamophilia' levelled against Henry, largely on the basis of the use of Moorish guards and attendants, clothing, and customs at the royal court. It has been pointed out that these were stock accusations, so that Alvaro of Luna's noble critics had attacked him for favouring 'infidels and heretics, enemies of our sacred laws and of our King and persons and wealth'. But the need to justify rebellion does not wholly account for the widespread distaste which led to such comments as those of the traveller Gabriel Tetzel. In his account of Leo of Rozmital's travels he reported that Henry 'eats and drinks and is clothed and worships in the heathen manner and is an enemy of Christians'. Tetzel's distaste for this behaviour was in tune with the feelings of many Castilians, and his comments reflected a highly significant change in opinion and attitudes which was sweeping through Castile, creating a dangerous gap between the life of the royal court and that of society at large. The most dramatic symptom of this change was a growing reaction against the practice of *convivencia*. The main victims of the reaction were the peninsula's Jews, who suffered increasing violence and discrimination after the pogroms of 1391. Those who converted (the *conversos*) were regarded with intense suspicion and became subject to popular riots, fuelled by the success which many *conversos* enjoyed in economic and political terms. Since few of them had any share in this prosperity, the Mudejars did not incur popular animosity to the degree that Jews and *conversos* did, but their religious privileges were inexorably eroded. In the early fifteenth century, for instance, Queen Catherine, Henry III's widow and regent for John II, attempted to segregate Mudejars as well as Jews in walled ghettos, while the Aragonese government forbade public manifestations of Islamic belief.

Castilian public opinion may have favoured all-out war with Granada, but until the nation achieved political stability this was clearly out of the question. In 1464 a rebel league was formed in defence of the claims of the *Infantes* Alfonso and Isabella, Henry's half-brother and half-sister,

[1] W. D. Phillips, *Enrique IV and the Crisis of Fifteenth-Century Castile, 1425–1480* (Cambridge, Mass., 1978), 55.

against Henry's daughter and heiress, Joanna (Juana). The rebels harnessed popular dissatisfaction with the 'Moorish' nature of the royal court, listing amongst their demands the expulsion of all the King's Moorish servants. Henry mismanaged his cause and in the autumn of 1468 he had to recognize Isabella as heiress to the throne. King John II of Aragon, desperate for allies against his rebellious Catalan subjects and their French supporters, proposed the marriage of Isabella to his eldest son, Ferdinand, and in October 1469 the wedding took place at Valladolid. Henry proceeded to disinherit Isabella, and after the King's death in 1474 civil war again broke out as Joanna's supporters called in Alfonso of Portugal, whom they betrothed to the Queen in May 1475. By 1477 the *Juanistas* were virtually defeated, and in 1479 peace was sealed between Castile and Portugal. In the same year John II died and Ferdinand succeeded to the throne of Aragon. Fifteen years of intermittent but traumatic civil conflict and foreign intervention thus ended with the dynastic union of the Crowns of Castile and Aragon. Just three years later, in 1482, Castile embarked on the series of campaigns which ended in the conquest of Granada.

Clearly the war with Granada has to be set against the background of Isabella's troubled accession, as well as that of the current of uniformist feeling described above. In fact it is best to consider the war's origins within a specifically Castilian context, since recent research has rather played down Aragon's contribution. Older views that the Renaissance classicism popular at the Aragonese court since Alfonso V's reign helped foster the ideal of peninsular unity, and hence revive the Reconquest impulse, now seem less convincing, as does the idea that the dynastic unification of the two peoples would somehow be 'sealed' by the conquest of Granada. Ferdinand's personal commitment to the conquest was strong, and his leadership of the Christian armies important; but it has been plausibly argued that his waging of the Granada war was the price Isabella exacted for the use of Castilian resources to back her husband's subsequent pursuit of more traditionally Aragonese goals in the north of the peninsula and in Italy. In 1526 Venice's ambassador at the court of Charles V claimed that 'all Spain' believed the initiative to have been Isabella's. Today it is clear that the union achieved by Ferdinand and Isabella was personal and fragile, and it may be that the chief link between that union and the conquest was that it robbed Granada of a potential Christian ally.

At this point it is worth quoting, at some length, the Catholic Monarchs' own explanation of the war, as it was set out in a letter to Pope Sixtus IV:

We have not been moved nor are we moved to this war by any desire to enlarge our realms and seigniories, nor by greed to obtain greater revenues than those we possess, nor by any wish to pile up treasures; for should we wish to increase our sovereignty and enrich our revenues, we could do this with much less danger and travail and expenditure than we are putting forth in this. But our desire to serve God, and our zeal for His holy Catholic faith, make us put all other interests aside and forget the constant travails and dangers which continue to increase for this cause; and although we could not only keep our treasures, and further have many more from the Moors themselves, which they would give us most willingly for the sake of peace, yet we refuse the treasures offered to us and pour out our own, hoping only that the holy Catholic faith will be multiplied and that Christendom will be quit of so constant a danger as she has here at her very doors, if these infidels of the kingdom of Granada are not uprooted and cast out from Spain.[2]

Granted its element of special pleading, and its general tone of self-righteousness, this remains a fair analysis of the motivation of Isabella and Ferdinand, as modern historians of the conquest have described it. It emphasizes the dual goals of ending Islamic government in the peninsula and eliminating a potential military threat. Both aims were important, the first in the realm of ideas, the now dominant royal policy of enforcing orthodoxy and unity in religious affairs; and the second in that of military reality, especially the new strategic agenda dictated by the Ottoman advance.

There can be no doubt that Isabella's reign in Castile affirmed and consolidated the rejection of *convivencia* and the triumph of its rival, what has been termed 'bellicose exclusivism'. The establishment of the Inquisition in 1478 was naturally the most striking sign of royal policy in this respect, and its chief victims were the *conversos*. But the connection between the Inquisition and the conquest of Granada is undeniable: the two were explicitly linked both by the Catholic Monarchs and by the papal Curia, and the Monarchs' sepulchral inscription refers to their 'prostrating the Mahomedan sect and extinguishing heretical perversity'. If, as Dr John Edwards has written, the *conversos* 'felt in their lives the power of the intellectual over the material', so too did the Moors of Granada. In this respect the Granada war resembles the First Crusade. For just as new currents of religious feeling in late eleventh-century Christendom caused contemporaries to find the longstanding Muslim occupation of Jerusalem intolerable, so late fifteenth-century Castile

---

[2] J. Goñi Gaztambide, 'The Holy See and the Reconquest of the Kingdom of Granada (1479–1492)', in R. Highfield (ed.), *Spain in the Fifteenth Century 1369–1516* (London, 1972), 361–2.

placed a premium on ending Islamic rule (though not, as yet, the Islamic religion) in the peninsula. As recent historians have stressed, both the Inquisition and the war were popular policies, a vitally important consideration in view of the war's heavy financial burden. Isabella thus managed, to a degree even more striking than in the case of Alfonso XI, to unite her subjects through war against the Moors, healing the wounds caused by decades of internal conflict. Furthermore, because the war took place in the context of rejuvenated royal prestige and authority, and in a period when firm structures of government were being created, victory in what Diego of Valera characteristically called 'this holy and necessary war', helped to fashion an enduring myth of royal policy in the service of religion, and to enmesh crusading institutions and ideas almost inextricably in the governmental structures and ideology of Early Modern Spain.

Military factors were of secondary importance, but should not be underestimated. The acute internal discord within the Emirate at the time of the war, which played a role in persuading the Catholic Monarchs to launch the conquest, should not disguise Granada's continuing military strength: in 1471 and 1477 the Emir Abu-l-Hasan took several hundred captives in raids on Murcia and Andalusia. More important, in the aftermath of the Turkish landing at Otranto in 1480, was the danger of Granada serving as a foothold for an Ottoman naval assault on Spain. Because of the Turkish threat to Aragonese Sicily Ferdinand was kept well aware of the Ottomans: in April 1480 he told the Grand Master of Santiago that naval preparations against the Turks had forced him to postpone an attack on Granada. There can be no doubt that the Catholic Monarchs played the Turkish card a great deal in their dealings with the papal Curia, arguing that unless the Granada war received proper Church funding, the defence of Sicily would be neglected, and promising assistance against the Turks once Granada was won. But their own concern was none the less for that.

The war with Granada developed into a programme of conquest, but it did not start as such. Its origins lay in Abu-l-Hasan's seizure of the frontier town of Zahara at the end of 1481, which provoked Rodrigo Ponce of León, Count of Cádiz, into leading a raid which managed to capture Alhama in February 1482. This unexpected success was reported to the King and Queen, who decided to hold Alhama and use it as a base for further conquests. The campaigns began in earnest in 1482 with the Castilian failure to take Loja, a humiliating defeat for Ferdinand but valuable schooling in Moorish tactics. In the following year a Christian defeat north of Málaga was balanced by victory over Abu-l-Hasan's son, Boabdil, near Lucena. The capture of Boabdil, who was in rebellion against his father, gave Ferdinand the chance to implement the traditional ploy of setting Boabdil up as a rival emir supported by Castile, 'to put Granada in division and destroy it', as the King expressed it. It may have been only at this point, in August 1483, that the possibility of total conquest was envisaged. Its achievement hinged on the taking, one after another, of Granada's great fortresses and cities; and this in turn entailed the application of constant pressure in the form of annual campaigns waged by huge armies, and the deployment of artillery on an unprecedented scale. What this meant in practice is best expressed, from the Muslim viewpoint, by an appeal which was directed to the Ottoman Sultan Bayezid II in about 1501 by the defeated Moors:

The Christians attacked us from all sides in a vast torrent, company after company, smiting us with zeal and resolution like locusts in the multitude of their cavalry and weapons . . . When we became weak, they camped in our territory and smote us, town after town, bringing many large cannons that demolished the impregnable walls of the towns, attacking them energetically during the siege for many months and days, with zeal and determination.[3]

A start on this arduous programme was made in 1484, with the capture of Alora and Setenil, but real progress was only made in 1485, when the Emirate's western bastion, Ronda, fell after a fifteen-day siege. The capture of Ronda gave Ferdinand about half of the Emirate's exposed western flank, besides yielding the valuable naval base of Marbella. Thus far Boabdil had been a disappointing ally: his support in Granada was limited and in 1485 Moorish resistance toughened when Abu-l-Hasan was dethroned by his brother al-Zagal, who proved to be a capable commander. In 1486 Boabdil came to terms with al-Zagal and volunteered to defend Loja against a powerful Castilian thrust which was robbing Granada of a series of towns north-west of the Emirate's capital. When Ferdinand took Loja Boabdil thus fell into Castilian hands for a second time. The two again came to terms, and during the next three years the conflict took on the appearance of a Granadan civil war, in which al-Zagal's resistance to the Christian advance was hindered by his nephew at every turn; Boabdil even fought against al-Zagal for control of the city of Granada itself, while his troops operated in the field alongside Ferdinand's army. Muslim division was thus fully as important as Ferdinand's artillery

---

[3] J. T. Monroe, 'A Curious Morisco Appeal to the Ottoman Empire', *Al-Andalus* 31 (1966), 296.

in bringing about Castilian success in the decisive campaigns of 1487, when the Christians first cut off Málaga's communications with Granada and then, throughout the summer months, besieged Málaga itself. The siege was contested with unrelenting determination by Málaga's mainly North African garrison, but the fall in August of Granada's second city and most important port completed the conquest of the Emirate's western flank.

By the close of 1487 the end seemed in sight, for apart from land in Christian hands, Boabdil now held all the city of Granada as well as the Emirate's north-eastern region, and during the siege of Málaga he had made a third treaty with Ferdinand in which he promised to surrender all that he held as soon as circumstances permitted. None the less, the war lasted for another four years. Initially, this was because al-Zagal continued to hold out from a strong position to the east of Granada. The siege of Baza in 1489 was thus on an even greater scale than that of Málaga. Paying and feeding the Castilian army of 52,000 combatants for almost six months posed financial and logistical problems which brought Ferdinand's war-administration to the brink of collapse. But food shortages, the persistence of the Castilian effort, and the hopelessness of any relief, led to the garrison's capitulation in December. Just a few days later al-Zagal concluded a treaty in which he consented to hand over his remaining towns, and in 1490 he joined forces with Ferdinand against Boabdil. For the latter, despairing of being able to persuade his subjects to surrender, now resisted Ferdinand, and it proved necessary to besiege Granada itself in 1491. Cut off from the coast, Boabdil had no hope of North African reinforcements; the Mamluks of Egypt had protested against Ferdinand's conquests but were not in a position to stop them. Military operations during the eight-month siege were therefore far fewer than at Málaga or Baza. Instead negotiations preoccupied both sides, and they resulted in the surrender of the city on 2 January 1492. The importance of the event eluded nobody. A Christian observer present at the surrender called it 'the most signal and blessed day there has ever been in Spain', while a contemporary Muslim lamented that it was 'one of the most terrible catastrophes which have befallen Islam', and Ferdinand himself, writing to Pope Innocent VIII, accurately commented that the fall of Granada brought to an end 780 years of Moorish government in Spain.

In the way it was fought the Granada war looked both backwards and forwards. Like their ancestors, the Catholic Monarchs raised their armies from a heterogeneous range of sources. Thus the greater nobility, bishops, and towns led or sent contingents, or money in lieu thereof, while the Military Orders provided soldiers, and there were troops supplied by the King and Queen themselves. Volunteers, numbering perhaps a few hundred, came at various points of the war from England, France, Italy, Germany, and Switzerland, and the Emperor Maximilian sent guns in 1487. In other respects Granada was the first of the great wars fought by Early Modern Spain. This applied, for example, to the decisive role played by artillery, the employment of *espingarderos* (early arquebusiers), the shifting emphasis from cavalry to foot, the growth in the overall numbers of troops deployed, and the greater attention paid to mobilizing, moving, feeding, lodging, and paying these armies. This required substantial effort and it was costly. In 1489, for instance, the Crown spent about eighty million *maravedís* in the purchase and transport of cereals for the army besieging Baza and the garrisons of conquered towns; only about a half of this sum was recouped from selling the cereals to the troops. The financial burden imposed on the monarchy by the long war was therefore enormous: one estimate stands at more than 800 million *maravedís*.

It was in this respect that the war's status as a crusade was crucially important. For a period of more than ten years the Castilian monarchy made continual demands on its subjects for troops or monetary substitutes, forced loans, and financial contributions from the *Hermandad*. In addition it requisitioned carts, mules, and cheap billeting in Andalusia, and generally concentrated its attention and resources on Granada. To make this palatable, especially in years marked by military stalemate or setbacks, the image of the war as a crusade was deliberately promoted. The publicists' task was facilitated by the background of enthusiasm for the war, nor was there a discrepancy between this 'official image' of the war and the behaviour of the army in the field, which eagerly took up the indulgences offered and celebrated success as a gift from God. When the propaganda song 'Setenil, ay Setenil', composed in 1484, voiced the hope that Ferdinand and Isabella would conquer 'as far as Jerusalem', it was a sentiment echoed by the Catholic Monarchs, their army, and Castile at large. But if the war was a release from the tension of years of civil conflict, a celebration of national unity, it was also a gruelling experience, and to fight it to its conclusion the Catholic Monarchs needed the emotional charge which its crusading character provided.

Even more significant, however, was the financial contribution made to the Crown's expenses by crusade taxes on the Church and the preaching of crusade indulgences. Throughout the war Castilian envoys kept the Curia under pressure to renew and extend crusading privileges. They used familiar arguments, especially the promise of victory, the shame of premature peace, and the offer of Spanish assistance against the Turks once Granada was won. Pope Sixtus IV granted the Catholic Monarchs their first crusade bull for war against Granada in November 1479, just two months after peace was reached with Portugal. Three years later the Pope levied a tenth on church revenues in Castile, Aragon, and Sicily; a third of the proceeds from both indulgences and tax was supposed to finance the war against the Ottomans, though the money never reached Rome. Crusade preaching was renewed by Sixtus in 1482, and by Innocent VIII at regular intervals from 1485 onwards. Precise figures for the proceeds raised are not known since the account books for the sale of indulgences prior to 1509 have disappeared, but all available indicators point to massive revenues. The Florentine ambassador Guicciardini later claimed that 800,000 ducats were collected from the sale of indulgences in 1487 alone. Proceeds from indulgences, in association with the money raised from the Church, paid nearly all the Crown's expenses. It is hard to avoid the conclusion that the war could not have been fought at all had it not been a crusade.

Earlier crusade preaching in Castile had been remunerative, but not on this scale, and it is necessary to ask how this financial breakthrough was made. The answer lies partly in the fervent atmosphere of national dedication within Castile, and partly in the nature of the bulls granted from 1482 onwards. For Sixtus IV, responding to a request from Ferdinand and Isabella for more generous terms, carried to a new extreme the gearing of his bulls' provisions to the raising of money. In particular, a scale of payments was established which allowed the poorest to secure the indulgence, together with a comprehensive list of privileges and exemptions, in exchange for a payment of just two silver *reales*, 'or as much as the treasurers [of the crusade] consider appropriate'. Even the rate of two *reales* was lowered at times of crisis, as during the siege of Baza in 1489. Other features of crusade preaching in Spain were clarified at this time, including the practice of issuing each recipient of the indulgence with a *buleta*, a sort of receipt which could be used to prove a claim to the crusader's privileges; this practice was of course enormously facilitated by printing, the oldest surviving printed *buleta* dating from 1483. Sixtus's long and detailed bull of 1482 thus became, as Goñi Gaztambide remarked, the prototype for the 'Bula de la cruzada'; and this, as we shall see, remained a feature of Spanish religious life for centuries to come.

The terms given to the conquered Moors of Granada were similar to those accorded in the wake of the great thirteenth-century advance. The civilians of Málaga, who were for the most part sold into slavery because of their town's long resistance, belonged to an unfortunate minority; elsewhere, although there was considerable variation between the terms of surrender reached with different towns and districts, the Moors were generally given the choice of assisted emigration to North Africa or remaining in Granada. If they chose to stay, they could usually practise their religion freely, and enjoyed a favourable legal status and financial condition. Initially, the resulting pattern resembled Valencia. The Muslim ruling class, including Boabdil and al-Zagal, found Christian rule unpalatable and emigrated *en masse*, but the majority of the Moors remained. Christian immigration was encouraged by the Crown, and by 1498 it had reached a total of about 40,000 people, mainly living in the cities and the neighbourhoods of castles. The first Archbishop of Granada, the Jeronimite Ferdinand of Talavera, who was given the task of converting the Mudejars, approached it with tact and psychological insight. He made a clear distinction between Islamic beliefs and Moorish customs, and prevented the Inquisition from working in Granada.

But within a few years the Mudejars of Granada were caught up in the general thrust towards religious orthodoxy. In 1492 the Catholic Monarchs issued their edict expelling all Jews from Castile and Aragon. Seven years later, dissatisfied with the slow progress made by Talavera in converting the Granadan Mudejars, they sent in Francis Jiménez of Cisneros, Archbishop of Toledo, to speed things up. Cisneros's controversial mass baptisms led to a series of rebellions in 1499–1501, and in 1501 the Monarchs decided to offer all the Mudejars of Granada a choice between conversion and emigration. The choice was contrary to the surrender capitulations, and the terms of emigration were much less favourable than they had been a decade previously. In 1502 the same alternatives were offered to Mudejars throughout Castile. The Mudejars of Aragon clung on to their religious rights until 1525. But in Habsburg Spain, a 'land of one religion' zealously guarded by the Inquisition, the converted Mudejars (*Moriscos*) were suspected of insincere belief in much the same way as the Jewish *conversos* of the fifteenth century, and in their case suspicion was aggravated by fear of their rebelling in conjunction with an attack by Spain's external enemies. A decree of 1567 which prohibited the speaking and writing of Arabic in Granada and tried to wipe out all vestiges of Moorish behaviour there, sparked off rebellion in 1568 and caused Philip II to expel the *Moriscos* from Granada to other parts of Spain in 1570. This tragic aftermath to the Reconquest therefore came to a close with the expulsion of the *Moriscos* from the entire peninsula in 1609–14.

As we have seen, the war against Granada gave expression to a deep-seated resurgence of Castilian crusading enthusiasm. In turn, the success which the war enjoyed, the thick matting of myths to which it gave rise, and the popularization of the conflict in royal propaganda, all helped to sustain that enthusiasm, while the 'Bula de la cruzada' gave it enduring institutional shape. It was therefore all but inevitable that the Spanish contribution to the crusading movement would assume new forms after 1492, and it would be quite wrong to see the raising of the cross over the Alhambra, Granada's royal palace, as the terminal point of Spanish crusading. Throughout the remainder of this chapter we will examine several areas of Spanish activity in the sixteenth century which can all be identified, in one way or another, as 'legatees' of the four centuries of crusading within the peninsula.

That the conquest of Granada was followed almost at once by the formulation of plans for a Castilian advance into North Africa is not surprising in view of past Castilian interest in the Maghrib, notably the detailed projects of Alfonso X in the mid-thirteenth century (see map 12). Since the Portuguese seizure of Ceuta in 1415, the Castilian government had watched with envy the success of their Iberian neighbours in building up a substantial group of towns on the Moroccan coast, comprising Ceuta, Alcácer-el Saghir (1458), Arzila (1471), and Tangier (1471). Although the Portuguese suffered several humiliating defeats in Morocco, including a disastrous failure at Tangier in 1437, the profits, particularly in terms of controlling the routes by which gold from sub-Saharan Africa reached the coast, seemed to make this expansion worth while. The Portuguese experienced no difficulty in persuading the popes to validate their Moroccan conquests as crusades, securing a flood of grants fully as impressive as those given to Castile for its war against Granada. These included the preaching of crusade indulgences, culminating in the issuing in 1486 of *Orthodoxe fidei*, a virtual duplicate of the great bull granted four years earlier to Ferdinand and Isabella for the conquest of Granada. Clerical taxes were also regularly levied, and the Curia made attempts, largely unsuccessful, to siphon off a percentage of the proceeds from both indulgences and taxes to its wars in Italy and against the Turks, just as we have seen it do in the case of Castile's crusades against Granada. Other important papal grants to the Portuguese comprised the legitimation of their conquests, approval for the administration of the Portuguese Military Orders by members of the royal house, and exemption from the ban on trading with the Muslims. The latter, a vital concession in view of the role expected of the ports, was even at times extended to arms exports: a highly unusual measure which shows how favourably Portugal's conquests were viewed by the Curia.

The temptation for Castile to contest the Maghrib with Portugal, once the ports of Granada were available, was overwhelmingly strong: quite apart from the lure of the gold routes, conquest of the coast between Ceuta and Tunis would remove the threat of a Moorish counter-attack in Granada, deprive the Ottomans of naval bases in the western Mediter-ranean, and consolidate Ferdinand's grip on Sicily, Sardinia, and the Balearic Islands. It was expected that the politically divided and militarily backward Muslim states of the Maghrib would be easy pickings compared with Granada. In crusading terms, the conquest of the Maghrib had long been regarded as an extension of the Reconquest on the grounds that North Africa had once been a Christian land. There was also the seductive argument, inapplicable in regard to Portugal's Moroccan conquests but plausible in the case of Spain's designs on Algeria, that this was the road to Jerusalem. It had already been put forward on several occasions by Aragon to validate its Maghriban interests, and acquired new force in the headily optimistic post-1492 atmosphere. Thus in 1493–4 Ferdinand of Zafra, the official placed in charge of Granada's defence, suggested an assault on North Africa. Since he needed King Ferdinand's assistance against Charles VIII's invasion of Italy, ironically also presented as a crusade, Alexander VI was prepared to support the venture. In 1494–5 the Pope granted the Catholic Monarchs clerical tenths, crusade preaching, *tercias*, and the requisite legitimation of their conquests. Manuel I of Portugal received similar grants in 1496, but Portugal's Maghriban expansion was now being overshadowed and to some extent barred by that of its mighty neighbour; as one historian has remarked, the Portuguese had to be content henceforth with 'collecting the crumbs which fell from the Spanish table'.

But North Africa had to contend with other areas calling for Spanish intervention, notably Italy. Thus, although Melilla was taken by the Duke of Medina Sidonia in 1497 and a garrison established there, it was not until Spanish troops had first suppressed the uprisings in Granada, and then conquered the Kingdom of Naples, that the advance could be resumed. Between 1505 and 1510 the conquest of a series of ports along the Maghriban coast dominated Spanish foreign policy. One reason for this was that Isabella, who died in November 1504, had urged in her testament that North Africa be conquered for the faith, partly in order that crusade funds raised for the conquest of Granada could be spent legitimately. The African campaigns also reconciled the Castilian magnate class to Ferdinand's 'diversion' of Castile's resources to Aragonese goals in Italy, while being fully in line with past instances of Aragonese intervention in the Maghrib. But it is arguable that the strongest motivation derived from Ferdinand himself, who made constant references in his later years to his desire to fight against the Muslims and regain Jerusalem. In February 1510, for instance, he wrote that 'the conquest of Jerusalem belongs to us and we have the title of that kingdom'. According to Peter of Quintana, his Secretary of State, 'the principal end and desire held by [Ferdinand] was general peace among Christians and war against the infidel . . . and he desired both these holy purposes like the salvation of his soul'. It is striking that Ferdinand and his youthful adversary Charles VIII of France, although belonging to different generations, both entertained as their highest political goal the recovery of Jerusalem, which each regarded as his by right.

Ferdinand's conquests were certainly spectacular. Mers-el-Kebir fell in 1505, Cazaza in 1506, Peñon del Vélez de la Gomera in 1508. The crusading status of the war was made clear when Pope Julius II gave grants of tenths and the *cruzada* in 1504 and 1506. The expedition to Mers-el-Kebir was financed by Cardinal Cisneros, a sort of Castilian John of Capistrano, and a dedicated exponent of Spanish advance into Africa. When an army of 10,000 men made a successful attack on Oran in 1509, Cisneros accompanied the troops and promoted an atmosphere of religious devotion in the field by his personal example and exhortation. The capture of Bougie and Tripoli, and the reduction of Algiers to vassal status, followed in 1510, and at the end of the year the Aragonese *cortes* voted over 500,000 pounds for the conquest of Tunisia. New grants of the *cruzada* were made by Julius II. Optimism was in the air. In 1505 Cisneros depicted the capture of Mers-el-Kebir as the first stage in the conquest of Greece, Turkey, Alexandria, and the Holy Land, and in 1510 Tunis was spoken of as a stepping-stone to Egypt and Palestine. In the early months of 1511 a fleet was prepared at Seville, and Spanish troops and English archers mustered in Andalusia, for an assault on Tunis, to be commanded by the King in person. Then the advance in North Africa fell victim for a second time to the burgeoning Franco-Spanish rivalry. The Seville fleet was diverted to the defence of the Kingdom of Naples, and in November 1511 Ferdinand announced that in view of the French threat, he was compelled to postpone his plans in Africa. Despite Cisneros's ardent lobbying, no further conquests were made in the reign of Ferdinand, though in his testament in 1516 the King echoed his wife's appeal for the crusade in Africa to be resumed.

Impressive as they looked on paper, this string of North African towns turned out to be less profitable in reality. Cisneros's ambitious but impracticable plans to settle immigrants along the coastal plain failed to win favour with the Crown, and in his last years Ferdinand came to see the ports not as springboards for further advance, or the bases for missionary activity, but as defensive positions against the Turks and their allies or clients, the corsairs, North African emirs, and Granadan exiles. The commercial gains were disappointing: by mid-century Spanish trade with Barbary yielded only 25,000 ducats a year in taxes, which in 1559 amounted to less than half the amount paid out in salaries to the Spanish soldiers in Oran alone. Seven years later the cost of wages for all the North African forts exceeded 200,000 ducats. Ferdinand's demand that the forts be self-financing proved impossible to implement. Isolated and expensive to maintain, the coastal forts had in fact come to look like a collection of Smyrnas, a striking fact in view of the resemblance between papal grants to Portuguese Ceuta and those earlier made by the Avignonese popes to the Anatolian outpost. None the less, in strategic terms Spain's North African possessions had a vital role to play in the great contest which now began between the Habsburg Charles V and the Ottomans for naval supremacy in the Mediterranean. From the very start of his reign Charles authorized operations against the corsairs who were attacking Bougie, securing the regular renewal of grants of the *cruzada* and the tenth for that purpose, despite the claims of the French that the money would be used against them. These campaigns were on a large scale—8,000 men were landed in an attempt to take Algiers in 1516, and 13,000 were used to destroy the pirate nest on Jerba in 1520—but they were overshadowed by the great conflict which developed after 1533, when a truce was sealed in the Balkans and the full attention of Habsburgs and Ottomans was given to the Maghrib.

The Mediterranean galley war which followed, lasting from Charles V's expedition to Tunis in 1535 to the battle of Lepanto in 1571, has been

described in Chapter 4.[4] There stress was laid on the crusading character
of Lepanto, and the fact that the Holy League was a lineal descendant of
earlier naval leagues against the Turks. Equally important, however, is the
fact that this protracted burst of naval warfare formed a continuum with
the North African crusades of Ferdinand, and hence with the conquest of
Granada and the last phase of the Reconquest. In leading the Tunis
crusade of 1535, for instance, Charles V carried out his grandfather's
aborted project of 1511. In military terms this continuum is readily
explained by the power vacuum which existed in the Maghrib at the end
of the fifteenth century, the dynamics of Ottoman expansion and the
rapid development of its naval arm, and Spain's fear, well-grounded
historically, of an invasion of the peninsula from North Africa. The
continuum is most striking in the institutional sense that there was
scarcely a break between the preaching of the *cruzada* and the levy of
church taxes for the war against Granada, and identical grants being
made for war against Muslim powers outside the peninsula. Given the
long-standing links between Christendom's two oldest crusading fronts,
the East and Iberia, it is peculiarly appropriate that in the last significant
period of crusading activity, the two should have merged.

One of North Africa's many rivals to the attention and resources of the
Spanish monarchy was the New World. Spain's inability to make conquests in Africa beyond the ports themselves, and the gruelling and
expensive defence of the coastal forts, contrasted sharply with its massive
territorial gains in America and the huge shipments of gold and silver
which resulted from them. Historians have long recognized the extent to
which these processes of conquest and settlement were based upon the
Reconquest experience: the debt is clear in a number of respects, ranging
from the system of *capitulaciones* used to formalize the subjugation of the
Indians, to the role of the Church and town corporations in colonization
and government, and the importance of sheep ranching in the colonial
economy. The links have recently been reaffirmed and elucidated in the
case of those 'laboratories' of nascent Iberian colonialism, Madeira, the
Canaries, and the Azores. Did the crusading aspect of the Reconquest
also have a part to play? Many contemporaries believed that it did. When
López of Gómara claimed that 'the conquest of the Indies began when
that of the Moors was over, for the Spanish have always fought against
infidels', he was expressing a common idea; it was accepted, for example,
in *Inter caetera* (1493), the bull in which Pope Alexander VI addressed

[4] Above, 131–42.

himself to the juridical problems created by Columbus's discoveries. But the very simplicity of this correlation between the end of holy war in Spain and the beginning of holy war overseas, enshrined in the fact that Columbus discovered the New World in the year Granada fell, warns us against too readily interpreting Spain's overseas conquests in crusade terms. A degree of initial scepticism is called for.

Institutional continuity is, as in the case of North Africa, impressive. On the basis of thorough research in the Vatican Archives, C.-M. De Witte showed that from the early fifteenth century onwards the Portuguese Crown gained a series of important crusade grants in support of its exploration off the western coast of Africa. Many of these grants were related to a hoped-for consolidation of Portugal's tenuous grip on the Atlantic coast of Morocco, but others extended papal backing to island conquests. Since these conquests could not be placed within the juridical context of the Reconquest, they posed a problem of interpretation for the Curia. The Canaries, a major archipelago of inhabited islands, proved to be the test case for papal thinking on the legitimacy of such activity, and hence on its claim to crusading status. When Clement VI made an abortive grant of the islands to a Spanish prince, Louis of la Cerda, in 1344, he took a confused stance: the Pope played with the extreme argument, first put forward in the thirteenth century by the canonist Hostiensis, that pagans could not enjoy political sovereignty; but, as if admitting the weakness of this argument, Clement also legitimized Louis's proposed expedition in terms of a dubious series of supposed acts of Canarian aggression against Christians, and infringements of natural law. A century later Eugenius IV rejected Hostiensis's argument in favour of the more moderate position adopted by that canonist's contemporary, Pope Innocent IV, that pagans had the right to govern themselves, but that this was overriden by the papal responsibility for their souls. A pope could thus authorize conquest if it would facilitate the work of missionary conversion; he could also, as Eugenius himself did, briefly, in 1434, prohibit conquest if it was impeding the work of missionaries. To this position, which avoided the heretical implications of Hostiensis's argument but enabled the popes to validate virtually any overseas conquest, the Curia clung well into the Early Modern period. So too did the Portuguese and Spanish. The effect was to create an association between conquest and conversion which had been largely absent from the justification of earlier crusading. *Dilatatio fidei* now firmly displaced *defensio fidei*, as for example in the bulls of Nicholas V and Alexander VI sanctioning overseas conquest.

The various phases of European conquest of the Canaries, actual or attempted, were thus nearly all backed by crusade privileges: this applied to Louis of la Cerda's plan in 1344–5, to the Norman expedition of John of Béthencourt and Gadifer of la Salle in the years following 1402, and to Castile's definitive conquest of Grand Canary, La Palma, and Tenerife in 1478–96. But the extent to which these grants corresponded to the motivation of those who made the initial Atlantic conquests has been hotly disputed. In a recent study, Dr Felipe Fernández-Armesto has made a distinction in this respect between Castile and Portugal. 'The evidence is overwhelming', he wrote, 'that the [Castilian] conquest of the Canaries was conceived and justified, not only by the monarchs and their advisers, but also at quite humble social and intellectual levels, as an extension of the "Reconquest", not much different in kind from the subjugation of Granada'. By contrast, he has argued, the motivation of Portugal's exploration and conquests along the coast of West Africa was chiefly, as in the case of her Moroccan conquests, the desire to establish a direct grip on the sources of African gold.

Any discussion of Portugal's overseas activity must hinge on the figure of Prince Henry, 'The Navigator', who merited his sobriquet even less than most medieval rulers (it was not in fact coined until the seventeenth century). Henry exerted a dominant influence on royal policy from the seizure of Ceuta in 1415 until his death in 1460, and in a famous passage inserted in his account of Portugal's exploration of the Guinea coast, Gomes Eannes of Zurara offered six reasons why Henry backed exploration so fervently. Two of these were related to the struggle against Islam, in that the Infante wanted to ascertain the exact extent of Muslim power in Africa, and discover hitherto unknown Christian rulers in Africa, especially the mythical Prester John, whose military assistance was hoped for on so many occasions in the later Middle Ages. A third reason was ' [Henry's] great desire to make increase in the faith of our lord Jesus Christ and to bring to him all the souls that could be saved'. Some historians have accepted, albeit with reservations, this picture of Henry as a crusading strategist and missionary, emphasizing his piety and passion for chivalric renown, especially in the Infante's last decades. George Holmes remarked that 'everything suggests that he was above all a dedicated crusader'. For Carl Erdmann, the great German historian of the crusades, Henry's career represented the late flowering of Portuguese crusade enthusiasm, while the Order of Christ, which helped to fund his maritime investments, formed a bridge between the Reconquest and

Portugal's overseas conquests. Others, most recently Dr Fernández-Armesto, have portrayed Henry as a pirate-slaver on a grand scale, whose goals (all unfulfilled) were gold, conquest, and a royal title, and who wrapped his ambitions up in the language of crusading in order to obtain papal support and deceive posterity. The question has yet to be resolved, and it is hard to see how it can be if all of Henry's own pronouncements are regarded as elaborate camouflage.

The view that Castile's discoveries were more inspired by crusading ideas and sentiments than those of Portugal derives a priori support from the career and writings of Columbus himself. Recent research has shown that Columbus shared fully in the atmosphere of millenial expectation that prevailed in Spain in the early 1490s. Throughout crusading history, success had been interpreted primarily as a divine stimulus and strategic springboard for more ambitious projects, and both the Admiral and his sponsors, the Catholic Monarchs, envisaged two goals of his voyages as the recovery of Jerusalem and the conversion of the world. Both were to be achieved by discovering a sea route to India and establishing contact with its peoples, who had reportedly shown interest in the Christian faith. These ideas were put forward with comparative restraint in 1492, but in his later years Columbus became, at times, obsessed with the eschatological expectations aroused by his reading of the works of Peter of Ailly, and in his remarkable and unjustly neglected 'Book of Prophecies' he cast himself in the role of Messiah of the Last Days, charged with the burden of recovering Jerusalem. As Columbus himself put it, 'In this voyage to the Indies Our Lord wished to perform a very evident miracle in order to console me and the others in the matter of this other voyage to the Holy Sepulchre.' It is probably going too far to say that this delusion of Columbus's later, disappointed, years, was the main motivation of his earlier voyages. None the less, the similarity to the rationale behind Castile's eastward expansion, along the Maghriban coast, is striking. But it is not altogether surprising: since the early twelfth century, Spaniards had worked the defence or liberation of the Holy Places into their own struggle against Islam, and the conquest of Granada, occurring in a period when prophetic and apocalyptic ideas were so popular, was bound to give rise to grandiose programmes of conquest. Columbus himself quoted the prophecy, made by Arnold of Villanova two centuries earlier, that 'he who will restore the ark of Zion will come from Spain'.

In the Indies themselves, the crusade was present less in the institutional or eschatological senses, than in what Professor Parry aptly termed the 'truculent missionary faith' of the *conquistadores*. The *cruzada* was certainly being preached in the Indies by 1516, but the money collected was destined for the homeland and its struggle against the Turks; Spain's massive mainland conquests seem to have been made too fast, and too far from royal and papal government, for crusade privileges to have played a major role. A slower conquest, more strictly directed by the Crown, would no doubt have been validated as a crusade, just as that of the Canaries had been. And yet the attitudes associated with Spanish crusading are constantly present in such key sources as the letters of Cortés, and Bernal Díaz's 'Conquest of New Spain'. Cortés's army carried banners inscribed with the cross; Christ, the Virgin, and St James were frequently appealed to, and made efficacious response; and, most interestingly, the *conquistadores* were obsessed with conversion, even occasionally at a cost to their military progress. Bernal Díaz's own analysis of his comrades' motives has often been disparagingly quoted: 'service of God and of His Majesty [Charles V], and to give light to those who sat in darkness—and also to acquire that wealth which most men covet'; and it is true that most of the Spanish conquerors would not have gone to the Indies had there not been the lure of gold, land, and slaves. But the hope of acquiring wealth had never been incompatible with crusading ideas: a papal bull of 1481, for instance, acknowledged that the Portuguese were undertaking conquests in Africa to secure the gold routes as well as to bring about conversions, without seeing any discrepancy or conflict between the two goals. And it is undeniable that crusading ideas were as deeply ingrained in the *conquistadores*' mentality as greed was, affording them confidence of victory and solace in defeat, and giving them an advantage over the Indians scarcely less important than their technical superiority in equipment.

The outpouring of energy and skill which made possible Spanish expansion into the Maghrib and conquests in the Americas, was characteristic of Spain's 'Golden Age', as was the persistence in both fields of at least some traditional features of Spanish crusading. Internally, the corresponding developments were the continuing roles played by the Military Orders and the 'Bula de la cruzada'. Their significance for the Spanish government was demonstrated by the establishment of royal advisory councils, in 1495 in the case of the Orders, and in 1509 in that of the *cruzada*. The history of the *cruzada* in the sixteenth century is a remarkable one in several respects. Since the start of the Granada war the *cruzada* had been granted to the Spanish Crown on such a regular basis that its proceeds had become a crucial feature of state finances. Gaspar Contarini, the Venetian ambassador, claimed in 1525 that three years' revenue from the *cruzada* amounted to 500,000 ducats, and the average annual profit during Charles V's reign seems to have been not much less than the Crown's income from America. Just as important as the amount which could be raised was its reliability; thus in 1570 the papal nuncio at Madrid wrote to Pius V's Secretary of State that the *cruzada* represented 'a large, immediate, and ever-present source of help'. Securing the *cruzada* had thus become as important for the financial health of Habsburg Spain as the clerical tenth had been for the early Valois kings of France.

The 'Bula de la cruzada' was, however, problematic. In order to maximize the profits, massive abuses had become integral to the way the *cruzada* was preached. The Crown farmed out each *Bula* to the highest bidder, usually a financier, who then hired 'preachers' (in practice not necessarily clerics) on a commission basis to hawk the *buletas*. The profit motive was thus ineradicably worked into the administration of the *Bula*. As successive Church councils complained, the 'preachers' became notorious for their use of coercion and lies to secure their sales. For example, labourers were forced to purchase a *buleta* in advance if they did not want to lose a day's work, sometimes in the middle of harvesting or grape-picking, as a result of compulsory attendance at sermons; and the idea was encouraged that salvation itself was impossible without a *buleta*. In order to persuade people to buy new *buletas*, each *Bula* was preached in three stages: the *suspensión*, when all existing privileges were nullified until the purchase of a new *buleta*, the *composición*, which consisted of the opportunity to settle ill-gotten gains, and the *ripredicatione*, when the *Bula* was preached again, with the addition of a few extra privileges. By mid-century there was widespread discontent with the *cruzada* within the Spanish church and among thoughtful laymen. Clerics in particular were appalled at this constant undermining of the penitential system, and irritated at the regular suspension of their own indulgences. The Bishop of Jaén waxed lyrical at Trent in 1546 about the 'numerous scandals' associated with the *cruzada*. But few Spanish critics dared openly to oppose a practice which worked to the benefit of their government. If the *cruzada* was to be reformed, the lead would have to be taken by the papacy.

The popes of the early sixteenth century were well aware of the abuses which were caused by the *cruzada* since it was also preached in Charles V's Italian lands, especially the Kingdom of Naples. None the less, they generally proved to be compliant towards the Emperor's demands for the regular renewal of the *cruzada*, either because they recognized the need for extraordinary financing of his war against the Turks, or because they needed Charles's support for other policies. When Paul III tried to suspend the *cruzada* in 1536, it was in order to replace it by the *fábrica*, the sale of indulgences in precisely the same way for the rebuilding of St Peter's. The struggle which ensued was settled by a compromise, by which the *cruzada* and *fábrica* alternated until 1552. The reforming atmosphere of the Council of Trent at first left the *cruzada* untouched, and Paul IV's suspension of the *cruzada* in 1555 and 1556 was again motivated less by reports of the abuses associated with it, than by the Pope's hatred for Charles V and Philip II. Pius IV's attempts at reform were unsuccessful, and it was only with the accession of Pius V in 1566 that the Spanish government encountered a pope who was determined to apply to the *cruzada* the ruling of the Council of Trent that indulgences should not be sold.

The conflict which ensued lasted for five years. Doctrinally the Spanish position was weak; when the court asked a group of leading archbishops and bishops for their advice on the *cruzada* in 1567, hoping for their support, the result was heavy criticism of many aspects of its administration. But Philip II's trump card was the fact that he was engaged in an appallingly expensive war against both the Turks in the Mediterranean and the Calvinists in the Low Countries. Without the *cruzada*, Philip's envoys repeatedly told Pius V, these conflicts could not be fought; and they were not far wrong, as it has been estimated that Pius's recalcitrance was costing the King 400,000 ducats a year. With extreme reluctance, the Pope granted a much restricted form of *cruzada* at the end of 1568, reverting to old formulae on the indulgence, stripping away many of the accumulated privileges, and failing to fix a payment rate for the indulgence. The Spanish rejected the bull as financially useless and negotiations got nowhere until, to save his beloved Holy League, Pius made important concessions. He adamantly refused to set a fixed rate of payment, 'because it seemed to him that he could not do that with a clear conscience, as it was expressly prohibited by the Council of Trent'. But his bull *Cum antea* of 21 May 1571, initially a two-year grant, was considered profitable enough for John Fernández of Espinosa to purchase the right of its administration in October for 684,000 ducats.

True to form, the Spanish government regarded *Cum antea* as merely a staging post on the road back to the old 'Bula de la cruzada', but it was made clear to Philip II's envoys in Rome that neither Pius V nor his successors would make more than minor changes to Pius's bull. Gregory XIII's bull *Cum alias* (15 July 1573) thus replaced Sixtus IV's bull of 1482 as the model for future *cruzada* grants. Partially reformed, and restored to a position of importance in Spanish governmental finance, the future of the *cruzada* was secure. For nearly three centuries grants of the *cruzada* were regularly made by the papal Curia, which earned its reward in the form of the sexennial payment of 100,000 ducats, a share rooted in the original compromise on the *fábrica*. Only in 1851 was the governmental post of 'Comisario general de la cruzada' abolished under the terms of Spain's new concordat with the papacy. From this point onwards the *cruzada* was administered by the Spanish church rather than the Crown, and its proceeds were spent on pastoral concerns. Only in 1915, when the Catholic Church's canon law was recodified, did there occur, in Jose Goñi Gaztambide's words, the final abandonment of 'the classic formula employed for the granting of the indulgence, the golden thread which linked the modern bulls with the most remote origins of the crusade'. The 'Bula de la cruzada' thus not only brought one of the crusading movement's basic features into the Early Modern period, but gave it residual life as late as the first decade of the present century.

In Chapter 4[5] it was noted that the *cruzada* was one of 'three graces' which the popes regularly granted to the Spanish Crown at the time of Lepanto, the other two being the clerical tax, or *subsidio*, and the *excusado*, which dated from 1567. By this point the *subsidio* was a tax of swingeing proportions, commonly a quarter of Church revenues in grants made to Philip II, and a half in the case of one grant to Charles V, though this was subsequently commuted to a lump sum. But it originated in the clerical tenth and must therefore be taken into account in any evaluation of what the Crown gained from traditional crusading sources. The *tercias reales*, which also originated in *Reconquista* finance, were treated as an ordinary Church tax by the Habsburgs and were collected alongside the *alcabala*, or sales tax. By contrast, the three graces were intended by the Curia to cover the military cost of Spain's struggle against infidels and heretics, the *excusado* being granted specifically for the suppression of the Dutch Revolt. This was more than a face-saving formula. The Spanish clergy objected vociferously in the 1550s when funds from the *subsidio* were used in the war against France, and Philip II had to pacify them by promising that the money would in future be stored separately, and used

[5] Above, 147–8.

only for the needs of the North African forts. Twenty years later the Habsburg administration again undertook to translate theory into practice, this time for budgeting reasons rather than on grounds of conscience. Proceeds from the *cruzada* were allocated to the provisioning and payment of the African garrisons, and the *subsidio* to the pay of the government's galleys. But constant fiscal problems normally caused all three graces to be deployed indiscriminately to cover advances from bankers and other expenses. A renewed attempt to divorce the three graces from other revenues, made by Philip III in 1602–3, also met with failure.

The value of the Military Orders to the Crown was, again, chiefly financial. In 1523 Pope Adrian VI, Charles V's former tutor, ratified the incorporation of the Orders in the Crown, formalizing the control of the various masterships (*maestrazgos*) built up by Ferdinand. The financial gain by the Crown was substantial and twofold, consisting of the rents from the Orders' lands in Spain, and of what has been termed a 'new mine of patronage' derived from the granting of titles and honours. Ferdinand himself believed the yield from the *maestrazgos* to be equal to that from the Kingdom of Naples; and at the start of the sixteenth century the Venetian ambassador Vincent Quirini estimated the combined annual value of Santiago, Calatrava, and Alcántara to be 111,000 ducats. What has already been said about the reliability of the *cruzada* applies even more strongly to the *maestrazgos*, which were not contingent upon papal grants of any kind. Taken together, the contribution made by *cruzada, subsidio, excusado*, and *maestrazgos* to Habsburg finances was clearly enormous. But there was a price to pay. In 1574 a complaint was made to Philip II that more than a half of Church revenues went to the Crown, and one indirect consequence of this very high level of Church taxation was capital starvation in the Spanish economy, since it was not in the government's interests to issue mortmain legislation to prevent property being bequeathed to the Church.

There were other important respects in which these institutions continued to exercise a formative impact on Spanish society. It is true that the *cruzada* was, in some respects, a distant relative of earlier crusade bulls: already by 1500 many of those who purchased *buletas* gave little thought to the reason they were being hawked, and were less interested in the indulgence than in the exemptions which accompanied it (such as the right to consume eggs and milk during Lent). Nevertheless, the *cruzada* remained, in the sixteenth century at least, identifiably a crusade bull, and its character has been radically misunderstood by those historians who have called it a 'tax'. At times of national crisis, when deployed in association with royal propaganda, it thus served as confirmation of the idea that the Spanish government was fighting on behalf of the faith. This was most clearly the case in the sixteenth century, though as late as 1898, when Cuba was lost, the Bishop of Segovia could call for a national crusade against the United States. But the perpetuation of the Military Orders was more important; as one historian commented, they 'served as an extant institutional embodiment' of the *Reconquista*, as 'the essential intellectual link between reconquest and conquest, crusade and empire'.

This was testimony to the Orders' important social role rather than to their military activity, which was nugatory. There were instances of individual brethren playing a part in Spain's expansion, such as Nicholas of Ovando, Knight Commander of Alcántara, who proved to be an energetic governor of Hispaniola in 1502–9. But the Spanish Orders generally displayed none of the flexibility displayed by the Hospitallers and Teutonic Knights. Proposals brought before the general chapter of Santiago in 1509, and the Castilian *cortes* in 1551 and 1576, that the Orders should be given the task of forwarding and defending Spain's possessions in North Africa, were not taken up; earlier attempts by both the papal and Portuguese courts to persuade Portugal's Military Orders to take part in the conquest of Morocco had been equally unsuccessful. In these circumstances the Orders themselves naturally became decadent: the brethren were allowed to own property, and to marry (in 1540 Paul III permitted the Knights of Calatrava and Alcántara to interpret the vow of chastity as entailing conjugal faithfulness). And when Olivares raised a regiment from the Knights of the Orders in 1640, the result was a débâcle.

On the other hand, acquisition of membership of an Order, the *hábito*, became a highly valued means of proving one's *limpieza* (purity of blood, the possession of solely Christian ancestry). This was because the three main Orders were extremely strict in excluding candidates of *converso* extraction. In 1661 Gerónimo Mascarenas described the role of the Council of the Orders as 'to conserve the Spanish aristocracy, to keep unsullied the purity of noble families, to give honour to persons who merit it, to distinguish the illustrious from the common herd, the noble from the base'. Satirists made fun of the anachronistic nature of the Orders, and the *hábitos* themselves were inexorably devalued as the hard-pressed Crown sold them to the patently unmilitary and non-noble, but prestige continued to be attached to the Orders well into the seventeenth century. Gonzalo Fernández of Córdoba, Spain's great commander in Italy, Hernan Cortés and Francis Pizarro, its leading *conquistadores*, and Don John of Austria, the victor of Lepanto, were all invested with *hábitos*. Investment with an *hábito* was regarded as a fitting tribute for the admiral Francis of Ribera in 1624, in recognition of a brilliant success against a vastly superior Turkish fleet. Much as they changed in nature, the Military Orders, like the *cruzada*, survived; by so doing they proved able to bridge and give inner coherence to several phases of Spanish history, including the Reconquest, the struggle against the Turks, and the expansion overseas.

But to conclude this survey of the later history of Spanish crusading ideas it is necessary to return to the theme of government. Two key goals of Spanish foreign policy in the reigns of Charles V and Philip II, the defeat of the Turks and the suppression of heresy, were traditional crusade objectives. As we have seen, the financing of that policy hinged on papal grants, including the 'Bula de la cruzada'. For these reasons the Spanish court's view of its role within Europe generally, formulated most forcefully in its correspondence with the papacy, laid emphasis upon the idea that Spain was serving God and Christendom, and that if the pope did not support Habsburg objectives he would be acting wrongly. It would be going too far to say that the Spanish regarded their foreign policy generally as a crusade, but at times, especially when the revolt in the Netherlands coincided with the height of the conflict against the Ottomans, the convergence was strong. The situation became in fact curiously reminiscent of the early fourteenth century, when the French court treated the conflict in Flanders as a holy war and accused the Flemings of impeding its project for a *passagium* against the Mamluks. The tone of injured self-righteousness sounded by Philip II, when the papacy gave him less than full support, thus reads remarkably like pronouncements of Philip the Fair of France and his immediate successors.

This might lead one to expect that Spain's military role in the Counter-Reformation would take on the appearance of a fully fledged crusade. Two sets of circumstances appear to have stopped this happening. One was Philip II's poor relations with the papal Curia; apart from constant clashes over ecclesiastical jurisdiction, taxation of the Spanish church, and the *cruzada*, there was understandable reluctance on the papacy's part to assist the further growth of Spain's enormous power. 'Great Christian princes', Sixtus V remarked, 'require a counterpoise', and even Protestant and Islamic rulers were sometimes acceptable in this capacity.

Nor would the Counter-Reformation Curia accept Philip II's assessment of his political role in Europe, viewing the King's constant claims to be preserving Catholicism as 'a pretext for His Majesty, whose principal aim is the security and aggrandisement of his dominions'. Secondly, although Philip II and his troops certainly saw the suppression of the Dutch revolt as a struggle for the defence of Catholicism, the King refused formally to treat the war as a crusade for the same reasons that his father had advanced in the case of German Lutheranism: that it would serve to unify the enemy, increase the danger of outside intervention, and make it impossible to hire Protestant troops. In fact the only clear instance of a 'Counter-Reformation crusade' appears to have been the Armada against England in 1588. It was able to enjoy clear crusade status since there were no political obstacles in the way, and the papal and Spanish courts had reached a consensus on ending English Protestantism by force. English Catholics like Nicholas Sanders and William Allen helped to provide an intellectual framework for the venture by updating traditional ideas on the validity of crusading against heretical rulers. The soldiers and sailors of the Spanish fleet thus enjoyed crusade indulgences, and there were traditional crusade ceremonies before the Armada sailed. The inscription on the Armada's banner, 'Arise, O Lord, and vindicate thy cause', had been used in crusades against recalcitrant Christians for centuries. But the agreement with Sixtus V which made all this possible proved to be fragile and short-lived.

These events have been recounted here, rather than in Chapter 8, because the launching of the Armada is best viewed as the last phase in the extraordinary burst of Spanish self-confidence which began in 1492. Decades of almost continual military successes, most of them won over infidels, pagans, and heretics and set against a background of *cruzada* preaching, had confirmed the firm belief amongst Spaniards that their government exercised a providential role. The temptation to interpret the parable of the feast in Luke 14: 16–24 ('compel them to come in') as 'an eschatological rationale for the universal monarchy of the Spanish Habsburgs' proved too strong for such men as the Franciscan missionary and thinker Gerónimo of Mendieta, who wrote, in his 'Historia eclesiástica indiana':

I am firmly convinced that as those Catholic Monarchs [Ferdinand and Isabella] were granted the mission of beginning to extirpate those three diabolical squadrons 'perfidious' Judaism, 'false' Mohammedanism and 'blind' idolatry along with the fourth squadron of the heretics whose remedy and medicine is the

Holy Inquisition, in like manner the business of completing this task has been reserved for their royal successors; so that as Ferdinand and Isabella cleansed Spain of these wicked sects, in like manner their royal descendants will accomplish the universal destruction of these sects throughout the whole world and the final conversion of all the peoples of the earth to the bosom of the church.[6]

Most recently, the battle of Lepanto, followed by Alexander Farnese's string of successes in the Low Countries in the early 1580s, combined to create the ethos of supreme optimism which underpinned the Armada project. 'I consider this enterprise the most important undertaken by God's church for many hundreds of years', was the comment of Peter of Ribadeneyra, a Jesuit priest.

Every conceivable pretext for a just and holy war is to be found in this campaign ... This is a defensive, not an offensive, war: one in which we are defending our sacred religion and our most holy Roman Catholic Faith; one in which we are defending the high reputation of our King and lord, and of our nation; defending, too, the land and property of all the kingdoms of Spain, and simultaneously our peace, tranquillity and repose.[7]

The storm which proved fatal to the Armada thus dealt a crushing blow to Spanish morale; a papal nuncio in Madrid reported that 'everybody is astounded to see the hand of God so openly against us'. The Armada's failure is often seen as a premonition of the ending of Habsburg Spain's 'Golden Age'; it certainly brought to a close a century during which Spanish military prowess had appeared to validate the impression, made so firmly in 1492, that what Spain did was the work of God.

In the past, attempts to trace the aftermath of the Spanish crusading tradition formed during the *Reconquista* have focused on the New World. It has been argued that, just as so many of the techniques of conquest and settlement employed in the Americas had their roots in the peninsular conquests, so the optimism, daring, and bravado which formed such essential weapons of the *conquistadores* derived from their crusading background. This may have been the case, although it is worth pointing out that the *conquistadores* were not alone amongst their contemporaries (Protestant as well as Catholic) in displaying courage and daring, nor need these qualities have derived solely from the peninsular crusading experience. I would argue that the Spaniards who remained, and who fought against the North African Moors, the Turks, and the

[6] J. L. Phelan, *The Millennial Kingdom of the Franciscans in the New World*, 2nd edn. (Berkeley, Calif., 1970), 13.
[7] J. H. Elliott, *Imperial Spain 1469–1716* (Harmondsworth, 1970), 288.

Protestants, were just as much the legatees of Reconquest crusading as those who went; they too marched behind banners portraying traditional crusade images, and enjoyed visions of St George and St James fighting alongside them in battle. Their thinking was, moreover, fully in harmony with a society in which a form of crusade bull continued to be preached, in which churchmen still paid to the Crown taxes rooted in the crusades, and in which both noblemen, and those who aspired to *hidalguía*, valued membership of the Military Orders. Above all, it was Charles V and Philip II who 'inherited' the crusade from Ferdinand and Isabella, in the sense that both rulers interpreted many of their political actions within a crusading context. In view of the efforts made by the Catholic Monarchs to prevent the Habsburg succession to their Spanish realms, this seems ironic. In many respects the creation of the Spanish overseas empire did form a continuation of the Reconquest as a whole; this was predictable, since many of the problems of conquest and colonization which the Spaniards faced were similar. But there is a strong case for arguing that the principal heir to the institutions, habits, and ideas of Spanish crusading was Habsburg imperial policy in the Old World.

11

The Crusade in North-Eastern Europe 1274–1382

✠

AMONGST the memoirs written in response to Pope Gregory X's plea of 1272 for advice on the crusade, one originated in Moravia. Its author, Bishop Bruno of Olmütz (Olomouc), was anxious to point out that it was just as important to defend the Church in eastern Europe from attack by pagans and schismatics, as it was to recover the Holy Land; otherwise, wishing to avoid Charybdis, the Christians would fall prey to Scylla. Bruno knew that the Curia had accepted, since the time of the Second Crusade, that crusades should be preached to further the Christian cause in eastern Europe. He also knew that while, in practice, nearly all these crusades had been associated with conquest, the Curia preferred to place crusading of all kinds within a just war framework, and that it was advisable to adopt a defensive stance; this was particularly true in the early 1270s, when the question was one of the relative needs facing the Holy Land and eastern Europe. Bruno therefore took care to enumerate the dangers to the Church in the East: the Cumans who raided Hungary, the Orthodox Russians and their Tatar lords, and the Prussians and Lithuanians who threatened the dioceses of Poland. We shall see that the relations between at least some of these peoples and their Latin Christian neighbours did indeed keep the crusading movement alive in the Baltic region for many decades to come. But viewed objectively, and over a long perspective, Bruno's attempt to portray eastern Europe as a region just as embattled as the Holy Land was tendentious in the extreme. The Bishop's lord, King Ottokar of Bohemia, was angling for the imperial crown, and a plausible argument to deploy at the Curia was that if he was granted it, he would be in a better position to help his beleagured fellow-Christians to the East. In reality the gains made by Christendom in this area since the start of the century had been almost as spectacular, and would prove to be just as enduring, as those made in the Iberian peninsula.

The most important conquests had been made in Livonia and Prussia (see maps 13 and 14). In Livonia the German commercial penetration of the Dvina valley had been viewed by Archbishop Hartwig II of Bremen, at the turn of the century, as an opportunity to convert the Livs. In 1200, after a series of misadventures, Hartwig sent his very capable nephew, Albert of Buxtehude, to undertake the task. In less than three decades Livonia, Lettigallia, southern Estonia, the island of Ösel, and the coastal plain of Curonia were subjugated. The driving force of conquest was undoubtedly the wealth of raw materials in the interior, which could be tapped along the Dvina; Riga, founded in 1201, became one of the key Baltic ports, shipping grain, furs, wax, and animals to Germany. Conquest was facilitated by the Germans' superiority in military technology, such as their armour, crossbows, catapults, and stone towers. Just as important as trade and technological advantage, however, were the two main instruments of conquest, and these would have been inconceivable without the crusading movement. The first was the service of bands of crusaders who came on an annual basis from Germany. They were recruited by Albert and his successors with the assistance of the crusade indulgences granted for Livonia by the popes of the period. The second instrument was the local Military Order of the Sword-Brethren, established by Albert in about 1202 on the model of the Knights Templar; the Order's Knights provided the garrisons for the forts which enforced German lordship over the natives, holding down lands won by the crusaders after they had returned to Germany.

In Prussia the role played by armed monks was even more important than in Livonia. The Prussians were a group of aggressive pagan tribes living east of the Vistula. Fruitless attempts at peaceful conversion in the early decades of the century were followed by a series of devastating Prussian raids against the Poles of Cujavia and Dobrzyn. After the failure of a large-scale crusade in 1222–3, Duke Conrad of Mazovia in desperation offered the southern part of Prussia, Kulmerland, to the Master of the Teutonic Knights, in return for the Order's defence of his frontiers. The 'Order of German Knights of the Hospital of St Mary at Jerusalem' was the last of the international Military Orders; it dated back to a field hospital established during the Third Crusade, which had been transformed into a Military Order in 1198 and recognized as such by

Innocent III in 1199. Although their chief commitment was to the defence of Palestine, the Teutonic Knights showed interest almost from the start in building up a territorial base in eastern Europe. The dual rationale for this was that the order would provide military assistance to Christian communities on the frontier, while helping to convert the pagans. Conrad of Mazovia's offer came at a point when the Order was being expelled from Hungary after more than a decade's service against the Cumans. The Master, Hermann of Salza, therefore tried to ensure that his Order's claim to Kulmerland would be watertight before undertaking the conquest of Prussia. In 1226 Frederick II, in the Golden Bull of Rimini, invested Hermann as an imperial prince for Kulmerland, and eight years later Pope Gregory IX accepted Prussia as a fief, to be held by the Order under papal suzerainty.

Starting at the isolated Polish fort of Kulm (Chelmno) in 1230, the Teutonic Knights advanced up the Vistula basin, with the goal of reaching the Frisches Haff. As in Livonia, groups and armies of crusaders arrived on a regular basis, in this case both Germans and Poles; the conquests which they helped the Order to make were subsequently maintained by stone keeps. Königsberg (Kaliningrad), one of the Knights' greatest castles, was built in 1254 in honour of King Ottokar of Bohemia, who had led one of the most important of these expeditions. By this point there were plans to link the territorial gains in Prussia to those in Livonia. For in 1237 the Livonian Sword-Brethren, who had been decimated by the Lithuanians in the previous year, were absorbed into the Teutonic Order and the latter assumed the military responsibility for Livonia. The northwards advance was co-ordinated with a southwards plunge from Memel in Curonia. But neither Prussia nor Livonia were to be won so easily. A serious Prussian revolt against the Order's rule in 1240 was followed by a well-organized rebellion there in 1260, itself coming in the wake of a severe defeat inflicted on the Order's Livonian branch by the Lithuanians. It was only in 1283, after the preaching of several crusades and the wholesale destruction or expulsion of the Scalovian, Nadrovian, and Sudovian tribes, that this second rebellion was finally suppressed. Although there were further attempts at revolt in 1286 and 1295, Prussia was now firmly in the Order's grip. By this point Livonia too was pacified as far south as Samogitia, which continued to separate it from Prussia.

By the time of the Second Council of Lyons, therefore, the Teutonic Order had effectively conquered vast tracts of the eastern Baltic littoral. For centuries to come the history of this region was closely shaped by the activities of the Order, as it defended and extended these gains, and worked with skill and pertinacity to implement its own methods of settlement and government there. It is thus necessary to ask how an international Order dedicated to the defence of the Holy Land became primarily associated with the government of Prussia (the *Ordensstaat* or 'Order-State'). Polish and Lithuanian historians, for historical reasons bitterly hostile towards the Order, have usually depicted it as pursuing a policy of territorial aggrandizement from the start. Some have claimed that as early as the 1220s Hermann of Salza entertained a 'grand plan' for an *Ordensstaat* modelled on the centralized autocracy supposedly practised by Frederick II, an outstanding patron of the Order, in his Kingdom of Sicily. More recently, the German historian Manfred Hellmann has proposed an explanation for the Order's territorial acquisitiveness couched in terms of contemporary German society. For in recruitment terms, the Order enjoyed its greatest success amongst the lesser nobility, especially the uniquely German group of 'service knights' (*ministeriales*). It has been suggested that many of them joined the Order as a means of social mobility, and the 'land hunger' of these men, their aspiration towards government and the status which accompanied it, have been seen as the chief driving force behind the Order's territorial ambitions.

An argument against this sociological explanation is the fact that all the international Military Orders were evincing a trend towards territorial government by the early thirteenth century; it is true that the Teutonic Order was both more persistent and more successful than the others, but this could have been because political circumstances in eastern Europe, towards which its landed holdings and patrons pulled it, were more propitious than those confronting the Hospitallers and Templars in Palestine and Syria. This said, Hellmann's explanation is plausible, provided it is accepted that the desire of many brethren for land and government, and, implicitly, for a concentration of resources on the Baltic rather than the Latin East, was opposed by a strong body of brethren who wanted to avoid the clashes with other Christian powers which this would lead to, and who continued to place the Holy Land first. It took a long time for this internal conflict to be resolved, and the slow and hesitant way in which the Order reorientated itself from the late thirteenth century counters any idea that it entertained a clear-cut view of what its future should be.

In the final decades of Christian rule in the Holy Land the Teutonic Knights faced a situation unique in the history of the Military Orders, for they were bearing simultaneous and massive military burdens along the Baltic and in the Holy Land, quite apart from their commitments in Armenia. One reason why the Order took so long to suppress the second Prussian revolt was that it needed all available men in the 1270s for the defence of Palestine. There are signs of an internal debate about priorities, which may be reflected in the extraordinary decision by Grand Master Burchard of Schwanden to join the Hospitallers on the eve of the Mamluk siege of Acre: it has been suggested that he was frustrated by opposition to his wish to reduce still further the military establishment in the Baltic. After 1291, when the Order's headquarters moved to Venice, the debate was little nearer to a solution; talk of recovery crusades was after all constant, and Venice was as conveniently placed as Cyprus for participating in one. The Prussian brethren grew more and more irritated at the absence of their Grand Master, forcing the abdication of Gottfried of Hohenlohe in 1303 and provoking an eight-year schism within the Order.

This stalemate was broken by three related sets of circumstances. One was the arrest of the Templars in 1307–8, which made the Grand Master aware both of his own physical isolation at Venice, and of the vulnerability of his Order to charges of misconduct or irrelevance. The second was the occupation of the port of Danzig (Gdańsk) and eastern Pomerelia (Pomorze) by the Prussian brethren in 1308. Called into Danzig by the Poles to resist aggression from neighbouring Brandenburg, the Teutonic Knights themselves seized the city and province on the excuse that the Poles did not reimburse them for their expenses. This flagrantly illegal move improved the lines of communication between Livonia, Prussia, and the Order's German bailiwicks, but it alienated Poland, which was robbed of its Baltic outlet and became a powerful and vociferous rival of the Order. Thirdly, the Curia was at this point investigating a formidable dossier of accusations levelled against the Livonian brethren by the Archbishop and townspeople of Riga. It would have been folly not to consolidate the territorial gains made in Pomerelia, at the same time establishing a position of military strength in the face of the Order's growing number of Christian enemies. It was therefore not surprising that in 1309 Siegfried of Feuchtwangen carried out a permanent move to Marienburg (Malbork). From this point onwards the Order was committed to the continuation of its work along the Baltic as its chief *raison d'être*.

The point to emphasize about these events is how powerful a build-up of pressure, much of it beyond the Order's control, was needed to effect the decision. And there is evidence that even so the move remained controversial. For example, in his account of the fall of Acre in the *Österreichische Reimchronik*, written in 1301–19, Ottokar of Styria portrayed Conrad, the irregularly chosen Grand Master who led the Teutonic Knights during the siege, swearing to avenge the fallen by destroying paganism in Prussia and Livonia. This was an interesting exercise in justification, and it is noteworthy that in his 'The Dream of the Old Pilgrim' (written *c*.1386), Philip of Mézières placed the Order's arrival in Prussia *after* 1291. Disagreement continued between some prominent brethren, who wanted to hand Pomerelia back to the Poles to maintain good relations, and the majority of the Knights, who wanted to keep it even at the cost of Polish hostility, fearing that the return of these lands would preface the Order's total expulsion from Prussia and consequent homelessness. Such internal bickering was a factor behind the short-lived abdication of Grand Master Charles of Trier in 1318, and the murder of his successor, Werner of Orseln, in 1330. Signs of stress like these should be borne in mind by those historians who still depict the Order's history as monothematic, and the brethren themselves as unthinking executants of a policy of aggrandizement.

Problematic as the definitive move to the Baltic had been, once carried out it enabled the Order to embark on its period of greatest achievement and renown, its *goldene Blütezeit*. One reason was that it created links between the front-line and the Order's donated estates, areas of recruitment, and chief patrons which were closer than those which any international Military Order had previously enjoyed. The Order's identification with the German nation had always been strong. Although brethren were admitted from other regions and the Order possessed lands as far afield as Greece and Castile, its heartland, in terms of both recruitment and landed holdings, was the twelve bailiwicks in the Empire. This association with Germany was tightened as the fourteenth century progressed. Non-German holdings were sold off or lost, and recruitment became almost exclusively German. As one fourteenth-century commentator remarked, 'This Order is the Order of the Germans and of the Blessed Mary of the Teutons, because they receive hardly anybody as a brother unless he is German-speaking.' Within Germany the Order's lands were concentrated in the south-west, especially in Swabia and western Franconia; its holdings in the north were fewer, though it was from here, in continuation of the tradition established by the Sword-Brethren, that the Order dispatched members to serve in Livonia. Working relations between the Prussian *Ordensstaat*, Livonia, and the German bailiwicks were generally good, partly because their mutual financial demands were light, and partly because a broad consensus on the Order's goals and government had been attained; it was not uncommon for members of the same noble family to serve simultaneously in Prussia and Germany.

In such circumstances it is not surprising that the Order's internal life flourished. The late thirteenth and fourteenth centuries were its heyday in spiritual and literary terms, and papal criticisms of the Order's political activities were rarely accompanied by the sort of complaints of conventual laxity and corruption which, as we have seen, were directed at the Hospitallers. Grand Master Luther of Brunswick (1331–5) epitomized the harmonious balancing of the Order's varied activities: as Commander of Christburg he had been an effective administrator and energetically sponsored settlement, but he also wrote religious verse and sang in the choir. Marian devotion, always a pronounced feature of the Order's spirituality, reached its peak: the Order normally started its summer and winter campaigns on the feast days of the Assumption (15 August) and Purification (2 February). The Annunciation and Nativity were also kept as high festivals, and in 1340 Grand Master Dietrich of Altenburg ordered that brethren should even honour the feast of the Conception, which was not generally observed in the West. Castles and towns named after the Virgin multiplied, and her cult permeated the prose histories, and verse chronicles and legends, which dominated the Order's impressive literary output, such as the anonymous Livonian Rhyme-Chronicle and Nicholas of Jeroschin's verse 'Chronicle of the Land of Prussia' ('Kronike von Pruzinlant'). In celebrating and justifying what had been won from the heathen, such works inspired brethren to emulate and continue the work of their predecessors.

In Prussia at least they certainly did so, for here the Order achieved, in the course of the fourteenth century, two remarkable successes. One was in the sphere of government. On the basis of the grants made to Hermann of Salza by Frederick II and Gregory IX, both Empire and papacy continued to exert a claim to suzerainty in Prussia, but this caused few problems; neither institution was strong enough to intervene effectively, and the Order was often able to play them off against each other. Within Prussia itself diarchical government by the Order and the bishops, which had been the papal Curia's goal, had been almost totally subverted by the Teutonic Knights by 1300. The chapters at Kulm, Pomesania, and Samland had been incorporated into the Order, and the bishops of Ermland alone retained their independence, leading such local criticism of the Order's rule as was voiced. The *Ordensstaat* was governed by the grand masters from Marienburg, in a highly centralized manner developed under Grand Master Werner of Orseln (1324–30), possibly in imitation of the Avignonese Curia. The grand masters took important decisions in association with a *Gebietigerrat* ('officers' council') composed of the Order's five chief officers in Prussia, the grand commander (a *de facto* lieutenant for the grand master), treasurer, marshal, and *Oberste Trapier* and *Oberste Spittler* (technically the officers bearing responsibility for the brethren's clothing and the Order's hospitaller function, but in practice honorific titles given to the commanders of Christburg and Elbing). Prussia was divided into commanderies (*Kommenden*), varying greatly in size, which were themselves subdivided into units called *Waldämter* or *Pflegerämter*. The brethren who managed these had wide-ranging duties: they furnished troops for campaigns, supervised the Order's demesne lands, presided over communities of brethren, and maintained the Order's castles, churches, and conventual houses.

This was an effective system of government, and its creation was the more remarkable in that the majority of the brethren came from southern Germany, where state-building was not progressing well in this period. It is true that the Order enjoyed a great initial advantage over nearly all its contemporaries in that it could call on the services of men bound by oaths of obedience, poverty, and chastity: these promoted efficiency, acted as a restraint on fraud, and prevented any clash between the interests of government and those of family or locality. But it built on this advantage with a series of astute institutional measures and practices. The *Ordensstaat* was one of the period's leading 'governments by paper', and written orders and reports were communicated through a postal system of exceptional rapidity which continued through the hours of darkness. An electoral process was devised which secured a relatively trouble-free succession at the death of each grand master. The problems which might have arisen from the concentration of power in the hands of the grand master were countered both by the vigilance of the *Gebietigerrat* and by the fact that his regular income was comparatively small: major expenditure entailed negotiations with the commanderies. And one of the Order's leading characteristics was the high degree of accountability at commandery level. The statutes specified that 'every officer shall show in writing how he found the possessions of the house and how he left it in ready cash and debts', and this was rigorously done from the grand mastership of Winrich of Kniprode (1351–82) onwards.

The Order's second great success lay in the field of economic management and advance. Under the terms of the treaty of Christburg (1249), all converted Prussians were supposed to enjoy the free possession of their lands, together with other civil liberties. Such an approach would have presented a virtually insuperable obstacle to the Order's economic utilization of Prussia, but the brethren argued that the series of rebellions between 1260 and 1283 rendered the native Prussians unworthy of these rights. The Order's subsequent treatment of those who were not killed, or driven into exile, varied in accordance with their stance during the revolts and their future usefulness. Many nobles were allowed to hold lands and retain their position of local superiority; of these some intermarried with immigrant Germans to form a new Prussian upper class, while others, especially on the eastern borders, remained identifiably 'Old Prussian' in their ways. The Order's success in defusing the hostility of the Old Prussian nobility is shown by the fact that in 1295 rebellious Prussian peasants planned to begin their revolt by murdering their local noblemen. For Prussian commoners, German rule generally brought seigneurial dependence, though its harshness was mitigated by the need to stop peasants migrating to better conditions elsewhere. Generalizations about the status of native Prussians are in fact as hazardous as in the case of the Spanish Mudejars, but in one crucial respect their fate was the same: military defeat entailed, in the long term, the destruction of their cultural identity, so that by 1500 Prussia, with the exception of parts of Samland and Carsovia, had been effectively 'Germanized'.

What brought this about was, of course, the influx of settlers. No previous phase of German *Ostsiedlung* had been so subject to direction as that of Prussia, and the terms offered by the Order were consistently generous; this approach was necessitated by the difficulty of working the land and the dangers from pagan Lithuania. The Order initially granted large estates to powerful nobles, but by 1300, for political as much as economic reasons, it had adopted a policy of making smaller grants to peasant settlers. The entrepreneurial linchpin in this process was the *Lokator*, who negotiated each new village's tenurial terms with the Order and invariably went on to become the village's hereditary mayor (*Schulz*). Bigger landowners were gradually bought out by the Order, and large estates restricted to the 'wilderness' of east Prussia, where continual warfare and vast forests reduced the value of the land anyway. As a result fourteenth-century Prussia contained very few great noble lineages, and was free from the disruption caused by their private castles and feuding.

The conditions under which peasant settlers lived were far superior to those in Germany and, after a slow start, Prussia was successfully colonized. By 1400 it contained about 1,400 villages covering 60,000 hides (about 2.25 million acres); it has been estimated that between 1280 and 1350 735 village churches were built. The pattern of settlement naturally favoured the richer soil, better communications, and more secure conditions of the Vistula basin. As early as 1287 the export of corn was anticipated, and in the course of the next century grain became an important constituent of Prussia's thriving export trade. It was claimed that more than 300 English ships loaded up with grain in 1392 in Danzig harbour alone. The towns which lay along the Vistula and the Baltic littoral—especially Thorn (Toruń), Kulm, Marienburg, and Elbing (El-blag)—became significant urban centres.

The Teutonic Order sponsored this burgeoning prosperity and gained enormously from it. Its own demesne lands produced grain for export and it had a number of officials responsible for monitoring trade, in particular the *Gross-Schäfer* (literally 'grand shepherd') of Marienburg, who supervised the grain market, and the *Gross-Schäfer* of Königsberg, who handled exports of raw materials from eastern Prussia. The grand master was a member of the Hanse. Revenues from exported goods, and from taxes on commerce, as well as other profits of lordship, are unquantifiable, but they enabled the Order not only to govern Prussia, wage its wars against Lithuania and provide entertainment for western knights who came to fight in them, but also to engage in a massive building programme. Dozens of castles and churches were built or rebuilt, largely in brick because of the lack of good stone, and modelled on well-known German examples. The castle at Marienburg was naturally the most impressive. As Eric Christiansen has put it, it was 'not only a fort but also a palace, a monastery, a parliament-house, a government office, an arsenal and a holy city, stunning the senses and awing the mind'. Within it the grand master kept an elaborate and costly court; it is not surprising that visitors from the West, used to rulers who could neither control their countries adequately nor pay for their outgoings, were somewhat astonished by a prince who could do both with apparent ease.

The Teutonic Knights could not expect to achieve the same degree of governmental or economic success in Livonia. Episcopal power was already well entrenched when the Order took over from the Sword-Brethren in 1237, and by the century's last decade there had developed a natural alliance between the archbishops of Riga and the chartered citizens of Riga, sometimes assisted by the bishops of Courland, Dorpat (Tartu), and Ösel. Friction over military obligations, trading rights on the Dvina, and civic affairs in Riga escalated into civil war in 1295. The Rigan alliance could not win a straightforward war against the Livonian branch of the Order, and it took steps which were to characterize this unequal conflict throughout the following decades: it called in Lithuanian soldiers to attack the Order in the rear, and it appealed to the Pope, Livonia's feudal suzerain. The dossiers presented to the Curia on this and later occasions by the Order and its enemies rehearsed in great detail the wide variety of incidents which were inevitable in a country where basic issues of government were unsettled, but overall the brethren were more to blame. Confronted with hostile papal verdicts, their response was invariably to lodge an immediate appeal, or, if that failed, to refuse to implement them. Consistently they taunted their enemies with their helplessness:

Don't you know that we are your pope? And even if your pope lived in this region with you, he would have to give you up to us whether he wanted to or not, and your pope is far away [1295] . . . You know that we are your pope, and we have a pope with us . . . The sword is our pope and it is a pope that is never far from you [1305] . . . If forty wagons came with papal letters in favour of the Archbishop and the Rigan church, the Rigans would still have to fulfil their promises [1359].[1]

The self-assurance of these comments does not disguise the fact that the brethren were failing to translate temporary military advantage into institutional control along the lines of the *Ordensstaat*. This was frustrating, but the Teutonic Knights also knew that Livonia offered less scope for economic management than Prussia. The harsh terrain attracted fewer immigrants, and the handful of lords who settled there in the thirteenth century as vassals of the bishops or Military Orders continued to hold sway. They used the civil conflict to extract concessions, in much the same way that the Order turned the papal-imperial dispute to its advantage. Under these masters, the native Livonians suffered seigneurial obligations severer than those endured by the Old Prussians. But if the Livonian feudatories, especially such well-established families as the Üxkülls, Thisenhusens, Ropes, and Rosens, held their lands under conditions notably better than their counterparts in Prussia, they also had heavier military duties to perform in defending a longer frontier. Its defence fell heaviest, however, on the Livonian brethren, who maintained

---

[1] W. Urban, *The Livonian Crusade* (Washington, DC, 1981), 33, 52, 121.

140 castles of varying sizes, perhaps two dozen of which called for substantial garrisons. Inevitably, the Livonian branch of the Order remained the poor relation of the Prussian brethren: an inventory of 1341 from the important castellany of Goldingen reveals a level of resources considerably lower than a convent of comparable size in Prussia would have been able to boast. Similarly, most of the money lent to the Livonian Master by Grand Master Dusemer in 1346 for the purchase of Danish Estonia had to be written off later. In economic terms, Livonia would not have been worth holding at all but for its trade routes to the Russian interior.

Prussia and Livonia were not the only territorial gains won by crusaders in the Baltic region during the thirteenth century. To the north the monarchies of Denmark and Sweden had also been active. In 1219 King Valdemar II of Denmark staked a claim to Estonia by building a fort, called Reval (Tallinn), guarding the country's best harbour. The King's naval dominance of the Baltic enabled him to pressurize the Sword-Brethren, and later the Teutonic Knights, into accepting Danish suzerainty over lands which they had conquered in southern Estonia; but neither Valdemar nor his successors could spare the resources to push their holdings further east than Narva, which marked the frontier with Novgorod. The Danish hold over Estonia was always tenuous. The country was colonized mainly by Germans whose rights of land tenure and self-government became steadily more advanced, until Valdemar IV acknowledged the hopelessness of trying to control this distant province by selling it to the Teutonic Knights for 10,000 marks in 1346. This was a natural move since the Estonian feudatories had always co-operated with the Order in military matters; three years previously the Livonian brethren had effectively rescued the Estonian Germans when the natives rebelled against their severe oppression, in the only fourteenth-century uprising which bears comparison with the Old Prussian revolts of 1260–83.

Denmark's gains in Estonia were thus little more than conquest by proxy, but Sweden's crusade against pagan Finland was much more substantial. In the early thirteenth century the Suomi (south-west Finns) had been converted by peaceful means, but attempts to bring conversion, and with it some form of political control, to the nomadic inland tribes of Tavastia and Karelia, brought the Swedes into collision with Novgorod, whose Orthodox princes were trying the same thing. In 1237 Gregory IX proclaimed a crusade against the Tavastians, and three years later the first major clash between Sweden and Novgorod ended in a decisive Russian victory. But in 1249 a Swedish crusade, which was later celebrated in colourful chivalric language in the 'Eric Chronicle', conquered the Tavastians. Novgorod saw the acute threat facing its trade routes through the Gulf of Finland and another Russo-Swedish war became inevitable. The Russians beat off a Swedish attack in 1256, and carried out successful raids in southern Finland in 1257 and Karelia in 1278. But in 1292 King Birger launched the biggest crusade yet. It took the twofold form of an attack on the Karelians and a thrust towards the Izhora, a tributary of the Neva which was only about seventy miles north of Novgorod itself. The crusade paved the way for the construction of the strategic fort of Viborg. The conquest of all coastal Finland, and much of the interior, was an accomplished fact.

The colonization of these new lands, which began in the 1250s, was closely controlled by the monarchy. The Swedish court realized that Finland's size and diversity made the imposition of a single pattern of settlement or government impracticable, and permitted a large degree of autonomy by local communities; on the other hand social groups, such as the magnates, burghers, and freehold peasants, were defined in terms of their royal privileges and obligations, upheld through the main royal castles at Abo (Turku), Tavastehus, and Viborg. Relations between the settlers and the native Finns were much better than those between the Germans and the conquered populations south of the Gulf. Many Finns were rapidly assimilated into the immigrant Swedish peasant class, while the inland tribes which lived by hunting, fishing, and trading continued their traditional way of life with relatively few changes. Finland in the fourteenth and fifteenth centuries was different from Sweden not because it was treated by the government, or regarded by incoming settlers, as a colonial appendage, but simply because its economy was more primitive, and its social and cultural mores more backward. It has been pointed out, for example, that when the Russians burnt Abo cathedral and the Bishop of Abo's castle at Kuusisto in 1318, 'they probably destroyed most of the books and records in Finland'; and that as late as 1460 there were only four churches in the whole of Swedish Karelia, outside Viborg.

In the century which followed the Second Lyons Council the recently conquered lands of the eastern Baltic were thus being subjected to processes of settlement and government which differed radically in nature. In much the same way, the crusades which were waged in this period against the pagan or schismatic neighbours of those lands do not fall into straightforward patterns; the political interweavings were manifold as alliances were formed and broken, and hostilities interrupted by truces and treaties. None the less it is both possible and convenient to examine crusading activity in terms of its two principal opponents, the schismatic Russian states and pagan Lithuania.

The former meant, principally, the great trading city and principality of Novgorod. With a population of about 22,000, Novgorod was by far the largest Russian town in the early fourteenth century. Its government was technically headed by the grand prince of Vladimir, but for most of this period Novgorod's policy was effectively in the hands of an oligarchy of leading boyars (nobles), and of its archbishop. Like their enemies at the Swedish court, they saw that economic control of the resources to be culled from Karelia—primarily animal furs, seal and whale oil, and fish—could best be secured by some form of lordship over the Karelians, with which conversion went hand-in-hand, and by the building of forts on the shores of Lake Ladoga, the Gulf of Finland, and at the mouths of the region's chief rivers. The war therefore took two forms: a constant frontier struggle waged between Lake Ladoga and the Gulf as each side built forts and used them for raiding purposes; and a series of more ambitious campaigns mounted when domestic circumstances became propitious. Such circumstances included, in the case of the Swedes, the securing of papal aid in the form of crusade privileges. These took the main form of grants of taxation on the Swedish clergy, and since the Curia normally expected a share from these for its own financial needs in Italy, it was the more ready to issue them when it required the money itself. On the other hand, Novgorod's military capacity hinged largely on the assistance it could obtain from the emerging Russian principalities of Tver and Moscow, and was thus tied up with the struggle for power between them, as well as their complicated relations with their Mongol overlords in the Golden Horde. Few crusades were so contingent upon such far-reaching factors.

In the years following the extension of Swedish power to Viborg there was brisk but inconclusive raiding by both sides, until the accession of the two-year-old Magnus II of Sweden in 1319 inaugurated a period of greater hostilities. Magnus also inherited Norway from his grandfather Hakon V, and this accretion of resources, coupled with the popularity of eastwards expansion amongst the Swedish and Norwegian nobility, brought renewed vigour to Swedish policy. The Swedish regency council requested, and received, crusade bulls, but it was the Russians who seized the initiative, as Muscovite aid to Novgorod reached its peak. They mounted a destructive raid on Finland in 1318, attempted to take Viborg in 1322, and in 1323 constructed a fort at Orekhov, giving them a hold on Lake Ladoga. In 1323 and 1326 first Sweden and then Norway made peace with Novgorod, but this was a mere pause in hostilities. Frontier raiding continued, and in the 1340s, when the political climate in his two Kingdoms was favourable, Magnus was tempted to take the offensive by the weakness of Novgorod, which was in an isolated position between Lithuania and Moscow. Political considerations aside, Magnus may have been influenced to undertake his expeditions by the religious exhortations of his cousin St Bridget; the procedure he adopted of offering the Russians a choice between conversion and conquest was similar to the ideas she was putting forward at this time.

The army which Magnus assembled at the end of 1347 was certainly on an impressive scale, but subsequent events were anticlimactic. Orekhov was besieged in June 1348 and fell two months later. Magnus now controlled the entire Neva basin, but he failed to provide Orekhov with an adequate garrison, and the army of Novgorod easily reoccupied it early in 1349. Despite the losses which Sweden suffered in the Black Death, Magnus resolved to mount another expedition in 1350. It proved no more successful than the 1348 campaign. Neither of these expeditions appears to have been preached as a crusade, and when, in 1351, papal bulls finally arrived decreeing crusade preaching and granting the King a half share of a four-year tenth on his clergy, they were too late to be of much help. Magnus could not organize a third army, and the help which he had relied upon from the Teutonic Knights and the Hanse failed to materialize. The King soon became embroiled in quarrels with his own magnates, and with the papal Curia, which was denied its due share of the 1351 tax and excommunicated Magnus in 1358. In retrospect it is clear that, even in the unique circumstances of Swedish–Norwegian dynastic union and political consensus which characterized the middle years of Magnus II's reign, this conflict was an over-ambitious extension of Swedish power. By the 1360s, moreover, the growth of Moscow's military power, and its influence at Novgorod, were making any attempt to encroach on the latter's lands hopeless. Not surprisingly, therefore, Magnus's campaigns were the last major exertions of Swedish might against Novgorod in the fourteenth century: crusade bulls were issued by Urban VI in 1378, but they came to nothing. It was not until 1495–6, when a brief but intense war broke out between Ivan III of Moscow and the Swedish regent Sten Sture, that a crusade bull was again granted for this region; and by this point the clergy were so unused to receiving crusading bulls that the Archbishop of Lund wondered what he should do with it.

When Magnus II tried to persuade the Livonian authorities in the winter of 1350–1 to support his war against Novgorod by enforcing a trade embargo, he met with no success. The incident is characteristic of the region's relations with its Russian neighbours. After their defeat at the hands of Alexander Nevsky in 1242 the Teutonic Knights resisted almost every temptation to push their Livonian frontier into Russian lands; the only significant exception was a war with Novgorod in 1268, which attracted crusaders from the West. Livonia's rulers were fully aware of their economic dependence on commerce with Novgorod, Pskov, and Polotsk, and they knew that the latter two cities were precariously balanced between Novgorod and Lithuania; any attempt at conquest might compel them to call on Lithuanian help. Disputes about frontiers and trading incidents did lead to occasional conflicts between Livonia and the Russians, such as the war with Novgorod and Pskov in 1367–71 and that with Polotsk in 1373, and there was even an attempted conquest of Polotsk in 1381, but Livonia's eastern frontier posed less danger than its southern one.

In fact, the war which the Teutonic Order waged from Livonia and Prussia against Lithuania was on a much more intense scale than any of the conflicts with the Russians; it formed one of the most important features of the crusading movement in the fourteenth century. Pagan Lithuania posed a more intractable challenge to the Order than either the Prussians or the Livs and Letts, for by the time the Teutonic Knights began to fight them in the 1270s, the Lithuanians had achieved an advanced degree of political organization and embarked on a phase of aggressive expansion. The former was the work of one of Lithuania's group of hereditary princes, Mindaugas, who reacted to the various external powers threatening Lithuania in the mid-thirteenth century— Alexander Nevsky's Novgorod, Poland, the Teutonic Knights, and the Mongols—by forcibly unifying and modernizing the country's fragmented tribal structure. He and his immediate successors then deployed their people's military skills and remarkable belligerence in conquering out-wards from the dense forests and river systems which formed Lithuania's heartlands, around its capital, Vilnius. Their most successful advance was towards the south and south-east, where the conquest of the rich agricultural lands and towns of 'Black Rus' brought in massive revenues, facilitating the import of scarce raw materials, up-to-date weapons, and advisers. The Poles suffered sixteen invasions between 1250 and 1325. To the north and west, to which they were pulled by the Dvina and Niemen, and above all by the Baltic coast, the Lithuanians found their way blocked by Prussia and Livonia. They were, however, successful in subjecting the Samogitians to their overlordship, and hence made land communications between the Order's two branches very tenuous.

Lithuanian paganism had its political uses, in that the grand princes on several occasions gained a respite from the threat of Latin Christian attack by opening negotiations with pope or emperor on baptism, while their Russian Orthodox subjects preferred the government of a heathen to that of a Catholic power. But it would be quite wrong to suggest that the pagan beliefs of the Lithuanians were residual or formal: western sources depict a vigorous, organized, and deeply felt pantheism. It powerfully contributed to the Lithuanians' martial culture through such practices as the ritual burning alive of their captured enemies, and the cremation of their own dead rulers in full warrior regalia, and in the company of their warhorses. When Grand Prince Gediminas allowed friars into his lands as part of his brief *rapprochement* with the papacy in 1323, they found the task of conversion a hard one; later events would prove that it took the full support of the Lithuanian state to bring about even the nominal conversion of the Lithuanians. They willingly borrowed or imitated the technical expertise of their Christian neighbours, and participated fully in their political manœuvrings, without showing any susceptibility to their religious ideas. The argument advanced by Humbert of Romans at the time of the Second Council of Lyons, that the Lithuanians could be peacefully converted, was largely without foundation: Europe's last substantial concentration of organized pagan belief was also its toughest.

It is thus not hard to see why Lithuania fought one of the fourteenth century's bitterest and longest wars—'the other Hundred Years War', as one historian has described it—against the Teutonic Order. Nor is it difficult to see how the Order was able to represent the conflict as a successor to the thirteenth-century crusades in this region: on the one hand, the expansionist ambitions of this massive state, which stretched from Smolensk to the Baltic, posed a clear threat to Latin Christian lands; and on the other, it was arguable that the conversion of the Lithuanians could only proceed once the Grand Principality had actually been conquered. The fact that this new war *contra paganos* provided the Order with a *raison d'être* at a time when it was under attack by its Christian opponents does not mean that it was provoked by the Order or kept going when peaceful relations were feasible: in this respect it is important to distinguish between the situation in the fourteenth and fifteenth centuries. The grand masters made skilful use of their new military obligations to provide the justification for ignoring the papacy's judicial rulings and promoting a glowing image of their Order's activities in Germany and elsewhere; as Hartmut Boockmann put it, 'with its wars against the Lithuanians the Order did what it was sent into this region to do—it fought against the heathens'. But the Order did not invent the formidable and bellicose Lithuanian state.

The drift towards war occurred in the course of the 1270s, when Lithuania had several hostile encounters with the Livonian brethren. The fighting abilities of the Lithuanians soon became clear; and their political adroitness was manifested when they intervened in the Livonian civil war in 1297 as allies of the Archbishop and citizens of Riga. Thereafter warfare was virtually continuous, but the region's appalling terrain and climate placed on it constraints of a kind unique in Europe. It has been estimated that between the cultivated heartlands of Lithuania, Livonia, and Prussia, there existed a belt of about 100 miles of forest, marsh, and bog, dubbed by the Germans the *Wiltnisse* (wilderness). This had to be penetrated before an attempt could even be made to plunder the enemy's lands or capture his forts, so armies had to take guides and sappers with them, as well as food and, in winter, fodder too: hence the distinctive name, *Reise* (journey), which the Christians gave to such campaigns. Many *Reisen* followed the river valleys, because these were the key to commercial wealth, and enormously facilitated the transport of men, materials, and supplies; on the other hand, they were also the places where the enemy was best-prepared. During the long winter a campaign (*Winterreise*) could only be mounted if temperatures were low enough to freeze the bogs and rivers, and make them passable to cavalry and wagons; unseasonably high temperatures made raging torrents of the rivers and their tributaries, while exceptionally low ones made any out-of-door activity impossible. And at any point between April and October heavy rain could make the terrain unmanageable, so that a *Sommerreise* demanded a period of hot sun to dry out the land. Whatever resources each side had temporarily at its disposal, and however strong their desire to fight the war to a finish, conditions were rarely propitious for doing so.

Most *Winterreisen* were on a small scale and had the limited objective of burning villages and capturing men and animals. Their perils were illustrated by events in the winter of 1375–6, when the Livonian brethren carried out a daring ten-day campaign against Wilkomierz, in snow so deep that they had to travel single file, and their Marshal died when a snow-laden tree fell on him; a Lithuanian counter-raid lost fifty men and 1,000 horses to the cold, and another fifty men died by falling through the ice near Gerzike. *Sommerreisen*, numbering many more men and lasting longer, also aimed to lay waste cultivated land and bring in prisoners, but they had strategic aims too, usually trying either to destroy an enemy fort, or to build and garrison one of their own; the Niemen valley became studded with the forts of both sides. Battles were infrequent since it was rarely possible for the defenders to get an army to the scene of operations before the invaders had achieved their objectives and started to withdraw, but the war was costly and destructive: Lithuanian attacks on Samland and Livonia in 1345 were so severe that Grand Master Ludolf König went mad with grief, while Master Burchard of Dreileben resigned in shame at a Marienburg grand chapter. It has been suggested that so many Samogitian captives were brought to Livonia that they flooded the labour market, stopping the native peasantry using the demographic losses of the period to improve their tenurial conditions. This large-scale displacement of civilian populations, occurring in circumstances of casual brutality, makes the war seem more familiar to the modern reader than almost any other medieval conflict.

Warfare of this magnitude placed a heavy strain even on the resources of the Teutonic Order, especially in terms of manpower. In the early fifteenth century the Order had only about 500 brethren in Livonia and 600–700 in Prussia; and the figures were probably not dissimilar in the period considered here. Neither the military service of feudatories nor the hiring of mercenaries could swell the Order's ranks sufficiently. As we shall see, it could not rely on Polish help because, although the Poles were sometimes hostile towards Lithuania, they were equally antagonistic towards the Order. The proclamation of a full-scale crusade, with its attendant apparatus of organized preaching, recruitment, and finance, was unsuited to the nature of the war, since nobody could predict the weather conditions at the time of the army's arrival. It would also make the Order too dependent on papal backing, and would probably lead to quarrels between the Order and the crusade's leaders on issues of strategy, and the disposal of conquered land, prisoners, and booty. But in

1245 Innocent IV had granted the Order the exceptional privilege of raising volunteers in Germany for the Prussian crusades 'without public preaching', and hence without the issue of a papal bull of crusade. This privilege was evidently used by the Order to advertise its need for help against the Lithuanians and to promise participants the status and rewards of the crusader; for while there appear to be no crusade bulls specifically addressed to the Order in this period, some volunteers who came were described in the sources as *crucesignati* and all regarded themselves as such. The *Reisen* therefore represented something new in crusading history (for despite the 1245 privilege the Prussian crusades had been preached in an orthodox manner): a sort of 'ongoing' crusade whose starting and finishing dates can only be reconstructed from the presence in Prussia or Livonia of the first, and last, groups of *crucesignati* recruited for this purpose in western Europe.

Taking part in one or more *Reisen* became a distinguishing characteristic of fourteenth-century chivalry, a process which was brilliantly encouraged by the Teutonic Order in the way it treated its guests. This will be examined in a later chapter when we shall explore the links between chivalry and crusading, in the context of popular feelings toward the crusade.[2] Here we shall focus on the role played by foreign crusaders in the war itself. It was an important one because of the sheer popularity of the *Reisen*. As had been the case with the Prussian crusades, recruitment was most successful in the Empire, and especially in those parts where the Teutonic Order's commanderies served to advertise its needs and to remind local families of their ancestral tradition of service to the Order. Erich Maschke has pointed out that the Teutonic Order was richly endowed with estates in the borderlands stretching from Burgundy to Flanders, where the great Church Reform movements had originated, the Holy Land crusade was consistently popular, and the Burgundian state, with its fascination for both crusading and chivalry, was at this point in the process of formation. On the basis of his work in the Burgundian archives, Oscar Halecki commented that the élite among Philip the Bold's knighthood 'made time and again the "voyage de Prusse", receiving generous rewards on their return'. Other key areas included Alsace, the tributaries of the upper Elbe, Austria, and Bohemia. King John of Bohemia made three journeys to Prussia. His *Reise* of 1328 was celebrated by the French poet William of Machaut, as was the 1377 *Reise* of Duke Albert III of Austria by Peter Suchenwirt.

[2] Below, 399–401.

But the appeal of the *Reisen* reached far beyond the Empire. Professor Paravicini was able to discover the names of about 450 noblemen from England and France who went on *Reisen*. The extent of English participation has recently been highlighted by Maurice Keen and Christopher Tyerman, against the background of the *Reise* which Chaucer included among the exploits of his Knight in the Prologue to 'The Canterbury Tales'; the fact that the term *reysa* was common in England when Chaucer wrote (*c*.1384) shows how well acquainted his contemporaries were with the Lithuanian war. 'A very high proportion of comital families ... prove to have a crusading veteran somewhere in their ranks', Dr Keen noted, and many of these were veterans of *Reisen*. Dr Tyerman has observed that English participation was at its greatest in the years following the Peace of Brétigny: between November 1367 and February 1368 royal licences to depart for Prussia were granted for no fewer than ninety-seven men. The French, like the English, flocked to Marienburg during intervals in the Anglo-French war. The exemplar of French chivalry, Marshal Boucicaut, served on three *Reisen* as a young man. The chance discovery of a notarial instrument of 1364 led Charles Higounet to identify a group of eight lords from Maine, Poitou, Aunis, and the Limousin who were in Prussia in the winter of 1362–3; they are representative of many others. At different times Italians, Scots, and men from the Low Countries were also present: Count William IV of Holland-Hennegau went three times, in 1336–7, 1343–4, and 1344–5, while Count William I of Guelderland undertook seven *Reisen* between 1383 and 1400. Such 'multiple *Reisen*' were commonplace. The *Winterreise* of 1344–5, which attracted two kings (John of Bohemia and Louis of Hungary) and a cluster of important princes, was exceptional but not unique.

The service of foreign crusaders against Lithuania was thus far more valuable than that of the groups which made their way to Granada at this time. They could make the difference between success and failure, and the chronicler Wigand of Marburg made it clear that such important undertakings as the capture of Kaunas, the siege of Pilenai, and the building of Bayerburg, were only possible because of the assistance of the *peregrini* from the West. Naturally the use which the Teutonic Knights were able to make of these volunteers depended to a large extent on the weather. In adverse conditions, when nothing ambitious could be undertaken, the Order was prepared to organize what were, effectively, nominal *Reisen* to please their guests, 'military excursions', one historian has remarked, 'that were not unlike modern luxury tours or hunting expeditions, except that the sights were Baltic forests and the prey was man'. But this was not what the Order intended. Princely contingents were often large—Duke Albert III of Austria brought 2,000 knights with him in 1377—and even commoners could be found duties in the field which made their services of value; so the arrival of large numbers of crusaders was, especially in summer, often the signal for a big *Reise*. Hard fighting could be expected, and if it was accompanied by the chivalric paraphernalia of challenges, jousting, and outdoor feasting, this does not mean that the *Reisen* constituted mock warfare, that they were a kind of 'super-tournament'. Had this been the case, Prussia would not have earned its reputation as a good place to learn, or improve, the profession of arms in preparation for wars in the West.

Most western volunteers made their way either overland or by sea to Marienburg or Königsberg, and took part in *Reisen* launched from Prussia. Relatively few undertook the longer and more arduous journey to Livonia, whose *Reisen* were on a less impressive scale anyway. Livonia tended to function as a 'second best' for knights whose hopes of service in Prussia were dashed and journeyed northwards in the expectation of seeing action there instead. It has been suggested that the Livonian brethren, as northern Germans, were less attuned to the chivalric ethos with which the *Reisen* were so intimately connected; and they certainly lacked the resources to cultivate visitors with the panache exhibited in Prussia. Some figures of importance did go to Livonia: the Count of Werl and Arnsberg arrived at Riga with a party of Rhenish knights to fight against Pskov in 1335, the Count of Loos brought thirty-six knights in 1341, and Engelbert III, Count of Mark, took part in the 1381 campaign against Polotsk. But in general the Livonian brethren acted in an auxiliary role throughout the Lithuanian war, and when the Order stepped up its campaigning into Samogitia in the 1360s, subsidies had to be sent northwards to secure an effective Livonian contribution.

Even with the assistance of its volunteers, who began to arrive as early as the winter of 1304–5, the Order came off worse in its struggle with Lithuania almost throughout the first half of the century. The Lithuanians were better placed for attacking their enemies' richest lands in both Prussia and Livonia; they had allies in Poland and the disaffected Christians of Livonia; and they possessed a series of highly able rulers in Grand Princes Vytenis, Gediminas, and Algirdas. In 1323, for example, after forcing a lull in hostilities with his offer of baptism to the Pope,

Gediminas executed a very successful raid into Prussia, capturing Memel, raiding as far south as Dobrzyn, and taking many thousands of prisoners. Gediminas died in 1341, but Algirdas and his brothers Kenstutis and Narimont attacked Samland in force each year from 1345 to 1347. In February 1348, however, substantial numbers of French and English crusaders enabled the Knights to win the battle of Strawen, fought in the course of an unusually large *Winterreise*. There were other important Christian victories in 1348, which were followed by a pause in hostilities as both sides were struck by the Black Death.

But it was during the long grand mastership of Winrich of Kniprode that the Order slowly gained the upper hand in the conflict. As Grand Commander, Kniprode had led the troops who won at Strawen. Following his election as Grand Master in 1351 he built a series of castles west of the Prussian *Wiltnisse* to guard the cultivated interior, and pushed the Order's hold on the Niemen as far upstream as Kaunas, which was reached in 1362. This afforded a reasonable degree of protection to Samland and Carsovia; and a defensive line of forts was also built in south-eastern Livonia. Meanwhile the Order's *Reisen* grew bolder as increasing numbers of volunteers arrived. There were co-ordinated attacks on Samogitia from both Prussia and Livonia, and raids into the lands lying between Vilnius and the Niemen. The Poles and Rigans were detached from their alliance with Lithuania. Most importantly, the Lithuanians began to suffer from the consequences of dynastic strife. After the death of Grand Prince Algirdas in 1377, his brother and successor Kenstutis was opposed by Algirdas's son Jogailo. In 1380 Kniprode formed an alliance with Jogailo, who took Vilnius itself two years later. By this point the Order had advanced as far as Trakai, just fourteen miles west of Vilnius. It seemed that the Lithuanian state was on the point of breaking up.

In the long run, however, the most serious enemy the Order faced was not pagan Lithuania but Christian Poland. The fragmentation of Poland, which compelled Conrad of Mazovia to call on the help of the Teutonic Knights against the Prussians, and enabled the Order to seize eastern Pomerelia in 1308, came to an end in January 1320 with the coronation of Wladyslaw Lokietek as King of Poland. The geo-political framework of eastern Europe shifted dramatically against the Teutonic Order, for the Polish *restauratio regni* was based in part on a surge of national sentiment which was accelerated by the events of 1308. Wladyslaw I and his heirs therefore viewed the recovery of this lost province, which included

Poland's sea outlet, as a central goal of their reigns. They had a valuable ally in the papal Curia, which from Boniface VIII onwards backed the attempt of Wladyslaw Lokietek to reunify Poland. Pope John XXII threw his weight behind the coronation of 1320 in exchange for an increase in Poland's payment of Peter's Pence. Earlier, Clement V had been shocked by the loss of life attending the Teutonic Knights' seizure of Danzig, regarding it in the same light as the scandal in Livonia. In 1319 John XXII set up a judicial enquiry into the Order's actions. The Order responded to the papal-Polish *entente* by cultivating its ties with Germany, both with the emperors, who were usually happy to ratify its political activities, and more importantly with the kings of Bohemia; they too faced Polish hostility over their conquest of Silesia, and they posed a useful threat to Poland's western flank.

Poland's new strength was thus mainly directed towards the redressal of its grievances in the north and west, and it viewed the Lithuanians as a potential ally against the Order. However, the situation Poland faced in the east was such as to make it, at times, just as important a crusading power as its main Christian enemy. Poland's neighbour here was Halicz-Vladimir (Ruthenia), a comparatively small principality uncomfortably sandwiched between the Tatar Golden Horde, the expanding Lithuanian state, and the Kingdoms of Poland and Hungary. Ruthenia's Orthodox rulers pursued a policy of placating all these powers while preserving their own neutrality, but the threat of the Horde absorbing Halicz-Vladimir and bordering directly on eastern Poland ('Little Poland') could not be ignored. The danger of a Lithuanian conquest was almost as great. One reason why the Curia welcomed Poland's reunification was the argument that the Kingdom could better deal with these threats, as well as promoting missionary activity in the East. The Polish court therefore knew that it could normally depend on the Curia to grant it crusade privileges against these schismatics and pagans, and it was not slow in asking for them. For this was crusading of a traditional kind, centring on the grant of indulgences, taxes, and the associated privileges valued by monarchies, chiefly as an assistance to their war finance. Poland's crusade was thus more akin to Magnus's campaigns against the Russians than to the Teutonic Order's war with Lithuania, and as in the case of the Swedish grants, the Curia usually demanded a share of the proceeds from the taxes which it levied on the Polish church.

Throughout the reigns of Wladyslaw I and his son Casimir III, Polish policy oscillated between the struggle against the Teutonic Order and the defence of Little Poland. Since the recovery of Pomorze was cherished above all by the nobility of Greater Poland, the oscillation reflected a continuing tension between the Kingdom's two main constituent territories. In the early years of Wladyslaw's reign it was the war in the east which dominated, so that indulgences were granted by John XXII in 1319 and 1325. In October 1325, however, came the dynastic marriage of Crown Prince Casimir to the Lithuanian Princess Aldona, after her conversion to Christianity. The marriage sealed an alliance based on the common hostility of the two countries towards the Teutonic Order. It inaugurated Poland's attempt to enforce a papal judicial verdict of 1321 that the Order should return Pomorze to Poland and pay an indemnity of 30,000 marks. Characteristically, the Order had ignored the verdict, and in 1329 the bizarre situation arose of Polish troops defending Dobrzyn and Plock against King John of Bohemia's crusaders, who had come to take part in a *Reise* but were deployed against Poland in response to Wladyslaw's attack on Kulm. Warfare continued until, in 1332, a truce was agreed. The Poles had suffered heavily from attacks launched from both Prussia and Bohemia, and King Casimir, who succeeded Wladyslaw in 1333, resorted to renewed papal intervention. In 1339 papal nuncios found on Casimir's behalf at the Process of Warsaw, but the ruling proved no more efficacious than that in John XXII's reign. The Teutonic Knights simply would not accept it, and in the treaty of Kalisz (1343) Casimir had to 'cede' Pomorze to the Order.

Poland's total failure in this eighteen-year struggle to regain its Baltic province had the one compensation that it released the monarchy's resources for what Professor Paul Knoll has dubbed 'the turn to the east'. This was Casimir's sustained attempt not just to defend his frontiers, but to conquer Halicz-Vladimir. The Polish invasion in 1340 was precipitated by the murder of the Catholicizing Prince Boleslaw-George at the hands of his own boyars, and by Casimir's fear of a Tatar takeover of Ruthenia. The King enjoyed striking initial success, but his gains had to be defended against Tatar counter-attacks, and it was to resist these that crusade preaching was granted him in August 1340, and a two-year tenth levied on the Polish church at the end of 1343. Even after the Golden Horde gave up the struggle for Ruthenia in the wake of the Black Death, Poland had to defend its new lands against Lithuanian attack, with the assistance of a new tax in 1351, renewed crusade preaching in 1352 and 1354, and another tax in 1355. More indulgences and taxes followed in 1363 and 1369. By that stage Casimir's success was clear: a treaty with Lithuania in

October 1366 allotted Poland about 25,000 square miles of land, 'the largest and perhaps the most valuable part' of Ruthenia.

In terms of territorial gains, this success was more impressive than the grinding war conducted by the Teutonic Order against the Lithuanians, let alone the ephemeral campaigning of Magnus of Sweden: indeed, Polish envoys in 1351 spoke of their conquests leading to the foundation of a total of eight new sees, one of them metropolitan. Casimir's wars in the east constituted one of the most important fourteenth-century crusades, and the privileges with which the Curia showered the King undoubtedly helped him shoulder the financial burden imposed by the war, for the taxes alone brought in between 10,000 and 15,000 Polish marks. More-over, the enjoyment of crusade status placed Casimir in a strong moral position *vis-à-vis* the Teutonic Order: in 1355 he called on the Knights to provide troops for his campaigns, and complained to Innocent VI when they refused to do so. In fact the Order had provided powerful, if indirect, assistance to Casimir, by tying down Lithuanian troops further north. But it tried hard to avoid doing this, knowing that Polish victory in Ruthenia would lead to the reassertion of claims in Pomerelia. In political terms, the crusades waged by the Teutonic Knights and the Poles against Lithuania were mutually exclusive; and at different times both powers were rebuked by the papal Curia for allying with pagan Lithuania against each other.

The two crusades also fed off, and stimulated, rather different ideologies. The Order's war was geared to the shared chivalric culture of Europe's nobility. When men like John of Bohemia, Louis of Hungary, and William IV of Holland came to fight in Prussia, they were acting as knights, not princes; appropriately, the main chronicler of the *Reisen*, Wigand of Marburg, was the Order's herald. By contrast, Poland's conflict was national, the ultimate rationale of the war being the security of Little Poland. Few if any volunteers came to take part in it from the West, where knowledge of Poland was superficial. In one respect, however, the two conflicts were similar. For some decades the Teutonic Order and its apologists had described the Knights acting as a wall, shield, or rampart for the Christian communities of Prussia and Livonia against the assault of the pagan Lithuanians, 'Christendom's most secure wall, and the marvellous propagator of the Christian Faith', as Pope Urban V described the Order to King Charles IV of Bohemia in 1366. The imagery was now transferred to Poland, giving the reunified Kingdom a specific role to play within the Christian community. For it was in the course of negotiations between the Polish and papal courts on the crusade that the idea was created of Poland forming 'Christendom's bulwark' (*antemurale Christianitatis*) against non-believers. As Professor Knoll has shown, the imagery seems to have originated in a petition from Wladyslaw, dated 1323, in which the King described Halicz-Vladimir as his country's shield against the Tatars. As Casimir's reign progressed, Poland itself began to be depicted as the defensive wall. This was a natural consequence of the conquest of Ruthenia, which reorientated the country eastwards, from the Vistula and Oder basins, which dominate respectively Little and Greater Poland, towards the basin of the Dniester. In 1364 even the foundation of the University of Cracow was related to the responsibilities arising from Poland's new frontiers: 'to bring about greater devotion in preaching, and a more effective teaching of the Catholic faith, for the conversion of the unbelieving pagans and schismatics who border on the said Kingdom'.

It was when the Ottomans reached Poland's southern flank in the fifteenth century that the new image came into its own. During the Varna campaign of 1444 the humanist Francis Filelfo wrote to King Wladyslaw 'All the nations and kings of Christendom pray God this day for your health and victory . . . Thou art a bulwark for the whole Christian Commonwealth.' By the end of the century, when Poland was actively fighting the Turks in Moldavia, the *antemurale* idea was significantly shaping both the Polish national consciousness, and the way Poland was viewed by foreigners. The triumphal arch erected at Paris in 1573 to celebrate Henry of Valois's election to the Polish throne described Poland as 'most steadfast fortress for the whole of Europe against the barbarian peoples', and in 1676 John III Sobieski wrote to Charles II of England to inform him how 'vast Multitudes of Turks and Tartars fell upone this Bulwarke of Christendome to destroy it'. The *antemurale* image was revived, briefly, when the Catholic troops of the newly formed Polish Republic fought Bolshevik Russia at the end of the First World War. It contributed to the atmosphere of religious and nationalist excitement which caused the Polish victories of August 1920 to be celebrated as 'the Miracle of the Vistula'.

The Teutonic Order's concern about Poland's territorial expansion could only be deepened by Casimir's internal achievements. The King built more than fifty new castles to symbolize and enforce royal authority. In 1347 his father's personal unification of Poland was given a legal foundation through the issuing of law codes for Greater and Little

Poland, 'the core round which Polish Law developed over the next four centuries'. While governmental administration grew more stable and assertive, an influx of Jews, who were being expelled from other countries but enjoyed royal protection in Poland, contributed to the expansion of the country's trade. Mineral deposits were extensively mined, and Poland became an exporter of finished cloth as well as raw materials and agricultural produce. Twenty-seven towns were enclosed by stone walls and Cracow, Poland's capital, was greatly embellished. When, in 1364, Casimir and four other monarchs assembled at the Congress of Cracow to debate, amongst other matters, eastern Europe's contribution to Peter of Cyprus's planned crusade, the occasion offered glittering proof of the prestige Casimir's eastern conquests had already brought him. By the end of Casimir's reign visitors from western Europe were beginning to remark on Poland's emergence as a great power with the same admiration they had previously reserved for the *Ordensstaat*.

Throughout the conflict for Ruthenia Casimir had not forgotten the lost lands of Pomerelia. But a visit to Marienburg in the autumn of 1366, when the Teutonic Knights confidently took him on a guided tour of their fortifications, persuaded the King that the Order was too strong to attack. Four years later Casimir died childless, and Poland entered a period of dynastic difficulties. Initially, the crown passed to Casimir's nephew, King Louis of Hungary. From the point of view of the eastern frontier Louis's accession made good sense, for the Hungarians had a fund of experience of fighting the Tatars and Lithuanians. The Avignonese Curia had granted both Louis and his father Charles-Robert crusade indulgences and taxes on several occasions; in particular, all the major instances of crusade preaching decreed for Casimir's campaigns in Halicz-Vladimir had been extended to Hungary, and Louis had led an army across the Carpathians in 1351–2. The personal union of the two Kingdoms had the advantage of combining their resources while settling the problem of Hungary's own claim to Ruthenia. But Louis neglected Poland and there were serious revolts, which the King attempted to deal with by granting the barons Crown lands and extensive fiscal rights. Typically, the one Polish campaign which he led was in 1377, in response to a Lithuanian raid which had taken advantage of the weakly defended frontiers to devastate Ruthenia and raid as far as Cracow.

Louis died, unexpectedly, in September 1382. He had no sons and he had effectively nominated one of his two daughters, Mary, as his successor in both his Kingdoms. The prospect of another absentee ruler was unacceptable to the Polish magnates, but they were divided between those who would take one of Louis's daughters, Mary or Jadwiga (Hedwig), provided she was Queen of Poland only, and those who elected a relative of Casimir, Ziemowit of Mazovia. Pursuing their usual policy of encouraging dissension amongst their enemies, the Teutonic Knights subsidized Ziemowit's cause. Poland seemed likely to be plunged into civil war, which would further erode the centralized strength achieved by Casimir, and put off the day when an attempt might be made to regain Pomorze. In the same year, as we have seen, the Teutonic Knights benefited from Lithuanian dynastic strife to gain control of Vilnius. The confusion caused to both of the Order's main enemies, Christian and pagan, by the problems of dynastic succession, must have seemed to confirm the advantages of ruling a monastic state. The contrast was especially apparent at a time when, in the words of one contemporary, 'Prussia shone with honour, peace, sternness, law, justice and discipline', while Philip of Mézières considered that the Teutonic Knights' practice of monastic knighthood 'put to great shame not only the other Military Orders of the Church, but all the Christian princes'. The tables would soon be turned, however, for the following decades would reveal that dynasticism had strengths just as formidable as its weaknesses, while the *Ordensstaat* suffered insoluble political problems arising from its very nature. The result would be a transformation of the political and religious situation in north-eastern Europe.

12

The End of the Baltic Crusade
1382–1562

✠

In the fifteenth and sixteenth centuries Iberia and the Baltic present, from the point of view of the crusades, an interesting study in contrasts. As we have seen, Spanish crusading enthusiasm attained new heights in the conquest of Granada, and went on to find novel channels of expression in both the Old and the New Worlds. By contrast, the Baltic region experienced what one historian has aptly termed 'the withering of the crusade'. By 1500 crusades had all but ceased to be preached, the *Ordensstaat* was in the last stages of decay, and the Teutonic Order itself faced a grave crisis. Few would have predicted such developments in 1382, when the Christian states of Iberia were enmeshed in internecine disputes, while the Teutonic Order was flourishing, and its war against Lithuania was regarded by almost all of Catholic Europe as a praiseworthy endeavour. Unlike the other fronts examined in this book, the Baltic crusade had no discernible life after about 1520. In this chapter we shall therefore be looking at the effective demise of a crusading tradition (see maps 13 and 14).

Historians have long recognized that the most important event leading to this demise was the marriage of Jadwiga of Poland and Jogailo of Lithuania in 1386. This dynastic union posed the same threat to the *Ordensstaat* which the marriage of Ferdinand and Isabella in 1469 would come to constitute for Granada: of three hostile powers, two were now united, their resources combined and directed against the third. In crusading terms, however, the result of the marriage of Jogailo and Jadwiga was precisely the opposite of that of Ferdinand and Isabella. For since the marriage of 1386 was preceded both by Jogailo's baptism, and by his promise to bring about the conversion of his subjects, it robbed the

Order of the crusading rationale which had characterized its war with Lithuania for a century, and had made possible its recruitment of volunteers in the West. In military and ideological terms the Teutonic Order had been outmanœuvred by the use of the only weapon with which it could not compete, the dynastic marriage. In broad outline, this traditional view of the Order's predicament in the fifteenth century remains correct, but in this chapter attention will also be paid to other aspects of the situation which faced the crusading movement in this region, and which recent research has greatly illuminated. For it is now clear both that the problems confronting the Order were extraordinarily complex, and that although the crusade was threatened it survived, in more than one form, for many decades after 1386.

The idea of converting the Lithuanian grand princes was as old as the Lithuanian state itself, for Mindaugas had been a baptized Christian for several years in the mid-thirteenth century. His conversion was notoriously nominal, but the problem was not really one of the grand princes' religious convictions, which could not be proved one way or the other; rather, it lay in offering them, in association with their own baptism, political benefits which were tangible and enduring, in order that the long-drawn-out process of converting their peoples might be undertaken. The papal Curia knew this well, so that Gregory XI wrote to the Lithuanians in 1373 that their terrible war with the Teutonic Knights would end if they accepted conversion. But the Lithuanians became expert at the game of entering negotiations to secure a respite from attack, then breaking them off. Thus in the summer of 1351 Kenstutis adroitly staved off Louis of Hungary's invasion by agreeing to return to Buda for baptism and to support the setting up of an archbishopric in Lithuania; he then escaped from the Hungarian camp in the middle of the night and reneged on his promises. Seven years later Kenstutis made a similarly disingenuous promise of conversion, this time to Charles IV, in the hope of securing Bohemian help against the Order. He even made the brazen suggestion that the Order should be transferred to southern Ruthenia to defend Lithuania against Tatar raids. Kenstutis's able son, Witold, permitted himself to be baptized five times, alternating between the Catholic and Orthodox churches as circumstances dictated.

Such episodes constituted valuable support for the Order's argument that the only way to bring Christianity to the Lithuanians was by conquering them first. Jogailo appeared to fit the familiar pattern, talking of baptism during his alliance with the Order after 1380. But when negotiations started in 1383 for his marriage to Jadwiga of Poland, it became clear that the temporary advantages which had been the sole aim of Gediminas, Kenstutis, and Jogailo himself, were being replaced by a dynastic union which would bring with it the Christianization of Lithuania. The union's foundations were solid, for the Polish magnates planned to use Lithuania's massive natural resources to promote their country's interests, while the Lithuanians hoped to benefit from Poland's more advanced government and economy. Jogailo was baptized as Wladyslaw, married, and crowned in the early months of 1386. Wladyslaw, as he now became known, then spent almost a year in his new Kingdom before returning to Lithuania in 1387. In February a cathedral was founded at Vilnius, the most important Lithuanian nobles were baptized, and a parish system was drawn up. The government of Lithuania was entrusted to Wladyslaw's kinsmen, under his brother Skirgailo, who had played a leading role in the political negotiations with the Polish magnates and now became Wladyslaw's lieutenant at Vilnius.

It seemed as if the political scenario had turned irreparably against the Teutonic Knights. To make matters worse, their own introduction of cannon into the war with Lithuania was at this point working against them, for as the downstream power they faced greater transportation problems than the Lithuanians. Thus Wladyslaw and his cousin Witold were able to take the recently built fort of Marienwerder in just six weeks in 1384, while in 1385 and 1388 invading armies led by Grand Master Zöllner were repulsed by artillery. But the Order was helped by the weaknesses of the Polish-Lithuanian union. These derived partly from the inevitable problems attending the dynastic union of two very different countries, and partly from a continuation of the internal strife which had afflicted both Poland and Lithuania after the deaths of Casimir and Algirdas. For example, the Order was able to occupy Dobrzyn after an agreement with the disaffected Prince Wladyslaw of Oppeln (Opole). More important were King Wladyslaw's unsettled relations with Witold, who followed in Wladyslaw's own footsteps by rebelling and forming an alliance with the Teutonic Knights in 1389. Witold's support enabled the Order to attempt sieges of Vilnius in 1390 and 1392, and although Wladyslaw came to terms with his cousin in 1392, the price was the virtual reconstitution of an independent Lithuania under Witold's control, subject only to Polish suzerainty.

There was no immediate prospect now of a united Polish-Lithuanian attack on the *Ordensstaat*. In fact, Witold turned his attention to the south-east, hoping to exploit the disruption caused to the Golden Horde by Tamerlane's advance, by extending Lithuania's borders to the Black Sea. In October 1398 Witold made peace with the Order at Sallinwerder, gaining the promise of its assistance in his planned campaign. He even secured a crusading bull, but his heterogeneous army of Lithuanians, Ruthenians, and Tatar deserters from the Horde was crushed in August 1399 on the Worskla, a tributary of the Dnieper. This put an end to Witold's Balkan plans. But the effective separation of Poland and Lithuania was confirmed early in 1401 when, following Jadwiga's death in July 1399, the constitutional situation in the two countries was clarified. Wladyslaw remained King of Poland and Grand Duke of Lithuania, but Witold governed Lithuania and exercised sole control over its foreign policy. If the Order could continue to play off Polish against Lithuanian interests, then the threat created in 1386 might be averted indefinitely. The Order even succeeded in finding a new malcontent to sponsor amongst Lithuania's ruling dynasty, this time Wladyslaw's youngest brother, Svitrigal. Profiting from Svitrigal's rebellion, the Order sealed a new treaty with both Wladyslaw and Witold at Raciaz in 1404, in which the terms of Kalisz (1343) and Sallinwerder (1398) were ratified.

In the century's final years it seemed as if the new religious circumstances created by the Polish-Lithuanian union need cause the Order no more difficulties than the political ones. Few people in the West appreciated what had taken place. In book three of his 'Dream of the Old Pilgrim', written very soon after Jogailo's baptism, Philip of Mézières envisaged a combined army of Teutonic Knights and Lithuanians marching together on Constantinople: 'And the lords of Prussia, together with the King of Lithuania, in all their power, will pass through the Kingdom of Russia and the surrounding lands towards Constantinople, and link up with the Germans to crush the might of the Turks.' Mézières thus not only accepted the conversion of the Lithuanians, but incorporated them forthwith into his crusading strategy; nothing could be more natural to this naive enthusiast for the Holy Land crusade than the creation of a crusading army linking these erstwhile heathens with their former enemies, who could now return to their Order's original *raison d'être*. But Mézières seems to have been exceptional amongst his contemporaries. Froissart, by contrast, depicted Sultan Bayezid I appealing to the Lithuanians for help on the eve of Nicopolis, and there were many who accepted the Order's argument that the conversion of Wladyslaw, and of increasing numbers of Lithuanians, was a sham. Thanks to the Order's dissimulation, it was only two years after Wladyslaw's baptism that Pope Urban VI formally congratulated the King and approved the steps he had taken towards establishing the Church in Lithuania. The reason was that the Poles still had no channels of communication with the West comparable with those long since established by the Order.

Wladyslaw's baptism therefore caused no immediate break in the flow of crusaders to Prussia. Indeed, the early 1390s witnessed some of the most important visitors there; the *Reisen* in 1390 and 1391 were especially well attended, partly because the Al-Mahdiya crusade stimulated a wave of crusade enthusiasm during a peaceful phase in Anglo-French relations. Henry Bolingbroke, the Earl of Derby and the most famous of all English participants in the *Reisen*, was in Prussia from August 1390 to March 1391. He took part in the *Sommerreise* of 1390, which won an engagement near Kaunas and besieged Vilnius for several weeks. Derby went to Prussia again in the summer of 1392. The ties between the English monarchy and the Teutonic Order, which were already close, were strengthened after Derby seized the crown in 1399; in 1407 he recalled with affection these adventures of his 'gadling days'. Boucicaut, like Derby, planned to go on the Duke of Bourbon's expedition to Al-Mahdiya in 1390. Forbidden to do so by King Charles VI, he went to Prussia instead, and although it was not cold enough for a *Winterreise* in 1390, Boucicaut was able to take part in Grand Master Conrad of Wallenrode's first *Reise* in the late summer of 1391. Margrave Frederick IV of Meissen brought 500 knights for the same campaign, which was considered to be a particularly splendid one. Gadifer of la Salle, the would-be conqueror of the Canaries, was one of Boucicaut's companions in 1391, and it was in the same year that Henry of Plauen, later to be the Order's saviour and grand master, arrived in Prussia as a crusader. Recruitment for the *Reisen* fell off after about 1394, but this was chiefly because of the stronger appeal of the Nicopolis crusade, and we have seen that even the organizers of that expedition initially considered taking their army to Prussia.

The last years of the fourteenth century were highly successful ones for the Order in military terms, as its grand masters reacted to the threat of the Polish-Lithuanian union by taking the offensive. Under the treaty of Sallinwerder (1398) Witold ceded to the Order his rights over Samogitia, and after a series of campaigns the territory was finally conquered in 1406. Also in 1398, Grand Master Conrad of Jungingen launched the only large-scale amphibious operation ever undertaken by the Order, an attempt to oust the pirates who had seized the island of Gotland as a base for disrupting trade in the Baltic. The Order's fleet of eighty-four ships, carrying 4,000 men, captured and held Gotland for ten years. It has been argued that the operation is less illustrative of territorial aggrandizement on Jungingen's part than of his awareness of the importance of protecting Prussia's maritime commerce. None the less, the chief characteristic of the Gotland campaign, as of the conquest of Samogitia, and the Order's purchase in 1400–1402 of the whole of the Brandenburg Neumark, was their expensiveness. Jungingen's ambitious policies undoubtedly strengthened the Order's links with Germany and constructed the longed-for bridge between Prussia and Livonia, but at the cost of flooding the *Ordensstaat* with mercenaries, and alienating the Prussian estates by his tax demands. As early as 1397 the disaffected nobility of Kulmerland formed the 'Lizard League' (*Eidechsengesellschaft*) to resist the Order's encroachments on its privileges. By the time Jungingen died in 1407, the ground was prepared for the internal problems which would prove crippling to his successors.

At this point Witold was engaged in a war against his own son-in-law, Vasilii I of Moscow, for the hegemony of western Russia. The war showed that Lithuania remained a formidable military power, and when this conflict was resolved in 1408 Witold's interest returned to Samogitia. In the following year he encouraged a rebellion there against the Order's rule. It became clear that Wladyslaw would support his cousin, just as he had in the Russian campaigns, and that the Order would have to fight against both its neighbours. Its diplomacy had failed. The first signs were now appearing, moreover, of a greater fluency by the Poles and Lithuanians in the propaganda conflict. This resulted largely from the study and teaching of canon and civil law at Cracow University, which was effectively refounded in 1400 and flourished in the following decades. Stanislaw of Skarbimierz, the University's Rector, wrote a detailed justification of Poland's war against the Order, 'On Just Wars' ('De bellis iustis'), in 1410. The Samogitians themselves had previously complained that 'the Order desires not our souls for God but our fields for itself', and in a manifesto written in August 1409 Wladyslaw and Witold reiterated the theme that the Teutonic Knights were simply engaged in territorial aggression; there were, after all, no more pagans left in this region. More than twenty years after Wladyslaw's baptism, the Order's claim that Lithuania's conversion was feigned was wearing thin. It was pursuing a policy which German historians have dubbed *Illusionismus*. As Eric

Christiansen has pointed out, the justificatory arguments used by the Poles and Lithuanians were also thin, but they did not depend on outside help and approval as the Order did.

The disaster which overwhelmed the Teutonic Knights in the summer of 1410 did not show that the bubble of illusion had burst, for several groups of crusaders, mainly from western Germany, came to offer their services. Two very different factors worked against the Order. One was its isolation, as its chief ally, King Sigismund of Hungary, failed to appear with his forces. It was not the last time that Sigismund was to prove an unreliable and expensive ally. The other factor was the purposeful and well-executed strategy adopted by Wladyslaw and Witold, who decided to march on Marienburg itself. Three years later Guillebert of Lannoy would remark on Marienburg's formidable strength: 'a very strong town and fortress, where resides the treasure, the might, and all the reserves of Prussia's lords'. But Grand Master Ulrich of Jungingen decided not to allow these fortifications to be put to the test, perhaps because it would have exposed Prussia's agricultural heartland, the *Grosse Werder*, to prolonged devastation. With his numerically inferior army of brethren and crusaders, Jungingen instead hurried to oppose the allied force and its Russian and Tatar auxiliaries. The Order's propagandists later made great play of the presence in the Polish army of these schismatics, pagans, and Muslims (Tatars who had converted to Islam), but the war was clearly a conflict between Catholic powers over territorial issues. Characteristically, both sides called on the help of the Virgin, the Poles, and Lithuanians through their great hymn *Bogurodzica*: 'Virgin, Mother of God, Maria, honoured by God, Your son's patroness, Maria, chosen Mother! Assist us. Kyrie Eleison.' On 15 July the two armies fought the battle of Tannenberg (Grünwald). The Lithuanians, positioned on the allies' right wing, were defeated and fled the field. They were pursued by the brethren in the Order's left wing, who on this occasion neglected to observe the 'corpse-like' obedience enjoined on them in their Rule. The Poles were then able to outflank and overwhelm the right and centre of Grand Master Jungingen's army. They resisted all the Order's desperate attacks, and by sunset the Grand Master, virtually all the Order's high command, and about 200 of its brethren, lay dead.

Tannenberg might have formed the prelude to the conquest of the entire *Ordensstaat*, had it not been for the energy displayed by Henry of Plauen, the Commander of Schwetz. Plauen, who had been entrusted with the defence of Pomerelia, was one of the few high-ranking officers to survive the battle, and he immediately took charge of the defence of Marienburg. He depended on being relieved by the Livonian brethren, who had not fought at Tannenberg, or by King Sigismund. On 19 September, after a two-month siege, Wladyslaw withdrew. Henry of Plauen had robbed him of the fruits of his great victory in much the same way that Conrad of Montferrat's defence of Tyre denied Saladin the full benefits of his success at Hattin in 1187. Another victory over the Order, at Koronowo on 10 October, failed to restore the situation. In February 1411 the First Peace of Thorn gave Samogitia to Lithuania until the deaths of Wladyslaw and Witold, after which the province was to return to the Order. Although the Teutonic Knights agreed to pay a massive war indemnity, these were, for Wladyslaw, unsatisfying terms after a victory on the scale of Tannenberg. But the battle's true significance soon emerged in the form of continuing Polish pressure on the Order, the permanent harm done to its military establishment, and a complex crisis within the *Ordensstaat*.

Before these developments occurred, however, the polemical counterpart to the battle of Tannenberg was fought when, at the end of 1414, both sides sent learned lobbyists to the Council of Constance. In the course of the next four years these intellectuals tried to resolve the question of whether the Teutonic Order's activity was still valid. Their debate was one of the most ambitious medieval attempts to apply legal criteria to political and military behaviour; in crusading history it was without precedent, or later parallel. There were several reasons why both protagonists placed high value on the Council's backing. The issue of the Order's western volunteers remained an important one. Fewer came after Tannenberg, despite the Order's desperate appeals, and only Germans seem to have come at all after 1413, partly because of the outbreak of the Anglo-French war; but, not surprisingly, the Poles resented their villages being burnt by crusaders, and themselves being termed *mescréans* or the 'allies of Saracens' (a generic term including pagans as well as Muslims). In addition, both sides hired mercenaries, especially in Silesia and Bohemia, and while wages and the expectation of booty were the key factors in attracting such men, they preferred, for the sake of their honour, to fight for a cause which had been validated as just. The decidedly mixed reaction in western Europe to the news of Tannenberg showed that the Teutonic Order's depiction of the struggle was already being questioned. Optimistic Poles therefore hoped to get the Order suppressed entirely, following the precedent of the Templars. Others, more realistically, aimed to secure a conciliar prohibition on the Order's use of the crusade, and a ruling against its territorial aggression. They considered that the Order should co-operate with themselves against the Russians and Tatars, a proposal first put forward, as we have seen, by the Lithuanians in the fourteenth century. To the Teutonic Knights, this meant helping their enemies gain extra power which they could then use to destroy the *Ordensstaat*. They wanted the Council to condemn their enemies for impeding the holy work of a religious Order, and even hoped for a full-scale crusade against the Poles, should they prove recalcitrant. The latter idea was not as fantastic as it seems, given the recent spate of crusades against Christian rulers, and the fact that crusading was already being discussed as a solution to Hussitism.

The key contributions to the Constance debate were made in 1415 by Peter Wormditt, the Grand Master's proctor, and the Polish canon lawyer Paul Vladimiri, and in 1416 by the pro-Order Dominican John Falkenberg. Wormditt contented himself with presenting a history of the Baltic region, carefully tailored to serve as a eulogy of the Teutonic Order's achievements. Like all the Order's apologists, he did not dwell on the principles underpinning the Baltic crusade, the *Ordensstaat*, or Military Orders generally; these could be assumed to form part of the common currency of Catholic belief. More controversially, he took for granted Lithuania's paganism, thus side-stepping the problem of the Order's future role. But if Wormditt failed to go far enough, Vladimiri went too far. Like his opponent, he presented a tendentious view of history, in which the Order became the villain and the Poles their victims. However, he also attacked the concept of a Military Order, declaring that as clerics the Teutonic Knights were prohibited from carrying arms, and even criticizing their practice of starting the *Reisen* on Marian feast days. The fact that Vladimiri found this objectionable shows how out of step he was with the crusading ideas expressed by the *Reisen*. Similarly, his daring argument that all the Order's early privileges were invalidated by its move from Palestine to Prussia fell flat in the light of the general acceptance of this development.

More importantly, Vladimiri caused a scandal by denying that previous popes and emperors had possessed the authority to grant the Order possession of lands ruled by the heathens; the many privileges on which Wormditt and the Order's other apologists relied were therefore valueless. There were no legal grounds, he claimed, for supposing that the western emperors possessed authority over lands other than those which they had inherited. As for the papacy, Vladimiri argued that pagans enjoyed lawful political authority which the popes could not, in normal circumstances, take away from them. This was in accordance with the mainstream juridical tradition of the Curia. What Vladimiri did not realize was that most of the papacy's privileges to the Order had assumed that the pagans had waived their rights by murdering missionaries and persecuting converts. The privileges therefore retained their validity even if Vladimiri's position was accepted. Moreover, as we saw in the case of crusades proclaimed in support of Iberian overseas expansion, by this point the Curia was moving beyond this moderate stance anyway, and accepting the argument that the pope could sanction conquest provided it brought conversions with it. Such, for example, was the argument expounded at Constance by the Benedictine Bishop of Ciudad Rodrigo, Andrew Escobar. It was ironical that Vladimiri's conservative stance not only placed him at odds with the emerging Catholic approach, but also put him in the awkward position of declaring that many past popes had exceeded their authority, as well as branding him as a 'friend of the pagans': 'You are a good advocate for pagans against Christians', was one critic's comment.

As Professor Frederick Russell has pointed out, Vladimiri recognized the importance of the crusade for the defence of Poland's south-eastern borders; he wanted to discredit only the Order's misuse of the crusade, not the crusade itself. Vladimiri's chief opponent, John Falkenberg, was much more extreme. By an astute conflation of Augustine and Aristotle, Falkenberg vindicated aggressive war on the heathen under imperial direction. He also launched a xenophobic assault on the Poles, criticizing them harshly for using pagan and schismatic troops in their war against the Teutonic Knights, and accusing them of harbouring designs to conquer as far as the Rhine. And in his *Satira*, a work written a few years earlier and revived at this point, Falkenberg put forward the case for a crusade against the Poles on the extraordinary grounds that they were not real Christians anyway. This was unacceptable, and Falkenberg was arrested and condemned in 1417 as the author of a scurrilous libel. It became clear to the Order's agents that the Poles were defending their corner far too ably to hope to get them branded as pariahs. Still, Falkenberg's views on war against the heathen formed an effective reply to Vladimiri, and his condemnation of the Polish use of pagan troops, although easily countered and in essence a red herring anyway, attracted much sympathy. Vladimiri's assault was also ably dealt with by the canonist John Urbach, who used the same assumptions and sources as Vladimiri to depict the Order as the victim of Polish aggression.

Most of the debate at Constance concerned the war between the Order and Poland, and its historical background. But the Poles also levelled against the Teutonic Knights the charge that they had failed to bring about the effective conversion of the pagan peoples whom they had conquered. This was a potentially damaging accusation since conversion had provided a large measure of the justification for the Order's conquests in Prussia and Livonia. At the end of 1415 Samogitian witnesses arrived at Constance, and they testified that the Order's aggression was actually a hindrance to their conversion, that they wanted to be 'baptized with water and not with blood'. It was a familiar and not altogether convincing argument, but there was much truth to the Polish claim that after generations of rule by the Order, Prussia itself remained a semi-pagan land. The same charge had been forcefully made at the enquiry established by Clement V a century earlier, and St Bridget had attacked the Order's poor record in converting its subjects. 'Lasset Preussen Preussen bleiben', 'let [Old, sc. pagan] Prussians stay that way' was quoted as a catch-phrase of the Order in 1427. In entrusting the conversion of the Samogitians to Poland-Lithuania, the Council showed that it was dissatisfied with the Order's achievements in this respect, and that it did not accept the brethren's claim that only constant military pressure brought about enduring conversion. But further than this the Council would not go, and when it ended in May 1418 the result was unsatisfactory for both sides. There was no crusade against the Poles, but there was also no condemnation of the Teutonic Order. Christendom's leading churchmen had declined the chance to pass judgement on what was happening on its north-eastern periphery, or to lay down guidelines for the future.

What did Constance prove? Manifestly the Poles failed to demonstrate to the Council that the religious situation in the Baltic region made any debate about the Order's war against heathens redundant. Instead, they allowed themselves to get bogged down in the backwaters of recent Baltic history, when virtually every event could be interpreted in radically different ways; the Order was a past master at this kind of haggling, with over a century's experience at it. Similarly, the Poles were lured into a theoretical discussion about the validity of warfare against the heathen. This they could not win, partly because, as the medieval adage quaintly put it, 'authorities have wax noses that can be bent in diverse directions', and more importantly because the Council was not prepared to condemn the values its forefathers had created and passed down to it. The Teutonic Order was thus able to retain the approval, though no longer the enthusiastic support, of the Church, on the basis largely of what it had done in the past. The question of what it should do in the future was not answered, and scarcely raised.

In practice, the failure of the Poles to secure a conciliar condemnation of the Order's habit of raising volunteers with the offer of crusader status did not matter, since the practice came to an end anyway soon afterwards. Following Tannenberg, Grand Master Henry of Plauen attempted to ameliorate his manpower problems by stimulating the recruitment of crusaders, promising his guests a warm welcome and the revival of the practice of the *Ehrentisch*, the table of honour set up in the fourteenth century to celebrate knights who performed especially well on the *Reisen*. When the Order was again plunged into war with Poland in 1422, appeals to Germany led to the arrival of bands of Rhenish crusaders under Count-Palatine Ludwig and Dietrich of Moers, the Archbishop of Cologne. These were the last important crusaders who went to Prussia. No doubt the decline of the Order's military reputation after Tannenberg, and its inability to entertain its guests as lavishly as in the past, contributed to ending the tradition. But the chief reason was the realization, at last, that the religious situation had irrevocably changed. In this respect it is possible that the Poles did win the Constance debate, in the indirect sense that the delegates, on their return home, spread the news that the Order's war was no longer one of religion. In 1429, for instance, the commanders of the German bailiwicks wrote to the Grand Master that people would not go to fight against the Poles and Lithuanians because they were Christians. Thereafter the *Reisen* retained their respectability only in literary form, where reality could be ignored or heavily disguised. In 'Le Petit Jehan de Saintré', written in 1456, Anthony of la Sale, who himself fought at Ceuta, made *Belle Cousine* comment that 'it seems to me that you could do nothing more holy or honourable than take part in this most sacred voyage to Prussia, and in the most holy battle which will occur when the Saracens are encountered'. Six years later the author of the 'Cent nouvelles nouvelles' had a character go to Prussia to fight alongside the Teutonic Knights, whom he praised as 'the good lords of Prussia, true champions and defenders of the most holy Christian faith'.

At the same time as, and to some extent for the same reasons that, the flow of volunteers from the West came to an end, the Order faced growing problems within its own ranks. During the first half of the century its national and social exclusiveness became more pronounced, only nobles of German descent now being admitted as brethren. A series of guidelines drawn up by the Order's senior officers in 1449 included the demand that

Item, the Provincial Commanders and Commanders in the German lands shall only admit counts, barons, good knights and service noblemen since that is good old custom. They shall not admit peasants or townsmen for money's sake. If it should happen that peasants or other people who are not of good birth should be admitted by the aforementioned Provincial Commanders etc. for money's sake or out of good will, and if one should come out to Prussia, then one shall send him back to Germany where he came from.[1]

In the following year, expelling a foreigner from the Order, the Grand Master wrote 'The Order is a German Order in which up to now no non-Germans, but only Germans, healthy and trained people, who are in all respects born to the shield, are customarily received.' By this point the Order was attracting very few members even of the higher nobility. All its grand masters between 1351 and 1498 belonged to the nobility's lower strata, and its association with Germany's lesser nobility is clear from the tendency for the German commanderies to align themselves with regional leagues of noble families in their struggles against the German towns.

But this attempt to preserve a distinctive social profile did not lead to harmony within the Order. Instead, Germany's acute regional antagonisms took destructive root there. Grand Master Henry of Plauen's attempt to break the monopoly of the Order's offices held by south Germans was a key motive behind his deposition in 1413. Grand Master Michael Küchmeister (1414–22) restored the Swabians, Bavarians, and Franconians to power, but his successor Paul of Rusdorf (1422–41) promoted Rhinelanders, and the factional strife thus created between the two groups persisted throughout the rest of the century. When much of Prussia had been lost, one Rhinelander composed a rueful verse to the effect that 'we said farewell to one another, and abandoned a fine land; nobody is to blame but the Bavarians, Swabians, and Franconians'. Similarly, Rusdorf's attempt to place Rhinelanders in key Livonian posts was resisted by the North German brethren who dominated the province; civil war broke out between Rhinelanders and Westphalians when heavy losses at the battle of Wilkomierz (Swienta) in 1435 created vacancies in

[1] M. Burleigh, *Prussian Society and the German Order: An Aristocratic Corporation in Crisis c.1410–1466* (Cambridge, 1984), 41.

many important Livonian offices. Soon afterwards the Livonian brethren denied the grand master any say in choosing their master; he was allowed only to receive the homage of the man they chose, who was always to be a Westphalian.

The cracks caused by regional factions thus contributed to the gradual divergence of the Order's various branches. In the decades following Tannenberg relations between Prussia, the German bailiwicks, and Livonia became strained as money was increasingly demanded, and denied, to meet the expenses of the *Ordensstaat*. In 1411 the Commander of Lorraine refused to send money on account of the devastation caused to his bailiwick by local wars; the Lotharingian nobility would not allow the sale or alienation of the Order's lands because 'they and their forefathers are remembered by it and divine service is increased by it'. The same excuses were offered by all the bailiwicks. Some years later Master Siegfried of Livonia refused to send help because 'our land in Livonia is so devastated and impoverished by hunger and pestilence, that God must know it and take pity on us. We can hardly man our Order's castles in Livonia, defend them and hold them if there is an emergency that comes unexpectedly.' By mid-century this loss of control had reached another level, as the grand master and masters could no longer expect obedience from individual commanders, or even castellans.

In these circumstances of internal tension and fissure, it is not surprising that the spiritual quality of conventual life suffered. Laxity in a religious Order is notoriously difficult to assess. But it is well attested in this instance, for example in an admonitory treatise, written probably by a Carthusian monk in 1426 or 1427, in which the brethren's failings were gloomily depicted. Since there were fewer brethren in Prussia—the total fell from about 700 in 1410, to 400 in 1437, and 300 in 1453—they were able to live in circumstances of greater comfort despite the Order's financial problems. Sources described them paying lip service at best to their monastic vows, and either preoccupied with personal ambition or living in purposeless indolence. Provincial commanders amassed private fortunes, kept mistresses, and engaged in large-scale nepotism. And as Dr Michael Burleigh has put it, the lives of many of the ordinary brethren were characterized by 'boredom, heavy drinking, trivial pranks, tough talk, violence and cliquishness'. A series of attempts at reform by the grand masters, especially in the second half of the century, were defeated by inertia and vested interest.

As remarked above, all these internal difficulties were related in some sense to the institutional displacement which afflicted the Teutonic Knights as their crusading role was shown to be illusionary. Although the German bailiwicks provided local hospitaller services to some degree, the need of the Order as a whole to find a new and specific function accelerated its close identification with the nobility. In 1453 Emperor Frederick III termed it 'the refuge of the German nobility', while in 1512 the Teutonic Knights claimed, in a letter to Emperor Maximilian I, that 'the Order alone is dedicated to the entire nobility of the German nation, of both high and low degree'. This limited and class-based function, which could not be expected to have wide social appeal, itself imposed obligations which added to the Order's problems. For example, when the Commander of Altenbiesen told the local nobility in 1449 that he could not admit any more of them as brethren at present, they indignantly asked 'why does one need the Order any more if it is not to be a hospital and abode for the nobility?' Similarly, both regional faction-fighting and the breakdown of the Order's hierarchy of command came about partly because there no longer existed a consensus of belief in the Order's goals. In such circumstances efforts were expended instead on a struggle for personal or group advance, or in the defence of the local unit's needs against what were seen as the intrusive and irrelevant demands of the grand master. The Order was falling apart.

From Tannenberg onwards, there were therefore numerous attempts to find the Order a new and more demanding role within the crusading movement. In the autumn of 1418 a summit conference assembled at Vilnius to deal with the problem of Samogitia, the outstanding territorial issue between the Order and the Polish monarchy. As Professor William Urban commented, 'this seemed to be the moment that the entire crusading movement in the Baltic region could be reshaped and redirected'. Geographically, there was little to prevent the Order assuming a part in the struggle against the schismatic Russians, the Hussites, or the Ottoman Turks, or some combination of the three. In practice, however, rival territorial claims remained an insuperable obstacle to peace on this and later occasions. The Order's main military efforts therefore continued to be directed against the Poles and Lithuanians. No amount of disguise could conceal the fact that the *Reisen*, always a particularly brutal form of warfare, were now being conducted against Christians. Nor did it help that in its desperate search for allies the Order at times turned to the Russians, a move it incongruously justified at the Council of Basle as a step towards the unification of the two churches.

A certain amount of reorientation did take place. As we shall see, the Livonian brethren fought important wars against Novgorod and Moscow. The Order became involved in the crusades against the Hussites, in support of its ally Sigismund of Hungary-Bohemia. The cost to its own lands and subjects was terrible, as the Hussites became in turn allies of Poland and raided western Prussia as far as the Baltic coast in 1433. And in 1429 the Grand Master responded to a request from Emperor Sigismund by taking over the defence of part of Transylvania against the Turks for six years. But none of these commitments were on the scale of the former wars against the Prussians and Lithuanians. In the course of the following decades proposals were advanced by many, including Sigismund, the Poles, representatives of the Order's German bailiwicks, and the Archbishop of Riga and Bishop of Ermland, that the Order invest its resources more fully in the conflict with the Turks. At the end of the century there was even a suggestion that the Teutonic Order should amalgamate with the Hospitallers for this purpose. These proposals were taken seriously: Pope Calixtus III excommunicated the Order's enemies on the grounds that they were hindering the crusade against the Turks. But none was followed up.

Apart from the paralysing effects of inertia and decay within the Order itself, the main obstacle to any major realignment of this kind remained the existence of the *Ordensstaat*. This was not only because its defence and government consumed the high command's resources and energies, but also because, while fighting crusades elsewhere might justify the Order, it would not provide the rationale for its ruling Prussia. Ironically, even this small-scale diversification of the Order's military efforts exacerbated internal tensions, by creating a dispute about priorities. Thus in the 1430s the German commanders wanted to concentrate on the Hussites, who were attacking some of their lands during their forays beyond Bohemia, at the cost of peace with Poland; and at the end of the 1490s Prussia's investment in the anti-Turkish conflict meant that it was unable to help Livonia resist the growing Russian threat. The Order thus again suffered, though to a smaller degree, the problem of crusade priorities which had afflicted it in the late thirteenth century.

Meanwhile it became clear that the Order could no longer rule Prussia effectively. The crisis which occurred there in the wake of Tannenberg came about partly because of economic circumstances, which were largely beyond the Order's control, but mainly because of the financial repercussions of defeat and the Teutonic Knights' poor political relations with their own subjects. In the early fifteenth century Prussia's agrarian economy suffered badly from depopulation caused by the Polish war, crop failures, and plague. Already in 1419 over 20 per cent of the Order's villages were deserted, and in the south-western Commandery of Schwetz the figure rose to 80 per cent by 1437–8. The symptoms of population decline included attempts to fix maximum wage rates, in 1407, 1417, and 1420, and harsh legislation against runaway serfs and servants. The Ordinances of 1494 specified that a runaway servant was to be nailed to the pillory by one ear and handed a knife with which to cut himself free. Above all, the century witnessed a remorseless increase in labour services; the most serious response to this was a major revolt by the peasants of the Ermland cathedral chapter in 1440. At the same time the Prussian towns, like all the members of the Hanse, fared badly from Dutch and English competition, and deteriorating profit margins. By 1422 Braunsberg, Elbing, Königsberg, and Thorn declared that they could not afford to send delegates to a Hanse meeting, and by 1500 Danzig alone continued to figure in long-distance trade. These developments hit the Order particularly hard because of its long-standing dependence on the profits gained from corn exports and commerce; and they increased the resistance mounted by the Prussian landowners and towns against the Order when it attempted to make up for its loss of revenue by raising taxes, debasing the currency, and rewriting the laws of inheritance in its own favour.

As the economic scenario grew harsher, events followed a pattern largely familiar to the student of late medieval government. Recent historians have discounted the idea that the Order's growing financial plight resulted from the war indemnity of 260,000 florins imposed by the First Peace of Thorn, pointing out that only ten months after the Peace was made the Order was prepared to pay a subsidy of 300,000 florins to its ally Sigismund. More important was the unremitting military pressure exerted by Poland. In the aftermath of the losses sustained at Tannenberg, and with the flow of volunteers from the West dwindling first to a trickle and then to nothing, this pressure compelled the Order to continue hiring expensive bands of mercenaries, who would mutiny if they were not paid. Ineffective and destructive as these hired soldiers were, the Order could not manage without them. As so often in military history, the threat of Polish attack was thus as harmful to the Order as invasion itself. The Prussians meanwhile formed into Estates, the towns in conscious imitation of their German colleagues in the Hanse, the knights and freemen as a political extension of their juridical co-operation in the country courts. When Henry of Plauen tried to levy a general tax in 1411 to pay the Order's war indemnity, he was presented with twenty-six articles of complaint, centring on the unfairness of the Order's commercial monopolies and privileges. Renewed war with Poland in 1414, 1422, and 1433, brought devastation to Prussia and induced in its civilian population overwhelming feelings of war weariness and political alienation. In December 1433 the Town Mayor of Thorn informed Grand Master Rusdorf that if he did not seek peace, 'your Grace should know that we will take it upon ourselves and seek out a lord who will give us peace and quiet'.

It was this open threat to transfer allegiance to Poland which points out the difference between the crisis in the Order's relations with its subjects, and the myriad other clashes over war taxation which characterized fifteenth-century Europe. As a monastic Order, the Teutonic Knights had failed to put down roots in Prussia. Significantly, the Prussian Estates claimed in 1453 that some of the Order's commanders had not taken the field in the Polish wars because 'they would not stick their necks out or let themselves be killed for our wives, children and property'. No ties of lineage or even region connected ruled and rulers, for Prussians were not welcome in the Order and the original settlers had come mainly from northern and central Germany. Mutual antagonism was fed by anti-clerical sentiments, which were rife throughout Europe in this period, but were sharpened in Prussia by the Order's aggressive clericalism, and stimulated by Hussite ideas imported by the Order's Bohemian mercenaries. Antagonism, in turn, crystallized into active hostility as the Prussian Estates became more assertive and resentful, while the Order responded with coarse and brutal disdain. Against the Order's claim that 'we were all pagans and that we were won by the sword and therefore we were more like serfs or people one bought', the Estates' reply was a justification for rebellion which combined crusading ideas with the traditional medieval concept of imperilled liberties:

Their forefathers and fathers came to Prussia to fight loyally against the heathen with loss of their blood in order to bring them into the Christian Faith and they helped master the land, as it exists today . . . and they helped bring other powerful lords and countries that border on Prussia to the Faith and they did this in praise of God and because of their liberty. Which liberty they have enjoyed for many years . . . But, from the moment the land of Prussia and the lands around it achieved peace and unity, the Order began to squander the good deeds, services and support of its subjects and burdened them with uncustomary taxes and unseemly charges when they had hoped for greater reward.[2]

In March 1440, after years of fiscal demands following the war of 1433, fifty-three Prussian noblemen and the delegates of nineteen towns formed a Union (*Bund*), with the goal of curtailing the Order's overween-ing lordship. At first the Order tried to contain the crisis with offers of concessions, and to split the Estates by exploiting the quarrels between towns and landowners, especially on the issue of migration. Then in 1449 the moderate and skilful Grand Master Conrad of Erlichshausen died, and after a comic interlude of papal and imperial interventions, open war between the Union and the Order broke out in 1454. Poland had naturally encouraged the Union since its formation, and in February 1454 King Casimir IV accepted its offer of the lordship of Prussia. His charter of incorporation granted the Estates all they could ask for. For the Prussian towns, this had the advantage of consolidating their status as entrepôts for Poland's booming exports; since the turn of the century Polish migration into the towns and villages of Prussia had increased markedly, while intermarriage between the Prussian and Polish border nobilities made closer political ties attractive. By 1454 there was thus a powerful lobby of incorporationists on both sides of the border. The logic of Polish–Prussian union should not be pushed too far, however. The alienation of the Prussian Estates represented a massive political failure on the part of the Order, brought about primarily by the overweening social contempt displayed by the Teutonic Knights towards their own subjects.

The Order was not prepared to surrender Prussia easily. There was no denying the military superiority of its opponents, but the strength of the Order's fortifications, its willingness to hire mercenaries in large numbers on expensive credit, and the comparative backwardness of Poland's forces, enabled the Teutonic Knights to stave off defeat for thirteen years. In September 1454 the Poles suffered a serious defeat at Konitz (Chojnice). But in contrast to Henry of Plauen's heroic defence of Marienburg in 1410, the Order ignominiously lost its capital to the enemy in 1457, when its unpaid mercenaries surrendered the fortress in exchange for money. In 1462 the Order was defeated at Puck, in 1463 it suffered a naval defeat off Elbing, and in 1464 the defection of the Bishop of Ermland cut the *Ordensstaat* in half. By then the devastation caused by the fighting was so

---

[2] Burleigh, *Prussian Society*, 140.

great that a delegation of peacemakers from neutral Lübeck noted that at one point, in what had previously been Prussia's agricultural heartland, 'there was not a living being, dog or cat for ten miles'. Two years later the Second Peace of Thorn was sealed. Poland annexed Pomorze, Elbing, Marienburg, Kulm, and Ermland. The Order retained Königsberg and east Prussia, but as a fief of the Polish Crown. The grand masters had to perform homage to the kings of Poland and render military service: ironically, it was the latter, rather than the Order's crusading obligations, which brought about its largest contribution to the struggle against the Turks, when Grand Master John of Tiefen took to the field with 4,000 troops to assist King John Albert in 1497.

The campaign of 1497 was the first major military engagement between the Poles and the Turks. A clash between Poland and the Ottomans had been predictable since the *voivode* of Moldavia paid homage to Wladyslaw II in 1387, and the *voivode* of Wallachia became his ally two years later. When western observers realized how powerful Poland had become, they quickly tried to harness its forces to the anti-Ottoman crusade. Philip of Mézières's suggestion, made at the time of Jogailo's baptism, that the Lithuanians join the Teutonic Knights in a crusade, has already been noted. In 1421 Henry V of England, who six years earlier had shown his high opinion of Poland's strength by inviting Wladyslaw to support his cause in the war against France, dispatched Guillebert of Lannoy to reconnoitre eastern Europe with a view to arranging Polish and Lithuanian assistance in a crusade against the Turks. The Polish court had far too many problems at this point to be interested, and although Wladyslaw III led the disastrous Varna crusade in 1444, this was regarded as a purely Hungarian enterprise, and few Polish troops were involved. In fact it was not until Bayezid II's capture of the Black Sea ports of Kilia and Akkerman in 1484, and his control over the Crimean Tatars, that Poland was pulled into the anti-Ottoman crusade. Thereafter it remained one of Christendom's 'front-line states': the destruction caused by two massive Turkish raids of southern Poland in 1498, carried out as a reprisal for John Albert's 1497 campaign, served as a lasting reminder of the fact, which was reflected in the stream of crusade bulls which were granted by the Curia.

Following the Second Peace of Thorn the rump of the *Ordensstaat* enjoyed something of an Indian Summer. Released from the crippling expenses of the war with Poland, and able to benefit to the full from its economic links with its neighbours, 'Ducal Prussia', as it was now known, experienced renewed prosperity and relative political stability. The Order's income and powers of government were substantially reduced both by its new feudal obligations to Poland, and by its grant of territories and associated public services to discharged mercenary captains whom it was unable to pay with cash. Since these captains came to form the backbone of the nobility, the immensely powerful and privileged Prussian *Junker* class of the Early Modern period can be considered as an indirect but indubitable consequence of the fading away of the Baltic crusade after Tannenberg, and of the manpower crisis which the Order suffered as a result. At the same time as the Order's grip slackened, the anomaly of government by a religious corporation became more jarring than ever. The secularization of the brethren's way of life proceeded apace, with senior officers treating their posts as private property to be bought and sold. But its natural culmination, the brethren's abandonment of their monastic vows, and their intermarriage with the Prussian nobility, was prevented by the Order's German ties. The sole rationale for the Order's holding lands within Germany was that it constituted an asylum for the younger sons of the nobility, and this would naturally cease if the richest pickings of lordship, the offices and privileges of government in Ducal Prussia, were vested permanently in existing brethren and their descendants. So in order to maintain a tenuous unity between the Order's various branches, a new policy of *Illusionismus* was created, this time relating to the corporation's very nature as a monastic Order. No sincere man could deny the need for change, but nobody had the power and the will to cut the Gordian knot holding Prussia and the German bailiwicks together.

Livonia meanwhile largely followed its own course, and it was here, after the Second Peace of Thorn, that the Order continued to display some military vigour and even to carry on its traditional crusading role. Politically, the first four decades of the fifteenth century were marked by a resurgence of those forces which had always resisted the Order's attempt to dominate the province; the archbishop of Riga and his suffragans in particular derived indirect benefits not only from the Order's military disasters, but also from the conciliarist movement, which encouraged the secular church everywhere to take the initiative. In 1428 a council of the Livonian church even proposed regular episcopal visitations of the Order's convents. Estates formed on lines similar to Prussia, and they used the Order's defeats to exact concessions in 1422 and 1435. These established Livonia as a confederation in which the Order had the status of senior partner rather than master, but they did not bring peace:

the Thirteen Years War had its equivalent in Livonia, and there was a further war between Riga and the Order between 1482 and 1491. Throughout the century the bishops of Dorpat conducted a separate foreign policy.

None the less, Livonia's economy remained healthier than Prussia's, and the Order's revenues were buoyant enough to enable it to invest heavily in cannon, usually imported by Hanseatic merchants. The Livonian brethren could not avoid assisting the embattled *Ordensstaat* in periods of crisis, such as the aftermath of Tannenberg, the war of 1433, and the Thirteen Years War. But they had fewer commitments in the south than in the fourteenth century, and despite the internal decay with which it had to contend, the high command in Livonia decided to use its extra resources to renew the push eastwards. The peaceful coexistence which had, for the most part, characterized Russo-Livonian relations since the mid-thirteenth century, was therefore succeeded by a period of warfare. The resulting conflict is reminiscent of King Magnus's earlier campaigns further north, but the Order's motivation was not simple expansionism; it was also attempting to consolidate its position in response to Moscow's alarming rise to power. There were *Reisen* against Pskov in 1406, 1407, and 1408, and an intermittent struggle against Novgorod in the following decades, centring on each side's attempts to take the enemy's frontier castles on Lake Chud, and along the Narva and Luga rivers.

Since the negotiations for the Union of the Catholic and Orthodox churches which took place at the Council of Ferrara-Florence in 1438–9 came to nothing, the war against Novgorod could be portrayed as a crusade against schismatics. Groups of German crusaders arrived to participate in it as late as the 1440s. In 1442, for example, the Grand Master wrote to his procurator at the papal Curia that 'we have . . . informed our Roman king and our lord electors and princes in Germany to see if anyone is willing to come on such a crusade at his own expense to praise God, honour his mother Mary, and extend the Christian faith'. Since the procurator was instructed to inform Pope Eugenius IV of this fact, it is clear that the Order was still making use of its thirteenth-century privilege to raise crusaders without specific papal permission. But while crusading volunteers were always welcome, the Order increasingly needed cash with which to hire mercenaries and buy artillery. For this papal indulgences were needed, with all the haggling, bribery, and financial compromise that procuring them entailed. In 1436 the Council of Basle decreed the preaching of indulgences to pay the expenses of negotiations about Union with the Greeks. Proceeds in Prussia and Livonia were used in the war against Novgorod, although in 1448 Nicholas V earmarked a third of the money to assist Hungary against the Turks. Nicholas then granted another indulgence in 1449 on a 50:50 basis. But when the war in Prussia broke out five years later the Pope refused renewal, probably fearing that the proceeds would be used there.

Between 1471 and 1489 Grand Prince Ivan III of Moscow showed that the Order's fears of his Principality's power were well justified by eroding, and then ending, Novgorod's position of semi-autonomy. Initially the Livonian brethren tried to counter Ivan's advance by themselves conquering Pskov, but they were then diverted by their war with Riga. And in 1492, a year after this dispute was finally settled, Ivan built the great castle of Ivangorod, challenging the Catholic fort of Narva across the Narva river. Walter of Plettenberg, elected Master in 1494, knew that war with Moscow was inevitable, and he prepared for it by forming an alliance with Lithuania in June 1501, and by hiring 2,000 German mercenary troops. But the Lithuanians let him down, and despite successes in August and September 1501, he could not prevent three Russian armies from ravaging eastern Livonia in the autumn. In the following summer Plettenberg raised the largest army possible and inflicted a defeat on the Muscovites at Lake Smolina. Fought, appropriately, on the eve of the Exaltation of the Cross (14 September), the battle gave Livonia a temporary respite from Russian attention. Ivan III needed his troops elsewhere, made peace with Plettenberg in 1503, and died two years later. Throughout the crisis the Order had received little help from the Curia, which entertained unrealistic hopes of securing Russian assistance against the Turks and feared to alienate Moscow. Constant petitioning for crusade indulgences only achieved success when the war had nearly ended, although the 40,000 ducats which were then raised, in preaching which went on for some years, did help to pay the Order's war debts. The burgeoning repercussions of the anti-Ottoman crusade thus had the opposite effect on the Baltic to that which they exercised on the western Mediterranean, where they gave Iberian crusading a new lease of life.

Before Livonia was again subjected to Russian attack, both it and Prussia faced the challenge of the Reformation. In a sense the Lutheran assault on the monastic way of life was a boon to the brethren governing Ducal Prussia, enabling them to abandon what had become, for most, the superficial trappings of conventual life. In choosing princes—Duke Frederick of Saxony and Margrave Albert of Brandenburg-Ansbach—as their last two grand masters, the brethren had already accelerated yet further the transformation of *Ordensstaat* into *Territorialstaat*. But if, in hindsight, the final stage in Prussia's secularization seems all but inevitable, at the time it was far from straightforward. By 1522 Lutheranism had become firmly entrenched amongst the Duchy's laity and secular clergy, but the brethren themselves were conservative. Most preferred both to rule Prussia and to continue enjoying the Order's ancient and splendid traditions. It was the devout and intelligent Grand Master Albert who, following a personal interview with Luther at Wittenberg in 1523, resolved that secularization was not only honourable, but also the only sure way to save the Duchy from anarchy. Accordingly he bullied the Prussian brethren into accepting the dissolution of the Order in Prussia in 1525. The *Ordensstaat* became an hereditary duchy. That this state would continue to be a Polish dependency was clear following Grand Master Albert's failure to win independence in the Order's last war with Poland, fought in 1519–21.

Walter of Plettenberg was still Master of the Livonian brethren when reform agitation reached the country, through such preachers as Andrew Knopken and Sylvester Tegetmeier at Riga, John Lange at Reval, and Hermann Marsow at Dorpat. Both Plettenberg and the Archbishop of Riga were sympathetic to reforming ideas, but Plettenberg was as conservative as most of the Prussian brethren and would not follow the Grand Master's lead. In 1526 he declined an offer to become the first duke of Livonia. Interestingly, Luther's response to Plettenberg's dilemma was accommodating: the Livonian brethren could retain their monastic regime, provided that Protestant doctrine was introduced into Livonian worship. Plettenberg was successful in bringing this about, and by 1526 the majority of the population were Lutheran, and a degree of toleration enforced. The Teutonic Knights still played a role in the country's government and defence, though there were by now fewer than 200 brethren left.

Within a generation, however, the Russian threat reappeared, and this time it could not be withstood. Ivan the Terrible invaded in 1558, taking Narva in May and Dorpat in July. In the following winter Russian armies ravaged Semigallia and Courland, and a truce in March 1559 was the signal for Poland, Sweden, and Denmark to intervene and secure their share of the spoils. Last minute appeals for imperial help proved fruitless. The secularization of the Livonian brethren in 1561–2, when Master Gotthard Kettler became the first Duke of Courland-Semigallia under Polish suzerainty, was little more than an incident in the protracted destruction of the Livonian confederation. Livonia suffered another twenty years of war before the Poles drove Ivan IV back, frustrating Russia's attempt to reach the Baltic. The religious confusion within Poland in these decades makes it highly unlikely that crusading indulgences were even sought for this war, and since the Russians' other enemies were Protestant, it is probable that the indulgences reluctantly issued to Plettenberg at the close of the previous war were the last ones granted for crusading along the Baltic.

Thus it was not the papacy's plans to forge a grand alliance of Catholic and Orthodox powers against the Turks, but the division of the Catholic world caused by the Reformation, which finally brought the Baltic crusade to a close. The Teutonic Order did not come to an end with the crusading tradition which it had so long promoted; in fact, although the German masters lost no opportunity, for generations to come, of lodging solemn protests against the illegality of what had occurred, the secularization of Prussia and Livonia gave the German bailiwicks a new freedom of action. The election of Master Kronberg of Germany as Grand Master in 1527, and his reforming measures, showed that a chapter had finished, not the whole book. Adaptation was not easy, for the Order's losses in the Reformation were severe. The peasants' uprising of 1525 did great damage to its estates, including the destruction of the Master's castle at Horneck on the Neckar. The Hussite Reformation had already cost the Order its Bohemian bailiwick, and by 1600 there were only seven Catholic bailiwicks left. Some of these, however, were persuaded or cajoled into playing a part in the war against the Ottomans. In 1565 the Imperial Counsellor Schwendi drew up a plan to hand the frontier over to the Order to defend. A similar project was presented to the Imperial Diet at Regensburg in 1576 by Maximilian II, who even proposed an interconfessional Order to fight against the Turks. In the new Rule drawn up in 1606, three years' military service on the Turkish frontier was prescribed for all entrants to the Order, and in 1696 the Order established its own regiment, to be commanded in the field by Teutonic Knights. The military role of the Austrian commanderies in particular remained notable throughout the Early Modern period, and recent historians of the Order have rightly stressed its similarity to the Hospitallers in the post-Prussian era of its long history. Both Orders successfully adapted to changing circumstances, and while the military establishment of the Hospitallers at Malta was greater, the achievement of the Teutonic Knights, who had to divest themselves of a dead crusading tradition, was just as notable.

13

Catholic Society and the Crusade
1274–1580

✠

W E have now looked at all the chief areas in which crusading occurred between 1274 and 1580, and are in a position to investigate more fully the relationship between the crusading movement and contemporary society and government. What place did the crusade hold in Catholic society between the Second Council of Lyons and the Habsburg–Ottoman truce of 1580? Historians have long ceased to believe that such a question can be answered easily, or with conviction. Indeed, one of the most important advances of recent years has been the realization that enthusiasm for the crusade varied enormously from country to country, and that instead of forming a straightforward pattern of growth followed by decline, it waxed and waned over the generations. For example, Dr Christopher Tyerman has recently shown that English enthusiasm remained strong until the disaster of Nicopolis, then declined sharply. By contrast, we have seen that the pulse of Castilian enthusiasm was almost at its weakest at the time of Nicopolis, but a century later it had undergone a revival which carried it into fresh enterprises beyond the peninsula. Again, the crusade itself changed in nature during these centuries, so that for most people enthusiasm ceased to result in personal participation. It was expressed instead in their readiness to contribute financially to a crusade, and in other displays of approval which do not lend themselves readily to analysis, let alone comparative quantification. There is the additional problem, familiar to all medievalists, that the bulk of the surviving sources emanated from, and relate to, the ruling élite and the educated minority; the opinions of the majority of the population can often only be surmised. Faced with these difficulties, it is tempting to abandon as impracticable any analysis of popular feeling and to concentrate, as so many historians have done in the past, on the governmental planning, diplomacy, and organization which present, by comparison, such reassuringly clear profiles. But to restrict one's attention to the courts and their executive bureaucracies would be to offer an unacceptably narrow picture of later crusading. Whatever the pitfalls and frustrations, the historian is obliged to look further, and to examine the range of contemporary attitudes which reveal themselves in terms of thought and behaviour.

Patterns of Thought

Old orthodoxies die hard, and the belief persists in some quarters that from the late thirteenth century onwards the crusade was no more than a residual ideal harboured by a few daydreaming theorists, backward-looking popes, and irresponsible rulers. This viewpoint is based to a large extent on the argument that the crusade was encountering increasing criticism, proof of its loss of both respectability and credibility. But recent studies by Elizabeth Siberry and Benjamin Kedar have effectively undermined the idea that by 1300 the crusade was subject to a growing barrage of hostility from vociferous opponents who demonstrated, and added to, the erosion of popular support for the movement. That some people questioned the validity of crusading and its military usefulness is apparent both from their writings and from those of apologists for the crusade, who, through their practice of rebutting points one by one, elucidate the arguments of their opponents. But unquestioning acceptance of the effectiveness of such criticism has led to its being greatly exaggerated.

Several important points are now clear. One is that fundamental questioning of the validity of crusading existed from the start of the movement, and was at its strongest in the mid-twelfth century, when the annalist of Würzburg went so far as to suggest that the Second Crusade was the creation of the Devil. Fewer such basic doubts were expressed in the thirteenth century, when the crusade was safely enclosed in the armour plating of a just war framework by such canonists as Hostiensis and Pope Innocent IV. If the crusading movement was not permanently damaged by the bitter disillusionment which resulted from the disasters of the Second Crusade, it is unlikely that its popularity would have been seriously impaired by the more limited criticism of the late Middle Ages. Another recent finding is that many of the so-called opponents of the crusade, such as Roger Bacon, William of Tripoli, and John Gower, were actually far more qualified in their criticism than had been supposed. Far from being opposed to the crusade, Bacon (d. 1292) was committed to the recovery of the Holy Places by force, suggesting the use of *opera sapientie*, including large mirrors to direct heat rays at the Muslims. As Professor Kedar noted, 'the advocacy of mirror warfare, like that of push-button warfare in another age, is not the hallmark of the pacifist'. And in the case of John Gower (*c.*1330–1408), comments in the *Confessio amantis* questioning the value of crusading—which may in any case be ironical—have to be set alongside the poet's earlier espousal of a crusade to reconquer the Holy Land in his *Vox clamantis*.

This is not to deny that dissent and debate persisted. This was unavoidable in the case of a movement which generated such powerful emotional currents, and which had such harsh military and political ramifications. But it is important to recognize that such criticism tended to run along narrow channels, in that people criticized specific crusades, or abusive practices which had sprung up in association with the organization of crusades. As we have seen in Chapters 8 and 12,[1] two types of crusade often singled out for criticism were expeditions against Christian enemies of the Church, and, at least following the baptism of Jogailo in 1386, the *Reisen* conducted against the Lithuanians by the Teutonic Knights. It is also worth mentioning an interesting attack on Clement VI's naval league, a letter purporting to come from the Turks themselves, and whose author was probably a Genoese opponent of the expedition; the letter obviously attracted some attention since it was tailored and circulated by Venice's enemies on later occasions when the Republic was at war with the Turks. But it is notable that few if any of this species of critic broadened their attack to comprise crusades other than the specific object of their animus. Indeed, some critics of the *crux cismarina* objected to crusading in the Christian heartlands precisely because they were enthusiastic promoters of crusades elsewhere. John Wyclif, the bitterest critic of Bishop Henry Despenser's Flanders crusade of 1383, does not appear to have disapproved of other forms of crusade. Similarly, Polish critics of the Teutonic Order, like Paul Vladimiri, lambasted the *Reisen* as a distortion of the genuine crusade, while the author of the tract attacking Clement VI's league argued only that this particular crusade was legally anomalous, on the spurious grounds that Turkish piracy was an invention of Venetian propaganda.

Much the same can be said of critical attacks on the scandals which occurred in the handling of crusade funds and the preaching of crusade

---

[1] Above, 262–6, and 358–62.

indulgences to raise money. As we shall see, the latter in particular provoked hostile comment, both because it formed a prominent aspect of the Church's commercialization of indulgences, which proved distasteful to the sensitive, and also because of the doors which it opened to dishonest preachers, the 'pardoners' whose excesses Protestant historians used to catalogue at length. In so far as the crusade had come to mean, for the vast majority of people, the purchase of indulgences, this criticism naturally entailed a frontal assault on the institution; for without the large-scale sale of indulgences there would be little point in declaring a crusade. But the fact remains that few of the critics of indulgences went so far as to say that granting of remission of sin for military purposes by the papacy, was wrong, or indeed that indulgences had no place in Catholic penitential practice. Even Erasmus, whose attacks on the abuse of indulgences were extreme, several times denied that he scorned indulgences *per se*; he insisted only on the folly of those who believed that the purchase of a piece of paper would, by itself, gain them entry into heaven, and on the wickedness of those who encouraged that belief. To this extent even criticism of the traffic in indulgences cannot be considered as criticism of the ideal of the crusade itself.

Apart from a muted but persistent pacifist minority, those who did confront the central issue of sacred violence usually belonged to heterodox groups. The cathars, Waldensians, Lollards, Hussites, and the Franciscan splinter-group known as 'fraticelli de opinione', were united in regarding the crusade itself as an unacceptable practice, symptomatic of the broader ills within the Church. Inquisitors were even instructed to ask suspected heretics their opinion of the crusade as a means of probing their orthodoxy. Dr Tyerman has shown that some English Lollard knights succeeded in squaring the circle by reconciling their heterodox beliefs with taking part in crusades; but such compromises were unusual and could not persist. The Protestant reformers were more thoroughgoing than their predecessors in their critique, as well as more effective politically. By denying the mediatory power of the Church in the forgiveness of sins, and by withdrawing obedience to Rome, they inevitably ended the crusade as an ideal and as an institution wherever they were successful.

The roots of the crusade went deep, and it took time to pull them up. In some cases, notably that of the Teutonic Order in Protestant Germany, there were actual or attempted compromises in dealing with powerful corporations or institutions associated with the crusade. But the Protestant impact was, in the long term, destructive and decisive. As Christopher

Tyerman has demonstrated, crusading ideas and imagery played an important role in the Pilgrimage of Grace in 1536, when Lord Darcy distributed amongst the pilgrims badges left over from his abortive crusade to North Africa in 1511; by 1569, by contrast, Catholic rebels could no longer hope to harness such ideas, as a new generation of Englishmen simply did not recognize the resonances. It was not only the central features of crusading which came to an end, but a whole cluster of associated traditions and practices. For example, by placing the conduct of warfare more fully than hitherto in the hands of the secular powers, the Protestants brought to a close the intervention of churchmen in military matters, which had been one of the crusading movement's most distinctive contributions to medieval society. The series of belligerent prelates whose exploits we have looked at in previous chapters, men like Peter Thomas, Julian Cesarini, Henry Despenser, Henry Beaufort, and Francis Jiménez of Cisneros, had no role to play in Protestant Europe. As Luther remarked, in typically colourful language, 'if I were a soldier and should see as the flag of my army the colours of a cleric or a cross, even if it were a crucifix, I would run away as if the devil himself were after me'. The same applied to fighting saints, the English Protestant John Foxe commenting that 'He that bringeth St George or St Denis, as patrons, to the field against the Turk leaveth Christ, no doubt, at home.' Significantly, Luther even dismissed the Holy Sepulchre as an irrelevance: what mattered was not 'the actual tomb, which the Saracens hold', but divine scripture, which had been murdered and buried by the papists, and whose body was guarded by the friars and inquisitors.

Until the formulation of the Protestant message in the second decade of the sixteenth century, however, it is the restraint of critics which remains most striking. It is unlikely that this derived from their fear of being branded as unorthodox for questioning one of the key attributes of papal authority, for some who took advantage of the *glasnost* of the conciliar period to express very radical criticisms of the papacy were silent on the subject of the crusade. But it is possible that they held fire for the practical reason that they recognized the indispensability of the crusade, albeit in a reformed condition, as a means of holding back the Ottoman menace. In this respect it is significant that both the Mamluks and the Ottomans were militantly Islamic as well as expansionist. This made it difficult to entertain realistic hopes of regaining the Holy Places, or defending Christendom, by converting the enemy. Potential critics of the crusade may have seen that there was no alternative to it.

Indeed, in the past a major error amongst historians of the late Middle Ages was to link the supposed decline in crusading enthusiasm with the idea of missionary activity amongst the Muslims, largely on the basis of the attractive idea put forward, for a few decades in the mid-thirteenth century, that conversion could replace crusade. For as Professor Kedar has shown, this optimism did not last in the face of the repeated failure of missionary efforts. By 1300 it had been superseded by the harsher, but more realistic link between crusade and mission, outlined by Innocent IV. This was the idea that, in view of the obstacles put in the way of peaceful preaching by the Islamic authorities, the conquest of non-believers was essential to open up the path for evangelizing. As St Thomas Aquinas put it in his *Summa Theologica* (1265–71), 'Christ's faithful frequently wage war against the infidels, not indeed to coerce them to believe . . . but in order to compel them not to hinder the faith of Christ.' It is true that as late as 1271 William of Tripoli argued that Muslims could be converted 'through the pure word of God, without philosophical arguments, without the arms of soldiers', but by that point he was in a minority. Many, if not most, missionaries in the fourteenth century viewed warfare against Islam as necessary; one of the most prominent amongst them, the Dominican William Adam, contributed to the genre of recovery literature a tract with the uncompromising title 'How to destroy the Saracens' ('De modo Sarracenos extirpandi'). In 1401 Pope Boniface IX even granted crusade indulgences to members of the Franciscan missionary society, the *Societas peregrinantium*, to help them organize the defence of converts along the Caspian coast against Tatar attack. Rather than replacing the crusade, hopes for conversion in the late Middle Ages therefore served to provide it with another *raison d'être*. As we have seen in Chapter 10,[2] this applied especially to Iberia, where the goal of extending Christendom's boundaries became a key rationale of crusading during the Age of Discoveries.

Missionary hopes were occasionally expressed by such men as John of Segovia and Nicholas of Cusa in the mid-fifteenth century, and by Erasmus in the early sixteenth; but they were inspired more by a sense of despair about the chances of a crusade in the East succeeding than by informed optimism regarding preaching to the Muslims. John of Segovia was depressed by the long history of crusading débâcles, and pinned his hopes on peaceful coexistence, followed by a patient exposition of the chief tenets of Christian belief. And as R. H. Schwoebel noted, Pius II's

[2] Above, 309.

famous letter to Mehmed II, in which the Pope eloquently pleaded with the Sultan to convert, followed the distressing events at Mantua, when 'he no doubt found it refreshing to reflect for a moment on the approach urged by those whom he normally regarded as theoreticians'. Laying aside the issue of Ottoman aggression, it is questionable whether many Catholics were becoming more sympathetic towards people who did not share their religious beliefs. Writing in about 1340, the English Dominican theologian Robert Holcot argued that if the Muslims declined to convert when the choice was offered to them, they should be killed; he compared the situation to a doctor cutting off a gangrenous foot which he could not heal. The popularity of Holcot's commentary, evinced by the number and diffusion of surviving manuscripts, is a powerful argument against the idea that later medieval society was either becoming more tolerant of divergent religious beliefs, or losing confidence in a violent approach to them.

Between the late fourteenth and sixteenth centuries many Europeans travelled extensively in the Ottoman Empire and wrote detailed accounts of Turkish society and government. More so than ever before, Christians were able to gain a clear impression of their leading enemy, and the popular image of the Turk naturally became a more complex one than hitherto. Perceived virtues of Ottoman society, such as the speedy and strict administration of justice, meritocratic social mobility, and the sobriety, piety, and honesty of most Turks, were admired and contrasted with the faults of Christian Europe. Ottoman military prowess in particular was commented on and discussed: indeed, if fighting the Turks was to have chivalric value then the enemy must be a worthy opponent, and it has been remarked upon the Feast of the Pheasant that 'there emerged from the vows sworn . . . an Ottoman nobility imbued with the qualities of chivalry'. One could even fight for such an enemy. In the course of a three-month sojourn at the Ottoman court in 1388 Marshal Boucicaut, the later hero of Nicopolis, and his companion, Renaud of Roye, offered their services to Sultan Murad I 'in the event that he made war on any Saracens'. Only when it was clear that no fighting was in prospect did the two make their way to the Hungarian court, after which they parted, Boucicaut going on pilgrimage to the Holy Land, while Roye went to take part in a *Winterreise* in Prussia. James of Créquy, lord of Heilly, who fought in Prussia and at Nicopolis, had actually served Murad I as a volunteer and spoke some Turkish.

But the idea that these proliferating contacts with the Turks, and the travel literature which resulted from them, eroded what remained of Christian animosity towards the Muslims is an erroneous one. In the first place, new stereotypes of the enemy—the 'cruel Turk', and the 'lascivious Turk'—were created which were hardly more favourable than those previously in circulation. Secondly, there existed among travellers themselves a wide spectrum of attitudes; some were noticeably tolerant, while others travelled the length and breadth of the Empire and returned with their contempt for the Turks confirmed. And thirdly, some of the most detailed accounts were written specifically to furnish background information for a hoped-for crusade. Thus John Lemaire de Belges wrote his 'Illustrations de Gaule et singularitez de Troie' (1500–12) in fulfilment of a vow which he had made on the altar of St Peter's, that he would write a guide on Turkish customs to advise nobles 'who resolved to take up arms and go to Greece and Turkey'. And William Postel wrote his influential 'De la république des Turcs' (1560) to 'provide, through a well-founded knowledge of the enemy, the means of resisting him'. Postel was prepared to grant credit to Islam for holding idolatry and paganism at bay; but this did not dilute his enthusiasm for an anti-Ottoman crusade. As so often in history, the liberal idea that deeper acquaintance necessarily nurtures tolerance proved to be misguided.

Clearly it is difficult enough to gauge the degree to which crusading was criticized, and the underlying attitudes. It is arguable that the absence of criticism can be attributed either to fear of the Turks or, in the case of those unaffected by the Ottoman advance, to simple lack of interest. How then can enthusiasm, or even approval, be identified, characterized, and measured? The problem can be approached by considering three important groups of sources which themselves formed a commentary on the crusade. The first of these is the genre of advisory and exhortatory literature. By comparison with the surviving instances of criticism—attenuated, spasmodic, and sometimes effectively answered by apologists like Humbert of Romans—the number of crusade tracts written between about 1270 and 1570 is remarkable. Thanks to the pioneering work of J. Delaville le Roulx almost exactly a hundred years ago, historians have long been aware of the plethora of 'recovery treatises': tracts written, chiefly in the two generations after 1291, to advise those hoping to launch a crusade to recover the Holy Land. Fidenzio of Padua, Peter Dubois, William of Nogaret, James of Molay, Fulk of Villaret, Henry II of Cyprus, Hetoum of Armenia, William Adam, William Durand, Ramon Lull, Marino Sanudo, Philip of Mézières, and

Emmanuel Piloti figure amongst the writers of the more significant treatises, some of whose recommendations were described in Chapter 1.[3]

Recently, however, it has become clear that the recovery treatises were equalled in number by the tracts later written to guide a hoped-for crusade against the Ottoman Turks: by John Torcello for the Council of Florence in 1439, by James Tedaldi and Lampo Birago in the wake of the fall of Constantinople in 1453, by Bertrandon of la Broquière, Geoffrey of Thoisy, Waleran of Wavrin, and others for Philip the Good of Burgundy. Nor was there any sign of a slackening of output in the century's last decades: in 1500 alone, the Bishops Alessio Celidonio and Stephen Taleazzi between them wrote six crusade tracts for the papal court. Even after the close of our period, in 1587–8, there appeared two lengthy projects for war against the Turks by Frenchmen whose backgrounds and views could hardly have formed a sharper contrast: the Huguenot and friend of Henry IV, Francis of la Noue, and the Catholic Savoyard, René of Lusinge. Despite the confessional divide, and the fact that their diagnosis of the Ottoman problem differed in many respects, both writers adhered to a pattern of thinking which dated back three centuries. And as Michael Heath has commented, the two tracts are evidence of the profound sense of cultural disorientation experienced by many Frenchmen aware of their country's crusading past, when they considered the Valois-Ottoman alliances of their age. On one occasion a canon against Christian alliances with the infidel dating back to the Third Lateran Council (1179) was quoted in rebuke of 'the Most Christian King'.

Akin to the advisory treatises were the *exhortatoria*, the more emotional and less finely detailed appeals for a crusade which usually took the form of a letter, speech, or sermon. These were often written in response to a disaster in the East; sometimes they constitute key sources for events there, as in the case of Thaddeo of Naples's account of the fall of Acre. Such appeals proliferated in the early fifteenth century, especially in the anti-Turkish orations, or 'exhortatoria ad bellum contra Turcos', which were written in large numbers by the Italian humanists. The humanist *exhortatoria* mark a new departure in crusading literature, both in the way they were structured and in the ideas they put forward. A distinctive rhetorical pattern was adopted. It was based on the principles of oratory in the Classical World, and had three sections. The justice and necessity of the proposed crusade were pinpointed; there followed a reassuring section on the expedition's viability ('ease'), in which Turkish weaknesses

[3] Above, 23–37, 45–6.

were lavishly depicted; and the orator concluded with an account of the profit, spiritual and material, which the crusade would bring to its participants.

Within this structure, as we noted in Chapter 3,[4] the humanists added two striking new themes to the traditional repertoire of crusading ideas. One was the point that the Ottoman advance threatened all Christians: crusading now entailed the defence of hearth and loved ones. The Horatian tag 'nam tua res agitur, paries cum proximus ardet' ('it is your business, when your neighbour's wall is ablaze') became beloved to the humanist crusaders as a convenient summary of this idea. Their second theme, one dear to their own hearts, was that the anti-Ottoman crusade constituted the defence of civilization against the new barbarians. The sack of Constantinople in 1453, and the subsequent occupation of Greece, confirmed for many humanists their worst fears of what Ottoman rule would mean. The lament for ravaged Greece, and the need to stop the Turks crossing the Adriatic, became stock themes; and the *devsirme*, or Ottoman levy of Christian children in the occupied Balkan countries, was henceforth the standard Ottoman atrocity. As Dr Robert Black has demonstrated, Italian humanists greeted every major political event, whether coronation, dynastic marriage, international congress, or meeting of Estates, with an outpouring of anti-Turkish appeals.

In sixteenth-century Austria and Germany the *exhortatoria* were mirrored in the series of printed anti-Turkish pamphlets (*Flugschriften*), which reached its height in 1541–2 in response to the most serious phase of the Ottoman advance. The contrast between the tabloid-style atrocity stories of the *Flugschriften* and the polished structure of the humanists' *exhortatoria* should not disguise the fact that the two genres together make a simple point: that the very vigour of the Ottoman thrust into the Balkans and East-Central Europe, coupled with the institutional survival of the crusade, were enough to keep the crusade in the minds of both rulers and ruled as a vital issue. This was particularly the case in areas threatened or overrun by that thrust: from exiled Croatian humanists alone there came a veritable bombardment of projects and pleas for a crusade against the Ottomans. It is interesting that Luther, who always abominated the idea of sacred violence, and started off by counselling non-resistance to the Turks on the grounds that they represented the wrath of God, came round to urging the German princes to resist them under the shattering impact of their advances in the 1520s; Erasmus's

---

[4] Above, 99–100.

thoughts on the Turks underwent a similar though more hesitant progression. One tract by a Lutheran went so far as to write of the Protestant soldier's participation in the anti-Turkish war as 'a good, holy work'. 'If anyone perish while performing it,' its author went on, 'he should not doubt that he dies in obedience to God; and if otherwise he truly believes in Christ, he will certainly attain eternal bliss.' In many respects, of course, Lutheran and Calvinist anti-Turkish tracts depart radically from the views of their Catholic contemporaries. The Huguenot la Noue, for example, had no specific spiritual reward to offer those who fought the Turks: he could offer only a tranquil conscience (though as Michael Heath has remarked, this was 'not to be despised, as the French civil wars approached their gruesome climax').

What broader conclusions can be drawn from this rich tradition of advisory and exhortatory literature? The manuscript or printing history of the tracts varied greatly, some being intended from the start only as guidance for rulers, and others representing no more than the views of their own authors. The latter point receives emphasis from the fact that some tracts, especially in the late fifteenth and sixteenth century, were hopelessly unpractical, their authors showing themselves to be woefully out of touch with political, military, and even geographical reality. The fantastic plans for conquest which take over some crusade projects are reminiscent of chapter 33 of Rabelais's *Gargantua*, and may even have inspired it. As for the *exhortatoria*, reference has often been made to the fact that many of the humanists' appeals for action were the kind of polished but superficial exercise in composition and style mocked by Erasmus in his 'Praise of Folly'. Benedict Colucci, in his *Declamationes*, represented Marsilio Ficino giving the composition of a crusading oration as practice to five of his pupils. The need first to argue the 'necessity' of crusading, and then to demonstrate its 'ease', set up an internal tension within many *exhortatoria* which rendered them ludicrously unconvincing. In addition, humanist crusaders had a living to make, and they were sometimes guilty of opportunism and insincerity. Giovanni Maria Filelfo's epic poem, *Amyris*, for example, began life as an encomium of Mehmed II; it was later rewritten as a crusade exhortation, and rededicated to Galeazzo Maria Sforza. Giovanni's father, Francis Filelfo, also tailored his writings to fit his audience's expectations, composing an appeal to Charles VII of France in 1451 to rescue Constantinople, and a Greek ode in celebration of Mehmed's great triumph after the city had fallen. But in Francis's case such events were less damning than they appear, as the ode was written with the purpose of facilitating the release of his mother-in-law from Turkish captivity, and in the course of a long career Francis's record as an activist for the crusade was a solid and consistent one.

Scepticism is healthy, but in the past it has been taken too far in judging this literature, and there are signs that historians are now adopting a more sympathetic attitude. It is hazardous to build an argument on something as potentially circumstantial as the number and diffusion of surviving manuscripts. But the full-scale crusade treatises at least were enough in number, existed in enough important libraries, and originated in a wide enough range of social groups and countries, for us to infer that they reflected far more than the views of isolated eccentrics. The case for the crusade which they argued could not be ignored by the powerful and influential in society. Similarly, historians of the Renaissance now accept that it was possible for the humanists to reconcile the new learning with deep religious convictions. A polished Latin prose style and genuine enthusiasm were not mutually exclusive attributes. And scholars are beginning to perceive that, when all due qualifications have been made, many of the crusading *exhortatoria* reflected commitment and reflection on the part of their authors.

The nexus between disaster and response, in the form of such writings, was always close, and the example of the fall of Negroponte in 1470 illustrates how the invention of printing enabled contemporaries to close the chronological gap. Cardinal Bessarion reacted to the terrible news by sending his *Orationes*, which were full of crusading appeals, to William Fichet, who had just founded a printing press at Paris. In mid-April 1471, just nine months after the Ottoman victory, the *Orationes* were published. Forty-six copies were distributed to important individuals, some accompanied by dedicatory letters in which Fichet made appeals tailored to the family history and personal circumstances of each recipient. Printing naturally not only speeded up the distribution of such appeals, but brought the Ottoman threat and the crusade closer to ordinary people. One of the earliest surviving specimens of modern printing is the indulgence which Nicholas V granted in 1451 to raise money for the relief of Cyprus. The popular thirst for up-to-date news of the Ottoman advance was a powerful incentive to the marketing of news-sheets in the Empire; indeed, the German word for newspaper probably first appeared in print in a report of the Veneto-Turkish conflict which was distributed in 1502, 'Newe zeytung von orient und auffgang'.

The invention of printing also made possible the almost immediate dissemination of detailed accounts of contemporary events in the East, the 'instant histories' which began to be marketed from the first siege of Rhodes (1480) onwards; together with the more considered, scholarly, histories of the crusades which were written in the fifteenth and sixteenth centuries, these constituted the second group of sources which are illustrative of popular feelings about crusading. The 'instant histories' were of course geared to the same market which would later enjoy the *Flugschriften*. Mehmed II's defeat in 1480 was celebrated by the printing of three separate histories; the most popular, that of William Caoursin, was printed ten times in 1480–3. Thereafter, the appearance of these popular histories followed the ebb and flow of the Turkish threat. In France, for example, there was an increase in 1565 and during the following years; as elsewhere, 1571 was an *annus mirabilis* for these pamphlets, with the printing of at least fifteen accounts of Lepanto at Paris, Lyons, and Rouen. Such *Turcica* cannot be dismissed as catering to mere curiosity. While they were not generally used as platforms for overt crusade propaganda, the pamphlets stimulated popular hostility towards the Ottomans and encouraged, as late as Lepanto, the idea that Christendom existed and needed active defending. Encomia of those who fought and died at Rhodes, Tunis, Prevesa, Malta, and Lepanto, appealed to those who bought and read these leaflets.

None the less, these 'instant histories' were probably less significant than the longer accounts of the crusading movement which were written by humanists from the 1440s onwards. Writers like Flavio Biondo, Aeneas Sylvius Piccolomini, and Benedict Accolti, saw in the 'classical period' of crusading (1095–1291) an age which had numerous lessons to teach their contemporaries, but which was also distant enough to be viewed with detachment and objectivity. Flavio Biondo's appeals to Frederick III, Alfonso V of Aragon, and the Doge of Genoa, in 1452 and 1453 to embark on a crusade were replete with references to past crusades, drawn from his own *Decades* (1439–50). Piccolomini produced a 'potted version' of Biondo's *Decades* which helped to disseminate the work. It also enabled Lodrisio Crivelli, Piccolomini's biographer, to begin his 'On the Expedition of Pius II against the Turks' ('De expeditione Pii papae II adversus Turcos') with a short history of earlier crusading expeditions. But the connection between earlier crusades and the present-day needs of Christendom was made with greatest force by the Florentine Benedict Accolti. Robert Black has shown that Accolti's decision to write a history of the First Crusade was intimately linked to his hopes—which were by no means unfounded—that the Republic which he served as Chancellor would respond with enthusiasm to the crusade plans of Pius II. As Pius had himself declared in an oration before Pope Nicholas V in 1452, the unexpected success of the First Crusade was the best possible answer to those cynics who responded to crusade appeals by sneering 'behold the old dream, the old delusion, the empty stories'. Faith had achieved miracles in the past and it could still do so. Bartholomew of Giano, Francis Filelfo, Flavio Biondo, and other humanists also turned hopefully to the First Crusade. Accolti's history, which was the most detailed since William of Tyre's, therefore had the twofold role of stimulating Florentine enthusiasm, and of demonstrating to the Pope that Florence was committed to his cause. Repeatedly in the letters which he wrote for the Republic, Accolti used phrases and ideas 'lifted' from his own history.

This renewed interest in crusading history on the part of Italian humanists, coupled with the firm belief that it offered a potent *exemplum* for their own times, was at its height in the decades following the fall of Constantinople. By the end of the fifteenth century the Ottoman threat to Italy had receded, and with it some of the humanists' curiosity about the great age of crusading. None the less, sixteenth-century German writers picked up the threads of earlier comparisons when confronted with Suleyman's offensives, and in general the fifteenth and sixteenth centuries displayed a greater awareness of the recurrent themes of crusading history than earlier generations had done. The most popular history of the First Crusade, that of Robert of Reims, survives in at least ninety-four manuscripts dating from the late Middle Ages, and was one of the earliest texts to be printed (Cologne, 1472). And in an edition of the letters of St Catherine of Siena printed in 1500, Aldo Manuzio noted that the saint's call to arms against the Turks was still relevant.

The third group of sources which are revealing of social attitudes towards crusading are those which placed the crusade within an eschatological context. Throughout its history the association between crusading and the fulfilment of a prophetic pattern of events had been a close one, and in the late Middle Ages it remained of great significance. At the close of the thirteenth century the Catalan physician Arnold of Villanova breathed new life into the Joachimist prophetic message, with his 'On the Time of the Coming of Antichrist' ('De tempore adventus antichristi' (1297)). Villanova asserted that the recovery of Jerusalem would occur only when the 'Last Emperor' had defeated Antichrist; he thereby made the identification of the 'Last Emperor' a profoundly political issue. Then in the third quarter of the fourteenth century Telesphorus of Cosenza produced what Marjorie Reeves described as 'a synthesis of the south-Italian Joachimist tradition and the French nationalist prophecy', writing of a French king who would defeat Antichrist, receive the imperial crown, and accomplish 'the seventh and final crusade for the Holy Land, which they will recover'. Predictably, this 'Second Charlemagne prophecy' was countered by a German prophecy in the early fifteenth century. This asserted that 'a great, last expedition to the Holy Land' would be accomplished by a German emperor.

Telesphorus's prophecy made a certain impact in the fourteenth century, and in the fifteenth writers like George of Trebizond fitted the Ottoman advance into a millenarian pattern. In 1445 a certain John Dubois tried to persuade Charles VII to assume the mantle of the Second Charlemagne and reconquer the Holy Land; as his reward for this suggestion he asked to be exempted from paying taxes. But it seems to have been in the decades around 1500 that prophecy and crusade converged most dramatically, when there appeared a cluster of credible candidates for the role of Last Emperor. As we have seen in previous chapters, the results were wide-ranging. They manifestly disprove the idea that this period was marked by a cold-blooded, *Realpolitik* approach to foreign policy on the part of Europe's rulers. In the first place, it is impossible to understand Charles VIII's expedition to Italy in 1494 without taking into account the Telesphoran prophecy. Charles himself appears to have been convinced that he was the 'Second Charlemagne' so long predicted, and references to Charlemagne abound in the sources for his campaign. The King was not alone in his conviction, for as Marjorie Reeves put it, 'there is no doubt that contemporaries were expecting a crisis of history which would see the fulfilment of prophecies'. Secondly, the achievements of the Castilians in conquering Granada, expanding into the Maghrib, and conquering the New World, were undoubtedly played out against a rich eschatological backcloth. As early as 1486 the Marquis of Cadiz enthused that Ferdinand of Aragon would 'not only . . . gain the Kingdom of Granada, but he will subdue all Africa . . . and he will take the Holy House of Jerusalem . . . and with his hands he will put the banner of Aragon on Mount Calvary'. The Spaniards were depicted as the heirs to the Israelites, and their rulers were seen as exercising an apostolic role as the converters of mankind. Such themes appealed most to the Franciscans, who broadcast them with energy.

But it was the dynastic union of Austria and Burgundy in 1477 which most excited such contemporaries as the astrologer John Lichtenberger. It fused the French and German prophetic traditions, reconciling the Lily with the Eagle. In the next generation but one, moreover, this union appeared to furnish, in the 'fifth Charles', an Emperor who not only fitted the prophetic bill dynastically, but had the resources required to act the part. For the whole of Charles V's career, prophetic programmes based on his role as the 'Last Emperor' were enthusiastically constructed, including the defeat of the Ottomans and the eventual recovery of Jerusalem. The hopes aroused, especially at the time of the imperial election in 1519, and during the Emperor's North African crusades in the 1530s, were greater than at any point since the thirteenth century. Unrealistic though they were, such expectations went deep, and there can be no question of their being entertained only by the unimportant or isolated. The sermon with which Giles of Viterbo opened the Fifth Lateran Council in May 1512, contained an overtly eschatological message: and its author was a cardinal, the General of the Augustinians, and a respected Church reformer. The German electors of 1519 took very seriously the possibility that the successful candidate might be the long-predicted Last Emperor. And in 1530 Giles of Viterbo continued to see vast hope in the sheer power wielded by Charles V, whom he characterized as a combination of Moses, Caesar, and David.

The Valois-Ottoman alliance and the onset of the Reformation naturally gave the pro-Habsburg prophets much useful material. The former, like the fact that only one sixteenth-century French king was called Charles, also proved a grave obstacle to the French tradition of 'Second Charle-magne' thinking. The last major prophecy formulated along these lines for many decades came in 1516 from Silvestro Meuccio, who wrote of a general council which would organize 'a crusade against the infidels and to recover holy Jerusalem', under the aegis of Francis I. But the Habsburgs did not entirely take over the prophetic tradition and its crusading implications. A prophecy relating to the reconquest of Jerusalem by a king of England circulated in England in about 1531, and French monarchs were reminded of their eschatological role well into the seventeenth century. Nor did belief in prophecy weaken as the century progressed. In the atmosphere of optimism which prevailed after Lepanto the linkage between crusade and prophecy was renewed; as Michael Heath has put it, 'there is . . . plenty of evidence that thoughts of . . . the "croisade apocalyptique" had not disappeared by the end of the sixteenth century, but coexisted with, and encouraged, plans for a secular war requiring meticulous preparation'.

In these three groups of sources, the needs of the present, the legacy of the past, and expectations of the future all established the continuing relevance of the crusade. There is no question of claiming that they 'represented' popular feeling, but it would be equally absurd to write off the many individuals involved as eccentric fanatics. For instance, Dr Black has shown that Benedict Accolti had the backing of an influential group of patricians in espousing the cause of the crusade at Florence in the 1450s and early 1460s. And Yvonne Labande-Mailfert has remarked that Charles VIII's interest in the crusade was far more than a court-based fantasy: 'it would be hard to exaggerate the diffusion of the crusading idea in the West at the end of the fifteenth century'. Interestingly, one crusade enthusiast who was a thoroughgoing eccentric, William Postel, was respected, honoured, and widely read by his contemporaries. The point about this large body of material is that, despite the contrasts in style and approach which characterize it, and the fact that it ranges over three centuries, it is positive and enthusiastic in its espousal of crusading.

This impression of approbation is firmly underlined by artistic and literary treatment of the crusade in the fourteenth, fifteenth, and early sixteenth centuries. It is only in recent years that such treatment has been given the attention it deserves, with the result that the pro-crusade sentiments expressed in the poetry of Petrarch, Eustace Deschamps, William of Machaut, and Leonard Dati, or in Anthony of la Sale's novel 'Le Petit Jehan de Saintré', can be compared with the wall paintings commissioned by Henry III of England to commemorate the First Crusade, Pleshey Castle's fifteen tapestries on the theme of Godfrey of Bouillon, and the Wilton Diptych, which was almost certainly commissioned to depict Richard II's crusading aspirations. Some Renaissance masterpieces, including Donatello's 'Judith and Holofernes' and Piero della Francesca's fresco cycle in the Bacci chapel of San Francesco in Arezzo, are open to a 'crusading' interpretation, and it is highly likely that the Sistine Chapel fresco of the drowning of Pharaoh in the Red Sea represents the great victories at Rhodes and Otranto in 1480–1. The middle decades of the fourteenth century saw the production of the second cycle of the great series of crusade epics; its four long poems constituted both the expression of continuing interest in the crusade, and in turn a stimulus to the revival of concern for the Holy Places. Typically, such crusade epics, and 'histories' which portrayed the struggle against the infidels, enjoyed great popularity at the court of Philip the Good in the 1450s.

In art and literature it was the First Crusade above all which appealed. This was partly because, as Pius II and Benedict Accolti realized, it was the most successful and inspirational, and partly because of the craze for Godfrey of Bouillon. Throughout the late Middle Ages visitors to the Abbey of St Denis, near Paris, were reminded of the First Crusade by the ambulatory's magnificent crusading window: it was hoped that they would also consider its relevance, in accordance with the dictum of Suger, the twelfth-century Abbot of St Denis, that 'by recollecting past events, we portray future ones'. A dramatic representation of the fall of Jerusalem to the First Crusade, possibly organized by the indefatigable Philip of Mézières, was performed at the court of Charles V in 1378 in honour of the visiting Emperor Charles IV. And when William Caxton printed an English translation of the romance 'Godfrey de Bouillon or the Siege and Conquest of Jerusalem' in 1481, he was well aware of the market which existed for such works, as well as its message: he claimed that he had decided to publish the work because of the lessons which it had to teach, in a world where the power of the Turks was more menacing than it had been in the eleventh century.

Of course it is necessary to keep these expressions of approval and interest in perspective. Crusading had always been an enthusiasm which some did not share, even in the extraordinary decades flanking the year 1200 when it was at its most intensive. And people who did feel the attraction of the crusade strongly were subject to the constraints of domestic conditions, political and economic in particular. For much of the fourteenth and fifteenth centuries, for example, it was impossible for most of the French nobility even to consider taking part in a crusade. But if in some periods internal considerations made crusading an unaffordable luxury, at others, such as the 1360s, 1390s, and 1450s, when there were disbanded soldiers who needed employment, they made it a highly attractive prospect. Philip of Mézières, for example, wrote of the crusade as an opportunity for Charles VI to rid France of 'the Companies and unholy relics ['reliques non saintes'] left over from the war in your realm'. The popularity of the crusade therefore waxed and waned as it always had done. But it is arguable that in the 1320s and 1330s, the 1390s, and the middle and last decades of the fifteenth century, at least some regions of Catholic Europe experienced a surge of interest in crusading which can reasonably be compared with the twelfth and thirteenth centuries.

Patterns of Behaviour

It remains true that no clear picture of how people regarded the crusade can ever be gained just by analysing the writings of contemporaries; we need also to examine the evidence left by their activity. And in this respect it is impossible to avoid the functional division of late medieval society into two groups, the military class and the civilian population. The first group poses fewer problems than the second, thanks largely to the work of Maurice Keen on chivalric culture in this period. In a series of studies, most notably a general survey of chivalry published in 1984, Keen has shown, first that chivalric values continued to exert an important influence on noble behaviour at least until the final decades of the fifteenth century; and secondly, that crusading was a vital constituent of those values. Amongst martial actions which earned a nobleman renown, Dr Keen has written, 'to take part in a crusade and to be armed against the infidel carries a special, sovereign honour'. As he admits, the precise gradations of honour are impossible to fix with certainty, and the evidence remains somewhat problematic. For example, Keen cites the statement by the Soldich of la Trau, one of Froissart's heroes, that he reckoned his presence at the siege of Al-Mahdiya in 1390 to be 'equally honourable as if I had been in three great battles'. It is probable, however, that the Soldich is referring to the fact that the crusaders had held at bay the armies of three *kings*: that they were *Muslim* kings (i.e. emirs) may have been incidental to his argument.

None the less, there is much strength in the general argument that crusading, 'God's great hunt', as Philip of Mézières quaintly termed it, epitomized chivalric behaviour, and that contemporary noblemen accepted Mézières's dictum that 'the first and principal glory of the dignity of true chivalry is to fight for the faith'. In the first place, there is the strong link often discernible between the secular orders of chivalry which flourished in the late Middle Ages, and participation in crusades. The link is most clear in the case of Peter I of Cyprus's Order of the Sword. The Order originated in the context of Peter's crusading plans, and subsisted for decades after the King's death as a loose association of foreign nobles who, while visiting Cyprus, had committed themselves to the island's defence against Muslim attack. The regulations for Louis of Taranto's Company of the Knot (1352), and Charles of Durazzo's Order of the Ship (1381), both had chapters obligating members to take part in a crusade to recover the Kingdom of Jerusalem, to which Louis and Charles exercised dynastic claims. The Order of the Ship had a complicated and rather bizarre hierarchy of augmentations to its badge, culminating in a third tiller which could be sported only by a man who distinguished himself in the reconquest of Jerusalem.

Crusading associations also characterized some fifteenth-century Orders, such as the Hungarian Society of the Dragon (1408), Ferrante of Naples's Order of Ermine (1465), and most notably Duke Albert V of Austria's Order of the Eagle (c.1430), which appears to have been dedicated to fighting both the Turks and the Hussites. Despite Professor Richard Vaughan's reservations, such associations are present too in the case of the most famous of these secular orders, that of the Golden Fleece, especially under the chancellorship of John Germain. For example, it was at a chapter-meeting of the Golden Fleece at Mons in May 1451 that Philip the Good first announced his intention personally to lead a crusade. More generally, some of the greatest chivalric set-pieces of the late Middle Ages were occasioned by the crusade, such as the eight days of cross-taking, weddings, and dubbings which occurred at Paris at Pentecost 1313, and the Feast of the Pheasant at Lille in 1454.

Membership of the secular orders of chivalry was reserved for a small élite. But the central place held by crusading in chivalric culture is clear from the lives of many individual noblemen. It has always been apparent that some noblemen in the late Middle Ages became obsessed with crusading, and the subsidiary activities of pilgrimage and foreign travel, in the same way that some nobles had since the inception of the movement. The Burgundian knight Guillebert of Lannoy seems to hold the palm in this respect, with his trip to the eastern Mediterranean in 1403, his travels to Granada in 1407 and 1410, his protracted trip to Prussia, Lithuania, and Poland in 1413–14, his lengthy perambulation of eastern Europe and the eastern Mediterranean basin in 1421, and his pilgrimage to Jerusalem in 1446. The limits of his travels were St Patrick's Cave in Ireland, Novgorod (on which Lannoy gives invaluable information), Granada, Caffa in the Crimea, and the Red Sea. An important advance of recent years, however, has been the realization that individuals like Lannoy were exceptional only in the extent of their travels, usually in the cause of crusade or pilgrimage. Recent controversy about the depiction of the Knight in 'The Canterbury Tales' has helped to elucidate the fact that Chaucer's Knight was not unrepresentative of the chivalric nobility in the fourteenth and early fifteenth centuries, either in the extent of his travelling or in his activities on Christendom's borders. When not prevented from doing so by military service to their kings, the pressures of office-holding, or domestic duties, it is clear that nobles frequently went to fight against the Moors in Granada and North Africa, the Turks and Mamluks in the East, and above all, the Lithuanians and Samogitians. Two examples, the Burgundian nobleman John of Roubaix and the Austrian Frederick of Kreisbach, can stand for countless others whose careers have been described in recent years. Roubaix went twice to Prussia, he fought at Al-Mahdiya and Nicopolis, he journeyed to Cyprus, and he went on pilgrimage to Jerusalem, Rome, and Santiago. Between 1346 and 1351 Kreisbach carried out a journey which took him to Armenia, Palestine, Cyprus and Constantinople, the Crimea, Russia, Poland, Mazovia, and Prussia. *En route* he fought for the Teutonic Order before Isborsk, and for King Magnus of Sweden at the siege of Orekhov.

Two key points are in fact now clear. One is that many dwellers in the pantheon of chivalric respect were characterized by the extent of their crusading service: Henry Grosmont, Gaston-Phoebus of Foix, and above all Marshal Boucicaut, with his trips to Prussia in 1384–5 and 1390–1, to the Holy Land in 1388–9, and to Constantinople in 1399, his participation in the Nicopolis crusade, and his raids on the Anatolian and Syrian coasts in 1403. The other point is that crusading, far from being an antique ideal cherished by the few, remained a living and important aspect of the behaviour and values of the nobility, and of those who wished to emulate them. It was still important in the fifteenth century, as shown by the career of John of Rebreviettes, who fought in Spain and Hungary in 1456 and 1460, and took a crusading vow at the Feast of the Pheasant in 1454, or that of Peter Vasquez of Saavedra, who was prominent at the Feast of the Pheasant, fought at least twice against the Turks, and joint-authored a crusade tract in 1451; 'this knight took part in many battles and encounters with infidels and others, at sea and on land', was a contemporary comment. Crusading appealed to bourgeois who aspired to noble status, so that one Cologne patrician in the mid-fourteenth century participated in no fewer than thirty-five campaigns against the Lithuanians. It also influenced the behaviour of the toughest and most ruthless men of the period. Gadifer of la Salle, who led an unsuccessful expedition to conquer the Canaries in 1402, had been on two *Reisen*, journeyed to Rhodes, and fought at Al-Mahdiya in 1390. Dr Keen has suggested that in Gadifer's astonishing career we can see a bridge between the age of chivalry and that of the *conquistador*, and that crusading influenced both. This is plausible, especially when we see the appeal which crusading undoubtedly possessed for those pariahs of the late Middle Ages, the captains and men of the mercenary companies. It was manifestly not something associated with the naïve or the *ingénu*.

When we look closely at the sources for such activities, and especially the most popular and best documented one, the *Reisen* against the Lithuanians, it becomes possible to pinpoint the nature of the appeal which the crusade exercised. It would be hard to exaggerate the import-ance of the past, the obligations imposed primarily by lineage, but also by national identity, and even by possession of the order of knighthood itself. Such obligations were deeply felt: indeed, they could hardly be ignored when popes, clerics, and propagandists for the crusade constantly referred to them. Kings were subjected to appeals set within a framework which Dr Simon Lloyd has aptly described as a 'compound of dynastic pride, regal dignity, and "national" honour'. It is no coincidence that the last medieval French kings to get anywhere near to leading a crusade against the Muslims, Philip VI and Charles VIII, were both obsessed by the image of Louis IX. Charles VIII informed Pope Alexander VI in 1494 that he was pursuing the crusade 'for the great favours I have received [from God], and to follow my ancestors'. Similarly, much of the florid speech delivered at Charles VII's court in 1451 by John Germain dwells on the crusading achievements of Charles' predecessors: 'Another con-sideration, Most Christian Prince, which should move you to undertake this holy work, is the fact that your predecessors undertook it, sparing neither their own persons nor their property.' There followed a roll-call which was mostly predictable—Charlemagne, the leaders of the First Crusade, Louis VII, Philip II, and Louis IX—except for the last name, Philip VI, who receives honourable mention for his aborted project.

Such dynastic name-dropping was not reserved for the French royal family. Henry III and Edward I of England were insistently reminded of what Richard I had achieved for the Holy Land. Indeed, given the amount of intermarriage between European royal houses, it was likely that any monarch would have at least one crusading ancestor whose image could be paraded before him. In 1452 Bernard Giustiniani reminded Emperor Frederick III of his fiancée's grandfather, John I of Portugal, who had seized Ceuta from the Moors. Because of Philip of Burgundy's marriage to Isabella of Portugal, John I's blood also flowed in the veins of Charles the Bold, so that Vasco of Lucena was able to refer to both John I and Duke John the Fearless setting examples which Charles ought to follow. Usually emulation was asked for; but in an interesting, though rather tactless, variation on this theme, Philip of Mézières, in his

'Letter to Richard II' (1395), included amongst the reasons why Richard should take part in a crusade the restitution of wrongs committed by his forefathers, who 'have impeded the holy passage overseas twice, during my lifetime, by the curse of their war [against the French]'.

At less exalted levels of aristocratic life lineage also played a key role; the existence of a family tradition of crusading was a powerful factor in shaping any nobleman's susceptibility to the appeal of the cross. But the exact nature of such influence naturally becomes harder to establish than in the case of royal dynasties. Certainly some noble houses, such as the Beauchamps, Percies, and Mowbrays in England, and the Beaujeus, Briennes, and Joinvilles in France, were well aware that their forebears had been prominent participants in crusades, and believed that this imposed obligations on them. The chronicler John of Joinville had crusading ancestors stretching back to the Second Crusade. His uncle Geoffrey V died at Krak when on the Fourth Crusade, and in 1253 John brought Geoffrey's shield back from Syria and hung it in the family chapel of St Lawrence at Joinville. In 1311 he composed the text for an epitaph to celebrate the crusading exploits of his ancestors. And a papal letter of 1455 intriguingly referred to a canon of Glasgow called Alexander Preston who had gone to fight the Turks, as had '[his] father and many others of his kinsmen' before him. Professor Paravicini has established the existence of several rich family traditions of participating in *Reisen*: members of the comital house of Jülich, to cite an extreme case, undertook no fewer than fifteen *Reisen* between 1321 and 1400.

As for national identity, the prominent role of the French in early crusading history, the 'Gesta Dei per Francos' theme, was constantly played on by popes and theorists in their appeals to the French Crown and nobility in the fourteenth and fifteenth centuries. But the French did not possess a monopoly in this respect. In 1455 Louis du Chesne, appealing to the Estates of Holland and Zeeland for financial assistance for Philip the Good's crusade, portrayed the Ottoman capture of Constantinople as a disgrace for the descendants of Baldwin of Flanders, the first Latin emperor of Constantinople, while Baldwin's capture of the city, and his subsequent coronation, were depicted in chivalric spectacle at Mons. The influence of past knighthood generally, irrespective of closer ties of lineage or nation, is shown by the *Le Canarien*, the chronicle written to celebrate the deeds of Gadifer of la Salle: 'Many are the knights who, hearing of the high adventures and fine deeds of those who in their time have undertaken distant voyages and of their battles fought against the infidel in the hope of turning them to the Christian faith, have taken heart and courage and wished to resemble them in their good work . . .'.

By imitating the past one acquired renown in the present. This meant, in the first place, *militia* itself, reception into the order of knighthood, for noblemen clearly believed that displaying *prouesse* in a crusade was the best way to establish one's worthiness to be dubbed. Examples are numerous. As one chronicler remarked of John of Nevers's participation in the Nicopolis expedition: 'Although his father [Philip the Bold] knew that the valorous youth had fought on several occasions under the banners of the King of France, he decided nevertheless that he should be girded with knighthood's belt while fighting against the enemies of the crucified one.' Duke Albert III of Austria was dubbed during the *Sommerreise* of 1377, on a day when, according to the poet Peter Suchenwirt, there were seventy-four dubbings in all. Guillebert of Lannoy received 'the order of knighthood' while on a sixteen-day *Reise* in 1413, and John of Rebreviettes was knighted by King Henry IV of Castile in 1456 in recognition of his prominence at the storming of Moorish Ximena. Connected with *militia* was *honor*, the renown acquired by a particularly impressive demonstration of *prouesse*. Again, the fact that the locations of most late medieval crusading were on the periphery of Christendom, in exotic areas such as southern Spain, North Africa, the eastern Balkans, Egypt, and Lithuania, undoubtedly contributed to its appeal, and not just to young knights or squires. 'To see the world' was one of Guillebert of Lannoy's favourite expressions. In 1410 he spent nine days admiring the palaces and pleasure gardens of Granada, 'which are beautiful and marvellous things to behold'; he seems to have been the first Frenchman to visit Nasrid Granada. Three years later, at the other end of the European continent, Lannoy observed 'another marvel', when the cold at Novgorod was so intense that a pot of water on the fire boiled at one side while freezing over at the other.

The *Reisen* held centre stage in the chivalric appeal of crusading not only because they offered so many of these attractions, but also because the Teutonic Order astutely and vigorously promoted their popularity. Werner Paravicini has commented that the time spent in Prussia before and after the campaign was 'scarcely less attractive than the *Reise* itself'. Dubbing was thus a standard practice on the *Reisen*; and knights who had performed especially well were permitted to leave their coats-of-arms depicted in the stained glass windows of Königsberg's Cathedral Church of St Mary. As Dr Keen put it, 'there must have been a time when a whole history of foreign crusading enterprise could be read in the armorial glass and blazoned memorials of the Marienkirche of Königsberg'. The *Reisen* were preceded and followed by carefully organized programmes of feasting, jousting, sightseeing, and hunting. Most importantly, there was the *Ehrentisch*, the table of honour at which, in the second half of the fourteenth century, those who had distinguished themselves in fighting against the Lithuanians were feasted and awarded prizes. The famous description of the *Ehrentisch* by the chronicler John Cabaret d'Orville, which is based on first-hand observation by John of Chastlemorand in 1375, is worth quoting at length:

And the Grand Master, seeing that this *Reise* had been honourably completed, on the day of Candlemas feasted the knighthood that were with him and that highly; and for the honour of the day, after Mass in his castle at Marienburg he had spread the Table of Honour, and it was his will that there should be seated at it twelve knights of the several kingdoms . . . and they were served, for the high dignity of the day, as was their due. And thanks be to God to those twelve they explained this order of the Table and how it came to be established. And then one of the knights of that religion gave to each of them a shoulder badge on which it was written in letters of gold 'Honneur vainc tout!'. And the next day the knights took their leave of the Grand Master, and returned each to his own country.[5]

The glitter and exuberance associated with the *Reisen* are seen at their most extreme in the accounts for Henry of Derby's expeditions of 1390–1 and 1392. Henry took with him a retinue of about 100 people. Although the first journey involved some gruelling fighting when the English assisted in the siege of Vilnius, the keynote of both enterprises was luxury. Henry and his household ate and drank well, and even the hunting falcons were fed on fresh chicken. Henry spent heavily, hosted banquets, and gave lavish presents. His expenses amounted to £4,438 on the first journey and £4,915 on the second. The money was paid primarily by his father, John of Gaunt, and at least some of it derived, appropriately enough, from the war indemnity which Gaunt had accepted to end his Castilian crusade in 1387. There is little indication that Henry regarded either journey as a penitential exercise. He disbursed money at Danzig to buy the plenary indulgence granted by Pope Boniface IX, but it is striking that while he lost £69 in gambling on his first journey, he spent only about £12 on alms. As Professor Du Boulay commented, the accounts reveal 'a

---

[5] Jean Cabaret d'Orville, *La Chronique du bon duc Loys de Bourbon*, ed. A. M. Chazaud (Paris, 1876), 65–6; the translation is that of M. Keen, in *Chivalry* (New Haven, Conn., 1984), 173.

man of physical competence and small sensibility', engaged on predominantly secular enterprises.

There is no need to regard Henry's trips to Prussia as typical of *Reisen*, let alone of chivalrous crusading generally. But they do raise the question of the part which *devotio* played in such activity. The desire to serve God is certainly put forward as one reason for a chivalric hero undertaking the crusade in the late Middle Ages. Louis of Bourbon is described as pleading for leadership of the Al-Mahdiya crusade by saying that 'it is the thing in the world that I have most desired, for after worldly activity it is a fine thing to serve God'. Similarly, Boucicaut's biographer wrote of John of Nevers's enthusiasm for the Nicopolis crusade that 'he considered that he could not employ himself better than by dedicating his youth to God's service by striving for the expansion of the faith'. At other times, as in the vows undertaken during and immediately after the Feast of the Pheasant in 1454, reference was constantly made to the honour of God, the Virgin, and all noble ladies. There is no reason to regard such devotion as insincere or superficial: chivalry continued to place a large emphasis on religious piety, and many nobles who went on crusades were noted for other acts of conspicuous and often thoughtful devotion. Henry Grosmont, for example, founded a collegiate church at Leicester and wrote a devotional treatise, the 'Livre de Seyntz Medicines'. But it is characteristic that in both the quotations just cited the emphasis is on the service of God by the demonstration of *prouesse*, rather than on the crusade's function as a penitential exercise; the latter only really exerted an influence in the case of planned *passagia* to the Holy Land, which were, as always, dominated by *imitatio Christi*.

From this several interesting things follow. One is that when noblemen decided to undertake a crusade to display their chivalric virtues, the precise location of the combat was of secondary importance: what mattered was fighting Christ's foes, the *inimici crucifixi*. At times they even displayed an odd nonchalance about where they would fight, and against whom. Between 1363 and 1365 Thomas Beauchamp, Earl of Warwick, seems to have considered several crusading fronts before settling on Prussia. As we saw in the previous chapter, Henry Bolingbroke and Marshal Boucicaut went to Prussia in 1390–1 because they could not secure permission from their kings to go to North Africa. In 1403 Boucicaut displayed the same attitude when he executed his series of daring raids on a number of ports in Anatolia and Syria, without any apparent regard for broader military or political considerations. According to Cabaret d'Orville, while returning from the Al-Mahdiya expedition, Louis of Bourbon asked his Genoese allies if there were any Christians nearby who traded with the Moors, against whom his crusaders could display their *prouesse*, in compensation for the relatively small amount of combat which they had enjoyed in Africa. Delighted, the Genoese supplied the names of several trading rivals, and the crusaders took the towns of Cagliari, Ogliastro, and Terracina. Most significant is the fact that the French and English organizers of the Nicopolis crusade were at first undecided whether to go to Prussia or Hungary; only when Grand Master Conrad of Jungingen declined their assistance in 1394 did they decide to fight the Turks.

In a sense, of course, all this was similar to the long-standing practice of vow commutation. But the fundamental difference was that whereas commutation was linked to the concept of a strategy directed by the pope through his exclusive control of the preaching of the crusade, this casual planning—or lack of it—made any kind of strategy difficult to work out, and with it any real papal direction of crusading endeavour. Other developments reinforce the impression that those who engaged in crusading because of the chivalric impulse had little understanding of, or interest in, the areas in which they fought: for example, the relative ease with which the Teutonic Knights were able to persuade western knights to continue taking part in *Reisen* after Jogailo's baptism in 1386. Using casuistic arguments similar to those we have seen Louis of Bourbon deploying in 1390, the Teutonic Knights justified the *Sommerreise* of 1413, in which Guillebert of Lannoy was a proud participant, on the grounds that the Poles 'favoured the Saracens'. And despite the background of intricate Anglo-French diplomacy which lay behind it, there is little developed sense of strategy even in the case of the Nicopolis crusade. Its chief function, in the eyes of its promoters, appears to have been to act as a symbol of Anglo-French peace under the common standard of chivalry. Thus in an important letter about the crusade which he wrote in 1395, Charles VI mentioned the defeat of the Ottomans as only one amongst a number of goals, some of them contradictory.

It is hardly surprising that the crusading movement in the late Middle Ages sometimes appears incoherent and diffuse. This is especially true of the fourteenth century, the golden age of chivalric crusading. There is a striking contrast between the deep thought given to crusade planning, to every aspect of strategy, logistics, organization, transportation, and finance, by the writers of the many treatises; and the shortsighted, and essentially limited, nature of the chivalric interest in crusading. The contrast is summed up by the fact that in 1390, one year after the severity of the Ottoman threat in the western Balkans had been made crystal clear by the crushing defeat of the Serbs and their allies at Kossovo, a crusade could set sail to Tunisia. And yet it is important to keep a sense of balance about the deficiencies of the chivalric impulse, in relation to crusading as in other respects. For as the crusade activities of the Burgundian court show, chivalry was not *ipso facto* incompatible with careful planning and preparation. And above all, the variety and vitality of crusading in the fourteenth and early fifteenth centuries owed a great deal to the enthusiasm of the nobility, which in turn was rooted in the continuing stimulus of chivalric ideals.

What of the civilian, non-noble majority of Catholics? In assessing their crusading activity, and using it as a pointer to their feelings about the crusade, it is essential to refer to the fundamental change which occurred in the procedure of crusade recruitment. By the time the Second Council of Lyons assembled, the Church was already turning its back on mass participation in crusading. It was responding partly to the débâcles which had attended the armed pilgrimages of the early phase of crusading history, but chiefly to the growing professionalism of warfare. We shall examine what the latter entailed for the crusade in the next chapter;[6] what concerns us here is the practical consequences of the restrictions which were increasingly placed on personal crusading. The movement away from mass participation is extremely difficult to date, and despite the clear signals coming from the papal Curia, probably varied in practice from country to country. There were important developments before 1274, springing from Innocent III's decision, enshrined in the bull *Quia maior* (1213), to encourage large-scale redemption of vows in order to maximize the financial receipts of crusade preaching. Recent study of the resulting practice in England has shown that in the 1230s vow redemption was systematically coupled to the energetic preaching of the new Orders of friars to achieve Innocent's goal, and that the procedure was not thereafter altered. But crusade organization and finance were more sophisticated in England than elsewhere, and by 1274 scandals in the practice of redemption had led the papal Curia generally to draw back from its use of vow redemptions as a means of raising money through preaching indulgences.

The century between the Second Lyons Council and the outbreak of

[6] Below, 430–44.

the Great Schism in 1378 in fact formed a transitional period. The Curia was well aware of the danger of licensing simony (the sale of holy things) by sanctioning the 'selling' of indulgences, and it wanted to avoid discouraging able-bodied recruits from taking the cross to fight in person. But the period's escalating military costs constituted an inexorable pressure towards using indulgences in order to raise money. In the mid-fourteenth century, moreover, Clement VI put the finishing touches to the concept of the 'Treasury of Merits', the great credit-balance of virtue believed to be at the disposal of the popes because of the lives of Christ and the saints. This furnished the theological basis for the dispensing of indulgences without reference to personal satisfaction for sins committed, provided that the recipient had confessed in full and was truly contrite. Gradually, therefore, the Curia edged towards the financial administration of indulgences. It is true that the majority of crusade bulls continued to offer the full indulgence only to people who went in person or arranged for deputies to fight in their stead: and those who went were granted a greater spiritual reward than those who sent. But on occasion, as during the preaching of the Hospitaller crusade of 1309–10, and Clement VI's naval league of 1343, the formula was used of granting the full indulgence to all who donated to crusade preachers what they would have spent had they gone in person. Sometimes, too, the Curia permitted its agents to substitute an agreed sum of money for the provision of deputies. And there are instances of these agents exceeding their brief, and selling indulgences in an open and scandalous fashion. In 1357, for example, the Bishop of Narni preached the crusade at Florence against the *routier* Great Company. He announced that Florentines could club together in groups of twelve; each group would pay the wages of one man-at-arms for six months. This amounted to the gaining of a crusade indulgence for just three-and-a-half florins. But the abuse went further, for the Bishop subsequently agreed to the Commune sending a force of troops to perform vicarious service against the Company. In exchange for this all Florentines, and their subjects, could claim the indulgence.

After 1378 the heightened financial exigencies weighing on both obediences of the Schism led them increasingly to incorporate into their crusade bulls explicit instructions for the selling of indulgences. This was one feature of a general trend towards the abuse of indulgences, which was accelerated by the Roman Pope Boniface IX (1389–1404) in particular. It was epitomized by the exploitation of the Jubilee Indulgence, which came to be regarded as the fullest possible indulgence and was often specified as the spiritual reward on offer in fifteenth-century crusade bulls. As Ludwig Von Pastor, a leading historian of the medieval papacy, put it, 'The real reason why indulgences were requested and granted was no longer the attainment of spiritual grace, but the need for money.' In the case of crusade bulls, this 'accursed sale of indulgences', as a Polish contemporary of Boniface IX termed it, usually took the form of a clause stating that the donation of an agreed sum of money could replace the provision of soldiers. The practice was not renounced after the Schism, with the result that the fifteenth and sixteenth centuries became the period when crusade preaching turned openly financial in its nature and goal. Crusade preachers were effectively collectors, and it was the financial aspects of crusade bulls which came to matter above all. Iron-bound wooden chests, which had occupied a corner in cathedral and parish churches since the twelfth century as repositories for donations to the crusade, now became the focal point of crusade preaching.

The change is most striking in the case of Spain, where it marked the emergence of the 'Bula de la cruzada' as a fiscal instrument of the Castilian government. Instead of previous euphemisms like donating a soldier's wages, or paying what would have been a year's expenses had the donor served in person, Pope Martin V (1417–31) established a straightforward rate of payment. This was not an innovation *per se*, for several of Martin's predecessors had done the same; the importance of the action lay in the fact that it became standard practice during following pontificates. All that Martin's successors had to do was to decide on the rate of payment, and in practice many delegated this to their commissioners. The latter thus enjoyed a tremendous boost to their power and influence, and the written guidance provided for preachers and confessors by such commissioners as Cardinal Branda in the case of the Hussite Crusade in 1421, and Cardinal Bessarion in that of the projected crusade against the Turks in 1463, had a key role to play in making preaching successful.

Further major changes came with Sixtus IV (1471–84). As we noted in Chapter 10,[7] his bull of 1482 for the Granada war laid down the procedure followed in *cruzada* preaching for centuries to come. The Pope still referred to the possibility of personal and vicarious service on crusade, but one of the bull's novelties lay in its graduated payments, ranging from 100 florins in the case of the King and Queen, to two *reales* or less in that of the poor. The *cruzada* has received close attention, but

---

[7] Above, 302.

there is no reason to doubt that other crusading fronts, especially of course the anti-Turkish crusade, did not experience parallel developments: indeed, Sixtus sanctioned the use of graduated payments for the preaching of the crusade in Scotland several years before his bull of 1482. On other occasions it was specified that the recipient of the indulgence should pay a week's household expenses, which had the advantage of flexibility over Sixtus's sliding scale. The innovations which the Curia made at this time were clarified and exploited by Raymond Peraudi, a French cleric whose contribution to indulgence preaching for the crusade was emphasized by Nikolaus Paulus, the finest modern scholar of indulgences. Peraudi was appointed commissioner for the indulgence which Sixtus IV granted to Saintes Cathedral in 1476, reserving a half of the proceeds for the crusade against the Turks. The bull was one of the first outside Iberia explicitly to extend indulgences to souls in Purgatory. Beginning with the *Summaria declaratio* which he wrote to clarify this matter, Peraudi produced a stream of printed manuals and guidelines which enormously facilitated the work of his preachers. He himself organized crusade preaching on several occasions in Germany between 1486 and 1504.

Peraudi proved to be an astute and resourceful commissioner. In November 1502, for example, he instructed his preachers to travel to small centres of population during Advent, rather than concentrating on the big towns, where indulgences were commonplace. Like other commissioners, he made great use of the Franciscan Observants. Their names recur with frequency on his printed letters of indulgence, and they clearly played the same key role in promoting the crusade in the fifteenth century as the early Franciscans had done in the thirteenth. Indeed, one of Peraudi's admirers, the Augustinian John of Paltz, later commented that he owed his success partly to his grasp of the importance of appointing suitable preachers, as well as to his *penchant* for dramatic effects.

Often papal nuncios who have been dispatched with [bulls of] jubilee and indulgences have handed out letters in corners, as it were, without solemnly raising the holy cross. Consequently they had little impact on the people. [Peraudi, on the other hand,] searched out the erudite, the renowned, and the devout in each and every university and college, selected them, appointed them, and sent them out. So he was able to persuade everybody, regardless of rank and sex, to look favourably on this most pious work, to convert the sinners and to free an infinite number of souls, both living and dead, from the penalties [of sin].[8]

---

[8] N. Paulus, 'Raimund Peraudi als Ablasskommissar', *Historisches Jahrbuch*, 21 (1900), 667 n. 5.

Peraudi's legations provide some of the most vivid descriptions of how the crusade was preached in the last decades of the fifteenth century. For example, at Erfurt in 1488

the legate ordered that a big red cross should be set up in the middle of the Church of Our Lady, with two banners bearing the papal arms; these were red, and there was a big iron chest nearby . . . And anybody who performed his confession there, would be a beneficiary of the Jubilee, just as if he had gone to Rome, and was released from punishment and guilt for all his sins, however great they were. Such an indulgence was without precedent in Erfurt. And each confessed person put whatever he could afford in the chest; people also put money into the chest for deceased persons, so that they too would benefit. Again, he had letters of indulgence (*Beichtbriefe*) given out, for which each person had to pay seven new *groschen*. So many confessions were made by the people and so many letters handed out that it cannot be described . . . It was also decreed, that a sermon about the indulgence would be preached each day in the Church of Our Lady by eminent and learned doctors, both clerical and lay . . . And the father confessors sat to hear confession from morning until night, and were exhausted from hearing confessions and preaching day in, day out. The indulgence was available at Erfurt for five whole weeks. Huge sums of money were raised from it and left the region.[9]

The overall trend towards the commercialization of indulgences for crusading is clear enough. But the reaction of the laity is much less so. The first point to make is that popular devotion to crusading could not simply be channelled into financial donation. On several occasions it burst these somewhat narrow banks, and a 'non-professional', predominantly civilian crusade was initiated akin to the old armed pilgrimage which remained, for many, the crusading ideal. This invariably happened because ordinary people reacted to crusade preaching by electing to serve in person, despite all the problems which this caused to rulers, for whom organizing a crusade of professional fighting men usually proved hard enough. Such a pattern emerged in France and elsewhere in 1309 and 1320. As we saw in Chapter 1,[10] both occasions were characterized by a background of intensive crusade planning and preaching, in 1309 for the Hospitaller *passagium* and in 1320 for the crusade proposals of Count Louis of Clermont and King Philip V. Thousands of people attempted to reach the Mediterranean ports to embark for the Holy Land, the result being unrest, crime, and (in 1320) serious outbreaks of anti-Semitic violence. The papacy and the clerical chroniclers of the period disapproved of both movements; but while they no doubt attracted criminal elements, they were mainly composed of ordinary people who resisted the official trend towards vicarious participation.

The 'People's Crusade' of 1309 and the *pastoureaux* of 1320 both related to plans to recover the Holy Land, and reflected a continuing devotion to that goal which was shared by all social classes in the early fourteenth century; it is apparent, for instance, in the Confraternity of the Holy Sepulchre which Louis of Clermont founded at Paris in 1317. Indeed, enthusiasm for the crusade, because of its heavy emphasis on penitential and Christ-centred *devotio*, could never be wholly detached from the dream of recovering Jerusalem and the Holy Land. But it would be wrong to deduce from this that Jerusalem remained central to popular enthusiasm once the thrust of crusade planning had shifted to the burgeoning problem of the Turks. Contemporary sources, some of them only recently given the attention they merit, show that it was possible to arouse a considerable degree of crusading zeal amongst non-chivalric classes outside the context of 'recuperatio terre sancte'. The Turks were not holding or threatening Christ's patrimony, but they were still felt to be his enemies because they abominated his name and enslaved his Church and people. The popular response to the preaching of the Smyrna crusade in 1344–6 shows this clearly, for the capture of Smyrna triggered off a wave of enthusiasm, especially in the cities of northern Italy. Clement VI himself was so excited by the success of his league that he sanctioned popular participation, without considering the detrimental military consequences; the latter were amongst the factors which doomed to failure the Dauphin Humbert's *passagium*.

By 1400 the movement away from personal participation had accelerated, and the fifteenth century gave rise to fewer instances of 'popular crusades'. The most significant was undoubtedly the crusade to defend Hungary against the Turks in 1456. As in 1344–6, Calixtus III, or his preachers, appear to have departed from the Curia's policy of excluding the civilian classes. They were perhaps prompted by the threat which Mehmed II posed to Belgrade, which was considered to be the strategic key to Central Europe. The result, the relief of Belgrade by an army of common crusaders led by John of Capistrano, has been sadly neglected by crusade historians because it does not fit into their pattern of decline, or at best, of the crusade surviving only because it was hitched to the chariot of chivalry. In a sense one can understand the unease of historians when confronted with events in 1456, for quite apart from the unexpected outcome of the crusade, what occurred was in every way extraordinary.

In the first place, there is the sheer success of the preaching, and the unusual character of the army which it produced. As the eyewitness John of Tagliacozzo wrote:

Many noblemen and their retainers had taken the cross, but the custom in Hungary is that such people set out for war with their lords, and since the lords did not come, none of them came either; or rather, to be more accurate, very few came. All those who assembled were commoners, peasants, the poor, priests, clerics, scholars, students, monks, mendicant friars of various Orders, members of the Third Order of St Francis, and hermits. Few of these people bore arms.[11]

Secondly, there is the impressive atmosphere of penitential devotion and brotherly charity in which the army lived in the field. John of Tagliacozzo commented that

There was no idleness, no weakness, no lax behaviour. Drunkenness, gluttony, dishonesty, and prostitution were absent. Idle gossip, gambling, theft, and pillaging were nowhere to be seen. Nobody complained about people who had not come, there was no grumbling or plotting, no quarrelling. Instead there was devotion, prayer, and frequent masses; for although many came to hear mass celebrated by the Blessed Father [John of Capistrano], each group (*turma*) had its own priest, a secular or a religious, from whom it often received the sacraments.[12]

The last point reflects the fact that, as in the case of previous 'people's crusades', the *crucesignati* of 1456, although poor, civilian, and originating in many different regions, none the less had their own cohesion and organization. Indeed, Tagliacozzo mentioned that the various *turmae* possessed banners, 'with the sign of the cross on one side, and the figures of St Francis, St Anthony, St Louis, or St Bernard on the other. This was either so that it could be perceived that the crusaders had been recruited by members of the Franciscan Order, or so that it could be understood that this crusade was intended for the poor, not the rich, and that their captain was a poor man.'

The cohesiveness of the crusaders of 1456, and their military success, can be partly accounted for by the fact that Hungary's peasants were accustomed to bearing arms because of their country's use of popular levies (the *militia portalis* system). None the less, Smyrna and Belgrade were not the only instances in the late Middle Ages of crusade preaching

---

[11] Giovanni da Tagliacozzo, 'Relatio de victoria Belgradensi', in L. Wadding, *et al.* (eds.), *Annales minorum* (25 vols.; Rome, 1731–1933), xii. 352–3.

[12] Ibid. 351.

against the Turks meeting with an enthusiastic response from a broad social base. Historians have written a great deal about the failure of Pius II to launch his planned crusade a few years after the relief of Belgrade, but have neglected the fact that some thousands of people did take the cross, and were either at Ancona or *en route* to the port when the Pope died. According to one source they included some 2,000 Saxons. A contingent from Ghent, several hundred strong, pressed on to the East regardless of the expedition's collapse, ceremonially placing their banner in the Church of St John at Ghent after their return. And in 1514 a large army of peasant crusaders was raised in Hungary to fight the Turks. Nor was it only against the Turks that people were prepared to serve. The preaching of the Bishop of Norwich's crusade against the Clementist schismatics of Flanders in 1383 enjoyed great success, bringing across the Channel large numbers of civilians whose presence was unwelcome to Despenser. In this instance, as in many others, historians have fixed their attention on the crusade's failure, and the abuses attending its preaching, taking scant notice of its undeniable popularity.

Such instances have much to teach us about popular feeling towards the crusade, but they remain exceptions to the general tendency to restrict actual crusading to professional fighters. Assessment of the attitude of the majority must therefore focus on the reception of preaching campaigns which had as their goal the raising of money. There is no denying that on occasion great sums could be raised, as in the case of the Jubilee and Livonia indulgences of 1501–6 in Germany. But we naturally want to know the overall record of indulgence campaigns, and this is a notoriously difficult matter to ascertain. The reasons are several: the relative scarcity of accounts showing how much was raised, the fact that such accounts rarely comprise only money collected from indulgences, and the many extraneous factors which could have shaped the success or failure of these fund-raising exercises. Similar problems surround the assessment of donations and legacies to crusading causes. Three areas which have received close attention from historians, Spain, England, and the Low Countries, show how complex the problem is, but also throw some light on it. The preaching of the *cruzada* in late fifteenth- and sixteenth-century Castile has already been described in Chapter 10.[13] It remains the outstanding example of success in adapting the crusade indulgence to government's financial needs, to such an extent that the Spanish Crown was prepared to fight a long battle against the forces of

[13] Above, 301–2, 312–15.

Catholic reform in order to retain it. But to what extent was Castile's experience mirrored elsewhere?

In England indulgences against the Turks were preached regularly throughout the fifteenth century, with twelve campaigns between 1444 and 1502 alone. Indulgences were also preached for other crusading causes, such as the Hospitallers' expenses at Rhodes, John XXIII's war against Ladislas of Naples, and the crusades against the Hussites. English participation in actual crusading had become minimal by this point, and the government either remained neutral or actively obstructed preaching. For these and other reasons the proceeds of the preaching, although at times respectable, were never very impressive. It is possible too that they declined in the course of the century. The papal collector Jasper Ponce, who sold indulgences in 1501, was described by Polydore Vergil as raising 'great sums of money' on behalf of Alexander VI's proposed crusade against the Turks. But even if true, this could simply reflect the fact that Ponce used fixed scales of payment which were notably elaborate, and must have made his task considerably easier. Most of the preaching campaigns in England were not even noted by chroniclers.

In the Low Countries too, indulgences, directed mainly against the Turks, were preached with frequency in the fifteenth and early sixteenth century. Whereas England's kings had relinquished any practical concern with crusading in this period, this region possessed, in Philip the Good and Charles V, two of the rulers who were most actively involved in the movement. The sale of indulgences, especially when it occurred in relation to their plans, was more successful than across the Channel. This was not least because the secular administration took a prominent role in the work of advertising the indulgences. In 1529–30, for example, crusade indulgences were twice preached to support the defence of Hungary by Charles V's brother Ferdinand, following the crushing defeat at Mohács. Margaret of Austria, the Emperor's regent in the Low Countries, promoted the cause, writing to local authorities in December 1529 that they should 'help the said agents in the publication of this crusade, be present at the preaching and processions, and give generously of your possessions, inducing the people in your jurisdiction to do the same'. The city authorities in Bruges organized a solemn procession to publicize the crusade; 500 copies of the bull of indulgence were printed, and 676 *livres* were eventually collected from the trunks which were set aside to hold the alms of the faithful.

But if preaching achieved a better result in the Low Countries than in contemporary England, it remained problematic. By this point, in the Low Countries as elsewhere, profits could only be sustained by offering sweeping privileges to the beneficiaries of the indulgence, as is clear from surviving examples of the printed indulgences which were issued. In 1508, for example, Henry and Bertha of Rhemen purchased indulgences on behalf of the Teutonic Order, 'for the protection of Livonia, in aid of the holy crusade against the most ferocious Russians, who are heretics and schismatics', from the collector Christian Bomhouwer. The indulgences could be enjoyed once during their lifetimes, and whenever they were in danger of death; the indulgences applied to all their offspring; and Henry and Bertha could choose their own confessors, who had the right to absolve them from virtually all offences. Despite such largesse, at the end of 1455 Pope Calixtus III was forced drastically to reduce the amount of money which the subjects of Philip the Good were required to pay for the crusade indulgence because the response so far had been disappointing. Instead of having to pay a tenth of their annual revenues for the indulgence, recipients could donate a hundredth each year that the Burgundian army remained in the field, or alternatively make a single payment of a hundredth of all their goods. Similarly, Margaret of Austria complained at the end of March 1530 that the indulgence had achieved little response ('little fruit has come of it'): and this in the wake of one of the most severe defeats ever suffered by a Christian army. In this instance respectable returns were eventually achieved by re-advertising the indulgences, but in general audiences in the Low Countries seem to have been ambivalent in their response to crusade indulgences. When the priest at Wageningen, in the Diocese of Utrecht, launched a vitriolic attack on indulgences in 1488, his parishioners were so sympathetic towards his onslaught that they would not permit the collector to take away the church's crusade chest.

Clearly local circumstances, especially the attitude assumed by the secular powers, counted for much in the preaching of indulgences. But there were general considerations too. Some of these related to all indulgences sold in this period; indeed, since recipients no longer took the cross, there was little difference in the procedure followed. Similarly, as no votive obligations were incurred, preaching campaigns for the crusade could last years: the indulgences issued in 1476 by Sixtus IV were in fact sold for more than a decade. Abuses were ineradicable, and there can be little doubt that they were resented even by people who benefited from the indulgences proffered, and regarded with enthusiasm the cause for which they were being sold. Controlling the preaching campaigns posed insuperable problems. Most contemporaries were not able to recognize a papal bull of crusade, let alone perceive that it had elapsed or been cancelled. There were therefore ongoing difficulties with false preachers, men who worked without licence for their own gain under the pretext of collecting money for the crusade. For example, Calixtus III complained in 1457 that they 'set a poor example and damaged the goods [given to the] crusade', and Stephen Taleazzi later claimed that these fake preachers had done great harm to Pius II's crusade project. Moreover, an alarming number of official preachers (*quaestores*) turned renegade in the course of their preaching. They ignored papal orders to stop preaching and hand in their proceeds, and involved the Curia and the local ecclesiastical authorities in lengthy correspondence and cross-country chases before they could be apprehended.

But the practices of bona fide preachers were not much better. They compelled people to attend their sermons under penalty of excommunication. Many falsified bulls and relics, misused their authority, and were ready, as contemporaries complained, to promise virtually anything 'as long as the money goes in the chest'. Even the diligent and highly respected Raymond Peraudi lamented that he could not contain the greed and disobedience of his agents. Possession of a crusade bull could be all but a licence to print money, and the Curia sometimes encouraged the use of unscrupulous sales techniques by farming out the right to organize a preaching campaign, and granting preachers a percentage of the take. When the papal commissioners for crusade preaching in France gave their preachers permission to retain a fifth of the collected money in 1517, the result was a flood of abuses so serious that the Sorbonne appealed to Francis I and the French episcopate to intervene. An echo of the measure is conserved in Panurge's comment, in Rabelais's *Gargantua*, 'Ha, my friend, if you knew how I feathered my nest from the crusade, you would be truly astonished. It was worth more than 6,000 florins to me.' The scandal which overtook this preaching, which was probably the last big occasion on which the crusade was preached in France, formed a sad finale to more than four centuries of French crusading effort.

From the middle of the fifteenth century onwards, virtually every year saw a church synod somewhere in Europe which bitterly criticized the practices of the 'pardoners', and passed ineffective decrees to curtail them. The *quaestores* became stock figures of fun and satire in the works of writers like Boccaccio, Chaucer, Langland, Brant, and Rabelais. The detrimental effect on collecting for crusades was undoubtedly serious. It was no wonder, the German Dominican George Schwarz commented in the early 1470s, that people did not give willingly to crusades, when they heard such lies, and could purchase indulgences every Sunday or feast-day for a few pence each. But if the grass-roots disrepute of indulgence marketing was to a large extent the responsibility of the *quaestores*, the Church's hierarchy was not blameless. The market for indulgences was simply saturated. There were too many causes which enjoyed plenary indulgences alongside the crusade. The German *Reichstags* of 1466, 1471, and 1474, and theorists like Stephen Taleazzi, argued that the Curia must suspend other indulgences and concentrate on preaching the crusade. The Curia sometimes took this advice, but could not resist the temptation to issue exemptions from the suspension to those who offered enough. In any case, suspension could work against the crusade as well as in its favour. Sixtus IV inaugurated a massive preaching campaign in 1480 to raise money to expel the Turks from Otranto, only to cancel it when it was in full swing, on the arrival of the news that the town had been recaptured.

In order to induce the secular authorities to permit preaching to take place, as well as to secure the co-operation of local churchmen, and to reconcile the latter to the suspension of their own indulgences, the Curia had to grant away sizeable percentages of the 'take'. As the German poet Thomas Murner put it,

> If the Pope gives out a pardon
> The local lord must have his share;
> If the Pope will not agree,
> The pardon just remains hot air.[14]

This practice added to the sordid impression that indulgences made. Erasmus's attack, in his 'Consultatio de bello Turcis inferendo' (1530), was particularly eloquent and acrid, but the points which he made were often put forward:

The same consideration has turned people almost completely against indulgences. It is clear, they say, that this is nothing but commerce. The justification changed all the time. At one moment it was war against the Turks, then the military needs of the Pope, then the Jubilee. The Jubilee was repeated, so that collection could occur again; under Alexander [VI] it was repeated twice, lest any opportunity for profit be lost. Then plenitude of power itself was surpassed, and Purgatory was

---

[14] N. Paulus, *Geschichte des Ablasses im Mittelalter* (3 vols.; Paderborn, 1922–3), iii. 463.

in danger of losing all its inhabitants . . . What more can one say? There was neither limit nor end to the haggling. Princes sliced off a part of the proceeds, as the price of their admitting the papal bulls; likewise deans and their officials; likewise commissioners; likewise those who did the preaching. Some were given money to talk; others to keep silence.[15]

In the case of the crusade, these abuses were compounded by the fact that the money raised did not even end up being used for the right cause. Numerous sources testify to the disillusionment, and subsequent suspicion, caused by this, but the most eloquent witnesses were Pius II and Erasmus. Their concurrence on this point is the more striking since one was a fervent advocate of crusading, and the other one of the movement's most prominent critics. Pius II's *Commentaries*, that invaluable testimony to the cloying deadweight of pessimism which had already begun to settle on crusading matters by the mid-fifteenth century, show that ordinary people were seen as no longer trusting the authorities, whether ecclesiastical or lay; as the Pope noted, in a famous passage quoted in Chapter 3, 'like insolvent tradesmen, we are without credit'.[16] But it is an acerbic passage in Erasmus's *Consultatio* which more than anything else sums up the fruits of a century of reiterated disappointments:

Every time that this farce has been acted out by the popes, the result has been ridiculous. Either nothing came of it, or the cause actually deteriorated. The money, people say, stays stuck to the hands of the popes, cardinals, monks, dukes, and princes. Instead of wages, the ordinary soldier is given licence to pillage. So many times we have heard the announcement of a crusade, of the recovery of the Holy Land; so many times we have seen the red cross surmounted on the papal tiara, and the red chest; so many times we have attended solemn gatherings and heard of lavish promises, splendid deeds, the most sweeping expectations. And yet the only winner has been money. We are informed by the proverb that it is shameful to hit yourself on the same stone twice; so how can we trust such promises, however splendid, when we have been tricked more than thirty times, misled so often and so openly?[17]

It was not surprising that in 1530, the same year that the *Consultatio* was published, Margaret of Austria instructed the civic authorities at Bruges to stress that every penny raised through the sale of indulgences would be employed in the defence of Hungary against the Turks.

---

[15] P. S. Allen, *et al.* (eds.), *Opus epistolarum Desiderii Erasmi Roterodami* (12 vols.; Oxford, 1906–58), viii. 384.

[16] Above, 107.

[17] Allen, *et al.*, *Opus epistolarum Desiderii Erasmi Roterodami*, viii. 384.

Scepticism about the sale of indulgences for crusades was probably at its greatest in the Empire, where the crusade was preached with great frequency in the second half of the fifteenth century. The *Reichstags* of 1458, 1460, 1518, and 1523 gave voice to widespread concern about the fate of money collected for crusading, and contemporaries like Nicholas of Siegen, Cornelius of Lopsen, and Paul Lang were suspicious of Raymond Peraudi's preaching campaigns. In 1502 the Strasburg cathedral preacher Geiler of Kaisersberg told Peraudi that the Curia had cried wolf too often in the past to be believed now; and in 1504 Peraudi himself predicted 'an incredible scandal' if the money which had been raised was stolen, as indeed it was. Most money raised for the crusade, in the fifteenth and sixteenth centuries as in the past, found its way into the coffers of princes. But, partly because the indulgences were sanctioned by the papal Curia, and partly because of the papacy's poor record of diverting crusade money, popular opinion concentrated on Rome. On the eve of the Reformation scandalous anecdotes about mores at the Curia found a ready audience in Germany; one of the best narrated how Cesare Borgia, having gambled away 100,000 ducats raised through crusade preaching in Germany, laughed off his losses with the jest 'There go the sins of the Germans.'

As late as November 1517, a commission of cardinals appointed by Pope Leo X to advise him on the crusade expressed the belief that this massive accumulation of mistrust could still be overcome:

Provided that war is waged in good faith, then great sums of money will be raised by publishing indulgences of the most holy crusade for people who contribute towards the defence of the holy faith. For faith is not dead in the hearts of believers, nor will they scorn the heavenly *patria*. There are many, and there will be many, who will gladly purchase eternal life for a small price, if they see that others are fighting for God in earnest, rather than pretending to do so.[18]

A few generations earlier the cardinals might have been proved right, for when we list the occasions on which indulgences did bring in a rich crop of money—such as in the preaching of the Hospitaller *passagium* of 1309–10, the defence of Genoese Caffa in 1456, or, most spectacularly, the campaigns against the Moors of Granada in the 1480s—we find that things were clearly happening: armies were being organized, or successes had already been achieved. There was, as Cardinal Bessarion put it in 1460, 'the possibility of war and the hope of victory'. Those who gave

---

[18] E. Charrière (ed.), *Négociations de la France dans le Levant* (4 vols.; Paris, 1848–50), i. 35.

money would therefore see it used for the purpose intended. They had a good chance of avoiding the problem which hovered like a black cloud over late medieval crusading, and doomed to failure other, equally well-planned and executed campaigns of preaching: the aborted crusade. It was this consideration which impelled Pius II to resolve to lead his crusade in person: people would respond 'when it once becomes known that the Pope of Rome . . . is marching straight on to win salvation for all and desires no man's silver since he is resolved to risk not only his own gold but his own person for Christ's sake'.

But by 1517 it was too late to turn back the tide, and the French reply to Leo X was probably nearer to the pulse of popular feeling than the cardinals were, in stating that disillusionment could not now be combatted.

The people's devotion has diminished to such a degree that almost nothing will come of [the offer of indulgences]. People have been deceived so often by such means, from which nothing has resulted, that they now regard them as a deception, clever tricks to extract their money.[19]

In any case, even if more crusading projects had materialized, and the donation of money had been seen as a viable means of supporting them, it is questionable whether the Church's attempt to channel enthusiasm into the purchase of indulgences could ever have attained the degree of popularity enjoyed, as late as the fourteenth century, by personal parti-cipation. First, personal service could not be expunged from a movement whose ties with pilgrimage were still strong. Inspiring preachers like Peraudi were, according to some sources, able to instil an atmosphere of piety and penitential devotion, especially in the case of the Jubilee Indulgence of 1501; but such men were few. How could the possession of a printed *buleta* compare with the sense of personal atonement and fraternal co-operation achieved by Capistrano's crusaders in 1456? And secondly, there would still have remained the abuses which were written into the financial administration of indulgences, however popular and pressing the military cause for which they were sold. Even after the Council of Trent had banned the use of *quaestores* and forbidden the sale of indulgences, Pius V's Holy League had to be financed by a crusade bull which, as Paulus remarked, was 'completely in accordance with the medieval pattern', and no doubt entailed the same squalid features in its administration. The success of *cruzada* preaching in Spain, where governmental patronage enabled abuses to coexist with profitability,

[19] Ibid. i. 43.

therefore remained an exception; and the massive revenues culled there could not be matched elsewhere, even in those parts of Italy which came under long-term Spanish control.

This decisive failure to make purchased indulgences a workable channel for crusading zeal can be located in the second half of the fifteenth century. Several other developments helped to make the fifteenth century a watershed in the decline of practical crusading. One was the fact that the opportunities for noblemen to fight diminished, as political circumstances closed, one after another, the most popular crusading fronts. Hopes for a recovery crusade had ended with the Mamluk-Cypriot treaty of 1370; the *Reisen* came to an end in the early 1420s; and the *Reconquista* had comparatively little to offer to foreign volunteers between the death of Alfonso XI in 1350, and the final assault on Granada in the 1480s. At the same time, the freedom of Europe's noblemen to express their chivalric aspirations in crusading perceptibly dwindled as the military demands of their own rulers grew, and the latter became less inclined to permit the freelance activities which had been so characteristic of the fourteenth century. And the dominance of the mounted nobility on the battlefield was challenged by the impact of changes in military techniques, especially the resurgence of infantry, the rise of hand-guns and cannon, and the beginnings of standing armies. Crusading ideas associated with chivalric culture persisted well into the sixteenth century, and even found practical expression at times. They inspired Englishmen who fought in the Granadan crusades, Frenchmen who went to assist the Order of St John during the siege of Malta, and the volunteers from several nations who fought at Lepanto. They also formed a cultural context for the diplomacy associated with the period's dynastic struggles, such as the famous meeting of Henry VIII and Francis I at the Field of the Cloth of Gold in 1520. But the impact was much less potent than it had been in its fourteenth-century heyday. The fifteenth century was therefore critical in establishing a gulf between enthusiasm for holy war and practical crusading.

Once it had persisted for long enough, this gulf was bound to change the way contemporaries viewed the crusade, and by 1500 such a change is clearly visible. It has been argued that Catholics in the late Middle Ages managed to come to grips with their inability to recover Palestine because the Holy Land itself was losing its centrality in their beliefs. The introduction of 'Stations of the Cross' in the fifteenth century is said to be symptomatic of a return to the symbolic in late medieval spirituality, which made the fate of the Holy Land less important. As Professor Bernard Hamilton has put it, 'Protestant and Catholic attitudes to relics and pilgrimages were . . . mirror images of each other, for both were more concerned with the cultivation of interior piety than with the performance of external acts of devotion.' An alternative, more pragmatic, argument is that the Holy Land ceased to exercise its former appeal because so many of its important relics had been brought to the West. Most spectacularly, the cult of the Holy House of Loreto, which was believed from the late fifteenth century to be the birthplace of the Virgin, miraculously transported to Italy by angels, enabled people to visit one key Palestinian shrine which was still in Christian hands. But these are somewhat tenuous arguments. Pilgrimage to Palestine lost none of its popularity in the late Middle Ages. And the transfer of relics to the West served not as a palliative for territorial losses in the East, but as a constant reminder of the Mamluk and Ottoman advances, and hence of the need to resist them. Pius II used the arrival of St Andrew's head from Greece in 1462 as the occasion for his most flamboyant promotion of the crusade. In any case, the Turkish onrush would not permit Catholics to lose interest in the East, as the East had come to their doorstep: the Holy House of Loreto itself seemed to be in danger when the Turks seized Otranto in 1480.

There is more substance to the view that although the crusade remained an inspirational ideal, commanding consistent interest and respect, it gradually ceased to be associated with military action. Too many people expected failure. In this respect one of the most characteristic features of late medieval crusading was the popularity of conditional vows, representing a transitional phase when noblemen continued to hope, but feared the worst. Even at the peak of Burgundian enthusiasm and commitment during and after the Feast of the Pheasant, it is notable how qualified were the vows made not just by the nobility of Philip the Good's lands in the Low Countries, but by the Duke himself. A corollary of this change was that the great age of crusading was beginning to be viewed as an extraordinary historical phenomenon, a series of marvellous events in the distant past. John Germain, for instance, appealed to Charles VII in 1451 'once again to place in motion the old expeditions overseas which we call "crusades" '. Similarly, as early as 1413 Guillebert of Lannoy referred to 'the time of the *Reisen*', showing his awareness that the practice's heyday was now past. From this point of view, constant references to the crusading achievements of the past by propagandists for crusading might have exercised a counter-productive effect on some of their targets, especially as one dominant *topos* of the period was that such achievements resulted from religious faith, and could therefore not be repeated in an age of decline. As Blaise of Monluc bluntly put it, 'it is no good reopening the conflict for the Holy Land, because we are not as devout as the good folk of former times'.

But the fact that the golden age of crusading was, by about 1450, beginning to be viewed in historical perspective, did not mean that the crusade itself had become history. The Turks saw to that. When the Basle historian John Herold published his account of the crusades, 'De bello sacro', in 1549, he indicated in the full title that he would be pursuing the subject 'up to our own times', and brought his sixth book up to 1521. In this and previous chapters, we have seen that such changes and advances as humanism, the invention of printing, and the Age of Discoveries all affected, and were influenced by, the crusading movement, without destroying it: only the religious revolution could do that. The crusade was carried into the sixteenth century as a factor in people's lives. For some, such as the English and Scots, its relevance was above all aspirational and cultural; but for others, especially those who lived in the Habsburg lands, it remained an issue of living political importance. The most apparent overall feature of the crusade's social impact by 1500 was, however, the disjuncture between the patterns of thought and behaviour which we have examined in this chapter: it was present throughout Catholic Europe to a greater or lesser degree. It was this, above all, which finally eroded enthusiasm, reducing it to sentiment, and finally to nostalgia. Given the nature of military organization in these centuries, the disjuncture can only be explained by reference to the activity (and inactivity) of government. It is, therefore, to Catholic Europe's authorities, ecclesiastical and secular, that we need to turn in order to understand what happened to the crusading movement.

14

Government and the Crusade
1274–1580

✠

'ALL the great expeditions which were made in times past beyond the sea, against the Saracens, were made with the consent of the holy father of Rome; and those who have read the histories of times past well know this.' This statement by the legal commentator Honoré Bonet in his 'The Tree of Battles' (c.1380) reflects the awareness amongst educated people in the late Middle Ages of the pivotal role played by the papal Curia in launching crusades. No crusade had taken place in the past, or could be set in motion in the future, without the clear authorization of the Curia. In the first place, the Curia retained its exclusive authority to grant the necessary indulgences and sanction the preaching of the cross, without which an expedition was not regarded as a crusade at all. Equally importantly, the papacy controlled the purse strings of crusade finance; without access to such funds major expeditions, to the East at least, could not be undertaken. But even apart from these basic functions of definition and financial support, the Curia's assistance was highly desirable in order to facilitate the intensive preliminary work which a crusade called for: the internal political ordering and military preparations, the external peacemaking and search for allies, which underpinned crusading of virtually any kind.

Even had it been possible to strip the Curia of its control over the issuing of crusade indulgences and privileges, and fully to secularize crusade finances, the crusade could not be dissociated from papal authority without effecting a revolution in religious and political thinking; the *negotium Christi* ('Christ's business') was bound to be seen as the peculiar responsibility of his Vicar. In 1462 George of Podiebrady, the heretical King of Bohemia, put forward a boldly innovative proposal for placing the struggle against the Turks in the hands of a 'League of

Princes' representing the chief powers whom they threatened. He was probably influenced by the growing weakness of Christendom's 'universal' authorities, the pope and emperor; this had recently been glaringly manifested at Mantua and a series of abortive *Reichstags*. Podiebrady and his advisers, Martin Mair and Anthony Marie, envisaged an assembly, executive council, and international court, with their own seal, treasury, and archives, and possessing the powers of taxation needed to raise forces with which to defeat the Turks. In accordance with much contemporary practice, Podiebrady suggested that the League's participants be grouped into 'nations', and that the assembly should move between these nations on a five-yearly pattern. The contribution made by the papacy would be limited to such matters as sanctioning clerical taxation and mediating between warring Christian powers which were not members of the League. Pius II was sufficiently alarmed by these proposals to invest renewed vigour in his own crusade activity, but with hindsight it is clear that Podiebrady's ideas were too radical to work. When the Protestant Reformers did successfully challenge the spiritual authority of the papacy, more than half a century later, they all but destroyed the crusade with it.

It is a truism that papal authority over the promulgation of a crusade was both consolidated, in terms of legal and theological ideas, and energetically exercised, by Innocent III (1198–1216). The Pope's major rulings on the crusade, together with the refinements and clarifications introduced by his immediate successors, were repeated for centuries after his death. This was true in the first place of the definitive approach to the crusade indulgence formulated in *Ad liberandam* (1215), and of other aspects of this decree, which were repeated in numerous papal and conciliar documents. But the Curia's response to many other issues found specific formulae, in some cases even a standard form of wording, at this time. For example, letters of absolution for misusing crusade funds, issued by Leo X to Francis I, were virtual duplicates of those granted three centuries earlier. In some cases, including this one, the practice indicates sterility of ideas, the tired resort to standard-form letters in dealing with problems which were simply intractable. At other times, on the contrary, it evidences the soundness with which Innocent handled the theology and practical requirements of crusading. Above all, it shows that in many fields relating to the crusade, including preaching, the securing of peace in Christendom, the financing of crusades and the handling of crusade funds, and diplomatic and economic relations with the Muslim powers, there existed a basic framework of activity which was enduring enough to withstand the convolutions which attended the transformation of Innocent III's papal monarchy into the Renaissance papacy of Pius II, or even the post-Tridentine Curia of Pius V.

But the Curia's possession of ultimate authority in crusading matters did not bring with it substantial power or influence over events. Papal sponsorship helped to invigorate the crusading movement, but it was not crucial to it; and the Curia was far from being able to dominate or direct all crusading efforts. There were popes whose personal interest in the crusade was minimal. The primary concern of Benedict XII (1334–42), for example, was for reform and financial retrenchment, and he was unenthusiastic in his response to the crusade proposals reaching him. Similarly, Nicholas V (1447–55) promoted the crusade mainly because his reign coincided with the final crisis of Byzantium; for all the praise lavished on the Pope by fellow-humanists like Piccolomini, he displayed little of the energy characteristic of other popes of his age, such as Eugenius IV and Calixtus III. Even popes who pursued the crusade with greater enthusiasm generally restricted their interest to the eastern Mediterranean, the Balkans, and Italy. By contrast, papal policy towards the *Reconquista*, and the struggle against Lithuania and Russia, was noticeably passive throughout the fourteenth and fifteenth centuries. The Curia usually displayed interest in these theatres of operation only when developments there impinged on Italy or the East, as when Alexander VI denied assistance to the Livonian branch of the Teutonic Order because he hoped to enlist Muscovite support against the Turks. Initiatives emanating from the Curia were rare, and crusade bulls dispatched to Catholic powers in Iberia and along the Baltic were usually laconic and generalized, and often inaccurate in their content. For example, a bull issued by Clement VI in 1352, in which he granted the Poles a crusade against the Tatars, was a virtual reissue of one dispatched by Benedict XII in 1340. The Curia lacked the detailed knowledge of local circumstances needed to pursue a fully fledged and consistent crusade policy here, even if it had possessed the time to do so, and if the local secular powers had permitted its intervention. Keeping track of developments in the East was hard enough. When, in 1369, Urban V ordered that a register should be compiled of all papal letters relating to eastern affairs dating back to Clement V's reign, he was probably responding to uncertainty at the Curia about its own past policy there.

The Curia's crusading policy in the East was active. If the sources sometimes give the impression that the Curia was only going through the motions of promoting the crusade, more often they portray concern, deliberation, and the conscious implementation of carefully conceived policy. But the failings of the papacy as an institution in the late Middle Ages meant that this policy was often shaped by crude financial considerations, vitiated by the intrusion of political factors relating to western, especially Italian, affairs, and characterized in practice by deception, inconsistency, and weakness. Motives were at best mixed when tenths were levied, and indulgences preached, with the proviso that a fixed proportion of the proceeds would be used for the needs of the Roman church. And they were tainted when the trade embargo on the Mamluk lands developed into a licensing system which benefited, above all, the papal *camera*. As we saw in Chapter 8,[1] money raised exclusively for the funding of a *passagium* to regain the Holy Land, or to hold back the Turks, was repeatedly siphoned off into the Curia's warfare in Italy. Newly elected popes caused confusion and dismay by changing the policies of their predecessors, as when Benedict XII reversed John XXII's generally benevolent attitude towards crusade proposals, and Clement VI in turn brought an end to Benedict's policy of retrenchment. Under Urban V the Curia pursued the incompatible objectives of promoting the crusade against both the Turks and the Mamluks. There was hypocrisy, as when criticisms were levelled against the Hospitallers on the grounds of extravagant living and absenteeism, from a Curia noted for its lavish life-style, which used the Knights of St John to govern its lands in Italy; or when praise was heaped on Scanderbeg for his military feats at the same time that essential funds were denied him.

More importantly, the Curia was constantly hampered in implementing its crusade policy by its own political and military weakness. This took the twofold form of vulnerability to diplomatic pressure exerted by leading secular powers in the West, and the possession of inadequate resources. The early Avignon popes, who were in any case inclined to view French petitions on the crusade with favour, were subject to intimidation, sometimes of the crudest kind, when they found these unacceptable. The pressure exerted on Clement V throughout the Trial of the Templars, particularly at Poitiers in 1308 and Vienne in 1312, was extraordinary; but in 1323 Charles IV executed one of John XXII's Gascon favourites in an attempt to force the Pope to agree to his crusade plans, and in 1335 there occurred an exchange of views on the crusade between Benedict XII and Philip VI's envoy which was so heated that it caused some

---

[1] Above, 262.

months of cold relations between the French and papal courts. It is no longer possible to view the Curia of the fourteenth century as a puppet of the French Crown, but it remains the case that the policies of Clement V and John XXII were thoroughly intertwined with those of the French court. The Curia regained its freedom of action when the Anglo-French war began, and it was not until the accretion of power in the hands of the Emperor Charles V that it faced comparable difficulties. But rulers whose services were indispensable to the Curia, whose lands provided substantial amounts of papal revenue, or who had powerful clients in the College of Cardinals, were still able to distort, manipulate, or frustrate the Curia's crusade policy.

Quite apart from the exertion of pressure, the Curia had to work with Christendom's secular powers in implementing its crusading goals in the East because it lacked the resources to execute almost anything but gestures itself. This was partly, of course, due to the priority invariably accorded to Italian affairs, which soaked up the attention and resources of the Curia like a sponge; but even if this had not been the case, the papacy's finances and, of equal importance, its administrative cadres, would probably have been too limited to permit it to take independent, large-scale action east of Greece. Operational difficulties were immense: when the great Tuscan banking houses collapsed in the mid-1340s, Clement VI had to resort to the Hospitallers to transfer funds for the galleys which he was maintaining in his crusading league in the East. To secure action on any noteworthy scale, the Curia had access to a limited range of options. It summoned councils and congresses to deliberate and agree on joint activity, but these assemblies became steadily less effective, a clear downwards trajectory manifesting itself from Lyons (1274), through Vienne (1311–12), Mantua (1459), and Rome (1490), to the Fifth Lateran Council (1512–17). The popes themselves were bitterly aware of their dwindling ability to arouse and mobilize concern. According to Alexander VI, the rulers of Europe did not even reply to his request for envoys to discuss the Turkish threat in October 1499, and eight years later, when Henry VII suggested that Julius II should convene a congress to debate the crusade, the Pope replied by reminding the King of the pathetic failure of the 1490 congress.

Other options proved to be not much more efficacious. The popes exhorted selected rulers to take action, promising liberal grants of taxes and other privileges if they agreed to do so; and they issued general appeals for action in the hope that individual nobles, cities, and groups of individuals would respond. Above all, the Curia worked with threatened powers to form alliances and leagues, making its own contribution and dispatching legates to provide coherence and encouragement. It was in this respect that the popes were most successful, the achievements of Clement VI, Eugenius IV, Calixtus III, and Pius V being especially notable. But the papacy's contributions to anti-Turkish leagues were throughout plagued by financial problems, management difficulties with its own legates and captains, and concern lest the leagues should be destroyed by the allies' mutual distrust, or by one ally (usually Venice) reaching an independent settlement with the Turks.

It would be misleading to dwell exclusively on deception and weakness; there were solid achievements too. The tradition of naval leagues organized by the papacy was itself a fine one. Similarly, the overall commitment of the papacy between Pius II and Pius V to countering the Turkish advance is striking: even Alexander VI rose above his particularist and dynastic obsessions at times. Doubtless the crusade enthusiasm of some fifteenth-century popes, especially Eugenius IV and Pius II, can be attributed in part to their desire to resist conciliarism by wielding one of the key attributes of papal monarchy. The energy with which other Renaissance popes tried to promote a crusade against the Ottomans can be explained in part by the fact that the Turks threatened Italy, and hence the papacy's temporal power: in this respect they had stepped into the shoes of the Staufen and the Ghibellines. And little can be said on behalf of Julius II, who relegated the anti-Ottoman crusade to the level of propaganda in the struggle for northern Italy, and did nothing to encourage the spontaneous if naïve enthusiasm of rulers like James IV of Scotland and Manuel of Portugal. But the richness of sixteenth-century papal documentation on the subject of the crusade against the Turks, which continued to be a major preoccupation of the Curia throughout the crisis of the Reformation, defies an explanation couched solely in terms of self-interest.

The Curia's crusading policy in the East was probably at its most coherent in the century between Nicopolis and Charles VIII's invasion of Italy (1396–1494). The nature of the enemy, their goals, and the severity of the threat which they posed, had become much clearer than in the second half of the fourteenth century, when a number of Anatolian emirates still jostled for hegemony, let alone the earlier generations, when *Romania* and the Holy Land competed for papal attention. The rulers of the threatened Balkan states, in particular Hungary, provided a reliable nucleus for the formation of crusading alliances. And the Hospitallers at Rhodes were in a somewhat similar position, since they were not only evolving into a front-line force, but were heavily dependent on papal support for the maintenance of their position. The comparative clarity and forceful-ness achieved in these circumstances did not, however, make the Curia's policy any more successful than previously, since the constraints imposed by the papacy's decline as a governmental institution remained as tight as ever. After 1494 the papacy's crusade policy was, for years at a time, almost wholly dominated by its deep involvement in the Franco-Spanish wars in Italy. And new political complications soon arose in the dangerous concentration of power in Habsburg hands, the Valois-Ottoman *entente*, and the onset of the Reformation.

No pope between 1274 and 1580 could wholly ignore the crusade. It was commingled with the Curia's grave responsibility for the plight of the eastern Christians, and later for the defence of Latin Christendom against the Hussites and the Turks; during the thirteenth and fourteenth centuries it was a major weapon in the defence and recovery of temporal power in Italy, and then in the defeat of rivals during the Great Schism; it represented some material advantage, in the shape of the *camera*'s share of crusade funds; and it was a key attribute in the Curia's self-perception, and in its projection of its role. But the political realities of the period inexorably transferred the bulk of crusading organization and imple-mentation into the sphere of secular government. For if the main problem facing the Curia was its inability to translate into action even the more consistent and altruistic facets of its crusading policy because of its political and military weaknesses, the most characteristic feature of secular government in this period was the tremendous growth in its resources, its control over its subjects, and its responsibility for military activity.

It was the second and third of these attributes which most clearly impinged on the crusade. If uncertainty still existed in the late Middle Ages about the precise meaning of such key terms as sovereignty, citizen-ship, and treason, it did not prevent governments in practice both making greater demands, and placing greater constraints, on the actions and resources of their subjects. The dictum 'each king is an emperor in his kingdom' ('rex in regno suo est imperator') well summarized a trend which had massive implications for traditional crusading. By 1335 secular powers of sovereignty were so advanced that Alfonso IV of Aragon was able to assert that despite the pope's possession of *plenitudo potestatis* in crusading affairs, in practice he needed to hold a meeting of secular rulers to gain their approval before launching a general passage. As we have seen, such attitudes were in part responsible for Philip the Fair's assault on the Templars; and they caused continual difficulties for the Hospitallers at Rhodes when the Convent attempted to garner money and supplies from the western priories. Rulers regarded this as the loss of indigenous resources, whether in the form of *specie* or goods, to a body which was not subject to their control and might even assist their Christian enemies.

In the West's advanced monarchies, fighting men could not take part in crusades without securing the permission of their rulers. Failure to secure such licences, together with general vetoes on fighting abroad, and refusals to countenance crusade preaching, form striking testimonies to the ability of the lay powers to cripple any crusade proposal, either by direct mandate or by more subtle methods. Naturally these powers were deployed most forcefully when a government itself had need of its fighting men. Thus in 1345 Clement VI agreed to Philip VI's request that the Smyrna indulgences should not be preached in France because of the Anglo-French conflict, and Alfonso of Portugal informed the Pope that none of his men-at-arms would be allowed to accompany Louis of la Cerda's crusade to the Canaries because they were all needed for the war against Granada. There were gains to be derived from allowing men-at-arms to fight in crusades, chiefly the military experience which they would acquire; but on many occasions these were counterbalanced by the expectation of imminent war at home, the fear of good soldiers being killed while on crusade, or suspicion that a crusade would benefit one's enemies, directly or indirectly.

It was perhaps Christendom's maritime powers, especially Venice, which showed most strikingly how the grip exerted by the lay powers on their subjects could hinder a crusade. This was not only because of their impressive ability to execute policy over fleets and territories scattered throughout the Mediterranean world, but also because their co-operation was crucial for a crusade to the East. Without them no trade embargo could be imposed, no troops or horses transported, no reinforcements hurried out. In 1366, for example, Venice responded furiously to the sack of Alexandria by forbidding the use of its ships to transport men, arms, and supplies to Cyprus, thereby rendering virtually impossible the organization of a 'follow-up' crusade to Peter I's *passagium*. In the fifteenth century the rhythm of the anti-Turkish crusade was all but determined by the state of Venetian relations with the Ottomans. Only when the city was at war with the Turks was a crusade on a large scale a practical possibility. Pius II raged in his *Commentaries* against the ingratitude, greed, and lack of crusading enthusiasm shown by Venice before its own entry into war with the Turks in 1463. But the Republic's approach, although more thinly disguised than that of other powers, was in essence not dissimilar.

The provision of men, equipment and supplies, even shipping, was overshadowed by the raising of money. The papal Curia's attempts to levy taxes, and sell indulgences, on behalf of a crusade venture in which the local ruler was not personally involved, met with the double objection that valuable resources were being exported and sovereignty infringed. Dr Robert Black and Professor Franco Cardini have demonstrated that these arguments played a dominant role in shaping the initially cold response of the Florentine government to Pius II's crusade programme, alongside fears that the Turks would undertake reprisals against the city's burgeoning eastern trade, and that the crusade would benefit Florence's enemy, Venice. Like Venice, Florence made ingenious use of its republican institutions in stalling on the crusade. Decisions on tenths and indulgences, it claimed, had to await the deliberations of several councils; and Cosimo Medici remarked that, as a private citizen in a free republic, there was nothing he could do to help things along. The Republic eventually allowed both preaching and taxation to take place within its territory, partly because of the pro-crusade lobby at Florence itself, and because it wanted to preserve Florence's reputation as a loyal Catholic city; but also because the *reggimento* calculated the political damage which it would incur by displeasing the Pope to be greater than the money lost by the city. Other crusade measures were taken, including the provision of three galleys, to be rowed by prisoners released from the city's prison. But it is noticeable that the proceeds of the taxes were to be used to pay the costs of a Florentine force of 1,000 horse and 500 foot, to serve for six months: thus the Republic was not ready simply to surrender the revenues raised. The example of Florence shows the wide spectrum of considerations which together forged the attitude taken by governments towards crusade proposals which they had not initiated. Florence, which was not a major European power and needed to remain on good terms with the Pope for reasons of Italian politics, was in a more vulnerable position than the West's emerging national kingdoms. But it is clear that the sensibilities of the Republic's rulers on the issues of sovereignty and the export of indigenous resources were fully as acute as those of any other power.

The natural corollary of these constraints was that lay rulers who did initiate proposals, and who committed themselves to leading crusades, gathered into their own hands virtually all the features of their military organization. The growth of governmental control over warfare, at least in advanced states, was, in Dr Christopher Allmand's words, 'one of the most striking developments in late medieval European society'. Chivalry itself was becoming, to quote Allmand again, 'life in the public service under the ruler's direction'. Inevitably the organization of crusading was included in the general trend, although historians of the movement have been surprisingly slow to recognize the fact and follow through its consequences. Let us take first the fundamental question of recruitment. By 1274 there was already in progress, throughout western Europe, an irreversible movement towards paid service. Sometimes this took the form of hired mercenaries (*stipendiarii*), who could be natives or foreigners; more often it meant that men with some form of legal obligation to serve, whether as vassals, subjects, or citizens, were rewarded according to established scales of payment. The object of the exercise was rarely to provide an exclusive reward for fighting, as wage rates tended to be low and were sometimes static for decades; they were probably less important as an inducement than was the expectation of booty, ransoms, prestige, and office. Rather, wages regulated service and made troops more willing to fight, and to remain in the field.

At the same time contractual service was increasing. Again, it was sometimes used as a means of raising troops, as in northern Italy, where the word *condotta* (contract) gave rise to the name *condottieri* for professional captains, who hired out the services of themselves and their men to the region's republics and despots. But in other instances, and perhaps more frequently, it was employed for reasons of administrative efficiency. In the case of England, for example, 'indentures' were first used to raise a whole army in 1337, when the King was not himself present, and the staff of his Wardrobe were therefore not available to handle payments to soldiers in the field. They were subsequently used on a large scale, though not invariably, during the Anglo-French war. In 1381, for example, Thomas Felton agreed to serve in Brittany for six months with 500 men-at-arms and 500 archers: he raised the troops through sub-contracts, of which fifteen survive, relating to 178 men-at-arms and 181 archers. In France the pressures of the Anglo-French war led the Valois monarchy to move from a clumsy combination of feudal service, conjoined with the use of the *arrière-ban* (the general obligation of all free adult males to serve), towards the issuing of 'lettres de retenue' which obligated captains to maintain troops in royal service for a specified period of time. By 1374 the practice was so advanced that Charles V issued an important ordinance which attempted to remedy its abuses by instituting regular inspections and formalizing payment procedures. The *condotta*, indenture, and 'lettre de retenue' were trend-setters, but all western European states were moving in the same direction.

Slowly and hesitantly, late medieval governments therefore tightened their grip on the process of military recruitment. The crusade mirrored secular warfare, with the same wide variations according to area. As Simon Lloyd has shown, England's precocity in the sphere of contractual service meant that the contract already served as one of the two main cohesive instruments of the Lord Edward's crusade of 1270. Indeed, since Edward was himself contractually bound to serve Louis IX, this crusade 'provides us with the fullest picture of a *passagium generale* structured throughout by means of contracts'. The other cohesive instrument was the extended households of Edward himself and the magnate *crucesignati* in his army. These households congealed on the basis of existing ties of kinship, neighbourhood, feudal obligation, and friendship; and they took shape so readily once the magnates had committed themselves to the crusade that, in Dr Lloyd's words, 'recruitment of participants looked after itself once the services of the great were secured'. So strong were the loyalties forged by such arrangements that Edward, like Henry IV later, could rely on the support of his old comrades-in-arms when he became king. One strength of the indenture system was its flexibility. Some indentures, like those between Earl Humphrey VIII of Hereford and Bartholomew of Enfield in 1306, and the Earl of Pembroke and John Darcy in 1310, envisaged the possibility of service in the Holy Land should the lord take part in a *passagium*; while others specifically excluded service on crusade.

France was less advanced in its recruitment practices, but the arrangements made or proposed for French crusade projects in the 1320s and 1330s included contractual service by at least a proportion of *crucesignati*, and payment of all who served. For example, in the scale drawn up for his *passagium generale* in August 1335, Philip VI promised twenty shillings a day for bannerets, ten shillings for knights, and five shillings for squires. The salary scales were of Burgundy's projected crusade: twenty crowns a month for each lance (i.e. fighting unit) from Burgundy, and fifteen for each from Picardy. The French kings and Philip the Good set great store by the crusade commitment of their higher nobility not only to secure a peaceful situation at home during their absence in the East, but also because they relied on the active co-operation of these individuals in recruiting for the *passagium* itself, by some combination of paid service, contract, and extended household. This was one reason for launching their projects in the full blaze of publicity, exemplified by the Feast of the Pheasant.

It was not only the recruitment of the great *passagia* to the East which was shaped by the movement towards paid, and often contractual, service. Papal legates like Bertrand du Poujet and Gil Albornoz raised forces for crusading in Italy by payments, which were duly written up in the account books of the *camera*, and Bishop Despenser used the indenture system to recruit for his Flanders crusade in 1383. It has been shown that English participants in the *Reisen* displayed a growing tendency, as the fourteenth century progressed, to join the retinues of magnates, who would pay their expenses, protect them, and increase the chance of their seeing action through the influence which they could exercise on the Teutonic Order. Peter I of Cyprus paid mercenaries to fight in his crusade of 1365, and Amedeo of Savoy's expedition took the form of an 'extended household' crusade. It is striking that although both Peter and Amedeo founded secular Orders of chivalry, and Peter specifically associated his with his crusading plans, neither ruler tried to use his Order as the organizational vehicle for his *passagium*. They knew that stronger and more proven techniques were needed, not least because the crusading recruits themselves would expect them. As Philip of Mézières perceptively put it at the end of the fourteenth century,

Any worthy knight who is bound for Outremer will want to know, firstly, how he will be sustained with food and drink and in the natural needs of the body; secondly, how he shall be supported with clothing, armour and horses to defend himself and to fight the enemies of the faith; thirdly, he will wish to be assured that in fighting for the faith he will be able to acquire just riches and true honour.[2]

One reason why recruitment was more closely organized was that it was becoming more specialized. During Edward III's war in France each of his units of 100 Welsh archers had its own chaplain, interpreter,

    [2] M. Keen, 'War, Peace and Chivalry', in B. P. McGuire (ed.), *War and Peace in the Middle Ages* (Copenhagen, 1987), 108.

standard-bearer, crier, and doctor. This was unusually advanced, but the technical innovations of warfare in the fourteenth and fifteenth centuries, especially the grouping of cavalry into lances, the increasing use of gunpowder weapons, more refined siege apparatus, and the re-emergence of infantry as a specialized combat arm, did accelerate the trend. The implications of this for the crusade were profound; and the much greater attention paid to naval warfare was bound to influence the planning of crusades to the East. By the mid-fifteenth century it was taken for granted that the personnel, both military and auxiliary, in a crusading army, would be highly specialized; and for budgeting reasons it was necessary to know how many of each category of fighter, sailor, or support personnel would be hired. A memorandum produced for Philip the Good's crusade in the mid-1450s was typical of many such projects in breaking down the proposed army into its constituent units. It was suggested that 400 lances would be recruited in Picardy and 300 in Burgundy. Each of the former would comprise a man-at-arms, a fighting valet, and a page (whose job was to mind the horses), while the latter included these three plus a crossbowman. Since the lances from Picardy lacked defensive cover, each lance would be accompanied by ten archers. In addition there would be 100 cannoneers and culverineers, 100 masons and smiths, 100 gunners, bowyers, fletchers, and crossbow-makers, and 300 pioneers and miners. As these 600 auxiliaries were expected to fight if needed, the army was to comprise 7,000 hired men, of whom 6,300 were combatants. The degree of specialization envisaged by these Burgundian administrators was striking, but it was exceeded by the exhaustive list of professionals whom Stephen Taleazzi regarded as necessary for a crusade in 1500: these included twenty *magistri*, together with their workers, to make lances and arrows, thirty doctors and surgeons, twenty tailors, and a contingent of 100 washerwomen.

So pronounced was this movement towards specialization that it found an echo in the period's crusade bulls, which in other respects remained very conservative in their format. Thus in his crusade bull of 1482 for the Granada war, Sixtus IV included amongst the beneficiaries of the indulgence

all doctors, apothecaries, surgeons, artisans, cobblers, butchers, workers in iron and wood, carpenters, those in charge of machinery and engaged on any kind of useful construction in the camps, suppliers and retailers bringing medicine, food and other necessary goods to the front line, or organizing and assisting in the supply system by help, advice or favour, those guiding the religious observances of the soldiers in camp or anywhere else, so that they fight more willingly, preachers of the word of God who publish these letters and indulgences and preach before the people, those who celebrate masses and the other divine offices in the army and hear the confessions of those present, and all others of whatever profession, trade, or occupation who remain there for at least three months, including women who tend the sick and wounded both in the army and elsewhere.[3]

It is probable that the Pope envisaged the indulgence in these instances as a bonus, rather than as the basic incentive to enlist; for as we saw in the previous chapter,[4] by this point crusade bulls were used to finance armies rather than recruit them. Indeed, the greatest indication of how far the crusade moved in the direction of military professionalism is the Spanish reaction to Pius V's attempt, at the end of 1568, to turn back the clock on the *cruzada* and restrict the availability of the indulgence to the terms decreed at the Fourth Lateran Council. The idea that the Duke of Alba's *tercios*, the best trained and most experienced soldiers in Europe, should be joined by crusading volunteers was greeted with alarm in Spain. 'As for the reference to somebody going in person: such an individual, neither skilled in military discipline nor selected by the captains, and therefore not subject to them, will be of no use at all. In fact those who know about these matters are convinced that this concession carries absolutely no value.'

'And so apart from the *crucesignati* who come because of their devotion, what we require is an army possessing solid strength, monetary sinews, authority, and confidence in victory.' Taleazzi's vision of an efficient, professional crusade was shared by nearly all the crusade theorists of the fourteenth and fifteenth centuries, notably Peter Dubois and Marino Sanudo. The theorists realized that recruitment was only the beginning of an arduous and continual process of maintenance and control; the larger the *passagium*, the greater the care needed in supplying, transporting, and directing the troops. It cannot be said that such organization was achieved. The Curia's policy of restricting personal participation appeared to make it viable, in so far as the promoters of a crusade could accept only those whom they wanted to serve, though even this was easier in theory than in practice. But military organization generally, even in the early sixteenth century, remained backward: payments and contracts by themselves were not enough. It is not

---

[3] J. Goñi Gaztambide, *Historia de la Bula de la cruzada en España* (Vitoria, 1958), 658–9.
[4] Above, 403–7.

surprising that the conglomerate armies which characterized combined crusading efforts in the fourteenth and fifteenth centuries, such as the Nicopolis and Varna campaigns, and the Hussite wars, were poorly disciplined, inadequately supplied, and prone to disobedience. In the case of the latter, the contrast between the ramshackle and dispirited performance of the German crusading forces and the efficiency of the Hussites led to attempts to imitate the ordered ways of the enemy: an imperial ordinance of 1431 prescribed that four or five priests should accompany each unit 'in order to preach to the people and teach them how to behave themselves and how to fight for the holy faith'. But even the comparatively refined forces which won Granada for the Catholic Monarchs lacked the efficiency which the Military Revolution of the Early Modern period would bring about. The future of course lay with standing armies akin to the Ottoman *kapi-kulus*. France, Burgundy, and Castile had all experienced standing armies by 1500, but they were on a small scale, provoked bitter resentment, and were not much more effective in practice than their *ad hoc* contemporaries.

Crusading forces, like all armies in the later Middle Ages, thus experienced fundamental changes in the way they were recruited, without undergoing advances, at least to the same degree, in the cognate spheres of discipline, control, and efficiency. The complicated strategic formulae nurtured by advocates of the Latin-Mongol alliance, and later by theorists like Philip of Mézières, who envisaged four great armies linking up after making their ways separately to the East, were sadly out of tune with reality. The Anglo-French war showed that it was difficult enough to coordinate the movements of two English armies in France. The realization of most planned *passagia* hinged on massive reforms in the military practices of the day, and eminently desirable as these were seen to be, they were not attainable. The truly streamlined crusade therefore remained a day-dream, as Philip of Mézières acknowledged in the title of his most substantial and ambitious tract: 'The Dream of the Old Pilgrim'.

Crusading not only became more difficult to organize: it also became much more expensive. Since the eleventh century, one of the key spurs to the growing fiscal demands of European governments had been the increasing cost of warfare. The pattern continued into, and beyond, the late Middle Ages. The extra financial burden imposed by the movement towards paid service was aggravated by the cost of such new technology as plate mail, which transformed warfare in the fourteenth century, and artillery, which did much the same in the fifteenth. By 1500 the French royal artillery numbered 149 pieces and needed hundreds of men and 2,250 horses to service it. The diversified role of naval warfare, and the constant salary and maintenance bills of fortress garrisons, added to the burden. Edward III needed 750 vessels to transport his army to France in 1346, while the cost of guarding France's land frontier was 57,000 *livres* a month in 1339. In the later fifteenth century armed forces began to grow in size and to remain in the field longer. As John of Bueil, a veteran of the Hundred Years War, remarked of the French army which assembled to resist the Burgundian invasion in 1471, 'war has become very different. In those days when you had eight or ten thousand men, you reckoned that you had a very large army: today it is quite another matter.'

England has received much attention, in the context of its prolonged wars with Scotland and France, and may be cited briefly as a convenient example of rising costs. By the accession of Edward I in 1271 obligatory vassalic service (*servitium debitum*) had shrunk so much that it ceased to provide more than a small proportion of the troops and money needed. In 1277, when Edward issued his first feudal summons, it raised only 228 knights and 294 sergeants; twenty-three years later a knight banneret who was serving the King for pay was able to discharge his *servitium debitum* by sending one sergeant for eight days. Similarly, the 1277 summons was worth just £1,500 to Edward, who was to spend one hundred times that sum each year in campaigns against Philip the Fair between 1294 and 1298. From this point onwards financial constraints became a key factor in determining the nature and course of the struggle with France. Edward III's campaigns of 1344-7 provoked expenditure of over £242,000 for the Wardrobe alone. When, following the treaty of Troyes in 1420, the English had to garrison Normandy, the financial strain became all but intolerable.

Growing costs undoubtedly affected crusades to a degree which, as in the case of recruitment, paralleled secular warfare. Whether payment was made in order to enlist fighters, or to establish control over *crucesignati*, wage bills existed in the case of virtually all crusades; and there were of course the additional expenses of planning, diplomacy, transportation, and provisioning. Almost a quarter of the French Crown's outlay on the Aragonese crusade of 1285 was spent on naval forces, and a century later Philip of Mézières argued that armed galleys had become prohibitively expensive, and that armies going to the East should be transported on other types of vessel. As a series of Avignonese popes remarked, after

1291 the planners of recovery *passagia* in particular faced heavier costs than the leaders of previous crusades to the Holy Land, because they had to gain an initial footing in Palestine. The securing of crusade status for a war did not normally make it any cheaper: if anything there were significant extra expenses involved, notably in the payments and hand-outs needed to secure the granting and efficient promulgation of crusade privileges. The financial benefit derived rather from the extra funds which were released. Rising costs were constantly referred to in negotiations about the crusade between secular rulers and the Curia; and while these comments were all too often vague and exaggerated, and always contained an element of special pleading, there is no reason to doubt that a serious problem lay behind them.

Medieval methods of accounting were so haphazard that it is very hard to quantify the problem of rising costs; but a reasonable impression can sometimes be gained from the attempts which were made to budget for proposed expeditions. Marino Sanudo Torsello provided detailed costings of his proposed, three-stage crusade in his 'Liber secretorum fidelium crucis' (1306–21). This resulted in figures of 102,000 florins a year for the preliminary blockade of Egypt, over two million florins for the *passagium particulare* which would effect a landing there, and two million florins a year for the culminating general passage. Characteristically, 70 per cent of the cost of the *passagium particulare* covered wages; and it is notable that although the Venetian's estimate for horses needed was remarkably small, the cost of forage was put at 4,800 florins a year, or two-thirds of the wages for the crew of a galley. After reviewing Marino Sanudo's intended expenditures, Franco Cardini raised the figures for both of the major *passagia* to three million florins each. As Cardini put it, 'Sanudo's tract, which was written as a guide to the crusade, in which the logistical and military imponderables would be minimized, becomes for us, simply because of its precision, a detailed analysis of exactly why a crusade of this type could never reach the point of organization.' At about the same time that Marino Sanudo wrote, Charles IV estimated the annual cost of his proposed *passagium particulare* as 1,600,000 *livres* of Tours. This was a considerably greater sum than Marino Sanudo's, and the papal Curia scaled down the King's figures to 1,200,000 *livres*. But both French and papal estimates were alarmingly high when compared with the 1,500,000 *livres* which had constituted the entire royal outlay for Louis IX's first crusade, an expedition which had lasted six years, and had been remarkable, in its day, for the meticulous preparation and organization involved.

The situation did not improve. Confronted by the growth of Ottoman military resources, most fifteenth-century planners conceived their projects on a vast and inflationary scale, in terms both of the numbers of troops and of the finance needed to support them. A constant theme was that the effort made had to be both enormous and sustained, or it would be pointless: a fair but discouraging observation. Pius II concluded that 88,000 men would take part in the crusade which was resolved on at Mantua in 1459. Innocent VIII, at the Congress of Rome in 1490, suggested 95,000 men, and Taleazzi, in 1500, reckoned on an army 130,000-strong, and a fleet of 300 vessels. At a time when military costs were rising anyway, these figures were bound to produce financial estimates as daunting as in Marino Sanudo's day, or more so. Pius II referred somewhat conservatively to the need for a million ducats a year, while Taleazzi estimated the initial cost as three million ducats, and in 1517 a working-party of cardinals appointed by Leo X put the cost of its proposals at eight million ducats. Of course these estimates related to projects which never materialized, so it is impossible to gauge whether the figures were exaggerated; but the costs incurred by the Catholic Monarchs in conquering Granada between 1482 and 1492, and by the participants in the Holy League of 1571–3, show how appallingly expensive crusading had become. As Thomas Fuller put it in 1639 in the first widely read history of the crusades, 'this warre was a quicksand to swallow treasure'.

In the case of secular wars, such developments compelled governments radically to advance their powers of taxation. In general they concentrated on indirect taxation (levies on goods and services), which was easier to adjust and collect than direct taxation on property or income. Historians have long perceived how heavy such taxation became, especially for those social groups which bore the brunt of it. In England, for example, Professor Michael Prestwich has shown that between 1294 and 1298 lay taxation absorbed about 20 per cent of the country's currency; it severely dislocated the market economy in many localities by denuding them of the *specie* necessary for normal commercial transactions. Similarly, a subsidy levied in Normandy in 1347–8 took the equivalent of a month's paid work from agricultural workers. Yet the situation subsequently became worse in both England and France. Public taxes, 'the people's blood' as John Juvenal des Ursins termed them, proved to be one of the most abiding legacies of the Anglo-French conflict. Just as important was the impact which they made on economic and political life in all major western states. Everywhere the collection and handling of taxes was the dynamo behind administrative expansion. In Valois France, for example, it led to the creation of the 'trésorier des guerres', the 'cour des aides', and the *élus* (district tax assessors). In some countries, such as England, the right to grant or refuse taxes proved to be a key feature in the success of representative bodies; while in others, like France, the power to tax was an instrument for the erosion of regional autonomy by centralizing governments.

Governments in our period were thus able to continue conducting large-scale warfare against their Christian neighbours because of their extraordinary exertions in the sphere of public finance. What occurred in the case of crusading? To answer this question we need to examine the chief sources of funding available for crusades. Naturally when a ruler decided to undertake a crusade money was found in a variety of ways; some of these, notably levies on Jewish communities, were connected, at least in the minds of contemporaries, with the cause being undertaken, while others, such as household and administrative economies, had little or no specific linkage with the crusade. Situations differed, but there were three major sources of funding which were specifically linked to crusading, and which were tapped in the case of nearly all projected or actual crusades. The first was the clerical tenth. It originated in the package of measures initiated by Pope Innocent III to facilitate the funding of crusades in the early thirteenth century. The tenth rapidly became the corner-stone of crusade finance; without it leaders like Louis IX would have found it impossible to organize major *passagia*. Equally rapidly, the Curia acknowledged the tenth's importance by directing collected funds into the hands of those who were shouldering the burdens of organization, leadership, and hence payment. Rulers liked the tenth because they knew from past experience how much they could expect to derive from it. There was the additional advantage that the crusade tenth could be imposed by the pope without seeking the consent of the clergy; their opposition could be overridden, and their resentment would be directed against the Curia rather than against the local lay power. The Curia accepted that the crusade was 'a matter of the Church' (*negotium ecclesiae*), and that it should be financed in large measure by the Church: 'he who serves the altar is entitled to live of the altar'. The popes were realistic enough to accept that without the guarantee of a sizeable tenth, no prince would undertake the commitment of crusading, and in the fourteenth century they were the more inclined to be generous in their grants since they adopted the practice of reserving a proportion of the collected money for their own needs.

The granting of a clerical tenth in their lands, and equally importantly, the terms under which it was to be levied, therefore became the single most important aspect of negotiations over proposed crusades between rulers and the Curia. Almost all the crusades documented in preceding chapters were underpinned by tenths, and most of these involved discussions which were invariably complex, often prolonged, and some-times acrimonious. Rulers naturally pressed for tenths granted over as many years as possible. They wanted up-to-date valuations, double tenths, the taxation of groups of clerics who were normally exempt (certain religious Orders and those seculars holding poor benefices), and the proceeds of tenths levied on previous occasions, which still existed in storage. They sought permission for their own officials to intervene in the process of collection to speed it up, and for the proceeds to be assigned to them as soon as they were assembled. Above all, they asked that tenths should be levied on their behalf in neighbouring states. For its part, the Curia attempted generally to place limits on the fiscal burden which would be faced by clerics, to retain the control exerted by the Church over the collection and storage of funds, and to secure the firmest possible guarantees against the funds being misused. It recognized that burgeoning attitudes towards sovereignty rendered the imposition of tenths in other states virtually impossible, unless strong political or dynastic ties existed between the two rulers involved, and it was unwilling to suffer the predictable rebuff.

From these conflicting, ultimately irreconcilable, positions innumerable compromises emerged. Each resulted from the particular circumstances of the day, but overall they clearly reflected the deteriorating position of the Curia when faced by the secular powers. The latter continued to accept that they must secure papal permission to levy crusade tenths. As late as the 1550s the Spanish clergy mounted the fiercest resistance when the government tried to deny this, less because of reverence for papal authority than because they knew that the need for papal sanction was the only thing keeping the government's rapacious demands in check. How-ever, the sheer pressure which governments were able to apply meant that in practice they could depend on solid and prolonged financial backing for any crusading project from the clergy within their lands. This victory carried an inevitable price in the loss of support from outside those lands, for the clergy in other countries would not be able to contribute against the wishes of their rulers. The fate of the Vienne tenth (1313–19), the last crusade tax which was levied and collected throughout Christendom, is illuminating in this respect. The proceeds were either taken over completely by the local lay power, divided between the secular authorities and the papacy, or used by the latter to fight its wars in Italy. After Vienne the assembly of a mass of money to pay the expenses of princes engaged on a *passagium generale* was inconceivable. Crusade finance had become fragmented in accordance with Christendom's political boundaries. As John XXII put it in 1325, 'we have been accustomed to grant no king a subsidy outside his own kingdom'.

This fragmentation aggravated the yawning gap which had opened up by the early fourteenth century between the expenses of crusading and the proceeds of the tenth. To some extent this resulted from the inbuilt deficiencies of the tenth itself, and of the machinery used in its collection. Like any direct tax, the value of the tenth hinged on the valuation employed; this needed regular revision to deal with inflation and economic trends generally, but new valuations were expensive and time-consuming. Collection itself was painfully slow and costly. In the case of the Castilian tenth of 1309–12, which has received close attention from Dr Peter Linehan, salaries and expenses absorbed 38 per cent of the revenue collected. This was exceptional, but the norm may not have been much less. Some collectors proved negligent or corrupt, although this did not become as serious a problem as in the case of preachers of indulgences. The main problem, however, was that the value of the tenth remained almost stagnant at a time of soaring costs. The French church, whose tenth was worth about 250,000 *livres* of Tours a year, paid two-thirds of the costs of Louis IX's first crusade in the form of a five-year tenth. Decades later, when Philip IV and his successors negotiated with the Curia, each year's tenth would pay only a fifth or a sixth of the annual cost of a *passagium particulare*. The situation was similar in contemporary Aragon, where the tenth was worth 20,000 pounds of Barcelona a year under the existing valuation. In 1332 Alfonso IV claimed that a three-year tenth would not even pay for three months' fighting.

To deal with the difficulty of the tenth's declining usefulness, both the Curia and secular powers with declared crusading intentions tried to extract money from the Church in a variety of ingenious ways. The tenth itself became virtually an annual levy, as at Venice in the sixteenth century, by which time the annual receipts of about 100,000 ducats were almost negligible in the context of the Republic's military expenditure.

Tenths were converted into fifths, thirds, or even halves; the proceeds of other benefice taxes, annates and intercalary fruits, were sometimes petitioned for and granted; and 'subsidies', grants 'voluntarily' made by individual clerics or by regional assemblies, were collected. As we saw in Chapter 9,[5] in Castile a third of church tithes (the *tercias reales*) was often granted to the kings alongside tenths, in accordance with a practice established in the time of Ferdinand III. But the general problem remained that the Church could no longer finance crusades by itself. The laity must be induced to make a bigger financial contribution.

Legacies, the proceeds of ill-gotten gains, and oblations formed continuous categories of crusade revenue from the thirteenth century onwards; as we noted in the previous chapter, they can rarely be quantified, and they were certainly inadequate as a major source of revenue. The proceeds of indulgences, first in the form of vow redemption payments and later in that of sold indulgences, were undoubtedly more substantial, and represent the second main source of crusade funding. Remy indeed concluded that indulgences sold in the Low Countries formed 'one of the main means by which the Turkish war was financed'. But, with the exception of preaching in Spain, where proceeds were steady enough for a system of *cruzada* farming to be implemented, indulgences were unreliable: governments did not regard it as viable to plan and finance military operations on the basis of revenues which were merely hoped for. Experience taught that if some preaching campaigns produced spectacular amounts, others scarcely met their costs. Besides, too much money was lost in practice through the compromises and deals needed to get the indulgences preached, and there were heavy losses because of the corruption of the *quaestores*. Secular powers certainly took care to petition for the preaching of indulgences, and they paid considerable attention to the precise terms on which they were offered. In 1309, for example, James II of Aragon asked Clement V to extend to his crusade against Granada the particularly liberal indulgences which the Pope had granted to the Hospitallers for their *passagium*; and a decade later Louis of Clermont also petitioned for the indulgences which the Hospitallers had enjoyed. Potentially at least, indulgences were too valuable a source of revenue to be neglected. But they could not replace the tenth as the corner-stone of crusade funding, or, even in association with the tenth, meet military needs.

The third main source of funding, lay taxation, was the most problematic one. The need for lay taxation was noted in nearly all crusade proposals, especially those put forward after about 1450, when the inadequacy of Church revenues was fully registered. It was usually suggested in the form of a percentage of income or property similar to, but less onerous than, the clerical tenth. For example, Podiebrady's proposal for a 'League of Princes' in 1462 specified the payment by all laymen of three days' income each year, and Innocent VIII spoke of the need for lay taxation at the Congress of Rome in 1490. Taleazzi took such taxation for granted in 1500, and the cardinals' memorandum of 1517 considered that nobles should pay a tenth, and other laymen a twentieth. However, such taxes signally failed to become the rule in the late Middle Ages. Gregory X attempted to impose a poll tax of one silver penny a year at the Second Council of Lyons in 1274, and at the Congress of Mantua Pius II proposed a lay thirtieth, payment of which would be rewarded by the grant of indulgences. But Gregory's tax was never imposed, and attempts to levy Pius's thirtieth met with failure even when, as at Bologna, refusal to pay was punished by withholding the sacraments. Burgundian negotiators in 1459 described Pius's thirtieth as 'a very new idea' and doubted its viability from the start.

Such failures, of course, reflected the decline of papal authority. But although secular rulers enjoyed more success in securing lay taxes for their crusading plans, even they found this to be one of the most problematic features of crusade organization. Philip V and Philip VI of France encountered massive resistance when they tried to impose taxes on the laity for their crusade projects, and fifteenth-century *Reichstags* proved notoriously reluctant to vote funds for crusading against the Turks and Hussites. The laity might pay taxes for crusading which involved the classic and acceptable tax justification of 'the defence of the realm' (*defensio regni*), as in the Spanish kingdoms, Poland, and Hungary. Elsewhere resistance proved too great, except in the states of Burgundy. Here arduous negotiations in 1394–5 and 1454–5 did bring in substantial sums of money for the organization of the Nicopolis crusade and the planned crusade of Philip the Good. In the case of Nicopolis, it appears that some 240,000 francs were raised from Flanders, Burgundy, and the other territories under Philip the Bold's rule, out of an estimated total of 520,000 francs available for the expedition. The importance of such *aides* to Burgundian planning is made clear by a comment, in a memorandum written for Philip the Good, that the recruitment of troops would have to await the Duke's decision, which hinged on the grant of *aides*.

There are a number of explanations why lay taxation for crusading proved generally unacceptable. First, lay taxation had become associated with the public community, and the crusade lacked the all-encompassing relevance to that community which would have made taxation viable. Secondly, even if a ruler was committed to the crusade, and the prestige of Crown and dynasty was therefore seen to be involved, there remained the resentment which greeted the levy of any tax; and this was the greater since, as we have seen, taxation for warfare at home accelerated tremendously in this period. Thirdly, and most importantly, attempts to tax for the crusade were viewed in the light of the many disappointments of the past. If crusade preaching increasingly met with suspicion, all the more so attempts to impose obligatory taxes, which were more open to the construction that crusading plans were merely serving as a pretext. A Bolognese chronicler wrote of Pius II (in this instance unjustly) that 'the Pope said that he wanted such payments [the lay thirtieth] to make war on the Turks, and this was not the truth, because he did otherwise. It was sheer robbery'. It was no coincidence that the response of some French towns to attempts to levy lay taxes for crusading was a canny offer of personal service once the *passagium* materialized, a ploy also employed by Castile's high nobility in 1527 when Charles V requested funds for a crusade. And it is striking that Burgundy, whose Valois dukes had a relatively clean record on the crusade, proved to be the only major state which accepted the practice of lay taxes. Lay taxation for crusading thus foundered on the same rock of disillusionment as the Church's attempt to channel enthusiasm into the sale of indulgences, though it usually foundered earlier and more emphatically. The results were disastrous: without a sound financial underpinning of the type which had become commonplace in the case of other wars, crusades became increasingly difficult to undertake.

It would be simplistic to claim that every crusade project which failed in the late Middle Ages did so solely because its secular planners realized and shunned the immense problems of finance involved. Other difficulties contributed their share, notably of course the crippling effects of rivalry and warfare in the West, which time and again brought about the postponement of projects. It has been pointed out that in the fourteenth and fifteenth centuries crusading was only possible during the interstices of Christendom's endemic 'civil wars'. Particularly problematic were the conflicting dynastic, jurisdictional, and territorial claims which bedevilled relations between such powers as France and England, Castile and Aragon, Poland and the Prussian *Ordensstaat*, Visconti Milan and the papacy: such issues were exceptionally complicated, and it is facile to assert that solutions could have been found had the will been there. But it is arguable that the central problem of war finance, within the context of the fundamental changes in military recruitment and techniques outlined earlier, constituted the greatest obstacle both to the realization of recovery projects in the period 1274–1336, and to the plans for defensive *passagia* against the Ottomans in the fifteenth century. The obstacle might prove destructive to planning at an early stage, during negotiations with the Curia, or later, when the protracted timetable required to gather in the financial resources allowed war to break out between Christian states; or it might come into play on the virtual eve of departure, when a realization of the problems still to be surmounted, combined with the temptation offered by the sums collected, proved too much.

As the last point suggests, the issue of sincerity is inseparably bound up with that of finance. It has sometimes been argued that in many or most cases of abandoned crusades, the projects were put forward with the sole intention of persuading the Curia to turn on the tap of crusade revenues. Such a viewpoint cannot of course be backed up directly by evidence—no ruler was likely to state in writing that he was practising deception—but it has a great deal of circumstantial evidence in its favour and demands consideration here. The issue is similar to the problem of the French government's motives in instigating the suppression of the Templars. Funds raised were certainly sequestered by the lay powers involved with great regularity, and at times they proved suspiciously handy for the realization of secular ambitions. The loss of the tenths levied throughout Christendom at Lyons in 1274 and Vienne in 1312 formed the most spectacular examples of funds being misused, but a catalogue of all funds which were diverted would be an extremely long one. Indeed, the seizure of crusade money by lay powers was on a greater scale than in the case of the papacy's diversion of funds for its Italian wars. There was, too, a whole history of diverted crusading fleets: from the galleys assembled by Philip VI for his *passagium generale*, which were moved from the Mediterranean to the Channel to engage the English in 1336, through John of Anjou's deployment of a squadron raised to fight the Turks in his attempt to conquer the *Regno* after the Congress at Mantua, to the diversions practised by Ferdinand of Aragon and Francis I of France.

The most elaborately phrased guarantees and solemnly sworn oaths failed to halt this inexorable process of diversion. Collected funds were sometimes centralized, and at others decentralized, in an attempt to provide security, but neither approach succeeded. Bishops and lay notables were ineffective guardians because they did not dare to stand in the way of their secular lords; while the transfer of collected money to the papal Curia only exposed it to the temptation which the papacy faced. Caught between the Scylla of secular confiscation and the Charybdis of papal diversion, there was simply no workable mechanism for keeping crusade resources intact. The popular disillusionment provoked by this amongst contemporaries was severe; expressions of discontent were as strongly put as in the parallel case of indulgences, examined in the previous chapter. There is no doubt that many people became openly cynical about the motives of their rulers. But this does not mean that they were right. For the issue of sincerity is far from being a black and white one: as a number of recent case studies for the late thirteenth and fourteenth centuries have amply shown, few if any rulers can be dealt with in simple terms.

It is useful to distinguish between the various political positions of rulers with stated crusading goals. At one end of the spectrum are those individuals who made fairly generalized statements of their crusade zeal, either in the form of a propaganda riposte to an enemy who himself emphasized the crusade, or in that of an essentially gestural response to papal or legatine appeals. The Declaration of Arbroath by Scotland's nobles in 1320, and the constant asseverations of crusading zeal by Edward III during the early phase of the Hundred Years War, may be cited as examples of the former: Pope Clement VI became so irritated by what he construed as Edward's rank hypocrisy, that he warned the King of the spiritual harm which he would incur by it. Similarly, the crusade enthusiasm expressed early in his reign by Henry VIII was typical of the empty offers which many of Europe's rulers became adept at making. The artificiality of the fervour expressed in such cases can be gauged from the fact that there was little or no follow-up in practical terms. If such individuals were pressed, they took refuge in the stance that they would take part once a crusade was planned, leaving the initiative to others in the safe expectation that nothing would come of it. Henry VIII, who offered 'our whole kingdom, our wealth, our authority, our goods, our prestige . . . yes, our very blood and body' to the cause of the crusade in August 1519, lost interest within a year. The Venetians were characteristically scathing about this tendency. In 1480 the Senate instructed its representative at the Curia to refrain from taking part in any negotiations for an expedition against the Turks, since these would, on past form, be pure fantasy.

If sincerity in such cases was clearly minimal, at least the rulers cannot be accused of practising deception on the matter of crusade revenues, since they shared with the Venetians the conviction that planning would not even reach the stage of funding measures being taken. In a rather different position were those rulers who energetically promoted and executed crusade projects, but whose projects were so enmeshed with their dynastic or national policies and requirements that the question arises whether the crusade was implanted in a calculated move to secure the revenues uniquely associated with it, or at least to gain the kudos or legitimizing gloss of crusading. The aggression of Charles I of Anjou and Charles of Valois against the Greeks, Charles VIII's invasion of Italy, and the series of wars conducted against the Turks by Charles V form clear examples of this type of crusade, in which the problem is not inactivity but the motivation and self-perception of the rulers involved. A similar problem relates to the place occupied by crusade ideas in the thinking of Henry the Navigator. Thanks to the strenuous efforts made by the papacy to finance crusading in an adequate manner, and its acceptance of a broad-based definition of crusading, it was both worthwhile and possible to depict a wide range of military activity in a crusade context. The Curia, pressurized to grant crusading status, and with its hands tied by the virtual sanctity of precedent, could hardly oppose such plans, even though it knew that the convergence between personal ambition and the *negotium Christi* might be far from perfect. All it could do was to try to ensure that money granted for crusading aims was spent in full on them, rather than being diverted to other policies which had no connection with the crusade.

In such cases the question of sincerity revolves around the psychology of the individuals involved, and concerns such issues as whether a late medieval ruler could have distanced himself from the ethos of crusading in such a way as consciously to manipulate its advantages. There are a very different set of problems in the case of those rulers whose crusading intentions were largely free of direct political advantage, but who cancelled their planned *passagia* and retained the crusade funds raised for them. These are indeed the crux cases. Although there are examples of this behaviour for all crusading fronts, the context is most frequently the recovery of the Holy Land, and instances are most dense in the decades between the Second Lyons Council and the outbreak of war between Philip VI and Edward III in 1337. The two monarchs who expressed the greatest interest in a recovery *passagium* were Edward I of England and

Philip VI of France, and in both cases the recent trend amongst historians has been exonerative. To some extent this is due to the fact that English and French crusade planning and diplomacy have received closer attention than ever before: a fuller awareness of how extensive and detailed these debates and negotiations were, has bred greater sympathy for the problems which both kings faced. Historians are consequently more willing to accept the sincerity of their fervently-expressed sentiments. It is true that neither ruler can be shown to have undertaken military preparations appropriate to the task which they claimed to be undertaking, but it is also the case that the old view of their cynically purloining crusade funds no longer holds water. Edward, it has been argued, made less from the crusade than used to be thought; and while Philip VI's government benefited to the tune of possibly 2,800,000 florins, the money was seized in the early stages of a conflict whose gravity was held to justify any fiscal measure. The crisis confronting France by the late 1330s could not have been foreseen during Philip VI's crusade negotiations.

Debate is likely to continue about Edward I and Philip VI, as it is about other figures, such as Henry III and Philip the Fair, who present problems of interpretation which are just as complex. The difference of views can be all but complete. The crusading plans of Charles VIII, for instance, were dismissed by Antonio Marongiu in 1970 as a combination of bait and camouflage, partly on the basis of a misreading of a passage in Philip of Commynes. A few years later they were viewed with much greater sympathy by Yvonne Labande-Mailfert, who convincingly placed them in the setting of the cultural forces of the age as well as the political ones. It is arguable that the sincerity of each ruler has to be decided on an individual basis. However, two general points which merit emphasis seem to emerge from recent studies. The first point is that the idea of such kings deliberately setting out to 'milk' the crusade for its funds, with no intention of keeping their promises, is growing increasingly difficult to accept. It is simply anachronistic in its portrayal of the way such men reasoned: adopting this approach to one of Christendom's most revered institutions would have been highly unorthodox, and most of the figures under consideration were thoroughly, if unoriginally, orthodox in their religious views. Even if they had been able to formulate policy in this way, it would have been clear to them that the potential gains did not balance out the heavy losses: not only papal disapproval and, possibly, sanctions, but also the resistance of the clergy in their own lands (which might lessen the amount which could be gained in any case), the resentment of their own subjects who took the cross in the expectation of action, and not least the damage done to their reputation, at home and abroad, and to that of their lineage after their death. The Curia had good reason to lay repeated stress on the public obloquy which rulers would incur by misusing crusade funds, and its warnings were taken seriously.

The second point is that Catholic rulers, up to at least 1500 and to some extent still in the sixteenth century, were not able to consider the crusade as simply another choice on the political menu, to be taken up or ignored. It was presented to them, with peculiar force and from several directions, as a solemn obligation. One source of pressure, that represented by ancestors who went on crusade, was discussed in the previous chapter, but there were others of equal importance. Charles the Bold, for instance, was propelled towards participation in the anti-Turkish crusade by his own vow at the Feast of the Pheasant (of which he was reminded by Pope Paul II as late as 1470), as well as by the hope of avenging Nicopolis, and by the glowing example of his father Philip the Good. But as Dr Richard Walsh showed, the Duke was also subject to such varied influences as the encouragement of a resident papal legate, the pleas of refugees like the exiled Despot of the Morea, the need to assist Burgundy's Italian allies, Venice and Naples, in their struggle against the Turks, and the undoubted prestige which continuation of the Burgundian crusade tradition would afford Charles in his political manœuvres, particularly *vis-à-vis* Louis XI. The crusade was therefore a unique compound of personal commitment to Christ, dynastic honour, prestige, and political benefit. It is misleading to emphasize the latter, or indeed any single factor. Nor should the tactical finesse with which Charles, like all able rulers of his times, turned the crusade to good propaganda use, lead us to suppose that he himself viewed it mainly in that light. For Charles, as for his descendants Charles V and Philip II, the crusade was less an instrument of policy than an inescapable part of the burden of Catholic rule.

The fact remains, however, that crusade funds were regularly diverted. If the manifold pressure to pursue the crusade was the chief reason why rulers were prepared, again and again, to take up the Sisyphean task of crusade planning and organization, why did they allow their veneration for the *negotium Christi* to crumble when it came to the disposal of funds raised on its behalf? First, no doubt, because of the sheer temptation presented by the existence of large amounts of *specie*, coupled with the fact that the most common reason for the postponement of a *passagium* was the outbreak of war with other Christians, which brought with it desperate financial needs. Secondly, because rulers believed their own pious claims that the money would be restored to the purpose of the crusade as soon as more immediate requirements were satisfied. And thirdly, because developing ideas of sovereignty, discussed above in the context of obstacles to crusading, made it easy to argue that the funds had been raised from the public community, clerical and lay, for the needs of government—albeit, in this case, related to Christendom as a whole—and that they could legitimately be spent on other governmental needs. In other words, the fact that crusading was increasingly organized along the lines of Catholic Europe's hardening political boundaries made it easier to justify, as well as bring about, the diversion of funds.

It was tempting for the apologists of secular government to go further. Kings who were prevented from leaving for the East by the actions of their Christian enemies had long been prone to assimilate those enemies with the Muslims, in order to justify their delay in fulfilling their crusade vows. The attitude manifested itself as early as the time of Orderic Vitalis; and in the late twelfth century it was reflected in Ralph of Diceto's comment, apropos the advice which Henry II received in 1185 on the question of his going to help Latin Syria: 'it seemed preferable to all, and more in the king's spiritual welfare, that he should govern his realm with due care, and protect it from the incursions of *barbari* and from foreign peoples, than take care for the deliverance of the Orientals in his own person'. A century later the idea that a war against Christian enemies could have some attributes of sanctity, even when not formally treated as a crusade by the Curia, had almost become a commonplace. Typical was the assertion, which the English claimed had been made by the Scottish clergy, that fighting against Edward I was more justified than fighting against the Muslims. The argument was still advanced most frequently when a war was being waged by a king who had assumed the cross, and who could be depicted as clearing a path to the East. But this was not a necessary precondition: thanks to papal crusade policy, contemporaries had become used to the idea of crusading against Christians, and the French court and its apologists in particular became adroit in borrowing arguments and phraseology from the *crux cismarina* to describe its wars in the West. As an anonymous French cleric put it in about 1302, 'he who wages war against the King [of France] works against the whole Church, against Catholic doctrine, against holiness and justice, and against the Holy Land'.

This tendency to 'sanctify' secular wars, especially when fought by identifiably national groups, inevitably became more pronounced in the fourteenth and fifteenth centuries. During the early phase of the Hundred Years War the English were alarmed, on several occasions, that the pro-French stance adopted by the Avignonese Curia might lead to an anti-English crusade. And as we observed in Chapter 8,[6] the Great Schism did make it possible, for a few years, for actual crusades to occur within the framework of the Anglo-French war. But such expeditions as those of Louis of Anjou and John of Gaunt were the institutionalized tip of an iceberg of sanctified warfare. Significantly, the link with planned *passagia* to the East became less frequent. This was partly because such planning was more sporadic, but also because the strong feelings aroused by such national conflicts as the Anglo-French war provided a surrogate enthusiasm in the form of nascent patriotism. The holiness of defending the realm thus became a theme of some importance in English, French, and Scottish sources. On occasion tentative moves were made towards appropriating features of the crusade itself, as when the English episcopate granted 'large indulgences' to all who rallied to the defence of the *patria* in 1360, but more common features were the employment of striking symbols, especially the cross itself, and the use of crusade language and ideas. Dr Christopher Tyerman has pointed out the cluster of associations with the crusade which became attached to such English victories as Neville's Cross (1346) and Agincourt (1415). In the case of the former, Henry Knighton wrote of a banner displaying the sign of the cross being carried in front of the English troops, who were prepared to die 'for the salvation of the Kingdom'. Accounts of Agincourt, and the organization of Henry V's subsequent victory procession into London, were characterized by strenuous references to the justice and sanctity of the King's cause, his personal piety, and England's religious past.

In both England and France, the Church was called upon to play a growing role in disseminating government propaganda and mobilizing public opinion in support of the war, and it is not surprising that representatives of the national churches were of particular importance in promoting this trend. High-ranking prelates fostered the beliefs that God was served by fighting for a just cause, that the soldier who fought for his lawful lord was performing a spiritually meritorious deed, and that the national community was special in God's eyes. Characteristically, Adam Houghton, Bishop of St David's, asserted before the English parliament in 1377 that 'God would never have honoured this land in the same way

[6] Above, 247–8.

as he did Israel through great victories over their enemies, if it were not that he had chosen it as his heritage'. On the other side, John Gerson was prepared to describe as 'martyrs of God' those men-at-arms who 'with good intent expose their lives in a righteous cause and in defence of justice and truth'. Men-at-arms naturally welcomed this idea, which facilitated their belief that, in John of Bueil's words, 'we poor soldiers will save our souls in arms just as well as we might by living in contemplation upon a diet of roots'.

This tendency to sanctify the Anglo-French war was not discouraged by the papacy, which in the fourteenth century embraced the idea that fighting in a just war on behalf of one's sovereign gave a soldier a status not dissimilar to that of a *crucesignatus*. It is not surprising that the ardently patriotic Clement VI granted Philip VI and Prince John of Normandy the plenary indulgence on all occasions when they faced death 'pro regni defensione', but it is interesting that Clement was also prepared to make an exception of fighting on the king's behalf, when he forbad an English *crucesignatus* from fighting against Christians while waiting to fulfil his vow. On Ash Wednesday 1338, when he was Archbishop of Rouen, Clement himself had preached a *collatio* on a passage from 1 Maccabees which formed a key text in the development of sacred violence *pro patria*: 'Arm yourselves and be valiant, men, and be prepared for the morning, so that you may fight against the nations which are gathered together to destroy us and our holy place.' And it was natural for Innocent VI and Urban V to grant indulgences to those Frenchmen who died fighting the *routiers*, those implacable transgressors of the *patria*'s peace.

The theme of 'sanctified patriotism' or 'national crusading' has received most recent attention from historians in relation to its ebullient emergence during the Anglo-French war. It has not been pursued very fully in the case of other countries, or into the later fifteenth or sixteenth centuries. Caution is necessary, but there is evidence that in this period too, contemporaries were encouraged to associate national or even dynastic warfare with neo-crusading ideas. We have seen that the conjunction between national war and crusade was a close one in Habsburg Spain; and the use of religion to coat warfare in a patina of pious justification was one of the characteristics of European warfare which most distressed Erasmus. At the time of Marignano and Pavia the French nobility appears to have regarded death in royal service as supremely honourable and meritorious. Given that the trend gathered pace in conjunction with the decline of the large-scale *passagium* to the East, it is possible to argue that this transfer of ideas fashioned an outlet for enthusiasm which could no longer find expression in actual crusading, at least against the Mamluks and Turks. Instead of the old argument that national feeling replaced, or even destroyed, crusading zeal, we have the idea that it was fertilized by it. As Dr Tyerman has put it in the case of England, 'By assuming for themselves and their followers the mantle of divinely sanctioned patriotism, monarchs appropriated some of the rhetoric, much of the emotion, and ultimately, in the sixteenth century and beyond, most of the traditional appeal of crusading . . . National wars could thus fill the vacuum left by the lack of opportunities to fight for the cross.'

The idea that the crusade, like so much else, was pressed into the service of the dynastic nation-state, is an engaging and, up to a point, a valid one. The growing emphasis placed on the holiness of warfare 'in defensione regni' undoubtedly helped to salve the consciences of rulers when they decided to abandon crusade projects; it may even have helped to justify, in their own eyes and those of their people, the use of crusade funds for such warfare. There is no reason to doubt that the abandonment of planned *passagia* often involved agonizing decisions. The elaborate financial provisions in favour of the crusade, which pepper the wills of monarchs who had earlier abandoned crusading projects, are ample testimony to this. Consciences required such surrogate measures as the provision of assistance to the Military Orders and to *crucesignati* leaving for the East, in groups or as individuals, the grant of pensions to refugees from the East, and donations for the maintenance of shrines in the Holy Land. But in the conflict which so often broke out between the needs of the realm and the obligation to crusade there was, despite the many pressures operating on behalf of the latter, little doubt as to the outcome. Pius II could use no stronger argument than his claim, when writing to Alfonso V of Portugal, that 'to obtain salvation you are obliged, as a prince and as a Christian, to assist with all your strength in defending the holy faith'. But it was not enough. The obligation faced by each subject to put service to prince before everything inevitably entailed a corresponding obligation on the prince's part to do nothing which would imperil the realm and his subjects.

By 1300 it was already clear that a big *passagium* was impossible without the continuing support of the West's rulers. Just as essential was the personal leadership of at least one of them. At the very start of our period, Edward I discovered not only that he could not leave the realm because of political problems, but also that the papal Curia would not release crusade funds for the leadership of his younger brother Edmund, on the grounds that planning would only generate sufficient enthusiasm and backing if the *passagium* was to be led by the King in person. Experience showed that the Curia was right to take this approach, but in practice it could not work. For after St Louis, monarchical leadership of a *passagium* to the East no longer proved viable. The papal nuncio Lionello Chieregato was thus not far from the truth when he informed Charles VIII and his court in 1488 that the failure of secular leadership was the main reason for the trail of abandoned crusade projects which had begun during Gregory X's reign more than two centuries earlier. Crusading came to an end in Iberia because it was successful, and in north-eastern Europe because of profound political and religious changes; but the crusade in the East fell victim to its own inherent weakness as the only expression of religious enthusiasm in Christian history which came to depend on large-scale secular organization.

The argument in this and the preceding chapter has been that crusading lost its practicality in the face of adverse developments in Europe's political, military, and financial structures: it was outgrown rather than overthrown or discredited. This meant that while the institution itself largely perished, beliefs and attitudes associated with it persisted. We have observed this at several points in this book, and in some respects it continued well past 1580. In governmental terms this persistence took the form of the continuing existence of Christendom (*Christianitas*), a community of powers and nations united by their shared religion. The idea of Christendom commanded respect even after the religious divide caused by the Reformation, when rulers had long since ceased going on crusade. Indeed, it is arguable that the concept of Christendom, the first to take shape among the various preconditions for the crusading movement, was also the last to vanish. Its chief manifestation was an a priori hostile view of the Turks, and the welcoming of their defeat, even when it was accomplished by a power which would normally, for political and religious reasons, be viewed with suspicion. For example, until relations between England and Spain worsened in the 1580s some of the warmest applause for Philip II's naval war against the Turks came from Protestant England. The historian Thomas Fuller wrote appreciatively that 'all West-Christendom oweth her quiet sleep to his [i.e. Philip's] constant waking, who with his galleys muzzleth the mouth of Tunis and Algiers'. It is true that King Sebastian's crusaders at Alcazar were killed by English guns, but prayers of thanksgiving were offered up in England in 1565 for the relief of Malta, and in 1566 for the defeat of the Turks in Hungary. Ralph Holinshed recorded the jubilant celebrations held in London on receipt of the news of Lepanto, 'a victorie of so great importance unto the whole state of Christian commonwealth'.

For decades after Lepanto the Turks continued to be regarded as pariahs in the diplomatic relations of the European powers. It was only in 1606 that the Habsburg–Ottoman treaty of Zsitvatorok showed the Sultan and Emperor recognizing each other as sovereign rulers. And although legal commentators like Grotius and Gentili argued in the following decades for the inclusion of the Turks within natural law, the prerequisite for ordinary diplomatic relations with Istanbul to occur, they recognized that in practice the Ottomans were implacably hostile to Christian Europe. Within Europe, public opinion regarding the Turks, although shaped less by fear and more by curiosity, was still marked by distaste and, at times, open animosity. Even Englishmen, who had strong political reasons for welcoming the inclusion of the Turks within the community of powers, found it hard to accept in practice. As late as the 1620s Sir Thomas Roe, ambassador at Istanbul for the pro-Spanish James I, was instructed to work for the good of all Christendom. The context was James I's hopes for Catholic–Protestant unity against the Ottomans, which Francis Bacon debated in 1622 in his 'An Advertisement Touching an Holy War'. James's hopes were undeniably quixotic, one character in 'An Advertisement' making the appropriate if unkind comment that the Holy War had become 'the rendezvous of cracked brains'. But the Ottomans remained a political force apart. Not until the Congress of Carlowitz in 1699 did they take part in a general assembly of the European powers.

It has been pointed out that by 1700 references to 'Christendom' had come to indicate above all a set of political, social, and cultural values which the Turks did not share, rather than the religious divide. Christendom had become synonymous with the civilized world, where a 'Christian gentleman' felt at ease. This change in meaning is a good example of the pitfalls which lie in wait for anyone who tries to trace the later history of crusade ideology, phraseology, and symbols. Similar problems attend the notion of a Protestant, even Puritan 'crusade'. Paul Rousset thought that he could detect convictions akin to those of the crusaders, especially the central concept of God's mandate for war, and His judgemental use of the battlefield, in the approach towards warfare of both Gustav Adolphus and Oliver Cromwell in the first half of the seventeenth century. Analogous convictions were expounded with enthusiasm in the writings of contemporary divines like Stephen Gosson, William Gouge, Alexander Leighton, and Thomas Barnes. It is arguable that the ideas found here, as in the earlier case of the Hussites, were generic ones of holy war rather than crusade; and that they came directly from the Protestants' reverence for the Old Testament, rather than being channelled through the crusading tradition. But traces of crusading thought are present, and there is substance in Rousset's general point about crusade ideology subsisting rather than disappearing. As he put it, 'its origin predated the institution of the crusade itself, and it continued its existence up to modern times'. So firm was the imprint made by the crusade on all Christian thinking about sacred violence that it was bound to exercise an influence for centuries.

The 'legacy of crusading' therefore remains a valid and important field of enquiry, in some ways more worth while than the search for 'the last crusade' itself. In the late fifteenth and sixteenth centuries practical crusading came to the end of its life as a widespread European practice: preaching was bogged down in the cul-de-sac of indulgence abuse; there were no effective solutions to the problems of inadequate resources, rampant misuse of funds, and the priority accorded to domestic political needs; and dynastic, national, and religious fissures meant that the *respublica christiana* had less tangible meaning than ever before. The Reformation and Counter-Reformation ended, except in Habsburg and Bourbon Spain, an institution which was already irreparably decayed. By 1580 most of the states and regions whose history was bound up with that institution, Lusignan and Venetian Cyprus, Latin *Romania*, the *Ordensstaat*, and Livonia, were already extinct or overrun by the Turks. But the ideas, iconography, and language associated with crusading survived, to fertilize the thinking and behaviour of all Christians engaged in military struggles which they considered to be inseparable from their religious beliefs, spanning time and space from Early Modern Europe to contemporary Latin America.

Appendix

Lists of Rulers

POPES

First date is that of election. An.=antipope. For popes during the Great Schism (1378–1417), R.=Roman obedience, A.=Avignonese obedience, P.=Pisan obedience.

Gregory X	1271–6	Alexander V (P.)	1409–10
Innocent V	1276	John XXIII (P.)	1410–15
Adrian V	1276	Martin V	1417–31
John XXI	1276–7	Eugenius IV	1431–47
Nicholas III	1277–80	Felix V (An.)	1439–49
Martin IV	1281–5	Nicholas V	1447–55
Honorius IV	1285–7	Calixtus III	1455–8
Nicholas IV	1288–92	Pius II	1458–64
Celestine V	1294	Paul II	1464–71
Boniface VIII	1294–1303	Sixtus IV	1471–84
Benedict XI	1303–4	Innocent VIII	1484–92
Clement V	1305–14	Alexander VI	1492–1503
John XXII	1316–34	Pius III	1503
Nicholas V (An.)	1328–33	Julius II	1503–13
Benedict XII	1334–42	Leo X	1513–21
Clement VI	1342–52	Adrian VI	1522–3
Innocent VI	1352–62	Clement VII	1523–34
Urban V	1362–70	Paul III	1534–49
Gregory XI	1370–8	Julius III	1550–5
Urban VI (R.)	1378–89	Marcellus II	1555
Boniface IX (R.)	1389–1404	Paul IV	1555–9
Innocent VII (R.)	1404–6	Pius IV	1559–65
Gregory XII (R.)	1406–15	Pius V	1566–72
Clement VII (A.)	1378–94	Gregory XIII	1572–85
Benedict XIII (A.)	1394–1423		

OTTOMAN SULTANS

Osman	d. 1326	Mehmed II	1451–81
Orhan	1326–62	Bayezid II	1481–1512
Murad I	1362–89	Selim I	1512–20
Bayezid I	1389–1403	Suleyman I	1520–66
Mehmed I	1413–21	Selim II	1566–74
Murad II	1421–51	Murad III	1574–95

BYZANTINE EMPERORS

(unless stated, all from Palaiologos dynasty)

Michael VIII	1261–82	John V (restored)	1379–90
Andronikos II	1282–1328	John VII	1390
Andronikos III	1328–41	John V (restored)	1390–1
John V	1341–7	Manuel II	1391–1425
John VI (Cantacuzene)	1347–54	John VIII	1425–48
John V (restored)	1354–76	Constantine XI	1448–53
Andronikos IV	1376–9		

KINGS OF HUNGARY

Ladislas III	1272–90	Ladislas IV	
Charles Martel*	1290–5	(Wladyslaw III	
Andrew III*	1290–1301	of Poland)	1439–44
Charles Robert	1310–42	Ladislas V	1444–57
Louis I	1342–82	Matthias Corvinus	1458–90
Sigismund	1387–1437	Ladislas VI	1490–1516
Albert I	1438–9	Louis II	1516–26

LUSIGNAN KINGS AND QUEENS OF CYPRUS

Hugh III	1267–84	Janus	1398–1432
John I	1284–5	John II	1432–58
Henry II	1285–1324	Charlotte	1458–64
Hugh IV	1324–59	James II	1464–73
Peter I	1359–69	James III	1473–4
Peter II	1369–82	Catherine	1474–89
James I	1382–98		

* disputed succession

MASTERS AND GRAND MASTERS OF THE HOSPITALLERS

Hugh Revel	1258–77	Peter Raymond	
Nicholas Lorgne	1277–84	Zacosta	1461–7
John of Villiers	1285–93	Giovanni Battista	
Odo of Pins	1294–6	Orsini	1467–76
William of Villaret	1296–1305	Peter of Aubusson	1476–1503
Fulk of Villaret	1305–19	Emery of Amboise	1503–12
Hélion of Villeneuve	1319–46	Guy of Blanchefort	1512–13
Dieudonné of Gozon	1346–53	Fabrizio del	
Peter of Corneillan	1353–5	Carretto	1513–21
Roger of Pins	1355–65	Philip Villiers of	
Raymond Berenger	1365–74	L'Isle Adam	1521–34
Robert of Juilly	1374–7	Pierino del Ponte	1534–5
John Fernández of		Didiers of St Jalle	1535–6
Heredia	1377–96	John of Omedes	1536–53
Philibert of Naillac	1396–1421	Claude of La Sengle	1553–7
Anton Fluvian	1421–37	John of La Valette	1557–68
John of Lastic	1437–54	Peter del Monte	1568–72
James of Milly	1454–61	John l'Aveque de la	
		Cassiere	1572–81

RULERS OF CASTILE

Alfonso X	1252–84	John II	1406–54
Sancho IV	1284–95	Henry IV	1454–74
Ferdinand IV	1295–1312	Isabella	1474–1504
Alfonso XI	1312–50	Ferdinand V	
Peter I	1350–69	(II of Aragon)	1475–1516
Henry II	1369–79	Charles I	
John I	1379–90	(V of Germany)	1516–56
Henry III	1390–1406	Philip II	1556–98

KINGS OF ARAGON

James I	1213–76	Martin I	1396–1410
Peter II	1276–85	Ferdinand I	
Alfonso III	1285–91	('of Antequera')	1412–16
James II	1291–1327	Alfonso V	1416–58
Alfonso IV	1327–36	John II	1458–79
Peter III	1336–87	Ferdinand II	
John I	1387–96	(V of Castile)	1479–1516

GRAND MASTERS OF THE TEUTONIC ORDER

Hartmann of		Paul of Rusdorf	1422–41
Heldrungen	1273–82	Conrad of	
Burchard of		Erlichshausen	1441–9
Schwanden	1282–90	Ludwig of	
Conrad of		Erlichshausen	1450–67
Feuchtwangen	1291–6	Henry Reuss of	
Gottfried of		Plauen	1469–70
Hohenlohe	1297–1303	Henry Reffle of	
Siegfried of		Richtenberg	1470–7
Feuchtwangen	1303–11	Martin Truchsess	
Charles of Trier	1311–24	of Wetzhausen	1477–89
Werner of Orseln	1324–30	John of Tiefen	1489–97
Luther of Brunswick	1331–5	Duke Frederick	
Dietrich of Altenburg	1335–41	of Saxony	1498–1510
Ludolf König	1342–5	Margrave Albert	
Henry Dusemer	1345–51	of Brandenburg-	
Winrich of Kniprode	1351–82	Ansbach	1511–25
Konrad Zöllner of		Walter of Kronberg	1527–43
Rotenstein	1382–90	Wolfgang Schutzbar	1543–66
Conrad of Wallenrode	1391–3	George Hund of	
Conrad of Jungingen	1393–1407	Wenckheim	1566–72
Ulrich of Jungingen	1407–10	Henry of	
Henry of Plauen	1410–13	Bobenhausen	1572–90
Michael Küchmeister			
of Sternberg	1414–22		

GRAND PRINCES AND GRAND DUKES OF LITHUANIA

Traidenis	c.1270–82	Witold	1401–30
Pukuveras	c.1282–92	Switrigailo	1430–2
Vytenis	1293–1315	Sigismund	1432–40
Gediminas	1315–41	Casimir (IV)	1440–92
Algirdas	1342–77	Alexander (I)	1492–1506
Kenstutis	1377–82	Sigismund (I)	1506–48
Jogailo (Wladyslaw II		Sigismund (II)	1548–69†
of Poland)	1382–1401		

† The Grand Duchy was incorporated into the Polish Crown in 1569 by the Union of Lublin

KINGS OF POLAND

Wladyslaw I	1320–33	John Albert	1492–1501
Casimir III	1333–70	Alexander I	1501–6
Louis I	1370–82	Sigismund I	1506–48
Jadwiga	1384–99	Sigismund II	1548–72
Wladyslaw II	1386–1434	Henry of Valois	1573–4
Wladyslaw III	1434–44	Stephen Bathory	1575–86
Casimir IV	1446–92		

KINGS OF FRANCE

Philip III	1270–85	Charles VII	1422–61
Philip IV	1285–1314	Louis XI	1461–83
Louis X	1314–16	Charles VIII	1483–98
John I	1316	Louis XII	1498–1515
Philip V	1316–22	Francis I	1515–47
Charles IV	1322–8	Henry II	1547–59
Philip VI	1328–50	Francis II	1559–60
John II	1350–64	Charles IX	1560–74
Charles V	1364–80	Henry III	1574–89
Charles VI	1380–1422		

VALOIS DUKES OF BURGUNDY

Philip the Bold	1363–1404	Philip the Good	1419–67
John the Fearless	1404–19	Charles the Bold	1467–77

FURTHER READING

My aim in compiling the following pages has been to provide, for the subject of each chapter, a reasonably comprehensive guide to further reading. Titles in foreign languages are given, but I have attempted to cite at least one work in English on each major theme, for the benefit of monoglots. Unless an English translation exists, primary sources are not normally given; similarly, I have not cited older (i.e. pre-1900) literature, except in cases when there is nothing else to recommend or the work in question remains important.

The full title of each item is cited in the section for each chapter; if repeated later in the section it is given in abbreviated form.

List of Abbreviations

AEM	*Anuario de estudios medievales*
AHP	*Archivum historiae pontificiae*
AHR	*American Historical Review*
AO	*Archivum ottomanicum*
Arbel, *et al.*, LGEM	B. Arbel, B. Hamilton, and D. Jacoby (eds.), *Latins and Greeks in the Eastern Mediterranean after 1204* (London, 1989)
ASI	*Archivio storico italiano*
ASPN	*Archivio storico per le provincie napoletane*
A[R]SRSP	*Archivio della [reale] Società romana di storia patria*
Bak and Király, FHR	J. M. Bak and B. K. Király (eds.), *From Hunyadi to Rákóczi: War and Society in Late Medieval and Early Modern Hungary* (New York, 1982)
Bartlett and MacKay, MFS	R. Bartlett and A. MacKay (eds.), *Medieval Frontier Societies* (Oxford, 1989)
BÉC	*Bibliothèque de l'École des chartes*
Benzoni, *Il Mediterraneo*	G. Benzoni (ed.), *Il Mediterraneo nella seconda metà del '500 alla luce di Lepanto* (Florence, 1974)
BF	*Byzantinische Forschungen*
BIHR	*Bulletin of the Institute of Historical Research*
BS	*Balkan Studies*
BSOAS	*Bulletin of the School of Oriental and African Studies*
Cardini, *Toscana*	F. Cardini (ed.), *Toscana e Terrasanta nel Medioevo* (Florence, 1982)

CH	Church History
CHR	Catholic Historical Review
CS	Collected Studies: Variorum Reprints
Edbury, CS	P. W. Edbury (ed.), Crusade and Settlement: Papers read at the First Conference of the Society for the Study of the Crusades and the Latin East and presented to R. C. Smail (Cardiff, 1985)
EHR	English Historical Review
Fleckenstein and Hellmann, GRE	J. Fleckenstein and M. Hellmann (eds.), Die geistlichen Ritterorden Europas (Sigmaringen, 1980)
Goss, MTW	V. P. Goss (ed.), The Meeting of Two Worlds: Cultural Exchange between East and West during the Period of the Crusades (Kalamazoo, Mich., 1986).
Highfield, SFC	R. Highfield (ed.), Spain in the Fifteenth Century 1369–1516 (London, 1972)
HJ	Historisches Jahrbuch
Holt, EMLPC	P. M. Holt (ed.), The Eastern Mediterranean Lands in the Period of the Crusades (Warminster, 1977)
Holt, et al., CHI	P. M. Holt, A. K. S. Lambton, and B. Lewis (eds.), The Cambridge History of Islam, i, The Central Islamic Lands (Cambridge, 1970)
HZ	Historisches Zeitschrift
JEH	Journal of Ecclesiastical History
JMH	Journal of Medieval History
MÂ	Le Moyen Âge
MÉFR	Mélanges de l'École française de Rome
OCP	Orientalia christiana periodica
Papadopoulos and Englezakis, Proceedings	T. Papadopoulos and B. Englezakis (eds.), Proceedings of the Second International Congress of Cypriot Studies (Nicosia, 1986)
PBSR	Papers of the British School at Rome
PP	Past and Present
QFIAB	Quellen und Forschungen aus italienischen Archiven und Bibliotheken
QSGDO	Quellen und Studien zur Geschichte des Deutschen Ordens
RBPH	Revue belge de philologie et d'histoire
RH	Revue historique
RHE	Revue d'histoire ecclésiastique
RHSEE	Revue historique du sud-est européen
ROL	Revue de l'orient latin
RQ	Römische Quartalschrift
SCH	Studies in Church History

SEER   *Slavonic and East European Review*
Setton, *HC*   K. M. Setton (gen. ed.), *A History of the Crusades*, 2nd
                edn. (6 vols.; Madison, Wis., 1969–90)
Setton, *PL*   K. M. Setton, *The Papacy and the Levant (1204–1571)*,
                Memoirs of the American Philosophical Society, 114, 127,
                161–2 (4 vols.; Philadelphia, 1976–84)
TRHS   *Transactions of the Royal Historical Society*

INTRODUCTION

For the pluralist approach, see J. Riley-Smith, *What were the Crusades?* (London, 1977); id., *The Crusades: A Short History* (London, 1987). The best introduction to the traditionalist approach is H. E. Mayer, *The Crusades*, 2nd edn. (Oxford, 1988). Christopher Tyerman's views are briefly outlined in his 'The Holy Land and the Crusades of the Thirteenth and Fourteenth Centuries', in Edbury, *CS*, and are often visible in his *England and the Crusades 1095–1588* (Chicago, 1988), but they are likely to become clearer in his forthcoming survey of the crusades for Cambridge University Press.

The only existing study of the later crusades, A. S. Atiya, *The Crusade in the Later Middle Ages* (London, 1938 and reprints), is almost wholly unsatisfactory. Work in progress on some of the lacunae mentioned at the end of the Introduction will be indicated in the following pages; but the best way to keep abreast of current research on the crusades is through the annual *Bulletin* of the Society for the Study of the Crusades and the Latin East (I can supply details).

A comparative approach towards frontier societies is adopted in Bartlett and MacKay, *MFS*.

CHAPTER 1

The Loss of the Holy Land, 1274–1370

For the situation in the Holy Land between c.1250 and 1291, see J. Richard, *The Latin Kingdom of Jerusalem*, tr. J. Shirley (Amsterdam, 1979); S. Runciman, 'The Crusader States, 1243–1291', in Setton, *HC*, ii. 557–98; J. Riley-Smith, *The Feudal Nobility and the Kingdom of Jerusalem, 1174–1277* (London, 1973); S. Schein, 'The Image of the Crusader Kingdom of Jerusalem in the Thirteenth Century', *RBPH* 64 (1986), 704–17. The rise of the Mamluks is examined in P. M. Holt, *The Age of the Crusades: The Near East from the Eleventh Century to 1517* (London, 1986); R. Irwin, *The Middle East in the Middle Ages: The Early Mamluk Sultanate 1250–1382* (London, 1986).

The Second Lyons Council has to be set in the broad context of thirteenth-century feelings and ideas on crusading. For the view that these had become negative and sterile, see P. Throop, *Criticism of the Crusade: A Study of Public Opinion and Crusade Propaganda* (Amsterdam, 1940, repr. 1975); M. Purcell, *Papal Crusading Policy: The Chief Instruments of Papal Crusading Policy and Crusade to the Holy Land from the Final Loss of Jerusalem to the Fall of Acre, 1244–1291* (Leiden, 1975); F. Cardini, 'La crociata nel Duecento. L" 'Avatara" di un ideale', *ASI* 135 (1977), 101–39. For the contrasting view that much enthusiasm and fruitful thinking remained, see E. Siberry, *Criticism of Crusading, 1095–1274* (Oxford, 1985); S. Lloyd, *English Society and the Crusade 1216–1307* (Oxford, 1988). Jean Richard has stressed the acceleration of thinking about the 'phased crusade' which occurred in the 1260s: 'La Croisade de 1270, premier "passage général"?', *Académie des inscriptions et belles-lettres, Comptes rendus* (1989), 510–23.

For Mamluk government and military techniques, see, in addition to the books by Holt and Irwin cited above, M. M. Ziada, 'The Mamluk Sultans, 1291–1517', in Setton, *HC*, iii. 486–512; P. M. Holt, 'The Position and Power of the Mamluk Sultan', *BSOAS* 38 (1975), 237–49; id., 'The Structure of Government in the Mamluk Sultanate', in Holt, *EMLPC*, 44–61; R. S. Humphreys, 'The Emergence of the Mamluk Army', *Studia islamica* 45 (1977), 67–99, 46 (1977), 147–82; D. Ayalon, *Studies on the Mamluks of Egypt (1250–1517)* (CS, London, 1977); id., *The Mamluk Military Society* (CS, London, 1979); B. Lewis, 'Egypt and Syria', in Holt, *et al.*, *CHI*, 175–230; I. Hrbek, 'Egypt, Nubia and the Eastern Deserts', in R. Oliver (ed.), *The Cambridge History of Africa*, iii, *From c.1050 to c.1600* (Cambridge, 1977), 10–97.

On recovery treatises in the period between the fall of Acre and the Council of Vienne, see J. Delaville le Roulx, *La France en Orient au XIVe siècle* (2 vols.; Paris, 1886); E. Stickel, *Der Fall von Akkon: Untersuchungen zum Abklingen des Kreuzzugsgedankens am Ende des 13. Jahrhunderts* (Bern, 1975); G. I. Bratianu, 'Le Conseil du roi Charles', *RHSEE* 19 (1942), 291–361; Pierre Dubois, *The Recovery of the Holy Land*, tr. W. I. Brandt (New York, 1956); E. A. Peers, *Ramon Lull: A Biography* (London, 1929); J. N. Hillgarth, *Ramon Lull and Lullism in Fourteenth-Century France* (London, 1971); H. Wieruszowski, 'Ramon Lull et l'idée de la Cité de Dieu: Quelques nouveaux écrits sur la croisade', *Estudis franciscans*, 47 (1935), 87–110. For recovery plans and attempts in these years, see S. Schein, '*Gesta Dei per Mongolos* 1300: The Genesis of a Non-Event', *EHR* 94 (1979), 805–19; F. Heidelberger, *Kreuzzugsversuche um die Wende des 13. Jahrhunderts* (Berlin, 1911); S. Schein, 'Philip IV and the Crusade: A Reconsideration', in Edbury, *CS*, 121–6; Lloyd, *English Society and the Crusade*; L. Thier, *Kreuzzugsbemühungen unter Papst Clemens V. (1305–1314)* (Werl, Westf., 1973); B. Z. Kedar and S. Schein, 'Un Projet de "passage particulier" proposé par l'Ordre de l'Hôpital, 1306–7', *BÉC* 137 (1979), 211–26; N. Housley, 'Pope Clement V and the Crusades of 1309–10', *JMH* 8 (1982), 29–43.

For the Council of Vienne and the crusade, see M. Barber, *The Trial of the*

Templars (Cambridge, 1978); E. Müller, *Das Konzil von Vienne (1311–1312): Seine Quellen und seine Geschichte* (Münster-i.-W., 1934).

On French projects in the period from 1313 to 1336, see the series of articles by C. J. Tyerman, 'Sed nihil fecit? The Last Capetians and the Recovery of the Holy Land', in J. Gillingham and J. C. Holt (eds.), *War and Government in the Middle Ages* (Woodbridge, 1984), 170–81; 'Philip V of France, the Assemblies of 1319–20 and the Crusade', *BIHR* 57 (1984), 15–34; 'Philip VI and the Recovery of the Holy Land', *EHR* 100 (1985), 25–51. Dr Tyerman also makes interesting comments on the projects in his *England and the Crusades 1095–1588* (Chicago, 1988). In addition, see M. Barber, 'The Pastoureaux of 1320', *JEH* 32 (1981), 143–66 and, for the attitude taken by the papal Curia towards the projects, N. Housley, *The Avignon Papacy and the Crusades, 1305–1378* (Oxford, 1986). For the fiscal background, see J. B. Henneman, *Royal Taxation in Fourteenth-Century France: The Development of War Financing 1322–1356* (Princeton, NJ, 1971).

For Marino Sanudo Torsello, see A. Magnocavallo, *Marin Sanudo il vecchio e il suo progetto di crociata* (Bergamo, 1901); C. J. Tyerman, 'Marino Sanudo Torsello and the Lost Crusade: Lobbying in the Fourteenth Century', *TRHS* 5th ser. 32 (1982), 57–73; F. Cardini, 'I costi della crociata: L'aspetto economico del progetto di Marin Sanudo il Vecchio (1312–1321)', in *Studi in memoria di Federigo Melis* (5 vols.; Naples, 1978), ii. 179–210; D. Jacoby, 'Catalans, Turcs et Vénitiens en Romanie (1305–1332): Un nouveau témoignage de Marino Sanudo Torsello', *Studi medievali*, 3rd ser. 15 (1974), 217–61. An up-to-date edition of the 'Liber secretorum fidelium crucis' is urgently needed. For the economic blockade of the Mamluk lands, see E. Ashtor, *Levant Trade in the Later Middle Ages* (Princeton, NJ, 1983); J. Trenchs Odena, ' "De Alexandrinis" (El comercio prohibido con los musulmanes y el Papado de Aviñón durante la primera mitad del siglo XIV)', *AEM* 10 (1980), 237–320.

On Peter I, Urban V, John II, and the Alexandria crusade, see P. W. Edbury, 'The Crusading Policy of King Peter I of Cyprus, 1359–1369', in Holt, *EMLPC*, 90–105; Housley, *The Avignon Papacy and the Crusades*; R. Cazelles, 'Jean II le Bon: Quel homme? Quel roi?', *RH* 232 (1974), 5–26; A. S. Atiya, *The Crusade in the Later Middle Ages* (London, 1938 and reprints); Setton, *PL*, i.

Relations between the Mamluks and the West after 1370 are handled in E. Ashtor and B. Z. Kedar, 'Una guerra fra Genova e i Mamelucchi negli anni 1380', *ASI* 133 (1975), 3–44; F. Gabrieli, 'Venezia e i Mamelucchi', in A. Pertusi (ed.), *Venezia e l'Oriente fra tardo Medioevo e Rinascimento* (Florence, 1966), 417–32. On Mamluk decline, see Holt, *The Age of the Crusades*; D. Ayalon, *Gunpowder and Firearms in the Mamluk Kingdom: A Challenge to a Medieval Society* (London, 1956).

For later recovery theorists and proposals, see Philippe de Mézières, *Le Songe du Vieil Pèlerin*, ed. and partially tr. G. W. Coopland (2 vols.; Cambridge, 1969);

N. Iorga, *Philippe de Mézières 1327–1405* (Paris 1896, repr. 1973); Emmanuele Piloti, *Traité sur le passage en Terre Sainte (1420)*, ed. P.-H. Dopp (Louvain, 1958); C.-M. De Witte, 'Un Projet portugais de reconquête de la Terre-Sainte (1505–1507)', *Congresso internacional de história dos descobrimentos, Actas, V(1)* (Lisbon, 1961), 419–49; N. Iorga, 'Un Projet relatif à la conquête de Jérusalem, 1609', *ROL* 2 (1894), 183–9. Pilgrimage to the Holy Land in the late Middle Ages is described in H. F. M. Prescott, *Jerusalem Journey: Pilgrimage to the Holy Land in the Fifteenth Century* (London, 1954).

CHAPTER 2

Greeks, Turks, and Latins: The Crusade in Romania, 1274–1396

For Byzantium in this period, and its relations with the West, see D. M. Nicol, *The Last Centuries of Byzantium 1261–1453* (London, 1972); id., *Byzantium and Venice: A Study in Diplomatic and Cultural Relations* (Cambridge, 1988); J. Gill, *Byzantium and the Papacy, 1198–1400* (New Brunswick, NJ, 1979); G. T. Dennis, *Byzantium and the Franks, 1350–1420* (CS, London, 1982). For the phase of active hostility, see D. J. Geanakoplos, *Emperor Michael Palaeologus and the West 1258–1282: A Study in Byzantine–Latin Relations* (Cambridge, Mass., 1959, repr. 1973); S. Runciman, *The Sicilian Vespers: A History of the Mediterranean World in the Later Thirteenth Century* (Cambridge, 1958); H. Moranvillé, 'Les Projets de Charles de Valois sur l'empire de Constantinople', *BÉC* 51 (1890), 63–86; A. E. Laiou, *Constantinople and the Latins: The Foreign Policy of Andronicus II 1282–1328* (Cambridge, Mass., 1972).

On the *ghazi* principalities, see P. Wittek, *Das Fürstentum Mentesche: Studien zur Geschichte Westkleinasiens im 13.–15. Jahrhundert* (Istanbul, 1934); O. Turan, 'Anatolia in the Period of the Seljuks and the *Beyliks*', in Holt, *et al.*, *CHI*, 231–62; H. Inalcik, 'The Rise of the Turcoman Maritime Principalities in Anatolia, Byzantium, and Crusades', *BF* 9 (1985), 179–217; S. Vryonis, *The Decline of Medieval Hellenism in Asia Minor and the Process of Islamization from the Eleventh through the Fifteenth Century* (Berkeley, Calif., 1971); P. Lemerle, *L'Émirat d'Aydin, Byzance et l'occident: Recherches sur 'La Geste d'Umur Pacha'* (Paris, 1957); E. A. Zachariadou, 'Holy War in the Aegean during the Fourteenth Century', in Arbel, *et al.*, *LGEM*, 212–25; Ibn Battuta, *Travels*, tr. H. A. R. Gibb (3 vols.; Cambridge, 1958–71). On relations between the Italian commercial powers and the Turks, see F. Thiriet, *La Romanie vénitienne au moyen-âge: Le Développement et l'exploitation du domaine colonial vénitien (XIIe–XVe siècles)* (Paris, 1959); A. Tenenti, 'Venezia e la pirateria nel Levante: 1300c.–1460c.', in *Venezia e il Levante fino al secolo XV* (2 vols.; Florence, 1973), ii. 705–71; M. Balard, *La Romanie génoise (XIIe–début du XVe siècle)* (2 vols.; Rome, 1978); E. A. Zachariadou, *Trade and Crusade: Venetian Crete and the Emirates of Menteshe* and Aydin (1300–1415) (Venice, 1983); ead., *Romania and the Turks (c.1300–c.1500)* (CS, London, 1985).

For anti-Turkish leagues, see A. Luttrell, 'The Crusade in the Fourteenth Century', in J. Hale, *et al.* (eds.), *Europe in the Late Middle Ages* (London, 1965), 122–54; id., 'The Hospitallers of Rhodes Confront the Turks: 1306–1421', in P. F. Gallagher (ed.), *Christians, Jews and Other Worlds: Patterns of Conflict and Accommodation* (Lanham, Md., 1988), 80–116; A. E. Laiou, 'Marino Sanudo Torsello, Byzantium and the Turks: The Background to the Anti-Turkish League of 1332–1334', *Speculum*, 45 (1970), 374–92; N. Housley, *The Avignon Papacy and the Crusades, 1305–1378* (Oxford, 1986); Setton, *PL*, i; Lemerle, *L'Émirat d'Aydin*; H. Ahrweiler, 'L'Histoire et la géographie de la région de Smyrne entre les deux occupations turques (1081–1317), particulièrement au XIIIᵉ siècle', *Travaux et mémoires*, 1 (1965), 1–204; F. J. Boehlke, *Pierre de Thomas: Scholar, Diplomat and Crusader* (Philadelphia, 1966).

The Latin–Greek *rapprochement* is examined by D. Geanakoplos, 'Byzantium and the Crusades, 1261–1354/1354–1453', in Setton, *HC*, iii. 27–68 and 69–103; O. Halecki, *Un Empereur de Byzance à Rome: Vingt ans de travail pour l'union des églises et pour la défense de l'empire d'orient 1355–1375* (Warsaw, 1930); W. De Vries, 'Die Päpste von Avignon und der christliche Osten', *OCP* 30 (1964), 85–128; R.-J. Loenertz, 'Ambassadeurs grecs auprès du pape Clément VI', *OCP* 19 (1953), 178–96.

On the Ottomans in this period, see F. Babinger, *Beiträge zur Frühgeschichte der Türkenherrschaft in Rumelien (14.–15. Jahrhundert)* (Munich, 1944); A. Bryer and H. Lowry (eds.), *Continuity and Change in Late Byzantine and Early Ottoman Society* (Birmingham, 1982); P. Lindner, *Nomads and Ottomans in Medieval Anatolia* (Bloomington, Ind., 1983); H. Inalcik, 'The Emergence of the Ottomans', in Holt, *et al.*, *CHI*, 263–91; V. L. Ménage, 'The Beginnings of Ottoman Historiography', in B. Lewis and P. M. Holt (eds.), *Historians of the Middle East* (London, 1962), 168–79; C. Imber, *The Rise of the Ottoman Empire 1300–1574* (London, forthcoming).

For *passagia* planned and realized between 1362 and 1390, see Setton, *PL*, i; E. L. Cox, *The Green Count of Savoy: Amadeus VI and Transalpine Savoy in the Fourteenth Century* (Princeton, NJ, 1967); N. Housley, 'King Louis the Great of Hungary and the Crusades, 1342–1382', *SEER* 62 (1984), 192–208; A. Luttrell, 'Popes and Crusades: 1362–1394', in *Genèse et débuts du Grand Schisme d'occident: 1362–1394* (Paris, 1980), 575–85; id., 'Gregory XI and the Turks', *OCP* 46 (1980), 391–417.

For the diplomatic background to Nicopolis, see the important study by J. J. N. Palmer, *England, France and Christendom, 1377–99* (London, 1972). On the campaign and battle, see A. S. Atiya, *The Crusade of Nicopolis* (London, 1934); J. Delaville le Roulx, *La France en orient au XIVᵉ siècle* (2 vols.; Paris, 1886); Setton, *PL*, i; R. Vaughan, *Philip the Bold: The Formation of the Burgundian State*

(London, 1962); P. Gautier, 'Un Récit inédit du siège de Constantinople par les Turcs (1394–1402)', *Revue des études byzantines*, 23 (1965), 100–17; R. Rosetti, 'Notes on the Battle of Nicopolis (1396)', *SEER* 15 (1937), 629–38; H. L. Savage, 'Enguerrand de Coucy VII and the Campaign of Nicopolis', *Speculum*, 14 (1939), 423–42. Older studies by A. Brauner, *Die Schlacht bei Nikopolis (1396)* (Breslau, 1876), and G. Köhler, *Die Schlachten von Nicopoli und Warna* (Breslau, 1882) retain some value.

CHAPTER 3

The Ottoman Threat, 1396–1502

Generally on the Ottomans in the fifteenth century, see H. Inalcik, *The Ottoman Empire: The Classical Age, 1300–1600*, tr. N. Itzkowitz and C. Imber (London, 1973); id., *The Ottoman Empire: Conquest, Organization and Economy* (CS, London, 1978); id., 'The Rise of Ottoman Historiography', in B. Lewis and P. M. Holt (eds.), *Historians of the Middle East* (London, 1962), 152–67; S. Shaw, *History of the Ottoman Empire and Modern Turkey*, i, *Empire of the Gazis: The Rise and Decline of the Ottoman Empire, 1280–1808* (Cambridge, 1976 and reprints); N. Itzkowitz, *Ottoman Empire and Islamic Tradition* (Chicago, 1980); N. Beldiceanu, *Le Timar dans l'état ottoman (début XIVe–début XVIe siècles)* (Wiesbaden, 1980); O. Turan, 'The Ideal of World Domination among the Medieval Turks', *Studia islamica*, 4 (1955), 77–90.

On the controversial views of Paul Wittek about the nature of the Ottoman state, see his *The Rise of the Ottoman Empire* (London, 1938); id., *La Formation de l'empire ottoman*, ed. V. L. Ménage (CS, London, 1982); C. J. Heywood, 'Wittek and the Austrian Tradition', *Journal of the Royal Asiatic Society*, (1988), 7–25; C. H. Imber, 'Paul Wittek's "De la défaite d'Ankara à la prise de Constantinople"', *Journal of Ottoman Studies*, 5 (1986), 65–81; id., 'The Ottoman Dynastic Myth', *Turcica*, 19 (1987), 7–27. On the conquered lands in the Balkans, see N. Beldiceanu, *Le Monde ottoman des Balkans (1402–1566): Institutions, société, économie* (CS, London, 1976); P. F. Sugar, *Southeastern Europe under Ottoman Rule, 1354–1804* (Seattle, 1977).

For Manuel II, see J. W. Barker, *Manuel II Palaeologus (1391–1425): A Study in Late Byzantine Statesmanship* (New Brunswick, NJ, 1969); D. M. Nicol, 'A Byzantine Emperor in England: Manuel II's Visit to London in 1400–1401', *University of Birmingham Historical Journal*, 12 (1971), 204–25; G. Schlumberger, 'Un Empereur de Byzance à Paris et à Londres', in *Byzance et croisades: Pages médiévales* (Paris, 1927), 87–147. On Tamerlane, see M.-M. Alexandrescu-Dersca, *La Campagne de Timur en Anatolie (1402)* (Bucharest, 1942); C. R. Markham (tr.), *Narrative of the Embassy of Ruy Gonzalez de Clavijo to the Court of Timour at Samarcand A.D. 1403–6*, Hakluyt Society, 26 (London, 1859).

Nobody can write about the crusades in the fifteenth century without reference to the tremendous compilation of sources by N. Iorga in *Notes et extraits pour servir à l'histoire des croisades au XVe siècle* (six series, Paris and Bucharest, 1899–1916). Setton, *PL*, ii, provides a detailed account of, and commentary on, papal crusade policy in this period.

Much has been written on the Varna crusade and its background. On the Curia's activity, see J. Gill, *The Council of Florence* (Cambridge, 1959); D. Caccamo, 'Eugenio IV e la crociata di Varna', *ASRSP* 79 (1956), 35–87; G. Valentini, 'La crociata da Eugenio IV a Calisto III (dai documenti d'archivio di Venezia)', *AHP* 12 (1974), 91–123. On Hungary's war against the Turks, see the important series of studies by F. Pall, 'Le condizioni e gli echi internazionali della lotta antiottomana del 1442–1443, condotta da Giovanni di Hunedoara', *Revue des études sud-est européennes*, 3 (1965), 433–63; id., 'Autour de la croisade de Varna: La Question de la paix de Szeged et de sa rupture (1444)', *Bulletin historique de l'Académie roumaine*, 22 (1941), 144–58; id., 'Un Moment décisif de l'histoire du Sud-Est européen: La Croisade de Varna (1444)', *Balcania*, 7 (1944), 102–20. The Ottoman crisis of 1444 is analysed in F. Babinger, 'Von Amurath zu Amurath: Vor- und Nachspiel der Schlacht bei Varna (1444)', *Oriens*, 3 (1950), 229–65; B. Cvetkova, 'Analyse des principales sources ottomanes du XVe siècle sur les campagnes de Vladislav le Varnénien et Jean Hunyadi en 1443–1444', *Studia albanica*, 5 (1968), 137–58. O. Halecki describes the campaign and battle in *The Crusade of Varna* (New York, 1943).

Hunyadi's campaigns against the Turks are described in J. Held, *Hunyadi: Legend and Reality* (New York, 1985). Bak and Király, *FHR*, contains several essays of importance for this period. For widely differing views on Scanderbeg, see F. Pall, 'Les Relations entre la Hongrie et Scanderbeg', *RHSEE* 10 (1933), 119–41; id., 'Die Geschichte Skanderbegs im Lichte der neueren Forschung', *Leipziger Vierteljahrschrift für Südosteuropa*, 6 (1942), 85–98; id., 'I rapporti italo-albanesi intorno alla metà del secolo XV', *ASPN* 83 (1966), 123–226; A. Gegaj, *L'Albanie et l'invasion turque au XVe siècle* (Louvain, 1937); A. Cutolo, *Scanderbeg* (Milan, 1940); F. S. Noli, *George Castrioti Scanderbeg (1405–1468)* (New York, 1947); W. Steltner, 'Zum Geschichtsbild des albanischen National-helden Georg Kastriota genannt Skanderbeg', *Zeitschrift für Geschichtswissenschaft*, 4 (1956), 1033–44; S. N. Naci, 'A propos de quelques truchements concernant les rapports de la papauté avec Skanderbeg durant la lutte albano-turque (1443–1468)', *Studia albanica*, 5 (1968), 73–86; A. Kostallari, *et al.* (eds.), *Deuxième conférence des études albanologiques à l'occasion du 5e centenaire de la mort de Georges Kastriote-Skanderbeg* (2 vols.; Tirana, 1969–70).

Jacques Paviot is preparing a book on the Dukes of Burgundy, the crusade, and the East in the fifteenth century; a detailed study is badly needed. Generally on Philip the Good and the crusade, see R. Vaughan, *Philip the Good: The Apogee of Burgundy* (London, 1970). On the Duke's activity before 1453, see

C. Marinesco, 'Philippe le Bon, duc de Bourgogne, et la croisade: Première partie (1419–1453)', in *Actes du VIe congrès international d'études byzantines*, i (Paris, 1950), 147–68; M. Izeddin, 'Deux voyageurs du XVe siècle en Turquie: Bertrandon de la Broquière et Pero Tafur', *Journal asiatique*, 229 (1951), 159–74; H. Taparel, 'Un épisode de la politique orientale de Philippe le Bon: Les Bourguignons en Mer Noire (1444–1446)', *Annales de Bourgogne*, 55 (1983), 5–29; id., 'Geoffrey de Thoisy: Une figure de la croisade bourguignonne au XVe siècle', *MÂ* 94 (1988), 381–93; J. D. Hintzen, *De kruistochtplannen van Philips den Goede* (Rotterdam, 1918); R. Degryse, 'De Bourgondische expedities naar Rhodos, Constantinopel en Ceuta', *Mededelingen der Akademie van Marine van Belgie*, 17 (1965), 227–52. W. Schulz, *Andreaskreuz und Christusorden: Isabella von Portugal und der burgundische Kreuzzug* (Freiburg, 1976), is an important analysis of the links between Burgundian and Portuguese crusade ideas. The reconnaissance reports by Bertrandon of la Broquière and Guillebert of Lannoy make fascinating reading: see la Broquière, *Le Voyage d'Outremer*, ed. C. Schefer (Paris, 1892, repr. Farnborough, 1972); Lannoy, *Œuvres*, ed. C. Potvin (Louvain, 1878), English translation by J. Webb in *Archaeologia Britannica*, 20 (1821), 281–444.

On the last years of Byzantium and the Ottoman capture of Constantinople, see D. M. Nicol, *The Last Centuries of Byzantium 1261–1453* (London, 1972); S. Runciman, *The Fall of Constantinople 1453* (Cambridge, 1965); *Byzantinoslavica*, 14 (1953), whole issue; H. Inalcik, 'The Policy of Mehmed II toward the Greek Population of Istanbul and the Byzantine Buildings of the City', *Dumbarton Oaks Papers*, 23 (1970), 231–49.

On the Ottomans between 1451 and 1502 see H. Inalcik, 'The Rise of the Ottoman Empire', in Holt, *et al.*, *CHI*, 295–323; F. Babinger, *Mehmed der Eroberer und seine Zeit: Weltenstürmer einer Zeitenwende* (Munich, 1953, Eng. tr., Princeton, NJ, 1978); H. Inalcik, 'Mehmed the Conqueror (1432–1481) and his Time', *Speculum*, 35 (1960), 408–27 (an extended review of Babinger); A. C. Hess, 'The Evolution of the Ottoman Seaborne Empire in the Age of the Oceanic Discoveries, 1453–1525', *AHR* 75 (1970), 1892–1919. R. F. Kreutel has translated some leading Ottoman sources into German: see his *Vom Hirtenzelt zur Hohen Pforte* (Graz, 1959), and *Der fromme Sultan Bayezid (1481–1512)* (Graz, 1978).

The crusading plans of Calixtus III, Philip the Good, and Alfonso V of Aragon in the years following the fall of Constantinople have received much attention. On Calixtus's policies, see C. Marinesco, 'Le Pape Calixte III (1455–1458), Alfonse V d'Aragon, roi de Naples et l'offensive contre les Turcs', *Bulletin historique de l'Académie roumaine*, 19 (1935), 77–97; M. Sciambra, G. Valentini, and I. Parrino, 'L'Albania e Skanderbeg nel piano generale di crociata di Callisto III (1455–1458)', *Bollettino della Badia greca di Grottaferrata*, NS 21 (1967), 83–136; J. Gill, 'Pope Callistus III and Scanderbeg the Albanian', *OCP* 33

(1967), 534–62; A. Bargellesi Severi, 'Nuovi documenti su Fr. Lodovico da Bologna, al secolo Lodovico Severi, nunzio apostolico in Oriente (1455–1457)', *Archivum franciscanum historicum*, 69 (1976), 3–22; L. Fumi, 'Il disinteresse di Francesco I Sforza alla crociata di Callisto III contro i turchi', *Archivio storico lombardo*, 39 (1912), 101–13.

On Burgundian planning, see C. Marinesco, 'Philippe le Bon, duc de Bourgogne, et la croisade: Deuxième partie (1453–1467)', *Bulletin des études portugaises de l'Institut français de Portugal*, NS 13 (1949), 3–28; Y. Lacaze, 'Philippe le Bon et les terres d'Empire, la diplomatie bourguignonne à l'œuvre en 1454–1455', *Annales de Bourgogne*, 36 (1964), 81–121; id., 'Politique "méditerranéenne" et projets de croisade chez Philippe le Bon: De la chute de Byzance à la victoire chrétienne de Belgrade (mai 1453–juillet 1456)', *Annales de Bourgogne*, 41 (1969), 5–42, 81–132; A. Grunzweig, 'Philippe le Bon et Constantinople', *Byzantion*, 24 (1954), 47–61; id., 'Le Grand Duc du Ponant', *MÂ* 62 (1956), 119–65; G. Doutrepont, 'Notice sur le manuscrit français 11594 de la Bibliothèque Nationale: La Croisade projetée par Philippe le Bon contre les Turcs', *Notices et extraits des manuscrits de la Bibliothèque nationale et autres bibliothèques*, 41 (1923), 1–28. The Feast of the Pheasant is examined by O. Cartellieri in 'Das Fasanenfest: Am Hofe der Herzöge von Burgund, 1454', *Historisch-politische Blätter für das katholische Deutschland*, 167 (1921), 65–80, 141–58, and see also Cartellieri's *Am Hofe der Herzöge von Burgund* (Basle, 1926; Eng. tr. London, 1929).

Alfonso V's involvement with the crusade and eastern politics is discussed in F. Cerone, 'La politica orientale di Alfonso di Aragona', *ASPN* 27 (1902), 3–93, 380–456, 555–634, 774–852, 28 (1903), 154–212; E. Pontieri, 'Alfonso I d'Aragona e la "crociata" di Callisto III', *Atti della Accademia nazionale dei Lincei, Rendiconti, Classe di scienze morali*, 8th ser. 29 (1974), 61–8. See also A. Ryder, *Alfonso the Magnanimous, King of Aragon, Naples, and Sicily, 1396–1458* (Oxford, 1990).

On events at Belgrade in 1456, see J. Hofer, *Giovanni da Capestrano: Una vita spesa nella lotta per la riforma della Chiesa* (L'Aquila, 1955); id., 'Der Sieger von Belgrad 1456', *HJ* 51 (1931), 163–212; F. Babinger, 'Der Quellenwert der Berichte über den Entsatz von Belgrade am 21–22. Juli 1456', *Sitzungsberichte der bayerischen Akademie der Wissenschaften*, 6 (1957), 1–69.

For Pius II and the crusade, see above all his own *Commentaries*: A. Van Heck (ed.), *Pii II Commentarii rerum memorabilium que temporibus suis contigerunt*, Studi e testi, 312–13 (2 vols.; Vatican City, 1984). There is an English translation by F. A. Gragg in Smith College Studies in History, 22, 25, 30, 35, 43 (5 vols.; Northampton, Mass., 1936–57), abridged as *Memoirs of a Renaissance Pope: The Commentaries of Pius II* (London, 1960). See also G. Valentini, 'La crociata di Pio II dalla documentazione veneta d'archivio', *AHP* 13 (1975), 249–82; G. Voigt, *Enea Silvio de' Piccolomini als Papst Pius II und sein Zeitalter* (3 vols.;

Berlin, 1856–63); A. Bryer, 'Ludovico da Bologna and the Georgian and Anatolian Embassy of 1460–1461', *Bedi Kartlisa*, 19–20 (1965), 178–98; H.-V. Sauerland, 'Rede des burgundischen Gesandten und Bischofs von Tournay Wilhelm Filastre in Sachen eines Kreuzzugs gegen die Türken, gehalten zu Rom am 8. October 1463 im öffentlichen Consistorium vor Papst Pius II', *RQ* 5 (1891), 352–63; F. Cardini, 'La repubblica di Firenze e la crociata di Pio II', *Rivista di storia della chiesa in Italia*, 33 (1979), 455–82; O. Cartellieri, 'Über eine burgundische Gesandschaft an den kaiserlichen and päpstlichen Hof im Jahre 1460', *Mitteilungen des Instituts für österreichische Geschichtsforschung*, 28 (1907), 448–64; G. Doutrepont, 'Épitre à la maison de Bourgogne sur la croisade turque projetée par Philippe le Bon (1464)', *Analectes pour servir à l'histoire ecclésiastique de la Belgique*, 3rd ser. 2 (1906), 144–95.

On two important promoters of crusading in the mid-fifteenth century, see Y. Lacaze, 'Un représentant de la polémique anti-musulmane au XVe siècle: Jean Germain, évêque de Nevers et de Chalon-sur-Saône', *Positions des thèses soutenues à l'École des chartes* (1958), 67–75; C. Schefer, 'Le Discours du voyage d'oultremer . . . prononcé en 1452 par Jean Germain, évêque de Chalon', *ROL* 3 (1895), 303–42; R. Manselli, 'Il cardinale Bessarione contro il pericolo turco e l'Italia', *Miscellanea francescana*, 73 (1973), 314–26; G. Schuhmann, 'Kardinal Bessarion in Nürnberg', *Jahrbuch für fränkische Landesforchung*, 34–5 (1975), 447–65.

For crusade planning between 1464 and 1502, see J. Delumeau, *L'Alun de Rome, XVe–XIXe siècle* (Paris, 1962); R. J. Walsh, 'Charles the Bold and the Crusade: Politics and Propaganda', *JMH* 3 (1977), 53–86; M. Viora, 'Angelo Carletti da Chivasso e la crociata contro i Turchi del 1480–81', *Studi francescani*, NS 11 (1925), 319–40; M. Izeddin, 'Un prince turc en France et en Italie au XVe siècle: Djem Sultan', *Orient*, 30 (1964), 79–99; H. Wiesflecker, *Kaiser Maximilian I: Das Reich, Österreich und Europa an der Wende zur Neuzeit,* i, *1459–1493* (Munich, 1971); id., 'Der Traum des Hans von Hermansgrün, eine Reformschrift aus dem Lager des Königs Maximilian I', in H. J. Mezler-Andelberg (ed.), *Festschrift Karl Eder zum siebzigsten Geburtstag* (Innsbruck, 1959), 13–32; J. Plösch, 'Der St. Georgsritterorden und Maximilians I. Türkenpläne von 1493/94', ibid. 33–56; H. F. Delaborde, *L'Expédition de Charles VIII en Italie: Histoire diplomatique et militaire* (Paris, 1888); P. Durrieu, 'La Délivrance de la Grèce projetée en France à la fin du quinzième siècle', *Revue d'histoire diplomatique*, 26 (1912), 333–51; Y. Labande-Mailfert, *Charles VIII et son milieu (1470–1498): La Jeunesse au pouvoir* (Paris, 1975).

Venice's conflicts with the Turks are given brief attention in F. C. Lane, *Venice: A Maritime Republic* (Baltimore, 1973), and D. S. Chambers, *The Imperial Age of Venice 1380–1580* (London, 1970). The development of Ottoman diplomatic relations with the western powers under Bayezid II is surveyed in S. N. Fisher, *The Foreign Relations of Turkey, 1481–1512* (Urbana, Ill., 1948);

H. Pfeffermann, *Die Zusammenarbeit der Renaissancepäpste mit den Türken* (Winterthur, 1946).

CHAPTER 4

The Anti-Turkish Crusade and European Politics, 1502–1580

As indicated at the start of the chapter, Setton, *PL*, iii–iv is the crucial text for the papacy's policy towards the Turks and the numerous political circumstances which helped to shape it. For the background of European politics see also G. R. Elton, *Reformation Europe 1517–1559* (London, 1963 and reprints), and J. H. Elliott, *Europe Divided 1559–1598* (London, 1968 and reprints).

For the Ottomans in this period, see, in addition to the books by Inalcik and Shaw cited in the previous section, Inalcik's 'The Heyday and Decline of the Ottoman Empire', in Holt, *et al.*, *CHI*, 324–53. Also important are A. C. Hess, 'Firearms and the Decline of Ibn Khaldun's Military Elite', *AO* 4 (1972), 173–200; id., 'The Ottoman Conquest of Egypt (1517) and the Beginning of the Sixteenth-Century World War', *International Journal of Middle East Studies*, 4 (1973), 55–76; C. H. Imber, 'The Navy of Suleyman the Magnificent', *AO* 6 (1980), 211–82; C. M. Kortepeter, 'Ottoman Imperial Policy and the Economy of the Black Sea Region in the Sixteenth Century', *Journal of the American Oriental Society*, 86 (1966), 86–113; id., *Ottoman Imperialism during the Reformation: Europe and the Caucasus* (London, 1973). On Safavid Persia, see R. M. Savory, 'Safavid Persia', in Holt, *et al.*, *CHI*, 394–429.

For crusading projects on the eve of the Reformation, see K. M. Setton, 'Leo X and the Turkish Peril', *Proceedings of the American Philosophical Society*, 113 (1969), 367–424; G. L. Moncallero, 'La Politica di Leone X e di Francesco I nella progettata crociata contro i Turchi e nella lotta per la successione imperiale', *Rinascimento*, 8 (1957), 61–109; R. J. Knecht, *Francis I* (Cambridge, 1982); J. Ursu, *La Politique orientale de François Ier (1515–1547)* (Paris, 1908); G. Wagner, 'Der letzte Türkenkreuzzugsplan Kaiser Maximilians I. aus dem Jahre 1517', *Mitteilungen des Instituts für österreichische Geschichtsforschung*, 77 (1969), 314–53; E. Laubach, 'Wahlpropaganda im Wahlkampf um die deutsche Königswürde 1519', *Archiv für Kulturgeschichte*, 53 (1971), 207–48; J. G. Russell, 'The Search for Universal Peace: The Conferences at Calais and Bruges in 1521', *BIHR* 44 (1971), 162–93.

On Mohács and the disintegration of Hungary, see the articles by Szakály, Kubinyi, Hess, Alföldi, and Domonkos in Bak and Király, *FHR*. For Charles V and the Turks, see H. Hantsch, 'Zum Ungarisch-Türkischen Problem in der allgemeinen Politik Karls V.', in H. J. Mezler-Andelberg (ed.), *Festschrist Karl Eder zum siebzigsten Geburtstag* (Innsbruck, 1959), 57–69; H. Duchhardt, 'Das Tunisunternehmen Karls V. 1535', *Mitteilungen des österreichischen Staatsarchivs*,

37 (1984), 35–72; K. Brandi, *The Emperor Charles V*, tr. C. V. Wedgwood (London, 1939 and reprints). The stance of the German Protestant princes is explored in A. Westermann, *Die Türkenhilfe und die politisch-kirchlichen Parteien auf dem Reichstag zu Regensburg (1532)* (Heidelberg, 1910); S. A. Fischer-Galati, 'Ottoman Imperialism and the Lutheran Struggle for Recognition in Germany, 1520–1529', *CH* 23 (1954), 46–67; id., 'Ottoman Imperialism and the Religious Peace of Nürnberg (1532)', *Archiv für Reformationsgeschichte*, 47 (1956), 160–79; id., *Ottoman Imperialism and German Protestantism 1521–1555* (Cambridge, Mass., 1959).

For the war at sea and in North Africa between the Ottomans and the Habsburgs, see J. F. Guilmartin, *Gunpowder and Galleys: Changing Technology and Mediterranean Warfare at Sea in the Sixteenth Century* (Cambridge, 1974); A. C. Hess, *The Forgotten Frontier: A History of the Sixteenth-Century Ibero–African Frontier* (Chicago, 1978); F. Braudel, *The Mediterranean and the Mediterranean World in the Age of Philip II*, tr. S. Reynolds (2 vols.; London, 1972 and reprints). The Habsburgs' imperial dilemma is examined in M. J. Rodríguez-Salgado, *The Changing Face of Empire: Charles V, Philip II and Habsburg Authority, 1551–1559* (Cambridge, 1988); G. Parker, 'Spain, her Enemies and the Revolt of the Netherlands 1559–1648', *PP* 49 (1970), 72–95; A. C. Hess, 'The Moriscos: An Ottoman Fifth Column in Sixteenth-Century Spain', *AHR* 74 (1968), 1–25. For the siege of Malta, see E. Bradford, *The Great Siege* (London, 1961).

For the Holy League, see L. Serrano, *La Liga de Lepanto entre España, Venecia, y la Santa Sede (1570–1573)* (2 vols.; Madrid, 1918–19); A. Tenenti, 'La Francia, Venezia e la Sacra Lega', in Benzoni, *Il Mediterraneo*, 393–408; H. Jedin, 'Papst Pius V., die Heilige Liga und der Kreuzzugsgedanke', ibid. 193–213. Benzoni's *Il Mediterraneo* contains many other valuable essays on the battle of Lepanto and its aftermath. Also of importance are J. De la Gravière, *La Guerre de Chypre et la bataille de Lépante* (2 vols.; Paris, 1888); G. A. Quarti, *La Guerra contro il Turco a Cipro e a Lepanto (1570–1571)* (Venice, 1935); A. C. Hess, 'The Battle of Lepanto and its Place in Mediterranean History', *PP* 57 (1972), 53–73; M. Lesure, *Lépante, la crise de l'empire ottoman* (Paris, 1972).

For Alcazar, see E. W. Bovill, *The Battle of Alacazar* (London, 1952); S. A. Skilliter, 'The Hispano-Ottoman Armistice of 1581', in C. E. Bosworth (ed.), *Iran and Islam: In Memory of the late Vladimir Minorsky* (Edinburgh, 1971), 491–515.

For the 'Long War' and the Austrian–Turkish border, see D. Caccamo, 'La Diplomazia della Controriforma e la crociata: dai piani del Possevino alla "lunga guerra" di Clemente VIII', *ASI* 128 (1970), 255–81; A. Tamborra, 'Dopo Lepanto: Lo spostamento della lotta antiturca sul fronte terrestre', in Benzoni, *Il Mediterraneo*, 371–91; G. E. Rothenberg, *The Austrian Military Border in Croatia, 1522–1747* (Urbana, Ill., 1960).

Key aspects of Ottoman decline are considered in C. M. Cipolla, *Guns and Sails in the Early Phase of European Expansion 1400–1700* (London, 1965); O. L. Barkan, 'The Price Revolution of the Sixteenth Century: A Turning Point in the Economic History of the Near East', *International Journal of Middle East Studies*, 6 (1975), 3–28; H. Inalcik, 'The Socio-Political Effects of the Diffusion of Fire-Arms in the Middle East', in V. J. Parry and M. E. Yapp (eds.), *War, Technology and Society in the Middle East* (London, 1975), 195–217.

CHAPTER 5

Latin Rule in Greece and the Aegean, 1274–1580

N. Cheetham provides a good introduction to the subject in *Mediaeval Greece* (New Haven, Conn., 1981). For greater detail see J. Longnon, 'The Frankish States in Greece, 1204–1311', in Setton, *HC*, ii. 235–74; P. Topping, 'The Morea, 1311–1364/1364–1460', ibid. iii. 104–40 and 141–66; K. M. Setton, 'The Catalans in Greece, 1311–1380', ibid. iii. 167–224; id., 'The Catalans and Florentines in Greece, 1380–1462', ibid. iii. 225–77; D. J. Wallace and T. S. R. Boase, 'The Arts in Frankish Greece', ibid. iv. 208–28. The works of W. Miller, *The Latins in the Levant: A History of Frankish Greece 1204–1566* (London, 1908), and *Essays on the Latin Orient* (Cambridge, 1921), are still worth consulting. A good introduction to current scholarship is Arbel, *et al.*, *LGEM*; the opening article by Jacoby is a particularly useful survey.

For the Latin Empire and Achaea, see J. Longnon, *L'Empire latin de Constantinople et la principauté de Morée* (Paris, 1949). The Morea's chief sources, the 'Chronicle of the Morea' and the 'Assizes of *Romania*', have both been translated: see H. Lurier (tr.), *Crusaders as Conquerors: The Chronicle of Morea* (New York, 1964: using the Greek version of the Chronicle); P. Topping (tr.), *Feudal Institutions as Revealed in the Assizes of Romania, the Law Code of Frankish Greece* (Philadelphia, 1949). Topping's translation and commentary are reprinted in his *Studies on Latin Greece A. D. 1205–1715* (CS, London, 1977), which contains other studies of importance. Two key collections of documents on the Morea are C. Perrat and J. Longnon (eds.), *Actes relatifs à la principauté de Morée 1289–1300* (Paris, 1967); J. Longnon and P. Topping (eds.), *Documents sur le régime des terres dans la principauté de Morée au XIVe siècle* (Paris, 1969). A. Bon, *La Morée franque: Recherches historiques, topographiques et archéologiques sur la principauté d'Achaie (1205–1430)* (2 vols.; Paris, 1969) is of value chiefly for its archaeological aspects.

Prof. David Jacoby has written extensively on the economy, society, and culture of the Morea and other regions of Latin Greece. See especially his *La Féodalité en Grèce médiévale. Les 'Assises de Romanie': Sources, application et diffusion* (Paris, 1971), and three volumes of collected studies, *Société et démographie à Byzance et en Romanie latine* (CS, London, 1975); *Recherches sur la Méditerranée orientale du XIIe au XVe siècle: Peuples, sociétés, économies* (CS, London, 1979); *Studies on the Crusader States and on Venetian Expansion* (CS, Northampton, 1989). His 'The Encounter of Two Societies: Western Conquerors and Byzantines in the Peloponnesus after the Fourth Crusade', *AHR* 78 (1973), 873–906, repr. in *Recherches*, is a good introduction to the issue of Greco-Latin relations.

For Venetian *Romania*, see F. Thiriet, *La Romanie vénitienne au moyen âge: Le Développement et l'exploitation du domaine colonial vénitien (XIIe–XVe siècles)* (Paris, 1959); id., *Études sur la Romanie greco-vénitienne (X^e–XVe siècle)* (CS, London, 1977). For Latin rule in the islands, see R.-J. Loenertz, *Les Ghisi dynastes vénitiens dans l'Archipel 1207–1390* (Florence, 1975).

The deeds of the Catalan Grand Company were chronicled by Ramon Muntaner: see Lady Goodenough (tr.), *The Chronicle of Muntaner*, Hakluyt Society, 2nd ser. 47, 50 (2 vols.; London, 1920–1). The chief source for the Catalans' conquest and government of Athens and Neopatras is A. Rubió y Lluch's monumental *Diplomatari de l'orient català (1301–1409)* (Barcelona, 1947). The main secondary studies are R. I. Burns, 'The Catalan Company and the European Powers, 1305–1311', *Speculum*, 29 (1954), 751–71; A. Rubió y Lluch, 'La Companyia catalana sota el comandament de Teobald de Cepoy, 1307–1310', in *Miscellània Prat De la Riba* (2 vols.; Barcelona, 1923), i. 219–70; K. M. Setton, *Catalan Domination of Athens 1311–1388*, rev. edn. (London, 1975); D. Jacoby, 'La "Compagnie catalane" et l'état catalan de Grèce: Quelques aspects de leur histoire', *Journal des savants* (1966), 78–103, repr. in *Société et démographie*; R. J. Loenertz, 'Athènes et Néopatras I: Regestes et notices pour servir à l'histoire des duchés catalans (1311–1394)', *Archivum fratrum praedicatorum*, 25 (1955), 100–212, 428–31; id., 'Athènes et Néopatras II: Regestes et documents pour servir à l'histoire ecclésiastique des duchés catalans (1311–1395)', *Archivum fratrum praedicatorum*, 28 (1958), 5–91; A. T. Luttrell, 'La Corona de Aragón y la Grecia catalana: 1379–1394', *AEM* 6 (1969), 219–52. All the articles by Loenertz cited in this section can also be found in his *Byzantina et Franco-graeca* (2 vols.; Rome, 1970 and 1978).

Specialist studies of the Morea in the confusing circumstances of the fourteenth century include R. J. Loenertz, 'Hospitaliers et Navarrais en Grèce (1376–1383): Regestes et documents', *OCP* 22 (1956), 319–60; id., 'Pour l'histoire du Péloponnèse au XIVe siècle (1382–1404)', *Études byzantines*, 1 (1943), 152–96; A. T. Luttrell, 'The Latins of Argos and Nauplia: 1311–1394', *PBSR* 34 (1966), 34–55; id., 'Intrigue, Schism, and Violence among the Hospitallers of Rhodes: 1377–1384', *Speculum*, 41 (1966), 30–48; id., 'Aldobrando Baroncelli in Greece: 1378–1382', *OCP* 36 (1970), 273–300.

For surrounding territories not under Latin control, see D. A. Zakythinos, *Le Despotat grec de Morée* (2 vols.; Paris, 1932 and 1953, repr. London, 1975);

D. Nicol, *The Despotate of Epiros 1267–1479: A Contribution to the History of Greece in the Middle Ages* (Cambridge, 1984); A. Ducellier, *L'Albanie entre Byzance et Venise (X^e–XVe siècles)* (CS, London, 1987). For studies of Palaiologan Byzantium and the Turks, see the sections for Chapters 2 and 3.

CHAPTER 6

The Kingdoms of Cilician Armenia and Cyprus, 1274–1573

For Cilician Armenia, see S. D. Nersessian, 'The Kingdom of Cilician Armenia', in Setton, *HC*, ii. 630–59; M. Chahin, *The Kingdom of Armenia* (London, 1987); T. S. R. Boase (ed.), *The Cilician Kingdom of Armenia* (Edinburgh, 1978).

Comprehensive and up-to-date treatment of Lusignan and Venetian Cyprus will be provided in the near future in book-length studies by Dr Peter Edbury and Dr Benjamin Arbel, and by the authors of a collaborative history of the island sponsored by the Archbishop Makarios III Foundation. For basic, detailed narrative, recourse must at present still be had to G. F. Hill, *A History of Cyprus* (4 vols.; Cambridge, 1940–52 and reprints), and to L. De Mas Latrie, *Histoire de l'île de Chypre sous le règne des princes de la maison de Lusignan* (3 vols.; Paris, 1852–61).

For the period before 1291, see E. C. Furber, 'The Kingdom of Cyprus, 1191–1291', in Setton, *HC*, ii. 599–629. The period between 1291 and 1489 is handled by H. Luke in two disappointing chapters in Setton, *HC*, iii. 340–60, 361–95. For the fourteenth century, see P. W. Edbury, 'The Crusading Policy of King Peter I of Cyprus, 1359–1369' in Holt, *EMLPC*, 90–105; J. Richard, 'La Révolution de 1369 dans le royaume de Chypre', *BÉC* 110 (1952), 108–23; P. W. Edbury, 'The Murder of King Peter I of Cyprus (1359–1369)', *JMH* 6 (1980), 219–33; id., 'Cyprus and Genoa: The Origins of the War of 1373–1374', in Papadopoulos and Englezakis, *Proceedings*, 109–26. The spectacular rise of Famagusta after 1291 is charted in D. Jacoby, 'The Rise of a New Emporium in the Eastern Mediterranean: Famagusta in the Late Thirteenth Century', in *Meletai kai hypomnemata, 1* (Nicosia, 1984), 145–79, repr. in his *Studies on the Crusader States and on Venetian Expansion* (CS, Northampton, 1989). For the Cypriot nobility under later Lusignan and Venetian rule, see B. Arbel, 'The Cypriot Nobility from the Fourteenth to the Sixteenth Century: A New Interpretation', in Arbel *et al.*, *LGEM*, 175–97.

Jean Richard has written a remarkable series of studies on the Church, economy, and social and political structures of the entire Lusignan period. See especially *Chypre sous les Lusignans: Documents chypriotes des archives du Vatican (XIVe et XVe siècles)* (Paris, 1962); and *Le Livre des Remembrances de la Secrète du royaume de Chypre (1468–1469)* (Nicosia, 1983). Some of Richard's articles on Cyprus were collected in his *Orient et occident au moyen âge: Contacts et relations* (CS, London, 1976); *Les Relations entre l'orient et l'occident au moyen âge* (CS, London, 1977); *Croisés, missionnaires et voyageurs* (CS, London, 1983). More recent articles by Prof. Richard include 'Agriculture in the Kingdom of Cyprus', in Setton, *HC*, v. 267–84; 'La Diplomatique royale dans les royaumes d'Arménie et de Chypre (XIIe–XVᵉ siècles)', *BÉC* 144 (1986), 69–86; 'Culture franque et culture grecque: Le royaume de Chypre au XVᵉᵐᵉ siècle', *BF* 11 (1987), 399–415; 'La Cour des Syriens de Famagouste d'après un texte de 1448', *BF* 12 (1987), 383–98. On the arts and fortifications, see T. S. R. Boase and A. H. S. Megaw, 'The Arts in Cyprus', in Setton, *HC*, iv. 165–207. Sir George Hill provided a good survey of relations between the Frankish conquerors and the Orthodox church in his *History of Cyprus*, iii. 1041–104.

For the Venetian period, see F. Thiriet, *La Romanie vénitienne au moyen âge: Le Développement et l'éxploitation du domaine colonial vénitien (XII–XVᵉ siècles)* (Paris, 1959), and the series of studies by B. Arbel, 'Cypriot Population under Venetian Rule (1473–1571): A Demographic Study', in *Meletai kai hypomnemata, 1* (Nicosia, 1984), 183–215; 'Urban Assemblies and Town Councils in Frankish and Venetian Cyprus', in Papadopoulos and Englezakis, *Proceedings*, 203–13; 'La Fiscalité vénéto-chypriote au miroir de la législation ottomane: Le Qanunname de 1572', *Turcica*, 18 (1986), 7–51; 'A Royal Family in Republican Venice: The Cypriot Legacy of the *Corner della Regina*', *Studi veneziani*, NS 15 (1988), 131–52; 'Résistance ou collaboration? Les Chypriotes sous la domination vénitienne', in M. Balard (ed.), *État et colonisation au moyen âge et à la Renaissance* (Lyons, 1989), 131–43.

CHAPTER 7

The Templars and the Hospitallers, 1274–1565: Disaster and Adaptation

On the international Military Orders in Palestine and Syria, see J. Riley-Smith, *The Knights of St John in Jerusalem and Cyprus c.1050–1310* (London, 1967); M. Melville, *La Vie des Templiers* (Paris, 1951); A. J. Forey, 'The Military Order of St Thomas of Acre', *EHR* 92 (1977), 481–503; J. Prawer, 'Military Orders and Crusader Politics in the Second Half of the XIIIth Century', in Fleckenstein and Hellmann, *GRE*, 217–29. Dr Malcolm Barber is writing a history of the Templars, which will be extremely welcome. For criticism of the Orders, see P. Amargier, 'La Défense du Temple devant le concile de Lyon en 1274', in *1274—Année charnière—Mutations et continuités* (Paris, 1977), 495–501; A. J. Forey, 'The Military Orders in the Crusading Proposals of the Late-Thirteenth and Early-Fourteenth Centuries', *Traditio*, 36 (1980), 317–45. A forthcoming study by Dr Helen Nicholson on the public image of the Orders in the twelfth and thirteenth centuries will clarify the issue of criticism.

For the trial and suppression of the Order of the Temple see M. Barber, *The*

Trial of the Templars (Cambridge, 1978); id., 'James of Molay, The Last Grand Master of the Order of the Temple', *Studia monastica*, 14 (1972), 91–124; id., 'The World Picture of Philip the Fair', *JMH* 8 (1982), 13–27; M. L. Bulst-Thiele, 'Der Prozess gegen den Templerorden', in Fleckenstein and Hellmann, *GRE*, 375–402; P. Partner, *The Murdered Magicians: The Templars and their Myth* (Oxford, 1982); S. Menache, 'Contemporary Attitudes concerning the Templars' Affair: Propaganda's Fiasco?', *JMH* 8 (1982), 135–47.

On the Hospitallers between 1291 and 1421, see the numerous studies by Anthony Luttrell. Many are most easily consulted in his two volumes of collected studies, *The Hospitallers in Cyprus, Rhodes, Greece and the West, 1291–1440* (CS, London, 1978), and *Latin Greece, the Hospitallers and the Crusades, 1291–1440* (CS, London, 1982). More recent articles include 'Greeks, Latins and Turks on Late-Medieval Rhodes', *BF* 11 (1987), 357–74; 'Rhodes and Jerusalem: 1291–1411', *BF* 12 (1987), 189–207; and 'The Hospitallers of Rhodes confront the Turks: 1306–1421', in P. F. Gallagher, *Christians, Jews and Other Worlds: Patterns of Conflict and Accommodation* (Lanham, Md., 1988), 80–116. Dr Luttrell's 'The Hospitallers of Rhodes: Prospectives, Problems, Possibilities', in Fleckenstein and Hellmann, *GRE*, 243–66, repr. in *Latin Greece*, is a stimulating overview of the fourteenth century, and his 'The Hospitallers at Rhodes, 1306–1421', in Setton, *HC*, iii. 278–313 is the best narrative account of the period, correcting and complementing J. Delaville le Roulx, *Les Hospitaliers à Rhodes jusqu'à la mort de Philibert de Naillac (1310–1421)* (Paris, 1913, repr. 1974).

The Hospitallers' relations with the Avignonese Curia are charted in N. Housley, *The Avignon Papacy and the Crusades, 1305–1378* (Oxford, 1986). For the papal inquest of 1373, see A.-M. Legras (ed.), *L'Enquête pontificale de 1373 sur l'Ordre des Hospitaliers de Saint-Jean de Jérusalem*, i, *L'Enquête dans le Prieuré de France* (Paris, 1987); J. Glénisson, 'L'Enquête pontificale de 1373 sur les possessions des Hospitaliers de Saint-Jean-de-Jérusalem', *BÉC* 129 (1971), 83–111. For the complex situation in Germany, see W. Rödel, *Das Grosspriorat Deutschland des Johanniter-Ordens im Übergang vom Mittelalter zur Reformation* (Cologne, 1972). On the Hospitallers at Nicopolis, see J.-C. Poutiers, 'Les Chevaliers de Rhodes à la croisade de Nikopol (1396)', *Études balkaniques*, 17 (1981), 89–123.

On the Hospital between 1421 and 1523, all that can be suggested is E. Rossi, 'The Hospitallers at Rhodes, 1421–1523', in Setton, *HC*, iii. 314–39; F. De Belabre, *Rhodes of the Knights* (Oxford, 1908); L. Butler, *The Siege of Rhodes in 1480* (London, 1980); Setton, *PL*, iii; E. Brockman, *The Two Sieges of Rhodes, 1480–1522* (London, 1969); T. S. R. Boase, 'The Arts in Rhodes' in Setton, *HC*, iv. 229–50; A. Gabriel, *La Cité de Rhodes MCCCX–MDXXII*, i, *Topographie, architecture militaire*; ii, *Architecture civile et réligieuse* (2 vols.; Paris, 1921–3).

For the Order's early decades on Malta, see E. W. Schermerhorn, *Malta of the*

Knights (London, 1929, repr. 1978); Setton, *PL*, iv; E. Bradford, *The Great Siege* (London, 1961 and reprints). A. Hoppen's monograph, *The Fortification of Malta by the Order of St John, 1530–1798* (Edinburgh, 1979) shows how the Order's history can, and should, be written for the post-1421 period.

CHAPTER 8

The Enemy Within: Crusading against Christians

On the origins of the *crux cismarina* and early instances of its application, see N. Housley, 'Crusades against Christians: Their Origins and Early Development, *c.*1000–1216', in Edbury, *CS*, 17–36; E. Kennan, 'Innocent III and the First Political Crusade: A Comment on the Limitations of Papal Power', *Traditio*, 17 (1971), 231–49; ead., 'Innocent III, Gregory IX and Political Crusades: A Study in the Disintegration of Papal Power', in G. F. Lytle (ed.), *Reform and Authority in the Medieval and Reformation Church* (Washington, DC, 1981), 15–35. For the Papal State, see D. P. Waley, *The Papal State in the Thirteenth Century* (London, 1961); P. Partner, *The Lands of St Peter: The Papal State in the Middle Ages and the Early Renaissance* (London, 1972).

For crusading between 1274 and 1343, see N. Housley, *The Italian Crusades: The Papal–Angevin Alliance and the Crusades against Christian Lay Powers, 1254–1343* (Oxford, 1982); id., 'Politics and Heresy in Italy: Anti-Heretical Crusades, Orders and Confraternities, 1200–1500', *JEH* 33 (1982), 193–208; J. Strayer, 'The Political Crusades of the Thirteenth Century', in Setton, *HC*, ii. 343–75; id., 'The Crusade against Aragon', *Speculum*, 28 (1953), 102–13; A. J. Forey, 'The Military Orders and Holy War against Christians in the Thirteenth Century', *EHR* 104 (1989), 1–24. On the War of the Sicilian Vespers, see M. Amari, *La guerra del Vespro siciliano*, ed. F. Giunta (2 vols. in 3 pts., Palermo, 1969); S. Runciman, *The Sicilian Vespers: A History of the Mediterranean World in the Later Thirteenth Century* (Cambridge, 1958); J. H. Pryor, 'The Naval Battles of Roger of Lauria', *JMH* 9 (1983), 179–216. T. S. R. Boase, *Boniface VIII* (London, 1933) is valuable both for the later phase of the Sicilian war and for the crusade against the Colonna.

Crusades in Italy between 1343 and 1378 are handled in N. Housley, *The Avignon Papacy and the Crusades, 1305–1378* (Oxford, 1986); id., 'The Mercenary Companies, the Papacy and the Crusades, 1356–1378', *Traditio*, 38 (1982), 253–80; F. Filippini, *Il cardinale Egidio Albornoz* (Bologna, 1933).

For crusades during the Great Schism, see R. N. Swanson, 'The Way of Action: Pierre d'Ailly and the Military Solution to the Great Schism', *SCH* 20 (1983), 191–200; E. Perroy, *L'Angleterre et le Grand Schisme d'occident* (Paris, 1933); P. E. Russell, *The English Intervention in Spain and Portugal in the Time of Edward III and Richard II* (Oxford, 1955); N. Housley, 'France, England and the

"National Crusade", 1302–1386', in G. Jondorf and D. Dumville (eds.), *France and the British Isles in the Middle Ages and Renaissance* (Woodbridge, 1991); C. Tyerman, *England and the Crusades 1095–1588* (Chicago, 1988).

On the Hussite revolution and wars, see H. Kaminsky, *A History of the Hussite Revolution* (Berkeley, Calif., 1967); F. G. Heymann, *John Žižka and the Hussite Revolution* (Princeton, NJ, 1955); F. M. Bartoš, *The Hussite Revolution 1424–1437*, tr. J. M. Klassen (Boulder, Colo., 1986); M. D. Lambert, *Medieval Heresy: Popular Movements from Bogomil to Hus* (London, 1977); F. Seibt, *Hussitica: Zur Struktur einer Revolution* (Cologne, 1965); id., 'Die Zeit der Luxemburger und der hussitischen Revolution', in K. Bosl (ed.), *Handbuch der Geschichte der böhmischen Länder*, i (Stuttgart, 1967), 351–536; F. Graus, 'The Crisis of the Middle Ages and the Hussites', tr. J. J. Heaney, in S. E. Ozment (ed.), *The Reformation in Medieval Perspective* (Chicago, 1971), 76–104; F. Von Bezold, *König Sigmund und die Reichskriege gegen die Hussiten* (3 vols.; Munich, 1872–7); J. Durdik, *Hussitisches Heerwesen* (Berlin, 1961); R. C. Hoffmann, 'Warfare, Weather, and a Rural Economy: The Duchy of Wroclaw in the Mid-Fifteenth Century', *Viator*, 4 (1973), 273–305.

The Hussite wars as crusading expeditions await their historian, whose linguistic attainments will have to be substantial. For the moment, see F. G. Heymann, 'The Crusades against the Hussites', in Setton, *HC*, iii. 586–646; Y. Lacaze, 'Philippe le Bon et le problème hussite: Un projet de croisade bourguignon en 1428–1429', *RH* 241 (1969), 69–98; G. A. Holmes, 'Cardinal Beaufort and the Crusade against the Hussites', *EHR* 88 (1973), 721–50.

For the crusade against George of Podiebrady, see F. G. Heymann, *George of Bohemia, King of Heretics* (Princeton, NJ, 1965); K. A. Fink, 'Der Kreuzablass gegen Georg Podiebrad in Süd-und Westdeutschland', *QFIAB* 24 (1932–3), 207–43.

The crusade of 1488 against the French Waldensians is examined in E. Cameron, *The Reformation of the Heretics: The Waldenses of the Alps, 1480–1580* (Oxford, 1984); J. Marx, *L'Inquisition en Dauphiné: Étude sur le développement et la répression de l'hérésie et de la sorcellerie du XIVe siècle au début du règne de François Ier* (Paris, 1914). For Francis Coppini's activity in England, see C. Head, 'Pope Pius II and the Wars of the Roses', *AHP* 8 (1970), 139–78.

'Political crusading' in the sixteenth century receives some treatment in K. Repgen, 'What is a "Religious War"?', in E. I. Kouri and T. Scott (eds.), *Politics and Society in Reformation Europe: Essays for Sir Geoffrey Elton on his Sixty-fifth Birthday* (London, 1987), 311–28; L. Romier, 'La Crise gallicane de 1551', *RH* 108 (1911), 225–50, 109 (1912), 27–55; P. Rousset, 'L'Idéologie de croisade dans les guerres de religion au XVIe siècle', *Schweizerische Zeitschrift für Geschichte*, 31 (1981), 174–84.

On papal policy and contemporary feelings about the *crux cismarina*, see Housley, *The Italian Crusades*; id., *The Avignon Papacy and the Crusades*;

C. Tyerman, 'The Holy Land and the Crusades of the Thirteenth and Fourteenth Centuries', in Edbury, *CS*, 105–112.

CHAPTER 9

The Iberian Peninsula:
The Rewards and Problems of Conquest, 1274–1415

Useful introductions to this period of Iberian history include J. N. Hillgarth, *The Spanish Kingdoms 1250–1516* (2 vols.; Oxford, 1976–8); A. MacKay, *Spain in the Middle Ages: From Frontier to Empire, 1000–1500* (London, 1977); J. F. O'Callaghan, *A History of Medieval Spain* (Ithaca, NY, 1975); T. N. Bisson, *The Medieval Crown of Aragon: A Short History* (Oxford, 1986). For the general problems of Spanish history in the Middle Ages, it is worth referring to A. Castro, *The Structure of Spanish History*, tr. E. L. King (Princeton, NJ, 1954); id., *The Spaniards: An Introduction to their History*, tr. W. F. King and S. Margaretten (Berkeley, Calif., 1971).

On the *Reconquista* itself, see C. J. Bishko, 'The Spanish and Portuguese Reconquest, 1095–1492', in Setton, *HC*, iii. 396–456; D. W. Lomax, *The Reconquest of Spain* (London, 1978). Crusading ideas in Iberia are discussed in P. Linehan, 'Religion, Nationalism and National Identity in Medieval Spain and Portugal', *SCH* 18 (1982), 161–99; C. Erdmann, 'Der Kreuzzugsgedanke in Portugal', *HZ* 141 (1930), 23–53. J. Goñi Gaztambide, *Historia de la Bula de la cruzada en España* (Vitoria, 1958), is a seminal work on the crusading features of the *Reconquista*; although flawed, it is one of the most important studies of crusading history, and should long ago have been translated into English.

Rev. Prof. R. I. Burns has written voluminously on the opportunities and problems of post-conquest settlement in Valencia. See, in particular, his *The Crusader Kingdom of Valencia: Reconstruction on a Thirteenth-Century Frontier* (2 vols.; Cambridge, Mass., 1967); *Islam under the Crusaders: Colonial Survival in the Thirteenth-Century Kingdom of Valencia* (Princeton, NJ, 1973); *Medieval Colonialism: Postcrusade Exploitation of Islamic Valencia* (Princeton, NJ, 1975). See also Burns's ongoing edition of Valencian documents, *Diplomatarium of the Crusader Kingdom of Valencia: The Registered Charters of its Conqueror, Jaume I, 1257–1276* (Princeton, NJ, 1985–). There are no comparable studies for Castile, for which the surviving documentation is much inferior, but see F. Fernández-Armesto, *Before Columbus: Exploration and Colonisation from the Mediterranean to the Atlantic, 1229–1492* (London, 1987); C. J. Bishko, 'The Castilian as Plainsman: The Medieval Ranching Frontier in La Mancha and Extremadura', in A. R. Lewis and T. F. McGann (eds.), *The New World looks at its History* (Austin, Tex., 1963), 47–69; R. I. Burns (ed.), *Alfonso the Learned, Emperor of Culture, 1284–1984* (New York, 1985); id. (ed.), *The Worlds of*

Alfonso the Learned and James the Conqueror: Intellect and Force in the Middle Ages (Princeton, NJ, 1985).

There is little to recommend for the Iberian Military Orders in this period. The *Actas del Congreso internacional hispano-portugues sobre 'Las Ordenes Militares en la peninsula durante la Edad media', 1971, AEM* 11 (1981), entire volume, gives an indication of the range of recent scholarship. F. Gutton provides a limp narrative in his series of studies jointly entitled 'La Chevalerie militaire en Espagne': *L'Ordre de Calatrava* (Paris, 1955), *L'Ordre de Santiago* (Paris, 1972), and *L'Ordre d'Alcántara* (Paris, 1975). For a good case study of one Order's political role, see J. F. O'Callaghan, 'The Masters of Calatrava and the Castilian Civil War 1350–1369', in Fleckenstein and Hellmann, *GRE*, 353–74.

On the Mudejars, *convivencia*, and acculturation, see, in addition to the books by Burns listed above, his volume of collected studies, *Muslims, Christians, and Jews in the Crusader Kingdom of Valencia: Societies in Symbiosis* (Cambridge, 1984). See also J. Boswell, *The Royal Treasure: Muslim Communities under the Crown of Aragon in the Fourteenth Century* (New Haven, Conn., 1977); T. F. Glick, 'Muhtasib and Mustasaf: A Case Study of Institutional Diffusion', *Viator*, 2 (1971), 59–81; T. F. Glick and O. Pi-Sunyer, 'Acculturation as an Explanatory Concept in Spanish History', *Comparative Studies in Society and History*, 11 (1969), 136–54; P. Wolff, 'The 1391 Pogrom in Spain: Social Crisis or Not?', *PP* 50 (1971), 4–18.

For Nasrid Granada, see M. A. Ladero Quesada, *Granada: Historia de un país islámico (1232–1571)* (Madrid, 1969); R. Arié, *L'Espagne musulmane au temps des Nasrides (1239–1492)* (Paris, 1973); J. Heers, 'Le Royaume de Grenade et la politique marchande de Gênes en occident (XVe siècle)', *MÂ* 63 (1957), 87–121. For the Marinids, and Christian relations with North Africa, see J. M. Abun-Nasr, *A History of the Maghrib* (Cambridge, 1971); C.-A. Julien, *History of North Africa*, tr. J. Petrie, ed. C. C. Stewart (London, 1970); A. Masiá De Ros, *La Corona de Aragón y los estados del norte de Africa* (Barcelona, 1951); C.-E. Dufourcq, 'Un projet castillan du XIIIe siècle: La "Croisade d'Afrique" ', *Revue d'histoire et de civilisation du Maghreb*, 1 (1966), 26–51; id., *L'Espagne catalane et le Maghrib aux XIIIe et XIVe siècles* (Paris, 1966); R. A. Messier, 'The Christian Community of Tunis at the Time of St Louis' Crusade, A.D. 1270', in V. P. Goss, *MTW*, 241–55.

For events in the *Reconquista* between the Council of Lyons and the fall of Algeciras, see A. Giménez Soler, *El Sitio de Almería en 1309* (Barcelona, 1904); id., *La Corona de Aragón y Granada* (Barcelona, 1908); H. Huici Miranda, *Las Grandes Batallas de la Reconquista durante las invasiones africanas* (Madrid, 1956); J. A. Robson, 'The Catalan Fleet and Moorish Sea-Power (1337–1344)', *EHR* 74 (1959), 386–408.

For the period between 1350 and 1415, see E. Mitre Fernández, 'De la Toma de Algeciras a la campagna de Antequera', *Hispania*, 32 (1972), 77–122; I. I.

Macdonald, *Don Fernando de Antequera* (Oxford, 1948); J. Torres Fontes, 'The Regency of Don Ferdinand of Antequera', in Highfield, *SFC*, 114–70; J. L. Vogt, 'Crusading and Commercial Elements in the Portuguese Capture of Ceuta (1415)', *Muslim World*, 59 (1969), 287–99.

The crusade of 1390 to Al-Mahdiya is discussed in L. Mirot, 'Une expédition française en Tunisie au XIVe siècle: Le Siège de Mahdia (1390)', *Revue des études historiques*, 97 (1931), 357–406; A. S. Atiya, *The Crusade in the Later Middle Ages* (London, 1938 and reprints); Setton, *PL*, i. For Clement VI and the Canary Islands, see E. Serra Ràfols and M. G. Martínez, 'Sermón de Clemente VI Papa acerca de la otorgación del Reino de Canarias a Luis de España, 1344', *Revista de historia canaria*, 29 (1963–4), 88–111; J. Vincke, 'Der verhinderte Kreuzzug Ludwigs von Spanien zu den Kanarischen Inseln', *Spanische Forschungen der Görresgesellschaft*, 1st ser. 17 (1961), 57–71.

For border relations, see J. De Mata Carriazo, *En la Frontera de Granada* (Seville, 1971); J. Torres Fontes, 'El Alcalde entre moros y cristianos del reino de Murcia', *Hispania*, 20 (1960), 55–80; D. Menjot, 'Le Poids de la guerre dans l'économie murcienne: L'Exemple de la campagne de 1407–1408 contre Grenade', *Miscelanea medieval murciana* (Murcia, 1976), 37–68; E. Mitre Fernández, 'La Frontière de Grenade aux environs de 1400', *MÂ* 78 (1972), 489–522; A. MacKay, 'The Ballad and the Frontier in Late Medieval Spain', *Bulletin of Hispanic Studies*, 53 (1976), 15–33; id., 'Religion, Culture, and Ideology on the Late Medieval Castilian–Granadan Frontier', in Bartlett and MacKay, *MFS*, 217–43; J. E. López De Coca Castañer, 'Institutions on the Castilian–Granadan Frontier 1369–1482', ibid. 127–50. Some frontier ballads are translated by R. Wright in his *Spanish Ballads* (Warminster, 1987).

CHAPTER 10

The End of the Reconquista: *Granada and Beyond*, 1415–1580

The final phase of the *Reconquista*, and its background in fifteenth-century Castile, receive treatment in the general surveys by Hillgarth, MacKay, O'Callaghan, Bishko, and Lomax, cited in the previous section. For Granada, see again M. A. Ladero Quesada, *Granada: Historia de un país islamíco (1232–1571)* (Madrid, 1969); R. Arié, *L'Espagne musulmane au temps des Nasrides (1239–1492)* (Paris, 1973). Goñi Gaztambide's *Historia de la Bula de la cruzada en España* remains the standard work for crusade preaching and indulgences, and for relations between the papacy and the Castilian Crown on the crusade.

For the period 1415–82, see A. MacKay, *Money, Prices and Politics in Fifteenth-Century Castile* (London, 1981); id., 'Popular Movements and Pogroms in Fifteenth-Century Castile', *PP* 55 (1972), 33–67; L. Suárez Fernández, *Juan II y la frontera de Granada* (Valladolid, 1954); W. D. Phillips, *Enrique IV and the*

Crisis of Fifteenth-Century Castile, 1425–1480 (Cambridge, Mass., 1978); R. H. Trame, *Rodrigo Sánchez de Arévalo, 1404–1470: Spanish Diplomat and Champion of the Papacy* (Washington, DC, 1958).

Amidst the vast literature on the Catholic monarchs and the Granada war, see in particular M. A. Ladero Quesada, *Castilla y la conquista del Reino de Granada* (Valladolid, 1967); id., *Milicia y economía en la guerra de Granada: El cerco de Baza* (Valladolid, 1964); id., *La Hacienda Real de Castilla en el siglo XV* (Seville, 1973); A. De la Torre, *Los Reyes Católicos y Granada* (Madrid, 1946); J. De Mata Carriazo, 'Historia de la guerra de Granada', in R. Menéndez Pidal (ed.), *Historia de España*, 17/1 (Madrid, 1969), 385–914; J. Goñi Gaztambide, 'La Santa Sede y la reconquista del Reino de Granada (1479–1492)', *Hispania sacra*, 4 (1951), 43–80 (partly translated in Highfield, *SFC*, 354–79); J. Vigón, *El Ejército de los reyes católicos* (Madrid, 1968); T. De Azcona, *Isabel la Católica, estudio crítico de su vida y su reinado* (Madrid, 1964); J. Edwards, 'War and Peace in Fifteenth-Century Castile: Diego de Valera and the Granada War', in H. Mayr-Harting and R. I. Moore (eds.), *Studies in Medieval History presented to R. H. C. Davis* (London, 1985), 283–95; M. Jiménes De la Espada, *La Guerra del Moro a fines del siglo XV*, 2nd edn. (Madrid, 1940); R. Menéndez Pidal, 'The Significance of the Reign of Isabella the Catholic, according to her Contemporaries', and 'The Catholic Kings according to Machiavelli and Castiglione', both in Highfield, *SFC*, 380–404 and 405–25; E. B. Ruano, 'Un Cruzado inglés en la guerra de Granada', *AEM* 9 (1974–9), 585–93; id., 'La Participacion extranjera en la guerra de Granada', *Revista de archivos, bibliotecas y museos*, 80 (1977), 679–701. Several contemporary accounts of the war are highly readable: see especially Diego de Valera, *Crónica de los reyes católicos*, ed. J. De Mata Carriazo (Madrid, 1927); Fernando del Pulgar, *Crónica de los reyes católicos*, ed. J. De Mata Carriazo (2 vols.; Madrid, 1943).

The decline of *convivencia* is discussed in J. Edwards, 'Religious Belief and Social Conformity: The "Converso" Problem in Late-Medieval Córdoba', *TRHS* 5th ser. 31 (1981), 115–28; id., 'Christian Mission in the Kingdom of Granada, 1492–1568', *Renaissance and Modern Studies*, 31 (1987), 20–33; A. MacKay, 'The Hispanic-*Converso* Predicament', *TRHS* 5th ser. 35 (1985), 159–79; R. Highfield, 'Christians, Jews and Muslims in the Same Society: The Fall of *Convivencia* in Medieval Spain', *SCH* 15 (1978), 121–46; M. A. Ladero Quesada, *Los Mudéjares de Castilla en tiempos de Isabel I* (Valladolid, 1969); J. Casey, 'Moriscos and the Depopulation of Valencia', *PP* 50 (1971), 19–40.

For Castile's advance into North Africa, see J. M. Abun-Nasr, *A History of the Maghrib* (Cambridge, 1971); C.-A. Julien, *History of North Africa*, tr. J. Petrie, ed. C. C. Stewart (London, 1970); N. Levtzion, 'The Western Maghrib and Sudan', in R. Oliver (ed.), *The Cambridge History of Africa*, iii, *From c.1050 to c.1600* (Cambridge, 1977), 331–462; J. M. Doussinague, *La Política internacional de Fernando el Católico* (Madrid, 1944). The works by A. C. Hess cited in the section for Chapter 4 are also relevant.

Stimulating introductions to the problems thrown up by European exploration are F. Fernández-Armesto's *Before Columbus: Exploration and Colonisation from the Mediterranean to the Atlantic, 1229–1492* (London, 1987); J. Muldoon, *Popes, Lawyers and Infidels: The Church and the Non-Christian World 1250–1550* (Liverpool, 1979); P. Chaunu, *L'Expansion européenne du XIIIe au XVe siècle* (Paris, 1969), English translation as *European Expansion in the later Middle Ages* (Amsterdam, 1979).

For the influence of crusading practices and ideas on Portugal's maritime exploration and discoveries, see C.-M. De Witte, 'Les Bulles pontificales et l'expansion portugaise au XVe siècle', *RHE* 48 (1953), 683–718, 49 (1954), 438–61, 51 (1956), 413–53, 809–36, 53 (1958), 5–46, 443–71; A. J. Dias Dinis, 'Antecedentes da expansão ultramarina portuguesa: Os diplomas pontifícios dos séculos XII a XV', *Revista portuguesa de história*, 10 (1962), 1–118; M. Barradas De Carvalho, 'L'Idéologie religieuse dans la "Crónica dos feitos de Guiné" de Gomes Eanes de Zurara', *Bulletin des études portugaises et de l'Institut français de Portugal*, NS 19 (1955–6), 34–63; J. L. Vogt, 'Crusading and Commercial Elements in the Portuguese Capture of Ceuta (1415)', *Muslim World*, 59 (1969), 287–99; B. X. Coutinho, 'L'Idée de croisade au Portugal au XVe siècle', *Miscellanea historia in honorem Alberti De Meyer* (2 vols.; Louvain-Brussels, 1946), ii. 737–47; J. Bensaude, *A Cruzada do Infante D. Henrique* (Lisbon, 1959); J. Vaz De Carvalho, 'O Ideal de Cruzada do Infante D. Henrique', *Broteria*, 71 (1960), 539–59; C. R. Beazley, *Prince Henry the Navigator*, 2nd edn. (London, 1923 and reprints); P. E. Russell, *Prince Henry the Navigator* (London, 1960); id., *Prince Henry the Navigator: The Rise and Fall of a Culture Hero* (Oxford, 1984); C. Erdmann, 'Der Kreuzzugsgedanke in Portugal', *HZ* 141 (1930), 23–53; C. R. Boxer, *The Portuguese Seaborne Empire, 1415–1825* (London, 1969).

Columbus's thinking is explored in A. Hamdani, 'Columbus and the Recovery of Jerusalem', *Journal of the American Oriental Society*, 99 (1979), 39–48; P. M. Watts, 'Prophecy and Discovery: On the Spiritual Origins of Christopher Columbus's "Enterprise of the Indies" ', *AHR* 90 (1985), 73–102; S. E. Morison, *The European Discovery of America: The Southern Voyages A.D. 1492–1616* (Oxford, 1974); and at some length in A. Milhou, *Colón y su mentalidad mesiánica en el ambiente franciscanista español* (Valladolid, 1983).

For links between the *Reconquista* and the Spanish conquest and settlement of the New World, see Bernal Díaz, *The Conquest of New Spain*, tr. J. M. Cohen (Harmondsworth, 1963 and reprints); P. Chaunu, *Conquête et exploitation des nouveaux mondes (XVIe siècle)* (Paris, 1969); H. B. Johnson (ed.), *From Reconquest to Empire: The Iberian Background to Latin American History* (New York, 1970); C. J. Bishko, 'The Iberian Background of Latin American History: Recent

Progress and Continuing Problems', *Hispanic American Historical Review*, 36 (1956), 50–80; J. H. Parry, *The Spanish Seaborne Empire* (London, 1966); I. A. Leonard, *Romances of Chivalry in the Spanish Indies* (Berkeley, Calif., 1933); M. De Lozoya, *La Prolongación de la Edad Media castellana en América Central en el siglo XVI* (Madrid, 1960). J. L. Phelan, *The Millenial Kingdom of the Franciscans in the New World*, 2nd edn. (Berkeley, Calif., 1970) is a fascinating account of the impact of eschatological ideas, many relating to Jerusalem.

For the 'three graces' and the Military Orders in Habsburg Spain, and other imprints made there by the crusade, see J. H. Elliott, *Imperial Spain 1469–1716* (London, 1963 and reprints); J. Lynch, 'Philip II and the Papacy', *TRHS* 5th ser. 11 (1961), 23–42; id., *Spain under the Habsburgs*, i, *Empire and Absolutism 1516–1598*, 2nd edn. (Oxford, 1981); I. A. A. Thompson, *War and Government in Habsburg Spain 1560–1620* (London, 1976); M. Steele, 'La Real Hacienda', in V. Vázquez De Prada (ed.), *Historia general de España y América*, vi, *La época de plenitud: Hasta la muerte de Felipe II (1517–98)* (Madrid, 1986), 143–67; L. P. Wright, 'The Military Orders in Sixteenth- and Seventeenth-Century Spanish Society: The Institutional Embodiment of a Historical Tradition', *PP* 43 (1969), 34–70; L. Van Der Essen, 'Croisade contre les hérétiques ou guerre contre les rebelles? La psychologie des soldats et des officiers espagnols de l'armée de Flandre au XVIᵉ siècle', *RHE* 51 (1956), 42–78; G. Mattingly, *The Defeat of the Spanish Armada* (London, 1959).

CHAPTER 11

The Crusade in North-Eastern Europe, 1274–1382

More than in any other field of crusading studies, nearly all research on this region was until recently distorted by nationalist and racial prejudices, especially on the part of German and Polish historians. For a masterly introduction to this polemic, see W. Wippermann, *Der Ordensstaat als Ideologie: Das Bild des Deutschen Ordens in der deutschen Geschichtsschreibung und Publizistik* (Berlin, 1979). Also useful are G. Labuda, 'A Historiographic Analysis of the German "Drang nach Osten" ', *Polish Western Affairs*, 5 (1964), 221–65; W. Wippermann, 'Die Ostsiedlung in der deutschen Historiographie und Publizistik. Probleme, Methoden und Grundlinien der Entwicklung bis zum Ersten Weltkrieg', in W. Fritze (ed.), *Germania slavica*, i (Berlin, 1980), 41–69; U. Arnold and M. Biskup (eds.), *Der Deutschordensstaat Preussen in der polnischen Geschichtsschreibung der Gegenwart*, QSGDO 30 (Marburg, 1982); M. Burleigh, 'The Knights, Nationalists and the Historians: Images of Medieval Prussia from the Enlightenment to 1945', *European History Quarterly*, 17 (1987), 35–55.

For general introductions to the region, see O. Halecki, *Borderlands of Western Civilization: A History of East Central Europe* (New York, 1952);

F. Dvornik, *The Slavs: Their Early History and Civilization* (Boston, 1956); M. Gimbutas, *The Balts* (London, 1963); ead., *The Slavs* (London, 1971); A. P. Vlasto, *The Entry of the Slavs into Christendom* (Cambridge, 1970).

Overall surveys of crusading along the Baltic are provided by E. N. Johnson, 'The German Crusade on the Baltic', in Setton, *HC*, iii. 545–85; E. Christiansen, *The Northern Crusades: The Baltic and the Catholic Frontier 1100–1525* (London, 1980). William Urban has provided detailed accounts of crusading up to *c*.1300 in *The Baltic Crusade* (De Kalb, Ill., 1975), and *The Prussian Crusade* (Washington, DC, 1980). For the Livonian crusades of the thirteenth century there are two excellent narrative sources in translation: Henry of Livonia, *Chronicle*, tr. J. A. Brundage (Madison, Wis., 1961); J. C. Smith and W. L. Urban (tr.), *The Livonian Rhymed Chronicle* (Bloomington, Ind., 1977).

The best overall introductory survey of the Teutonic Order is H. Boockmann, *Der Deutsche Orden: Zwölf Kapitel aus seiner Geschichte* (Munich, 1981 and reprints). There are also M. Tumler, *Der Deutsche Orden im Wenden, Wachsen, und Wirken bis 1400* (Vienna, 1955); M. Tumler und U. Arnold, *Der Deutsche Orden von seinem Ursprung bis zur Gegenwart* (Marburg, 1981); E. Maschke, *Der Deutsche Ordensstaat: Gestalten seiner grossen Meister* (Hamburg, 1935); id., *Domus hospitalis Theutonicorum: Europäische Verbindungslinien der Deutschordensgeschichte*, QSGDO 10 (Bonn, 1970); W. Hubatsch, *Quellen zur Geschichte des Deutschen Ordens* (Göttingen, 1954). In English there is only C. Krollmann, *The Teutonic Order in Prussia*, tr. E. Horstmann (Elbing, 1938), which is tainted at times by Nazi ideology. The pre-1291 period is surveyed by I. Sterns in 'The Teutonic Knights in the Crusader States', in Setton, *HC*, v. 315–78. Other, more specific studies, include M. Hellmann, 'Bemerkungen zur sozialgeschichtlichen Erforschung des Deutschen Ordens', *HJ* 80 (1961), 126–42; K. Gorski, 'L'Ordre Teutonique: Un nouveau point de vue', *RH* 230 (1963), 285–94; id., 'The Teutonic Order in Prussia', *Medievalia et humanistica*, 17 (1966), 20–37; W. Zeisemer, *Die Literatur des Deutschen Ordens in Preussen* (Breslau, 1928); C. H. G. Helm and W. Zeisemer, *Die Literatur des Deutschen Ritterorden* (Giessen, 1951); M. E. Goenner, *Mary-Verse of the Teutonic Knights* (Washington, DC, 1943).

Settlement and government in Prussia, Livonia, Estonia, and Finland is discussed in H. Helbig and L. Weinrich (eds.), *Urkunden und Erzählende Quellen zur deutschen Ostsiedlung im Mittelalter* (2 vols.; Darmstadt, 1968–70); G. Labuda, 'Geschichte der deutschen Ostkolonisation in den neueren westdeutschen Forschungen', *Polish Western Affairs*, 2 (1961), 260–83; H. Boockmann, 'Die mittelalterliche deutsche Ostsiedlung: Zum Stand ihrer Erforschung und zu ihrem Platz im allgemeinen Geschichtsbewusstsein', in H. Boockmann, K. Jürgensen, and G. Stoltenbert (eds.), *Geschichte und Gegenwart* (Neumünster, 1980), 131–47; F. L. Carsten, *The Origins of Prussia* (Oxford, 1954); R. Wenskus, 'Das Ordensland Preussen als Territorialstaat des 14. Jahrhunderts', in H. Patze (ed.), *Der Deutsche Territorialstaat im 14. Jahrhundert* (2 vols.; Sigmaringen, 1970–1), i. 347–82; M. Biskup, 'Polish Research Work on the History of the Teutonic Order State Organization in Prussia (1945–1959)', *Acta Poloniae historica*, 3 (1960), 89–113; H. Samsonowicz, 'Der Deutsche Orden und die Hanse', in Fleckenstein and Hellmann, *GRE*, 317–28; W. Urban, 'The Organization of Defense of the Livonian Frontier in the Thirteenth Century', *Speculum*, 48 (1973), 525–32; id., *The Livonian Crusade* (Washington, DC, 1981); F. D. Scott, *Sweden: The Nation's History* (Minneapolis, 1977); E. Jutikkala and K. Pirinen, *A History of Finland*, tr. P. Sjöblom (London, 1962).

For Sweden's wars against Novgorod and their ramifications, see J. L. I. Fennell, *The Crisis of Medieval Russia 1200–1304* (London, 1983); id., *The Emergence of Moscow 1304–1359* (London, 1968); id., 'The Campaign of King Magnus Eriksson against Novgorod in 1348: An Examination of the Sources', *Jahrbücher für Geschichte Osteuropas*, 14 (1966), 1–9; R. O. Crummey, *The Formation of Muscovy 1304–1613* (London, 1987); G. Vernadsky, *The Mongols and Russia* (New Haven, Conn., 1953); Christiansen, *The Northern Crusades*; N. Housley, *The Avignon Papacy and the Crusades, 1305–1378* (Oxford, 1986).

For the Teutonic Order's relations with the Russian principalities, see Urban, *The Livonian Crusade*; K. Forstreuter, *Preussen und Russland im Mittelalter* (Königsberg, 1938); id., *Preussen und Russland von den Anfängen des Deutschen Ordens bis zu Peter dem Grossen* (Göttingen, 1955). On the conflict between the Teutonic Order and Lithuania, see K. Forstreuter, *Deutschland und Litauen im Mittelalter* (Cologne, 1962); E. Weise, 'Der Heidenkampf des Deutschen Ordens', *Zeitschrift für Ostforschung*, 12 (1963), 420–73, 622–72, 13 (1964), 401–20; J. Jakstas, 'Das Baltikum in der Kreuzzugsbewegung des 14. Jahrhunderts. Die Nachrichten Philipps de Mézières über die baltischen Gebiete', *Commentationes balticae*, 6/7 (1958–9), 139–83; W. Urban, 'Martin of Golin', *Lituanus*, 22 (1976), 45–59. A detailed study of Lithuania itself under Mindaugas and his successors is a desideratum.

On the *Reisen*, the definitive study will be that of W. Paravicini, *Die Preussenreisen des europäischen Adels* (3 vols.; Sigmaringen, 1989–). Also important are W. Paravicini, 'Die Preussenreisen des europäischen Adels', *HZ* 232 (1981), 25–38; U. Arnold, 'Engelbert III. Graf von der Mark, seine Kreuzfahrten ins Heilige Land, nach Livland und nach Preussen', *Beiträge zur Geschichte Dortmunds und der Grafschaft Mark*, 64 (1968), 79–95; K. Conrad, 'Der dritte Litauerzug König Johanns von Böhmen und der Rücktritt des Hochmeisters Ludolf König', in *Festschrift für H. Heimpel*, ii (Göttingen, 1972), 382–401; H. Koeppen, 'Die englische Rente für den Deutschen Orden', ibid. 402–21; C. Higounet, 'De La Rochelle à Torun: Aventure de barons en Prusse et relations économiques (1363–1364)', *MÂ* 69 (1963), 529–40; M. Keen, 'Chaucer's Knight, the English Aristocracy and the Crusade', in V. J. Scattergood and J. W. Sherborne (eds.), *English Court Culture in the Later Middle Ages* (London,

1982), 45–61; W. Urban, 'When was Chaucer's Knight in "Ruce"?', *Chaucer Review*, 18 (1984), 347–53.

For Poland and its relations with Prussia and Lithuania, see W. F. Reddaway, *et al.* (eds.), *The Cambridge History of Poland (to 1696)* (Cambridge, 1950); N. Davies, *God's Playground: A History of Poland*, i, *The Origins to 1795* (Oxford, 1981 and reprints); P. W. Knoll, *The Rise of the Polish Monarchy: Piast Poland in East Central Europe, 1320–1370* (Chicago, 1972); id., 'Poland as *Antemurale Christianitatis* in the Late Middle Ages', *CHR* 60 (1974), 381–401; Housley, *The Avignon Papacy and the Crusades*; G. Rhode, *Die Ostgrenze Polens: Politische Entwicklung, kulturelle Bedeutung, und geistige Auswirkung*, i (Cologne, 1955).

CHAPTER 12

The End of the Baltic Crusade, 1382–1562

Many works cited in the previous section are relevant for this one: see especially the books by Christiansen, Boockmann, Maschke, and Reddaway. For the period between 1382 and 1410, see H. Gersdorf, *Der Deutsche Orden im Zeitalter der polnisch-litauischen Union: Die Amtszeit des Hochmeisters Konrad Zöllner von Rotenstein (1382–1390)* (Marburg, 1957); F. R. H. Du Boulay, 'Henry of Derby's Expeditions to Prussia 1390–1 and 1392', in Du Boulay and C. M. Barron (eds.), *The Reign of Richard II: Essays in Honour of May McKisack* (London, 1971), 153–72; R. H. Schmandt, 'The Gotland Campaign of the Teutonic Knights, 1398–1408', *Journal of Baltic Studies*, 6 (1975), 247–58.

On Tannenberg, see S. Ekdahl, *Die Schlacht bei Tannenberg, 1410. Quellenkritische Untersuchungen*, i, *Einführung und Quellenlage* (Berlin, 1982). G. C. Evans's *Tannenberg 1410:1914* (London, 1970) is cursory, C. R. Jurgela's *Tannenberg* (New York, 1961) obtrusively nationalistic.

The debate at Constance is discussed by E. Weise (ed.), *Die Staatsschriften des Deutschen Ordens in Preussen im 15. Jahrhundert*, i, *Die Traktate vor dem Konstanzer Konzil (1414–1418) über das Recht des Deutschen Ordens am Lande Preussen* (Göttingen, 1970); H. Boockmann, *Johannes Falkenberg, der Deutsche Orden und die polnische Politik* (Göttingen, 1975); S. F. Belch, *Paulus Vladimiri and his Doctrine concerning International Law and Politics* (2 vols.; The Hague, 1965); F. H. Russell, 'Paulus Vladimiri's Attack on the Just War: A Case Study in Legal Polemics', in B. Tierney and P. Linehan (eds.), *Authority and Power: Studies on Medieval Law and Government presented to Walter Ullmann on his Seventieth Birthday* (Cambridge, 1980), 237–54.

M. Burleigh, *Prussian Society and the German Order: An Aristocratic Corporation in Crisis c.1410–1466* (Cambridge, 1984) is an excellent analysis of the Teutonic Order's internal crisis after Tannenberg. See also id., 'Anticlericalism in Fifteenth-Century Prussia: The Clerical Contribution Reconsidered', in

C. M. Barron and C. Harper-Bill (eds.), *The Church in Pre-Reformation Society: Essays in Honour of F. R. H. Du Boulay* (Woodbridge, 1985), 38–47; A. Czacharowski, *Études sur l'histoire de l'Ordre Teutonique et de son état* (Toruń, 1984); W. Nöbel, *Michael Küchmeister Hochmeister des Deutschen Ordens 1414–1422*, QSGDO 5 (Bonn, 1969); H. Koeppen, 'Das Ende der englischen Preussenfahrten', *Preussenland*, 8 (1970), 10–52; C. A. Lückerath, *Paul von Rusdorf, Hochmeister des Deutschen Ordens 1422–1441*, QSGDO 15 (Bonn, 1969); K. E. Murawski, *Zwischen Tannenberg und Thorn: Die Geschichte des Deutschen Ordens unter dem Hochmeister Konrad von Erlichshausen (1441–1449)* (Göttingen, 1953).

For Livonia's wars against Novgorod and Muscovy, see W. Urban, *The Livonian Crusade* (Washington, DC, 1981); id., 'The Origin of the Livonian War, 1558', *Lituanus*, 29 (1983), 11–25; L. Arbusow, 'Die Beziehungen des Deutschen Ordens zum Ablasshandel seit dem 15. Jahrhundert', *Mitteilungen aus dem Gebiete der Geschichte Liv-, Ehst-, und Kurland*, 20 (1910), 367–457; K. Forstreuter, *Preussen and Russland von den Anfängen des Deutschen Ordens bis zu Peter dem Grossen* (Göttingen, 1955); R. O. Crummey, *The Formation of Muscovy 1304–1613* (London, 1987); J. L. I. Fennell, 'Russia, 1462–1583', in G. R. Elton (ed.), *The New Cambridge Modern History*, ii, *The Reformation 1520–1559* (Cambridge, 1958 and reprints), 534–61; id., *Ivan the Great of Moscow* (London, 1961); W. Kirchner, *The Rise of the Baltic Question* (Newark, NJ, 1954).

The impact of the Reformation in Prussia and Livonia is discussed in K. Forstreuter, *Vom Ordensstaat zum Fürstentum; Geistige und politische Wandlungen im Deutschordenstaate Preussen unter den Hochmeistern Friedrich und Albrecht (1498–1525)* (Kitzingen/Main, 1951); M. Biskup, 'Das Ende des Deutschordensstaates Preussen im Jahre 1525', in Fleckenstein and Hellmann, *GRE*, 403–16; L. Arbusow, *Die Einführung der Reformation in Liv-, Est-, und Kurland* (Darmstadt, 1964). The development of the Teutonic Order after 1525 can be traced in M. Tumler and U. Arnold, *Der Deutsche Orden von seinem Ursprung bis zur Gegenwart* (Marburg, 1981). For plans to entrust the Order with the Turkish frontier-lands, see H. Von Zwiedeneck-Südenhorst, 'Über den Versuch einer Translation des Deutschen Ordens an die ungarische Grenze', *Archiv für österreichische Geschichte*, 56 (1877), 405–64; W. Erben, 'Die Frage der Heranziehung des Deutschen Ordens zur Vertheidigung der ungarischen Grenze', ibid. 81 (1895), 516–98.

CHAPTER 13

Catholic Society and the Crusade, 1274–1580

Material used in this and the following chapter has to a large extent been culled from books and articles cited in previous sections. Titles are given here either because they have not been cited before, or because, although previously cited, they form indispensable guides to the topics discussed in the chapter.

Patterns of Thought

For criticism of crusading, see E. Siberry, *Criticism of Crusading, 1095–1274* (Oxford, 1985); ead., 'Criticism of Crusading in Fourteenth-Century England', in Edbury, *CS*, 127–34. Erasmus's views are discussed by J.-C. Margolin, *Guerre et paix dans la pensée d'Érasme* (Paris, 1973); id., 'Érasme et la guerre contre les Turcs', *Il pensiero politico*, 13 (1980), 3–38; M. Cytowska, 'Érasme et les Turcs', *Eos*, 62 (1974), 311–21; M. J. Heath, 'Erasmus and War against the Turks', in J.-C. Margolin (ed.), *Acta conventus neo-latini turonensis* (Paris, 1980), 991–9; L.-E. Halkin, 'Érasme, la guerre et la paix', in *Krieg und Frieden im Horizont des Renaissancehumanismus* (Weinheim, 1986), 13–44, repr. in his *Érasme: Sa pensée et son comportement* (CS, London, 1988).

The Protestant critique of crusading has received some attention. Generally, see K. M. Setton, 'Lutheranism and the Turkish Peril', *BS* 3 (1962), 133–68. For Luther, see H. Lamparter, *Luthers Stellung zum Türkenkrieg* (Munich, 1940); G. W. Forell, 'Luther and the War against the Turks', *CH* 14 (1945), 256–71; H. Buchanan, 'Luther and the Turks 1519–1529', *Archiv für Reformationsgeschichte*, 47 (1956), 145–59; R. Mau, 'Luthers Stellung zu den Türken', in H. Junghans (ed.), *Leben und Werk Martin Luthers von 1526 bis 1546* (2 vols.; Göttingen, 1983), i. 647–62, ii. 956–66. For Calvin, see J. Pannier, 'Calvin et les Turcs', *RH* 180 (1937), 268–86. For Thomas Müntzer, see J. Irmscher, 'Das Türkenbild Thomas Müntzers', in M. Steinmetz (ed.), *Der deutsche Bauernkrieg und Thomas Müntzer* (Leipzig, 1976), 137–42.

For crusading and missions, see B. Z. Kedar, *Crusade and Mission: European Approaches toward the Muslims* (Princeton, NJ, 1984); M. W. Baldwin, 'Missions to the East in the Thirteenth and Fourteenth Centuries', in Setton, *HC*, v. 452–518; R. I. Burns, 'Christian–Islamic Confrontation in the West: The Thirteenth-Century Dream of Conversion', *AHR* 76 (1971), 1386–1434; E. R. Daniel, 'Apocalyptic Conversion: The Joachite Alternative to the Crusades', *Traditio*, 25 (1969), 127–54; R. H. Schwoebel, 'Coexistence, Conversion, and the Crusade against the Turks', *Studies in the Renaissance*, 12 (1965), 164–87.

For the Turkish 'image' in the West in the fifteenth and sixteenth centuries, see R. C. Schwoebel, *The Shadow of the Crescent: The Renaissance Image of the Turk (1453–1517)* (Nieuwkoop, 1967); H. J. Kissling, 'Die Türkenfrage als europäisches Problem', *Südostdeutsches Archiv*, 7 (1947), 39–57; id., 'Türkenfurcht und Türkenhoffnung im 15./16. Jahrhundert: Zur Geschichte eines "Komplexes" ', ibid. 23 (1964), 1–18; C. Göllner, 'Die Türkenfrage im Spannungsfeld der Reformation', *Südost-Forschungen*, 24 (1975), 61–78; id., *Turcica: Die Türkenfrage in der öffentlichen Meinung Europas im 16. Jahrhundert* (Bucharest,

1978); S. H. Moore, 'The Turkish Menace in the Sixteenth Century', *Modern Language Review*, 40 (1945), 30–6; D. M. Vaughan, *Europe and the Turk, 1350–1700* (Liverpool, 1954); A. Mas, *Les Turcs dans la littérature espagnole du siècle d'or* (2 vols.; Paris, 1967); C. D. Rouillard, *The Turk in French History, Thought, and Literature (1520–1660)* (Paris, 1941); S. C. Chew, *The Crescent and the Rose: Islam in England during the Renaissance* (Oxford, 1937).

Such literature as exists on specific crusade treatises and their authors is given in the sections for Chapters 1 and 3. For comparative treatment of the recovery treatises, J. Delaville le Roulx, *La France en Orient au XIVe siècle* (2 vols.; Paris, 1886), retains some value, but it will be largely superceded by S. Schein, *Fideles Crucis: Europe and the Crusade, 1274–1314* (forthcoming). Schwoebel, *The Shadow of the Crescent*, is useful for fifteenth-century tracts. On the humanist contribution, see M. B. Petrovich, 'The Croatian Humanists and the Ottoman Peril', *BS* 20 (1979), 257–73; F. Babinger, 'Maometto il Conquistatore e gli umanisti in Italia', in A. Pertusi (ed.), *Venezia e l'Oriente fra tardo Medio Evo e Rinascimento* (Florence, 1966), 433–49; L. Gualdo Rosa, 'Il Filelfo e i Turchi: Un inedito storico dell'Archivio Vaticano', *Università di Napoli: Annali della Facoltà di Lettere e Filosofia*, 11 (1964–8), 109–65. M. J. Heath, *Crusading Commonplaces: La Noue, Lucinge and Rhetoric against the Turks* (Geneva, 1986) is an important study of the humanist approach to crusading oratory. On la Noue, see also P. Rousset, 'Un Huguenot propose une croisade: Le Projet de François de la Noue (1580–1585)', *Revue d'histoire ecclésiastique suisse*, 72 (1978), 333–44.

On the *Flugschriften* and 'instant histories', see R. Ebermann, *Die Türkenfurcht: Ein Beitrag zur Geschichte der öffentlichen Meinung in Deutschland während der Reformationszeit* (Halle, 1904); C. Göllner, *Turcica: Die europäischen Türkendrucke des XVI. Jahrhunderts* (2 vols.; Bucharest, Berlin, and Baden-Baden, 1961–8); J. W. Bohnstedt, *The Infidel Scourge of God: The Turkish Menace as seen by German Pamphleteers of the Reformation Era* (Philadelphia, 1968). For the humanists' treatment of crusading history, see L. Schmugge, *Die Kreuzzüge aus der Sicht humanistischer Geschichtsschreiber* (Basle, 1987); R. Black, 'La storia della Prima Crociata di Benedetto Accolti e la diplomazia fiorentina rispetto all'Oriente', *ASI* 131 (1973), 3–25; id., *Benedetto Accolti and the Florentine Renaissance* (Cambridge, 1985).

For prophecy and the crusade, see M. Reeves, *The Influence of Prophecy in the Later Middle Ages: A Study in Joachimism* (London, 1969); M. Chaume, 'Une Prophétie relative à Charles VI', *Revue du moyen âge latin*, 3 (1947), 27–42; N. Valois, 'Conseils et prédictions adressés à Charles VII, en 1445 par un certain Jean du Bois', *Annuaire-Bulletin de la Société de l'histoire de France*, 46 (1909), 201–38; J. Deny, 'Les pseudo-prophéties concernant les Turcs au XVIe siècle', *Revue des études islamiques*, 10 (1936), 201–20; A. Olivieri, 'Il significato escatologico di Lepanto nella storia religiosa del Mediterraneo del Cinquecento', in Benzoni, *Il Mediterraneo*, 257–77.

On the second cycle of the series of crusade epics, see R. F. Cook and L. S. Crist, *Le Deuxième Cycle de la Croisade: Deux études sur son développement* (Geneva, 1972); K.-H. Bender (ed.), *Les Epopées de la Croisade: Premier colloque international* (Stuttgart, 1987). Generally on literature and crusading, see G. Doutrepont, *La Littérature française à la cour des ducs de Bourgogne* (Paris, 1909).

Patterns of Behaviour

Two key primary sources for chivalry and crusading are Jean Cabaret d'Orville, *La Chronique du bon duc Loys de Bourbon*, ed. A. M. Chazaud (Paris, 1876), and D. Lalande (ed.), *Le Livre des fais du bon messire Jehan le Maingre, dit Bouciquaut* (Geneva, 1985). Maurice Keen's arguments are contained in *Chivalry* (New Haven, Conn., 1984); 'Huizinga, Kilgour and the Decline of Chivalry', *Medievalia et humanistica*, NS 8 (1977), 1–20; 'Chaucer's Knight, the English Aristocracy and the Crusade', in V. J. Scattergood and J. W. Sherborne (eds.), *English Court Culture in the Later Middle Ages* (London, 1982), 45–61; 'Gadifer de La Salle: A Late Medieval Knight Errant', in C. Harper-Bill and R. Harvey (eds.), *The Ideals and Practice of Medieval Knighthood* (Woodbridge, 1986), 74–85; 'War, Peace and Chivalry', in B. P. McGuire (ed.), *War and Peace in the Middle Ages* (Copenhagen, 1987), 94–117. Other important studies on chivalry and crusading include D'A. J. D. Boulton, *The Knights of the Crown: The Monarchical Orders of Knighthood in Later Medieval Europe 1325–1520* (Woodbridge, 1987); E. Maschke, 'Burgund und der preussische Ordensstaat: Ein Beitrag zur Einheit der ritterlichen Kultur Europas im späten Mittelalter', in his *Domus hospitalis Theutonicorum*, QSGDO 10 (Bonn, 1970), 15–34; E. Porter, 'Chaucer's Knight, the Alliterative *Morte Arthure*, and Medieval Laws of War: A Reconsideration', *Nottingham Medieval Studies*, 27 (1983), 56–78.

For Guillebert of Lannoy's travels, see his *Œuvres*, ed. C. Potvin (Louvain, 1878); R. Arié, 'Un seigneur bourguignon en terre musulmane au XVe siècle: Ghillebert de Lannoy', *MA* 85 (1977), 283–302; O. Halecki, 'Gilbert de Lannoy and his Discovery of East Central Europe', *Bulletin of the Polish Institute of Arts and Sciences in America*, 2 (1943–4), 314–31. On the importance of family traditions of crusading, see E. Mason, 'Fact and Fiction in the English Crusading Tradition: The Earls of Warwick in the Twelfth Century', *JMH* 14 (1988), 81–95; S. Lloyd, *English Society and the Crusade 1216–1307* (Oxford, 1988); C. Tyerman, *England and the Crusades 1095–1588* (Chicago, 1988).

For literature on the *Reisen*, see the section for Chapter 11. Henry of Derby's expeditions are documented in L. Toulmin-Smith (ed.), *Expeditions to Prussia and the Holy Land made by Henry, Earl of Derby*, Camden Society, 2nd ser. 52 (London, 1894), and described in F. R. H. Du Boulay, 'Henry of Derby's Expeditions to Prussia 1390–1 and 1392', in Du Boulay and C. M. Barron (eds.), *The Reign of Richard II: Essays in Honour of May McKisack* (London, 1971), 153–72.

For the development of papal policy on indulgences, see N. Paulus, *Geschichte des Ablasses im Mittelalter* (3 vols.; Paderborn, 1922–3); id., 'Raimund Peraudi als Ablasskommissar', *HJ* 21 (1900), 645–82; L. Mohler, 'Bessarions Instruktion für die Kreuzzugspredigt in Venedig (1463)', *RQ* 35 (1927), 337–49; J. Goñi Gaztambide, *Historia de la Bula de la cruzada in España* (Vitoria, 1958); M. Purcell, *Papal Crusading Policy: The Chief Instruments of Papal Crusading Policy and Crusade to the Holy Land from the Final Loss of Jerusalem to the Fall of Acre, 1244–1291* (Leiden, 1975); N. Housley, *The Avignon Papacy and the Crusades, 1305–1378* (Oxford, 1986).

On 'popular' crusades, see M. Barber, 'The Crusade of the Shepherds in 1251', in J. F. Sweets (ed.), *Proceedings of the Tenth Annual Meeting of the Western Society for French History* (Lawrence, Kan., 1984), 1–23; G. Dickson, 'The Advent of the *pastores* (1251)', *RBPH* 66 (1988), 249–67; id., 'The Flagellants of 1260 and the Crusades', *JMH* 15 (1989), 227–67; M. Barber, 'The Pastoureaux of 1320', *JEH* 32 (1981), 143–66; J. Hofer, 'Der Sieger von Belgrad 1456', *HJ* 51 (1931), 163–212; A. Borosy, 'The *militia portalis* in Hungary before 1526', in Bak and Király, *FHR* 63–80; J. Held, 'Peasants in Arms, 1437–1438 and 1456', ibid. 81–101.

On financial returns from indulgences, and the problems of indulgence abuse, see W. E. Lunt, *Financial Relations of the Papacy with England* (2 vols.; Cambridge, Mass., 1939–62); F. Remy, *Les Grandes Indulgences pontificales aux Pays-Bas à la fin du moyen âge (1300–1531)* (Louvain, 1928); L. Gilliodts-Van Severen, 'La Croisade de 1530 ordonnée par Charles-Quint', *Bulletins de la Commission royale d'histoire*, 4th ser. 16 (1889), 261–82; Paulus, *Geschichte des Ablasses*, iii; J. Heers, 'La Vente des indulgences pour la Croisade, à Gênes et en Lunigiana, en 1456', in *Miscellanea storica ligure*, 3 (1963), 71–101, repr. in his *Société et économie à Gênes (XIVᵉ–XVᵉ siècles)* (CS, London, 1979); L.-E. Halkin, 'La Place des indulgences dans la pensée religieuse d'Érasme', *Bulletin de la Société de l'histoire du protestantisme français*, 129 (1983), 143–54, repr. in his *Érasme: Sa pensée et son comportement* (CS, London, 1988).

For western sensibilities about the Holy Land in the late Middle Ages, see B. Hamilton, 'The Ottomans, the Humanists and the Holy House of Loreto', *Renaissance and Modern Studies*, 31 (1987), 1–19; A. Benvenuti Papi, ' "Margarita filia Jerusalem": Santa Margherita da Cortona e il superamento mistico della crociata', in Cardini, *Toscana*, 117–37; R. Rusconi, 'Gerusalemme nella predicazione popolare quattrocentesca tra millennio, ricordo di viaggio e luogo sacro', ibid. 285–98.

CHAPTER 14

Government and the Crusade, 1274–1580

Y. Renouard, *The Avignon Papacy 1305–1403*, tr. D. Bethell (London, 1970), and J. A. F. Thomson, *Popes and Princes, 1417–1517: Politics and Polity in the*

Late Medieval Church (London, 1980) form useful introductions to the late medieval papacy and its problems. In addition to Setton's magisterial survey in *PL*, there are a number of studies of papal crusading policy which handle individual popes or specific periods of papal history. For the period between 1274 and 1378, see M. Purcell, *Papal Crusading Policy: The Chief Instruments of Papal Crusading Policy and Crusade to the Holy Land from the Final Loss of Jerusalem to the Fall of Acre, 1244–1291* (Leiden, 1975); N. Housley, *The Avignon Papacy and the Crusades, 1305–1378* (Oxford, 1986); L. Thier, *Kreuzzugsbemühungen unter Papst Clemens V. (1305–1314)* (Werl, Westf., 1973); F. Giunta, 'Benedetto XII e la crociata', *AEM* 3 (1966), 215–34; J. Gay, *Le Pape Clément VI et les affaires d'orient (1342–1352)* (Paris, 1904); F. Giunta, 'Sulla politica orientale di Innocenzo VI', in *Miscellanea in onore di Roberto Cessi* (2 vols.; Rome, 1958), i. 305–20; A. T. Luttrell, 'Gregory XI and the Turks: 1370–1378', *OCP* 46 (1980), 391–417; P. Thibault, 'Pope Gregory XI (1370–1378) and the Crusade', *Canadian Journal of History*, 20 (1985), 313–35.

For papal policy during the early phase of the Great Schism see, for the moment, A. Luttrell, 'Popes and Crusades: 1362–1394', in *Genèse et débuts du Grand Schisme d'occident: 1362–1394* (Paris, 1980), 575–85; a study of the crusading policies pursued by all the obediences during the Schism is a desideratum. For the fifteenth century, see D. Caccamo, 'Eugenio IV e la crociata di Varna', *ASRSP* 3rd ser. 10 (1956), 35–87; J. Gill, 'Pope Callistus III and Scanderbeg the Albanian', *OCP* 33 (1967), 534–62; M. Sciambra, *et al.*, 'L'Albania e Skanderbeg nel piano generale di crociata di Callisto III (1455–1458)', *Bollettino della Badia greca di Grottaferrata*, NS 21 (1967), 83–136. F. Cardini, 'La repubblica di Firenze e la crociata di Pio II', *Rivista di storia della chiesa in Italia*, 33 (1979), 455–82, makes some cogent observations about Pius II's crusade plans. For sixteenth-century popes, see K. M. Setton, 'Leo X and the Turkish Peril', *Proceedings of the American Philosophical Society*, 113 (1969), 367–424; H. Jedin, 'Papst Pius V., die Heilige Liga und der Kreuzzugsgedanke', in Benzoni, *Il Mediterraneo*, 193–213; D. Caccamo, 'La diplomazia della Controriforma e la crociata: dai piani del Possevino alla "lunga guerra" di Clemente VIII', *ASI* 128 (1970), 255–81.

For Podiebrady's proposed League, see H. Markgraf, 'Über Georgs von Podiebrad Project eines christlichen Fürstenbundes', *HZ* 21 (1869), 245–304; F. G. Heymann, *George of Bohemia, King of Heretics* (Princeton, NJ, 1965); O. Odložilík, *The Hussite King: Bohemia in European Affairs 1440–1471* (New Brunswick, NJ, 1965).

Useful introductory surveys of the state in the late Middle Ages, and of changes in military techniques and organization, are B. Guenée, *States and Rulers in Later Medieval Europe*, tr. J. Vale (Oxford, 1985); P. Contamine, *War in the Middle Ages*, tr. M. Jones (Oxford, 1984 and reprints); id., *Guerre, état et société à la fin du Moyen Âge: Études sur les armées des rois de France 1337–1494* (Paris, 1972); M. Prestwich, *The Three Edwards: War and State in England 1272–1377*

(London, 1980 and reprints); C. T. Allmand, *The Hundred Years War: England and France at War c.1300–c.1450* (Cambridge, 1988). Several essays in Bak and Király, *FHR*, deal with Hungary's experience of these changes. The impact of ideas of sovereignty can be seen in A. Luttrell, 'The Aragonese Crown and the Knights Hospitallers of Rhodes: 1291–1350', *EHR* 76 (1961), 1–19.

Recruitment for crusading to the East receives attention in S. Lloyd, *English Society and the Crusade 1216–1307* (Oxford, 1988), and C. Tyerman, *England and the Crusades 1095–1588* (Chicago, 1988). On the Granada war, see P. Stewart, 'The Soldier, the Bureaucrat, and Fiscal Records in the Army of Ferdinand and Isabella', *Hispanic American Historical Review*, 49 (1969), 281–92. For the memorandum prepared for Philip the Good, see J. Finot, 'Projet d'expédition contre les Turcs préparé par les conseillers du duc de Bourgogne Philippe-le-Bon', *Mémoires de la Société des sciences de Lille*, 4th ser. 21 (1895), 161–206, and for Taleazzi's proposals, B. Feliciangeli, 'Le proposte per la guerra contro i Turchi presentate da Stefano Taleazzi, vescovo di Torcello, a papa Alessandro VI', *ARSRSP* 40 (1917), 5–63.

J. Favier, *Finance et fiscalité au bas moyen âge* (Paris, 1971), is a good introduction to the development of state finance under the pressure of military costs. For the expense of crusading, see F. Cardini, 'I costi della crociata: L'aspetto economico del progetto di Marin Sanudo il Vecchio (1312–1321)', in *Studi in memoria di Federigo Melis* (5 vols.; Naples, 1978), ii. 179–210; E. Carusi, 'Preventivi di spese per la spedizione contro il Turco al tempo di Pio II', *Archivio muratoriano*, 16 (1915), 273–9; M. A. Ladero Quesada, *Milicia y economía en la guerra de Granada: El cerco de Baza* (Valladolid, 1964); id., *Castilla y la conquista del Reino de Granada* (Valladolid, 1967); G. Parker and I. A. A. Thompson, 'The Battle of Lepanto, 1571: The Costs of Victory', *The Mariner's Mirror*, 64 (1978), 13–21; F. Ruiz Martin, 'Las finanzas de la monarquia hispanica y la Liga Santa', in Benzoni, *Il Mediterraneo*, 325–70.

On clerical taxes for the crusade, see W. E. Lunt, *Papal Revenues in the Middle Ages* (2 vols.; New York, 1934); id., *Financial Relations of the Papacy with England* (2 vols.; Cambridge, Mass., 1939–62); H. Möhring, 'Geld zum Kampf gegen Ungläubige: Die Finanzierung der Kreuzzüge und die Besteuerung des Klerus', in U. Schultz (ed.), *Mit dem Zehnten fing es an: Eine Kulturgeschichte der Steuer* (Munich, 1986), 87–99; P. Linehan, 'The Church, the Economy and the Reconquista in Early Fourteenth-Century Castile', *Revista española de teologia*, 43 (1983), 275–303. For negotiations with the Curia on clerical taxes, see N. Housley, 'The Franco-Papal Crusade Negotiations of 1322–3', *PBSR* 48 (1980), 166–85; id., *The Avignon Papacy and the Crusades*; J. Vincke, *Staat und Kirche in Katalonien und Aragon während des Mittelalters*, i (Münster-i.-W., 1931); O. Cartellieri, 'Über eine burgundische Gesandtschaft an den kaiserlichen und päpstlichen Hof im Jahre 1460', *Mitteilungen des Instituts für österreichische Geschichtsforschung*, 28 (1907), 448–64.

Lay taxation for the crusade can be approached through C. H. Taylor, 'French

Assemblies and Subsidy in 1321', *Speculum*, 43 (1968), 217–44; C. Tyerman, 'Philip V of France, the Assemblies of 1319–20 and the Crusade', *BIHR* 57 (1984), 15–34; E. A. R. Brown, 'Customary Aids and Royal Fiscal Policy under Philip VI of Valois', *Traditio*, 30 (1974), 191–258; P. Moraw, 'Der "Gemeine Pfennig": Neue Steuern und die Einheit des Reiches im 15. und 16. Jahrhundert', in Schultz (ed.), *Mit dem Zehnten fing es an*, 130–42; W. Steglich, 'Die Reichstürkenhilfe in der Zeit Karls V.', *Militärgeschichtliche Mitteilungen*, 11 (1972), 7–55.

On the sincerity issue, see S. Lloyd, *English Society and the Crusade*; M. Prestwich, *Edward I* (London, 1988); S. Schein, 'Philip IV and the Crusade: A Reconsideration', in Edbury, *CS*, 121–6; C. Tyerman, 'Sed nihil fecit? The Last Capetians and the Recovery of the Holy Land', in J. Gillingham and J. C. Holt (eds.), *War and Government in the Middle Ages* (Woodbridge, 1984), 170–81; id., 'Philip VI and the Recovery of the Holy Land', *EHR* 100 (1985), 25–51; A. Marongiu, 'Carlo VIII e la sua crociata (come problema storiografico)', in L. De Rosa (ed.), *Ricerche storiche ed economiche in memoria di Corrado Barbagallo* (2 vols.; Naples, 1970), ii. 237–58; Y. Labande-Mailfert, *Charles VIII et son milieu (1470–1498): La Jeunesse au pouvoir* (Paris, 1975); R. J. Walsh, 'Charles the Bold and the Crusade: Politics and Propaganda', *JMH* 3 (1977), 53–86.

For 'sanctified patriotism', see E. H. Kantorowicz, '*Pro patria mori* in Mediaeval Political Thought', *AHR* 56 (1950–1), 472–92; G. Post, 'Two Notes on Nationalism in the Middle Ages: I. *Pugna pro patria*, II. *Rex imperator*', *Traditio*, 9 (1953), 281–320; J. Strayer, 'France: The Holy Land, the Chosen People, and the Most Christian King', in T. K. Rabb and J. E. Seigel (eds.), *Action and Conviction in Early Modern Europe* (Princeton, NJ, 1969), 3–16; C. Tyerman, *England and the Crusades*; N. Housley, 'France, England and the "National Crusade", 1302–1386', in G. Jondorf and D. Dumville (eds.), *France and the British Isles in the Middle Ages and Renaissance* (Woodbridge, 1991). I shall also be handling this theme in a chapter in P. Contamine (ed.), *Guerre et compétition dans la croissance des états européens (XIIIᵉ–XVIIIᵉ siècle)*.

On the concept of Christendom in the sixteenth and seventeenth centuries, see D. Hay, *Europe: The Emergence of an Idea*, 2nd edn. (Edinburgh, 1968); F. Autrand, *et al.* (eds.), *La Conscience européenne au XVᵉ et au XVIᵉ siècle* (Paris, 1982); F. Le Van Baumer, 'The Church of England and the Common Corps of Christendom', *Journal of Modern History*, 16 (1944), 1–21; id., 'England, the Turk and the Common Corps of Christendom', *AHR* 50 (1944–5), 26–48; id., 'The Conception of Christendom in Renaissance England', *Journal of the History of Ideas*, 6 (1945), 131–56; J. V. Polisensky, 'Bohemia, the Turk and the Christian Commonwealth (1462–1620)', *Byzantinoslavica*, 14 (1953), 82–108.

The 'Protestant crusade' is discussed in P. Rousset, 'La "Croisade" puritaine de Cromwell', *Schweizerische Zeitschrift für Geschichte*, 28 (1978), 15–28; id., 'L'Idéologie de croisade dans les guerres de religion au XVIᵉ siècle', *Schweizerische*

Zeitschrift für Geschichte, 31 (1981), 174–84; J. R. Hale, 'Incitement to Violence? English Divines on the Theme of War, 1578 to 1631', in J. G. Rowe and W. H. Stockdale (eds.), *Florilegium historiale: Essays presented to Wallace K. Ferguson* (Toronto, 1971), 369–99, repr. in his *Renaissance War Studies* (London, 1983), 487–517. See also A. Wang, *Der 'Miles Christianus' im 16. und 17. Jahrhundert und seine mittelalterliche Tradition. Ein Beitrag zum Verhältnis von sprachlicher und graphischer Bildlichkeit* (Berne, 1975).

INDEX